PROBLEMS AND MATERIALS ON

THE TAXATION OF SMALL BUSINESS ENTERPRISE:
INDIVIDUAL, PARTNERSHIP, AND CORPORATION

By

Philip F. Postlewaite
Professor of Law
Northwestern University

John H. Birkeland
Shareholder Lentz, Evans and King P.C.

AMERICAN CASEBOOK SERIES®

WEST PUBLISHING CO.
ST. PAUL, MINN., 1997

COPYRIGHT © 1997 By WEST PUBLISHING CO.
610 Opperman Drive
P.O. Box 64526
St. Paul, MN 55164–0526
1–800–328–9352

ISBN 0–314–06603–9

 *TEXT IS PRINTED ON 10% POST CONSUMER RECYCLED PAPER*

"The most important thing a father can do for
his children is to love their mother."

Theodore Hesburgh

To Matthew
I love you!

P.F.P.

*

To
Mom, Joy, John, and Sarah
and in remembrance
of Dad

J.B.

*

Preface

This text differs from most current tax casebooks in a number of respects. Many tax texts, with their particularized analysis of the law's subtle twists, are more akin to treatises than casebooks. Unfortunately, when inundated by detail on entering the complex world of income taxation, readers often become confused and frustrated. This text seeks to mitigate that problem by focusing on major concepts and their underlying policies.

The text stresses a problem-solving approach through the use of numerous, short problems interspersed among the relevant materials. This problem-solving approach parallels a "real world" experience and thus helps to develop legal and analytic skills.

The text is organized around the life cycles, i.e., the organization, operation, and disposition, of the sole proprietorship, the partnership, and the corporation in the small business context. While it is still technically possible to receive partnership treatment through the use of a corporation, i.e., the Subchapter S corporation, minimal coverage of this alternative is presented since, in the future, most settings where an S corporation would prove valuable can now be accomplished through the use of a limited liability enterprise taxed as a partnership.

The material in this text and accompanying teacher's manual, both of which are current through April 1, 1996, reflect the valuable assistance of a variety of people to whom the authors express their thanks. Initially, the authors wish to thank the fine staffs of their respective institutions, the law firm of Lentz, Evans and King P.C. and Northwestern University School of Law. All have been particularly helpful and cooperative, in particular Cheri Zweig and Kathy Croan. Without their assistance, the project would still be in its embryonic stage. We further wish to thank the members of the Spring 1996 Partnership and Corporate Taxation class at Northwestern, on whom we inflicted a draft of this text. That usage, accompanied by student comments and reactions to the materials, permitted a far better refinement of the product than we would have attained operating in a vacuum. Particular thanks are due to John Pennell and Tom Manolakas for their assistance in the preparation of earlier versions of some of the partnership problems.

In order to ease the reading of the cases, some citations have been omitted without the use of ellipses, and in some instances footnotes in cases and other quoted material have been eliminated without indication. Any footnotes that were not edited retain their original numbers.

In this text, the word "section" or a section symbol (§) refers to sections of the Internal Revenue Code and the Regulations promulgated thereunder; Regulations or Reg., Proposed Regulations or Prop. Reg. refers to Treasury Department Regulations; Revenue Ruling or Rev. Rul.

refers to Rulings published by the Internal Revenue Service; Revenue Procedure or Rev. Proc. refers to Service-published Procedures; and Private Letter Ruling or Priv. Let. Rul. refers to Private Rulings (without precedential value) issued by the Service.

P.F.P.
J.H.B.

October, 1996

Acknowledgments

We would like to thank the following copyright holders for permission to use portions of their works which originally appeared in their publications.

Little, Brown and Company, Problems and Materials in Federal Income Taxation and the accompanying teacher's manual (4th edition 1994) by Guerin and Postlewaite.

Shepard's/McGraw-Hill, Partnership Taxation—Student Edition, Cases, Materials and Problems and the accompanying teacher's manual (1994 edition) by Willis, Pennell, and Postlewaite.

*

Summary of Contents

Table of Contents

*

Table of Cases

The principal cases are in bold type. Cases cited or discussed in the text are roman type. References are to pages. Cases cited in principal cases and within other quoted materials are not included.

Table of Internal Revenue Code Sections

Table of IRS Rulings and Procedures

*

Table of Treasury Regulations

*

PROBLEMS AND MATERIALS ON

THE TAXATION OF SMALL BUSINESS ENTERPRISE:

INDIVIDUAL, PARTNERSHIP, AND CORPORATION

*

Chapter 1

FORMATION OF SOLE
PROPRIETORSHIP

A. CHOICE OF ENTITY

For federal income tax purposes, the three major pillars of business activity have historically been the sole proprietorship, the partnership, and the corporation. In recent years, however, various hybrid entities have been authorized by state legislation. The most prevalent of these new entity types is the limited liability company. Some states also permit such entities as limited liability partnerships, limited liability limited partnerships, and other similar organizations.

The choice among organizing a business under state law as a sole proprietorship, as a partnership, as a hybrid entity such as a limited liability company, or as a corporation is governed primarily by three considerations: the applicable commercial law, the tax treatment of the business form chosen, and the investment and business preferences of the parties involved.

The principal commercial law difference between the legal status of a sole proprietorship or a traditional partnership and the legal status of a limited liability company or a corporation is the extent to which participants are held personally liable to business creditors. In a sole proprietorship or a general partnership, all entrepreneurs are jointly liable for debts and obligations of the enterprise. Additionally, even as regards a limited partnership in which the limited partners are immune from liability, there may be an individual general partner who is personally liable for the debts of the enterprise. Many states have modified this traditional treatment by allowing general partnerships or limited partnerships with individual limited partners to elect limited liability status for all of the members by merely filing a document of registration with the Secretary of State. Such registration makes a general partnership a "limited liability partnership" and a limited partnership a "limited liability limited partnership."

By way of contrast to the traditional partnership rules, all shareholders of a corporation are generally protected from creditors' claims regardless of their management activity. Where the principal participants are to manage the business and its creditors potentially could have claims beyond what they could collect from the business, the selection of the corporate vehicle has traditionally held a strong attraction. In addition, the limited liability feature protects a manager/shareholder's assets from claims against his co-owner's negligence, unlike a traditional partnership.

This fundamental commercial law distinction between partnerships and corporations has been blurred by the recent emergence of the limited liability company and the other similar types of entities noted above. Such a hybrid enterprise is a businessman's delight since it bestows immunity from liability on all of its members, yet, as discussed in Chapter 4, the Service has generally classified such entities as a partnership for tax purposes. Whether Congress will act to prevent this previously enigmatic treatment remains to be seen. The Internal Revenue Code does not create a separate status for these new entities, but instead taxes them as either a partnership or a corporation. The following discussion assumes that such hybrid entities will be taxed as partnerships rather than corporations for federal tax purposes.

The principal difference in the tax treatment of the three types of business organizations is the "pass-through" characteristic of sole proprietorships and partnerships. Corporations generally do not afford "pass through" treatment but instead are taxed as separate taxpayers. With regard to sole proprietorships, as the enterprise is commensurate with the individual status of its owner, all tax consequences are taken into account at the individual level. The pass through treatment of partnerships permits each item of income, gain, loss, deduction, or credit of the partnership to retain its character as determined at the partnership level when reported by the partner, without first being taxed at the partnership level. However, a corporation is taxed as an entity that exists independently of its shareholders and thus must report income and take tax credits and deductions as an entity, separate and distinct from its shareholders. Consequently, corporate income may be taxed twice by the time it reaches the pockets of its owners—once when earned by the corporation and a second time when distributed to the shareholders. While certain small business corporations can avoid this separate tax by electing "S Corporation" status for tax purposes; such usage will dramatically decline in the future due to the emergence of limited liability enterprises. Although the same state law protection against liability is available to such entities, greater flexibility for tax purposes arises through the use of a limited liability enterprise classified as a partnership. Thus, the election of S Corporation treatment should be the exception, not the rule.

1. SOLE PROPRIETORSHIPS

In most ways, given its pass through nature, a sole proprietorship resembles a partnership. Thus, much of the discussion which follows regarding partnerships is equally applicable to sole proprietorships.

Possibly the only distinguishing characteristic between the two is the fact that the sole proprietor resembles the recluse in societal terms. He/she does not join with others. The sole proprietor may not want to confront the difficulties associated with taking in a partner. From a tax and economic standpoint, the sole proprietor acts independently and vividly understands the maxim that "one eats what one kills." He or she will report the business activities on a separate schedule of the individual tax return form. As the sole proprietorship is no more than an individual engaged in income generating activity, the income derived therefrom is subject to the graduated rates, with a top bracket of 39.6 percent. See generally Guerin and Postlewaite, *Problems and Materials in Federal Income Taxation* ch. 10 (Little Brown 5th ed. 1997).

2. PARTNERSHIPS

Whenever two or more individuals associate in a common business for joint profit, they constitute a partnership. The partnership has no particular form and, in fact, is no more than a contract between the parties engaged in conducting the partnership business.

As with the selection of the corporate form of business, the selection of the partnership form is governed by considerations of commercial law and tax consequences. The most notable business disadvantage of the general partnership has traditionally been that it subjects all of the partners to joint liability for the debts of the partnership. In a business requiring considerable borrowing of funds, however, the owners may find that the distinction between the corporate form and the partnership form is more theoretical than practical in this area. In a corporate setting, the lenders may demand that the stockholders personally guarantee loans, in which case they are subject to personal liability on those loans just as if they were partners. They are also liable for their own acts of negligence. Thus, the limited liability feature of the corporation may provide little protection for personal assets. In addition, the new limited liability entities which are taxed as partnerships may make the use of a corporation unnecessary for obtaining liability protection.

The principal income tax characteristic of the partnership is that it is a conduit through which the various items of partnership income, gain, loss, deduction, or credit are passed to the partners unchanged. The partnership itself is not subject to tax. Thus, for example, if the partnership realizes tax-exempt interest or capital gain, those items of income retain their tax status when the partners report them as part of their distributive shares of partnership income. See generally Willis, Pennell, and Postlewaite, *Partnership Taxation* (Warren, Gorham & Lamont 6th ed. 1996).

3. CORPORATIONS - ℓ or ^

Both the commercial law and the tax rules may influence the decision of whether to conduct business as a corporation rather than as a partnership or sole proprietorship. A commercial law consideration that has frequently led to the decision to incorporate is the insulation the corporation provides its shareholders from personal liability for debts and tort claims of the business operation. An important tax factor in making such a decision is whether the corporate tax rates on business income are lower than those faced by individuals.

The distinctions in the commercial law governing the various forms of conducting business may now prove significantly less dramatic in practice than they were in the past. For example, although stockholders are not liable personally for the corporate debts, the reality of this protection as a practical matter should be investigated before deciding to incorporate. If the principal exposure to business creditors will be borrowing by the business, the stockholders may be required by the lenders to personally guarantee the loans. If so, the corporate shield from personal liability may not be material. Consideration also should be given to whether the business can be insured adequately against tort claims so that the investors face minimal exposure. On the other hand, liability protection may now be acquired through the selection of a limited liability company or similar entity without forfeiting the pass through benefits of partnership taxation.

The lowering of overall tax rates in recent years has reversed the impact of the Code rate structure on the choice of business organization. Prior to 1978, the maximum corporate tax rate was 48 percent on taxable income over $25,000 compared to a maximum individual rate of 70 percent for taxable income exceeding $215,400. At those rates, it often was wise to incorporate, pay tax on business operating income at the lower corporate level, retain the net proceeds, and hope eventually to realize, at the maximum capital gains tax rate of 28 percent, the investment appreciation through the sale of the corporate stock or the liquidation of the corporation.

The recent Congressional tampering with the tax rates for individuals and corporations, however, reduced the incentive to incorporate. Individual rates have been reduced to a maximum of 39.6 percent while the maximum corporate rate is 35 percent. The capital gain rate remains at 28% and may be lowered. Thus, corporate income for wealthy shareholders is subject to a maximum ultimate rate of 53.20 percent (35 percent as earned by the corporation and 28 percent capital gain rate on the remaining 65 percent on the sale or the liquidation of the stock) or 60.74 percent if the corporate income after taxes is distributed as a dividend, which is nondeductible to the distributing corporation and taxed at ordinary, rather than capital gain, rates to the individual recipients. See generally Bittker and Eustice, *Federal Income Taxation of Corporations and Shareholders* (Warren, Gorham, and Lamont 6th ed. 1994).

B. SOLE PROPRIETORSHIPS—LACK
OF SEPARATE EXISTENCE

The concept of a sole proprietorship as a business enterprise builds on the student's study of the introductory tax class. See generally Guerin and Postlewaite, *Problems and Materials in Federal Income Taxation* chs. 1–10 (Little Brown 5th ed. 1997). The individual tax provisions of the Code address and encompass sole proprietorship activity. However, nowhere in the Code is the concept of a sole proprietorship separately addressed. Instead, a sole proprietorship and the economic activities attendant thereto are covered by the general taxing provisions for individuals. For tax purposes, the sole proprietorship does not possess a separate existence.

For example, assume that an individual is a lawyer engaged in practice by herself. Her billings for the year are $80,000 in fees, offset by expenses of $25,000 (rent of $12,000, salary for her secretary of $8,000, and other expenses of $5,000). Additionally, assume that her nonbusiness, investment income from dividends and interest totals $10,-000. While one typically would describe the lawyer as earning $55,000 from her business and $10,000 from her investment efforts, the Code combines these amounts for tax purposes.

Employing the taxing formula for individuals mandated by the Code, the taxpayer first determines her gross income. Under § 61(a)(2), gross income includes the gross, not net, income derived from business activities. Additionally, § 61(a)(4) and (5) force the inclusion of interest income and dividend income in gross income. Thus, the taxpayer has gross income of $90,000.

Moving further through the taxing formula, § 62(a)(1) permits the deduction of trade or business expenses under § 162 in arriving at the taxpayer's adjusted gross income. Under § 162, her expenses of $25,000 for rent, salary, and other items should meet the requirements for deductibility. Consequently, the taxpayer's adjusted gross income equals $65,000. Thereafter, the taxpayer's itemized deductions (or standard deduction if greater) and personal exemptions will be taken into account in determining her taxable income. The appropriate individual tax rate would then be applied to such taxable income to determine her tax due.

C. TRANSFER OF PROPERTY TO
A SOLE PROPRIETORSHIP

As discussed in B. above, the sole proprietorship is not an entity separate and distinct from the individual sole proprietor. Thus, many of the tax recognition issues which attend the transfer of property to a partnership or a corporation do not exist in the formation of a sole proprietorship. When a taxpayer "transfers" an asset from his personal or investment capacity to his sole proprietorship, few, if any, income tax consequences will arise.

The one area for such "transfers" where rules *are* specified by the Regulations is the conversion of personal assets to business or investment assets where such assets become, by such conversion, subject to depreciation and loss allowance. Personal assets are not depreciable and may not generate an allowable tax loss on disposition. In order to prevent manipulation of these rules upon conversion of such assets from personal to business usage, the Regulations provide that the basis for depreciation and loss purposes of a personal asset "contributed" to a sole proprietorship is its fair market value at the time of conversion if that amount is less than its tax adjusted basis. If the property's fair market value is greater than its tax adjusted basis, the property's adjusted basis is used for computing the depreciation deduction and for loss purposes.

Chapter 2

OPERATIONS OF SOLE PROPRIETORSHIP

A. INTRODUCTION

As previously noted, a sole proprietorship for tax purposes is not separate and distinct from its owner. Once formed, the operational activities of the sole proprietorship continue to be governed by the concepts encountered by the reader in his or her introductory tax class. See generally Guerin and Postlewaite, *Problems and Materials in Federal Income Taxation* (Little Brown 5th ed. 1997). Given the tendency of many introductory tax courses to treat lightly the income tax consequences of business and property transactions, this textbook pauses to discuss and/or review some of these basic tax concepts as they apply to the daily operational activities of a sole proprietorship. Many of these concepts are foundational for a thorough understanding of partnership taxation and corporate taxation.

The primary concepts arising in the operational business context are (1) the acquisition of property and the determination of its basis for purposes of depreciation or amortization as well as for calculating gain or loss upon its disposition, (2) the deductibility of business expenses, (3) the recognition and timing of income or loss from the disposition of inventory property or property used in the trade or business of the sole proprietorship, and (4) the characterization and the allowance of the income or loss from these activities.

B. ACQUISITION OF PROPERTY— ADJUSTED BASIS

A typical sole proprietorship conducting business activities will require the acquisition of numerous assets essential to the business. These assets may run the gamut from office machinery to plant and equipment. The assets may be contributed by the business owner from his own pool of property acquired outright for cash or may be acquired by employing various financing techniques.

7

Contributed personal property takes a basis for gain purposes equal to its basis in the hands of the owner and a basis for loss purposes equal to the lesser of its fair market value or its basis in the hands of the owner. Under § 1012, the basis for an acquired asset is determined by its cost. In the case of a cash acquisition, basis is easily determined as it equals the purchase price. The more difficult issue is the determination of the taxpayer's basis when the acquisition of such property is financed either by the extension of credit by the seller or the procurement of a loan from a third party lender. See generally Guerin and Postlewaite, *Problems and Materials in Federal Income Taxation* ch. 2 (Little Brown 5th ed. 1997).

1. DEBT INCURRED IN THE ACQUISITION OF PROPERTY

In *Crane v. Commissioner,* 331 U.S. 1 (1947), the Supreme Court propounded one of the most important principles of tax law—the entire amount of any debt incurred in the acquisition of property generally is included in the purchaser's cost basis at the time the property is acquired. The increase need not await a later date when the debt is paid. For example, if the taxpayer purchases property worth $100,000 in exchange for $20,000 cash plus an $80,000 note secured by a first mortgage to the seller, the taxpayer-purchaser has a $100,000 cost basis at the time of acquisition. The taxpayer's subsequent mortgage payments have no impact on the tax basis of the property.

The *Crane* rule is premised on the assumption that the purchaser will satisfy the debt over time. Thus, regardless of when the purchaser pays the $80,000, the long-term consequences are the same as if the property had been purchased for cash. If, however, the obligation is not discharged by the time the purchaser disposes of the property, the unsatisfied amount of the obligation is debt relief and typically is included in the amount realized upon the property's disposition. In summary, debt incurred on acquisition and debt relief on disposition are treated respectively as cash paid and received.

Debt incurred on an acquisition may take several forms. The purchaser may (1) provide the seller with the purchaser's promissory note, in which case, barring a provision to the contrary, the buyer is personally liable to the seller in case of default; (2) assume an existing debt of the seller, in which case the buyer becomes personally liable to a third party; (3) acquire the property with funds obtained from a third party bank or other lender, upon which debt the purchaser is personally liable; (4) merely acquire the property subject to an existing debt to a third party without becoming personally liable, in which case only the purchaser's rights to the property are affected on default; or (5) acquire the property from the seller for a down payment and the execution of a promissory note to the seller or to a third party lender without recourse against the purchaser. The debt in the first three situations may entitle the lender to reach the borrower's personal assets if there is a default on the loan (a recourse debt), while in the last two situations only the property itself can be reached for payment in the case of default (a nonrecourse debt).

Some commentators have argued that nonrecourse debt should not be included in the cost basis of property because the debtor can abandon the property and lose only his rights in the encumbered asset. Other commentators contend that as long as the fair market value of the encumbered property exceeds the amount of the outstanding nonrecourse debt, the obligor has equity in the property and generally will continue to service the debt to protect this interest. Based on this latter view and the economic reality it reflects, courts have held that a nonrecourse purchase money debt is included in the purchaser's cost of acquiring property.

CRANE v. COMMISSIONER

331 U.S. 1 (1947).

MR. CHIEF JUSTICE VINSON delivered the opinion of the Court.

The question here is how a taxpayer who acquires depreciable property subject to an unassumed mortgage, holds it for a period, and finally sells it still so encumbered, must compute her taxable gain.

Petitioner was the sole beneficiary and the executrix of the will of her husband, who died January 11, 1932. He then owned an apartment building and lot subject to a mortgage,[1] which secured a principal debt of $255,000.00 and interest in default of $7,042.50. As of that date, the property was appraised for federal estate tax purposes at a value exactly equal to the total amount of this encumbrance. Shortly after her husband's death, petitioner entered into an agreement with the mortgagee whereby she was to continue to operate the property—collecting the rents, paying for necessary repairs, labor, and other operating expenses, and reserving $200.00 monthly for taxes—and was to remit the net rentals to the mortgagee. This plan was followed for nearly seven years, during which period petitioner reported the gross rentals as income, and claimed and was allowed deductions for taxes and operating expenses paid on the property, for interest paid on the mortgage, and for the physical exhaustion of the building. Meanwhile, the arrearage of interest increased to $15,857.71. On November 29, 1938, with the mortgagee threatening foreclosure, petitioner sold to a third party for $3,000.00 cash, subject to the mortgage, and paid $500.00 expenses of sale.

Petitioner reported a taxable gain of $1,250.00. Her theory was that the "property" which she had acquired in 1932 and sold in 1938 was only the equity, or the excess in the value of the apartment building and lot over the amount of the mortgage. This equity was of zero value when she acquired it. No depreciation could be taken on a zero value.[2]

---

1. The record does not show whether he was personally liable for the debt.

2. This position is, of course, inconsistent with her practice in claiming such deductions in each of the years the property was held. The deductions so claimed and allowed by the Commissioner were in the total amount of $25,500.00.

Neither she nor her vendee ever assumed the mortgage, so, when she sold the equity, the amount she realized on the sale was the net cash received, or $2,500.00. This sum less the zero basis constituted her gain * * *.

The Commissioner, however, determined that petitioner realized a net taxable gain of $23,767.03. His theory was that the "property" acquired and sold was not the equity, as petitioner claimed, but rather the physical property itself, or the owner's rights to possess, use, and dispose of it, undiminished by the mortgage. The original basis thereof was $262,042.50, its appraised value in 1932. Of this value $55,000.00 was allocable to land and $207,042.50 to building. During the period that petitioner held the property, there was an allowable depreciation of $28,045.10 on the building, so that the adjusted basis of the building at the time of sale was $178,997.40. The amount realized on the sale was said to include not only the $2,500.00 net cash receipts, but also the principal amount of the mortgage subject to which the property was sold, both totaling $257,500.00. The selling price was allocable in the proportion, $54,471.15 to the land and $203,028.85 to the building * * *.

Logically, the first step under this scheme is to determine the unadjusted basis of the property, and the dispute in this case is as to the construction to be given the term "property." If "property," as used in that provision, means the same thing as "equity," it would necessarily follow that the basis of petitioner's property was zero, as she contends. If, on the contrary, it means the land and building themselves, or the owner's legal rights in them, undiminished by the mortgage, the basis was $262,042.50.

We think that the reasons for favoring one of the latter constructions are of overwhelming weight. In the first place, the words of statutes—including revenue acts—should be interpreted where possible in their ordinary, everyday senses. The only relevant definitions of "property" to be found in the principal standard dictionaries are the two favored by the Commissioner, i.e., either that "property" is the physical thing which is a subject of ownership, or that it is the aggregate of the owner's rights to control and dispose of that thing. "Equity" is not given as a synonym, nor do either of the foregoing definitions suggest that it could be correctly so used. Indeed, "equity" is defined as "the value of a property * * * above the total of the liens * * *." The contradistinction could hardly be more pointed. Strong countervailing considerations would be required to support a contention that Congress in using the word "property," meant "equity" * * *.

A further reason why the word "property" should not be construed to mean "equity" is the bearing such construction would have on the allowance of deductions for depreciation and on the collateral adjustments of basis.

Section 23(1) permits deduction from gross income of "a reasonable allowance for the exhaustion, wear and tear of property * * *." Section 23(n) declare[s] that the "basis upon which exhaustion, wear and tear

* * * are to be allowed" is the basis "for the purpose of determining the gain upon the sale" of the property, which is the basis "adjusted ... for exhaustion, wear and tear * * * to the extent allowed (but not less than the amount allowable). * * * "

Under these provisions, if the mortgagor's equity were the basis, it would also be the original basis from which depreciation allowances are deducted. If it is, and if the amount of the annual allowances were to be computed on that value, as would then seem to be required, they will represent only a fraction of the cost of the corresponding physical exhaustion, and any recoupment by the mortgagor of the remainder of that cost can be effected only by the reduction of his taxable gain in the year of sale. If, however, the amount of the annual allowances were to be computed on the value of the property, and then deducted from an equity basis, we would in some instances have to accept deductions from a minus basis or deny deductions altogether. The Commissioner also argues that taking the mortgagor's equity as the basis would require the basis to be changed with each payment on the mortgage, and that the attendant problem of repeatedly recomputing basis and annual allowances would be a tremendous accounting burden on both the Commissioner and the taxpayer. Moreover, the mortgagor would acquire control over the timing of his depreciation allowances.

* * * It may be added that the Treasury has never furnished a guide through the maze of problems that arise in connection with depreciating an equity basis, but, on the contrary, has consistently permitted the amount of depreciation allowances to be computed on the full value of the property, and subtracted from it as a basis. Surely, Congress' long-continued acceptance of this situation gives it full legislative endorsement.

We conclude that the proper basis is the value of the property, undiminished by mortgages thereon, and that the correct basis here was $262,042.50. The next step is to ascertain what adjustments are required * * * in making any depreciation adjustments whatsoever.

* * * The Tax Court found on adequate evidence that the apartment house was property of a kind subject to physical exhaustion, that it was used in taxpayer's trade or business, and consequently that the taxpayer would have been entitled to a depreciation allowance, except that, in the opinion of that Court, the basis of the property was zero, and it was thought that depreciation could not be taken on a zero basis. As we have just decided that the correct basis of the property was not zero, but $262,042.50, we avoid this difficulty, and conclude that an adjustment should be made as the Commissioner determined.

Petitioner urges to the contrary that she was not entitled to depreciation deductions, whatever the basis of the property, because the law allows them only to one who actually bears the capital loss, and here the loss was not hers but the mortgagee's. We do not see, however, that she has established her factual premise. There was no finding of the Tax Court to that effect, nor to the effect that the value of the property was ever less than the amount of the lien. Nor was there evidence in the record, or any indication that petitioner could produce evidence, that this was so. * * *

* * * At last we come to the problem of determining the "amount realized" on the 1938 sale. * * * If the "property" to be valued on the date of acquisition is the property free of liens, the "property" to be priced on a subsequent sale must be the same thing.

Starting from this point, we could not accept petitioner's contention that the $2,500.00 net cash was all she realized on the sale except on the absurdity that she sold a quarter-of-a-million dollar property for roughly one percent of its value, and took a 99 percent loss. Actually, petitioner does not urge this. She argues, conversely, that because only $2,500.00 was realized on the sale, the "property" sold must have been the equity only, and that consequently we are forced to accept her contention as to the meaning of "property." We adhere, however, to what we have already said on the meaning of "property," and we find that the absurdity is avoided by our conclusion that the amount of the mortgage is properly included in the "amount realized" on the sale.

Petitioner concedes that if she had been personally liable on the mortgage and the purchaser had either paid or assumed it, the amount so paid or assumed would be considered a part of the "amount realized." The cases so deciding have already repudiated the notion that there must be an actual receipt by the seller himself of "money" or "other property," in their narrowest senses. It was thought to be decisive that one section of the Act must be construed so as not to defeat the intention of another or to frustrate the Act as a whole, and that the taxpayer was the "beneficiary" of the payment in "as real and substantial [a sense] as if the money had been paid it and then paid over by it to its creditors."

Both these points apply to this case. The first has been mentioned already. As for the second, we think that a mortgagor, not personally liable on the debt, who sells the property subject to the mortgage and for additional consideration, realizes a benefit in the amount of the mortgage as well as the boot.[37] If a purchaser pays boot, it is immaterial as to our problem whether the mortgagor is also to receive money from the purchaser to discharge the mortgage prior to sale, or whether he is merely to transfer subject to the mortgage—it may make a difference to the purchaser and to the mortgagee, but not to the mortgagor. Or put in another way, we are no more concerned with whether the mortgagor is, strictly speaking, a debtor on the mortgage, than we are with whether the benefit to him is, strictly speaking, a receipt of money or property. We are rather concerned with the reality that an owner of property, mortgaged at a figure less than that at which the property will sell, must and will treat the conditions of the mortgage exactly as if they were his

37. Obviously, if the value of the property is less than the amount of the mortgage, a mortgagor who is not personally liable cannot realize a benefit equal to the mortgage. Consequently, a different problem might be encountered where a mortgagor abandoned the property or transferred it subject to the mortgage without receiving boot. That is not this case.

personal obligations. If he transfers subject to the mortgage, the benefit to him is as real and substantial as if the mortgage were discharged, or as if a personal debt in an equal amount had been assumed by another.

Therefore we conclude that the Commissioner was right in determining that petitioner realized $257,500.00 on the sale of this property.

Petitioner contends that the result we have reached taxes her on what is not income within the meaning of the Sixteenth Amendment. If this is because only the direct receipt of cash is thought to be income in the constitutional sense, her contention is wholly without merit. If it is because the entire transaction is thought to have been "by all dictates of common sense * * * a ruinous disaster," as it was termed in her brief, we disagree with her premise. She was entitled to depreciation deductions for a period of nearly seven years, and she actually took them in almost the allowable amount. The crux of this case, really, is whether the law permits her to exclude allowable deductions from consideration in computing gain. We have already showed that, if it does, the taxpayer can enjoy a double deduction, in effect, on the same loss of assets. The Sixteenth Amendment does not require that result any more than does the Act itself.

Affirmed.

Problem 2–1

Frances agrees to acquire Sam's printing business and operate it as a sole proprietorship. What would Frances' cost basis be in each of the following examples if she purchased equipment for her sole proprietorship worth $100,000 from Sam for the stipulated consideration?

a. Frances paid Sam $100,000 cash, which she had borrowed minutes earlier from the First National Bank.

b. Frances agreed to personally assume a $100,000 debt secured by the acquired property.

c. Frances gave a $100,000 nonrecourse note to Sam.

d. Frances assumed an $80,000 obligation encumbering the acquired property and gave Sam a nonrecourse note for $20,000.

e. Frances did not assume the $80,000 obligation in *d* above but agreed to acquire the property "subject to" the debt. In addition, she paid $12,000 cash, which she had borrowed from the First National Bank on a nonrecourse basis, and agreed to pay a debt of $8,000 owing to Sam's paper supplier.

2.   DEBT INCURRED AFTER PROPERTY ACQUISITION

As the *Crane* decision illustrates, the basis of property acquired by purchase generally equals the purchase price—that is, cash plus liabilities incurred in acquiring the property. Although the *Crane* case decided the issue for debt incurred in the acquisition of property, it did not provide any guidance concerning debt incurred after the date of acquisition. For example, what is the tax result when a taxpayer purchases property to be used in his sole proprietorship for $100,000 cash on January 1, 1996, and on January 1, 1998, after the property has appreciated in value to $200,000, borrows $140,000 from the bank by executing a first mortgage on the property? This example raises the important issue of whether the property's basis increases by the $140,-000 post-acquisition debt incurred. Is the post-acquisition loan considered a "cost" of acquiring the property pursuant to § 1012?

Woodsam Associates, Inc. v. Commissioner, 198 F.2d 357 (2d Cir. 1952), held that when property is mortgaged as security for a loan for a purpose other than the property's acquisition, no current tax consequences arise because there has been no sale, exchange, or other disposition. The same result occurs if the liability is a nonrecourse debt in excess of the basis of the encumbered property. Such debt does not represent the cost of the property; thus, it is not included in basis.

In *Woodsam*, the taxpayer refinanced real property by giving the lender a nonrecourse mortgage in excess of the property's basis. Arguing that refinancing constituted a taxable disposition, the taxpayer urged the court to find taxable gain on the transaction, with a concomitant increase in basis to the extent of that gain. The court disagreed with the taxpayer's theory and held that the refinancing was not a taxable event. Because the taxpayer had not disposed of the property but remained its owner after the refinancing, the court concluded that no gain was realized and the basis of the property was unaffected. It should be noted, however, that if the loan proceeds were utilized to improve or otherwise enhance the property, a basis increase would occur to the extent thereof.

C. DEPRECIATION AND AMORTIZATION EXPENSES AND OTHER BUSINESS DEDUCTIONS

Code References: §§ 167(a), (c); 168(a)–(e); 179; 197(a)–(e); 263(a).

Regulations: §§ 1.167(a)–1, (a)–3, (a)–10, (b)–0, (b)–1, (b)–2, (g)–1; Prop.Reg. § 1.168–1.

In order to stimulate economic growth, encourage investment in technological innovations, and permit a recoupment of business—or profit-oriented expenditures, Congress has provided a means by which taxpayers can recover capital invested in certain assets that have a finite physical or technological life. The depreciation and amortization provisions, § 167, § 168, and § 197, allow a deduction over a period of time for the costs of most business-related capital expenditures of a sole proprietorship. Section 167 was the predecessor of § 168, which incorporated many of the concepts and provisions of § 167. Expenditures for tangible or intangible property that will be used for more than one year and are incurred in producing income are classified as capital expenditures. Examples of capital expenditures include the acquisition of a typewriter, delivery van, or office furnishings. See generally Guerin and Postlewaite, *Problems and Materials in Federal Income Taxation* ch. 6 (Little Brown 5th ed. 1997). This allowable deduction for depreciation and amortization often provides one of the major offsets to proprietorship revenues in determining the taxable income of the business.

1. THE CONCEPT OF DEPRECIATION

The underlying rationale for the § 167 depreciation allowance is similar to that for the § 162 business expense deduction. Both sections permit deductions in an attempt to reflect the costs that a business incurs in producing income, thereby ensuring that net income rather than gross income is taxed.

A tenet of general financial accounting and of tax accounting requires the matching of expenses with the income they generate. The only way to properly match a capital expenditure to the annual income it generates is to capitalize and amortize the cost of the asset over its useful life. Thus, the entire cost of a capital expenditure is not expensed or deducted in the year in which it is incurred. Instead, a portion of the cost is matched with a particular accounting period and gradually expensed as a depreciation deduction. Depreciation deductions are taken over the property's useful life—i.e., the years in which the property is expected to be used in the business. Accordingly, the useful life of the asset must be finite or ascertainable. Assets such as land, which have an infinite useful life, are not depreciable.

The following example illustrates the depreciation concept. Assume that a calendar-year taxpayer, Harry, starts a new business selling legal outlines to law students. Harry purchases new business equipment for $20,000. Harry assumes that the equipment will be obsolete in this particular business in four years (its useful life), after which time its estimated salvage value will be $5,000. Because Harry plans to dispose of the equipment at the end of four years, before it has lost all value, only $15,000 of its cost will have been used. This $15,000 represents the depreciable cost of the asset.

How is the depreciable cost to be allocated to the four accounting periods in which the equipment is used? One alternative would be to allocate the entire cost to the first year as a current deduction. Section 263 prevents this result, which would have the effect of understating the first year's income and overstating the income in years 2, 3, and 4. If Harry were permitted a current deduction for the entire cost of the equipment, year 1 would reflect a deduction for the total cost of an expense that was not depleted in that year. In years 2, 3, and 4, the business would receive the benefit of a working asset without bearing any of its cost. Because the new business equipment has a useful life of more than one year, the cost of acquiring the equipment is a capital expenditure and not currently deductible.

Section 167(b), before amendment, listed the methods by which a "reasonable allowance" for depreciation could be computed. Harry could, for example, have elected the straight-line method of depreciation, which had the effect of evenly allocating the expense over the useful life of the asset. The annual allowable straight-line depreciation deduction was computed by dividing the depreciable cost of the asset by its useful life according to the following formula:

$$\text{Annual straight-line depreciation} = \frac{\text{Adjusted basis of asset—Salvage value}}{\text{Useful life}}$$

Thus, Harry would have been entitled to an annual deduction of $3,750:

$$\frac{\$20,000 - \$5,000}{4} = \$3,750$$

Section 167(b) also allowed accelerated methods of depreciation including the declining balance method. Accelerated depreciation provides a potential benefit to small business by allowing deductions to be taken earlier than if straight line depreciation were used. If Harry elected to use such a method, his rate of deduction was determined by the nature of the asset being depreciated and the rate of allowable straight-line depreciation. Under that method, the depreciation rate was calculated by multiplying the applicable percentage, depending on whether the property was new or used, by the straight-line rate. If Harry acquired used property, he was limited to a rate of 150 percent or less of allowable straight-line depreciation. The rate permitted for new tangible property with a useful life of three years or more was 200 percent or double declining balance.

In the above hypothetical, Harry's equipment, which was new when purchased, had a four-year useful life. Harry therefore was entitled to elect the double declining balance method. Under that method, depreciation for a given year was determined by applying twice the straight-line rate to the adjusted basis (original cost less depreciation taken in prior years) as of the beginning of that year. Harry's straight-line rate of depreciation was 25 percent per year. His rate of depreciation for the first year under the double declining balance method, therefore, was 50 percent (2 × 25%). The declining balance method did not deduct the salvage value from the adjusted basis of the asset. However, the salvage value limited the total amount of deductions that could be taken with regard to the depreciable asset.

Harry's deductions over the useful life of the new business equipment therefore was computed as follows. In the year of purchase, Harry deducted 50 percent of his $20,000 purchase price, or $10,000. His declining balance (adjusted basis) thereafter was $10,000. In year 2, his deduction was $5,000 (50% × $10,000) and his balance declined to $5,000. Thus, in year 3, Harry reached the salvage value limitation and could take no further depreciation deductions on his new business equipment.

2. THE ACCELERATED COST RECOVERY SYSTEM

The accelerated cost recovery system (ACRS), enacted in 1981 and modified in 1986, illustrates Congressional efforts to manipulate the depreciation rules in order to achieve economic goals by permitting taxpayers to depreciate assets at a more rapid rate than existed under pre–1982 law. In addition to focusing on economic goals, the ACRS eliminates two areas of controversy that existed under § 167: the determinations of useful life and salvage value.

Previously, a taxpayer would contend that the salvage value of the asset was low in order to maximize deductions. In response, the Service would, of course, argue for a higher salvage value. Section 168 disregards salvage value in computing cost recovery, removing it as a potential issue for litigation. See § 168(b)(4). A similar area of controversy existed with regard to the useful life of an asset. Taxpayers favored short useful lives (to accelerate deductions to earlier years), while the Service argued for long ones (to defer deductions). ACRS eliminates this area of conflict by providing statutory periods over which allowable deductions may be taken. See § 168(c).

TAX REFORM ACT OF 1986

H.R.Rep. No. 841, 99th Cong., 2d Sess. II–38 (1986).

CAPITAL COST PROVISIONS

A. COST RECOVERY: DEPRECIATION * * *

1. Accelerated Depreciation

a. Cost Recovery Classes * * *

Conference Agreement

In General

The conference agreement modifies the Accelerated Cost Recovery System (ACRS) for property placed in service after December 31, 1986 * * *.

The conference agreement provides more accelerated depreciation for the revised three-year, five-year and 10–year classes, reclassifies certain assets according to their present class life (or "ADR * midpoints," Rev.Proc. 83–35, 1983–1 C.B. 745), and creates a seven-year class, a 20–year class, a 27.5–year class, and a [39.5]–year class. The conference agreement prescribes depreciation methods for each ACRS class * * *. Eligible personal property and certain real property are assigned among a three-year class, a five-year class, a seven-year class, a 10–year class, a 15–year class, or a 20–year class.

The depreciation method applicable to property included in the three-year, five-year, seven-year, and 10–year classes is the double de-

---

* The generally employed depreciation method prior to the enactment of § 168.— Eds.

clining balance method, switching to the straight-line method at a time to maximize the depreciation allowance. For property in the 15–year and 20–year class, the conference agreement applies the 150–percent declining balance method, switching to the straight-line method at a time to maximize the depreciation allowance. For property in the 15–year and 20–year class, the conference agreement applies the 150–percent declining balance method, switching to the straight-line method at a time to maximize the depreciation allowance. The cost of section 1250 real property generally is recovered over 27.5 years for residential rental property and [39.5] years for nonresidential property, using the straight-line method.

Classes of Property

Property is classified as follows:

Three-year class.—ADR midpoints of 4 years or less, except automobiles and light trucks, and adding horses which are assigned to the three-year class under present law.

Five-year class.—ADR midpoints of more than 4 years and less than 10 years, and adding automobiles, light trucks, qualified technological equipment, computer-based telephone central office switching equipment, research and experimentation property, and geothermal, ocean thermal, solar, and wind energy properties, and biomass properties that constitute qualifying small power production facilities (within the meaning of section 3(17)(C) of the Federal Power Act).

Seven-year class.—ADR midpoints of 10 years and less than 16 years, and adding single-purpose agricultural or horticultural structures and property with no ADR midpoint that is not classified elsewhere.

10–year class.—ADR midpoints of 16 years and less than 20 years.

15–year class.—ADR midpoints of 20 years and less than 25 years, and adding municipal wastewater treatment plants, and telephone distribution plant and comparable equipment used for the two-way exchange of voice and data communications.

20–year class.—ADR midpoints of 25 years and more, other than section 1250 real property with an ADR midpoint of 27.5 years and more, and adding municipal sewers.

27.5–year class.—Residential rental property (including manufactured homes that are residential rental property and elevators and escalators).

[39.5]–year class.—Nonresidential real property (section 1250 real property that is not residential rental property and that either does not have an ADR midpoint or whose ADR midpoint is 27.5 years or more, including elevators and escalators) * * *.

c. *Changes in classification* * * *

Under the conference agreement, the Treasury Department has the authority to adjust class lives of most assets (other than residential rental property and nonresidential real property) based on actual experience. Any new class life will be used for determining the classification of such property and in applying an alternative depreciation system.

Any class life prescribed under the Secretary's authority must reflect the anticipated useful life, and the anticipated decline in value over time, of an asset to the industry or other group. Useful life means the economic life span of property over all users combined and not, as under prior law, the typical period over which a taxpayer holds the property. Evidence indicative of the useful life of property which the Secretary is expected to take into account in prescribing a class life includes the depreciation practices followed by taxpayers for book purposes with respect to the property. It also includes useful lives experienced by taxpayers, according to their reports. It further includes independent evidence of minimal useful life—the terms for which new property is leased, used under a service contract, or financed—and independent evidence of the decline in value of an asset over time, such as is afforded by resale price data. If resale price data is used to prescribe class lives, such resale price data should be adjusted downward to remove the effects of historical inflation. This adjustment provides a larger measure of depreciation than in the absence of such an adjustment. Class lives using this data should be determined such that the present value of straight-line depreciation deductions over the class life, discounted at an appropriate real rate of interest, is equal to the present value of what the estimated decline in value of the asset would be in the absence of inflation.

Initial studies are expected to concentrate on property that now has no ADR midpoint. * * *

4. *Accounting Conventions*

a. *Half–Year Convention*

Conference Agreement

* * * All property placed in service or disposed of during a taxable year is treated as placed in service or disposed of at the midpoint of such year. In the case of a taxable year less than 12 months, property is treated as being in service for half the number of months in such taxable year. * * *

7. *Expensing* * * *

The Senate amendment provides a [$17,500] ceiling for expensing for taxpayers whose total investment in tangible personal property is $200,000 or less. For other taxpayers, for every dollar of investment in excess of $200,000, the [$17,500] ceiling is reduced by one dollar. The amount eligible to be expensed is limited to the taxable income derived from the active trade or business in which the property is used. The difference between expensing and ACRS deductions is recaptured if property is converted to nonbusiness use at any time before the end of the property's recovery period. * * *

The conference agreement generally follows the Senate amendment, but provides that the amount eligible to be expensed is limited to the taxable income derived from any trade or business. Married individuals filing separate returns are treated as one taxpayer for purposes of determining the amount which may be expensed and the total amount of investment in tangible personal property.

Note

Once a taxpayer determines that property is subject to § 168, the provisions are mandatory unless straight-line depreciation is elected under § 168(b)(5). Consider the effect of § 168 on the above described (p. 15) Harry. Under those facts, the applicable depreciation method, the applicable convention, and the applicable recovery period must be determined. Assume that the class life of Harry's new asset is 3–year property as defined in § 168(e)(1). Under § 168(b)(1), Harry must determine the amount of his recovery according to the 200 percent declining balance, switching to straight line at that time when it produces a larger allowance unless he elects to depreciate the asset under the optional straight-line method of § 168(b)(5). Under § 168(d)(1), the applicable convention is the half-year convention. As a result, a half-year of depreciation is allowed in the first year, regardless of when the property was placed in service. Thus, in year 1, Harry's allowable deduction is $6,667 (66⅔% × ½ × $20,000). In year 2, he can deduct $8,889 (66⅔% × $13,334). In year 3, he can deduct $2,963 (66⅔ % × $4,444). In year 4, he can deduct $1,482 (the greater of 66⅔% × $1,482 ($988) or the straight-line amount of $1,482). Harry will, therefore, have deducted 100 percent of the cost of the asset. At the end of the recovery period, Harry's basis in the asset is $0 because he has recovered his entire investment. See § 1016(a)(2). The property's salvage value is irrelevant under § 168.

Problem 2–2

On January 1, 1997, William paid $12,500 for an asset to be used in his sole proprietorship trade or business. Assuming the asset has a useful life of four years and a salvage value of $2,500, compute William's annual depreciation deduction and accumulated depreciation at the end of each of the four years under the following methods.

a. Straight-line method. See Reg. § 1.167(b)–1(a).

b. Double declining balance method. See Reg. § 1.167(b)–2(a).

c. Accelerated cost recovery method assuming the asset is three-year class property. See § 168.

d. Same as *c,* but William elects a three-year straight-line approach.

e. Same as *c,* but William elects to apply § 179.

f. In *a* through *e,* what basis adjustments are required? See § 1016(a)(2).

3. AMORTIZATION OF INTANGIBLE ASSETS
Code Reference: §§ 197(a)–(e); 1060.

It has long been recognized that the cost of an intangible asset may be amortized over its useful life. Reg. § 1.167(a)–3. Historically, the problem in the area was evidencing the useful life of the intangible asset. As a consequence, assets incapable of precise measurement did not qualify for a recoupment of costs under the Regulations. By way of contrast, a purchased asset susceptible of precise valuation and an accurate determination of its useful life (such as a three-year covenant not to compete) qualified for straight-line amortization. Further complicating the valuation issue was the fact that many intangible assets were purchased as part of an overall business rather than as a separate independent asset. As a consequence, a determination of the purchase price attributable to the asset was more difficult.

In response to many of these problems, Congress enacted § 197 in 1993 to permit the amortization of many intangible assets, including goodwill, over a statutorily stipulated 15–year useful life. This change in the tax law eliminates the burdensome requirements of establishing the useful life of the asset, proving that the intangible asset is separate from goodwill, and in conjunction with § 1060 determining the portion of the purchase price allocable to the amortizable intangible asset.

While helpful in clarifying amortization procedure for intangible assets, § 197 presents various new advantages and disadvantages to the business enterprise. For instance, an intangible asset such as a three-year covenant not to compete, which may have previously been amortized over a useful life of three years, is now required to be amortized over the considerably longer 15–year period, even though the cash paid to the noncompeting party may have been paid over the three years or even entirely when the agreement was executed. On the other hand, an intangible asset such as a patent, which was typically amortized over a useful life of 17 years, can now be amortized in full over 15 years. Goodwill, which previously could not be amortized at all because of its indeterminable useful life, is now subject to the 15–year rule.

It is important to note that § 197 is not applicable to many self-created and certain other intangible assets. § 197(c)(2). Consequently, even after the enactment of § 197, not all intangible assets qualify for amortization.

OMNIBUS RECONCILIATION ACT OF 1993

H.Rep. No. 213, 103rd Cong., 1st Sess. 689 (1993).

F.   TREATMENT OF INTANGIBLES

1.   *Amortization of Goodwill and Certain Intangibles*

Present Law

In determining taxable income for Federal income tax purposes, a taxpayer is allowed depreciation or amortization deductions for the cost or other basis of intangible property that is used in a trade or business or held for the production of income if the property has a limited useful life that may be determined with reasonable accuracy. Treas.Reg. sec. 1.167(a)–(3). These Treasury Regulations also state that no depreciation deductions are allowed with respect to goodwill.

The U.S. Supreme Court recently held that a taxpayer able to prove that a particular asset can be valued, and that the asset has a limited useful life which can be ascertained with reasonable accuracy, may depreciate the value over the useful life regardless of how much the asset appears to reflect the expectancy of continued patronage. However, the Supreme Court also characterized the taxpayer's burden of proof as "substantial" and stated that it "often will prove too great to bear." Newark Morning Ledger Co. v. United States, 507 U.S. 546, at 566 (1993).

Reasons for Change

The Federal income tax treatment of the costs of acquiring intangible assets is a source of considerable controversy between taxpayers and the Internal Revenue Service. Disputes arise concerning (1) whether an amortizable intangible asset exists; (2) in the case of an acquisition of a trade or business, the portion of the purchase price that is allocable to an amortizable intangible asset; and (3) the proper method and period for recovering the cost of an amortizable intangible asset. These types of disputes can be expected to continue to arise, even after the decision of the U.S. Supreme Court in Newark Morning Ledger Co. v. United States, supra.

It is believed that much of the controversy that arises under present law with respect to acquired intangible assets could be eliminated by specifying a single method and period for recovering the cost of most acquired intangible assets and by treating acquired goodwill and going concern value as amortizable intangible assets. It is also believed that there is no need at this time to change the Federal income tax treatment of self-created intangible assets, such as goodwill that is created through advertising and other similar expenditures.

Accordingly, the bill requires the cost of most acquired intangible assets, including goodwill and going concern value, to be amortized ratably over a [15]–year period. It is recognized that the useful lives of certain acquired intangible assets to which the bill applies may be shorter than [15] years, while the useful lives of other acquired intangible assets to which the bill applies may be longer than [15] years.

Explanation of Provision

In general

The bill allows an amortization deduction with respect to the capitalized costs of certain intangible property (defined as a section 197 intangible) that is acquired by a taxpayer and that is held by the taxpayer in connection with the conduct of a trade or business or an activity engaged in for the production of income. The amount of the deduction is determined by amortizing the adjusted basis (for purpose of determining gain) of the intangible ratably over a [15]–year period that begins with the month that the intangible is acquired. No other depreciation or amortization deduction is allowed with respect to a section 197 intangible that is acquired by a taxpayer.

In general, the bill applies to a section 197 intangible acquired by a taxpayer regardless of whether it is acquired as part of a trade or business. * * * The bill generally does not apply to a section 197 intangible that is created by the taxpayer if the intangible is not created in connection with a transaction (or series of related transactions) that involves the acquisition of a trade or business or a substantial portion thereof.

Except in the case of amounts paid or incurred under certain covenants not to compete (or under certain other arrangements that have substantially the same effect as covenants not to compete) and certain amounts paid or incurred on account of the transfer of a franchise, trademark, or trade name, the bill generally does not apply to any amount that is otherwise currently deductible (i.e., not capitalized) under present law.

* * *

Definition of section 197 intangible

In general

The term "section 197 intangible" is defined as any property that is included in any one or more of the following categories: (1) goodwill and going concern value; (2) certain specified types of intangible property that generally relate to workforce, information base, know-how, customers, suppliers, or other similar items; (3) any license, permit, or other right granted by a governmental unit or an agency of instrumentality thereof; (4) any covenant not to compete (or other arrangement to the extent that the arrangement has substantially the same effect as a covenant not to compete) entered into in connection with the direct or indirect acquisition of an interest in a trade or business (or a substantial portion thereof); and (5) any franchise, trademark, or trade name.

Certain types of property, however, are specifically excluded from the definition of the term "section 197 intangible." The term "section 197 intangible" does not include: (1) any interest in a corporation, partnership, trust, or estate; (2) any interest under an existing futures contract, foreign currency contract, notional principal contract, interest rate swap, or other similar financial contract; (3) any interest in land; (4) certain computer software; (5) certain interests in films, sound recordings, video tapes, books, or other similar property; (6) certain rights to receive tangible property or services; (7) certain interests in patents or copyrights; (8) any interest under an existing lease of tangible property; (9) any interest under an existing indebtedness (except for the deposit base and similar items of a financial institution); (10) a franchise to engage in any professional sport, and any item acquired in connection with such a franchise; and (11) certain transaction costs.

In addition, the Treasury Department is authorized to issue regulations that exclude certain rights of fixed duration or amount from the definition of a section 197 intangible.

Problem 2–3

McKenzie, interested in operating a graphic design studio, purchased such a business from its original owner, Harvey, for $200,000. As a result of protracted negotiations, McKenzie and Harvey agreed that the purchase price was properly allocated to the following assets—$10,000 for equipment, $50,000 for the building, $30,000 for land, $40,000 for goodwill, $20,000 for a three-year covenant not to compete, $35,000 for computer software, and $15,000 for a specialized design process.

    a.   With regard to Harvey's ownership of these assets prior to the sale to McKenzie, how did he treat each of those assets for purposes of § 167, § 168, § 179, and § 197?

    b.   With regard to McKenzie, how must she treat each of these assets for purposes of § 167, § 168, § 179, and § 197?

4. BUSINESS DEDUCTIONS IN GENERAL

Code References: §§ 162(a); 212; 262; 263(a); 263A(a) to (c), (h).

Regulations: §§ 1.162–1; 1.162–4; 1.262–1; 1.263(a)–1, 1.263(a)–2; 1.263A–1(a), (b)(1)–(4).

The deductibility of business expenditures of a sole proprietorship is governed by the familiar standards of § 162. Section 162 authorizes the deduction of "all the ordinary and necessary expenses paid or incurred during the taxable year in carrying on any trade or business." Section 162 is the most broadly written of the deduction-granting provisions and encompasses most expenditures encountered in operating a business. See generally Guerin and Postlewaite, *Problems and Materials in Federal Income Taxation* ch. 6 (Little Brown 5th ed. 1997).

The generous language of § 162 focuses on the distinction between deductible business expenses and nondeductible personal or cost of living expenses. Although broad in language and scope, the business expense provision is not without limits. Section 162 specifies three criteria for deductibility: (1) The item must be ordinary and necessary, (2) the item must be incurred in a trade or business, and (3) the item must be an expense rather than a capital expenditure.

a. Ordinary and Necessary

For an expense to be deductible under § 162(a), it must be an expense that is ordinary and necessary in the taxpayer's particular trade or business. The ordinary and necessary standard is used in determining the deductibility of legitimate business expenses. It is therefore important to define the two items. In Deputy v. du Pont, 308 U.S. 488 (1940), the Supreme Court provided the following definition of "ordinary:"

Ordinary has the connotation of normal, usual, or customary. To be sure, an expense may be ordinary though it happen but once in the taxpayer's lifetime ... Yet the transaction which gives use to it must be of common or frequent occurrence in the type of business involved.

"Necessary" merely requires that the expense be appropriate and helpful in the taxpayer's business. *Commissioner v. Tellier,* 383 U.S. 687 (1966).

Although, at first glance, the necessary requirement appears more difficult to apply because it is dependent on subjective factors such as appropriateness and helpfulness while ordinary appears to be a more objective, clear-cut requirement, this is not the way the courts have approached the problem. Most courts have focused on the ordinary half of the test because the ordinary requirement is more difficult to define and thus to establish. Attempts to deduct business expenses that are not customary or are unusual have led the courts to look for a workable definition of ordinary in an attempt to outline the parameters of allowable deductions. Despite some definitional issues, § 162 is clearly broad enough to provide for many typical expenses incurred by a sole proprietorship such as rent, employee salaries, professional fees, repairs, and materials and supplies used in the business.

b. *Incurred in a Trade or Business*

The second explicit statutory requirement for a permissible § 162 deduction is that the expenditure arise in the taxpayer's "trade or business." In general, two problem areas arise under the trade or business requirement: (1) the taxpayer's activities must constitute a trade or business, not merely investment activity; and (2) to be deductible, the expense must be incurred pursuant to that trade or business and not to some other venture or to a personal activity. In the absence of a statutory or regulatory definition of a trade or business, the courts have formulated various interpretations of the phrase.

In *Deputy v. du Pont,* 308 U.S. 488 (1940), Justice Frankfurter in his concurring opinion stated that carrying on any trade or business "involves holding one's self out to others as engaged in the selling of goods or services." In *du Pont,* the taxpayer, who held 16% of a corporation's shares, incurred interest expenses and other costs in accommodating the corporation in its plan to sell stock to nine employees appointed to a new executive committee. The Court held that the shareholder's expenses were not incurred in connection with his trade or business, even though they may have been related to the *corporation's* business interests.

The *du Pont* goods and services concept was developed at a time when courts were struggling to decide whether certain activities, not traditionally business in nature, were included within the phrase "trade or business." In 1941, the Supreme Court finally settled the issue when it held that managing one's stock investments, even as continuous activity, did not constitute the carrying on of a trade or business. Thus, expenses related thereto were nondeductible. *Higgins v. Commissioner,* 312 U.S. 212 (1941).

Congress responded to *Higgins* by enacting § 212, which allows the deduction of expenses arising from the production or collection of income or the management, conservation, or maintenance of property held for the production of income. Thus, for many nonbusiness investment activities, including securities investments, expenses are now deductible under § 212. Although the allowance of § 212 expenses is significant, the issue of where in the taxing formula such expenses are deducted is equally important. With the sole exception of § 62(a)(4) expenses, expenses incurred in the production of income are itemized deductions which are subject to various limitations not applicable to amounts deductible under § 62.

In addition to its preoccupation with distinguishing business activities from investor activities, the Supreme Court struggled to provide a workable definition of "carrying on any trade or business." It revisited the issue in *Commissioner v. Groetzinger,* 480 U.S. 23 (1987), in which it held that a full-time gambler who makes wagers solely for his own account was engaged in a trade or business for purposes of § 162. The court rejected the goods and services test of *du Pont.* Instead, it relied on an examination of the relevant facts and circumstances and stated the test as follows:

> We accept the fact that to be engaged in a trade or business, the taxpayer must be involved in the activity with continuity and regularity and that the taxpayer's primary purpose for engaging in the activity must be for income or profit. A sporadic activity, a hobby, or an amusement diversion does not qualify.

c. *Current Expenses versus Capital Expenditure*

Section 162 requires that to be currently deductible by a sole proprietor an item must be an expense as opposed to a capital expenditure. Thus, expenses may be currently deductible under § 162, whereas deductions for capital expenditures must be postponed at least partially to future taxable years. Section 263(a)(1) and (2) provides that capital expenditures include "any amount paid out for new buildings or for permanent improvements or betterments made to increase the value of any property or estate" and amounts "expended in restoring property or in making good the exhaustion thereof for which an allowance is or has been made." Capital expenditures are not limited to costs incurred in the acquisition of buildings but also encompass capital improvements to such buildings as well as the acquisition of "machinery and equipment, furniture and fixtures, and similar property having a useful life substantially beyond the taxable year." Reg. § 1.263(a)–2(a). Section 263A provides that capital expenditures include the costs of real or tangible property produced by the taxpayer.

In deciding how to treat capital expenditures, at least three possible cost recoupment alternatives were available to Congress: (1) the taxpayer could take no deduction in the year of acquisition, and any decline in value realized on final disposition would be deducted as a loss at that later date; (2) the taxpayer could deduct the entire expenditure in the year of acquisition, leaving the asset with a basis of zero; or (3) the taxpayer could allocate and deduct the asset's cost over the asset's expected useful life in the taxpayer's business. Congress selected the third recoupment alternative, commonly known as a depreciation or amortization deduction, which, as discussed previously, allows deductions for the purchase price (or cost of improvements) over the useful life of the acquired or improved asset.

D. DISPOSITION OF INVENTORY AND PROPERTY USED IN THE TRADE OR BUSINESS

Code References: §§ 1001; 1012; 1016.

Regulations: §§ 1.167(a)–8(a)(4); 1.1001–2(a) to (c) examples (1), (2), (6), (7), (8); 1.1012–1(a); 1.1016–2(a), (b).

1. GAINS OR LOSSES ON THE DISPOSITION OF PROPERTY

On the sale or exchange of appreciated property by a sole proprietor, regardless of whether the property disposed of is inventory, plant and equipment, land, or intangible assets, gain or loss is determined by comparing the adjusted basis of the property transferred with the amount realized by the taxpayer on the disposition. A gain is realized to the extent the amount realized exceeds the adjusted basis. Losses arise where basis for the property exceeds the amount realized. Thus, to calculate income or loss arising on the sale of property, the transferor must determine both the amount realized on the disposition and the adjusted basis of the property transferred. See generally Guerin and Postlewaite, *Problems and Materials in Federal Income Taxation* ch. 2 (Little Brown 5th ed. 1997).

Section 1001(b) defines the amount realized as the sum of money received plus the fair market value of any property received. Whether the transferor receives cash, property, or services, a benefit has been realized, and this benefit is measured by the value of any cash, property, or services received. Thus, the amount realized represents the total economic benefit received in exchange for the property transferred.

Similarly, because an economic benefit accrues whenever the transferee cancels or assumes the transferor's indebtedness or acquires the property subject to a debt, the amount realized typically includes the amount of the debt cancelled or assumed. In general, it makes no difference whether the debt is related to the property or whether the seller is personally liable for the debt. The seller is relieved of an obligation, and the amount of debt relief is therefore included as an amount realized. In effect, the seller is treated as receiving cash and using it to settle the preexisting obligation.

For example, assume that Rose sells land to Sandy. In return, Sandy pays Rose $20,000 cash, transfers title to an automobile worth $8,000, and assumes a $150,000 mortgage encumbering the acquired property. Sandy also agrees to pay Rose's $5,000 orthodontist bill. Rose's total amount realized on the sale is:

Cash	$20,000
Fair market value of automobile	8,000
Debt relief	
Mortgage assumed	150,000
Orthodontist bill assumed	5,000
	$183,000

After computing the amount realized on the disposition, the taxpayer's next step in computing the gain (or loss) realized is determining the adjusted basis of the transferred property. As previously discussed, the taxpayer's adjusted basis is typically the cost of the property. In the above example, if Rose had purchased the land for $100,000, then the sale to Sandy results in Rose's realization of an $83,000 gain ($183,000 amount realized minus the $100,000 adjusted basis).

Conversely, the concept of adjusted basis is *not* relevant in determining gross income earned from the rendition of services. The reason for the difference is logical—any amount realized in exchange for services rendered creates an economic gain, whereas an amount realized on the transfer of property creates economic gain only to the extent that amount exceeds the transferor's cost for the property sold. Thus, in property dispositions, the adjusted basis concept results in a tax-free return of capital. Only if the sale proceeds exceed such capital does a taxable gain result.

Adjusted basis is a term of art that, as a broad generalization, represents the taxpayer's investment in the property. Section 1012 provides the general rule applicable to most purchases of property: Initial basis equals the taxpayer's cost of acquiring the property. On the purchase of property, cost includes not only cash paid by the taxpayer but also the fair market value of other property transferred or services rendered in exchange for the property received. In addition, a cost basis includes certain acquisition expenses, such as broker's and attorney's fees. This initial basis is "adjusted" or reduced by depreciation or amortization allowed or allowable for such asset.

The taxpayer's basis depends on the manner in which the property was acquired. Different rules apply in order to determine the basis of property acquired by purchase, gift, inheritance, or exchange. Moreover, although these rules determine the initial or unadjusted basis of property, that basis must be adjusted for certain subsequent events. For instance, depreciation deductions decrease basis (see § 1016(a)(2)), whereas capital improvements to the property increase basis (see § 1016(a)(1)).

Problem 2–4

On February 7, Delores purchased ten shares of IBM stock for $10 per share. She sold the shares for $12 per share on August 1. Delores incurred a 75 cents per share broker's fee both in acquiring and selling the stock.

 a. What is her basis in the IBM stock?

 b. What is her amount realized on the sale of the IBM stock?

 c. What is her gain realized on the sale of the IBM stock?

2. AMOUNT REALIZED FROM DEBT RELIEF

a. *Nonrecourse Indebtedness*

Regulation § 1.1001–2 provides the general rule that the amount realized on the disposition of encumbered property includes the full amount of any debt relief. The rule applies without regard to whether the amount of the discharged liability was incurred in conjunction with the purchase or after the date of the property's acquisition.

The reason for including debt relief as an amount realized was addressed by the Supreme Court in *Crane*. The Court reasoned that because the debt had been included in the seller's basis, thereby increasing the amount of depreciation deductions and the measure for determining gain, it was essential to equalize this tax and economic benefit by including the amount of debt relief as an amount realized by the seller. Without this adjustment to the amount realized, the true amount of economic gain or loss would not be taxed.

For example, assume that Emily purchases property worth $100,000 in exchange for $20,000 cash plus the assumption of an $80,000 mortgage. Emily's basis is $100,000. If Emily subsequently sells that property for $110,000, with the purchaser paying $30,000 and assuming the $80,000 mortgage, Emily realizes an economic gain of $10,000. If, however, the amount realized only included the $30,000 cash received, Emily would realize a $70,000 tax loss. To correct this potential loophole, case law treats the $80,000 debt relief as an amount realized, resulting in a total amount realized of $110,000 and a $10,000 taxable gain. It should be noted, however, that only the unsatisfied balance of the obligation constitutes debt relief, not the entire face amount of the original obligation. Thus, in the above example, if prior to sale Emily had discharged $30,000 of the $80,000 mortgage debt, only the remaining $50,000 unpaid balance would be included as an amount realized on the disposition. The taxpayer would therefore incur a $20,000 loss which comports with economic reality since she put $50,000 cash in the property and only received back $20,000.

Despite the language of *Crane*, the true rationale for including all debt relief arising from a refinancing or after-acquired indebtedness as an amount realized is not based on a prior tax benefit because the amount of the debt was never included in basis. Instead, the economic benefit lies in the taxpayer's economic gain or increased net worth. Proceeds from the refinancing were received tax free. The purchaser ultimately pays the note to the lender. Consequently, if such debt relief is not considered an amount realized, the taxpayer's life-long net worth has increased without any concomitant taxable gain.

Although § 1.1001–2 of the Regulations reflects the *Crane* holding, as well as the above policies, it does not incorporate footnote 37 of the *Crane* opinion. In footnote 37, the Court indicated that if a nonrecourse liability exceeds the value of the property on the date of disposition, the excess amount might not be included as an amount realized. The footnote implies that because the transferor would receive an economic benefit only to the extent of the value of the property, the amount realized might be limited to that amount.

The Fifth Circuit in *Tufts v. Commissioner,* 651 F.2d 1058 (5th Cir.1981), adopted the reasoning of the *Crane* footnote by limiting the amount realized from nonrecourse debt relief to the fair market value of the taxpayer's encumbered property. In a nonrecourse debt situation, the creditor and debtor agree in advance that the creditor may seek satisfaction of his debt only from the mortgaged property and not from the debtor's other assets. The following examples illustrate the tax benefits available if the Fifth Circuit's approach in *Tufts* is controlling. Assume that Able purchases his $100,000 building in return for his $100,000 nonrecourse note payable to the seller. Further, assume that in the following year, Able is allowed a $20,000 depreciation deduction and Able pays no principal on the note. The next year, at a time when the property's value has declined to $50,000, Able abandons the property subject to the $100,000 obligation. The analysis employed by the Fifth Circuit in *Tufts* would allow Able to recognize a $30,000 tax loss on the transaction ($50,000 value less adjusted basis of $80,000). Thus, not only would Able have a $30,000 deductible loss, but he also would have been permitted a $20,000 depreciation deduction at no tax or economic cost. In order to account for previous depreciation deductions, Able must include as an amount realized the full $100,000 of debt relief and realize a gain of $20,000 ($100,000 amount realized less $80,000 adjusted basis).

In its review of *Tufts,* which follows, the United States Supreme Court reversed the Fifth Circuit.

COMMISSIONER v. TUFTS

461 U.S. 300 (1983).

Justice Blackmun delivered the opinion of the Court.

Over 35 years ago in Crane v. Commissioner, 331 U.S. 1 (1947), this Court ruled that a taxpayer, who sold property encumbered by a nonrecourse mortgage (the amount of the mortgage being less than the property's value), must include the unpaid balance of the mortgage in the computation of the amount the taxpayer realized on the sale. The case now before us presents the question whether the same rule applies when the unpaid amount of the nonrecourse mortgage exceeds the fair market value of the property sold.

I

On August 1, 1970, respondent Clark Pelt, a builder, and his wholly owned corporation, respondent Clark, Inc., formed a general partnership. The purpose of the partnership was to construct a 120–unit apartment complex in Duncanville, Tex., a Dallas suburb. Neither Pelt nor Clark, Inc., made any capital contribution to the partnership. Six days later, the partnership entered into a mortgage loan agreement with the Farm & Home Savings Association (F & H). Under the agreement, F & H was committed for a $1,851,500 loan for the complex. In return, the partnership executed a note and a deed of trust in favor of F & H. The partnership obtained the loan on a nonrecourse basis: neither the partnership nor its partners assumed any personal liability for repayment of the loan. Pelt later admitted four friends and relatives, respondents Tufts, Steger, Stephens, and Austin, as general partners. None of them contributed capital upon entering the partnership.

The construction of the complex was completed in August 1971. During 1971, each partner made small capital contributions to the partnership; in 1972, however, only Pelt made a contribution. The total of the partners' capital contributions was $44,212. In each tax year, all partners claimed as income tax deductions their allocable shares of ordinary losses and depreciation. The deductions taken by the partners in 1971 and 1972 totalled $439,972. Due to these contributions and deductions, the partnership's adjusted basis in the property in August 1972 was $1,455,740.

In 1971 and 1972, major employers in the Duncanville area laid off significant numbers of workers. As a result, the partnership's rental income was less than expected, and it was unable to make the payments due on the mortgage. Each partner, on August 28, 1972, sold his partnership interest to an unrelated third party, Fred Bayles. As consideration, Bayles agreed to reimburse each partner's sale expenses up to $250; he also assumed the nonrecourse mortgage.

On the date of transfer, the fair market value of the property did not exceed $1,400,000. Each partner reported the sale on his federal income tax return and indicated that a partnership loss of $55,740 had been sustained. The Commissioner * * *, on audit, determined that the sale resulted in a partnership capital gain of approximately $400,000. His theory was that the partnership had realized the full amount of the nonrecourse obligation. * * *

II

* * * At issue is the application of [§ 1001(b)] to the disposition of property encumbered by a nonrecourse mortgage of an amount in excess of the property's fair market value.

A

In Crane v. Commissioner, this Court took the first and controlling step toward the resolution of this issue. Beulah B. Crane was the sole beneficiary under the will of her deceased husband. At his death in

January 1932, he owned an apartment building that was then mortgaged for an amount which proved to be equal to its fair market value, as determined for federal estate tax purposes. The widow, of course, was not personally liable on the mortgage. She operated the building for nearly seven years, hoping to turn it into a profitable venture; during that period, she claimed income tax deductions for depreciation, property taxes, interest, and operating expenses, but did not make payments upon the mortgage principal. In computing her basis for the depreciation deductions, she included the full amount of the mortgage debt. In November 1938, with her hopes unfulfilled and the mortgagee threatening foreclosure, Mrs. Crane sold the building. The purchaser took the property subject to the mortgage and paid Crane $3,000; of that amount, $500 went for the expenses of the sale.

Crane reported a gain of $2,500 on the transaction. She reasoned that her basis in the property was zero (despite her earlier depreciation deductions based on including the amount of the mortgage) and that the amount she realized from the sale was simply the cash she received. The Commissioner disputed this claim. He asserted that Crane's basis in the property [under § 1014] was the property's fair market value at the time of her husband's death, adjusted for depreciation in the interim, and that the amount realized was the net cash received plus the amount of the outstanding mortgage assumed by the purchaser.

In upholding the Commissioner's interpretation, the Court observed that to regard merely the taxpayer's equity in the property as her basis would lead to depreciation deductions less than the actual physical deterioration of the property, and would require the basis to be recomputed with each payment on the mortgage. The Court rejected Crane's claim that any loss due to depreciation belonged to the mortgagee. The effect of the Court's ruling was that the taxpayer's basis was the value of the property undiminished by the mortgage.

The Court next proceeded to determine the amount realized [under § 1001(b)]. In order to avoid the "absurdity" of Crane's realizing only $2,500 on the sale of property worth over a quarter of a million dollars, the Court treated the amount realized as it had treated basis, that is, by including the outstanding value of the mortgage. To do otherwise would have permitted Crane to recognize a tax loss unconnected with any actual economic loss. The Court refused to construe one section of the Revenue Act so as "to frustrate the Act as a whole."

Crane, however, insisted that the nonrecourse nature of the mortgage required different treatment. The Court, for two reasons, disagreed. First, excluding the nonrecourse debt from the amount realized would result in the same absurdity and frustration of the Code. Second, the Court concluded that Crane obtained an economic benefit from the purchaser's assumption of the mortgage identical to the benefit conferred by the cancellation of personal debt. Because the value of the property in that case exceeded the amount of the mortgage, it was in Crane's economic interest to treat the mortgage as a personal obligation;

only by so doing could she realize upon sale the appreciation in her equity represented by the $2,500 boot. The purchaser's assumption of the liability thus resulted in a taxable economic benefit to her, just as if she had been given, in addition to the boot, a sum of cash sufficient to satisfy the mortgage.

In a footnote, pertinent to the present case, the Court observed:

> Obviously, if the value of the property is less than the amount of the mortgage, a mortgagor who is not personally liable cannot realize a benefit equal to the mortgage. Consequently, a different problem might be encountered where a mortgagor abandoned the property or transferred it subject to the mortgage without receiving boot. That is not this case. Id., at 14, n. 37.

B

This case presents that unresolved issue. We are disinclined to overrule *Crane,* and we conclude that the same rule applies when the unpaid amount of the nonrecourse mortgage exceeds the value of the property transferred. *Crane* ultimately does not rest on its limited theory of economic benefit; instead, we read *Crane* to have approved the Commissioner's decision to treat a nonrecourse mortgage in this context as a true loan. This approval underlies *Crane*'s holdings that the amount of the nonrecourse liability is to be included in calculating both the basis and the amount realized on disposition. That the amount of the loan exceeds the fair market value of the property thus becomes irrelevant.

When a taxpayer receives a loan, he incurs an obligation to repay that loan at some future date. Because of this obligation, the loan proceeds do not qualify as income to the taxpayer. When he fulfills the obligation, the repayment of the loan likewise has no effect on his tax liability.

Another consequence to the taxpayer from this obligation occurs when the taxpayer applies the loan proceeds to the purchase price of property used to secure the loan. Because of the obligation to repay, the taxpayer is entitled to include the amount of the loan in computing his basis in the property; the loan, under § 1012, is part of the taxpayer's cost of the property. Although a different approach might have been taken with respect to a nonrecourse mortgage loan,[5] the Commissioner

---

5. The Commissioner might have adopted the theory, implicit in *Crane*'s contentions, that a nonrecourse mortgage is not true debt, but, instead, is a form of joint investment by the mortgagor and the mortgagee. On this approach, nonrecourse debt would be considered a contingent liability, under which the mortgagor's payments on the debt gradually increase his interest in the property while decreasing that of the mortgagee. Because the taxpayer's investment in the property would not include the nonrecourse debt, the taxpayer would not be permitted to include that debt in basis.

We express no view as to whether such an approach would be consistent with the statutory structure and, if so, and *Crane* were not on the books, whether that approach would be preferred over *Crane*'s analysis. We note only that the *Crane* Court's resolution of the basis issue presumed that when property is purchased with proceeds from a nonrecourse mortgage, the purchaser becomes the sole owner

has chosen to accord it the same treatment he gives to a recourse mortgage loan. The Court approved that choice in *Crane,* and the respondents do not challenge it here. The choice and its resultant benefits to the taxpayer are predicated on the assumption that the mortgage will be repaid in full.

When encumbered property is sold or otherwise disposed of and the purchaser assumes the mortgage, the associated extinguishment of the mortgagor's obligation to repay is accounted for in the computation of the amount realized. Because no difference between recourse and nonrecourse obligations is recognized in calculating basis,[7] *Crane* teaches that the Commissioner may ignore the nonrecourse nature of the obligation in determining the amount realized upon disposition of the encumbered property. He thus may include in the amount realized the amount of the nonrecourse mortgage assumed by the purchaser. The rationale for this treatment is that the original inclusion of the amount of the mortgage in basis rested on the assumption that the mortgagor incurred an obligation to repay. Moreover, this treatment balances the fact that the mortgagor originally received the proceeds of the nonrecourse loan tax-free on the same assumption. Unless the outstanding amount of the mortgage is deemed to be realized, the mortgagor effectively will have received untaxed income at the time the loan was extended and will have received an unwarranted increase in the basis of his property. The Commissioner's interpretation of § 1001(b) in this fashion cannot be said to be unreasonable.

C

The Commissioner in fact has applied this rule even when the fair market value of the property falls below the amount of the nonrecourse obligation. Because the theory on which the rule is based applies equally in this situation, we have no reason, after *Crane,* to question this treatment.[11]

---

of the property. Under the *Crane* approach, the mortgagee is entitled to no portion of the basis. The nonrecourse mortgage is part of the mortgagor's investment in the property, and does not constitute a coinvestment by the mortgagee.

7. The Commissioner's choice in *Crane* "laid the foundation stone of most tax shelters," by permitting taxpayers who bear no risk to take deductions on depreciable property. Congress recently has acted to curb this avoidance device by forbidding a taxpayer to take depreciation deductions in excess of amounts he has at risk in the investment. Real estate investments, however, are exempt from this prohibition. Although this congressional action may foreshadow a day when nonrecourse and recourse debts will be treated differently, neither Congress nor the Commissioner has sought to alter *Crane's* rule of includ-

ing nonrecourse liability in both basis and the amount realized.

11. Professor Wayne G. Barnett, as amicus in the present case, argues that the liability and property portions of the transaction should be accounted for separately. Under his view, there was a transfer of the property for $1.4 million, and there was a cancellation of the $1.85 million obligation for a payment of $1.4 million. The former resulted in a capital loss of $50,000, and the latter in the realization of $450,000 of ordinary income. Taxation of the ordinary income might be deferred under § 108 by a reduction of respondents' bases in their partnership interests.

Although this indeed could be a justifiable mode of analysis, it has not been adopted by the Commissioner. Nor is there anything to indicate that the Code requires the Commissioner to adopt it. We note

Respondents received a mortgage loan with the concomitant obligation to repay by the year 2012. The only difference between that mortgage and one on which the borrower is personally liable is that the mortgagee's remedy is limited to foreclosing on the securing property. This difference does not alter the nature of the obligation; its only effect is to shift from the borrower to the lender any potential loss caused by devaluation of the property. If the fair market value of the property falls below the amount of the outstanding obligation, the mortgagee's ability to protect its interests is impaired, for the mortgagor is free to abandon the property to the mortgagee and be relieved of his obligation.

This, however, does not erase the fact that the mortgagor received the loan proceeds tax-free and included them in his basis on the understanding that he had an obligation to repay the full amount. When the obligation is canceled, the mortgagor is relieved of his responsibility to repay the sum he originally received and thus realizes value to that extent within the meaning of § 1001(b). From the mortgagor's point of view, when his obligation is assumed by a third party who purchases the encumbered property, it is as if the mortgagor first had been paid with cash borrowed by the third party from the mortgagee on a nonrecourse basis, and then had used the cash to satisfy his obligation to the mortgagee.

Moreover, this approach avoids the absurdity the Court recognized in *Crane.* Because of the remedy accompanying the mortgage in the nonrecourse situation, the depreciation in the fair market value of the property is relevant economically only to the mortgagee, who by lending on a nonrecourse basis remains at risk. To permit the taxpayer to limit his realization to the fair market value of the property would be to

that Professor Barnett's approach does assume that recourse and nonrecourse debt may be treated identically.

The Commissioner also has chosen not to characterize the transaction as cancellation of indebtedness. We are not presented with and do not decide the contours of the cancellation-of-indebtedness doctrine. We note only that our approach does not fall within certain prior interpretations of that doctrine. In one view, the doctrine rests on the same initial premise as our analysis here—an obligation to repay—but the doctrine relies on a freeing-of-assets theory to attribute ordinary income to the debtor upon cancellation. See United States v. Kirby Lumber Co., 284 U.S. 1, 3 (1931). According to that view, when nonrecourse debt is forgiven, the debtor's basis in the securing property is reduced by the amount of debt canceled, and realization of income is deferred until the sale of the property. Because that interpretation attributes income only when assets are freed, however, an insolvent debtor realizes income just to the extent his assets exceed his liabilities

after the cancellation. Lakeland Grocery Co. v. Commissioner, 36 B.T.A. 289, 292 (1937). Similarly, if the nonrecourse indebtedness exceeds the value of the securing property, the taxpayer never realizes the full amount of the obligation canceled because the tax law has not recognized negative basis.

Although the economic benefit prong of *Crane* also relies on a freeing-of-assets theory, that theory is irrelevant to our broader approach. In the context of a sale or disposition of property under § 1001, the extinguishment of the obligation to repay is not ordinary income; instead, the amount of the canceled debt is included in the amount realized, and enters into the computation of gain or loss on the disposition of property. According to *Crane,* this treatment is no different when the obligation is nonrecourse: the basis is not reduced as in the cancellation-of-indebtedness context, and the full value of the outstanding liability is included in the amount realized. Thus, the problem of negative basis is avoided.

recognize a tax loss for which he has suffered no corresponding economic loss. Such a result would be to construe "one section of the Act ... so as ... to defeat the intention of another or to frustrate the Act as a whole."

In the specific circumstances of *Crane,* the economic benefit theory did support the Commissioner's treatment of the nonrecourse mortgage as a personal obligation. The footnote in *Crane* acknowledged the limitations of that theory when applied to a different set of facts. *Crane* also stands for the broader proposition, however, that a nonrecourse loan should be treated as a true loan. We therefore hold that a taxpayer must account for the proceeds of obligations he has received tax-free and included in basis. Nothing in either § 1001(b) or in the Court's prior decisions requires the Commissioner to permit a taxpayer to treat a sale of encumbered property asymmetrically, by including the proceeds of the nonrecourse obligation in basis but not accounting for the proceeds upon transfer of the encumbered property.   * * *

IV

When a taxpayer sells or disposes of property encumbered by a nonrecourse obligation, the Commissioner properly requires him to include among the assets realized the outstanding amount of the obligation. The fair market value of the property is irrelevant to this calculation. We find this interpretation to be consistent with Crane v. Commissioner, 331 U.S. 1 (1947), and to implement the statutory mandate in a reasonable manner.

The judgment of the Court of Appeals is therefore reversed.

It is so ordered.

JUSTICE O'CONNOR, concurring.

I concur in the opinion of the Court, accepting the view of the Commissioner. I do not, however, endorse the Commissioner's view. Indeed, were we writing on a slate clean except for the decision in Crane v. Commissioner, 331 U.S. 1 (1947), I would take quite a different approach—that urged upon us by Professor Barnett as amicus.

Crane established that a taxpayer could treat property as entirely his own, in spite of the "coinvestment" provided by his mortgagee in the form of a nonrecourse loan. That is, the full basis of the property, with all its tax consequences, belongs to the mortgagor. That rule alone, though, does not in any way tie nonrecourse debt to the cost of property or to the proceeds upon disposition. I see no reason to treat the purchase, ownership, and eventual disposition of property differently because the taxpayer also takes out a mortgage, an independent transaction. In this case, the taxpayer purchased property, using nonrecourse financing, and sold it after it declined in value to a buyer who assumed the mortgage. There is no economic difference between the events in this case and a case in which the taxpayer buys property with cash; later obtains a nonrecourse loan by pledging the property as security; still later, using cash on hand, buys off the mortgage for the market value of the devalued property; and finally sells the property to a third party for its market value.

The logical way to treat both this case and the hypothesized case is to separate the two aspects of these events and to consider, first, the ownership and sale of the property, and, second, the arrangement and retirement of the loan.   Under *Crane,* the fair market value of the property on the date of acquisition—the purchase price—represents the taxpayer's basis in the property, and the fair market value on the date of disposition represents the proceeds on sale.   The benefit received by the taxpayer in return for the property is the cancellation of a mortgage that is worth no more than the fair market value of the property, for that is all the mortgagee can expect to collect on the mortgage.   His gain or loss on the disposition of the property equals the difference between the proceeds and the cost of acquisition.   Thus, the taxation of the transaction *in property* reflects the economic fate of the *property*.   If the property has declined in value, as was the case here, the taxpayer recognizes a loss on the disposition of the property.   The new purchaser then takes as his basis the fair market value as of the date of the sale.

In the separate borrowing transaction, the taxpayer acquires cash from the mortgagee.   He need not recognize income at that time, of course, because he also incurs an obligation to repay the money.   Later, though, when he is able to satisfy the debt by surrendering property that is worth less than the face amount of the debt, we have a classic situation of cancellation of indebtedness, requiring the taxpayer to recognize income in the amount of the difference between the proceeds of the loan and the amount for which he is able to satisfy his creditor. The taxation of the financing transaction then reflects the economic fate of the loan.

The reason that separation of the two aspects of the events in this case is important is, of course, that the Code treats different sorts of income differently.   A gain on the sale of the property may qualify for capital gains treatment, §§ 1202, 1221, while the cancellation of indebtedness is ordinary income, but income that the taxpayer may be able to defer.   §§ 108, 1017.   Not only does Professor Barnett's theory permit us to accord appropriate treatment to each of the two types of income or loss present in these sorts of transactions, it also restores continuity to the system by making the taxpayer-seller's proceeds on the disposition of property equal to the purchaser's basis in the property.   Further, and most important, it allows us to tax the events in this case in the same way that we tax the economically identical hypothesized transaction.

Persuaded though I am by the logical coherence and internal consistency of this approach, I agree with the Court's decision not to adopt it judicially.   We do not write on a slate marked only by *Crane.*   The Commissioner's long-standing position, Rev.Rul. 76–111, 1976–1 Cum. Bull. 214, is now reflected in the regulations.   Treas.Reg. § 1.1001–2. In the light of the numerous cases in the lower courts including the amount of the unrepaid proceeds of the mortgage in the proceeds on sale or disposition, it is difficult to conclude that the Commissioner's interpretation of the statute exceeds the bounds of his discretion. As the Court's opinion demonstrates, his interpretation is defensible. One can reasonably read § 1001(b)'s reference to "the amount realized *from* the sale or other disposition of property" (emphasis added) to permit the Commissioner to collapse the two aspects of the transaction. As long as his view is a reasonable reading of § 1001(b), we should defer to the regulations promulgated by the agency charged with interpretation of the statute.

Accordingly, I concur.

b. Recourse Indebtedness

In Revenue Ruling 90–16, which follows, the Service held that § 61(a)(3) income from dealings in property and § 61(a)(12) income from debt cancellation arose in a transfer of property to a bank in satisfaction of a debt. Can the Revenue Ruling be reconciled with the *Tufts* decision?

REV.RUL. 90–16

1990–1 C.B. 12.

ISSUE

A taxpayer transfers to a creditor a residential subdivision that has a fair market value in excess of the taxpayer's basis in satisfaction of a debt for which the taxpayer was personally liable. Is the transfer a sale or disposition resulting in the realization and recognition of gain by the taxpayer under sections 1001(c) and 61(a)(3) of the Internal Revenue Code?

FACTS

X was the owner and developer of a residential subdivision. To finance the development of the subdivision, X obtained a loan from an unrelated bank. X was unconditionally liable for repayment of the debt. The debt was secured by a mortgage on the subdivision.

X * * * defaulted on the debt. X negotiated an agreement with the bank whereby the subdivision was transferred to the bank and the bank released X from all liability for the amounts due on the debt. When the subdivision was transferred pursuant to the agreement, its fair market value was 10,000x dollars, X's adjusted basis in the subdivision was 8,000x dollars, and the amount due on the debt was 12,000x dollars which did not represent any accrued but unpaid interest. * * *

LAW AND ANALYSIS

Section 61(a)(3) and 61(a)(12) of the Code provide that, except as otherwise provided, gross income means all income from whatever source derived, including (but not limited to) gains from dealings in property and income from discharge of indebtedness. * * *

Section 1.61–6(a) of the Income Tax Regulations provides that the specific rules for computing the amount of gain or loss from dealings in property under section 61(a)(3) are contained in section 1001 and the regulations thereunder.

Section 1001(a) of the Code provides that gain from the sale or other disposition of property shall be the excess of the amount realized therefrom over the adjusted basis provided in section 1011 for determining gain.

Section 1001(b) of the Code provides that the amount realized from the sale or other disposition of property shall be the sum of any money received plus the fair market value of the property (other than money) received.

Section 1001(c) of the Code provides that, except as otherwise provided in subtitle A, the entire amount of the gain or loss, determined under section 1001, on the sale or exchange of property shall be recognized.

Section 1.1001–2(a)(1) of the regulations provides that, except as provided in section 1.1001–2(a)(2) and (3), the amount realized from a sale or other disposition of property includes the amount of liabilities from which the transferor is discharged as a result of the sale or disposition. Section 1.1001–2(a)(2) provides that the amount realized on a sale or other disposition of property that secures a recourse liability does not include amounts that are (or would be if realized and recognized) income from the discharge of indebtedness under section 61(a)(12). *Example (8)* under section 1.1001–2(c) illustrates these rules as follows:

> *Example (8).* In 1980, *F* transfers to a creditor an asset with a fair market value of $6,000 and the creditor discharges $7,500 of indebtedness for which *F* is personally liable. The amount realized on the disposition of the asset is its fair market value ($6,000). In addition, *F* has income from the discharge of indebtedness of $1,500 ($7,500 − $6,000).

In the present situation, *X* transferred the subdivision to the bank in satisfaction of the 12,000*x* dollar debt. To the extent of the fair market value of the property transferred to the creditor, the transfer of the subdivision is treated as a sale or disposition upon which gain is recognized under section 1001(c) of the Code. To the extent the fair market value of the subdivision, 10,000*x* dollars, exceeds its adjusted basis, 8,000*x* dollars, *X* realizes and recognizes gain on the transfer. *X* thus recognizes 2,000*x* dollars of gain.

To the extent the amount of debt, 12,000*x* dollars, exceeds the fair market value of the subdivision, 10,000*x* dollars, *X* realizes income from the discharge of indebtedness. * * *

If the subdivision had been transferred to the bank as a result of a foreclosure proceeding in which the outstanding balance of the debt was discharged (rather than having been transferred pursuant to the settle-

ment agreement), the result would be the same. A mortgage foreclosure, like a voluntary sale, is a "disposition" within the scope of the
gain or loss provisions of section 1001 of the Code.

HOLDING

The transfer of the subdivision by X to the bank in satisfaction of a
debt on which X was personally liable is a sale or disposition upon which
gain is realized and recognized by X under sections 1001(c) and 61(a)(3)
of the Code to the extent the fair market value of the subdivision
transferred exceeds X's adjusted basis. * * *

Problem 2–5

On January 1, 1994, Wyatt purchased an office computer from Computo–Tech, Inc. for $10,000. Wyatt gave the seller $1,000 cash and his
nonrecourse note for $9,000.

For the taxable year ending December 31, 1994, Wyatt claimed the
appropriate $1,000 depreciation deduction. On December 15, 1995, Wyatt
received an offer from Sam to purchase the computer for $15,000, its market
value at the time. Sam's offer, which was accompanied by a $2,000 deposit
check, was not subject to any conditions other than the transfer of clear title.
Wyatt refused the offer and returned the check, although he orally agreed
with Sam that the property was worth $15,000. On December 30, 1995,
Wyatt borrowed $4,000 from National Bank, securing the loan by giving the
bank a second nonrecourse mortgage on the computer. For the taxable year
ending December 31, 1995, Wyatt claimed $1,000 of depreciation. On
January 2, 1996, Wyatt used the $4,000 loan proceeds from the second
mortgage to reduce the balance of the principal amount of his Computo–
Tech, Inc. loan from $9,000 to $5,000.

During 1996, the value of Wyatt's computer decreased from $15,000 to
$8,000. For the taxable year ending December 31, 1996, Wyatt claimed
$1,000 of depreciation. Wyatt, realizing that the computer was subject to
more debt than its current value, abandoned the property at the main
headquarters of Computo–Tech, Inc. on January 1, 1997.

   a. What was Wyatt's adjusted basis in the computer on January 1,
      1994?

   b. What was Wyatt's adjusted basis in the computer on January 1,
      1995?

   c. What was the tax effect of Sam's offer on December 15, 1995?

   d. What was the tax effect of the agreement executed between National
      Bank and Wyatt on December 30, 1995?

   e. What was the tax effect of Wyatt's repayment, on January 2, 1996,
      of $4,000 of the $9,000 loan from Computo–Tech, Inc.?

   f. What was the tax effect of Wyatt's abandonment of the computer on
      January 1, 1997?

   g. What result if, instead of abandoning the computer, Wyatt found
      someone to purchase it for $10,000 on January 1, 1997, with the
      purchaser paying Wyatt $1,000 and acquiring the property subject to

the $9,000 debt ($5,000 to Computo–Tech and $4,000 to National Bank)?

Problem 2–6

On January 1, 1994, Rose purchased a parcel of undeveloped land from Morgan for use in his sole proprietorship in exchange for $100,000 cash and Rose's $900,000 promissory note. Rose was unconditionally personally liable for repayment of the note, which was secured by the parcel of land. On January 15, 1997, after making a total of $25,000 principal payments on the note, Rose informed Morgan that because the property had declined in value to $850,000, Rose would not make any additional payments. What result to Rose if:

a. Morgan foreclosed on the property and received $850,000 at a foreclosure sale. Rose had a $25,000 deficiency judgment assessed against him.

b. Rose deeded the property to Morgan in lieu of foreclosure. Morgan accepted the property in cancellation of only $850,000 of Rose's $875,000 personal obligation.

c. Rose deeded the property to Morgan in lieu of foreclosure. Morgan accepted the property in cancellation of the entire $875,000 obligation.

25000 Indebtness Relief

3. DEFERRED PAYMENT SALES OF PROPERTY

Deferred payment sales arise whenever property is sold and all or a portion of the sales proceeds are to be received at a future date. When future payments are to be received after the close of the taxable year of sale, tax accounting problems surface. Should all payments, even those to be received in future years, be included in gross income for the year of sale, or should only the payments received in any one year be included in gross income at annual intervals?

To illustrate this problem, assume that Marcia transfers property with a $20,000 adjusted basis and a $100,000 fair market value, in return for $10,000 cash and the purchaser's promise (in the form of a promissory note) to pay $30,000 in each of the three succeeding years. If payment is made as promised, Marcia's income from the transaction will be $80,000 ($100,000 amount realized less $20,000 adjusted basis). If the entire $100,000 is "recognized" in the year of the sale, Marcia will have $80,000 of gross income in year 1. If, on the other hand, the payments are to be "recognized" annually as they are received, how should Marcia report the $80,000 of income: in one year or prorated over three years?

There are three ways to report deferred payment sales: (1) closed transaction reporting; (2) open transaction reporting; and (3) installment reporting. Closed transaction and installment reporting are based on § 1001 and § 453, respectively, while open transaction reporting (that is, cost recovery) is a judicial creation of very limited application.

a. *Closed Transaction Reporting*

Code References: § 1001(a) to (d).

Regulations: § 1.1001–1(a).

As a general rule, gross income includes all income derived from any source, including gains from dealings in property. Thus, under § 1001(c), unless a nonrecognition provision applies, the entire gain or loss realized on the sale or exchange of property is to be recognized. If all gain realized in a deferred payment sale is recognized in the year of sale, the transaction is referred to as a "closed transaction" because the tax consequences are established and finalized at the time of the sale. In this case, a taxpayer generally recognizes gain to the extent the amount realized exceeds the adjusted basis of the property sold.

For the taxpayer using the cash receipts and disbursements method of accounting, items are included in gross income when cash or its equivalent, services, or property is actually or constructively received. If a purchaser's promissory note is considered "property received," the taxpayer must determine the fair market value of the note and include that value in the amount realized. See § 1001(b). Thus, a cash method seller who closes a transaction and recognizes gain in the year of sale may have a tax liability in excess of cash received in the year of sale.

For the taxpayer using the accrual method for reporting a closed transaction, "income is includible in gross income when all the events have occurred which fix the right to receive such income and the amount thereof can be determined with reasonable accuracy." Reg. § 1.451–1(a). Thus, an accrual method seller who receives a purchaser's note must generally include the face amount of the note as an amount realized at the time of sale because the obligation to pay that amount is fixed.

For example, compare two taxpayers, Arthur and Cort. Arthur is an accrual method taxpayer; Cort uses the cash method. Arthur and Cort each sell a coin collection worth $10,000 and each receives a $2,000 down payment and a solvent purchaser's $8,000 note bearing market interest for the balance. Assume that both Arthur and Cort have a $1,000 basis in their collection.

In the year of the sale, Cort will have an amount realized of $2,000 plus the fair market value of the note. Assuming that the fair market value of the note is $6,000 (because of the buyer's poor financial condition) and Cort's gain of $7,000 is taxed in the 30 percent marginal tax bracket, Cort will have a resulting tax liability of $2,100 ($100 more than the cash he received). Arthur will fare even worse. As an accrual method taxpayer, Arthur must include the entire face amount of the note received ($8,000) as an amount realized, in addition to the $2,000 cash down payment. Thus, in the year of the sale, Arthur realizes a $9,000 gain on the sale. If his gain is taxed in the 30 percent marginal tax bracket, then his resulting tax liability will be $2,700—$700 more than the cash he actually received in the year of the sale.

WARREN JONES CO. v. COMMISSIONER

524 F.2d 788 (9th Cir.1975).

ELY, J. * * *

I. BACKGROUND

On May 27, 1968, the [cash method] taxpayer, a family-held corporation chartered by the State of Washington, entered into a real estate contract for the sale of one of its Seattle apartment buildings, the Wallingford Court Apartments, to Bernard and Jo Ann Storey for $153,000. When the sale closed on June 15, 1968, the Storeys paid $20,000 in cash and took possession of the apartments. The Storeys were then obligated by the contract to pay the taxpayer $1,000 per month, plus 8 percent interest on the declining balance, for a period of fifteen years. The balance due at the end of fifteen years is to be payable in a lump sum. The contract was the only evidence of the Storeys' indebtedness, since no notes or other such instruments passed between the parties. Upon receipt of the full purchase price, the taxpayer is obligated by the contract to deed the Wallingford Apartments to the Storeys.

The Tax Court found, as facts, that the transaction between the taxpayer and the Storeys was a completed sale in the taxable year ending on October 31, 1968, and that in that year, the Storeys were solvent obligors. The court also found that real estate contracts such as that between the taxpayer and the Storeys were regularly bought and sold in the Seattle area. The court concluded, from the testimony before it, that in the taxable year of sale, the taxpayer could have sold its contract, which had a face value of $133,000, to a savings and loan association or a similar institutional buyer for approximately $117,980. The court found, however, that in accordance with prevailing business practices, any potential buyer for the contract would likely have required the taxpayer to deposit $41,000 of the proceeds from the sale of the contract in a savings account, assigned to the buyer, for the purpose of securing the first $41,000 of the Storeys' payments. Consequently, the court found that in the taxable year of sale, the contract had a fair market value of only $76,980 (the contract's selling price minus the amount deposited in the assigned savings account).

On the sale's closing date, the taxpayer had an adjusted basis of $61,913 in the Wallingford Apartments. In determining the amount it had realized from the sale, the taxpayer added only the $20,000 downpayment and the portion of the $4,000 in monthly payments it had received that was allocable to principal. Consequently, on its federal income tax return for the taxable year ending October 31, 1968, the taxpayer reported no gain from the apartment sale. * * *

* * * The question presented is whether section 1001(b) requires the taxpayer to include the fair market value of its real estate contract

with the Storeys in determining the "amount realized" during the taxable year of the sale.

Holding that the fair market value of the contract was not includable in the amount realized from the sale, the Tax Court majority relied on the doctrine of "cash equivalency." * * *

The Tax Court majority adopted the following as its definition of the phrase, "equivalent of cash":

> if the promise to pay of a solvent obligor is unconditional and assignable, not subject to set-offs, and is of a kind that is frequently transferred to lenders or investors at a discount not substantially greater than the generally prevailing premium for the use of money, such promise is the equivalent of cash.

Applying the quoted definition, the Tax Court held that the taxpayer's contract, which had a face value of $133,000, was not the "equivalent of cash" since it had a fair market value of only $76,980. Had the taxpayer sold the contract, the discount from the face value, approximately 42 percent, would have been "substantially greater than the generally prevailing premium for the use of money."[4]

The Tax Court observed that requiring the taxpayer to realize the fair market value of the contract in the year of the sale could subject the taxpayer to substantial hardships. The taxpayer would be taxed in the initial year on a substantial portion of its gain from the sale of the property, even though it had received, in cash, only a small fraction of the purchase price. To raise funds to pay its taxes, the taxpayer might be forced to sell the contract at the contract's fair market value, even though such a sale might not otherwise be necessary or advantageous. Most importantly in the Tax Court's view, if the taxpayer were required to realize the fair market value of the contract in the year of the sale, the sale transaction would be closed for tax purposes in that year; hence, the taxpayer's capital gain on the transaction would be permanently limited to the difference between its adjusted basis and the contract's fair market value plus the cash payments received in the year of sale. If the taxpayer did retain the contract, so as to collect its face value, the amounts received in excess of the contract's fair market value would constitute ordinary income. The Tax Court also noted that requiring the cash basis taxpayer to realize the fair market value of the real estate contract would tend to obscure the differences between the cash and accrual methods of reporting.

[T]he Commissioner contends that since, as found by the Tax Court, the contract had a fair market value, section 1001(b) requires the taxpayer to include the amount of that fair market value in determining the amount realized.[6]

---

4. The taxpayer's argument on appeal that to be a cash equivalent, a debt instrument must be negotiable is untenable.

6. The Commissioner's theoretical approach to the result for which he contends is not altogether clear. He may be rejecting the doctrine of cash equivalency altogether

II. STATUTORY ANALYSIS

The first statutory predecessor of section 1001(b) was section 202(b) of the Revenue Act of February 24, 1919, which stated:

> When property is exchanged for other property, the property received in exchange shall for the purpose of determining gain or loss be treated as the equivalent of cash to the amount of its fair market value, if any.

We have no doubt that under that statute, the taxpayer would have been required to include the fair market value of its real estate contract as an amount realized during the taxable year of sale.

Only three years later, however, in the Revenue Act of November 23, 1921, Congress replaced the language of the statute enacted in 1919 with the following:

> On an exchange of property, real, personal or mixed, for any other such property, no gain or loss shall be recognized unless the property received in exchange has a readily realizable market value.

The original statute had created "a presumption in favor of taxation." In the 1921 Act, Congress doubtless intended a policy more favorable to the taxpayer. Interpreting the 1921 statute, the Treasury Regulations provided that

> [p]roperty has a readily realizable market value if it can be readily converted into an amount of cash or its equivalent substantially equal to the fair value of the property.

The law established in 1921 appears to have been substantially in accord with the position taken in this case by the Tax Court majority.

Notwithstanding the foregoing, in the Revenue Act of 1924, ch. 234, § 202(c), Congress again changed the law, replacing the 1921 statute with the language that now appears in section 1001(b) of the current Code. Of the 1921 statute, and its requirement of a "readily realizable market value," the Senate Finance Committee wrote in 1924:

> The question whether, in a given case, the property received in exchange has a readily realizable market value is a most difficult one, and the rulings on this question in given cases have been far from satisfactory * * *. The provision cannot be applied with accuracy or consistency.

Under the 1924 statute, "where income is realized in the form of property, the measure of the income is the fair market value of the property at the date of its receipt."

or he may be contending that any property with a fair market value is the equivalent of cash in the amount of its fair market value. Since as to a cash basis taxpayer, with which we are here concerned, both theories would achieve the same result, we need not distinguish between them.

The taxpayer contends that the basic question before us is one of fact. We disagree. The question is essentially one of statutory construction and it therefore presents an issue of law.

* * * We cannot avoid the conclusion that in 1924 Congress intended to establish the more definite rule for which the Commissioner here contends and that consequently, if the fair market value of property received in an exchange can be ascertained, that fair market value must be reported as an amount realized.

Congress clearly understood that the 1924 statute might subject some taxpayers to the hardships discussed by the Tax Court majority. In the Revenue Act of 1926, ch. 27, § 212(d), Congress enacted the installment basis for reporting gain that is now reflected in section 453 of the current Code. * * *

By providing the installment basis, Congress intended " * * * to relieve taxpayers who adopted it from having to pay an income tax in the year of sale based on the full amount of anticipated profits when in fact they had received in cash only a small portion of the sales price." For sales that qualify, the installment basis also eliminates the other potential disadvantages to which the Tax Court referred. Since taxation in the year of the sale is based on the value of the payments actually received, the taxpayer should not be required to sell his obligation in order to meet his tax liabilities. Furthermore, the installment basis does not change the character of the gain received. If gain on an exchange would otherwise be capital, it remains capital under section 453. Finally, the installment basis treats cash and accrual basis taxpayers equally.

We view section 453 as persuasive evidence in support of the interpretation of section 1001(b) for which the Commissioner contends. The installment basis is Congress's method of providing relief from the rigors of section 1001(b). In its report on the Revenue Act of 1926, the Senate Finance Committee expressly noted that in sales or exchanges not qualifying for the installment basis, "deferred-payment contracts"

> are to be regarded as the equivalent of cash if such obligations have a fair market value. In consequence, that portion of the initial payment and of the fair market value of such obligations which represents profit is to be returned as income as of the taxable year of the sale * * *.

III. Case Law

The prior decisions of our own court support the conclusion we have reached. On several occasions, we have held that if the fair market value of a deferred payment obligation received in a sale or other exchange can be ascertained, that fair market value must be included as an amount realized under section 1001(b). * * * In Heller Trust v. Commissioner, 382 F.2d 675, 681 (9th Cir.1967), our court affirmed a Tax Court decision requiring a taxpayer to include the fair market value of real estate contracts as an amount realized in the year of a sale, even though the fair market value of the contracts there involved was only 50 percent of their face value.

There are, of course, "rare and extraordinary" situations in which it is impossible to ascertain the fair market value of a deferred payment obligation in the year of sale. See Treas.Reg. § 1.1001–1(a). The total amount payable under an obligation may be so speculative, or the right to receive any payments at all so contingent, that the fair market value of the obligation cannot be fixed. If an obligation is not marketable, it may be impossible to establish its fair market value. * * *

The Tax Court found, as a fact, that the taxpayer's real estate contract with the Storeys had a fair market value of $76,980 in the taxable year of sale. Consequently, the taxpayer must include $76,980 in determining the amount realized under section 1001(b). * * *

Reversed and remanded, with directions.

Problem 2–7

Geraldine reports income on the cash method. On January 1, 1997, Geraldine sold a tractor for $10,000, in which she had a $2,000 adjusted basis. The purchaser, Harry, paid Geraldine $1,000 cash plus his $9,000 promissory note. The note required interest at the market rate of 10 percent per annum, for nine years, beginning on January 1, 1999. Harry's promissory note was freely assignable and was secured by the tractor. Because Harry's current net worth was meager, he had been rejected by each of the seven banks he had contacted for financial assistance. What was Geraldine's taxable income for 1997 if she "elected out" of installment reporting and:

a.   The fair market value of the note was $7,500?

b.   The fair market value of the note was $4,800?

c.   The fair market value of the note was $500?

d.   The note had not been assignable or transferable but was worth $4,000?

e.   What result in a through d if Geraldine was an accrual method taxpayer?

f.   What result when the note is paid in full?

b. Open Transaction Reporting

Code References: §§ 1001(a) to (c); 1011(a).

Regulations: § 1.1001–1(a).

Occasionally, a purchaser's obligation may not have a specific face amount and may be incapable of valuation. In such "rare and extraordinary" cases, if it is virtually impossible to determine the amount to be realized under § 1001(b), open transaction reporting may be permitted. In those limited situations in which open transaction reporting is available, the seller is permitted to hold the transaction open, treating payments received as a tax-free recovery of basis to the extent of the basis of the property sold and thereafter treating any payments received in excess of basis as taxable gain in the year received. Consequently, open reporting permits total deferral of gain until basis has been completely recovered. This is generally favorable treatment and one sought to be achieved by taxpayers and denied by the Service.

Under *Burnet v. Logan,* which follows, the touchstone for open transaction reporting was the inability to value the consideration received with reasonable certainty.   In that case, the Supreme Court found that the value of the taxpayer's right to receive future payments, based on the recovery of iron ore, would become apparent only with time and that the tax assessment should therefore be deferred until basis was fully recovered.   In considering the timing of taxation, the Court was concerned not only with the practical difficulties associated with valuing the consideration received but also with the fairness to the seller.   At the time of sale, the seller was not assured that the total payments to be received would actually exceed her basis in the property.   Accordingly, the Court ruled that the taxpayer would be allowed to hold the transaction open and report the income received on the cost recovery method.

BURNET v. LOGAN

283 U.S. 404 (1931).

MR. JUSTICE MCREYNOLDS delivered the opinion of the Court.   * * *

Prior to March, 1913, and until March 11, 1916, respondent, Mrs. Logan, owned 250 of the 4,000 capital shares issued by the Andrews & Hitchcock Iron Company.   It held 12 percent of the stock of the Mahoning Ore & Steel Company, an operating concern.   In 1895 the latter corporation procured a lease for 97 years upon the "Mahoning" mine and since then has regularly taken therefrom large, but varying, quantities of iron ore.   * * * Through an agreement of stockholders (steel manufacturers) the Mahoning Company is obligated to apportion extracted ore among them according to their holdings.

On March 11, 1916, the owners of all the shares in Andrews & Hitchcock Company sold them to Youngstown Sheet & Tube Company, which thus acquired, among other things, 12 percent of the Mahoning Company's stock and the right to receive the same percentage of ore thereafter taken from the leased mine.

For the shares so acquired the Youngstown Company paid the holders $2,200,000 in money and agreed to pay annually thereafter for distribution among them 60 cents for each ton of ore apportioned to it. Of this cash Mrs. Logan received 250/4000ths—$137,500; and she became entitled to the same fraction of any annual payment thereafter made by the purchaser under the terms of sale.   * * *

During 1917, 1918, 1919 and 1920 the Youngstown Company paid large sums under the agreement.   * * *

Reports of income for 1918, 1919 and 1920 were made by Mrs. Logan upon the basis of cash receipts and disbursements.   They included no part of what she had obtained from annual payments by the Youngstown Company.   She maintains that until the total amount actually received by her from the sale of her shares equals their [basis], no taxable income will arise from the transaction.   * * *

The Commissioner ruled that the obligation of the Youngstown Company to pay 60 cents per ton had a fair market value of $1,942,-111.46 on March 11, 1916; that this value should be treated as so much cash and the sale of the stock regarded as a closed transaction with no profit in 1916. He also used this valuation as the basis for apportioning subsequent annual receipts between income and return of capital. * * *

The 1916 transaction was a sale of stock—not an exchange of property. We are not dealing with royalties or deductions from gross income because of depletion of mining property. Nor does the situation demand that an effort be made to place according to the best available data some approximate value upon the contract for future payments. * * * As annual payments on account of extracted ore come in they can be readily apportioned first as return of capital and later as profit. The liability for income tax ultimately can be fairly determined without resort to mere estimates, assumptions and speculation. When the profit, if any, is actually realized, the taxpayer will be required to respond. The consideration for the sale was $2,200,000.00 in cash and the promise of future money payments wholly contingent upon facts and circumstances not possible to foretell with anything like fair certainty. The promise was in no proper sense equivalent to cash. It had no ascertainable fair market value. The transaction was not a closed one. Respondent might never recoup her capital investment from payments only conditionally promised. Prior to 1921 all receipts from the sale of her shares amounted to less than their [basis]. She properly demanded the return of her capital investment before assessment of any taxable profit based on conjecture.

"In order to determine whether there has been gain or loss, and the amount of the gain, if any, we must withdraw from the gross proceeds an amount sufficient to restore the capital value that existed at the commencement of the period under consideration." Doyle v. Mitchell Bros. Co., 247 U.S. 179, 184, 185. Ordinarily, at least, a taxpayer may not deduct from gross receipts a supposed loss which in fact is represented by his outstanding note. And, conversely, a promise to pay indeterminate sums of money is not necessarily taxable income. "Generally speaking, the income tax law is concerned only with realized losses, as with realized gains." Lucas v. American Code Co., 280 U.S. 445, 449. * * *

The judgments above are affirmed.

Problem 2–8   *for Web.*

Damino, a calendar year, cash method taxpayer, owned a specially modified 1989 Porsche 911 Turbo in which she had a $60,000 adjusted basis. Damino's 17–year–old friend, Washington, believed that with Damino's "one of a kind" car, he could become a successful Grand Prix driver. Washington proposed to buy the car, but because he had little cash or collateral, he offered only $5,000 cash as a down payment, plus installments for six years equal to 40% of his winnings from racing the car. In January 1997, Damino accepted Washington's offer, despite the fact that Washington had never raced a car before, because she felt that the fair market value of her unusual car depended solely on its earning capacity.

The first installment of $25,000 was paid in December 1997, and a second installment of $20,000 was paid in December 1998. Assume that Damino elected out of § 453 reporting.

a. If Washington's promise had no ascertainable value, how much income should Damino report in 1997?

    1. How much income should she report in 1998?

    2. Assume that a third installment of $45,000 was received on December 31, 1999. How much income should Damino report in 1999?

    3. How should Damino report the future installments for taxable years 2000 through 2003?

b. Assume that the ascertainable fair market value of Washington's promise was $85,000. What was the result in 1997, when the $5,000 down payment and $25,000 first installment were received?

    1. What would be the result in 1998 if a $20,000 installment had been received?

    2. What would be the result in 1999 if a $45,000 installment had been received?

    3. What would be the result in 2000 if a $30,000 installment had been received?

c. *Installment Reporting*

Code References: §§ 453(a)–(g), (i); 453B(a), (b); 1001(c), (d); 1041(a).

Regulations: §§ 15A.453–0; 15A.453–1(a), (b)(1) to (3)(i), (c)(1) to (2)(i), (3), (4), (d)(1) to (2), (e)(1).

The most widely used deferred payment reporting method is § 453 installment reporting. It provides relief for the tax consequences of closed transaction reporting. Installment sale reporting is designed (1) to relieve taxpayers from having to pay an income tax in the year of sale based on the sale price and (2) to avoid the difficult task of appraising the value of the purchaser's promissory obligations in uncertain markets. Thus, § 453 installment reporting, which automatically applies unless the taxpayer "elects out," eliminates the hardship often created by the general tax accounting methods. This is accomplished by placing the seller on a hybrid tax reporting method: As payments are collected, the seller treats a portion of each payment as a return of basis and a portion as income. After the total sales proceeds have been collected, the entire gain will be taxed, but the seller will generally incur his tax liability gradually at the time cash or other payments are received.

The mechanics of § 453(c), which divides payments between income and return of basis, require the identification of three items: (1) payments received in a taxable year; (2) gross profit; and (3) total contract price. For each taxable year, taxable gain equals the total payments received in that year multiplied by the gross profit percentage (that is, the gross profit divided by the contract price). Gross profit generally equals the selling price minus the adjusted basis of the property sold. Thus, income to be recognized from an installment sale is computed each year as follows:

$$\text{Income recognized} = \text{Payment} \times \frac{\text{Gross profit}}{\text{Total contract price}}$$

For example, assume that Grace sells property with a $100,000 value and a $30,000 adjusted basis. In return, the purchaser agrees to pay Grace $10,000 in the year of sale and the balance in three equal annual installments of $30,000. If § 453 applies, the gross profit percentage is 70 percent, computed as follows:

$$\text{Gross profit percentage} = \frac{\text{Gross profit}}{\text{Total contract price}} = \frac{\$100,000 - \$30,000}{\$100,000} = 70\%$$

Thus, in the year of sale, there is $7,000 of gross income and a $3,000 return of basis attributable to the $10,000 cash payment received. Moreover, the same 70 percent gross profit percentage will be applied as the three remaining $30,000 payments are received, producing an additional $63,000 (70% × $90,000) of taxable gain.

By using § 453 installment reporting, the seller may discharge the resulting tax liability from the proceeds collected each year, spread the tax liability over the payment period, and maintain a positive after-tax cash position. It should be noted, however, that the installment method is not available for the disposition of inventory property. § 453(b)(2).

INSTALLMENT SALES REVISION ACT OF 1980
S.Rep. No. 1000, 96th Cong., 2d Sess. 7 (1980).

EXPLANATION OF THE BILL * * *

F. RELATED PARTY SALES

Present Law

Under present law, the installment sale statutory provision does not preclude installment sale reporting for sales between related parties. Further, the statutory provision does not preclude installment sale reporting for sales of marketable securities although the seller might readily obtain full cash proceeds by market sales.[11]

Under the existing statutory framework, taxpayers have used the installment sale provision as a tax planning device for intra-family

---

11. The receipt of the buyer's obligation payable on demand or a readily tradable evidence of indebtedness is treated as the receipt of payment by the seller. For this purpose readily tradable items include bonds and notes issued by a corporation or governmental unit with interest coupons attached or in registered form or in any other form designed to make the bond or note readily tradable in an established securities market.

transfers of appreciated property, including marketable securities. There are several tax advantages in making intra-family installment sales of appreciated property. The seller would achieve deferral of recognition of gain until the related buyer actually pays the installments to the seller, even if cash proceeds from the property are received within the related party group from a subsequent resale by the installment buyer shortly after making the initial purchase. In addition to spreading out the gain recognized by the seller over the term of the installment sale, the seller may achieve some estate planning benefits since the value of the installment obligation generally will be frozen for estate tax purposes. Any subsequent appreciation in value of the property sold, or in property acquired by reinvestment of the proceeds from the property sold on the installment basis, would not affect the seller's gross estate since the value of the property is no longer included in his gross estate.

With respect to the related buyer, there is usually no tax to be paid if the appreciated property is resold shortly after the installment purchase. Since the buyer's adjusted basis is a cost basis which includes the portion of the purchase price payable in the future, the gain or loss from the buyer's resale would represent only the fluctuation in value occurring after the installment purchase. Thus, after the related party's resale, all appreciation has been realized within the related group but the recognition of the gain for tax purposes may be deferred for a long period of time. * * *

In the leading case, Rushing v. Commissioner, [441 F.2d 593 (5th Cir.1971)], the test was held to be that, in order to receive the installment benefits, the "seller may not directly or indirectly have control over the proceeds or possess the economic benefit therefrom." In this case, a sale of corporate stock was made to the trustee of trusts for the benefit of the seller's children. Since the sales were made to trusts created after the corporations had adopted plans of liquidation, the Government made an assignment of income argument. The Court upheld installment sale treatment for the stock sold to the trustee under the "control or enjoyment" test because the trustee was independent of the taxpayer and owed a fiduciary duty to the children. The Court rejected the assignment of income argument because it found that no income was being assigned.

The *Rushing* case has been followed in another case where the stock sold to a family trust was that of a corporation which was to be liquidated after the sale. The liquidation was formally authorized after the sale to the trust. In other cases, the Tax Court has rejected the Service's substance over form and constructive receipt arguments and held that sales to a family trust qualified for installment method reporting. In the *Pityo* case [Pityo v. Commissioner, 70 T.C. 225 (1978)], the taxpayer's wife was the beneficiary of one of the trusts to which the installment sale was made. In the *Roberts* case [Roberts v. Commissioner, 71 T.C. 311 (1978)], the trustees were the seller's brother and personal accountant. In both cases, installment sale reporting was allowed because the Tax Court held that the trustees were independent of the seller and satisfied the *Rushing* control or enjoyment test.

In another case, installment method reporting was allowed for a sale of marketable stock by a wife to her husband although a resale by the husband was contemplated. In this case, the Court held that the husband could not be considered a mere conduit for the wife's sale of the stock since both were "very healthy economic entities" and the husband had an independent purpose for obtaining needed funds for an investment at a low rate of interest.

In the few cases in which the Service has prevailed, installment method reporting has been denied with respect to transactions involving a controlled corporation, a sale to a son where the son was forced to resell the stock and invest the proceeds in other securities held in escrow, and, in the case of a sale by a husband to his wife where the Court found there was no bona fide purpose for the transaction other than tax avoidance.

Reasons for Change

[T]he committee believes that the application of the judicial decisions * * * to intra-family transfers of appreciated property has led to unwarranted tax avoidance by allowing the realization of appreciation within a related group without the current payment of income tax.

Explanation of Provision

The bill prescribes special rules for situations involving installment sales to certain related parties who also dispose of the property and for situations involving installment sales of depreciable property. * * *

Sales Other Than Sales of Depreciable Property
Between Certain Closely–Related Parties

Under the bill, the amount realized upon certain resales by the related party installment purchaser will trigger recognition of gain by the initial seller, based on his gross profit ratio, only to the extent the amount realized from the second disposition exceeds actual payments made under the installment sale. Thus, acceleration of recognition of the installment gain from the first sale will generally result only to the extent additional cash and other property flows into the related group as a result of a second disposition of the property. In the case of a second disposition which is not a sale or exchange, the fair market value of the property disposed of is treated as the amount realized for this purpose. For these purposes, the portion of the amount realized from a second disposition will not be taken into account to the extent attributable to any improvements which had been made by the related installment purchaser.

The excess of any amount realized from resales over payments received on the first sale as of the end of a taxable year will be taken into account. Thus, the tax treatment would not turn on the strict chronological order in which resales or payments are made. If, under these rules, a resale results in the recognition of gain to the initial seller, subsequent payments actually received by that seller would be recovered tax-free until they have equaled the amount realized from the resale which resulted in the acceleration of recognition of gain.

In the case of property other than marketable securities, the resale rule will apply only with respect to second dispositions occurring within two years of the initial installment sale. For this purpose, the running of the two-year period would be suspended for any period during which the related purchaser's risk of loss with respect to the property is substantially diminished. This rule will apply with respect to the holding of a put, the holding of an option by another person, a short sale, or any other transaction which has the effect of substantially diminishing the risk of loss. However, for this purpose, a typical close corporation shareholders' agreement is not intended to be taken into account. Further, the holding of an option is not to be considered to have the effect of substantially diminishing risk of loss if the option purchase price is to be determined by reference to the fair market value of the property at the time the option is exercised. * * *

* * *

The bill also contains several exceptions to the application of these rules. * * * Further there would be no acceleration of recognition of gain from a second disposition which occurs after the death of the installment seller or purchaser. Generally, it is intended that this exception will apply after the death of either spouse when the spouses hold their interests in the installment obligation or the purchased property as community property or as equal undivided joint interests. Finally the resale rules will not apply in any case where it is established to the satisfaction of the Internal Revenue Service that none of the dispositions had as one of its principal purposes the avoidance of Federal income taxes.

In the exceptional cases to which the nonavoidance exception may apply, it is anticipated that regulations would provide definitive rules so that complicated legislation is not necessary to prescribe substituted property or taxpayer rules which would not be of general application. In appropriate cases, it is anticipated that the regulations and rulings under the nontax avoidance exception will deal with certain tax-free transfers which normally would not be treated as a second disposition of the property, e.g., charitable transfers, like-kind exchanges, gift transfers, and transfers to a controlled corporation or a partnership. Generally it is intended that a second disposition will qualify under the nontax avoidance exception when it is of an involuntary nature, e.g., foreclosure upon the property by a judgment lien creditor of the related purchaser or bankruptcy of the related purchaser. In addition it is intended that the exception will apply in the case of a second disposition which is also an installment sale if the terms of payment under the installment resale are substantially equivalent to, or longer than, those for the first installment sale. However, the exception would not apply if the resale terms would permit significant deferral of recognition of gain from the initial sale when proceeds from the resale are being collected sooner.

Under the bill, the period for assessing a deficiency in tax attributable to a second disposition by the related purchaser will not expire before the day which is two years after the date the initial installment seller furnishes a notice that there was a second disposition of the property. The notice is to be furnished in the manner prescribed by regulations. Under the bill, a protective notification may be filed to prevent the tolling of the period of limitations for assessing a deficiency in cases where there are questions as to whether a second disposition has occurred (e.g., a lease which might be characterized as a sale or exchange for tax purposes) or whether there is a principal purpose of Federal income tax avoidance. * * *

It is to be understood that the provisions governing the use of the installment method to report sales between related parties, and the definition of such relationships, are not intended to preclude the Internal Revenue Service from asserting the proper tax treatment of transactions that are shams.

Sales of Depreciable Property Between Certain Closely–Related Parties

Under the bill, the accrual method of accounting in effect is required for deferred payment sales of depreciable property between certain closely-related parties. In general, this rule is intended to deter transactions which are structured in such a way as to give the related purchaser the benefit of depreciation deductions (measured from a stepped-up basis) prior to the time the seller is required to include in income the corresponding gain on the sale. For transactions to which the special rule will apply, the deferred payments will be deemed to be received in the taxable year in which the sale occurs. In the case of sales for contingent future payments, it is intended that, in general, the amount realized in the year of sale will be equal to the value of the property sold. * * *

J. Sales Subject to a Contingency

Present Law

As a general rule, installment reporting of gain from deferred payments is not available where all or a portion of the selling price is subject to a contingency. The case law holds that the selling price must be fixed and determinable for section 453(b) to apply. An agreement, however, to indemnify the purchaser for breach of certain warranties and representations by offset against the purchase price will not disqualify an installment sale under section 453(b). Exactly how broad such contingencies can be is unclear.

Where an installment sale is subject to a contingency with respect to the price and the installment method is not available, the taxpayer is required to recognize all of the gain in the year of the sale with respect to all of the payments to be made, even though such payments are payable in future taxable years. In the case of a cash-method taxpayer where the future payments have no readily ascertainable fair market value, the taxpayer may treat the transaction with respect to those payments as "open" and use the cost-recovery method under Burnet v. Logan, 283 U.S. 404 (1931).

Reasons for Change

The committee believes that a taxpayer should be permitted to report gain from a deferred payment sale under the installment method even if the selling price may be subject to some contingency.

Explanation of Provision

The bill permits installment sale reporting for sales for a contingent selling price. In extending eligibility, the bill does not prescribe specific rules for every conceivable transaction. Rather, the bill provides that specific rules will be prescribed under regulations.

However, it is intended that, for sales under which there is a stated maximum selling price, the regulations will permit basis recovery on the basis of a gross profit ratio determined by reference to the stated maximum selling price. For purposes of this provision, incidental or remote contingencies are not to be taken into account in determining if there is a stated maximum selling price. In general, the maximum selling price would be determined from the "four corners" of the contract agreement as the largest price which could be paid to the taxpayer assuming all contingencies, formulas, etc., operate in the taxpayer's favor. Income from the sale would be reported on a pro rata basis with respect to each installment payment using the maximum selling price to determine the total contract price and gross profit ratio. If, pursuant to standards prescribed by regulations, it is subsequently determined that the contingency will not be satisfied in whole or in part, thus reducing the maximum selling price, the taxpayer's income from the sale would be recomputed. The taxpayer would then report reduced income, as adjusted, with respect to each installment payment received in the taxable year of adjustment and subsequent taxable years. If the maximum price is reduced in more than one taxable year, e.g., because of successive changes in the status of the contingency, each such year of reduction would constitute an adjustment year.

Where the taxpayer has reported more income from installment payments received in previous taxable years than the total recomputed income, the taxpayer would be permitted to deduct the excesses in the adjustment year as a loss.

In cases where the sales price is indefinite and no maximum selling price can be determined but the obligation is payable over a fixed period of time, it is generally intended that basis of the property sold would be recovered ratably over that fixed period. In a case where the selling price and payment period are both indefinite but a sale has in fact occurred, it is intended that the regulations would permit ratable basis recovery over some reasonable period of time. Also, in appropriate cases, it is intended that basis recovery would be permitted under an income forecast type method.[31]

The creation of a statutory deferred payment option for all forms of deferred payment sales significantly expands the availability of installment reporting to include situations where it has not previously been permitted. By providing an expanded statutory installment reporting option, the Committee believes that in the future there should be little incentive to devise convoluted forms of deferred payment obligations to attempt to obtain deferred reporting. In any event, the effect of the new rules is to reduce substantially the justification for treating transactions as "open" and permitting the use of the cost-recovery method sanctioned by Burnet v. Logan. Accordingly, it is the Committee's intent that the cost-recovery method not be available in the case of sales for a fixed price (whether the seller's obligation is evidenced by a note, contractual promise, or otherwise), and that its use be limited to those rare and extraordinary cases involving sales for a contingent price where the fair market value of the purchaser's obligation cannot reasonably be ascertained. * * *

Problem 2–9   2-9

Walter and his daughter, Jenny, were calendar-year, cash method taxpayers. On May 1, 1997, Walter sold a 1970 Mercedes to Jenny for its $16,000 fair market value. Jenny made a $1,000 down payment and executed a 15–year negotiable promissory note, bearing a face amount of $15,000, payable $1,000 per year commencing in 1998, plus interest at the market rate of 10 percent per annum. Walter, who had used the car only for weekend outings, had purchased it in 1990 for $4,000. On January 1, 1998, before making any payments on the note to Walter, Jenny sold the car to Gage for $17,000 in cash.

   a.   What were the tax consequences to Walter in 1997 as a result of the sale of the car to Jenny?

   b.   What were the tax consequences to Walter and Jenny in 1998 when Jenny sold the car to Gage for $17,000 cash?

   c.   Would it make a difference in b if Jenny had sold the car to Gage on May 5, 1999? What would be the result to Walter?

---

31. In general the income forecast method for basis recovery is considered appropriate for a transaction with respect to which it may be demonstrated that receipts will be greater for the earlier years of the payment period and then decline for the later years of the payment period. It is intended that the regulations will deal with the application of this method with respect to sales of property qualifying for depreciation under the income forecast method (e.g., movies), mineral rights when the selling price is based on production, a sale under which the amount payable to the seller is based on a declining percentage of the purchaser's revenues, and similar sales. In developing these regulations, the committee intends that the Treasury Department will prescribe rules for this method to avoid, whenever possible, leaving a seller with an unrecovered basis in the obligation, and thereby creating a capital loss, after the final payment is received. For qualifying transactions, a more rapid basis recovery under this method is to be allowed even if there is a fixed period over which payments are to be received.

d. Would it make a difference in a and b if Walter had sold the car to his brother instead of Jenny?

e. Assume that Jenny sold the car to Gage on January 1, 1998, for a $7,000 down payment, plus a five-year balloon payment note having a $9,000 face amount, bearing interest at the market rate of 10 percent per annum and a $6,000 fair market value, and that she did not "elect out" of § 453. What result? What result if she had elected out of § 453?

f. What result in e if Gage paid no cash and gave her a $16,000 note due in 20 years instead of five years?

g. What result in a if Walter had sold the car to his wholly owned corporation?

h. What result in a if Walter had sold the car to his wife?

E. CHARACTER OF INCOME—DISPOSITIONS

1. INTRODUCTION

Generally, taxpayers want gains to be classified as capital gain rather than ordinary income because capital gains are afforded preferential tax treatment. See § 1(h). On the other hand, taxpayers prefer losses to be characterized as ordinary losses in order to avoid the statutory limitations on capital loss deductions. See § 1211. These goals are not easily met, however, because the characterization of gains and losses recognized on the disposition of property is determined by the interaction of ever changing Code sections, case law, and administrative Rulings. One of the primary functions of a tax advisor is to guide the client and structure the transaction so that the appropriate, and possibly most favorable, characterization is achieved.

a. *Background*

The Supreme Court in *Burnet v. Harmel,* 287 U.S. 103, 106 (1932), cited two policies justifying the preferential tax treatment afforded capital gains: "to relieve the taxpayer from ... [the] excessive tax burdens on gains resulting from a conversion of capital investments, and to remove the deterrent effect of those burdens on such conversions [that is, realization]." The first policy is commonly known as the bunching problem, and the second policy is often referred to as the lock-in effect.

The preference afforded capital gains currently resides primarily in the rate structure. The maximum federal rate on ordinary income for individuals (excluding FICA, FUTA, and Medicare contributions) currently is 39.6 percent while the maximum rate on capital gains for individuals is 28 percent under § 1(h). Thus, a premium is placed on deriving capital gain rather than ordinary income.

b. *Overview of Capital Gain and Loss Analysis*

A three-step process assists in determining the nature of property gains and losses under the present taxing structure and helps organize the myriad of rules involved. The first step is the characterization phase. This phase employs three important statutory concepts: (1) the definition of a capital asset, (2) the sale or exchange requirement, and (3) the taxpayer's holding period in the capital asset that is sold or exchanged. The second step, the recharacterization phase, considers several specific statutory exceptions that serve to prevent unduly favorable tax treatment resulting from the application of the general capital gain rules. The third step in the treatment of gains and losses from property transactions is the netting phase. Rules contained in § 1222 require the netting of capital gains and losses, which may lead to the unfavorable limitation rules reserved for capital losses (§ 1211). See generally Guerin and Postlewaite, *Problems and Materials in Federal Income Taxation* ch. 7 (Little Brown 5th ed. 1997).

Finally, it is important to note that the role of the § 1211 capital loss limitation is to allow or disallow deductions from gross income. The deduction for capital losses is an adjusted gross income (AGI) deduction under § 62(a)(3). As with other AGI deductions, Code sections other than § 62 must be consulted to determine the rules for their deductibility.

2. MECHANICS OF CAPITAL GAIN AND LOSS

Code References: §§ 61(a)(3); 62(a)(3); 165(a), (b), (c), (f); 1211(b); 1212(b); 1222.

a. *Statutory Overview*

In general, all recognized gains, capital or otherwise, are included in gross income. The amount of capital gains and losses must be computed and compared. This process is called netting. The rules found in § 1222, the primary definitional section for capital gains and losses, dictate which gains and losses are to be netted together in determining if, and to what extent, there is either a net capital gain or capital loss. These netting processes may produce (1) a net capital gain, (2) a net capital loss that is deductible subject to limitations prescribed by § 1211(b), or, in some cases, (3) a net capital loss that is not currently deductible as a result of the § 1211(b) limitations but may be carried forward by § 1212 to later years.

Sections 1211, 1212(b), and 1222 do not independently include capital gains in gross income, nor do they deduct a portion of net capital losses from gross income. Other Code provisions control these determinations. Section 61(a)(3) includes in gross income all gains recognized from dealings in property, regardless of whether they are capital, short-term or long-term, or ordinary.

Section 62(a)(3), which authorizes a deduction from gross income for losses from the sale or exchange of property, cross-references to § 165, which adds requirements to capital loss deductibility not present for capital gain inclusion. Gains require realization and recognition before characterization; losses, in addition to these two conditions, require allowability under § 165(c). Section 165(c) allows losses for "individuals" only if they arise in a trade or business, a production of income activity, or from a casualty loss. As a result, losses from the sale of personal use property, such as a principal residence or automobile, are nondeductible capital losses. After the allowance of the loss has been established under § 165(c), § 165(f) applies and refers to § 1211 and § 1212, which govern by limitation the amount and method for computing a capital loss deduction. Thus, although § 165(c) and § 165(f) perform different functions, both subsections' requirements must be met before an AGI deduction for capital losses is allowed under § 62(a)(3).

b. Definitions and Netting Rules

The foregoing description of the treatment of capital gains and losses highlights the importance of the definitional and netting provisions. Section 1222(1) through (4) defines capital gains and losses as either short-term or long-term. A short-term asset is a capital asset held for one year or less; a long-term capital asset is one held for more than one year. Thus, long-term capital gain or loss is gain or loss recognized on the sale or exchange of a capital asset held for more than one year. Short-term capital gain or loss is defined similarly, except that the holding period is one year or less.

Section 1222(5) through (11) provides the bulk of the netting rules. Net short-term capital gain or loss and net long-term capital gain or loss are aggregate amounts derived from comparing gains and losses from all transactions in one particular holding period. Thus, a taxpayer with a $10,000 long-term capital gain and a $4,000 long-term capital loss has a $6,000 net long-term capital gain.

c. Capital Loss Deduction

Section 1211(b) provides the rules for determining the maximum capital loss deduction in a particular taxable year. In considering the § 1211(b)(1) limitation, it is helpful to divide its application into two parts.

First, all capital losses can be deducted to the extent of all capital gains. If, for example, capital losses (short-term and long-term) for the taxable year total $8,000 and capital gains (short-term and long-term) for the taxable year total $10,000, the § 1211(b) deduction is $8,000 regardless of the long-term or short-term composition of the $8,000 of losses or the $10,000 of gains. In such a case, since all capital losses are deductible, no further computation would be necessary under § 1211(b). If, however, capital losses in the above example total $15,000, then $10,000 of the capital losses would be deductible under the first part of the § 1211(b)(1) limitation, with the remaining $5,000 of capital losses subject to the limitation rules under the second part of § 1211(b)(1).

The second part of § 1211(b)(1) (the clause following the word "plus") applies only to the portion of capital losses that exceed the total amount of capital gains. The applicable limitation (that is, amount deductible) is the smaller of (1) $3,000 or (2) the excess of capital losses over capital gains. This rule often provides an incentive for a taxpayer to generate capital gains at year end (such as through a sale of stock) in order that it be "sheltered" by otherwise non-deductible capital losses.

When capital losses exceed the amount currently deductible under § 1211(b)(1), § 1212(b) applies to carry forward the excess net capital loss to the subsequent taxable years, where it retains its character as a short-term or long-term loss.

d. Carryover of Capital Losses

Section 1212(b) permits excess capital losses to be carried forward to subsequent taxable years. Losses carried forward retain their original character as either long-term or short-term and are treated as though they were sustained in the year to which they are carried. Thus, a net long-term capital loss carryover first reduces long-term capital gain recognized in the carryover year, then reduces net short-term capital gain, with the unused portion reducing ordinary income up to the $3,000 limitation. In the carryover year, short-term capital losses carried forward from a prior year continue to be applied against the $3,000 ordinary income limit first. If the deduction limit against ordinary income has not been reached after offsetting by the net short-term capital losses, the long-term capital losses are then applied against the limit. Consider the following examples.

> Example 1. Dana has taxable income of $60,000 in 1997, a $1,000 net short-term capital loss, and a $6,000 net long-term capital loss. Dana must first use the $1,000 net short-term capital loss against $1,000 of ordinary income, and then $1,000 of the net long-term capital loss to offset the remaining $2,000 of ordinary income ($3,000 limit). The remaining $4,000 ($6,000–$2,000) long-term capital loss is carried over to a future year, retaining its long-term character.

> Example 2. Hilda has $60,000 of taxable income in 1997, a $1,000 net short-term capital gain, a $100 net long-term capital gain, and a short-term capital loss carryover of $5,000 from 1996. Because § 1212 requires that the loss carryover be treated as if incurred in the year to which it is carried, Hilda will first offset the short-term loss carryover by the current $1,000 net short-term capital gain; next, the current $100 net long-term capital gain will offset $100 of the loss carryover. Finally, the resulting second stage deduction for 1997 would be to the extent of the $3,000 ordinary income deduction limit. The $900 remaining from the 1996 carryover may again be carried forward for use as a short-term capital loss in post–1997 taxable years.

Problem 2–10

Burbach has the following gains and losses in 1997: $10,000 long-term capital gain; $15,000 long-term capital gain; $5,000 short-term capital gain;

$7,000 short-term capital loss; $1,000 long-term capital loss; and a $2,000 long-term capital loss.

   a.   What is the amount of net long-term capital loss or gain?

   b.   What is the amount of net short-term capital loss or gain?

   c.   What is the net capital gain?

   d.   How much capital gain in included in Burbach's gross income for 1997?

   e.   Is Burbach entitled to a capital loss deduction under §§ 165(f) and 1211(b)?

   f.   What is Burbach's adjusted gross income?

   g.   Assume that Burbach did not have any short-term capital loss but that all other facts are the same. What is the net capital gain?

Problem 2–11

In 1997, Adam has the following capital gains and losses from stock sales: long-term capital gain of $5,000; long-term capital loss of $3,000; long-term capital gain of $15,000; short-term capital loss of $2,000; short-term capital gain of $12,000; short-term capital loss of $14,000; and a long-term capital loss of $25,000. Assume that Adam's taxable income without including capital gains and losses is $40,000.

   a.   What is the amount of net short-term capital loss?

   b.   What is the amount of net long-term capital loss?

   c.   What is Adam's capital loss deduction for 1997?

   d.   What is the amount of net capital loss?

   e.   What is the amount and character of Adam's capital loss carryforward?

   f.   What is Adam's adjusted gross income for 1997?

3.　DEFINITION OF A CAPITAL ASSET

Code References: §§ 1221; 1235(a), (b).

Regulations: § 1.1221–1.

a.　Statutory Analysis

Capital characterization arises when a capital asset is sold or exchanged, with the resulting capital gain or loss being long-term or short-term depending on the asset's holding period. Thus, the threshold issue is the definition of a capital asset.

Section 1221 broadly defines a capital asset as "property held by the taxpayer (whether or not connected with his trade or business)" except for items described in § 1221(1) through (5). Thus, the capital asset definition includes all property with the exception of five types. The exceptions of § 1221(1) through (5) necessarily become the focus of the initial statutory inquiry.

The first two exceptions to the broad language of § 1221 list property generally found in a small business. Section 1221(1) excludes from the definition of capital assets stock in trade, inventory, and property held primarily for sale to customers in the ordinary course of a trade or business. Section 1221(2) excludes real or depreciable property used in a trade or business. For example, a taxpayer's personal use automobile is a capital asset, but a car held as inventory or a car that the taxpayer uses in a trade or business is not. It should be noted that although § 1221(2) disqualifies property used in a trade or business from capital treatment, § 1231(b) (discussed at section 4 of this chapter) may qualify such property for preferential tax treatment.

The third exception, § 1221(3), excludes certain property created by the holder's personal efforts, such as copyrights, music, paintings, and so forth. Treating the type of property listed in § 1221(3) as noncapital in the hands of its creator is consistent with taxing wages and salaries as ordinary income—gains from personal effort or services are generally taxed as ordinary income, whereas gains from capital appreciation are not.

The fourth exception from the definition of capital assets closes a loophole otherwise available on the sale of § 1221(1) property (or the rendition of taxpayer's services) in exchange for notes or accounts receivable instead of cash. On receipt of a note or account receivable, a cash method taxpayer might not be required to report income. When payment is received on the note, the cash method taxpayer reports ordinary income. If however, the note or account is sold prior to discharge, it arguably might constitute a sale of property that could qualify for capital treatment. To prevent circumvention of the purpose and intent of § 1221, § 1221(4) classifies notes and accounts receivable for services rendered or for the sale of § 1221(1) property as noncapital assets. The § 1221(4) exclusion, therefore, prevents conversion of ordinary income into capital gains.

The final exception, a minor one, is for federal publications acquired for less than their fair market value.

b. *Property Held Primarily for Sale*

The most commonly encountered property excluded by the statutory definition of a capital asset is business property. Three categories of business assets are listed in § 1221(1): inventory, stock in trade, and property held primarily for sale. Although the first two are relatively straightforward and can usually be easily identified through general accounting principles, the third category is a catchall with ill-defined boundaries.

Due to its uncertain scope, the phrase "property held by the taxpayer primarily for sale to customers in the ordinary course of his trade or business" has been the subject of as much litigation as any phrase in the Code. In determining the parameters of this phase, courts initially struggled with the meaning of the word "primarily." The

Supreme Court, in *Malat v. Riddell,* 383 U.S. 569 (1966), held that primarily should be given its "literal" interpretation to mean "of first importance" or "principally." Although *Malat* failed to resolve definitively which property is to be excluded from capital asset treatment because the Court addressed only the meaning of one word in the phrase, *Malat* clearly articulated the intended policy of § 1221(1):

> The purpose of [§ 1221(1)] is to differentiate between the "profits and losses arising from the everyday operation of a business" on the one hand * * * and "the realization of appreciation in value accrued over a substantial period of time" on the other.

Although the difference between everyday business profits and losses and appreciation because of the passage of time may be readily apparent in some cases, in many others it is difficult to determine which factor was the catalyst for the taxpayer's gain or loss. Reacting to the limited application of *Malat*'s "first importance" or "principally" test, courts developed a more comprehensive analysis of § 1221(1). Under this analysis, property is excluded from capital asset treatment if it is (1) held primarily for sale (2) to customers (3) in the ordinary course of a trade or business.

The first element considers whether the property is held primarily for sale or primarily for investment. In practical business parlance, the issue focuses on whether the proprietor's activities have risen to the level of becoming a "dealer" in the property sold. Numerous factual determinations, none of which is controlling, make this the most difficult of the three elements in the analysis. Initially, the § 1221(1) limitation was applied as a one-question dealer versus investor test in order to determine whether property was a capital asset. This single question test was developed because it was reasoned that if taxpayers are classified as holding property primarily for sale rather than investment, they may be presumed to be selling the property in the ordinary course of business. As more challenging factual situations arose, however, it became apparent that this perfunctory assumption was a misconception and the dealer versus investor inquiry supplies only the first of the three statutory elements.

The second element of the statutory language requires examination of the phrase "to customers." This phrase was added to § 1221(1) to distinguish stock investors (regardless of how active) from professional securities dealers and brokers. Thus, securities investors are not regarded as having customers, and their losses and gains are generally capital.

The third element of the statutory formula requires an analysis of the words "in the ordinary course of his trade or business," as well as their impact on a taxpayer's classification as an investor or a dealer. For instance, if property is held primarily for sale, but not in a trade or business, the asset should not be excluded by § 1221(1). On the other hand, even when property is not held primarily for sale, if it is used in a trade or business the asset is excluded from the definition of a capital asset by § 1221(2). Similarly, if property is held for sale in the taxpayer's trade or business, but only in an extraordinary context, it may be excluded from the definition.

In determining whether sales or exchanges are in the ordinary course of a trade or business, the resolution turns on whether the sale or exchange was a routine transaction in the course of the taxpayer's everyday affairs of business. For example, a used car dealer who sells a used car to a customer has made a sale in the ordinary course of business, but a used car dealer who sells his or her used office equipment to a neighbor has not.

UNITED STATES v. WINTHROP

417 F.2d 905 (5th Cir.1969).

GOLDBERG, J.

We must emerge with a solution to the "old, familiar, recurring, vexing and ofttimes elusive" problem concerning capital gains versus ordinary income arising out of the sale of subdivided real estate. Finding ourselves engulfed in a fog of decisions with gossamer like distinctions, and a quagmire of unworkable, unreliable, and often irrelevant tests, we take the route of ad hoc exploration to find ordinary income.

I

The taxpayer, Guy L. Winthrop, was the owner of certain property in the environs of Tallahassee, Florida, known as Betton Hills. The property had been in his family since 1836. Winthrop first received a share of the property in 1932 upon the death of his mother. Additional portions of the property were received by him in 1946, 1948, and 1960 through inheritance and partition. As the city of Tallahassee expanded, its city limits were extended to incorporate most of the Winthrop property and the taxpayer began to sell lots for homesites. The first subdivision was undertaken in 1936, and the first sales were made in that year. Thereafter, eight other subdivisions were platted and developed by the taxpayer. Each subdivision was platted separately and the taxpayer endeavored to sell most of the lots in one subdivision before another was developed. The process was one of gradual orderly development of the property through the various subdivisions. Each was surveyed and platted. The streets were graded and paved at Winthrop's expense. Electricity and water facilities were installed; and in some subdivisions sewer lines were built, again at Winthrop's expense, although this was eventually repaid out of the utility bills incurred by homeowners who moved into the subdivisions. Moreover, the taxpayer participated in building five houses for sale in the addition in order to assist other purchasers in obtaining F.H.A. loans to finance their homes.

In selling the lots Winthrop neither advertised nor engaged brokers. The customers primarily came to his home to conduct the sale negotiations since he did not even have an office. He did however, purchase an annual occupational license as a real estate broker from the City of

Tallahassee from 1948 through 1963. Despite this low pressure and informal selling technique, the parties stipulated that Winthrop was primarily engaged in selling the Betton Hills property and that though he was a civil engineer by profession, he did little work of this type during the period in question save that done on the Betton Hills property. Furthermore, Winthrop's technique, although unorthodox, was apparently effective. Commencing with the year 1945 and ending in December, 1963, approximately 456 lots were sold in Betton Hills. The profit and other income realized by Winthrop from the sale of these lots from 1951 through 1963 was $483,018.94 or 52.4 percent of his total income during that period. * * *

II

The government's first argument in support of its contention that the district court erred in granting capital gains treatment to the taxpayer is founded upon the proposition that capital gains treatment is available only where the appreciation in value is the result of external market changes occurring over a period of time. In other words, the government argues that where the appreciation is due to the taxpayer's efforts, all profit should be reported as ordinary income. In statutory terms the government argues that the subdivided land ceased to be a "capital asset" when the taxpayer improved the land through his own efforts by platting the lots, paving streets, and installing utilities. Although recognizing that subdivided land is not expressly removed from the "capital asset" category by the exclusionary provisions of I.R.C. § 1221 unless such land is held primarily for sale to customers in the ordinary course of business, the government, nevertheless, maintains that its taxpayer efforts rule has, in effect, been read into the statute by the courts. * * *

* * * As this court said in *Barrios' Estate,* [265 F.2d 517 (5th Cir.1959)]:

> The idea of selling a large tract of land in lots embraces necessarily the construction of streets for access to them, the provision of drainage and the furnishing of access to such a necessity as water. It is hardly conceivable that taxpayer could have sold a lot without doing these things. To contend that reasonable expenditures and efforts, in such necessary undertakings are not entitled to capital gains treatment is to reject entirely the established principle that a person holding lands under such circumstances may subdivide it for advantageous sale.

265 F.2d at 520. We therefore conclude that this blanket interdiction of capital gains treatment where there has been any laying on of hands is belied by the past decisions of this court.

III

While we are in disagreement with the government's first argument concerning taxpayer efforts, we find its second argument, that the land in question was primarily held for sale in the ordinary course of business and, therefore, was not a capital asset under § 1221, persuasive.   In holding against the government on this point the court below appears to have placed particular emphasis upon the following facts: (1) the proceeds from the sales of the property were not reinvested in real estate; (2) the taxpayer had other investments, none of which involved the sale of real estate; (3) the subdivided property was acquired by inheritance, not by purchase for the purpose of resale; (4) the taxpayer's holding period was twenty-five years; (5) the taxpayer maintained no office, made most of the sales from his home, spent no time whatever promoting sales and did not advertise; and (6) the purchasers came to him and he was selective in making the sales.

In relying on these factors the court below was obviously following earlier suggestions by this court that such facts are relevant in determining the ultimate question of whether or not the land in question was held primarily for sale to customers in the ordinary course of business. In condensed form the tests mentioned most often are: (1) the nature and purpose of the acquisition of the property and the duration of the ownership; (2) the extent and nature of the taxpayer's efforts to sell the property; (3) the number, extent, continuity and substantiality of the sales; (4) the extent of subdividing, developing, and advertising to increase sales; (5) the use of a business office for the sale of the property; (6) the character and degree of supervision or control exercised by the taxpayer over any representative selling the property; and (7) the time and effort the taxpayer habitually devoted to the sales.

Despite their frequent use, this court has often declared that these seven pillars of capital gains treatment "in and of themselves ... have no independent significance, but only form part of a situation which in the individual case must be considered in its entirety to determine whether or not the property involved was held primarily for sale in the ordinary course of business (source cited)."   Cole v. Usry, 294 F.2d at 427.   * * *

In the instant case the trial court found that these test facts, about which there is no disagreement, compelled a finding of the ultimate fact that the holding was not primarily for sale in the ordinary course of the taxpayer's business.   In weighing the arguments on this point this court recognizes that the characterization of the taxpayer's manner of holding lands is a question of fact.   * * *

We think, therefore, that even though we accept as true the fact findings of the court below, it is nevertheless incumbent upon this court to inquire into the ultimate conclusion of law reached by that court. * * *

* * * We therefore approach first the issue of whether or not Winthrop held the property "primarily for sale" as that phrase is used in § 1221.

It is undisputed that Winthrop inherited the first portion of the Betton Hills land in 1932.   By 1936 the first sales had been made and further subdivisions were under way.   Mrs. Winthrop's testimony indicates that, except for the subdividing and selling, the land was not used by the taxpayer. * * * On the other hand, her testimony was equally clear in showing that the taxpayer's activities regarding the land, such as paving the streets and having utilities installed, were done with the express purpose of making it more saleable. She testified that he built houses on some of the lots in order to make FHA financing available to prospective purchasers of other lots. Moreover, he built some houses on the lots because "if a person built a house and there was a house nearby, somebody wanted the lot, because people like neighbors."

There were, therefore, no multiple, dual, or changes of purpose during the relevant years of Winthrop's Betton Hills sales. The taxpayer, long before the tax years in question, had as his sole motivation the sale of Betton Hills, lot by lot, year by year, transaction by transaction. The evidence is clear and uncontradicted that the lots were at all times held by Winthrop "primarily for sale" as that phrase was interpreted by the Supreme Court in Malat v. Riddell, 1966, 383 U.S. 569.

Holding primarily for sale, however, is by itself insufficient to disqualify the taxpayer from capital gains privileges. The sales must also be made in the ordinary course of the taxpayer's trade or business. The next issue, therefore, is whether the taxpayer's activities constituted a trade or business. We think that they did. The magnitude and continuity of his operations and design all point to these sales being part of a business. This was a planned program of subdividing and selling, lasting over a quarter of a century. It constituted Winthrop's principal activity and produced over one-half of his income during the years in question. This was no minuscule operation in terms of transactions or profits. * * * [T]he taxpayer here devoted a substantial amount of his time, skill and financial resources to developing and selling the property. He thereby became engaged in the business of subdividing real estate for sale. One need not be a static holder to qualify for capital gains treatment, but the flexing of commercial muscles with frequency and continuity, design and effect does result in disqualification because it indicates one has entered the business of real estate sales.

The taxpayer has made much over the fact that no office was used, no brokers were employed, no time was spent promoting sales, and no advertising was used. While advertising, solicitation and staff are the usual components of a business, they are not a necessary element in either the concept or the pragmatics of selling. Here it is evident that the taxpayer was quite successful in selling the lots without the assistance of these usual props. It is not necessary that customers be actively and fervently and frenetically sought. Winthrop had lots to sell and not mousetraps, so they beat a way to his door to buy his lots. As the court remarked in Thompson v. Commissioner, supra, which involved a similar lack of promotional activity, "merely because business was good, indeed brisk, does not make it any less in the ordinary course of such a good business." Winthrop was in the business of selling lots in Betton Hills, even though his salesmanship was unorthodox and low pressure. The sales were out of his lots, and were made to customers, though these customers sought him out rather than having been pursued.

In addition, we think the sales were ordinary in the course of this business. The concept of normalcy requires for its application a chronology and a history to determine if the sales of lots to customers were the usual or a departure from the norm. History and chronology here combine to demonstrate that Winthrop did not sell his lots as an abnormal or unexpected event. He began selling shortly after he acquired the land; he never used the land for any other purpose; and he continued this course of conduct over a number of years. Thus, the sales were not only ordinary, they were the sole object of Winthrop's business. It is this singleness of purpose which distinguishes Winthrop's sales from those in *Barrios' Estate* * * * relied on by the taxpayer. It is true, as the taxpayer asserts, that in each of these cases there was considerable sales activity. However, in each the property had been used for some other purpose and the sales ensued only when this primary purpose was abandoned. Here there was no change of purpose.

* * * Sale was the prime purpose of the holding and the sales were made in the ordinary course of the taxpayer's business. We conclude, therefore, that the taxpayer is not entitled to capital gains treatment on the profit made from the sales of land during the years 1959 through 1963. The judgment of the district court is reversed.

c. *Nonstatutory Analysis*

The preceding *Winthrop* decision illustrates the role that judicial opinions have played in establishing the parameters of the Code's broad definition of a capital asset. Another significant judicial focus is on the congressional intent for the term "capital asset." In the decision of *Arkansas Best,* which follows, the Supreme Court addressed the definition of a capital asset. Focusing on the nature of the taxpayer's business, the Court in its earlier decision in *Corn Products* held that the purchase and sale of corn futures constituted an integral part of the taxpayer's business and, therefore, the gain was ordinary, not capital. In essence, the Court held that the exclusions from capital asset status should be broadly interpreted. Subsequent expansion of the *Corn Products* doctrine by the lower courts, however, forced the Supreme Court to confront the issue again in *Arkansas Best.*

ARKANSAS BEST CORP. v. COMMISSIONER

485 U.S. 212 (1988).

JUSTICE MARSHALL delivered the opinion of the Court.

The issue presented in this case is whether capital stock held by petitioner Arkansas Best Corporation (Arkansas Best) is a "capital asset" as defined in § 1221 of the Internal Revenue Code regardless of whether the stock was purchased and held for a business purpose or for an investment purpose.

I

Arkansas Best is a diversified holding company. In 1968 it acquired approximately 65% of the stock of the National Bank of Commerce (Bank) in Dallas, Texas. Between 1969 and 1974, Arkansas Best more than tripled the number of shares it owned in the Bank, although its percentage interest in the Bank remained relatively stable. These acquisitions were prompted principally by the Bank's need for added capital. Until 1972, the Bank appeared to be prosperous and growing, and the added capital was necessary to accommodate this growth. As the Dallas real estate market declined, however, so too did the financial health of the Bank, which had a heavy concentration of loans in the local real estate industry. In 1972, federal examiners classified the Bank as a problem bank. The infusion of capital after 1972 was prompted by the loan portfolio problems of the bank.

Petitioner sold the bulk of its Bank stock on June 30, 1975, leaving it with only a 14.7% stake in the Bank. On its federal income tax return for 1975, petitioner claimed a deduction for an ordinary loss of $9,995,-688 resulting from the sale of the stock. The Commissioner of Internal Revenue disallowed the deduction, finding that the loss from the sale of stock was a capital loss, rather than an ordinary loss, and that it therefore was subject to the capital loss limitations in the Internal Revenue Code.

Arkansas Best challenged the Commissioner's determination in the United States Tax Court. The Tax Court, relying on cases interpreting Corn Products Refining Co. v. Commissioner, 350 U.S. 46 (1955), held that stock purchased with a substantial investment purpose is a capital asset which, when sold, gives rise to a capital gain or loss, whereas stock purchased and held for a business purpose, without any substantial investment motive, is an ordinary asset whose sale gives rise to ordinary gains or losses. The court characterized Arkansas Best's acquisitions through 1972 as occurring during the Bank's " 'growth' phase," and found that these acquisitions "were motivated primarily by investment purpose and only incidentally by some business purpose." The stock acquired during this period therefore constituted a capital asset, which gave rise to a capital loss when sold in 1975. The court determined, however, that the acquisitions after 1972 occurred during the Bank's " 'problem' phase," and, except for certain minor exceptions, "were made exclusively for business purposes and subsequently held for the same reasons." These acquisitions, the court found, were designed to preserve petitioner's business reputation, because without the added capital the Bank probably would have failed. The loss realized on the sale of this stock was thus held to be an ordinary loss.

The Court of Appeals for the Eighth Circuit reversed the Tax Court's determination that the loss realized on stock purchased after 1972 was subject to ordinary-loss treatment, holding that all of the Bank stock sold in 1975 was subject to capital-loss treatment. The court reasoned that the Bank stock clearly fell within the general definition of "capital asset" in Internal Revenue Code § 1221, and that the stock did not fall within any of the specific statutory exceptions to this definition. The court concluded that Arkansas Best's purpose in acquiring and holding the stock was irrelevant to the determination whether the stock was a capital asset. * * *

II

Section 1221 of the Internal Revenue Code defines "capital asset" broadly, as "property held by the taxpayer (whether or not connected with his trade or business)," and then excludes five specific classes of property from capital-asset status. In the statute's present form, the classes of property exempted from the broad definition are (1) "property of a kind which would properly be included in the inventory of the taxpayer"; (2) real property or other depreciable property used in the taxpayer's trade or business; (3) "a copyright, a literary, musical, or artistic composition," or similar property; (4) "accounts or notes receivable acquired in the ordinary course of trade or business for services rendered" or from the sale of inventory; and (5) publications of the Federal Government. Arkansas Best acknowledges that the Bank stock falls within the literal definition of capital asset in § 1221, and is outside of the statutory exclusions. It asserts, however, that this determination does not end the inquiry. Petitioner argues that in Corn Products Refining Co. v. Commissioner, supra, this Court rejected a literal reading of § 1221, and concluded that assets acquired and sold for ordinary business purposes rather than for investment purposes should be given ordinary-asset treatment. Petitioner's reading of *Corn Products* finds much support in the academic literature and in the courts. Unfortunately for petitioner, this broad reading finds no support in the language of § 1221.

In essence, petitioner argues that "property held by the taxpayer (whether or not connected with his trade or business)" does not include property that is acquired and held for a business purpose. In petitioner's view an asset's status as "property" thus turns on the motivation behind its acquisition. This motive test, however, is not only nowhere mentioned in § 1221, but it is also in direct conflict with the parenthetical phrase "whether or not connected with his trade or business." The broad definition of the term "capital asset" explicitly makes irrelevant any consideration of the property's connection with the taxpayer's business, whereas petitioner's rule would make this factor dispositive.

In a related argument, petitioner contends that the five exceptions listed in § 1221 for certain kinds of property are illustrative, rather than exhaustive, and that courts are therefore free to fashion additional exceptions in order to further the general purposes of the capital-asset provisions. The language of the statute refutes petitioner's construction. Section 1221 provides that "capital asset" means "property held by the taxpayer[,] * * * but does not include" the five classes of property listed as exceptions. We believe this locution signifies that the listed exceptions are exclusive. The body of § 1221 establishes a general definition of the term "capital asset," and the phrase "does not include" takes out of that broad definition only the classes of property that are specifically mentioned. The legislative history of the capital asset definition supports this interpretation ("[T]he definition includes all property, except as specifically excluded"), ("[A] capital asset is property held by the taxpayer with certain exceptions"), as does the applicable Treasury regulation.

Petitioner's reading of the statute is also in tension with the exceptions listed in § 1221. These exclusions would be largely superfluous if assets acquired primarily or exclusively for business purposes were not capital assets. Inventory, real or depreciable property used in the taxpayer's trade or business, and accounts or notes receivable acquired in the ordinary course of business, would undoubtedly satisfy such a business-motive test. Yet these exceptions were created by Congress in separate enactments spanning 30 years. Without any express direction from Congress, we are unwilling to read § 1221 in a manner that makes surplusage of these statutory exclusions.

In the end, petitioner places all reliance on its reading of Corn Products Refining Co. v. Commissioner, 350 U.S. 46 (1955)—a reading we believe is too expansive. In *Corn Products,* the Court considered whether income arising from a taxpayer's dealings in corn futures was entitled to capital-gains treatment. The taxpayer was a company that converted corn into starches, sugars, and other products. After droughts in the 1930's caused sharp increases in corn prices, the company began a program of buying corn futures to assure itself an adequate supply of corn and protect against price increases. The company "would take delivery on such contracts as it found necessary to its manufacturing operations and sell the remainder in early summer if no shortage was imminent. If shortages appeared, however, it sold futures only as it bought spot corn for grinding." The Court characterized the company's dealing in corn futures as "hedging." As explained by the Court of Appeals in *Corn Products,* "[h]edging is a method of dealing in commodity futures whereby a person or business protects itself against price fluctuations at the time of delivery of the product which it sells or buys." In evaluating the company's claim that the sales of corn futures resulted in capital gains and losses, this Court stated:

> Nor can we find support for petitioner's contention that hedging is not within the exclusions of [§ 1221]. Admittedly, petitioner's corn futures do not come within the literal language of the exclusions set out in that section. They were not stock in trade, actual inventory, property held for sale to customers or depreciable property used in a trade or business. But the capital-asset provision of [§ 1221] must not be so broadly applied as to defeat rather than further the purpose of Congress. Congress intended that profits and losses arising from the everyday operation of a business be considered as ordinary income or loss rather than capital gain or loss * * *. Since this section is an exception from the normal tax requirements of the Internal Revenue Code, the definition of a

capital asset must be narrowly applied and its exclusions interpreted broadly.

The Court went on to note that the hedging transactions consistently had been considered to give rise to ordinary gains and losses, and then concluded that the corn futures were subject to ordinary-asset treatment.

The Court in *Corn Products* proffered the oft-quoted rule of construction that the definition of capital asset must be narrowly applied and its exclusions interpreted broadly, but it did not state explicitly whether the holding was based on a narrow reading of the phrase "property held by the taxpayer," or on a broad reading of the inventory exclusion of § 1221. In light of the stark language of § 1221, however, we believe that *Corn Products* is properly interpreted as involving an application of § 1221's inventory exception. Such a reading is consistent both with the Court's reasoning in that case and with § 1221. The Court stated in *Corn Products* that the company's futures transactions were "an integral part of its business designed to protect its manufacturing operations against a price increase in its principal raw material and to assure a ready supply for future manufacturing requirements." The company bought, sold, and took delivery under the futures contracts as required by the company's manufacturing needs. As Professor Bittker notes, under these circumstances, the futures can "easily be viewed as surrogates for the raw material itself." The Court of Appeals for the Second Circuit in *Corn Products* clearly took this approach. That court stated that when commodity futures are "utilized solely for the purpose of stabilizing inventory cost[,] * * * [they] cannot reasonably be separated from the inventory items," and concluded that "property used in hedging transactions properly comes within the exclusions of [§ 1221]." This Court indicated its acceptance of the Second Circuit's reasoning when it began the central paragraph of its opinion, "Nor can we find support for petitioner's contention that hedging is not within the exclusions of [§ 1221]." In the following paragraph, the Court argued that the Treasury had consistently viewed such hedging transactions as a form of insurance to stabilize the cost of inventory, and cited a Treasury ruling which concluded that the value of a manufacturer's raw-material inventory should be adjusted to take into account hedging transactions in futures contracts. This discussion, read in light of the Second Circuit's holding and the plain language of § 1221, convinces us that although the corn futures were not "actual inventory," their use as an integral part of the taxpayer's inventory-purchase system led the Court to treat them as substitutes for the corn inventory such that they came within a broad reading of "property of a kind which would properly be included in the inventory of the taxpayer" in § 1221.

Petitioner argues that by focusing attention on whether the asset was acquired and sold as an integral part of the taxpayer's everyday business operations, the Court in *Corn Products* intended to create a general exemption from capital-asset status for assets acquired for business purposes. We believe petitioner misunderstands the relevance of the Court's inquiry. A business connection, although irrelevant to the initial determination of whether an item is a capital asset, is relevant in determining the applicability of certain of the statutory exceptions, including the inventory exception. The close connection between the futures transactions and the taxpayer's business in *Corn Products* was crucial to whether the corn futures could be considered surrogates for the stored inventory of raw corn. For if the futures dealings were not part of the company's inventory-purchase system, and instead amounted simply to speculation in corn futures, they could not be considered substitutes for the company's corn inventory, and would fall outside even a broad reading of the inventory exclusion. We conclude that *Corn Products* is properly interpreted as standing for the narrow proposition that hedging transactions that are an integral part of a business' inventory-purchase system fall within the inventory exclusion of § 1221. Arkansas Best, which is not a dealer in securities, has never suggested that the Bank stock falls within the inventory exclusion. *Corn Products* thus has no application to this case.

It is also important to note that the business-motive test advocated by petitioner is subject to the same kind of abuse that the Court condemned in *Corn Products*. The Court explained in *Corn Products* that unless hedging transactions were subject to ordinary gain and loss treatment, taxpayers engaged in such transactions could "transmute ordinary income into capital gain at will." The hedger could garner capital-asset treatment by selling the future and purchasing the commodity on the spot market, or ordinary-asset treatment by taking delivery under the future contract. In a similar vein, if capital stock purchased and held for a business purpose is an ordinary asset, whereas the same stock purchased and held with an investment motive is a capital asset, a taxpayer such as Arkansas Best could have significant influence over whether the asset would receive capital or ordinary treatment. Because stock is most naturally viewed as a capital asset, the Internal Revenue Service would be hard pressed to challenge a taxpayer's claim that stock was acquired as an investment, and that a gain arising from the sale of such stock was therefore a capital gain. Indeed, we are unaware of a single decision that has applied the business-motive test so as to require a taxpayer to report a gain from the sale of stock as an ordinary gain. If the same stock is sold at a loss, however, the taxpayer may be able to garner ordinary-loss treatment by emphasizing the business purpose behind the stock's acquisition. The potential for such abuse was evidenced in this case by the fact that as late as 1974, when Arkansas Best still hoped to sell the Bank stock at a profit, Arkansas Best apparently expected to report the gain as a capital gain.

III

We conclude that a taxpayer's motivation in purchasing an asset is irrelevant to the question whether the asset is "property held by a taxpayer (whether or not connected with his business)" and is thus within § 1221's general definition of "capital asset." Because the capital stock held by petitioner falls within the broad definition of the term "capital asset" in § 1221 and is outside the classes of property excluded from capital-asset status, the loss arising from the sale of the stock is a capital loss. Corn Products Refining Co. v. Commissioner, supra, which we interpret as involving a broad reading of the inventory exclusion of § 1221, has no application in the present context. Accordingly, the judgment of the Court of Appeals is affirmed.

Problem 2–12

Jason, a retired lawyer and ardent wine taster, collected rare wines for his personal consumption. In 1993, Jason had his wine collection appraised, and much to his astonishment, the value of many of the bottles had appreciated significantly. This revelation prompted Jason to stop drinking many of the wines and, instead, to begin holding the collection for investment.

Jason continued his investment in wine for the next four years, occasionally selling less valuable wines and replacing them with more precious vintages. In 1997, Jason hired a winebroker and began advertising the wine collection in a trade publication. In 1997, Jason sold 25 percent of his collection and reported the resulting profits as long-term capital gain. In 1998, he sold another 55 percent of his total collection for an aggregate gain of $100,000.

    a.   Should Jason report ordinary gain in 1997? Briefly explain the Service's and the taxpayer's arguments. May he report a portion of these profits as capital gain?

    b.   What effect if, instead of individual sales, Jason sold his entire wine collection to one purchaser in one transaction?

    c.   Assume that in 1996 Jason developed cirrhosis of the liver and sold his wine in 1997 and 1998 pursuant to his doctor's orders.

    d.   Are there any arguments that either Jason or the Service may make to distinguish 1997 from 1998?

Problem 2–13.

Fluff–Up Down (FUD), a major processor of goose down, has recently seen two discouraging economic events take place in the down products industry. First, goose down has fluctuated both in price and supply, making it difficult for major users, like FUD, to supply their customers. Second, the innovation of polar guard, a synthetic substitute for goose down, and its popularity with cold weather garment manufacturers have threatened to put FUD out of business.

To prevent its demise, as well as the collapse of the goose down industry, FUD expanded its operations and diversified its holdings. In 1995, FUD paid $100,000 to acquire 60% of Goose, Inc., the third largest goose ranch in the country. FUD was the main customer of the ranch and believed that owning a sizable portion of the ranch would help stabilize its source of down and that the ranch would eventually become a profitable, dividend-paying enterprise.

FUD had previously purchased goose down futures. After it purchased the goose ranch, however, it was unnecessary for FUD to retain the majority of the futures for use in its processing operations. It therefore sold 70% of its contracts and planned to pursue this practice as long as profitable trading continued.

FUD's final economic venture was to acquire a popular down garment manufacturer that was threatening to switch to polar guard. On July 1, 1995, FUD purchased Boiler Works Garments (BWG) stock for $1,000,000. This takeover prevented BWG from switching to the synthetic fillings and also guaranteed FUD a future buyer for 40% of the down that it processed and sold.

These acquisitions coupled with the industry's recent return to down-filled garments have enabled FUD to enlarge its enterprise and sell some of its earlier acquisitions. In 1997, FUD's sale of all of its stock in Goose, Inc., resulted in a loss of $50,000, and its sale of BWG resulted in a profit of $1.5 million. In 1997, FUD also sold 80% of the goose down futures (which it purchased a year and a half earlier) at a gain of $250,000.

    a.   What is the character of the loss on the sale of Goose, Inc. stock?

    b.   What is the character of the gain on the sale of goose down futures?

    c.   What is the character of the gain on the sale of BWG?

d. Sale or Exchange Requirement

Code References: §§ 1001(a), (b), (c); 1222; 1234(a).

Regulations: §§ 1.167(a)–8(a)(4); 1.1001–2(a), (b); 1.1002–1; 1.1234–1.

The "sale or exchange" requirement for capital gain or loss characterization is statutorily embodied in § 1222. The sale or exchange language in § 1222 establishes a requirement that must be satisfied before a realized gain or loss may be characterized as capital.

Not all transactions can be easily classified as a sale or exchange. For instance, in *Helvering v. William Flaccus Oak Leather Co.*, 313 U.S. 247 (1941), the Supreme Court held that insurance compensation received for the loss of a building destroyed by fire did not constitute a § 1222 sale or exchange. Other transactions that may not neatly comport with the ordinary meaning of the phrase "sale or exchange" include abandonments, foreclosures, and the granting of options. For example, in *Freeland v. Commissioner*, 74 T.C. 970 (1980), the taxpayer reconveyed encumbered property to the vendor-mortgagee by a quitclaim deed. At the time of reconveyance, the nonrecourse debt on the property ($41,000) exceeded the fair market value of the property ($27,000) and the taxpayer (vendee-mortgagor) received no consideration on reconveyance. The taxpayer argued that the reconveyance by deed in lieu of foreclosure was equivalent to an abandonment, which may not constitute a sale or exchange. The court held that "voluntary reconveyance of the property to the mortgagee for no monetary consideration (boot) was a sale within the meaning of sections 1211 and 1212, ... even though petitioner had no personal obligation on the mortgage debt." If abandonment treatment had been allowed, there would have arguably been no "sale or exchange" and the taxpayer's loss would not have been limited by the restrictions of § 1211.

e. Holding Period

Code References: §§ 1015(a); 1222(1) to (4); 1223(1), (2), (5), (6), (7), (11); 7701(a)(42) to (44).

Regulations: §§ 1.1012–1(c)(1); 1.1222–1(a); 1.1223–1(a), (b), (f), (g), (i).

The third factor in characterizing gains and losses is the asset's holding period. The holding period serves a different function than the capital asset and sale or exchange requirements. The two latter requirements are essential to labeling an asset as capital or ordinary. The holding period is relevant, however, only if the asset (1) receives capital status under § 1221 or (2) does not attain capital asset status because of § 1221(2). In the first instance, the asset's holding period determines whether the gain or loss is short-term or long-term; in the second, the holding period determines whether the asset qualifies as a § 1231 asset.

Generally, the two relevant dates in computing an asset's holding period are the date of acquisition and the date of disposition. The day of acquisition is excluded from the calculation while the day of disposition is included. Thus, if a capital asset is purchased February 1 and sold on February 1 of the next year, it cannot qualify for long-term treatment. But if the asset is sold on or after February 2 of the next year, it has been held for more than one year and is classified as long term.

Crucial to ascertaining the holding period is the determination of when the sale or exchange was consummated. The Supreme Court addressed this issue in *McFeely v. Commissioner,* 296 U.S. 102 (1935), stating: "In common understanding, to hold property is to own it. In order to own or hold one must acquire. The date of acquisition is, then, that from which to compute the duration of ownership or the length of holding." For example, the mere execution of a contract to sell real estate on a specified date in the future is generally not a conveyance requiring the realization of gain or loss, even if a nominal payment was made, because a sale or exchange has not yet occurred. Thus, realization of gain or loss occurs on the delivery of a deed or on the transfer, from a practical standpoint, of the benefits and burdens of ownership to the buyer, not by virtue of the execution of a sales contract.

Tacking. Although the holding period requirements are inflexible, a taxpayer may nevertheless qualify for long-term treatment for an asset actually held for less than one year. A deemed holding period may be added ("tacked on") to the taxpayer's actual holding period of an asset. Section 1223 prescribes situations, most often where an "exchanged" (§ 1223(1)) or "transferred" (§ 1223(2)) basis applies to the property, in which either the taxpayer's holding period in a prior asset or the prior owner's holding period is tacked on to the taxpayer's actual holding period of the newly acquired asset. See § 7701(a)(42)–(44). Exchanged basis refers to a basis determined by reference to the basis of property transferred (such as § 1031 like-kind exchange), whereas transferred basis refers to property with a basis in a transferee's hands that is determined by reference to the basis the transferor had in the property (such as § 1015 gift basis).

4. SECTION 1231—PROPERTY USED IN A TRADE OR BUSINESS

Code References: §§ 165(c); 1221(2); 1231.

Regulations: §§ 1.1221–1(b); 1.1231–1.

Definitions and mechanics. The first step in taxing gains and losses arising on the disposition of property requires their characterization. The initial inquiry in the characterization phase concerns whether the property falls within the § 1221 definition of capital asset. Section 1221(2) excludes real or depreciable property used in a trade or business from the definition of a capital asset. However, the characterization of property meeting the § 1221(2) disqualification is not complete until the effect of § 1231 has been assessed. Section 1231(b) modifies § 1221(2) by permitting capital treatment on the disposition of certain § 1221(2) property. In addition, § 1231 can apply to other capital assets and affect the character of their gain or loss. See generally Guerin and Postlewaite, *Problems and Materials in Federal Income Taxation* ch. 7 (Little Brown 5th ed. 1997).

To some extent, § 1231 provides the best of both worlds: It may provide long-term capital treatment for gains and ordinary treatment for losses on transfers of the same types of assets. This favorable treatment results from the two-tier consolidation, or netting, of recognized gains and losses from the sale of § 1231 property. In general, if the netting process results in gains exceeding losses, each item of gain or loss is treated as though derived from the sale or exchange of a long-term capital asset. If, however, losses exceed gains, each gain and loss item is treated as ordinary income and loss. Consequently, long-term capital gain benefits are generally available when there is a net gain, and ordinary loss benefits are available when there is a net loss.

It is important to understand that § 1231 netting determines only the characterization of each item of § 1231 property as either ordinary or capital; the net figure derived by § 1231 netting has no independent significance with regard to the amount included in gross income. Finally, because it is easy to become lost in the § 1231 maze, it may be helpful to remember that § 1231 involves a series of interrelationships between three basic concepts: (1) § 1231 property, (2) § 1231 events, and (3) the two-tier netting process.

The categories of gains and losses subject to § 1231 netting are (1) any recognized gain or loss from the sale or exchange of property used in trade or business (that is, § 1231(b) property), and (2) any recognized gain or loss from the compulsory or involuntary conversion of property used in trade or business or of any capital asset that is held for more than one year and held in connection with a trade or business or a transaction entered into for profit. § 1231(a)(3).

Section 1231(b) defines property used in a trade or business. Section 1231(b) assets are strictly limited to property, used in a trade or business and held for more than one year, that is not inventory or property held primarily for sale to customers. Thus, real property and depreciable property used in a trade or business may receive the benefits of long-term capital treatment even though they are not capital assets. This is a crucial and favorable factor in determining the tax treatment of a sole proprietor who disposes of certain business assets.

The second category of property subject to § 1231 netting, long-term capital assets held in connection with a trade or business or a transaction entered into for profit, receives § 1231 treatment only if it is the object of condemnation or involuntary conversion (such as theft, fire, storm, shipwreck, or other casualty). If property held for personal use, such as a home, clothing, or automobile, is subject to condemnation or involuntary conversion, it is not included in the § 1231 netting process. Furthermore, if a long-term capital asset held in connection with a trade or business or for profit is disposed of by sale or exchange, those gains or losses are not netted in § 1231 because § 1231 only includes gains and losses from sales or exchanges of § 1231(b) property.

There are three types of transactions or events to which § 1231 may apply—involuntary conversions, sales or exchanges, and condemnations. Characterization of the gain or loss from these transactions involves a two-tier process (see Figure 2–2).

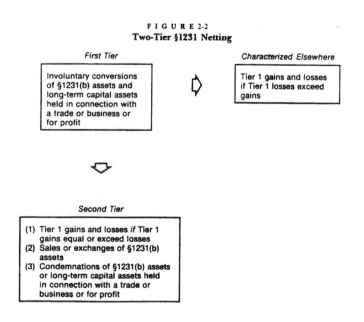

FIGURE 2-2
Two-Tier §1231 Netting

First Tier

Involuntary conversions of §1231(b) assets and long-term capital assets held in connection with a trade or business or for profit

Characterized Elsewhere

Tier 1 gains and losses if Tier 1 losses exceed gains

Second Tier

(1) Tier 1 gains and losses *if* Tier 1 gains equal or exceed losses
(2) Sales or exchanges of §1231(b) assets
(3) Condemnations of §1231(b) assets or long-term capital assets held in connection with a trade or business or for profit

Involuntary conversions due to fire, theft, storm, shipwreck, or other casualty are first netted in tier 1. Both § 1231(b) assets and long-term capital assets held in connection with a trade or business or a transaction entered into for profit are included in tier 1. Tier 1 losses receive two opportunities within the framework of the two-tier netting process to have losses treated as ordinary. First, if the tier 1 losses exceed the tier 1 gains, none of the tier 1 assets will be subject to characterization under § 1231. Thus, the characterization of such gains and losses will retain their original, non–§ 1231 status and will be governed by the normal rules, which should yield ordinary gain or loss because there has not been a sale or exchange of the asset. The second chance for an ordinary loss arises if the tier 1 gains equal or exceed the losses, in which case all tier 1 gains and losses are renetted in tier 2.

Tier 2 netting includes sales or exchanges of § 1231(b) property, gains and losses arising from condemnations and, if required, tier 1 involuntary conversions. All gains and losses included in the second tier are netted together. If the total gains exceed total losses, all tier 2 gains and losses are individually characterized as either long-term capital gains or long-term capital losses. If tier 2 losses equal or exceed gains, all of the tier 2 assets will receive ordinary gain or loss treatment.

The rules described above apply only if the taxpayer had no § 1231 netting transactions in which losses exceeded gains in the prior five years. To preclude manipulation of § 1231, particularly with regard to the sale of property used in a trade or business, § 1231 provides that net § 1231 gains will be treated as ordinary income to the extent of "unre-captured net section 1231 losses" for the preceding five years. Thus, if in any of the preceding five years § 1231 losses exceeded gains resulting in ordinary characterization and if for the current year § 1231 gains exceed losses, then § 1231(c) requires characterization of all or part of the gain as ordinary. If the net gain for the year exceeds the nonrecap-tured § 1231 losses, the excess will receive capital characterization.

INTERNATIONAL SHOE MACHINE
CORP. v. UNITED STATES
491 F.2d 157 (1st Cir.1974).

COFFIN, C.J.

Appellant taxpayer contends that the Commissioner of Internal Revenue erroneously treated income realized from the appellant's sales of certain shoe machines as "property held by the taxpayer primarily for sale to customers in the ordinary course of his trade or business," § 1231(b)(1)(B), thereby taxing it as ordinary income instead of treating it under the capital gains provisions of the Code. * * *

It is undisputed that during the years in question, 1964 through 1966, appellant's main source of income derived from the leases of its shoe machinery equipment, rather than from their sales. The revenue from sales of the leased machinery comprised, respectively, only 7 percent, 2 percent, and 2 percent of appellant's gross revenues. In fact, because the appellant preferred the more profitable route of leasing its machines, it never developed a sales force, never solicited purchases, set prices high to make purchasing unattractive, and even attempted to dissuade customers from purchasing them.

Yet the district court found that, beginning in 1964, when the investment tax credit made it more attractive for shoe manufacturers to buy shoe machinery rather than to lease it, the selling of machinery became an accepted and predictable, albeit small, part of appellant's business. Since appellant's chief competitor was selling leased shoe machines, it was necessary for appellant to offer its customers the same option. During the years in issue, appellant never declined to quote a price, nor did it ever decline to make a sale if the customer was persistent. Unlike previous years, purchase inquiries were referred to the appellant's vice president for sales, normally charged with selling new, nonleased machines, whereupon a price was negotiated. A schedule was prepared, indicating the sales price of leased machines, based upon the number of years that the machines had been leased. In total, 271 machines were sold to customers who, at the time of the sales, had been leasing the machines for at least six months.

The case raises what has become a repeating source of difficulty in applying § 1231(b)(1)(B), which denies * * * capital gains tax treatment to "property held * * * primarily for sale to customers in the ordinary course of his trade or business." In particular, does the word "primarily" invoke a contrast between sales and leases, as the appellant contends, or between sales made in the ordinary course of business and nonroutine sales made as a liquidation of inventory? And, if the latter, how can sales made in the ordinary course of business be distinguished from a liquidation of inventory?

In support of its contention that "primarily" refers to a contrast between sales and leases, appellant relies upon Malat v. Riddell, 383 U.S. 569 (1966). There, the taxpayer purchased a parcel of land, with the alleged intention of developing an apartment project. When the taxpayer confronted zoning restrictions, he decided to terminate the venture, and sold his interest in the property, claiming a capital gain. The lower courts found, however, that the taxpayer had had a "dual purpose" in acquiring the land, a "substantial" one of which was to sell if that were to prove more profitable than development. Therefore, since the taxpayer had failed to establish that the property was not held primarily for sale to customers in the ordinary course of his business, his gain was treated as ordinary income. The Supreme Court vacated and remanded the case, stating that the lower courts had applied an incorrect legal standard when they defined "primarily" as merely "substantially" rather than using it in its ordinary, everyday sense of "first importance" or "principally." Although the Court in *Malat* was dealing with § 1221, rather than § 1231, the same clause appears in both sections. Appellant argues that the present case is analogous, since the "first" and "principal" reason for holding the shoe machinery was clearly for lease rather than for sale.

We cannot agree that *Malat* is dispositive. Even if "primarily" is defined as "of first importance" or "principally," the word may still invoke a contrast between sales made in the "ordinary course of * * * business" and those made as liquidations of inventory, rather than between leases and sales. *Malat* itself concerned the dual purposes of developing an apartment complex on the land and selling the land. Although these two possible sources of income might be characterized as income from "lease" or "sale," a more meaningful distinction could be made between on-going income generated in the ordinary course of business and income from the termination and sale of the venture. * * *

[T]o rest the word "primarily" on the distinction between lease and sale income would lead to the absurd result that whenever lease income exceeded sale income on the same item, the sale income could be treated as capital gain.

The real question, therefore, concerns whether or not the income from the sales of appellant's shoe machinery should have been characterized as having been generated in the "ordinary course of * * * business." Appellant contests the conclusion of the district court that selling was "an accepted and predictable part of the business" by pointing out that sales were made only as a last resort, after attempts to dissuade the customer from purchasing had failed. We think that the district court was correct in its finding. While sales were made only as a last resort, it seems clear that after 1964 such sales were expected to occur, on an occasional basis, and policies and procedures were developed for handling them. Purchase inquiries were referred to the vice president for sales, a price schedule was drawn up, and discounts were offered to good customers. Appellant may not have desired such sales. It is likely that appellant would never have developed a sales policy for its leased machines had it not been forced to do so by the pressure of competition. But it was justifiable to find that such occasional sales were indeed "accepted and predictable."

Even "accepted and predictable" sales might not, however, occur in the "ordinary course of * * * business." For example, a final liquidation of inventory, although accepted and predictable, would normally be eligible for capital gains treatment. Appellant's final contention, therefore, is that the sales in question represented the liquidation of an investment. Appellant points out that the machines were leased for an average of eight and one half years before they were sold, during which time depreciation was taken on them and repairs were made. Thus, appellant seeks to bring itself within the scope of the "rental-obsolescence" decisions, which hold that the sale of rental equipment, no longer useful for renting, is taxable at capital gains rates. * * *

In the "rental obsolescence" decisions, however, equipment was sold only after its rental income-producing potential had ended and "such sales were * * * the natural conclusion of a vehicle rental business cycle." Moreover, the equipment was specifically manufactured to fit the requirements of lessees; it was sold only when lessees no longer found the equipment useful. In the present case, however, the shoe manufacturing equipment was sold, not as a final disposition of property that had ceased to produce rental income for the appellant, but, rather, as property that still retained a rental income producing potential for the appellant. Had appellant chosen not to sell the shoe machinery, the machinery would have continued to generate ordinary income in the form of lease revenue. Thus, the sale of such machinery, for a price which included the present value of that future ordinary income, cannot be considered the liquidation of an investment outside the scope of the "ordinary course of * * * business."

Affirmed.

Problem 2–14

Lee is the owner of a secretarial counseling and management firm. The following occurred in 1997: Machine A, which had been used in Lee's business for more than one year, was sold for a gain of $13,000; an automobile held for more than one year and used in her business was destroyed by a flood, resulting in an uninsured loss of $6,000; business machine B held for more than one year was sold for a loss of $1,000; Lee's business typewriter, purchased in the Orient two years before, was stolen, but insurance proceeds resulted in a gain of $5,000; her business tape recorder, held for three months, was also stolen, resulting in a loss of $500; business machine C was held for less than one year and sold at a gain of $4,000; IBM stock, held for more than one year and having no connection to Lee's firm, was sold at a loss of $2,000; Lee's yacht, acquired two years before and used for personal purposes, was sold, resulting in a loss of $15,000; business machine D was abandoned after three years of use, resulting in a loss of $10,000; raw land, acquired 16 months before and held for profit, was sold under the threat of condemnation at a loss of $3,000.

a. Which events are subject to § 1231 netting?

b. Which of the § 1231 events fall into either tier 1 or tier 2 for netting purposes?

c. What is the character of each item of gain or loss?

5. RECAPTURE OF DEPRECIATION—GENERAL PRINCIPLES

Code References: §§ 1245(a)(1) to (3), (b)(1) to (4), (c), (d).

Regulations: §§ 1.1245–1(a) to (d); 1.1245–2(a)(1) to (4); 1.1245–3; 1.1245–4(a)(1).

Tax avoidance schemes may evolve from unintended statutory consequences inherent in the taxation of property transactions. To prevent abuse, Congress has enacted exceptions to the general rules discussed in preceding sections of this chapter. In general, these exceptions create a statutory mechanism by which one Code section supersedes another.

See generally Guerin and Postlewaite, *Problems and Materials in Federal Income Taxation* ch. 7 (Little Brown 5th ed. 1997).

For example, on the sale of a capital asset which is personal property, § 1245 (a depreciation and amortization recapture provision) may override the capital gain provisions by requiring gain to be characterized as ordinary income. The § 1245 depreciation recapture provision may characterize as ordinary income all or a portion of the gain recognized on the sale or disposition of certain depreciable property. In addition, § 1245 may also require recognition of gain on dispositions that would otherwise be nontaxable under other provisions of the Code. Furthermore, even if the property is not depreciable in the hands of the taxpayer who sells or exchanges it, it may be subject to depreciation recapture if it has a substituted basis, such as a gift, and was depreciable in the hands of the taxpayer's transferor.

The recapture provisions frequently arise in small business transactions and are integrally related to the depreciation and amortization provisions of § 167, § 168, and § 197, which, as described in section C of this chapter, allow an annual deduction over the useful life of an asset or over a statutorily prescribed period representing the recovery of the capital investment in the asset. By permitting these deductions, Congress has provided an economic incentive for business and industry to modernize plants and other facilities. The investment incentive can be statutorily manipulated either by increasing the percentage of investment recovered annually, by shortening the recovery period, or by a combination of the two.

Real property, however, is generally immune from the recapture of depreciation deductions upon its sale. See §§ 12250, 168. This occurs because § 1250 typically recaptures only excess depreciation, i.e., that taken in excess of the straight-line amount, and under § 168 most real property must be depreciated on a straight-line basis.

The amount realized on the disposition of depreciable assets often exceeds the taxpayer's basis in the asset because the projected decline in value estimated by § 167, § 168, or § 197 is excessive or nonexistent. Although the mandatory § 1016 basis adjustment ensures the taxation of the proper amount of excessive depreciation or amortization, characterization of the resulting gain under § 1221 or § 1231 may nevertheless be unduly favorable to the taxpayer. If the entire gain receives capital treatment, the Service may not be made whole because the benefit to the taxpayer from depreciation or amortization deductions (that is, less ordinary income) might not be offset by the recoupment of that amount as long-term capital gain. Congress, therefore, enacted § 1245 to remedy this deficiency in the personal property context. Consequently, gain attributable to depreciation or amortization recapture of business personal property will be characterized as ordinary income. Any gain in excess of the recaptured depreciation is unaffected by § 1245. As noted, the recapture of depreciation on the sale of real property is generally capital gain even though the § 168 deductions sheltered ordinary income.

The following examples demonstrate the operation of the recapture rules of § 1245 and § 1250.

1. On January 1, 1996, Abel purchased machinery, § 1245 recovery property, for use in his manufacturing business. His basis for depreciation was $10,000. After properly claiming depreciation deductions totaling $4,000, Abel sold the asset on January 2, 1997, for its fair market value of $7,500. Abel, therefore, realized a gain of $1,500 ($7,500 amount realized—$6,000 adjusted basis). Section 1245 requires Abel to recapture that gain as ordinary income to the extent of his depreciation deductions ($4,000). Thus, the entire $1,500 gain is treated as ordinary income under § 1245(a)(1) and not as gain from the sale or exchange of § 1231 property.

2. If Abel sold the property in example 1 for $10,500, his gain would be $4,500. Section 1245 would require recharacterization of $4,000 of the gain as ordinary income. The remaining $500 would, however, be treated as the gain from the sale or exchange of a § 1231 asset.

3. In 1997, Carl, a farmer, gave his son, Don, a rototiller that he no longer needed. The rototiller, purchased in 1995 for $1,500, had been totally depreciated. Don used the rototiller once to prepare his front yard for reseeding and then sold it for $450 in 1998. Because the rototiller was a gift from Carl to Don, Don took a substituted basis in the machine. Thus, under § 1015, Don's basis was zero, and he realized a $450 gain on his sale. Because Don had a substituted basis, the recapture taint that attached to the asset in Carl's hands carried over to Don and the $450 gain is recaptured as ordinary income, despite the fact that Don held the rototiller as personal, nondepreciable property.

4. On January 1, 1995, Donald purchased a building for $117,-000 for use in his business. The building constitutes nonresidential real property depreciable over 39 years. The depreciation allowance for 1995 and 1996 was $3,000 per year as such property is limited to straight-line depreciation. On January 1, 1997, when the building's basis was $111,000, Donald sold the building for $120,000. None of the $9,000 gain would be subject to § 1250 since only excess depreciation (that which exceeds the straight-line amount) is recaptured. Thus, the $9,000 gain would be characterized under § 1231.

LEGISLATIVE HISTORY OF § 1245 (GAIN FROM THE DISPOSITION OF CERTAIN DEPRECIABLE PROPERTY)

S.Rep. No. 1881, 87th Cong., 2d Sess. 95 (1962).

Under present law, in the case of depreciable property the taxpayer may write off the cost or other basis of the property over the period of the useful life of the asset in his hands. This cost or other basis can be written off evenly (i.e., in a "straight line" over the asset's life), under the declining balance method, under the sum-of-the-years digits method, or under any other consistent method which does not during the first two thirds of the useful life of the property exceed the allowances which would have been allowed under the declining balance method. The depreciation deduction is a deduction against ordinary income. If either the useful life of the asset is too short, or the particular method of depreciation allows too much depreciation in the early years, the decline in value of the asset resulting from these depreciation deductions may exceed the actual decline. Wherever the depreciation deductions reduce the basis of the property faster than the actual decline in its value, then when it is sold there will be a gain. Under present law this gain is taxed as a capital gain, even though the depreciation deductions reduced ordinary income. The taxpayer who has taken excessive depreciation deductions and then sells an asset, therefore, has in effect converted ordinary income into a capital gain.

The President stated that our capital gains concept should not encompass this kind of income. He indicated that this inequity should be eliminated. * * * He states that we should not encourage the further acquisition of such property through tax incentives as long as the loophole remains.

This problem also is of major significance in connection with the recent depreciation liberalization announced by the Treasury Department. Under this new approach, many taxpayers will be permitted to depreciate assets faster for tax purposes than has previously been the case. Therefore, additional ordinary income would be converted into capital gain if this were not dealt with in the provision. * * *

The general rule (in sec. 1245) provides that ordinary income is to be recognized in the case of sales or exchanges to the extent the so-called recomputed basis, or the amount realized in the sale or exchange, whichever is lesser, exceeds the basis of the property in the hands of the person making the sale or exchange. "Recomputed basis" is defined generally as equaling the adjusted basis plus the depreciation deductions previously taken. The excess of the amount realized over the adjusted basis is, of course, the amount presently recognized as capital gain. Since the rule requires that the smaller of these two amounts be treated as ordinary income, this in effect means that the ordinary income in the usual case is to be the gain realized or the sum of the depreciation deductions taken, whichever is smaller. Where there is a disposition of an asset without a sale or exchange, gain is determined by reference to the fair market value of the asset.

Problem 2–15

Bayless is a salesman who travels throughout the country by automobile. On January 1, 1994, he purchased a Volare station wagon for $10,000 to be used exclusively for business purposes. On January 2, 1997, Bayless sold the car for $7,000. The total depreciation taken to the date of sale was the entire $10,000.

On January 1, 1994, Bayless received a Ford van as a gift from his father. His father had purchased the van for $15,000 one year earlier and used it as a delivery vehicle in his restaurant supply business. His father claimed one year of depreciation totaling $1,500 on the van. Bayless used the van in his sales business for three years, during which time he did not claim any depreciation deductions. The amount of depreciation properly allowable on the straight-line method for the three-year period was $9,000. He sold the van on January 2, 1997, for $11,000.

    a.   What is Bayless's adjusted basis in the station wagon on the date of sale?

    b.   What is Bayless's recomputed basis in the station wagon?

    c.   What is the amount realized on the sale of the station wagon?

    d.   How much depreciation recapture must Bayless recognize on the sale of the station wagon, and what is the amount of the § 1231 gain?

    e.   Assume that Bayless sold the station wagon for $12,000; what is the answer to d?

    f.   What is his father's adjusted basis in the van on January 1, 1994?

    g.   Does the father recognize § 1245 recapture on the date of the gift?

    h.   What is Bayless's basis in the van on January 1, 1994?

    i.   What is Bayless's adjusted basis on January 2, 1997?

    j.   What is Bayless's recomputed basis in the van?

    k.   What is the amount and character of any gain that Bayless must recognize on the sale of the van?

Chapter 3

DISPOSITION ASPECTS OF SOLE PROPRIETORSHIP

A. INTRODUCTION

At some point in time during the life cycle of a sole proprietorship, the entrepreneur begins to consider partial or complete retirement. Depending upon the degree to which he or she wishes to retain some participation in the enterprise, numerous options are available at that time. In addition, there is always the possibility that the owner's participation in the business will end because of his or her death.

The most extreme option for the retiring owner is an outright sale of the enterprise to third parties for cash. A middle ground involves giving the business to the sole proprietor's children or other objects of affection. This option may permit some continued involvement, typically in the role of a well-paid consultant. Death of the owner will cause passage of the business to those beneficiaries designated in the sole proprietor's will. The final option is the transfer of the business to a corporation or a partnership in return for an equity interest therein (usually a majority interest). Under this last alternative, the entrepreneur continues ownership in the enterprise to some degree, either as an active or passive member of the acquiring entity.

B. SALE OF BUSINESS—COVENANTS AND GOODWILL

Code References: §§ 1221(1), 1060(a) to (c).
Regulations: § 1.167(a)–3.

A going business usually consists of diverse elements including, but not limited to, goodwill, real property, fixtures, machinery, and inventory. When a business is sold, there are at least two possibilities as to how the transaction will be treated for tax purposes. The entire business entity could be viewed as a single asset of its owner, similar to a shareholder's interest in a corporation. If this were the case, the entire gain or loss on the sale would typically be capital, regardless of the character of the business's underlying assets. See discussion at Chapter 2.

The Service, however, views the sale of a sole proprietor's business differently. It treats such a sale as a sale of the underlying assets, not a single piece of property. The Service's position was adopted by the courts in the *Williams* decision, which follows. Therein, the Second Circuit analyzed the sale of an unincorporated going business and enunciated the generally accepted rule—a sale of a going business is to be treated as a separate sale of each of the component parts of the business. See also discussion at Chapter 31. See generally Guerin and Postlewaite, *Problems and Materials in Federal Income Taxation* ch. 7 (Little Brown 5th ed. 1997).

WILLIAMS v. McGOWAN

152 F.2d 570 (2d Cir.1945).

L. Hand, J. * * *

Williams, the taxpayer, and one, Reynolds, had for many years been engaged in the hardware business in the City of Corning, New York. On the 20th of January, 1926, they formed a partnership, of which Williams was entitled to two-thirds of the profits, and Reynolds, one-third. They agreed that on February 1, 1925, the capital invested in the business had been $118,082.05, of which Reynolds had a credit of $29,029.03, and Williams, the balance—$89,053.02. At the end of every business year, on February 1st, Reynolds was to pay to Williams, interest upon the amount of the difference between his share of the capital and one-third of the total as shown by the inventory; and upon withdrawal of one party the other was to have the privilege of buying the other's interest as it appeared on the books. The business was carried on through the firm's fiscal year, ending January 31, 1940, in accordance with this agreement, and thereafter until Reynolds' death on July 18th of that year. Williams settled with Reynolds' executrix on September 6th in an agreement by which he promised to pay her $12,187.90, and to assume all liabilities of the business; and he did pay her $2,187.98 in cash at once, and $10,000 on the 10th of the following October. On September 17th of the same year, Williams sold the business as a whole to the Corning Building Company for $63,926.28—its agreed value as of February 1, 1940—"plus an amount to be computed by multiplying the gross sales of the business from the first day of February, 1940 to the 28th day of September, 1940," by an agreed fraction. This value was made up of cash of about $8,100, receivables of about $7,000, fixtures of about $800, and a merchandise inventory of about $49,000, less some $1,000 for bills payable. To this was added about $6,000 credited to Williams for profits under the language just quoted, making a total of nearly $70,000. Upon this sale Williams suffered a loss upon his original two-thirds of the business, but he made a small gain upon the one-third which he had bought from Reynolds' executrix; and in his income tax return he entered both as items of "ordinary income," and not as transactions in "capital assets." This the Commissioner disallowed and recomputed the tax accordingly. * * * The only question is whether the business was "capital assets."

It has been held that a partner's interest in a going firm is for tax purposes to be regarded as a "capital asset." * * * If a partner's interest in a going firm is "capital assets" perhaps a dead partner's interest is the same. We need not say. When Williams bought out Reynolds' interest, he became the sole owner of the business, the firm had ended upon any theory, and the situation for tax purposes was no other than if Reynolds had never been a partner at all, except that to the extent of one-third of the "amount realized" on Williams' sale to the Corning Company, his "basis" was different. The judge thought that, because upon that sale both parties fixed the price at the liquidation value of the business while Reynolds was alive, "plus" its estimated earnings thereafter, it was as though Williams had sold his interest in the firm during its existence. But the method by which the parties agreed upon the price was irrelevant to the computation of Williams' income. * * * We have to decide only whether upon the sale of a going business it is to be comminuted into its fragments, * * * or whether the whole business is to be treated as if it were a single piece of property.

Our law has been sparing in the creation of juristic entities; it has never, for example, taken over the Roman "universitas facti";[1] and indeed for many years it fumbled uncertainly with the concept of a corporation. One might have supposed that partnership would have been an especially promising field in which to raise up an entity, particularly since merchants have always kept their accounts upon that basis. Yet there too our law resisted at the price of great and continuing confusion; and, even when it might be thought that a statute admitted, if it did not demand, recognition of the firm as an entity, the old concepts prevailed. And so, even though we might agree that under the influence of the Uniform Partnership Act a partner's interest in the firm should be treated as indivisible, and for that reason a "capital asset" we should be wary about extending further so exotic a jural concept. Be that as it may, in this instance the section itself furnishes the answer. It starts in the broadest way by declaring that all "property" is "capital assets," and then makes three exceptions. The first is "stock in trade * * * or other property of a kind which would properly be included in the inventory"; next comes "property held * * * primarily for sale to customers"; and finally, property "used in the trade or business of a character which is subject to * * * allowance for depreciation." In the face of this language, although it may be true that a "stock in trade," taken by itself, should be treated as a "universitas facti," by no possibility can a whole business be so treated; and the same is true as to any property within the other exceptions. Congress plainly did mean to comminute the elements of a business; plainly it did not regard the whole as "capital assets."

---

1. "By universitas facti is meant a number of things of the same kind which are regarded as a whole; e.g., a herd, a stock of wares." Mackeldey, Roman Law § 162.

As has already appeared, Williams transferred to the Corning Company "cash," "receivables," "fixtures" and a "merchandise inventory." "Fixtures" are not capital because they are subject to a depreciation allowance; the inventory, as we have just seen, is expressly excluded. So far as appears, no allowance was made for "good will." * * * There can of course be no gain or loss in the transfer of cash; and, although Williams does appear to have made a gain of $1,072.71 upon the "receivables," the point has not been argued that they are not subject to a depreciation allowance. That we leave open for decision by the district court, if the parties cannot agree. The gain or loss upon every other item should be computed as an item in ordinary income.

Judgment reversed.

FRANK, J. (dissenting in part).

I agree that it is irrelevant that the business was once owned by a partnership. For when the sale to the Corning Company occurred, the partnership was dead, had become merely a memory, a ghost. To say that the sale was of the partnership's assets would, then, be to indulge in animism.

But I do not agree that we should ignore what the parties to the sale, Williams and the Corning Company, actually did. They did not arrange for a transfer to the buyer, as if in separate bundles, of the several ingredients of the business. They contracted for the sale of the entire business as a going concern. Here is what they said in their agreement: "The party of the first part agrees to sell and the party of the second part agrees to buy, *all of the right, title and interest* of the said party of the first part *in and to the hardware business* now being conducted by the said party of the first part, including cash on hand and on deposit in the First National Bank & Trust Company of Corning in the A.F. Williams Hardware Store account, in accounts receivable, bills receivable, notes receivable, merchandise and fixtures, including two G.M. trucks, good will and all other assets of every kind and description used in and about said business * * *. Said party of the first part agrees not to engage in the hardware business within a radius of twenty-five miles from the City of Corning, New York, for a period of ten years from the 1st day of October 1940."

To carve up this transaction into distinct sales—of cash, receivables, fixtures, trucks, merchandise, and good will—is to do violence to the realities. I do not think Congress intended any such artificial result. In the Senate Committee Report it was said: "It is believed that this Senate amendment will be of material benefit to businesses which, due to depressed conditions, have been compelled to dispose of their plant or equipment at a loss. The bill defines property used in a trade or business as property used in the trade or business of a character which is subject to the allowance for depreciation, and real property held for more than six months which is not properly includable in the inventory of the taxpayer if on hand at the close of the taxable year or property held by the taxpayer primarily for sale to customers in the ordinary course of his trade or business. If a newspaper purchased the plant and equipment of a rival newspaper and later sold such plant and equipment at a loss, such plant and equipment, being subject to depreciation, would constitute property used in the trade or business within the meaning of this section." These remarks show that what Congress contemplated was not the sale of a going business but of its dismembered parts. Where a business is sold as a unit, the whole is greater than its parts. Businessmen so recognize; so, too, I think, did Congress. Interpretation of our complicated tax statutes is seldom aided by saying that taxation is an eminently practical matter (or the like). But this is one instance where, it seems to me, the practical aspects of the matter should guide our guess as to what Congress meant. I believe Congress had those aspects in mind and was not thinking of the nice distinctions between Roman and Anglo–American legal theories about legal entities.

Problem   3–1

Sheldon wishes to sell his successful retail clothing business. The assets that will be sold include goodwill, building, land, and inventory. Sheldon also will execute a covenant not to compete with the purchaser.

a. How might Sheldon wish to allocate the sales proceeds?

b. Assuming the same facts, how might a potential purchaser wish to allocate the purchase price?

C.   GIFTS AND BEQUESTS

1.   SECTION 1015—BASIS FOR PROPERTY RECEIVED AS A GIFT

Code References: § 1015(a), (d)(1), (2), (4), (6).

Regulations: §§ 1.1015–1(a), (c), (d); 1.1015–4; 1.1015–5(a)(1)(i), (a)(2).

An attraction of employing a gift of the business to favored offspring is that neither the donor nor the donee typically will be subject to *income* tax consequences from the transfer. The combination of § 102 and § 1015 insulates both parties from the reach of the income tax collector. See generally Guerin and Postlewaite, *Problems and Materials in Federal Income Taxation* ch. 3 (Little Brown 5th ed. 1997). Obviously, gift tax considerations might present themselves, but that topic is beyond the scope of this casebook. In practice, gifts of businesses are often made gradually through the annual transfer of minority interests in operating entities such as corporations, partnerships, or similar hybrid forms. This allows a "minority interest discount" for gift tax purposes. Such a technique is obviously not available in the sole proprietorship context.

Once it is determined that the transferee has received a gift, an issue arises if the gift is one of property other than cash: What is the transferee's tax basis in the acquired property? Pursuant to § 1015, a taxpayer who receives a gift acquires a transferred or "carryover" basis in the gift property—that is, the donee's basis is generally the donor's basis in the property at the time of the transfer. See § 7701(a)(43). One effect of the carryover basis is that the appreciation in value that accrued while the property was held by the donor is not taxed to the donor but is taxed to the donee on a subsequent taxable disposition of that property. See Taft v. Bowers, 278 U.S. 470 (1929).

As is evident from § 1015, the appreciation in value of property transferred by gift is not permanently excluded from income but is taken into account by the donee if he or she subsequently sells the property for a gain. Nevertheless, a parent/donor can often reduce the family unit's total income tax liability by transferring appreciated property to a child in a lower tax bracket. Such transfers must, however, be examined in light of potential gift tax liabilities and the possible application of the "kiddie tax" of § 1(g) if the child is under the age of 14.

Because the inherent gain generally is not realized at the time the gift is made, potential advantages exist for transferring appreciated property. However, Congress has chosen not to allow a similar transfer of tax losses. As a result, the rule for computing the basis of property received by gift is dependent on whether the donee's subsequent disposition of the property results in gain, or in loss, or in neither gain nor loss.

Section 1015 sets forth the rules for determining the basis of property acquired by gift. The first step in calculating a donee's basis is to determine whether the fair market value of the property at the time of the gift is greater or less than the donor's adjusted basis in the property. If the fair market value is greater than or equal to the donor's adjusted basis, the donee's basis will be the donor's adjusted basis increased (but not above the property's fair market value) by the gift tax paid (if any), which is attributable to the net appreciation in the property. See § 1015(d). These carryover basis rules preserve any inherent gain in the property until a subsequent recognition event. Thus, the donee who eventually disposes of the property in a sale or other taxable exchange realizes a gain equal to the total appreciation since the last taxable disposition of that property. For example, assume that parent (Paula) transferred to her child (Cassie) property with a fair market value of $20,000. Assume that no gift tax is incurred on the transaction and that Paula's basis in the property was $8,000. The transfer is therefore of appreciated property, and under § 1015(a), Cassie's basis in the property for determining gain or loss is $8,000. If Cassie subsequently sells the property for $25,000, she will recognize a $17,000 gain—the $12,000 of appreciation in Paula's hands plus $5,000 of appreciation in Cassie's hands.

If the value of the property at the time of the gift is less than the donor's adjusted basis (that is, if there is an inherent loss), the rules become more complex. In such cases, the donee will have two bases in the property: a basis for determining gain and a basis for determining loss. The basis for gain is, as above, the donor's adjusted basis. The basis for loss, however, is the fair market value of the property at the time of the gift. (This is the method by which § 1015 prevents a donor from transferring a tax loss to the donee.) If the donee sells the property for more than the gain basis, the excess is a realized gain. If the property is sold for less than the loss basis, the excess is a realized loss.

Thus, if Al gives property with a $3,000 fair market value and a $5,000 adjusted basis to Bob, who subsequently sells the property for $6,000, Bob's basis for computing gain is $5,000. Bob will realize a $1,000 gain. If Al gives the same property to Bob, who sells it for $2,000, Bob's basis for computing loss is $3,000—the property's fair market value at the time of the gift. B therefore realizes only a $1,000 loss, and $2,000 of the tax loss inherent in the property at the time of transfer disappears. If, however, the donee sells the property for an amount greater than the loss basis (fair market value at the time of the gift), but less than the gain basis (donor's basis), the donee realizes neither gain nor loss. As noted above, Al's basis was $5,000 when he gave Bob property with a $3,000 fair market value. If Bob subsequently sells the property for $4,000, the amount realized is less than the gain basis ($5,000) and more than the loss basis ($3,000); therefore, Bob will realize neither gain nor loss on the disposition.

Problem 3–2

Larry purchased two non-depreciable properties in 1989 for use in his sole proprietorship trade or business for the following amounts: property A, $10,000, and property B, $14,000. In 1997, the properties were valued at $15,000 and $9,000, respectively.

    a.   In 1997, Larry gave property A to his daughter Monica incurring a $1,000 gift tax liability as a result of the transfer. Monica sold the property one month later for $17,000. What was Monica's gain or loss from the sale?

    b.   In 1997, Larry gave property B to his younger daughter, Pearl, incurring a $750 gift tax liability as a result of the transfer. Pearl sold the property one month later for $8,000. What was Pearl's gain or loss from the sale?

    c.   What result in *b* if Pearl had sold property B for $12,000? Assume that there was no gift tax liability on the original transfer to her.

2. PART SALE/PART GIFT TRANSACTIONS

Code References: §§ 1015; 1011(b).

Regulations: §§ 1.1015–4; 1.1001–1(e); 1.1001–2(a)(1), (4)(iii).

A part sale/part gift arises when property is transferred in return for consideration totaling less than the property's fair market value. For example, a parent operating the business might agree to transfer it to his child for a bargain price. To the extent that consideration is received, the transaction is treated as a sale. To the extent that the fair market value of the property exceeds the consideration, the transaction is generally treated as a gift. The rules for determining the basis of property acquired in a part sale/part gift transaction are, as one might expect, a hybrid of the cost basis and gift basis rules. These rules are set forth in Regulation § 1.1015–4.

Generally, in a sale, the transferee takes a "cost" basis in the acquired property pursuant to § 1012, whereas in a gift transaction the transferee takes the donor's basis (carryover basis) pursuant to § 1015. Where the transaction is a part sale/part gift, however, the transferor is deemed to have sold the property for the amount of consideration received. Reg. § 1.1015–4(a). In such cases, the transferee takes a basis in the property received equal to the amount paid or the transferor's adjusted basis, whichever is greater, increased by the gift tax attributable to the net appreciation on the gift portion of the transfer.

By selling property to a family member for an amount below fair market value, the taxpayer can recoup his or her original investment. For example, assume that John sells property with a $100,000 fair market value and $40,000 adjusted basis to a third party, Joy, for $100,000. John realizes a gain of $60,000. If, on the other hand, he sells the property to his son, Terry, for $35,000, he realizes no gain on the transaction because his amount realized does not exceed his adjusted basis. Yet he recoups $35,000 of his original investment. Although it might initially appear that John could have deducted a $5,000 loss as a result of the transaction, no loss deduction is permitted to the transfer on a part sale/part gift. Reg. § 1.1001–1(e).

Under Regulation § 1.1015–4(a), Terry in the example above has a basis of $40,000—the greater of (1) the amount Terry paid ($35,000) or (2) John's adjusted basis at the time of the transfer ($40,000). It is assumed that no gift tax was due on the transfer. The $60,000 of potential gain not taxed as income to John will be realized by Terry, if he later sells the property for $100,000 or more.

As in the pure gift situation, in determining whether a loss is realized on the transferee's subsequent sale of property acquired in a part sale/part gift, the calculation of basis differs from the computation of basis for gain purposes. Regulation § 1.1015–4(a) provides that the basis in such situations is the lesser of (1) the transferee's basis (the greater of cost or the transferor's adjusted basis) or (2) the fair market value of the property at the time of the transfer.

DIEDRICH v. COMMISSIONER

457 U.S. 191 (1982).

Chief Justice Burger delivered the opinion of the Court. * * *

I * * *

In 1972 petitioners Victor and Frances Diedrich made gifts of approximately 85,000 shares of stock to their three children, using both a direct transfer and a trust arrangement. The gifts were subject to a condition that the donees pay the resulting federal and state gift taxes. There is no dispute concerning the amount of the gift tax paid by the donees. The donors' basis in the transferred stock was $51,073; the gift tax paid in 1972 by the donees was $62,992. Petitioners did not include as income on their 1972 federal income tax returns any portion of the gift tax paid by the donees. After an audit the Commissioner of Internal Revenue determined that petitioners had realized income to the extent that the gift tax owed by petitioners but paid by the donees exceeded the donors' basis in the property. Accordingly, petitioners' taxable income for 1972 was increased by $5,959.[1] * * *

II

A

Pursuant to its constitutional authority, Congress has defined "gross income" as income "from whatever source derived," including "[i]ncome from discharge of indebtedness." This Court has recognized that "income" may be realized by a variety of indirect means. In Old Colony Trust Co. v. Commissioner, 279 U.S. 716 (1929), the Court held that payment of an employee's income taxes by an employer constituted income to the employee. Speaking for the Court, Chief Justice Taft concluded that "[t]he payment of the tax by the employe[r] was in consideration of the services rendered by the employee and was a gain derived by the employee from his labor." The Court made clear that the substance, not the form, of the agreed transaction controls. "The discharge by a third person of an obligation to him is equivalent to receipt by the person taxed." The employee, in other words, was placed in a better position as a result of the employer's discharge of the employee's legal obligation to pay the income taxes; the employee thus received a gain subject to income tax.

The holding in *Old Colony* was reaffirmed in Crane v. Commissioner, 331 U.S. 1 (1947). In *Crane* the Court concluded that relief from the obligation of a nonrecourse mortgage in which the value of the property exceeded the value of the mortgage constituted income to the taxpayer. The taxpayer in *Crane* acquired depreciable property, an apartment building, subject to an unassumed mortgage. The taxpayer later sold the apartment building, which was still subject to the nonrecourse mortgage, for cash plus the buyer's assumption of the mortgage. This Court held that the amount of the mortgage was properly included in the amount realized on the sale, noting that if the taxpayer transfers subject to the mortgage, "the benefit to him is as real and substantial as if the mortgage were discharged, or as if a personal debt in an equal amount had been assumed by another." Id., at 14. Again, it was the "reality," not the form, of the transaction that governed. The Court found it immaterial whether the seller received money prior to the sale in order to discharge the mortgage, or whether the seller merely transferred the

---

1. Subtracting the stock basis of $51,073 from the gift tax paid by the donees of $62,992 the Commissioner found that petitioners had realized a long-term capital gain of $11,919. After a 50 percent reduction in long-term capital gain, 26 U.S.C. § 1202, the Diedrichs' taxable income increased by $5,959.

property subject to the mortgage. In either case the taxpayer realized an economic benefit.

B

The principles of *Old Colony* and *Crane* control. A common method of structuring gift transactions is for the donor to make the gift subject to the condition that the donee pay the resulting gift tax, as was done in each of the cases now before us. When a gift is made, the gift tax liability falls on the donor. When a donor makes a gift to a donee, a "debt" to the United States for the amount of the gift tax is incurred by the donor. Those taxes are as much the legal obligation of the donor as the donor's income taxes; for these purposes they are the same kind of debt obligation as the income taxes of the employee in *Old Colony.* Similarly, when a donee agrees to discharge an indebtedness in consideration of the gift, the person relieved of the tax liability realizes an economic benefit. In short, the donor realizes an immediate economic benefit by the donee's assumption of the donor's legal obligation to pay the gift tax.

An examination of the donor's intent does not change the character of this benefit. Although intent is relevant in determining whether a gift has been made, subjective intent has not characteristically been a factor in determining whether an individual has realized income. Even if intent were a factor, the donor's intent with respect to the condition shifting the gift tax obligation from the donor to the donee was plainly to relieve the donor of a debt owed to the United States; the choice was made because the donor would receive a benefit in relief from the obligation to pay the gift tax.

Finally, the benefit realized by the taxpayer is not diminished by the fact that the liability attaches during the course of a donative transfer. It cannot be doubted that the donors were aware that the gift tax obligation would arise immediately upon the transfer of the property; the economic benefit to the donors in the discharge of the gift tax liability is indistinguishable from the benefit arising from discharge of a preexisting obligation. Nor is there any doubt that had the donors sold a portion of the stock immediately before the gift transfer in order to raise funds to pay the expected gift tax, a taxable gain would have been realized. The fact that the gift tax obligation was discharged by way of a conditional gift rather than from funds derived from a pregift sale does not alter the underlying benefit to the donors.

C

Consistent with the economic reality, the Commissioner has treated these conditional gifts as a discharge of indebtedness through a part gift and part sale of the gift property transferred. The transfer is treated as if the donor sells the property to the donee for less than the fair market value. The "sale" price is the amount necessary to discharge the gift tax indebtedness; the balance of the value of the transferred property is treated as a gift. The gain thus derived by the donor is the amount of the gift tax liability less the donor's adjusted basis in the entire property. Accordingly, income is realized to the extent that the gift tax exceeds the donor's adjusted basis in the property. This treatment is consistent with § 1001 of the Internal Revenue Code, which provides that the gain from the disposition of property is the excess of the amount realized over the transferor's adjusted basis in the property.

III

We recognize that Congress has structured gift transactions to encourage transfer of property by limiting the tax consequences of a transfer. Congress may obviously provide a similar exclusion for the conditional gift. Should Congress wish to encourage "net gifts," changes in the income tax consequences of such gifts lie within the legislative responsibility. Until such time, we are bound by Congress' mandate that gross income includes income "from whatever source derived." We therefore hold that a donor who makes a gift of property on condition that the donee pay the resulting gift taxes realizes taxable income to the extent that the gift taxes paid by the donee exceed the donor's adjusted basis in the property. * * *

JUSTICE REHNQUIST, dissenting.

It is a well-settled principle today that a taxpayer realizes income when another person relieves the taxpayer of a legal obligation in connection with an otherwise taxable transaction. See Crane v. Commissioner, 331 U.S. 1 (1947) (sale of real property); Old Colony Trust Co. v. Commissioner, 279 U.S. 716 (1929) (employment compensation). In neither *Old Colony* nor *Crane* was there any question as to the existence of a taxable transaction; the only question concerned the amount of income realized by the taxpayer as a result of the taxable transaction. The Court in this case, however, begs the question of whether a taxable transaction has taken place at all when it concludes that "[t]he principles of *Old Colony* and *Crane* control" this case.

In *Old Colony,* the employer agreed to pay the employee's federal tax liability as part of his compensation. The employee provided his services to the employer in exchange for compensation. The exchange of compensation for services was undeniably a taxable transaction. The only question was whether the employee's taxable income included the employer's assumption of the employee's income tax liability.

In *Crane,* the taxpayer sold real property for cash plus the buyer's assumption of a mortgage. Clearly a sale had occurred, and the only question was whether the amount of the mortgage assumed by the buyer should be included in the amount realized by the taxpayer. The Court rejected the taxpayer's contention that what she sold was not the property itself, but her equity in that property.

Unlike *Old Colony* or *Crane,* the question in this case is not the amount of income the taxpayer has realized as a result of a concededly taxable transaction, but whether a taxable transaction has taken place at all. Only *after* one concludes that a partial sale occurs when the donee agrees to pay the gift tax do *Old Colony* and *Crane* become relevant in ascertaining the amount of income realized by the donor as a result of the transaction. Nowhere does the Court explain why a gift becomes a partial sale merely because the donor and donee structure the gift so that the gift tax imposed by Congress on the transaction is paid by the donee rather than the donor.

In my view, the resolution of this case turns upon congressional intent: whether Congress intended to characterize a gift as a partial sale whenever the donee agrees to pay the gift tax. Congress has determined that a gift should not be considered income to the donee. Instead, gift transactions are to be subject to a tax system wholly separate and distinct from the income tax. Both the donor and the donee may be held liable for the gift tax. Although the primary liability for the gift tax is on the donor, the donee is liable to the extent of the value of the gift should the donor fail to pay the tax. I see no evidence in the tax statutes that Congress forbade the parties to agree among themselves as to who would pay the gift tax upon pain of such an agreement being considered a taxable event for the purposes of the income tax. Although Congress could certainly determine that the payment of the gift tax by the donee constitutes income to the donor, the relevant statutes do not affirmatively indicate that Congress has made such a determination.

I dissent.

Problem 3–3

Shaun transferred property with an adjusted basis of $30,000 and a fair market value of $90,000 to his son, Michael, in return for $60,000. One year later, Michael sold the property for $100,000.

    a. Ignoring gift tax implications, what was Michael's gain or loss from the sale?

    b. What result in a if Michael sold the property for $25,000?

    c. Assume that Shaun transferred other property to Michael having an adjusted basis of $60,000 and a fair market value of $90,000, in return for $30,000. One year later, Michael sold the property for $100,000. Ignoring gift tax implications, what was Michael's gain or loss from the sale?

    d. What result in c if Michael sold the property for $25,000?

3. BASIS OF PROPERTY ACQUIRED BY INHERITANCE OR DEVISE

Code References: § 1014(a), (b)(1), (2), (e).

Regulations: §§ 1.1014–1(a), (b); 1.1014–2(b)(1); 1.1014–3(a).

Sometimes a relative inherits an unincorporated operating business previously owned by a decedent. The new owner will need to determine the tax basis of the assets received. Section 1014(a) provides the general rule that the basis of property received from a decedent is the fair market value of the property on the date of death. When the fair market value of the property at the date of death is greater than its adjusted basis, the devisee receives a "stepped-up" basis. In such cases, although the value of the property may be subject to estate tax, the difference between the decedent's basis and the stepped-up basis effectively escapes *income* (but not estate) taxation. If, however, the property had a basis in excess of its fair market value on the date of death, there is a step-down in basis and neither the decedent nor the person receiving the property may recognize the inherent tax loss. Thus, tax planners generally recommend that economically depreciated property (with a value less than its adjusted basis) be sold prior to death in order to recognize the tax loss, whereas appreciated property should be held until death so that the beneficiary receives a § 1014 step-up in basis and predeath appreciation escapes income taxation.

As an illustration of the dramatic effects of § 1014, consider the following hypothetical. Two taxpayers, Tim and Paul, own identical assets, each having a $1 million value and a $400,000 adjusted basis. Each begins negotiations for a sale to a common purchaser for $1 million. Tim's sale is completed at noon on April 13, while Paul's sale is still in the process of negotiation. On their way to dinner on the evening of April 13, both are killed in an auto accident. Paul's nephew, Marty, inherits Paul's asset and sells the asset several months later, on the above terms.

Tim's sale, completed during his life, results in a $600,000 gain realized ($1,000,000 amount realized, less $400,000 adjusted basis). Paul's heir, however, realizes no gain on his disposition of the inherited property. On inheriting the asset, Marty received a step-up in basis to the $1,000,000 fair market value at the time of Paul's death. The amount realized on the sale therefore does not exceed Marty's adjusted basis. Thus, no income tax is due.

Carryover basis, however, is required for one limited situation set forth in § 1014(e) and described by the following statement from that section's legislative history:

> [T]he stepped-up basis rules contained in section 1014 will not apply with respect to appreciated property acquired by the decedent through gift within [one year] of death (including the gift element of a bargain sale), if such property passes, directly or indirectly, from the donee-decedent to the original donor or the donor's spouse. The denial of a stepped-up basis applies where the donor receives the benefit of the appreciated property regardless of whether the bequest by the decedent to the donor is a specific bequest, a general bequest, a pecuniary bequest, or a residuary bequest.

H.R.Rep. No. 201, 97th Cong., 1st Sess., 188–189 (1981).

This rule is obviously designed to prevent the giving of property to a dying person who then wills it back to the original owner in an effort to increase the original owner's basis.

Problem 3–4

a. Randolph purchased business property for $10,000. Five years later, when the property was valued at $40,000, Randolph died, leaving the property to his trusted employee, Veronica. One month later, Veronica sold the property for $40,000. Did Veronica have gross income on receipt of the bequest? What was Veronica's gain or loss from the sale? What if she had sold the property for $15,000?

b. Assume that, prior to death, Randolph purchased other non-depreciable business property for $25,000. Three years after the purchase, when the property was valued at $10,000, he was on his deathbed. Should he allow this property to pass to his heirs through his estate or should he sell it prior to his death?

c. Tom gave his father, Jack, property with an adjusted basis of $5,000 and a fair market value of $50,000, incurring a gift tax liability of $10,000 as a result of the transfer. One month later, Jack died, and bequeathed the property to Tom. Three months later, Tom sold the property for $80,000. What was Tom's gain or loss from the sale?

d. What result in *c* if Jack had bequeathed the property to Tom's son (i.e., Jack's grandson)?

D. NONRECOGNITION TRANSFERS TO ANOTHER ENTITY

1. TO A PARTNERSHIP

One option in terminating a sole proprietor's status as such is to either form a partnership with another or to transfer the business to another pre-existing partnership in exchange for an interest in that partnership. Such transfers are typically granted nonrecognition treatment under § 721, subject to a few noteworthy exceptions. However, the inherent gain or loss is preserved for future recognition through the carryover of basis rule under § 722. This topic is discussed in detail at Chapters 5 and 6. See generally, Willis, Pennell, and Postlewaite, *Partnership Taxation* (Warren, Gorham & Lamont, 6th ed. 1996).

2. TO A CORPORATION

A similar pattern exists under the Code for the transfer of assets, including those of a sole proprietorship, to a corporation. Nonrecognition may be provided under § 351; however, a larger number of exceptions to nonrecognition exist in the corporate area than the partnership area. Thus, the transfer of sole proprietorship assets to an existing corporation in exchange for its stock is less likely to qualify under § 351 than a similar transfer to an existing partnership. If § 351 applies, a carryover of basis concept is provided in § 358. This topic is discussed in greater detail in Chapters 22 and 24. See generally Bittker and Eustice, *Federal Income Taxation of Corporations and Shareholders* (Warren, Gorham & Lamont, 6th ed. 1994).

Chapter 4

PARTNERSHIP CLASSIFICATION

Code References: §§ 701; 761(a)–(b); 7701(a)(1)–(3); 7704(a)–(c), (f).

Regulations: §§ 1.701–1; 1.761–1; 1.761–2(a)–(b); 301.7701–1; 301.7701–2(a)–(e); 301.7701–3.

A. INTRODUCTION

As discussed in Chapter 1, business activity may occur in a number of different forms ranging from the conduct of operations as a sole proprietorship to the use of a corporation. Along this continuum, for the small entrepreneur, there are various choices available to him/her as to how those operations are conducted—as a sole proprietorship, a tenancy in common, a joint tenancy, a joint venture, a general partnership, a limited partnership, an S corporation, a limited liability company, a professional corporation, and a C corporation. In some state jurisdictions, there is even a broader range of choices including such hybrid entities as limited liability partnerships, limited liability limited partnerships, and limited partnership associations.

The choice between organizing a business as a noncorporate or corporate entity is governed primarily by three considerations: the applicable commercial law, the income and estate tax treatment of the business form chosen, and the investment and business preferences of the parties involved.

The major commercial law difference between the legal status of noncorporate and corporate entities has traditionally been the extent to which participants are held personally liable to business creditors. In a general partnership as well as a sole proprietorship, all members of the enterprise are liable for its debts and obligations. In a limited partnership, the limited partners are shielded from liability to creditors if they do not manage the business. However, barring state statutes to the contrary, the general partner of a limited partnership remains fully liable for the debts of the organization. In a corporation or a limited liability company, all owners are protected from creditors' claims (except those arising from their own personal conduct) regardless of the extent of their management activity.

For tax purposes, the relevant classification categories of a business enterprise are three: (1) a sole proprietorship, (2) a partnership, and (3) a corporation. There are no separate taxing categories for hybrid entities. They must be classified for tax purposes as one of the designated three. Although trusts are a separate category for tax purposes, trusts are not business operating entities. Given the focal point of this casebook, i.e. the selection of the proper vehicle for the conduct of small business activity, all three categories require consideration. This casebook has discussed the tax consequences of conducting business operations as a sole proprietorship in Chapters 1–3.

The classification issues at one end of the spectrum (sole proprietorship and tenancy in common versus partnership) are not particularly significant. While classification standards exist for distinguishing a sole proprietorship or a tenancy in common from a partnership, the consequences thereof are not particularly critical. This is so because sole proprietors, tenants in common, and members of a partnership are treated similarly for most tax purposes. No entity tax is imposed on the use of a partnership and therefore a single tax imposed at the individual level will arise regardless of how the enterprise is classified. While the treatment of various tax elections might differ depending upon how the enterprise is classified (e.g., the nonrecognition of gain from the involuntary conversion of an asset must be elected by the partnership, not the partners, while in a tenancy in common each individual would make the election), on the whole the tax consequences between the two classifications are minimal.

Of far greater importance are the lines of demarcation and the governing standards for classifying an enterprise as either a partnership or a corporation. See generally Willis, Pennell, and Postlewaite, *Partnership Taxation* ch. 3 (Warren, Gorham & Lamont, 6th ed. 1996). The distinction between a partnership and a C corporation is dramatic in terms of overall tax liability. Income of a partnership is taxed but once, yet a C corporation, recognized as an entity separate and distinct from its members, is subject to tax as the income is earned and its shareholder members are taxed again as earnings are distributed—the much feared "double taxation" feature of corporations. Additionally, the distinction between the two forms is material as regards the utilization of losses. A loss incurred by a C corporation can only offset corporate income (either currently or through a loss carryback or carryover to other taxable years); it is of little or no value to the shareholders of the corporation. By way of contrast, losses generated by a partnership, with certain exceptions, flow through to its members who may offset income from other sources with them.

The Code broadly defines a partnership to include "a syndicate, group, pool, joint venture, or other unincorporated organization through or by means of which any business, financial operation, or venture is carried on, and which is not, within the meaning of this [subtitle] a corporation or a trust or estate." §§ 761(a), 7701(a)(2). A business entity is classified for federal income tax purposes as either a partnership or a corporation under the "resemblance" test first enunciated by the Supreme Court in *Morrissey v. Commissioner,* 296 U.S. 344 (1935), and subsequently adopted in modified form by the Regulations. Reg. § 301.7701–2(a)(1). This standard is subject to congressional alteration. For example, S corporations (§§ 1361–1371) are treated as the functional equivalent of a partnership regardless of how they might otherwise fare under the standards of the Regulations. All other hybrid business entities, however, such as limited liability companies, limited partnerships, limited liability partnerships, limited liability limited partnerships, and limited partnership associations must be measured against this test to determine their tax classification. If an entity more closely resembles a corporation than another type of business organization, it will be classified as such and taxed accordingly.

The Regulations identify six characteristics associated with the corporate form of doing business. They are:

1. Associates.

2. An objective to carry on business for profit as a common enterprise.

3. Continuity of life.

4. Centralized management.

5. Limited liability.

6. Free transferability of interests.

Under the Regulations, an entity will be treated as a corporation, rather than a partnership, for federal income tax purposes if *more* corporate characteristics than noncorporate characteristics are present. Because the first two characteristics are common to both partnerships and corporations, they are ignored and the entity's status for tax purposes is determined by the remaining four factors. Therefore, unless the entity possesses more than two corporate characteristics, it will be classified as a partnership. However, as evidenced by *Zuckman v. United States,* 524 F.2d 729 (Ct.Cl.1975), it may be that all partnerships classified as such under state law (other than those described in § 7704) will be taxed as such regardless of the nature, composition, or relationship between or among its partners. Under a *Zuckman* analysis, it would appear virtually impossible for a limited partnership to possess the corporate characteristics of limited liability and continuity of life. In such a case, given the certainty of at least a "2–2 tie" on the controlling characteristics, partnership status would be assured. Most of the hybrid entities lack continuity of life and either free transferability of interest or centralized management. Thus, they also are generally taxed as partnerships.

B.　TENANCY IN COMMON AND OTHER RELATIONSHIPS v. PARTNERSHIP

At one end of the spectrum, a line of demarcation is required to distinguish the partnership from enterprises which do not rise to that level. The case law and the Regulations parrot the definition of a partnership utilized in the Uniform Partnership Act. A partnership arises when two or more parties join together as co-owners of a business for profit. Reg. § 1.761–1(a). Three requisites arise from the definition. First, the enterprise must be seeking a profit. As noted by the Regulations, a mere expense-sharing arrangement does not constitute a partnership as it lacks the objective of producing a profit. Once a profit orientation is found, the issue is whether the parties share that profit as co-owners. If the parties are sharing the profit in a relationship other than co-ownership, for example employer-employee, seller-purchaser, etc., the co-ownership element will be lacking and a partnership will not exist. Co-ownership is a factual determination focusing upon the rendition of services or the contribution of capital to the enterprise, the sharing of management duties, and the sharing in profits and losses. Co-ownership is also the issue in those states which allow single member limited liability companies. Although such an entity lacks the corporate characteristics of continuity of life and centralized management, dictating non-corporate status, it cannot be a partnership with only one owner. It is apparently a sole proprietorship for tax purposes.

If a profit objective exists and co-ownership thereof is found, the final requirement for partnership status is a finding that the enterprise is engaged in business, rather than passive or investment, activities. Thus, under the Regulations, a cotenancy which merely leases its property to others is not a partnership. However, if significant, non-customary services are provided, partnership status is assured.

LUNA v. COMMISSIONER

42 T.C. 1067 (1964).

Drennen, Judge.

* * * Petitioner, an experienced life insurance agent who had conceived a special 15–year life insurance, investment fund policy, became employed by Pioneer in 1952 and entered into a contract with Pioneer in 1953 whereby he was appointed manager of Pioneer's expansion department. Pioneer issued the policy devised by petitioner, and petitioner's duties as manager of the expansion department entailed generally the promotion of the policy and the recruiting and training of agents to sell the policy. Petitioner was to receive, as a commission, the first year's premiums on the policies, which was to be shared with agents selling the policies and with general agents in whose territories the policies were sold. He was also to receive renewal commissions from premiums paid on the policies after the first year. The contract provided that if the agreement was terminated petitioner was to continue to receive commissions on business written prior to the date of termination. As of June 1, 1955, petitioner terminated the contract with Pioneer, gave up his position with the corporation, and thereafter had no contact with agents selling the policy or the variations of it which petitioner had also conceived.

After petitioner terminated the contract in 1955, he continued to receive payments from Pioneer. He testified that these payments included commissions from first-year premiums paid for the special policies sold after June 1, 1955, but we think he may have been mistaken in this testimony, and that the payments included only renewal commissions on policies sold before June 1955. Under his contract and the termination notice petitioner was not entitled to commissions on business written after termination of the contract, and there was no reason why petitioner, who performed no services after June 1, 1955, would have been paid a commission from the first-year premium on policies sold after he severed all connection with Pioneer and with the agents selling the policies. The special policy which petitioner had devised was not unique; it was merely a variation of other policies which were being written when petitioner conceived the idea of combining investment and life insurance features in a 15–year policy. Petitioner does not contend, and the evidence does not support the theory, that he had any property rights in the policy for which Pioneer would have had to compensate him.

In any event, the evidence shows that petitioner was entitled only to renewal commissions when he entered into the settlement with Pioneer in 1959 and that Pioneer paid him solely for cancellation of his rights. Lebo calculated the amounts to which petitioner would be entitled after December 31, 1958 (if there were no lapses of the policies), to be $148,905.77. Lebo's computation is set forth in our findings. Lebo had been authorized by Pioneer's board of directors to negotiate with petitioner to pay him 30 percent of the total commissions which might be payable to him in the future. In 1959 Lebo and petitioner arrived at a settlement by which petitioner was paid $45,000—an amount almost exactly 30 percent of the potential renewal commissions to which petitioner was entitled as calculated by Lebo.

We conclude, therefore, that the $45,000 paid petitioner by Pioneer in 1959 was an amount representing the negotiated present value of potential renewal commissions on the special policies negotiated prior to termination of petitioner's contract with Pioneer.

In their petition petitioners alleged that the $45,000 was "realized from the sale of a contract which was a capital asset in their hands." On brief, however, petitioner's entire argument is directed to the proposition that petitioner and Pioneer were joint venturers, that petitioner sold his interest in the venture to Pioneer, and that the $45,000 he received in 1959 was taxable as an amount received upon the sale or exchange of an interest in a partnership. * * *

Under petitioner's view of the case, as we understand the argument, he and Pioneer associated in 1952 in a joint venture which existed until June 1, 1955; this joint venture, by virtue of section 761 of the Code of 1954, must be deemed a partnership for income tax purposes, and petitioner and Pioneer must be treated as partners; petitioner sold to Pioneer on June 1, 1955, his interest in the joint venture, receiving therefor the right to share in premium income from special policies sold after that date; on March 31, 1959, he sold, for $45,000, payment rights to which he became entitled when he was a "partner" and other payment rights based on policies sold after he ceased being a "partner"; the amount of $18,000 of the total selling price must be allocated to "payment rights" resulting from policies sold between March 9, 1954 (the effective date of section 735), and June 1, 1955, and is ordinary income because it results from the sale of unrealized receivables; and, finally, the remaining portion of the $45,000 must be allocated to other payment rights which were not unrealized receivables and constitutes capital gain.

We think that petitioner's argument, founded as it is on the premise that petitioner and Pioneer were engaged in a joint venture, contorts the facts, and we do not necessarily agree with petitioner's conclusions even if his premise be granted. But it is clear that petitioner and Pioneer were not joint venturers.

In *Beck Chemical Equipment Corporation*, 27 T.C. 840, extensive consideration was given to the issue of whether the petitioner had associated with another party in a joint venture during the year in controversy. We said (pp. 848, 849):

> The legal relationship known as a joint venture has been defined as a "special combination of two or more persons, where in some specific venture a profit is jointly sought without any actual partnership or corporate designation," and also as "an association of persons to carry out a single business enterprise for profit." * * *

Whether parties have formed a joint venture is a question of fact to be determined by reference to the same principles that govern the question of whether persons have formed a partnership which is to be accorded recognition for tax purposes. Therefore, while all circumstances are to be considered, the essential question is whether the parties intended to, and did in fact, join together for the present conduct of an undertaking or enterprise.

We are not convinced by petitioner's argument that he and Pioneer were joint venturers under Alabama law even though they were unaware of the relationship. But, in any event, their status under local law would not be determinative, since the Internal Revenue Code prescribes its own standards for qualification of an unincorporated association as a partnership and supersedes local law. However, it is relevant in deciding whether Pioneer did enter into the joint venture for the issuance of the special policies, that petitioner was not licensed or authorized to underwrite insurance or to engage in the insurance business except as an agent selling policies.

The following factors, none of which is conclusive, bear on the issue. The agreement of the parties and their conduct in executing its terms; the contributions, if any, which each party has made to the venture; the parties' control over income and capital and the right of each to make withdrawals; whether each party was a principal and coproprietor, sharing a mutual proprietary interest in the net profits and having an obligation to share losses, or whether one party was the agent or employee of the other, receiving for his services contingent compensation in the form of a percentage of income; whether business was conducted in the joint names of the parties; whether the parties filed Federal partnership returns or otherwise represented to respondent or to persons with whom they dealt that they were joint venturers; whether separate books of account were maintained for the venture; and whether the parties exercised mutual control over and assumed mutual responsibilities for the enterprise.

The contract between Pioneer and petitioner is unambiguous; it was an employment contract by which petitioner was hired by Pioneer in an executive capacity to recruit and supervise agents to sell the special policies, and he was to receive commissions from sales in return for his services. The agents were to be employees of Pioneer, not of petitioner or of any joint venture or other association. The parties' conduct with respect to the terms of the contract was consistent with its clear import. Petitioner indicated in his testimony that he was an employee of Pioneer. Carter testified that, in negotiating the contract with petitioner, a partnership was never discussed or contemplated, and implicit in his testimony is the fact that petitioner was considered an employee of Pioneer. Petitioner was furnished an office at Pioneer's headquarters as would have been any executive employee.

Profits from the policies would have resulted from two sources: (1) Underwriting profits for life insurance features of the policies; and (2) a share of gains and profits from the investment accounts established with a portion of the premiums paid. Pioneer was to receive 10 percent of the latter gains and profits at the end of the contract term as its compensation for managing the account. Of course, petitioner in no manner shared in these profits, nor did he have anything to do with the funds held by Pioneer. He was not to share losses.

Petitioner had no control over, or responsibility with respect to, the issuance of the special policies. He had no proprietary interest in the net profits from issuance of the policies or from investment of premiums.

There is no evidence that petitioner and Pioneer ever held themselves out as joint venturers. No Federal partnership returns were ever filed for the purported joint venture, and apparently neither party represented to respondent that a joint venture existed. In fact, we conclude that the notion that petitioner and Pioneer formed a joint venture is an afterthought. Undeniably, neither party considered during the period involved that a joint venture had been established.

We conclude that petitioner and Pioneer were not partners or joint venturers and that no part of the $45,000 paid to petitioner was for the sale or exchange of an interest in a partnership. This conclusion obviates the necessity of discussing other phases of petitioner's rather complicated argument on brief. * * *

We conclude that the $45,000 paid to petitioner by Pioneer in 1959 was taxable to petitioners as ordinary income.

Decision will be entered for the respondent.

Problem 4–1

Saul is producing a Broadway play and approaches Stockard to participate in the lead role. Stockard agrees to accept the position in return for 20% of the gross receipts. What is their relationship for tax purposes?

Problem 4–2

Donald and Lester each own an undivided one-half interest in a tract of raw land. Under the following facts, how should the operation be classified for tax purposes? Would it make any difference if Donald and Lester each owned individually a part of the tract instead of each owning an undivided interest in the whole?

> a. Donald and Lester constructed a parking lot on the property, which they leased to Lorraine for $2,000 per month. Lorraine operates the parking business. Donald and Lester divided the profit equally.

> b. Some time later, Donald and Lester constructed an apartment building on their property which they leased through an agent. The agent provided customary tenant amenities and services such as electricity, hot and cold water, parking stalls, heat, maintenance, cleaning of the public areas, and the like.

C. PARTNERSHIP VERSUS ASSOCIATION

As one moves along the business enterprise continuum, passing from cotenancy and joint tenancy into partnership classification, further movement will soon test the other boundary of partnership classification. At some point, the enterprise under consideration begins to resemble a corporation. While at first glance one would expect the determinative characteristic between a partnership and a corporation to be the existence of limited liability, such has not been the standard constructed by the Service and embraced by the courts. Instead the equal-weighted, four-factor test of the Regulations has governed the classification of such an enterprise. The Regulations require a determination of whether the enterprise possesses any or all of the governing corporate characteristics: continuity of life, centralized management, limited liability, and free transferability of interests. As each of the factors carries the same weight and as the Regulations have adopted a pro-partnership orientation ("ties" go to the partnership status), an enterprise need only show that it possesses two partnership characteristics in order for partnership status to be assured. Under the Regulations, the lack of continuity of life is virtually assured for any limited partnership seeking partnership status. Similarly, state statutes generally ensure that the other hybrid entities will dissolve upon the death or bankruptcy of an owner. After the *Zuckman* decision, which follows, is there any limited partnership which would not ultimately be classified as a partnership for tax purposes?

ZUCKMAN v. UNITED STATES

524 F2d 729 (Cl Ct 1975).

COWEN, CHIEF JUDGE.

* * * The parties are generally in agreement as to the material facts. The stated purpose of Towne House, formed as a limited partnership under Missouri law by an agreement dated June 10, 1964, was to acquire a specific parcel of real property in St. Louis, Missouri, known as the Lindell property, and to construct and operate an apartment building on that property. The original partners of Towne House and their respective interests before and after completion of construction were as follows:

Partner	Interest Before Construction (percent)	Interest After Construction (percent)
Forest Park of Missouri, Inc.	51	69.577
J.H. Kanter	47	29.331
Robert Blatt	1	.546
Plaintiff George Zuckman	1	.546

The limited partnership agreement designated Forest Park as the sole general partner, and J.H. Kanter, Mr. Blatt, and the plaintiff as limited partners.

Forest Park, incorporated under Missouri law on July 17, 1963, was the wholly-owned subsidiary of Kanter Corporation, which in turn was wholly owned by J.H. Kanter. During the period in question, Kanter Corporation had net assets in excess of $3,500,000. From the time of Towne House's formation on June 10, 1964, through the taxable year ending March 31, 1968, Forest Park remained capitalized at only $500, had no substantial assets other than its interest in Towne House, and engaged in no activities beyond those directly related to Towne House. On August 7, 1963, J.H. Kanter, as president and sole shareholder of Kanter Corporation, received from the directors of that corporation a continuing proxy to vote all of the stock of Forest Park "as though he owned the stock in his individual capacity." By use of this proxy, J.H. Kanter elected all of the Forest Park directors during the period in suit. Three of Forest Park's five officers and directors served concurrently as officers and full-time employees of Kanter Corporation. None of these latter officers received any compensation from Forest Park during the fiscal year 1968.

In October 1963, Forest Park acquired the Lindell property from Millstone Construction, Inc., for $574,500, payable pursuant to a promissory note executed jointly by Forest Park and Kanter Corporation. Shortly thereafter, Kanter Corporation pledged all of its Forest Park stock to Millstone Construction as security for the promissory note. A principal payment of $424,500 was made on the note in July 1967, and a new note for $150,000 was executed by Forest Park and Kanter Corporation.

Construction of the apartment building was financed by a loan of $7,873,300 from the Central Trust Company to Towne House. The loan was evidenced by a Deed of Trust Note dated June 24, 1964, secured by the deed of trust executed that same date by Towne House, and insured by the Federal Housing Administration pursuant to Towne House's execution of an FHA Regulatory Agreement. This latter agreement, in part, prohibited voluntary dissolution of Towne House absent FHA approval, so long as the Towne House property remained subject to the FHA insured mortgage. The agreement further provided that none of the partners of Towne House would be personally liable for repayment of the FHA loan. Towne House defaulted on its mortgage payments in 1967 and, on September 27, 1967, an agreement restoring the mortgage to current status was executed among Towne House, the FHA, and Kanter Corporation, whereunder Kanter Corporation assumed a potential liability to the FHA of $78,333.

Plaintiff and Mr. Blatt were the largest shareholders and highest officers of Towne Construction, Inc., which was incorporated in Missouri on June 4, 1964, to serve as general contractor for the Towne House construction project. In the contract between Towne Construction and Towne House, dated June 22, 1964, Towne House reserved the right to approve all subcontracts. Beginning in June 1964, Kanter Corporation rendered services to Towne Construction for which it was paid $53,000.

Additional limited partners were added at various times during 1967 and 1968. These new partners were all subcontractors on the Towne House construction project. Thereafter, the partners and their respective interests for the taxable year ending March 31, 1968, were as follows:

Partner	Interest (percent)
Forest Park	61.829
J.H. Kanter	21.798
Robert Blatt	1.014
Plaintiff	1.014
Burroughs Glass Co.	.355
Metal Trims, Inc.	.811
Ray R. Dolan, Sr.	.253

Partner	Interest (percent)
Daniel F. Shedran	.253
Milton J. Ortbal	.169
Stephen Gorman Bricklaying Co., Inc.	6.759
Thomas J. Dolan	1.690
Daniel E. Siegel	4.055
	100.000

For its fiscal year ending March 31, 1968, Towne House had a net operating loss of $1,050,759. In computing this loss, Towne House took deductions for depreciation in the amount of $533,302 and for interest in the amount of $426,333. As of March 31, 1968, plaintiff had contributed a total of $7,500 to Towne House as a limited partner. Plaintiff's distributive share of Towne House's loss for the fiscal year ending March 31, 1968, was $10,655. This loss was claimed by plaintiff on his Federal income tax return for calendar year 1968. By letter dated January 12, 1970, the District Director of Internal Revenue, Cincinnati, Ohio, issued a proposed assessment, disallowing plaintiff's claimed deductions for the stated reason that Towne House, during the applicable period, was to be considered an association, and not a partnership, for tax purposes. On November 30, 1970, plaintiff paid the full amount of the proposed assessment, plus statutory interest, and on December 14, 1970, filed a timely claim for refund. After more than six months had elapsed without action on the claim, plaintiff instituted this suit.

I

The Classification Regulations

The Internal Revenue Code defines a partnership to include "a syndicate, group, pool, joint venture, or other unincorporated organization * * * which is not, within the meaning of this title a trust or estate or a corporation." Section 7701(a)(2). A corporation is defined to include "associations, joint-stock companies, and insurance companies." Section 7701(a)(3). To clarify and effectuate these rather broadly drawn definitions, the Internal Revenue Service promulgated a series of regulations embodying standards for each of the three major classes of business organizations—associations (taxable as corporations), partnerships and trusts. Reg. §§ 301.7701–2 (1960) (associations), –3 (partnerships), and –4 (trusts).

The regulation applicable to partnerships states that an organization qualifying as a limited partnership under state law may be classified for tax purposes as an association if, after the standards in the regulation dealing with associations are considered, the limited partnership more closely resembles a corporation than a partnership. Reg. § 301.7701–3(b). The regulation dealing with associations articulates six corporate characteristics: (1) associates, (2) an objective to carry on business and divide the gains therefrom, (3) continuity of life, (4) centralization of management, (5) liability for corporate debts limited to corporate property, and (6) free transferability of interests. Reg. § 301.7701–2(a)(1). Since (1) associates and (2) an objective to carry on a business and divide the gain are characteristics common to both partnerships and corporations, they are generally disregarded in distinguishing between the two. Reg. § 301.7701–2(a)(2). Thus, the classification of a limited partnership with a corporate general partner as either a partnership or a corporation for income tax purposes must turn on the remaining four characteristics. * * *

II

Continuity of Life

The first of the four corporate characteristics, continuity of life, is defined by the regulation to exist when "the death, insanity, bankruptcy, retirement, resignation, or expulsion of any member will not cause a dissolution" of the organization. Reg. § 301.7701–2(b)(1). As a shorthand route to this determination, the final sentence of the regulation— added as part of the 1960 amendments—provides, in blanket fashion, that "a general partnership subject to a statute corresponding to the Uniform Partnership Act and a limited partnership subject to a statute corresponding to the Uniform Limited Partnership Act both lack continuity of life." Reg. § 301.7701–2(b)(3). The State of Missouri has adopted without material change both the Uniform Partnership Act (hereinafter referred to as the "UPA") and the Uniform Limited Partnership Act (hereinafter referred to as the "ULPA"). In addition, there is no dispute that Towne House was formed as a limited partnership pursuant to the Missouri statute. Accordingly, were the regulation to be literally applied, a finding that Towne House lacked the corporate characteristic of continuity of life would be inescapable.

Defendant argues, however, that two factors in this case present a unique circumstance not provided for by either the regulation or the ULPA: (1) the existence of a sole corporate general partner, and (2) an amendment to the limited partnership agreement, executed pursuant to a separate FHA underwriting agreement, expressly prohibiting the partnership's voluntary dissolution. By virtue of these two factors, defendant contends, literal application of the regulation's shorthand test would be inappropriate, inasmuch as the remainder of the regulation dictates inquiry into the substance, not merely the form, of a particular entity. We disagree with defendant and hold, in express accordance with the regulation, that a limited partnership subject to a ULPA-type statute cannot have the corporate characteristic of continuity of life.

Even had the last sentence of the regulation been omitted, however, the same result would necessarily follow under the detailed standards set forth in the remainder of the regulation. The regulation provides that:

> If the retirement, death, or insanity of a general partner of a limited partnership causes a dissolution of the partnership, unless the remaining general partners agree to continue the partnership or unless all remaining members agree to continue the partnership, continuity of life does not exist.

Reg. § 301.7701–2(b)(1). The regulation further states that, even if the partnership agreement provides for continuation of the business by the remaining partners in the event of a member's death or withdrawal, such agreement will not establish continuity of life "if, under local law, the death or withdrawal of any member causes a dissolution of the organization." Reg. § 301.7701–2(b)(2).

Looking first to local law, Section 20 of the ULPA (Mo.Ann.Stat. § 359.200) articulates the causes of dissolution as follows:

> The retirement, death or insanity of a general partner dissolves the partnership, unless the business is continued by the remaining general partners
>
> > (1) Under a right so to do stated in the certificate; or
> >
> > (2) With the consent of all members.

Under its Limited Partnership Agreement of June 10, 1964, Towne House was to continue in existence until the year 2010 unless sooner terminated in accordance with the agreement's other terms. Paragraphs (14) and (15) of the Agreement provide for such earlier termination under the following circumstances:

> (b) *Managing Partner.* In the event of the adjudication of bankruptcy or the forfeiture of the corporate charter of the Managing Partner, the Partnership shall be dissolved.

> 15. *Causes of Dissolution of Partnership.* The Partnership shall be dissolved upon the happening of any of the following events:
>
> > (a) The adjudication of bankruptcy, or the forfeiture of the Charter of the Managing Partner.
> >
> > (b) The decision of Partners owning a majority of the participation units then owned by all Partners to dissolve the Partnership.

Thus, even were we to find that Forest Park, the sole corporate general partner, were subject to the complete control of J.H. Kanter, making its voluntary withdrawal unlikely, it could still become bankrupt and, in such event, Towne House's dissolution would automatically result. See 11 U.S.C. § 23 (when all general partners are adjudged bankrupt, so is the partnership).

Nor, for several reasons, could dissolution be avoided by means of a right to continue the business. First, such right is unequivocally eliminated by paragraph (13) of the Towne House Certificate of Limited Partnership, which states that:

> Under the partnership agreement no right is given to the general partner or the limited partners to continue the business on the retirement, or disability or forfeiture of charter of the general partner.

Second, since the withdrawal of Forest Park would leave no remaining general partners exclusively entitled under the ULPA to continue the business, there could be no continuation in any event. Finally, under the rule announced in *Glensder Textile Co. v. Commissioner,* 46 B.T.A. 176, 185–86 (1942), expressly adopted by the Treasury in its final regulations, Reg. § 301.7701–2(b)(1), the mere reservation in the limited partnership agreement of a power in the remaining general partners to continue the business on a general partner's withdrawal, constitutes only a "contingent continuity of existence," insufficient to satisfy the regulation's corporate standard.

Notwithstanding the above, defendant argues that the amendment to the Towne House Limited Partnership Agreement (hereinafter referred to as the "FHA amendment"), in consideration for which the FHA undertook to insure a non-recourse loan to Towne House of nearly $8,000,000, is controlling here. The amendment provides, in pertinent part, that:

> * * * 2. There is added to section 15b the following provision. There shall be no voluntary dissolution of the partnership so long as the property of the partnership is subject to an FHA insured mortgage without the express prior written approval of the Commissioner of the Federal Housing Administration.

Defendant also cites the Regulatory Agreement itself, which states that:

> Owners shall not file any petition in bankruptcy, or for a receiver, or in insolvency, or for reorganization or composition, or make any assignment for the benefit of creditors or to a trustee for creditors; or permit an adjudication in bankruptcy, the taking possession of the mortgaged property or any part thereof by a receiver, or the seizure and sale of the mortgaged property or any part thereof under judicial process or pursuant to any power of sale and fail to have such adverse actions set aside within 45 days.

Defendant contends that the effect of these agreements was to deprive the owners of Towne House of their right lawfully to dissolve the partnership and, hence, that Towne House thereby contractually assumed the corporate characteristic of continuous existence.

We agree with defendant that by the FHA amendment, Forest Park relinquished its right voluntarily to withdraw from Towne House, or otherwise to act, or fail to act, in such a way as to cause dissolution of the partnership under Missouri law. In this respect, the FHA amendment was little different in effect from a provision in a partnership agreement that the firm is to be continued for a definite term, or until accomplishment of a particular undertaking. Under such circumstances, it has long been held in Missouri, as elsewhere, that no partner has the right to dissolve the partnership until the term has ended or the undertaking been accomplished.

It does not follow, however, as defendant further contends, that because Forest Park surrendered its *right* to voluntarily dissolve the Towne House partnership, it also and simultaneously surrendered its *power* to do so. The Treasury Regulation, the Uniform Acts and the weight of relevant decisions are to the contrary. They consistently distinguish between a partner's right and his power to dissolve the partnership entity, notwithstanding the existence of an agreed term or transaction to be completed. As the regulation states:

> In determining whether any member has the *power* of dissolution, it will be necessary to examine the agreement and to ascertain the effect of such agreement under local law * * * [I]f the agreement provides that the organization is to continue for a stated period or until the completion of a stated transaction, the organization has continuity of life if the effect of the agreement is that no member has the *power* to dissolve the organization in contravention of the agreement. Nevertheless, if, notwithstanding such agreement, any member has the *power* under local law to dissolve the organization, the organization lacks continuity of life.

Reg. § 301.7701–2(b)(3) [Emphasis added].

The significance of this distinction was well expressed in the early case of *Karrick v. Hannaman,* 168 U.S. 328, 334–37, 18 S.Ct. 135, 138, 42 L.Ed. 484 (1897), where the Supreme Court, addressing the question of whether one partner, without the assent of the other, has the power to dissolve a partnership for a specified term before the expiration thereof, stated as follows:

> A contract of partnership is * * * in effect, a contract of mutual agency, each partner acting as a principal in his own behalf and as agent for his co-partner. [Citation omitted.] No partnership can efficiently or beneficially carry on its business without the mutual confidence and co-operation of all the partners. Even when, by the partnership articles, they have covenanted with each other that the partnership shall continue for a certain period, the partnership may be dissolved at any time, at the will of any partner, so far as to put an end to the partnership relation and to the authority of each partner to act for all but rendering the partner who breaks his covenant liable to an action at law for damages, as in other cases of breaches of contract. [Citations omitted.] [T]he only difference, so far as concerns the right of dissolution by one partner, between a partnership for an indefinite period and one for a specified term, is this: In the former case, the dissolution is no breach of the partnership agreement, and affords the other partner no ground of complaint. In the latter case, such a dissolution before the expiration of the time stipulated is a breach of the agreement, and as such to be compensated in damages; but in either case the action of one partner does actually dissolve the partnership.

This recognition in *Karrick* of a partner's power to dissolve, although the right to dissolve does not exist, has been followed by a majority of American jurisdictions, see Crane & Bromberg on Partnership § 75, at 427–28 (1968), and has been incorporated in the Uniform Partnership Act, Sections 31(2) and 38(2)(a)(II).

In sum, whether Forest Park had the right, voluntarily or involuntarily, to cause dissolution of the partnership, i.e., could do so without breaching the partnership agreement and incurring liability therefore, is immaterial.   Since Forest Park had the power under Missouri law to dissolve the partnership, irrespective of the consequences, we conclude that—even absent the final unequivocal sentence of the regulation, Reg. § 301.7701–2(b)(3)—Towne House lacked the corporate characteristic of continuity of life.

III

Centralization of Management

The second corporate characteristic, centralization of management, is defined by the regulation as "a concentration of continuing exclusive authority to make independent business decisions on behalf of the organization which do not require ratification by members of such organization."   Reg. § 301.7701–2(c)(3).   As with continuity of life, the final sentences of the regulation, added in 1960, ostensibly furnish a shorthand test for application to limited partnerships "subject to a statute corresponding to the Uniform Limited Partnership Act."   Reg. § 301.7701–2(c)(4).   Such partnerships, the regulation states, "*generally* do not have centralized management, but centralized management *ordinarily* does exist in such a limited partnership if substantially all the interests in the partnership are owned by the limited partners."   Id. [Emphasis added].

As the words "generally" and "ordinarily" imply, limited partnership status does not in itself preclude centralized management, as it does continuity of life.   Unlike a general partnership, wherein the mutual agency relationship between partners empowers each partner to act on behalf of the entity and to bind all partners by his acts, notwithstanding any agreement vesting management in a selected few, limited partners typically lack virtually all management control rights.   Thus, insofar as "continuing exclusive authority to make independent business decisions" is concentrated in the hands of the general partners, a limited partnership may be said always to possess centralized management.

This was essentially the position adopted by the Treasury in its proposed regulations, issued in December 1959.   24 Fed.Reg. 10450.   In response to these, substantial objections were raised on the ground that the regulation had long observed a distinction between centralized management in the corporate sense and the limited partnership sense, respectively.   In the corporate context, there could be no centralized management unless the management power is held and exercised in a representative capacity, i.e., by directors, acting as representatives of the stockholders.   In the limited partnership context, however, centralized management meant that the general partner has the exclusive management power, ULPA § 9, and acts primarily in his own behalf, subject only to the fiduciary duty he owes to the other partners.   UPA §§ 18–23. Association status for tax purposes under the regulations turns upon an organization's resemblance to a corporation.   Reg. § 301.7701–2(a)(1). The focus of inquiry must therefore be on the "representative," rather than the "centralized," character of management, inasmuch as centralization *per se* is generally common to both corporations and limited partnerships and, hence, immaterial in distinguishing between the two. Reg. § 301.7701–2(a)(2).

The characteristic of centralized management held in a representative capacity was recognized as a corporate trait in the *Morrissey* decision from which the present regulations derive, 296 U.S. at 359, 56 S.Ct. 289, and was incorporated into the definitional sentence of the regulation, which states: "Centralized management means a concentration of continuing exclusive authority to make independent business decisions *on behalf* of the organization * * *." Reg. § 301.7701–2(c)(3) [Emphasis added]. The final regulation, promulgated in 1960, bears out this continuing focus on the representative character of an organization by providing that centralized management will ordinarily obtain in a limited partnership "if substantially all the interests in the partnership are owned by the limited partners." Reg. § 301.7701–2(c)(4). The rationale for this ownership test, as suggested by the foregoing analysis, is that if the limited partners own substantially all the partnership's interests, then the general partner can only be acting on their behalf, i.e., in a representative capacity, and, hence, the partnership must possess the corporate management characteristic.

In applying this test, defendant contends that, since J.H. Kanter indirectly owned and controlled Forest Park, "it is entirely appropriate for present purposes to consider Forest Park's ownership interest in Towne House as in substance owned by J.H. Kanter." By means of such attribution, defendant's argument runs, J.H. Kanter should be considered the owner of 98 percent of the interests in Towne House (Forest Park's 51 percent plus J.H. Kanter's 47 percent) up to the time of the admission of additional limited partners (i.e., to at least December 15, 1967), and the owner of 83 percent thereafter. Accordingly, Towne House must possess the corporate characteristic of centralized management since, under the regulation, "substantially all the interests in the partnership are held by the limited partners" (i.e., J.H. Kanter). This argument is adroit but unacceptable.

First, we can find no authority, nor has any been cited by defendant, for applying a constructive ownership rule to the determination of the locus of substantial ownership and control in a limited partnership. Certainly no such rule can expressly be found among the pertinent statutes and regulations. Experience likewise suggests that where such a rule has been considered appropriate, defendant has proven adept at making such appropriateness known other than by resort to mere inference and analogy. See, e.g., Int.Rev.Code §§ 267, 318, 544 and 554. In arguing for the applicability of a constructive ownership rule, defendant is in effect challenging its own regulation. It is well settled, however, that "Treasury regulations must be sustained unless unreasonable and plainly inconsistent with the revenue statutes."

In a recent case, moreover, we expressly held that the instant regulations "are reasonable and conform to the revenue statutes, and are, therefore, valid." *Outlaw v. United States,* 494 F.2d 1376, 1386, 204 Ct.Cl. 152, 169 (1974), *cert. denied,* 419 U.S. 844, 95 S.Ct. 78, 42 L.Ed.2d 73 (1974). Under these circumstances, the regulations must be considered as binding on the Government as they are on the taxpayer. The express language of the regulation neither directly nor otherwise contemplates application of a constructive ownership rule. Absent such a rule, Forest Park's undoubtedly substantial interest in Towne House's capital and profits would ordinarily preclude a finding that the latter possessed centralized management.

Even were Forest Park's interest attributable to J.H. Kanter on some theory, the result—under our reading of the regulation—would be the same. Centralized management, taken in the abstract, is common to both corporations and limited partnerships. The regulation's ownership (or "substantial interest") test applicable to limited partnerships is only a shorthand means of ascertaining, in the ordinary case, whether or not the centralized management power is held and exercised in a representative capacity, i.e., by directors acting on behalf of the stockholders. Where substantially all the interests in an organization are owned by the limited partners, i.e., distributed broadly among a comparatively large number of limited partners *qua* stockholders, then the regulation erects a presumption that the centralized management power (in the hands of the general partner or partners) will generally be exercised on the limited partners' behalf. Were Forest Park's interest attributable to J.H. Kanter, however, as defendant contends, J.H. Kanter's resultant 98 percent (or 83 percent) interest in Towne House would in itself effectively rule out any possibility of representative management.

IV

Limited Liability

The regulation states that an organization has the third corporate characteristic, limited liability, if there is no member who is personally liable for the debts of and claims against the organization under local law. Reg. § 301.7701–2(d)(1). Personal liability is defined as existing when a creditor or tort victim may seek personal satisfaction from a member of the organization to the extent that the assets of the organization are insufficient to satisfy his claim. Id. In this case, these are essentially two members as to whom personal liability may exist for the debts of and claims against Towne House: Forest Park and J.H. Kanter.

Defendant argues that personal liability cannot exist as to Forest Park since, under the regulation, it has no substantial assets (other than its interest in the partnership) which could be reached by a creditor of Towne House and is merely a "dummy" acting as the agent of the limited partners (i.e., J.H. Kanter). Plaintiff, while conceding that Forest Park had no substantial assets, counters that determination of the corporate partner's "dummy" status involves questions of fact which, if critical to the outcome, would be inappropriate for resolution on this motion for summary judgment.

With respect to J.H. Kanter, the second party as to whom personal liability may exist for Towne House's debts, the parties reach a similar impasse. Both agree, and plaintiff vigorously supports the fact, that "beyond question J.H. Kanter completely ran the Towne House show," and that he "was the single person in charge of all of Towne House's business decisions." Plaintiff argues, however, that these facts alone, insofar as they establish that J.H. Kanter was in "control" of Towne House, are sufficient to make J.H. Kanter personally liable for the partnership's debts. In support of this contention, plaintiff relies on Section 7 of the Uniform Limited Partnership Act (Mo.Ann.Stat. § 359.070) and Missouri decisions construing it. Section 7 states that:

> A limited partner shall not become liable as a general partner unless, in addition to the exercise of his rights and powers as a limited partner, *he takes part in the control of the business.*

[Emphasis added]. Plaintiff also relies on the applicable portion of the regulation, which provides that:

> Notwithstanding the formation of the organization as a limited partnership, when the limited partners act as the principals of such general partner, personal liability will exist with respect to such limited partners.

Reg. § 301.7701–2(d)(2).

Defendant, relying on the same statute and regulation and generally identical decisions, counters that J.H. Kanter's control of the business, although conceded, is not in itself sufficient to make him a general partner in fact, or otherwise to render him personally liable for Towne House's obligations. For personal liability to exist, according to defendant, plaintiff must show not only that J.H. Kanter was in control of Towne House but, in addition, that his words or actions have actually and reasonably led third parties to believe that he was generally liable, and to act on that belief. Such requisite third party reliance, defendant contends, simply cannot be shown in this case, inasmuch as "J.H. Kanter at all times was held out as only a limited partner."

Clearly if, as plaintiff contends, the fact of "control" alone constitutes a sufficient basis in law for holding J.H. Kanter personally liable, then we must conclude that Towne House lacks the corporate characteristic of limited liability. If, however, as defendant argues, third party reliance constitutes a necessary and material factor in the limited liability equation, we are presented, as in the case of Forest Park's disputed "dummy" and agency status, with a genuine issue of material fact inappropriate for resolution on these cross motions for summary judgment.

However, we have concluded that it is unnecessary to remand either of these factual issues for trial in order to determine that Towne House lacks the corporate characteristic of limited liability, inasmuch as the regulation itself, albeit none too lucidly, mandates such a finding as a matter of law.

The portion of the regulation dealing with limited liability, added *in toto* as part of the 1960 amendments, incorporates by reference applicable provisions of the ULPA as a shorthand test similar to those tests, earlier discussed, bearing upon centralized management and continuity of life. As the history of the 1960 amendments suggests, the intent of the drafters was to make it as difficult as possible for the then-burgeoning medical and legal partnerships to achieve association status for tax purposes. In this aim, particularly with respect to the characteristic of limited liability, the drafters were eminently successful.

Paragraph 2(d), subparagraph (1) of the regulation provides, in pertinent part, that:

> * * * [I]n the case of a limited partnership subject to a statute corresponding to the Uniform Limited Partnership Act, personal liability exists with respect to each general partner, except as provided in subparagraph (2) of this paragraph.

After stating the general rule that a limited partnership does not normally possess limited liability, subparagraph (2) merely describes four specialized situations to which this general rule will nonetheless apply, one situation to which it will not, and one in which personal liability will exist with respect to limited partners. Thus, subparagraph (2) states that personal liability will exist with respect to a general partner where (1) such general partner is a corporation having substantial assets which can be reached by creditors; (2) the general partner contributes only services, but still has substantial assets; (3) the general partner has substantial assets, although insufficient to satisfy the obligations of an organization engaged in large-scale financial transactions; and (4) the general partner has no substantial assets and is not merely a "dummy" acting as the agent of the limited partners. Since Forest Park, the sole general partner of Towne House, concededly has no substantial assets, we are concerned here only with (4). Thus, if Forest Park is *not* a "dummy," it is personally liable.

In only one situation does the regulation provide an exception to the general rule of personal liability with respect to the general partners of a limited partnership. If the general partner has no substantial assets (as here), and *is* merely a "dummy" acting as the agent of the limited partners, it is not personally liable. However, in that situation, the following provision of subparagraph (2), previously quoted above, becomes pertinent: "Notwithstanding the formation of the organization as a limited partnership, when the limited partners act as the principals of such general partner, personal liability will exist with respect to such limited partners." Thus, although the general partner is not personally liable when it is a "dummy" and acts merely as an agent, the limited partners as principals of the general partner are personally liable. In short, the regulation draws a tight, albeit opaque, circle by declaring that where the general partner of a limited partnership has no assets, only two alternatives may follow: (1) if it is not a "dummy", then it is personally liable; or (2) if it *is* a "dummy", then the limited partners for whom it acts as agent and who in turn serve as its principal, are personally liable. In either case, the limited partnership cannot have limited liability, inasmuch as at least one of its "members"—whether general or limited—must at all times bear personal liability.

In view of the foregoing, it is unnecessary to proceed further to determine whether third party reliance existed in this case. Such determination would have bearing only upon the question of which party, Forest Park or J.H. Kanter, must ultimately bear personal responsibility for Towne House's obligations. For tax classification purposes, it is sufficient to conclude that either one or the other would have to bear such responsibility. Accordingly, we hold that, under the applicable regulation, Towne House lacks the corporation characteristic of limited liability.

V

Free Transferability of Interests

The fourth and last major corporate characteristic, free transferability of interests, is defined by the regulation to exist with respect to an organization when "[e]ach of its members or those members owning substantially all of the interests in the organization have the power, without the consent of other members, to substitute for themselves in the same organization a person who is not a member of the organization * * * [and] to confer upon [their] * * * substitute all the attributes of [their] * * * interest in the organization." Reg. § 301.7701–2(e)(1). See also Reg. § 301.7701–3(b)(2), example (1) (limited partner who may transfer his entire interest only with unanimous consent of general partners will not have a freely transferable interest).

Also added as part of the 1960 amendments, this portion of the regulation is perhaps the simplest and most straight-forward in operation and, accordingly, its application presents little difficulty. While the term "substantially all" is not defined in the regulation, we may fairly and reasonably conclude that the 61 percent (and, after the admission of new limited partners, 49 percent) interest held by Forest Park, taken alone, would be insufficient. Accordingly, in order for Towne House to possess the corporate characteristic of free transferability, it is necessary to show that not only Forest Park's interest, but J.H. Kanter's interest as well, was freely transferable.

In determining, first, whether J.H. Kanter had the power, without the consent of other members of Towne House, to substitute for himself a non-member of the organization, we must look to the pertinent provisions of the ULPA as adopted in Missouri. Section 19, subsection (4) thereunder (Mo.Ann.Stat. § 359.190(4)) provides that an assignee shall have the right to become a substituted limited partner if (i) all the members consent thereto, or (ii) the limited partnership certificate empowers the assignor to transfer all his interest to a substituted limited partner. Paragraph (10) of the Towne House Limited Partnership Certificate provides that:

A limited partner has the right under the Partnership Agreement to substitute an assignee as contributor in his place *with the prior consent of the general partner* and upon execution by the assignee of the Partnership Agreement.

[Emphasis added]. Similarly, the Towne House Limited Partnership Agreement provides that "[N]o * * * transferee of the interest of a Limited Partner shall become a substituted limited partner without first obtaining the written consent of Managing Partner, and executing a copy of the Partnership Agreement."

Plaintiff contends that since under the statute and partnership certificate, J.H. Kanter's interest could be fully assigned only with the consent of Forest Park, J.H. Kanter's interest was therefore not freely transferable within the meaning of the regulation.

Defendant counters that, inasmuch as J.H. Kanter indirectly owned Forest Park, and held a continuing proxy from the Kanter Corporation directors to vote all of Forest Park's stock, the requirement of consent by Forest Park to any assignment of J.H. Kanter's partnership interest was a matter of form, not substance; therefore, J.H. Kanter's interest must be considered as freely transferable. We agree with defendant's contention.

While J.H. Kanter's *de facto* control of Forest Park could not in itself constitute corporate centralized management, which as earlier discussed additionally requires that such control be exercised in a representative capacity, the consequence of such control is different with respect to the characteristic of free transferability. So long as a member has the power, *unconditional* as between that member and the remaining members, to fully substitute a non-member for himself in the organization, the existence of a mere formal or nominal condition will not prevent such member's interest from being freely transferable within the meaning of the regulation.

Defendant further maintains, by reason of J.H. Kanter's *de facto* control of Forest Park, that J.H. Kanter also had complete discretion to fully transfer the Towne House interests of Forest Park. Accordingly, defendant argues that, since the combined interests of J.H. Kanter and Forest Park constituted "substantially all" of Towne House's outstanding interests, Towne House must be deemed to have the corporate characteristic of free transferability. We disagree.

In the absence of an agreement to the contrary, a sole general partner of a limited partnership may assign his interest and substitute another for himself without the consent of the limited partners, but such assignment and substitution will result in a technical dissolution of the partnership unless the right to continue the business is specifically accorded the substituted general partner by the limited partnership certificate. ULPA § 9 (Mo.Ann.Stat. § 359.090). Paragraph (13) of the Towne House Certificate provides that:

Under the partnership agreement no right is given the general partner or the limited partners to continue the business on the *retirement* or disability or forfeiture of charter of the general partner. [Emphasis added].

Thus, for a substitute general partner to have the power, without dissolution, to continue the business on the retirement or withdrawal of the original general partner, there must be unanimous ratification by the limited partners. As stated in Section 9 of the ULPA (Mo.Ann.Stat. § 359.090):

A general partner shall have all the rights and powers and be subject to all the restrictions and liabilities of a partner in a partnership without limited partners, except that without the written consent or ratification of the specific act by all the limited partners, a general partner or all of the general partners have no authority to . . .

(7) Continue the business with partnership property on the death, retirement or insanity of a general partner, unless the right to do so is given in the certificate.

Accordingly, since Forest Park's transfer of its Towne House interests and substitution of a new general partner in its place would require either the consent of all the limited partners (i.e., not merely J.H. Kanter), or—absent such consent—would result in technical dissolution of the firm, Forest Park's interests are not freely transferable. As stated in the regulation:

[A]lthough the agreement provides for the transfer of a member's interest, there is no power of substitution and no free transferability of interest if under local law a transfer of a member's interests results in the dissolution of the old organization and the formation of a new organization.

In sum, although J.H. Kanter's interests were, in effect, freely transferable within the meaning of the regulation, we find that Forest Park's interests were not. Hence, inasmuch as J.H. Kanter's interests alone could not constitute "substantially all" of the outstanding interests in the firm, we find that Towne House lacked the corporate characteristic of free transferability of interests.

VI

Additional Characteristics

Relying on the regulation and our recent decision in *Outlaw v. United States,* 494 F.2d 1376, 1385, 204 Ct.Cl. 152, 169 (1974), *cert. denied,* 419 U.S. 844, 95 S.Ct. 78, 42 L.Ed.2d 73 (1974), defendant's final argument is that certain corporate characteristics other than those expressly identified and described in the regulations may be significant in determining whether an entity is a partnership or an association for tax purposes. The additional corporate characteristics as claimed by defendant are: (1) Forest Park had unilateral power to admit additional limited partners, and (2) Forest Park had exclusive discretion to determine when and if any of Towne House's available funds should be distributed to itself and the limited partners. Inasmuch as we have already found that Towne House lacked all four of the "major" corporate characteristics expressly treated in the regulation, it is plainly unnecessary to consider additional ones in this case.

Moreover, it should be emphasized that our discussion herein of each of the four major corporate characteristics is in no way intended to suggest that an absence of all four characteristics must be found in order to hold a partnership taxable as such under the regulation. On the contrary, the regulation unequivocally states that if an organization "has more corporate characteristics than noncorporate characteristics," Reg. § 301.7701–2(a)(3), it will be classified as an association. Since the regulation specifically covers only four "major" corporate characteristics which are not common to both partnerships and corporations, we interpret the foregoing test to mean that, as a general rule, any partnership *lacking two or more* of these characteristics will not be classified as an association. Conversely, any partnership *having three or more* of these characteristics will be classified as an association.

This is not to say that a taxpayer claiming classification as a partnership will be entitled to prevail in every conceivable situation merely by showing that the organization lacks two of the four major corporate characteristics. As the regulation itself states:

> In addition to the major characteristics set forth in this subparagraph, other factors may be found *in some cases* which may be significant in classifying an organization as an association, a partnership, or a trust. * * *

> For example, if a limited partnership has centralized management and free transferability of interests but lacks continuity of life and limited liability, *and if the limited partnership has no other characteristics which are significant in determining its classification,* such limited partnership is not classified as an association.

Reg. § 301.7701–2(a)(1), (3) [Emphasis added].

But this is not such a case, nor can a contrary interpretation of this regulation be derived from our recent decision in *Outlaw*. At issue in *Outlaw* was whether a particular trust should be classified as a trust or a corporation for tax purposes. As such, the dispositive questions under the regulation were whether the trust had associates and an objective to carry on business and divide the gains therefrom. The remaining four major corporate characteristics—those addressed in the case presently before us—are treated by the regulation as common to both corporations and trusts and, hence, immaterial in distinguishing between the two. As the pertinent portion of the regulation states:

> Some of the major characteristics of a corporation are common to trusts and corporations, and others are common to partnerships and corporations. Characteristics common to trusts and corporations are not material in attempting to distinguish between a trust and an

association, and characteristics common to partnerships and corporations are not material in attempting to distinguish between an association and a partnership. For example, since centralization of management, continuity of life, free transferability of interests, and limited liability are *generally common* to trusts and corporations, the determination of whether a trust which has such characteristics is to be treated for tax purposes as a trust or as an association depends on whether there are associates and an objective to carry on business and divide the gains therefrom. On the other hand, since associates and an objective to carry on business and divide the gains therefrom are *generally common* to both corporations and partnerships, the determination of whether an organization which has such characteristics is to be treated for tax purposes as a partnership or as an association depends on whether there exists centralization of management, continuity of life, free transferability of interests, and limited liability.

As the term "generally" implies, the regulation clearly contemplates—as under its provision for consideration of "other factors"—that situations may arise where characteristics *generally* common to both corporations and partnerships, or corporations and trusts, may arguably be lacking in a particular case. Plaintiff has not argued, nor would it have been fruitful for him to argue, that the characteristics of associates and an objective to carry on business and divide the gains therefrom, are lacking in the instant case. Precisely because plaintiff in *Outlaw did* so argue, however (*i.e.,* against the regulation's presumption that the four partnership characteristics are generally common to trusts and corporations), it was necessary in that case to consider factors other than those which the regulation deems normally dispositive in distinguishing between corporations and trusts for tax purposes. Such a problem is not presented in this case.

Conclusion

Since we find that Towne House should be classified as a partnership for tax purposes under Reg. § 301.7701–2, we conclude that plaintiff was entitled to deduct his distributive share of the Towne House losses for the calendar year 1968. Accordingly, it is ordered that plaintiff's motion for summary judgment is granted; defendant's cross motion for summary judgment is denied; and judgment is hereby entered in favor of plaintiff for the sum of $6,299.56, plus interest thereon as provided by law.

D. ADMINISTRATIVE RULING REQUIREMENTS

While no limited partnership in the modern era has failed to be classified by the courts as a partnership for tax purposes (i.e., in the two litigated cases, *Zuckman* and *Larson,* the taxpayers won), the Service has not totally capitulated on the issue. While its judicial victories have been nonexistent, the Service has used the in terrorem effect of administrative pronouncements through which to announce its views as to the requirements for evidencing noncorporate characteristics. In Revenue Procedure 89–12, which follows, the Service under the guise of prerequisites to the issuance of a Ruling established its own requirements for evidencing a lack of the corporate characteristics of continuity of life, centralized management, and limited liability. While such guidelines are confined to the Ruling process, do they become the governing standards for audit purposes? Do the guidelines find support in the Regulations? Is a court bound to follow such standards?

REVENUE PROCEDURE 89–12
1989–1 CB 798.

Section 1. Purpose

.01 This revenue procedure specifies the conditions under which the Internal Revenue Service will consider a ruling request that relates to classification of an organization, for federal tax purposes, as a partnership. * * *

.02 Organizations covered by this revenue procedure include both those formed as partnerships and other organizations seeking partnership classification. In the case of an organization not formed as a partnership, references to "partnership" documents, including the "partnership agreement," apply to the organization's comparable documents, however designated. Any reference to a "limited partnership" includes an organization formed as a limited partnership under applicable state law and any other organization formed under a law that limits the liability of any member for the organization's debts and other obligations to a determinable fixed amount. References to "general partners" and "limited partners" apply also to comparable members of an organization not designated as a partnership under controlling law and documents; the "general partners" of such an organization will ordinarily be those with significant management authority relative to the other members. In the case of a foreign organization, "state" and "federal" references in the information requirements of section 3 apply to any relevant foreign jurisdictions. This revenue procedure does not apply to a publicly traded partnership treated as a corporation under section 7704 of the Internal Revenue Code.

.03 The provisions of this revenue procedure are not intended to be substantive rules for the determination of partner and partnership status and are not to be applied upon audit of taxpayer's returns.

.04 The Service may decline to issue a ruling under this revenue procedure whenever warranted by the facts and circumstances of a particular case and whenever appropriate in the interest of sound tax administration.

Section 2. Background

.01 Section 7701(a)(2) of the Code defines the term "partnership" to include a syndicate, group, pool, joint venture, or other unincorporated organization, through or by means of which any business, financial operation, or venture is carried on, and which is not, within the meaning of the Code, a trust or estate or a corporation. Sections 301.7701–2 and 301.7701–3 of the Procedure and Administration Regulations set forth rules for determining whether an organization is classified, for federal tax purposes, as a partnership or as an association taxable as a corporation.

.02 Rev.Proc. 89–1, 1989–1 I.R.B. 8, as updated annually, sets forth procedures for the taxpayer request and Service issuance of advance rulings. The Service generally issues rulings on prospective transactions and on completed transactions for which the applicable return has not been filed. Section 5.01 of Rev.Proc. 89–1, however, provides that the Service will also consider ruling requests concerning the classification of an existing organization as a partnership. A ruling issued in response to such a request will be effective prospectively.

SECTION 3. INFORMATION TO BE SUBMITTED

.01 Section 8 of Rev.Proc. 89–1 outlines general requirements concerning the information to be submitted as part of a ruling request, including a classification ruling request. For example, a partnership classification ruling request must contain a complete statement of all the facts relating to the classification issue. Among those facts are the items of information specified in this revenue procedure. The ruling request must therefore provide all items of information specified below, or at least account for all such items. As an example of accounting for an item, if no registration statement is required to be filed with the Securities and Exchange Commission (section 3.04(3)), the ruling request should so state.

.02 Submission of the documents and supplementary materials required by section 3.04 herein does not satisfy the information requirements contained in section 3.03 herein or in section 8 of Rev.Proc. 89–1. Thus, all material facts in documents, including those items required by section 3.03, must be included in the letter requesting a ruling and not merely incorporated by reference. All submitted documents and supplementary materials must contain applicable exhibits, attachments, and amendments.

.03 Required General Information.

(1) The name and identification number of the organization.

(2) The business of the organization.

(3) The date and place of filing the partnership certificate, or the anticipated date and place.

(4) The state whose law controls the formation and operation of the organization, and whether or not the controlling law is a statute corresponding to, as applicable, the Uniform Partnership Act, the Uniform Limited Partnership Act (1916), or the Revised Uniform Limited Partnership Act (1976) with or without amendments.

(5) If the Service has not determined that the controlling state statute corresponds to the applicable Uniform Act for purposes of section 301.7701–2 of the regulations, a list of all substantial differences.

(6) A representation that the organization has been, and will be at all times, in conformance with the controlling state statute.

(7) The nature, amount, and timing of the capital contributions made and to be made by both the general partners and the limited partners.

(8) The extent of participation of the general partners and the limited partners in profits and losses, including any possible shift in the profit and loss sharing ratios over time.

(9) A description of the relationships, direct and indirect, between the limited partners and the general partners that suggest that the general partners, individually or in the aggregate, may not at all times act independently (because of individual or aggregate limited partner influence or control). Such relationships include: (a) ownership by limited partners of 5 percent or more of the stock or other beneficial interests in a general partner; (b) control by limited partners of 5 percent or more of the voting power in a general partner; (c) ownership of 5 percent or more of the stock or other beneficial interests in any general partner and in any limited partner by the same person or persons acting as a group; and (d) control of 5 percent or more of the voting power in any general partner and in any limited partner by the same person or persons acting as a group. For purposes of the preceding sentence, a person shall be considered to own any beneficial interest owned by a related person and shall be considered to control any voting power controlled by a related person; a person shall be treated as related to another person if they bear a relationship specified in section 267(b) or section 707(b)(1) of the Code. The relationships defined in the first sentence of this section 3.03(9) may also include a debtor-creditor relationship and an employer-employee relationship.

(10) A representation of the net worth (based on assets at current fair market value) of each general partner, excluding interests in the partnership, a description of all general partner assets and liabilities arising from transactions with the partnership or with a person related to any general partner under section 267(b) or section 707(b)(1) of the Code, and a description of all other partnerships in which any of the general partners has an interest.

(11) If, and to the extent that, section 4 of this revenue procedure applies to the organization, a detailed description of how each of the applicable provisions therein is satisfied.

.04   Required Copies of Documents and Supplementary Materials.

(1) The partnership agreement.

(2) The partnership certificate filed or to be filed with the state in which the organization is formed.

(3) The registration statement filed or to be filed with the Securities and Exchange Commission. (A draft is acceptable.)

(4) If a registration statement is not required to be filed with the Securities and Exchange Commission, then documents filed or to be filed with any federal or state agency engaged in the regulation of securities and any private offering memorandum. (Drafts are acceptable.)

(5) A copy of the applicable state statutes, and amendments, under which the organization was or will be formed.

(6) An outline or copies of all promotional material used to sell interests in the organization, highlighting statements about probable tax consequences and the effect of the requested ruling upon the tax consequences.

SECTION 4.   PROVISIONS APPLICABLE TO LIMITED PARTNERSHIPS

The Service will ordinarily consider a ruling request that relates to classification of a limited partnership as a partnership, for federal tax purposes, only if the conditions in this section 4 are satisfied. Section 4.05, however, relates solely to the corporate characteristic of continuity of life described in section 301.7701–2(b) of the regulations. Similarly, section 4.06 relates solely to the corporate characteristic of centralization of management described in section 301.7701–2(c). Therefore, failure to satisfy section 4.05 or section 4.06 will preclude a specific ruling that continuity of life or centralized management is lacking, but will not necessarily preclude the issuance of a partnership classification ruling. Section 4.07 provides a safe harbor, generally applicable to a limited partnership with at least one corporate general partner, that relates to the corporate characteristic of limited liability described in section 301.7701–2(d).

.01   Unless exempted by section 4.02 below or the provisions of this section 4.01, the interests (including limited partnership interests) of all the general partners, taken together, in each material item of partnership income, gain, loss, deduction, or credit must be equal to at least 1 percent of each such item at all times during the existence of the partnership, and the partnership agreement must expressly so provide. If the 1–percent standard will not be satisfied because of a temporary allocation required under section 704(b) of the Code, section 704(c), or corresponding Income Tax Regulations (a qualified income offset or minimum gain chargeback, for example), this will generally not be considered a violation of this section 4.01, but the ruling request must describe any such allocation and explain why the allocation is required under section 704(b) or (c), as appropriate. Any other temporary non-conformance with the 1–percent standard will be considered a violation of this section 4.01 unless it is demonstrated that the general partners' interest in net profits and losses over the anticipated life of the partnership is material. For this purpose, a profits interest generally will not be considered material unless it is substantially in excess of 1 percent and will be in effect for a substantial period of time during which it is reasonably expected that the partnership will generate profits. For example, a 20–percent interest in profits that begins 4 years after partnership formation and continues for the life of the partnership would generally be considered material if the partnership is expected to generate profits for a substantial period beyond the 4 years.

.02   If the limited partnership has total contributions exceeding $50 million, the general partners need not meet the 1–percent standard in section 4.01. However, except for a temporary allocation or nonconformance specified in section 4.01, the general partners' aggregate interest at all times in each material item must be at least 1 percent divided by the ratio of total contributions to $50 million, and the partnership agreement must expressly incorporate at least the computed percentage. For example, if total contributions are $125 million, the interest in each material item must be at least .4 percent, that is, 1 percent divided by 125/50. In no event, however, other than as a result of a temporary allocation or nonconformance specified in section 4.01, may the general partners' aggregate interest at any time in any material item be less than .2 percent.

.03   Unless section 4.04 applies, the general partners, taken together, must maintain a minimum capital account balance equal to either 1 percent of total positive capital account balances for the partnership or $500,000, whichever is less. Whenever a limited partner makes a capital contribution, the general partners must be obligated to contribute immediately capital equal to 1.01 percent of the limited partner's capital contribution or a lesser amount (including zero) that causes the sum of the general partners' capital account balances to equal the lesser of 1 percent of total positive capital account balances for the partnership or $500,000. If no limited partner capital account has a positive balance, the general partners, taken together, need not have a positive capital account balance to satisfy this section 4.03. Capital accounts and the value of contributions are determined by application of the capital accounting rules in section 1.704–1(b)(2)(iv) of the regulations.

.04   If at least one general partner has contributed or will contribute substantial services in its capacity as a partner, apart from services for which guaranteed payments under section 707(c) of the Code are made, then the general partners need not meet the capital account standard in section 4.03. However, the partnership agreement must expressly provide that, upon the dissolution and termination of the partnership, the general partners will contribute to the partnership an amount equal to: (a) the deficit balances, if any, in their capital accounts; or (b) the excess of 1.01 percent of the total capital contributions of the limited partners over the capital previously contributed by the general partners; or (c) the lesser of (a) or (b). Those services that do not relate to day-to-day operations in the partnership's primary business activity, such as services relating to organization and syndication of the partnership, accounting, financial planning, and general business planning, and those that are in the nature of investment management will be closely scrutinized to determine if they are in fact substantial services. In making this determination, the Service will consider the nature of the partnership and its activities.

.05 For a limited partnership formed in a state with a statute corresponding to the Uniform Limited Partnership Act or the Revised Uniform Limited Partnership Act, in the case of the removal of a general partner, the partnership agreement may not permit less than a majority in interest of limited partners to elect a new general partner to continue the partnership, or the Service will not rule that the partnership lacks continuity of life.

.06 Limited partner interests, excluding those held by general partners, may not exceed 80 percent of the total interests in the partnership, or the Service will not rule that the partnership lacks centralized management. In addition, the Service will consider all the facts and circumstances, including limited partner control of the general partners (whether direct or indirect), in determining whether the partnership lacks centralized management.

.07 If the net worth of corporate general partners at the time of the ruling request equals at least 10 percent of the total contributions to the limited partnership and is expected to continue to equal at least 10 percent of the total contributions throughout the life of the partnership, then, for advance ruling purposes, the partnership will generally be deemed to lack limited liability. In the case of a limited partnership in which the only general partners are corporations that do not satisfy the safe harbor described in the preceding sentence, close scrutiny will be applied to determine whether the partnership lacks limited liability. In that connection, it must be demonstrated either that a general partner has (or the general partners collectively have) substantial assets (other than the partner's interest in the partnership) that could be reached by a creditor of the partnership or that the general partners individually and collectively will act independently of the limited partners. * * *

Problem 4–3

A limited partnership was formed for the purpose of developing tracts of land, with Art, Bill and Charlie as individual limited partners and Zeus, Inc. an unrelated corporation, as the general partner. The corporation has a 20% interest in the partnership and has substantial assets other than its partnership interest.

The partnership agreement provides that limited partners can transfer income interests only with the consent of the general partner and further provides that the limited partners can freely transfer their capital interests only after first offering such interests to other members of the partnership at fair market value. The partnership agreement also provides that the partnership will continue for 30 years.

a. How should the organization be classified for tax purposes?

 b. Assume alternatively that Zeus, Inc. has a 15% interest in the organization and has no assets other than its interest in the partnership.

 c. Same as b, except that Art and Bill own all of the stock of Zeus, Inc.

E. LIMITED LIABILITY COMPANIES

A recent development in the classification arena is the rise of the limited liability company and its progeny (the limited liability partnership, the limited liability limited partnership, and the limited partnership associations). As evidenced by Revenue Ruling 88–76, which follows, this business form may be classified as a partnership for tax purposes notwithstanding the existence of the corporate trait of limited liability. While a limited partnership for practical purposes affords many of its participants limited liability, there is a general partner which in name, if not reality, possesses personal liability. However, the limited liability company vehicle affords *all* of its members limited liability. Nevertheless, the Service has permitted partnership classification in certain settings, since the typical limited liability company statute ensures the lack of continuity of life (i.e., dissolution upon the death or bankruptcy of a member) and a lack of free transferability of interests (i.e., consent of all members required for a transferee to become a substitute member). In addition, centralized management may be lacking if the entity is managed by its members. While Congress has effectively permitted partnership treatment with respect to S corporations, is something inappropriate about an administrative agency making such a decision? Has the Service given up on the classification issue? Will Congress respond by enacting prohibitive legislation?

REVENUE RULING 88–76
1988–2 C.B. 360.

ISSUE

Whether a Wyoming limited liability company, none of whose members or designated managers are personally liable for any debts of the company, is classified for federal tax purposes as an association or as a partnership.

FACTS

M was organized as a limited liability company pursuant to the provisions of the Wyoming Limited Liability Company Act (Act). The purpose of *M* is to acquire, own, and operate improved real property. *M* has 25 members, including *A, B,* and *C.*

The Act provides that a limited liability company may be managed by a designated manager or managers, or by its members. If the limited liability company is managed by its members, management authority is vested in its members in proportion to their capital contributions to the company. *M* is managed by its designated managers, *A, B,* and *C.*

Under the Act, neither the members nor the designated managers of a limited liability company are liable for any debts, obligations, or liabilities of the limited liability company.

The Act also provides that the interest of a member in a limited liability company is part of the personal estate of the member; however, each member can assign or transfer the member's respective interest in the limited liability company only upon the unanimous written consent of all the remaining members. In the event that the remaining members fail to approve the assignment or transfer, the assignee or transferee has no right to participate in the management or become a member of the limited liability company. However, the assignee or transferee is entitled to receive the share of profits or other compensation and the return of contributions to which the transferring member would otherwise be entitled.

A limited liability company formed under the Act is dissolved upon the occurrence of any of the following events: (1) when the period fixed for the duration of the company expires; (2) by the unanimous written consent of all the members; or (3) by the death, retirement, resignation, expulsion, bankruptcy, dissolution of a member or occurrence of any other event that terminates the continued membership of a member, unless the business of the company is continued by the consent of all the remaining members under a right to do so stated in the articles of organization of the company. Under M's articles of organization, the business of M is continued by the consent of all the remaining members.

LAW AND ANALYSIS

Section 7701(a)(2) of the Internal Revenue Code provides that the term "partnership" includes a syndicate, group, pool, venture, or other unincorporated organization, through or by means of which any business, financial operation, or venture is carried on, and which is not a trust or estate or a corporation.

Section 7701(a)(3) of the Code provides that the term "corporation" includes associations, joint-stock companies, and insurance companies.

Section 301.7701–1(b) of the Procedure and Administration Regulations states that the Code prescribes certain categories, or classes, into which various organizations fall for purposes of taxation. These categories, or classes, include associations (which are taxable as corporations), partnerships, and trusts. The tests, or standards, that are to be applied in determining the classification of an organization are set forth in sections 301.7701–2 through 301.7701–4.

Section 301.7701–2(a)(1) of the regulations sets forth the following basic characteristics of a corporation: (1) associates, (2) an objective to carry on business and divide the gains therefrom, (3) continuity of life, (4) centralization of management, (5) liability for corporate debts limited to corporate property, and (6) free transferability of interests. Whether a particular organization is to be classified as an association must be determined by taking into account the presence or absence of each of these corporate characteristics. In addition to the six major characteristics, other factors may be found in some cases which may be significant in classifying an organization as an association, a partnership, or a trust.

Section 301.7701–2(a)(2) of the regulations further provides that characteristics common to partnerships and corporations are not material in attempting to distinguish between an association and a partnership. Since associates and an objective to carry on business and divide the gains therefrom are generally common to corporations and partnerships, the determination of whether an organization which has such characteristics is to be treated for tax purposes as a partnership or as an association depends on whether there exists centralization of management, continuity of life, free transferability of interests, and limited liability.

Section 301.7701–2(a)(3) of the regulations provides that if an unincorporated organization possesses more corporate characteristics than noncorporate characteristics, it constitutes an association taxable as a corporation.

In interpreting section 301.7701–2 of the regulations, the Tax Court, in *Larson v. Commissioner,* 66 T.C. 159 (1976), *acq.,* 1979–1 C.B. 1, concluded that equal weight must be given to each of the four corporate characteristics of continuity of life, centralization of management, limited liability, and free transferability of interests.

In the present situation, *M* has associates and an objective to carry on business and divide the gains therefrom. Therefore, *M* must be classified as either an association or a partnership. *M* is classified as a partnership for federal tax purposes unless the organization has a preponderance of the remaining corporate characteristics of continuity of life, centralization of management, limited liability, and free transferability of interests.

Section 301.7701–2(b)(1) of the regulations provides that if the death, insanity, bankruptcy, retirement, resignation, or expulsion of any member will cause a dissolution of the organization, continuity of life does not exist. Section 301.7701–2(b)(2) provides that an agreement by which an organization is established may provide that the business will be continued by the remaining members in the event of the death or withdrawal of any member, but such agreement does not establish continuity of life if under local law the death or withdrawal of any member causes a dissolution of the organization.

Under the Act, unless the business of *M* is continued by the consent of all the remaining members, *M* is dissolved upon the death, retirement, resignation, expulsion, bankruptcy, dissolution of a member or occurrence of any other event that terminates the continued membership of a member in the company. If a member of *M* ceases to be a member of *M* for any reason, the continuity of *M* is not assured, because all remaining members must agree to continue the business. Consequently, *M* lacks the corporate characteristic of continuity of life.

Under section 301.7701–2(c)(1) of the regulations an organization has the corporate characteristic of centralized management if any person (or group of persons that does not include all the members) has continuing exclusive authority to make management decisions necessary to the conduct of the business for which the organization was formed.

Under the Act, a limited liability company has the discretion to be managed either by a designated manager or managers, or to be managed by its members. Because M is managed by its designated managers, A, B, and C, M possesses the corporate characteristic of centralized management.

Section 301.7701–2(d)(1) of the regulations provides that an organization has the corporate characteristic of limited liability if under local law there is no member who is personally liable for the debts of, or claims against, the organization. Personal liability means that a creditor of an organization may seek personal satisfaction from a member of the organization to the extent that the assets of such organization are insufficient to satisfy the creditor's claim.

Under the Act, neither the managers nor the members of M are personally liable for its debts and obligations. Consequently, M possesses the corporate characteristic of limited liability.

Under section 301.7701–2(e)(1) of the regulations, an organization has the corporate characteristic of free transferability of interests if each of the members or those members owning substantially all of the interests in the organization have the power, without the consent of other members, to substitute for themselves in the same organization a person who is not a member of the organization. In order for this power of substitution to exist in the corporate sense, the member must be able, without the consent of other members, to confer upon the member's substitute all the attributes of the member's interest in the organization. The characteristic of free transferability does not exist if each member can, without the consent of the other members, assign only the right to share in the profits but cannot assign the right to participate in the management of the organization.

Under the terms of the Act, a member of M can assign or transfer that member's interest to another who is not a member of the organization. However, the assignee or transferee does not become a substitute member and does not acquire all the attributes of the member's interest in M unless all the remaining members approve the assignment or transfer. Therefore, M lacks the corporate characteristic of free transferability of interests.

M has associates and an objective to carry on business and divide the gains therefrom. In addition, M possesses the corporate characteristics of centralized management and limited liability. M does not, however, possess the corporate characteristics of continuity of life and free transferability of interests.

HOLDING

M has associates and an objective to carry on business and divide the gains therefrom, but lacks a preponderance of the four remaining corporate characteristics. Accordingly, *M* is classified as a partnership for federal tax purposes.

Problem 4–4

Exports, LLC is organized as a limited liability company under the provisions of the New Jersey Limited Liability Company Act. Under its operating agreement, Exports, LLC may engage in any and all business activity permitted by New Jersey. It has 25 members and three of them are elected as managers. Under the Act, management is vested in its members in proportion to their percentage in the profits of the organization, unless otherwise specified in the operating agreement of the company. Exports' operating agreement grants exclusive management authority to its designated managers.

Under the New Jersey Act, no member, manager, employee, or agent is obligated personally for any of the organization's debts, obligations, or liabilities. Furthermore, the organization is dissolved upon the death, retirement, resignation, expulsion, or bankruptcy of any member unless the business is continued upon the vote of all members and the operating agreement contains such a provision. Under Exports' operating agreement, upon the assignment of a membership interest, the assignee of the interest has no right to participate in Exports or become a member without the written consent of all of Exports' members other than the assignor member. How will Exports be classified for tax purposes?

F.   THE FUTURE OF THE CLASSIFICATION ISSUE

Given the elaborate judicial and administrative labyrinth which has been constructed for classification issues, a student of the field should inquire as to the wisdom and rationale for such efforts. Over the past 20 years while taxpayers and the Service parried regarding classification issues, the Treasury and Congress took a more direct approach aiming a frontal assault on those areas which lead taxpayers to prefer one classification over the other. For example, previously the corporate form was preferred over the partnership form in order to enjoy greater latitude in deducting pension and profit sharing contributions, while the partnership form was superior to the corporate form if the enterprise generated losses. With the passage of retirement plan reform legislation equalizing the deferral and deduction benefits regardless of the type of business selected and the adoption of the at risk rules of § 465 and passive loss rules of § 469 which dramatically limit the loss flow through benefits of a partnership, the tax attributes of a particular classification have been minimized. If so, why is the Service as late as 1989 promulgating detailed classification guidelines? The Service is currently considering the elimination of the entire classification analysis by allowing a taxpaying entity to merely "check a box" to inform the Service which type of tax entity it selects. See Notice 95–14, which follows. As this casebook went to press, the Service issued Proposed Regulations to this effect. See Prop.Reg. §§ 301.7701–1 to –3.

SIMPLIFICATION OF ENTITY CLASSIFICATION RULES

Notice 95–14.
1995–14 I.R.B. 7.

The Internal Revenue Service and the Treasury Department are considering simplifying the classification regulations to allow taxpayers to treat domestic unincorporated business organizations as partnerships or as associations on an elective basis. The Service and Treasury also are considering adopting similar rules for foreign business organizations. Comments are requested regarding this and other possible approaches to simplifying the regulations.

BACKGROUND

Section 7701(a)(2) of the Internal Revenue Code defines a partnership to include a syndicate, group, pool, joint venture, or other unincorporated organization, through or by means of which any business, financial operation, or venture is carried on, and which is not a trust or estate or a corporation. Section 7701(a)(3) defines a corporation to include associations, joint-stock companies, and insurance companies. In addition, certain business entities are taxed as corporations under various sections of the Code, such as publicly traded partnerships under § 7704 and taxable mortgage pools under § 7701(i).

Sections 301.7701–2 and 301.7701–3 of the Procedure and Administration Regulations (the classification regulations) provide rules for determining whether an unincorporated organization that has associates and an objective to carry on business and divide the gains therefrom is classified as a partnership or as an association for federal tax purposes. These regulations classify such an organization as an association if it has a preponderance of four specified corporate characteristics: (1) continuity of life, (2) centralization of management, (3) liability for organization debts limited to the organization's assets, and (4) free transferability of interests. The classification regulations, together with numerous revenue rulings and revenue procedures, provide guidance in determining when an unincorporated organization possesses these characteristics.

The existing classification regulations are based on the historical differences under local law between partnerships and corporations. However, many states recently have revised their statutes to provide that partnerships and other unincorporated organizations may possess characteristics that have traditionally been associated with corporations, thereby narrowing considerably the traditional distinctions between corporations and partnerships. For example, some partnership statutes have been modified to provide that no partner is unconditionally liable for all of the debts of the partnership. Similarly, almost all states have enacted statutes allowing the formation of limited liability companies. These entities are designed to provide liability protection to all members and to otherwise resemble corporations, while generally qualifying as partnerships for federal tax purposes. See, e.g., Rev.Rul. 88–76, 1988–2 C.B. 360.

One consequence of the narrowing of the differences under local law between corporations and partnerships is that taxpayers can achieve partnership tax classification for a non-publicly traded organization that, in all meaningful respects, is virtually indistinguishable from a corporation. Taxpayers and the Service, however, continue to expend considerable resources in determining the proper classification of domestic unincorporated business organizations. For example, since the issuance of Rev.Rul. 88–76, the Service has issued seventeen revenue rulings analyzing individual state limited liability company statutes, and has issued several revenue procedures and numerous letter rulings relating to classification of various unincorporated organizations under the classification regulations. In addition, small unincorporated organizations may not have sufficient resources and expertise to apply the current classification regulations to achieve the tax classification they desire.

POSSIBLE SIMPLIFICATION OF THE CURRENT CLASSIFICATION RULES

A. Domestic Unincorporated Business Organizations

The Service and Treasury are considering simplifying the existing classification regulations to allow taxpayers to elect to treat certain domestic unincorporated business organizations as partnerships or as associations for federal tax purposes. This approach would apply to all such organizations that have two or more associates and an objective to carry on business and divide the gains therefrom, unless the organization's classification is determined under another Code provision. For example, an entity that is treated as a partnership, but which is publicly traded and is taxed as a corporation under § 7704, would continue to be taxed as a corporation under this approach. Similarly, a taxable mortgage pool under § 7701(i) would continue to be taxed as a corporation, and an entity that makes an election to be a real estate mortgage investment conduit (REMIC) under § 860D(b) would continue to be taxed under the REMIC rules. This approach generally would not affect the existing rules for classifying trusts (other than trusts that are classified as associations or partnerships under §§ 301.7701–2 and 301.7701–3).

Under this approach, all affirmative elections would be prospective from the date the election is filed or a later date designated in the election. Retroactive elections would not be permitted. The elections would have to be executed by all members of the organization and would be binding on all members thereafter, until superseded by a subsequent election.

The Service and Treasury recognize that there is considerable flexibility under the current rules to effectively change the classification of an organization at will (for example, by forming a new organization with different factors that would result in a different classification, and merging the old organization into it). On the other hand, the purpose of this approach is to simplify the rules in order to reduce the burdens on both taxpayers and the Service. The Service and Treasury are concerned that allowing taxpayers to change their classification simply by filing an election could result in a significant increase in the number of organizations changing their classification, thereby increasing burdens for some taxpayers and the Service. Accordingly, the Service and Treasury will consider whether the elections provided under this approach should be restricted.

Under this approach, an election to change the classification of an organization would have the same federal tax consequences as a change in classification under current law. For example, if an organization were classified as an association taxable as a corporation and later elected to be classified as a partnership, the election would be treated as a complete liquidation of the corporation and a formation of a new partnership. Thus, a final return for the corporation and a first-year return for the partnership each would have to be filed. In addition, the new partnership would have to ensure that its allocations were in compliance with § 704(b) and the regulations thereunder.

This approach would include mechanisms for classifying organizations that do not make affirmative classification elections. Because the Service and Treasury believe that domestic unincorporated business organizations typically are formed to obtain partnership classification, those organizations generally would be classified as partnerships for federal tax purposes unless the organization files an election to be classified as an association taxable as a corporation. However, because the Service and Treasury believe that the current classification of existing organizations should be altered only by affirmative election, those organizations that are in existence on or prior to the effective date of the revised regulations would retain their current classification unless an affirmative election to be classified differently is filed. * * *

REQUEST FOR COMMENTS AND HEARING

The Service and Treasury invite comments on simplification of the current classification regulations, including alternate methods for simplifying those regulations. In addition, comments are invited on the approach described in this notice, including (1) whether adoption of the simplified approach described in this notice would be appropriate; (2) whether this approach would result in a greater proportion of newly formed businesses choosing unincorporated organizations rather than state-law corporations; (3) the mechanics of this approach, including the election requirements, the classification of organizations that do not file an affirmative election, and transition issues; (4) whether the ability to elect to change the classification of an organization should be restricted, and if so, in what manner; and (5) the proper treatment of unincorporated organizations that have a single owner or member. * * *

EFFECT ON CURRENT LAW

While the Service and Treasury consider simplifying the current classification regulations, the Service will continue to apply the current rules without regard to the approach described in this notice. No inference is intended concerning the proper interpretation and application of the current rules. * * *

Chapter 5

PARTNERSHIP FORMATION—ACQUISITION OF A PARTNERSHIP INTEREST IN EXCHANGE FOR A CONTRIBUTION OF PROPERTY

Code References: §§ 721; 722; 723; 705(a)(2); 731(a)(1); 733; 752(a)–(b). **See briefly:** §§ 168(i)(7)(A), (B); 1223(1), (2); 1245(b)(3).

Regulations: §§ 1.721–1; 1.722–1; 1.723–1; 1.453–9(c)(2); 1.752–1(b), (c), and (f).

A. INTRODUCTION

Two or more entrepreneurs may desire to form a partnership, or an entity taxed as a partnership, in several settings. They might be contributing money or property to a newly formed, start-up business. Alternatively, they might be combining two businesses formerly operated as proprietorships. Additionally, an existing partnership may receive an injection of cash or property from a new or existing participant. In any of these situations, a partner can acquire his or her partnership interest (upon formation of the partnership by joining or adding to an existing partnership) in exchange either for a contribution of property or for the rendition of services. This chapter focuses on the tax consequences of a receipt of a partnership interest in return for contribution of property. Chapter 6 addresses the tax consequences of the receipt of a partnership interest in return for services.

One of the dominant themes in the tax area is the concept of the recognition of gain or loss on the exchange of property for cash or other property. Upon the formation of a partnership, each partner exchanges something of significance (e.g., money, property, or services) in return for his or her partnership interest. As that partnership interest typically has a value equal to the contribution, the issue is whether the contributing partner must recognize gain or loss under the general operative rule of § 1001. While *realization* of income by the contributor arises on such a transfer, sound tax policy acknowledges that *recognition* of gain or loss by the contributor in such a setting would act as a deterrent to the formation of partnerships. The principles of tax neutrality should minimize the role of the tax law in choosing among alternate tax modes of conducting business operations (sole proprietorship, partnership, or corporation).

In effectuating this policy, Subchapter K through § 721(a) provides that "no gain or loss shall be recognized to a partnership or to any of its partners in the case of a contribution of property to the partnership in exchange for an interest in the partnership." A limited exception to this nonrecognition treatment for gains arises under § 721(b) for contributions to an investment partnership. This exception is premised upon the existence of a relatively passive and stable vehicle (the investment partnership), as opposed to an operating business entity, and the partner's assumed ability to diversify his investment and, therefore, "cash in" through the relinquishment of his 100% ownership interest in the contributed assets in return for a lesser percentage interest in all of the investment partnership's assets. This text focuses on partnerships which are operating active small businesses. See generally Willis, Pennell, and Postlewaite, *Partnership Taxation* ch. 4 (Warren, Gorham and Lamont, 6th ed. 1996).

B. DEFINITION OF PROPERTY

For a contribution to qualify for nonrecognition of gain or loss under § 721, the partner must transfer "property" to the partnership. Neither § 721 nor its Regulations define the term. Money clearly is considered property, but gain or loss is never inherent in the holding of domestic, as opposed to foreign, currency. Real property and tangible personal property qualify as such if title is transferred to the partnership. However, as discussed at Chapter 6, services do not constitute property for § 721 purposes. This line of demarcation is a familiar one previously considered in the basic tax course. The statutory opposition to nonrecognition on the receipt of a partnership interest in return for services stems from the fear that ordinary income (compensation for services rendered) may be converted into capital gain (the typical characterization of the gain generated on the sale of a partnership interest).

Other types of rights and interests are not as easily classified. For example, in *Oden v. Commissioner,* which follows, a personal promissory note was held to constitute property for purposes of § 721. The taxpayer had a zero basis in the note which carried over to the partnership and, as payments were made on the note, the taxpayer's basis for his partnership interest increased. Intangible rights, frequently termed "intellectual property," pose similar classification issues. The latter class of assets has had their claim to property status bolstered by the enactment of § 197 in 1993 which specifically defines many of those assets and provides an amortization period of 15 years.

ODEN v. COMMISSIONER

41 T.C.M. 1285 (1981).

IRWIN, JUDGE.

OPINION

* * * The Issue presented for our determination focuses upon the propriety of petitioners' claimed partnership loss of $30,789. This loss was mainly attributable to alleged intangible drilling costs deducted by the Ohio Producers partnership pursuant to an election under section 263(c).

Respondent bases his denial of the claimed partnership loss in excess of $16,250 on the following grounds: (1) Petitioner has not established that intangible drilling costs in an amount in excess of $65,000 were actually incurred in connection with the Chamberlain well. Thus, petitioner, with a one-fourth interest in the well, may not deduct more than $16,250 for intangible drilling costs; (2) petitioner, according to respondent, did not acquire an operating interest in the Chamberlain well until after the well had been drilled to production. Thus, respondent relies on Haass v. Commissioner, 55 T.C. 43 (1970) which holds that a working or operating interest in a specific well must be acquired prior to the incursion of drilling and development expenses in order that expenses be deductible to the holder of such an interest; and (3) petitioner has not established that he had a higher basis than $16,250 in his partnership interest.

Petitioner argues that the issue of the amount of intangible drilling costs incurred by the Ohio Producers partnership was not raised in the notice of deficiency and hence constitutes new matter regarding which the burden of proof rests on respondent. This burden, petitioner asserts, has not been satisfied. Petitioner further maintains that he acquired his partnership interest prior to the time that intangible drilling costs were incurred respecting the Chamberlain well. Petitioner claims that his basis in the Ohio Producers partnership was $35,000 and accordingly the claimed partnership loss of $30,789 is allowable.

We hold for respondent for the reason that petitioner's basis in his partnership interest has not been shown to be greater than $16,250 and accordingly any partnership loss in excess of that amount must be disallowed.

Section 722 provides in pertinent part that the basis of an interest in a partnership acquired by a contribution of property, including money, to the partnership shall be the amount of such money and the adjusted basis of such property to the contributing partner at the time of the contribution. A partner's distributive share of partnership loss (including capital loss) shall be allowed only to the extent of the adjusted basis of such partner's interest in the partnership at the end of the partnership year in which the loss occurred. Section 704(d). Petitioner's cash contribution to the Ohio Producers partnership was $16,250. Additionally, he argues that he tendered a note for $18,750 at the time of the creation of the partnership. Petitioner claims that under section 742 he is entitled to a $35,000 basis in his partnership interest.

Petitioner's application of section 742 to the instant case is in error. That section provides that a transferee's initial basis in his partnership interest is determined under the rules generally applicable to acquisitions of other types of property. See section 1.742–1, Income Tax Regs. Accordingly, if a partnership interest is purchased or acquired in a taxable exchange, the transferee's basis is his cost under section 1012. Where, however, the partnership interest is acquired by a contribution of property to the partnership, the contributor's basis in the acquired interest is determined by reference to the adjusted basis of the property so contributed.

Petitioner urges that we determine that his basis in the Ohio Producers partnership includes the face amount ($18,750) of a note allegedly executed and delivered by him to the partnership. Petitioner has not shown that any payments were made on the note during 1971.

Petitioner advances an elaborate argument which points to the alleged transfer of his own note to the partnership. He emphasizes that the note created a bona fide indebtedness to the partnership, while he minimizes the importance of the question of whether the note was recourse or nonrecourse. While we agree that it is irrelevant in the present context whether the note was either recourse or nonrecourse, we believe that such irrelevancy stems from the fact that petitioner's basis in his partnership interest is to be determined under section 722. Since petitioner incurred no cost in making the note, its basis to him was zero. Petitioner has not shown that any payments on the note were made in 1971. Thus, pursuant to the mandate of section 722, petitioner is not entitled to increase his partnership basis by the face amount of the allegedly transferred note. Accordingly, petitioner is not entitled to deduct any partnership loss in excess of his cash contribution of $16,250. Section 704(d).

Other arguments aired by the parties are rendered moot by our holding above and thus we do not address them.

Decision will be entered for the respondent.

C. STATUTORY AND JUDICIAL SAFEGUARDS

The nonrecognition treatment of § 721 may be undercut by other judicial and statutory doctrines. For example, the potential application of § 1245, regarding recapture of depreciation on the transfer of depreciable assets, and § 453B, regarding the disposition of an installment obligation, must be considered. If such assets are transferred to a partnership in return for an interest therein, do these sections apply to force gain recognition notwithstanding the literal provisions of § 721?

Additionally, judicial doctrines, such as the assignment of income doctrine, may appear ripe for application in such a setting. As noted by the Staff of the Joint Committee regarding the legislative changes to Subchapter K in 1984: "These changes were not intended to override the anticipatory assignment of income doctrine in those situations in which such doctrine would apply to a cash-method partner's contribution of accrued but unpaid items to a partnership." However, in light of § 704(c), discussed in Chapter 10, can an argument be fashioned that, in the partnership context, the assignment of income doctrine should be inapplicable to partners' contributions?

D. BASIS AND HOLDING PERIOD DETERMINATIONS

When a contribution of property to a partnership qualifies under § 721, the contributing partner's basis in his partnership interest is determined under § 722. Accordingly, the basis of the partnership interest is equal to the amount of money contributed plus the adjusted basis of any property contributed. An increase in basis is available only for the amount of any gain recognized under § 721(b) by the contributing partners. Such policies follow solid tax precepts witnessed previously in the gift area discussed in Chapter 3. Once nonrecognition is bestowed on a transaction involving the transfer of property, a carryover of basis is required to preserve the preexisting appreciation or depreciation for future recognition.

Similarly, § 723 provides for the determination of the partnership's basis for the contributed assets. Notwithstanding the fact that the partners, not the partnership, are responsible on their personal returns for the earnings or losses from partnership operations, an entity approach is employed whereby the partners possess and maintain a basis for their partnership interests. A tax return is filed at the partnership level although the entity itself pays no tax. The basis of a partner in his or her partnership interest is reflected in the tax return and is required for the determination of gain or loss upon a subsequent disposition of the interest. Also, the application of the gain recognition provisions of § 731 and the loss allowance provisions of § 704(d) turn upon the amount of the partner's basis for the partnership interest.

The partnership's basis for contributed property is the adjusted basis of the property to the contributing partner at the time of the contribution. Essentially, the partnership takes a transferred basis from the partner and will recognize gain or loss upon the ultimate disposition of the property. Such recognition will flow through to the partners of the partnership in accordance with their percentage partnership interests. Additionally, the amount, if any, of depreciation or amortization expense available to the partnership is dependent upon its basis in the asset. The effect of these rules is that the total of the partnership's bases in its assets, i.e., "inside basis," initially equals the total of the partners' bases in their partnership interests, i.e., "outside basis," and will generally run in tandem and may remain equal after years of operations.

The rules of § 1223 generally provide for tacking when calculating the holding period for both the property contributed to the partnership and for the partner's partnership interest.   The partnership's holding period in contributed property will include that of the contributing partner in a given asset.   Similarly, the partnership interest of the contributing partner generally will include the holding period of the contributed asset.   The holding period is relevant in determining whether the sale of the subject asset yields long-term or short-term capital gain or loss.   What result if various assets with different holding periods are contributed?

McDOUGAL v. COMMISSIONER

62 T.C. 720 (1974).

FAY, JUDGE.

* * * Mutual concessions having been made, the following issues remain to be decided:

(1) Did the McDougals' transfer of a one-half interest in the racehorse, Iron Card, to Gilbert McClanahan constitute a gift, or alternatively, did the aforesaid transfer constitute a contribution to an oral partnership or joint venture previously or contemporaneously formed by the McDougals and Gilbert McClanahan; * * *

FINDINGS OF FACT

F.C. and Frankie McDougal maintained farms at Lamesa, Tex., where they were engaged in the business of breeding and racing horses. Gilbert McClanahan was a licensed public horse trainer who rendered his services to various horse owners for a standard fee.   He had numbered the McDougals among his clientele since 1965.

On February 21, 1965, a horse of exceptional pedigree, Iron Card, had been foaled at the Anthony Ranch in Florida.   Title to Iron Card was acquired in January of 1967 by one Frank Ratliff, Jr., who in turn transferred title to himself, M.H. Ratliff, and John V. Burnett (Burnett). The Ratliffs and Burnett entered Iron Card in several races as a 2–year–old; and although the horse enjoyed some success in these contests, it soon became evident that he was suffering from a condition diagnosed by a veterinarian as a protein allergy.

When, due to a dispute among themselves, the Ratliffs and Burnett decided to sell Iron Card for whatever price he could attract, McClanahan (who had trained the horse for the Ratliffs and Burnett) advised the McDougals to make the purchase.   He made this recommendation because, despite the veterinarian's prognosis to the contrary, McClanahan believed that by the use of home remedy Iron Card could be restored to full racing vigor.   Furthermore, McClanahan felt that as Iron Card's allergy was not genetic and as his pedigree was impressive, he would be valuable in the future as a stud even if further attempts to race him proved unsuccessful.

The McDougals purchased Iron Card for $10,000 on January 1, 1968. At the time of the purchase McDougal promised that if McClanahan trained and attended to Iron Card, a half interest in the horse would be his once the McDougals had recovered the costs and expenses of acquisition. This promise was not made in lieu of payment of the standard trainer's fee; for from January 1, 1968, until the date of the transfer, McClanahan was paid $2,910 as compensation for services rendered as Iron Card's trainer.

McClanahan's home remedy proved so effective in relieving Iron Card of his allergy that the horse began to race with success, and his reputation consequently grew to such proportion that he attracted a succession of offers to purchase, one of which reached $60,000. The McDougals decided, however, to keep the horse and by October 4, 1968, had recovered out of their winnings the costs of acquiring him. It was therefore on that date that they transferred a half interest in the horse to McClanahan in accordance with the promise which McDougal had made to the trainer. A document entitled "Bill of Sale," wherein the transfer was described as a gift, was executed on the following day.

Iron Card continued to race well until very late in 1968 when, without warning and for an unascertained cause, he developed a condition called "hot ankle" which effectively terminated his racing career. From 1970 onward he was used exclusively for breeding purposes. That his value as a stud was no less than his value as a racehorse is attested to by the fact that in September of 1970 petitioners were offered $75,000 for him; but after considering the offer, the McDougals and McClanahan decided to refuse it, preferring to exploit Iron Card's earning potential as a stud to their own profit.

On November 1, 1968, petitioners had concluded a partnership agreement by parol to effectuate their design of racing the horse for as long as that proved feasible and of offering him out as a stud thereafter. Profits were to be shared equally by the McDougals and McClanahan, while losses were to be allocated to the McDougals alone. * * *

We shall now turn our attention to those returns and amended returns filed in April of 1970. The McDougals explicitly claimed by way of amendment to have transferred the half interest in Iron Card to McClanahan as compensation for services rendered and thus to be entitled to a $30,000 business expense deduction, computed by reference to the last offer to purchase Iron Card received prior to October 4, 1968. Furthermore, the McDougals acknowledged that they had recognized a gain on the aforesaid transfer. By charging the entire depreciation deduction of $1,390 against the portion of their unadjusted cost basis allocable to the half interest in Iron Card which they retained, the McDougals computed this gain to be $25,000 and characterized it as a long-term capital gain under section 1231(a) of the Internal Revenue Code of 1954.

McClanahan simultaneously increased his income arising out of the transfer from $5,000 to $30,000. He could thus claim to have a tax cost basis of $30,000 in their half interest in the horse. Finally, purporting to have transferred the horse to a partnership in concert on November 1, 1968, petitioners computed the partnership's basis in the horse to be $33,610 under section 723. This increase in basis led the partnership to claim a depreciation deduction of $934 for 1968 instead of $278 and to report only $81 of taxable income for that year. The McDougals thereupon reduced their distributive share of partnership income for 1968 from $405 to $40, while McClanahan reduced his share from $332 to $41. For the year 1969 the partnership claimed a deduction for depreciation on Iron Card in the amount of $5,602, closing the year with a loss of $8,911. * * *

ULTIMATE FINDINGS OF FACT

The transfer of October 4, 1968, gave rise to a joint venture to which the McDougals are deemed to have contributed Iron Card and in which they are deemed to have granted McClanahan an interest in the capital and profits thereof, equal to their own, as compensation for his having trained Iron Card. * * *

OPINION

Respondent contends that the McDougals did not recognize a $25,-000 gain on the transaction of October 4, 1968, and that they were not entitled to claim a $30,000 business expense deduction by reason thereof. He further contends that were Iron Card to be contributed to a partnership or joint venture under the circumstances obtaining in the instant case, its basis in Iron Card at the time of contribution would have been limited by the McDougals' cost basis in the horse, as adjusted. Respondent justifies these contentions by arguing that the transfer of October 4, 1968, constituted a gift.

In the alternative, respondent has urged us to find that at some point in time no later than the transfer of October 4, 1968, McDougal and McClanahan entered into a partnership or joint venture to which the McDougals contributed Iron Card and McClanahan contributed services. Respondent contends that such a finding would require our holding that the McDougals did not recognize a gain on the transfer of October 4, 1968, by reason of section 721, and that under section 723 the joint venture's basis in Iron Card at the time of the contribution was equal to the McDougals' adjusted basis in the horse as of that time.

We dismiss at the outset respondent's contention that the transfer of October 4, 1968, constituted a gift, * * *. The relationship of the parties concerned was essentially of a business nature, and the transfer itself was made conditional upon the outcome of an enterprise which McDougal had undertaken at McClanahan's suggestion and in reliance upon McClanahan's ability to render it profitable. These factors instead bespeak the presence of an arm's-length transaction.

With respect to respondent's alternative contention, we note firstly that the law provides no rule easy of application for making a determination as to whether a partnership or joint venture has been formed but rather directs our attention to a congeries of factors relevant to the issue, of which none is conclusive.

A joint venture is deemed to arise when two or more persons agree, expressly or impliedly, to enter actively upon a specific business enterprise, the purpose of which is the pursuit of profit; the ownership of whose productive assets and of the profits generated by them is shared; the parties to which all bear the burden of any loss; and the management of which is not confined to a single participant.

While in the case at bar the risk of loss was to be borne by the McDougals alone, all the other elements of a joint venture were present once the transfer of October 4, 1968, had been effected. Accordingly, we hold that the aforesaid transfer constituted the formation of a joint venture to which the McDougals contributed capital in the form of the horse, Iron Card, and in which they granted McClanahan an interest equal to their own in capital and profits as compensation for his having trained Iron Card. We further hold that the agreement formally entered into on November 1, 1968, and reduced to writing in April of 1970, constituted a continuation of the original joint venture under section 708(b)(2)(A). Furthermore, that McClanahan continued to receive a fee for serving as Iron Card's trainer after October 4, 1968, in no way militates against the soundness of this holding. However, this holding does not result in the tax consequences which respondent has contended would follow from it.

When on the formation of a joint venture a party contributing appreciated assets satisfies an obligation by granting his obligee a capital interest in the venture, he is deemed first to have transferred to the obligee an undivided interest in the assets contributed, equal in value to the amount of the obligation so satisfied. He and the obligee are deemed thereafter and in concert to have contributed those assets to the joint venture.

The contributing obligor will recognize gain on the transaction to the extent that the value of the undivided interest which he is deemed to have transferred exceeds his basis therein. The obligee is considered to have realized an amount equal to the fair market value of the interest which he receives in the venture and will recognize income depending upon the character of the obligation satisfied. The joint venture's basis in the assets will be determined under section 723 in accordance with the foregoing assumptions. Accordingly, we hold that the transaction under consideration constituted an exchange in which the McDougals realized $30,000.

In determining the basis offset to which the McDougals are entitled with respect to the transfer of October 4, 1968, we note the following: that the McDougals had an unadjusted cost basis in Iron Card of $10,000; that they had claimed $1,390 in depreciation on the entire horse for the period January 1, to October 31, 1968; and that after an agreement of partnership was concluded on November 1, 1968, depreciation on Iron Card was deducted by the partnership exclusively.

* * *

In determining their adjusted basis in the portion of Iron Card on whose disposition they are required to recognize gain, the McDougals charged all the depreciation which they had taken on the horse against their basis in the half in which they retained an interest. This procedure was improper. As in accordance with section 1.167(g)–1, Income Tax Regs., we have allowed the McDougals a depreciation deduction with respect to Iron Card for the period January 1 to October 4, 1968, computed on their entire cost basis in the horse of $10,000; so also do we require that the said deduction be charged against that entire cost basis under section 1016(a)(2)(A).

As the McDougals were in the business of racing horses, any gain recognized by them on the exchange of Iron Card in satisfaction of a debt would be characterized under section 1231(a) provided he had been held by them for the period requisite under section 1231(b) as it applies to livestock acquired before 1970. In that as of October 4, 1968, Iron Card had been used by the McDougals exclusively for racing and not for breeding, we do now hold that they had held him for a period sufficiently long to make section 1231(a) applicable to their gain on the transaction. This is the case although the McDougals may have intended eventually to use Iron Card for breeding purposes.

The joint venture's basis in Iron Card as of October 4, 1968, must be determined under section 723 in accordance with the principles of law set forth earlier in this opinion. In the half interest in the horse which it is deemed to have received from the McDougals, the joint venture had a basis equal to one-half of the McDougals' adjusted cost basis in Iron Card as of October 4, 1968, i.e., the excess of $5,000 over one-half of the depreciation which the McDougals were entitled to claim on Iron Card for the period January 1 to October 4, 1968. In the half interest which the venture is considered to have received from McClanahan, it can claim to have had a basis equal to the amount which McClanahan is considered to have realized on the transaction, $30,000. The joint venture's deductions for depreciation on Iron Card for the years 1968 and 1969 are to be determined on the basis computed in the above-described manner.

When an interest in a joint venture is transferred as compensation for services rendered, any deduction which may be authorized under section 162(a)(1) by reason of that transfer is properly claimed by the party to whose benefit the services accrued, be that party the venture itself or one or more venturers, sec. 1.721–1(b)(2), Income Tax Regs. Prior to McClanahan's receipt of his interest, a joint venture did not exist under the facts of the case at bar; the McDougals were the sole owners of Iron Card and recipients of his earnings. Therefore, they alone could have benefited from the services rendered by McClanahan prior to October 4, 1968, for which he was compensated by the transaction of that date. Accordingly, we hold that the McDougals are entitled to a business expense deduction of $30,000, that amount being the value of the interest which McClanahan received. Respondent has contended that a deduction of $30,000 would be unreasonable in amount in view of the nature of the services for which McClanahan was being compensated. But having found that the transaction under consideration was not a gift but rather was occasioned by a compensation arrangement which was entered upon at arm's length, we must reject this contention. * * *

Problem 5–1

Phyllis, Vicki, Alice, and Bruce are sole proprietors, each individually engaged in the business of freelance court reporting. All four individuals report their income on the cash method. They decide to form an equal, cash method, general partnership with capital contributions of $30,000 each. Phyllis contributes $30,000 cash. Vicki contributes stock in Speed Reporting, Inc., held for two weeks, value of $12,000 and adjusted basis of $10,000 and real property used in her business valued at $18,000, adjusted basis of $7,000, and a holding period of five years. Alice contributes a Xerox duplicator held for several years with a value of $30,000, purchased for $40,000, and adjusted basis of $10,000. Bruce contributes $25,000 in § 453 installment obligations acquired two years ago from the sale of property with a value of $20,000 and adjusted basis of $15,000 as well as accounts receivable from his sole proprietorship valued at $10,000.

1. What gain or loss is recognized to each partner as a result of these contributions?

2. What is the tax basis of each partner's interest in the partnership?

3. What is the partnership's basis in each asset?

4. a. What is each partner's holding period for his or her partnership interest?

   b. What is the partnership's holding period for its assets?

   c. Would it make any difference if Alice has held the Xerox duplicator for five months?

E. GAIN RECOGNITION THROUGH LIABILITY RELIEF

Gain may arise in the formation context through the shifting of, and the assumption by, the partnership of the liabilities of the partners. This could occur in the initial formation context if certain of the assets contributed were mortgaged. It could also occur in the context of an ongoing partnership if a newly-admitted partner assumed, or were deemed to assume, his or her share of existing partnership debt. Notwithstanding the nonrecognition provision of § 721(a), the excess of any money that is distributed or deemed distributed to a partner in connection with the contribution of property to the partnership over the adjusted basis of the partner's partnership interest constitutes taxable gain under § 731(a). The underlying policy for such treatment reflects notions of the discharge of the indebtedness doctrine of the basic tax law and the *Crane* and *Tufts* doctrines of tax consequences arising through liability relief.

As discussed more thoroughly in Chapter 7, under § 752(a), a partner is deemed to contribute money to a partnership to the extent of his or her share of the partnership's liabilities. Additionally, under § 752(b), if the partnership (i.e. the other partners) assumes the liability of a partner, e.g., by the acceptance of a contribution of encumbered property to the partnership, the contributing partner is deemed to receive a distribution of money in that amount. Thus, when the amount of the *net* liability relief arising to a partner exceeds the basis for the partner's partnership interest, gain will be generated under § 731.

Problem 5–2

Assuming the same facts as Problem 5–1, what are the tax consequences (i.e., gain recognition and character and basis) to Alice if the partnership assumed a recourse liability on the Xerox machine of (a) $9,000? (b) $18,000? Assume, in both situations, that the gross value of the Xerox machine increases (i.e., $39,000 and $48,000) so that the net value remains a $30,000 contribution.

Chapter 6

PARTNERSHIP FORMATION—
ACQUISITION OF A
PARTNERSHIP INTEREST IN
EXCHANGE FOR A CONTRIBUTION
OF SERVICES

Code References: §§ 83(a), (b), (c), and (h); 263(a)(1); 707(c); 721; 723.

Regulations: § 1.721–1(b), Prop.Reg. § 1.721–1(b)(1); § 1.83–1(a)(1), (b)(2), –2, –6.

A. INTRODUCTION

Partnership business ventures often are formed between a money partner and a service partner. The former may not have the skill, time, or desire to operate the business. The latter may lack capital, but is willing to earn his or her share of the activity by a contribution of special talent or hard work (frequently described as "sweat equity"). A service partner may acquire a partnership interest in exchange for a contribution of past, present, or promised future services. In contrast to a contribution of property in return for a partnership interest which qualifies for nonrecognition treatment, a contribution of services rendered, or a promise of services to be rendered, to a partnership in exchange for an interest therein may result in a taxable event. Such a contribution is not protected by § 721.

Among the major themes in partnership taxation are the issues of deferral versus current recognition and, upon recognition, the derivation of capital gain versus ordinary income. If a partner's promise to perform services were treated as property and hence the receipt thereof entitled to nonrecognition treatment, the service partner would secure the benefits of deferral. Such a tax result would be highly unusual as regards the rendition of services for which aggressive safeguards such as the assignment of income doctrine have been fashioned by the courts

154

and Congress. The receipt of unrestricted corporate stock for services, for instance, clearly results in immediate income to its recipient.

The other rationale for requiring immediate recognition of income on the receipt of a partnership interest in exchange for the rendition of services is to prevent a character conversion from ordinary income to capital gain. If the service partner were permitted deferral, he would be given a $0 basis for the partnership interest which by definition possesses value. Under the governance of § 741, a disposition of a partnership interest is generally entitled to capital gain treatment. Thus, the policy of immediate income recognition by the service partner prevents both deferral *and* conversion benefits.

A confusing aspect of the services issue in the partnership context is the distinction between the concept of income recognition to a partner for the rendition of services and the concept of imputed income. As regards imputed income (the value of rendering services to oneself, e.g., mowing one's own lawn), character conversion can occur. For example, if a taxpayer who is knowledgeable and mechanically proficient improves an automobile and increases its value through his personal efforts, he may convert the services component of the sales price (the increased value not reflected in the basis of the asset because he, rather than an outside auto mechanic, did the work) into capital gain. Such a conversion is equally possible in the partnership context since any or all of the partners may expend their efforts on various projects of the partnership. The critical distinction between unrecognized imputed income and income recognition for the rendition of services under § 721 is that in the latter setting the partner is receiving established value for which he was not instrumental either in producing or in being associated (as a partner) with those who were.

B. CAPITAL INTEREST FOR SERVICES

Interests in a partnership include an interest in capital (i.e., a member's rights to proceeds upon liquidation) and an interest in profits and losses (i.e., a member's share of future realized gain or loss). Regulation § 1.721–1(b)(1) provides that the value of an interest in partnership *capital* transferred to a partner as compensation for services constitutes immediate income to the partner under § 61. In such a setting, the service partner has received something of value for which he should be held accountable. If the partnership were liquidated in proportion to capital accounts the day following the receipt of the capital interest, the service partner would receive cash or property.

The time for determining the value of a partnership interest and the time for including the value of the interest in the gross income of the service partner is specified under Regulation § 1.721–1(b)(1). The receipt of a capital interest is includable when the interest is received unless unfettered ownership is conditioned upon the rendition of services in the future. The amount includable in gross income is its fair market value at the time for inclusion. Additionally, to the extent that the partnership interest in capital is transferred for deductible services to be rendered by the service partner to the enterprise, a corresponding deduction is available to the partnership in return for granting the service partner his partnership interest.

Many difficulties are encountered in conceptualizing the transfer. The generally accepted view is that the share of partnership assets to which the service partner would be entitled upon liquidation of his or her capital interest is considered to have been distributed to the partner. If the partnership's sole asset is cash (e.g., money partner combines with service partner), the liquidation consequences are easy to visualize. If other assets or property are involved, however, the issue is more complicated. Gain or loss to the partnership will arise if the assets are appreciated or depreciated when "distributed" to the service partner. The transaction is conceptualized as the property which is "distributed" is then contributed by the distributee/service partner to the partnership in return for his or her partnership interest. In such a configuration, interesting allocation issues of gain or loss and the corresponding deduction arise, i.e., does the incoming service partner share in either the gain or loss recognized by the partnership on the transfer of the property or the deduction available to the partnership for the payment of deductible services to be performed by the recipient service partner.

For transfers of a capital interest, Proposed Regulation § 1.721–1(b) provides that § 83 governs the tax consequences. Thereunder, the interest is includable in the partner's gross income at an amount equal to the fair market value of the partnership interest determined when the partner's rights in the interest are not subject to a substantial risk of forfeiture. Under § 83, while such restrictions or conditions are in force, the service partner is not treated as a partner for tax purposes. The Proposed Regulation has been neither adopted nor withdrawn but has continued as "proposed" for over 25 years, suggesting some hesitancy on the part of the Service to fully embrace this doctrine. Nonetheless, in most major respects the result will be the same under either current Regulation § 1.721–1(b) or Proposed Regulation § 1.721–1(b) which adopts § 83. The major difference between the two is the existence of the § 83(b) election under which the time for including the value of the capital interest in gross income may be accelerated and the amount of income potentially minimized.

In the *Diamond* case, which follows, did the taxpayer receive a profits interest or a capital interest? In the General Counsel Memorandum, is the Service's logic and rationale sound? If so, why was the proposed Revenue Ruling never published?

DIAMOND v. COMMISSIONER

492 F.2d 286 (7th Cir.1974).

FAIRCHILD, CIRCUIT JUDGE.

This is an appeal from a decision of the Tax Court upholding the commissioner's assessment of deficiencies against Sol and Muriel Diamond for the years 1961 and 1962. The deficiencies for each year were consolidated for trial, but are essentially unrelated. The Tax Court concluded that Diamond realized ordinary income on the receipt of a right to a share of profit or loss to be derived from a real estate venture (the 1962 partnership case), * * *

THE 1962 PARTNERSHIP CASE

During 1961, Diamond was a mortgage broker. Philip Kargman had acquired for $25,000 the buyer's rights in a contract for the sale of an office building. Kargman asked Diamond to obtain a mortgage loan for the full $1,100,000 purchase price of the building. Diamond and Kargman agreed that Diamond would receive a 60% share of profit or loss of the venture if he arranged the financing.

Diamond succeeded in obtaining a $1,100,000 mortgage loan from Marshall Savings and Loan. On December 15, 1961 Diamond and Kargman entered into an agreement which provided:

(1) The two were associated as joint venturers for 24 years (the life of the mortgage) unless earlier terminated by agreement or by sale;

(2) Kargman was to advance all cash needed for the purchase beyond the loan proceeds;

(3) Profits and losses would be divided, 40% to Kargman, 60% to Diamond;

(4) In event of sale, proceeds would be devoted first to repayment to Kargman of money supplied by him, and net profits thereafter would be divided 40% to Kargman, 60% to Diamond.

Early in 1962, Kargman and Diamond created an Illinois land trust to hold title to the property. The chief motivation for the land trust arrangement was apparently to insulate Diamond and Kargman from personal liability on the mortgage note.

The purchase proceeded as planned and closing took place on February 18, 1962. Kargman made cash outlays totalling $78,195.33 in connection with the purchase. Thus, under the terms of the agreement, the property would have to appreciate at least $78,195.33 before Diamond would have any equity in it.

Shortly after closing, it was proposed that Diamond would sell his interest and one Liederman would be substituted, except on a 50–50 basis. Liederman persuaded Diamond to sell his interest for $40,000. This sale was effectuated on March 8, 1962 by Diamond assigning his interest to Kargman for $40,000. Kargman in turn then conveyed a similar interest, except for 50–50 sharing, to Liederman for the same amount.

On their 1962 joint return, the Diamonds reported the March 8, 1962 $40,000 sale proceeds as a short term capital gain. This gain was offset by an unrelated short term capital loss. They reported no tax consequences from the February 18 receipt of the interest in the venture. Diamond's position is that his receipt of this type of interest in partnership is not taxable income although received in return for services. He relies on § 721 and Reg. § 1.721–1(b)(1). He further argues that the subsequent sale of this interest produced a capital gain under § 741. The Tax Court held that the receipt of this type of interest in partnership in return for services is not within § 721 and is taxable under § 61 when received. The Tax Court valued the interest at $40,000 as of February 18, as evidenced by the sale for that amount three weeks later, on March 8.

Both the taxpayer and the Tax Court treated the venture as a partnership and purported to apply partnership income tax principles. It has been suggested that the record might have supported findings that there was in truth an employment or other relationship, other than partnership, and produced a similar result, but these findings were not made. It has also been suggested (and argued, alternatively, by the government) that although on the face of the agreement Diamond appeared to receive only a right to share in profit (loss) to be derived, the value of the real estate may well have been substantially greater than the purchase price, so that Diamond may really have had an interest in capital, if the assets were properly valued. This finding was not made. The Tax Court suggested the possibility that Diamond would not in any event be entitled to capital gains treatment of his sale of a right to receive income in the future, but did not decide the question.

Taking matters at face value, taxpayer received, on February 18, an interest in partnership, limited to a right to a share of profit (loss) to be derived. In discussion we shall refer to this interest either as his interest in partnership or a profit-share.

The Tax Court, with clearly adequate support, found that Diamond's interest in partnership had a market value of $40,000 on February 18. Taxpayer's analysis is that under the regulations the receipt of a profit-share February 18, albeit having a market value and being conferred in return for services, was not a taxable event, and that the entire proceeds of the March 8 sale were a capital gain. The Tax Court analysis was that the interest in partnership, albeit limited to a profit-share, was property worth $40,000, and taxpayer's acquisition, thereof on February 18 was compensation for services and ordinary income. Assuming that capital gain treatment at sale would have been appropriate, there was no gain because the sale was for the same amount.

There is no statute or regulation which expressly and particularly prescribes the income tax effect, or absence of one, at the moment a partner receives a profit-share in return for services. The Tax Court's holding rests upon the general principle that a valuable property interest received in return for services is compensation, and income. Taxpayer's argument is predicated upon an implication which his counsel, and others, have found in Reg. § 1.721–1(b)(1), but which need not, and the government argues should not, be found there.

26 U.S.C. § 721 is entitled "Nonrecognition of gain or loss on contribution," and provides: "No gain or loss shall be recognized to a partnership or to any of its partners in the case of a contribution of property to the partnership in exchange for an interest in the partnership." Only if, by a strained construction, "property" were said to include services, would § 721 say anything about the effect of furnishing services. It clearly deals with a contribution like Kargman's, of property, and prescribes that when he contributed his property, no gain or loss was recognized. It does not, of course, explicitly say that no income accrues to one who renders services and, in return, becomes a partner with a profit-share.

Reg. § 1.721–1 presumably explains and interprets § 721, perhaps to the extent of qualifying or limiting its meaning. Subsec. (b)(1), particularly relied on here, reads in part as follows:

> "Normally, under local law, each partner is entitled to be repaid his contributions of money or other property to the partnership (at the value placed upon such property by the partnership at the time of the contribution) whether made at the formation of the partnership or subsequent thereto. To the extent that any of the partners gives up any part of his right to be repaid his contributions (as distinguished from a share in partnership profits) in favor of another partner as compensation for services (or in satisfaction of an obligation), section 721 does not apply. The value of an interest in such partnership capital so transferred to a partner as compensation for services constitutes income to the partner under section 61...."

The quoted portion of the regulation may well be read, like § 721, as being directly addressed only to the consequences of a contribution of money or other property. It asserts that when a partner making such contributions transfers to another some part of the contributing partner's right to be repaid, in order to compensate the other for services or to satisfy an obligation to the other, § 721 does not apply, there is recognition of gain or loss to the contributing partner, and there is income to the partner who receives, as compensation for services, part of the right to be repaid.

The regulation does not specify that if a partner contributing property agrees that, in return for services, another shall be a partner with a profit-share only, the value of the profit-share is not income to the recipient. An implication to that effect, such as is relied on by taxpayer, would have to rest on the proposition that the regulation was meant to be all inclusive as to when gain or loss would be recognized or income would exist as a consequence of the contribution of property to a partnership and disposition of the partnership interests. It would have to appear, in order to sustain such implication, that the existence of income by reason of a creation of a profit-share, immediately having a determinable market value, in favor of a partner would be inconsistent with the result specified in the regulation.

We do not find this implication in our own reading of the regulation. It becomes necessary to consider the substantial consensus of commentators in favor of the principle claimed to be implied and to look to judicial interpretation, legislative history, administrative interpretation, and policy considerations to determine whether the implication is justified.

The Commentators: There is a startling degree of unanimity that the conferral of a profit-share as compensation for services is not income at the time of the conferral, although little by way of explanation of why this should be so, or analysis of statute or regulation to show that it is prescribed.

One of the most unequivocal statements, with an explanation in terms of practicality or policy, was made by Arthur Willis in a text:

> "However obliquely the proposition is stated in the regulations, it is clear that a partner who receives only an interest in future profits of the partnership as compensation for services is not required to report the receipt of his partnership interest as taxable income. The rationale is twofold. In the first place, the present value of a right to participate in future profits is usually too conjectural to be subject to valuation. In the second place, the service partner is taxable on his distributive share of partnership income as it is realized by the partnership. If he were taxed on the present value of the right to receive his share of future partnership income, either he would be taxed twice, or the value of his right to participate in partnership income must be amortized over some period of time."

Judicial Interpretation: Except for one statement by the Tax Court no decision cited by the parties or found by us appears squarely to reach the question, either on principle in the absence of the regulations, or by application of the regulations. In a footnote in Herman M. Hale, 24 T.C.M. 1497, 1502 (1965) the Tax Court said: "Under the regulations, the mere receipt of a partnership interest in future profits does not create any tax liability. Sec. 1.721-1(b), Income Tax Regs." There was no explanation of how this conclusion was derived from the regulations.

Legislative History: The legislative history is equivocal.

An advisory group appointed in 1956 to review the regulations evidently felt concern about whether the provision of Reg. § 1.721-1 that the value of an interest in capital transferred to a partner in compensation for services constitutes income had a statutory basis in the light of § 721 providing that there shall be no recognition of gain or loss in the case of a contribution of property. The group proposed enactment of a new section to provide such basis, and legislation introduced into the 86th Congress in 1959 incorporated this recommendation. The bill, H.R. 9662, would have created a new § 770 providing specifically for the taxation of a person receiving an interest in partnership capital in exchange for the performance of services for the partnership. However, neither proposed § 770 nor anything else in H.R. 9662 dealt with the receipt merely of a profit-share. The lack of concern over an income tax impact when only a profit-share was conferred might imply an opinion that such conferring of a profit-share would not be taxable under any circumstances, or might imply an opinion that it would be income or not under § 61 depending upon whether it had a determinable market value or not.

Several statements in the course of the hearings and committee reports paralleled the first parenthetical phrase in Reg. § 1.721–1(b) and were to the effect that the provision did not apply where a person received only a profit-share. There was, however, at least one specific statement by the chairman of the advisory group (Mr. Willis) that if the service partner "were to receive merely an interest in future profits in exchange for his services, he would have no immediate taxable gain because he would be taxed on his share of income as it was earned." H.R. 9662 passed the House of Representatives, and was favorably reported to the Senate by its finance committee, but never came to a vote in the Senate. Even had the bill become law, it would not have dealt expressly with the problem at hand.

Administrative Interpretation: We are unaware of instances in which the Commissioner has asserted delinquencies where a taxpayer who received a profit-share with determinable market value in return for services failed to report the value as income, or has otherwise acted consistently with the Tax Court decision in *Diamond*. Although the consensus referred to earlier appears to exist, the Commissioner has not by regulation or otherwise acted affirmatively to reject it, and in a sense might be said to have agreed by silence.

Consideration of partnership principles or practices: There must be wide variation in the degree to which a profit-share created in favor of a partner who has or will render service has determinable market value at the moment of creation. Surely in many if not the typical situations it will have only speculative value, if any.

In the present case, taxpayer's services had all been rendered, and the prospect of earnings from the real estate under Kargman's management was evidently very good. The profit-share had determinable market value.

If the present decision be sound, then the question will always arise, whenever a profit-share is created or augmented, whether it has a market value capable of determination. Will the existence of this question be unduly burdensome on those who choose to do business under the partnership form?

Each partner determines his income tax by taking into account his distributive share of the taxable income of the partnership. Taxpayer's position here is that he was entitled to defer income taxation on the compensation for his services except as partnership earnings were realized. If a partner is taxed on the determinable market value of a profit-share at the time it is created in his favor, and is also taxed on his full share of earnings as realized, there will arguably be double taxation, avoidable by permitting him to amortize the value which was originally treated as income. Does the absence of a recognized procedure for amortization militate against the treatment of the creation of the profit-share as income?

Do the disadvantages of treating the creation of the profit-share as income in those instances where it has a determinable market value at that time outweigh the desirability of imposing a tax at the time the taxpayer has received an interest with determinable market value as compensation for services?

We think, of course, that the resolution of these practical questions makes clearly desirable the promulgation of appropriate regulations, to achieve a degree of certainty. But in the absence of regulation, we think it sound policy to defer to the expertise of the Commissioner and the Judges of the Tax Court, and to sustain their decision that the receipt of a profit-share with determinable market value is income. * * *

GENERAL COUNSEL MEMORANDUM 36346
July 23, 1975.

SOL DIAMOND

Lawrence B. Gibbs
Assistant Commissioner (Technical)
Attention: Director, Individual Tax Division

Your memorandum of April 18, 1975 (T:I:I:P) referred a proposed revenue ruling (Control No. 75 1 30944) for our concurrence or comment. The proposed ruling concludes that the fair market value of an interest in the profits and losses of a partnership is includible in the gross income of the recipient if it was received as compensation for services he had performed for another individual, citing Sol Diamond, 56 T.C. 530 (1971), aff'd, 492 F.2d 286 (7th Cir.1974).

The proposed revenue ruling is being returned to you without comment pursuant to the agreement reached by representatives of our respective offices at our July 21, 1975 meeting. It was the consensus of opinion that publication of the proposed ruling should be deferred pending further discussion of the alternative positions available to the Service in resolving the issue involved. Such alternatives are to be set forth in a memorandum to be prepared by this office.

As you may be aware this Office has been considering the proper treatment of the receipt of a profits interest in a partnership as compensation for services. This consideration stems from the decision in Sol Diamond, 56 T.C. 530 (1971), aff'd, 492 F.2d 286 (7th Cir.1974), holding that the fair market value of an interest in partnership profits received as compensation for services is taxable under Int.Rev.Code of 1974, § 61(a)(1) (hereinafter cited as Code). This decision has been widely criticized as being contrary to Treas.Reg. § 1.721–1, as creating severe valuation problems and as resulting in double taxation to the recipient partner. See, e.g., A. Willis, Partnership Taxation, § 11.04 (2d ed. 1976). Previously it has been proposed that the Service not follow Diamond when a profits interest is received as compensation for services rendered in a capacity as partner. O.M. 18281, Receipt of a Profits Interest in a Partnership for Services Rendered: The Sol Diamond Problem, I–176–75 (Sept. 29, 1975): amplifying O.M. 18205, Receipt of a Partnership Interest by One Who Renders Services: The Sol Diamond Problem. I–190–74 (June 4, 1975). This approach was found unacceptable because it seemed to place a premium on whether the partnership is formed before or after the services are rendered.

The position of this Office is set forth in the attached proposed revenue ruling which states that the Service will not follow Diamond to the extent that it holds that the receipt of an interest in future partnership profits as compensation for services results in taxable income. Having conceded this question, the ruling generally preserves the result in Diamond by concluding that most of the interest the taxpayer received was an interest in capital, as distinguished from an interest in future profits. In addition the ruling seeks to limit the conversion of compensation into capital gain upon the receipt and sale of a profits interest by emphasizing that the renderer of services must be a partner rather than an employee or independent contractor. Whether an interest is a capital interest or an interest in future profits and whether the recipient is a partner rather than an employee or independent contractor are primarily factual questions.

Arguably the only rationale for not taxing a profits interest received as compensation is that Treas.Reg. § 1.721–1(b) was apparently designed to reach such a result. See A. Willis, supra at § 11.01. It is difficult to quarrel with the Tax Court's finding that such an interest is property under Treas.Reg. § 1.61–2(d)(1). When a profits interest is defined to preclude any interest in partnership assets, as is done in the proposed revenue ruling, such an interest becomes analogous to an unfunded, unsecured promise to pay deferred compensation. Such a promise is not taxable upon receipt and, in fact, is not considered to be property. See Treas.Reg. § 1.83–3(e). An analogy of a partnership profits interest to an unfunded, unsecured promise to pay deferred compensation is imperfect, however, because amounts received pursuant to or upon assignment of such a promise are taxable as compensation whereas the character of partnership profits or the character of the gain on a sale of a profits interest is determined under Code § 702(b) and Code § 741.

It must be emphasized that in holding that the receipt of a "profits" interest is not taxable, the proposed revenue ruling is limited to interests that give the holder no rights to existing partnership assets upon the liquidation of his interest. Correspondingly, a "capital" interest, which is taxable, includes any interest in earned but unrealized gains. This broad definition of a capital interest is simply an extension of the rule in Treas.Reg. § 1.61–2(d)(1) that property received as compensation is taxed at its fair market value. This rule is reflected in both Treas.Reg. § 1.704–1(e) and Treas.Reg. § 1.721–1(b)(1). In addition, support for including unrealized appreciation in partnership capital may be found in the proposed Trust and Partnership Income Tax Revision Act of 1960, H.R. 9662, 86th Cong., 2d Sess. (1960). That Act would have added a section 770 to the Code to govern the treatment of an exchange of an interest in partnership capital for services rendered to the partnership. The Senate Report states as follows:

> It is important to note that the section does not deal with the transfer of a partnership interest which gives the service partner merely the right to share in appreciation in partnership assets which occurs, or in partnership profits which are earned, subsequent to the date of transfer. Thus, for example, assume that a person who has been associated with a cash basis partnership as an employee is admitted as a partner in the partnership, and acquires an interest in the appreciation then existing in partnership assets, as well as an interest in profits of the partnership which have been earned as of that time, but not yet taken into partnership income. Such preexisting appreciation and previously earned profits are considered to be an interest in partnership capital, and section 770 is applicable. However, if such service partner had acquired only an interest in the appreciation occurring subsequent to his admission and in profits of the partnership earned after such time, the rules of section 770 would have no application. S.Rep. No. 1616, 86th Cong.2d Sess. 117 (1960).

It should be noted that unrealized accounts receivable are also considered partnership capital. This can be important for professional partnerships. Perhaps a separate revenue ruling should be published to demonstrate this point.

The partner or partnership for whom services are performed may be entitled to a deduction for the value of the capital interest transferred. Treas.Reg. § 1.721–1(b)(2) See also Rev.Rul. 75–214, 1975–1 C.B. 185. However, if such value exceeds the basis of the interest, the transferor will be required to recognize gain. F.C. McDougal, 62 T.C. 720 (1974), acq. 1975–1 C.B. 2.

When a partner receives an interest in unrealized appreciation or unrealized receivables, he could be taxed not only at that time but also when appreciation or receivables are actually realized. This potential double taxation may be avoidable if the partnership elects under Code § 754 to make the optional basis adjustments provided for in Code § 743(b).

Finally, the distinction between a profits interest received as a partner rather than as an employee or independent contractor is a major issue in movie tax shelters. See, e.g., G.C.M. 36961, * * * I–277–76 (Dec. 21, 1976); G.C.M. 36436, * * *, I–359–73 (Sept. 25, 1975); O.M. 18034, * * *, I–514–73 (May 15, 1974). We believe that recognizing the taxpayer as a partner in the proposed revenue ruling is consistent with our position in the movie area. * * *

Proposed Revenue Ruling

Advice has been requested concerning the treatment, for Federal income tax purposes, of the receipt of an interest in a partnership as compensation for services under the circumstances described below.

On May 15, 1976, X entered into a contract to purchase an apartment building on June 15, 1976 for $300,000. On June 1, 1976 A, an individual, purchased X's interest in the contract for $10,000.

At the time A was negotiating with X, A asked B, a mortgage broker, if B could obtain financing for the entire $300,000 purchase price. In return, A offered to give B an interest in the building. B agreed to obtain the financing in exchange for a 25 percent interest in a partnership to be formed by A and B to own and operate the building.

On June 10, 1976, A and B entered into a partnership agreement under which B was to receive, as compensation for services rendered in arranging the financing, 25 percent of the operating profits from the apartment building. B was also chargeable with 25 percent of the losses. When the building was sold, the proceeds of the sale were to be used first to satisfy any mortgages and to repay A the $10,000 A had paid to X for the right to purchase the property and the remaining proceeds were to be distributed 75 percent to A and 25 percent to B. A was to manage the building for the partnership and was to receive compensation in addition to a 75 percent distributive share of profits and losses for such managerial services. B was to render no services in connection with the building other than to arrange the financing and such services were performed both before and after formation of the partnership. The approval of both A and B was required for a sale of the property.

On June 15 the building was purchased in the names of A and B for $300,000 and contributed to the partnership. The entire purchase price was financed by the lender. An independent appraisal concluded that with 100 percent financing the fair market value of the property on June 15 was $360,000. On July 1, 1977 B sold his interest in the partnership to an unrelated third party for $15,000.

Under section 61 of the Internal Revenue Code of 1954 gross income means all income from whatever source derived, unless specifically excluded from gross income by law.

Section 1.61–2(d)(1) of the Income Tax Regulations provides, in part, that if services are paid for other than in money, the fair market value of the property or services taken in payment must be included in income.

Section 721 of the Code provides that no gain or loss shall be recognized to a partnership or to any of its partners in the case of a contribution of property to the partnership in exchange for an interest in the partnership.

Section 1.721–1(b)(1) of the regulations provides, in part, that normally under local law, each partner is entitled to be repaid his contributions of money or other property to the partnership (at the value placed upon such property by the partnership at the time of the contribution) whether made at the formation of the partnership or subsequent thereto. To the extent that any of the partners gives up any part of his right to be repaid his contributions (as distinguished from a share in partnership profits) in favor of another partner as compensation for services (or in satisfaction of an obligation), section 721 of the Code does not apply.

For purposes of section 1.721–1(b)(1) a partner's right to be repaid his contributions consists of the value of any property that would be distributable to him on liquidation of his interest. Thus, under the regulations the value of an interest in such partnership capital so transferred to a partner as compensation for services constitutes income to the partner under section 61.

Correspondingly, a partner who receives a partnership interest as compensation for services is treated as receiving a capital interest to the extent of the fair market value of partnership assets that would be distributable to such partner if the partner withdrew from the partnership or if the partner's interest were liquidated immediately after it was acquired. For example, an interest in any unrealized appreciation of partnership assets is a capital interest. A service partner who receives only an interest in the appreciation occurring subsequent to such partner's admission receives an interest the value of which is attributable to the right to participate in the partnership's future profits. Whether an interest in a partnership is a capital interest as distinguished from an interest in future partnership profits, must be determined on the facts and circumstances of each case.

Section 741 of the Code provides that gain or loss on the sale or exchange of an interest in a partnership shall be considered as gain or loss from the sale of a capital asset, except as otherwise provided in section 751 (relating to unrealized receivables and inventory items which have appreciated substantially in value).

In the case of Sol Diamond, 56 T.C. 530 (1971), aff'd 492 F.2d 286 (7th Cir.1974), the court held the receipt of an interest in a partnership as compensation for services results in taxable income without regard to whether the interest represented an interest in capital as distinguished from an interest in future partnership profits. The Internal Revenue Service will not follow the decision in Sol Diamond to the extent that it holds that the receipt by a partner of an interest in future partnership profits as compensation for services results in taxable income.

However, the fact that a person holds the right to a share of the future profits of a venture does not necessarily mean that such person is a joint venturer or partner for Federal income tax purposes. An examination of the facts and circumstances of each case is necessary in order to determine whether an interest in the future profits of a venture was acquired as compensation for services rendered by a partner as distinguished from an employee or an independent contractor. See Rev.Rul. 75–43, 1975–1 C.B. 383, for a discussion of some of the factors considered in determining whether a person who has a right to a share of profits is a partner.

In addition to the factors in Rev.Rul. 75–43, a person who acquires an interest in the future profits of a venture as compensation for services rendered or to be rendered will not be treated as a partner unless there is an intent to invest his services in the enterprise. In other words, it must be intended that the return for the services be contingent upon the future success of the venture. The fact that a future profits interest acquired as compensation for services is sold shortly after it is acquired may be evidence that the seller of the interest intended to receive a fixed amount for the services rather than investing the services in the enterprise and that, therefore, it was not intended that the seller become a partner.

When an interest in the future profits of an enterprise is acquired as compensation for services by someone other than a partner, such interest is not considered property for purposes of section 61 of the Code and Treas.Reg. 1.61–2(d)(1). See Treas.Reg. § 1.83–3(e); Rev.Rul. 60–31, 1960–1 C.B. 174. Any profits subsequently received and any gain on the sale of the profits interest is taxable as compensation for services.

In the instant case, A and B referred to the venture as a partnership in their agreement. Since title to the building was in the names of A and B, a sale of the building would have required B's approval. B had a proprietary interest in any profits and had an obligation to share any losses. Although B sold his interest after acquiring it, the sale was not prearranged. B did not intend to sell his interest upon receiving it but instead contemplated an investment of his services the return on which would be contingent upon the future success of the venture. Thus, based on all the facts and circumstances, B acquired his interest in the venture as a joint venturer or partner, rather than as an employee or independent contractor.

In the instant case, B's interest in the venture entitled B to 25 percent of the value of the building in excess of $310,000, its basis on the date B received the interest. Because the building was in fact worth $360,000 on the date B received the 25 percent interest as compensation, B acquired a capital interest having a value of $12,500 ($360,000 − 310,000 × 25%).

Accordingly, for 1976 B must recognize $12,500 of compensation income under Code § 61 and Treas.Reg. § 1.721–1(b)(1). Upon the sale of B's interest for $15,000 in 1977, B also must recognize gain to the extent the amount realized exceeds B's adjusted basis in the partnership interest (which includes the $12,500 compensation taxed to him in 1976). This gain will be considered as gain from the sale of an interest in a partnership and, therefore, is treated as capital gain under Code § 741 except as provided in Code § 751. * * *

Problem 6–1

Since October, 1994, April and Larry have operated an equal law partnership. Each partner contributed $30,000 to the partnership's formation with which it purchased the small office building (basis $60,000, current fair market value $120,000) where they practice in a suburban community. In December, 1997, the partners seek to persuade Joan, a highly respected tax attorney, to join them as a partner. Joan has no money or property to contribute. Nevertheless, April and Larry are willing to give her a one-third interest in the capital, profits, and losses of the partnership. Joan agrees to join the firm and to establish and conduct a tax department.

1. What are the tax consequences to Joan on the transfer to her of the partnership capital interest, including:

   a. The amount of income and its character for tax purposes,

   b. The adjusted basis and holding period of the interest received?

2. What are the tax consequences to the partnership on the transfer, including:

   a. Gain or loss realized,

   b. Gain or loss recognized and its character,

   c. Adjusted basis and holding period of partnership property after the transfer,

   d. Deductions?

3. What are the tax effects to Joan and the partnership if the partnership agreement provides that Joan cannot sell her partnership interest unless she has performed services for the partnership until the earlier of her death or five years from the date she entered the partnership?

C. PROFITS INTEREST FOR SERVICES

In contrast to the receipt of a capital interest, in some cases the partnership conveys only an interest in partnership profits to the incoming service partner. In such a setting, the apparent intention of the transferor partners is to retain fully their interests in the pre-admission value of the partnership assets. Additionally, by awarding a profits interest, the partners have more likely ensured the service partner's continued participation in the endeavor. In such a setting, the service partner would have no initial liquidation property rights. Depending upon the precise wording of the agreement, the service partner's termination of his or her relationship with the partnership in the future may result in a forfeiture of any accumulated property rights. If the economic rights are conditioned upon continued participation at the time any profits arise, the interest in partnership profits will be of little or no capital value upon departure. Thus, as regards a true profits interest, it may be subject to an implicit, never-ending substantial risk of forfeiture.

Notwithstanding the apparent exclusion of such a receipt from gross income under the language of Regulation § 1.721–1(b), the courts have had great difficulty in delineating an acceptable line between taxable and nontaxable receipts of a profits interest. As the normal earnings process of the partnership should suffice to ensure that a partner with a profits interest will be taxed on those profits as earned, from a tax policy perspective, the rationale of taxing the receipt of such an interest by a partner appears to be in error.

What is the significance of the Service's issuance of Revenue Procedure 93–27, which follows? What is the tax policy basis for excepting the three specified types of transactions from its coverage?

REVENUE PROCEDURE 93–27

1993–2 C.B. 343.

Section 1.　Purpose

This revenue procedure provides guidance on the treatment of the receipt of a partnership profits interest for services provided to or for the benefit of the partnership.

Section 2.　Definitions

The following definitions apply for purposes of this revenue procedure.

.01 A capital interest is an interest that would give the holder a share of the proceeds if the partnership's assets were sold at fair market value and then the proceeds were distributed in a complete liquidation of the partnership. This determination generally is made at the time of receipt of the partnership interest.

.02 A profits interest is a partnership interest other than a capital interest.

Section 3.　Background

Under section 1.721–1(b)(1) of the Income Tax Regulations, the receipt of a partnership capital interest for services provided to or for the benefit of the partnership is taxable as compensation. On the other hand, the issue of whether the receipt of a partnership profits interest for services is taxable has been the subject of litigation. Most recently, in *Campbell v. Commissioner,* 943 F.2d 815 (8th Cir.1991), the Eighth Circuit in dictum suggested that the taxpayer's receipt of a partnership profits interest received for services was not taxable, but decided the case on valuation. Other courts have determined that in certain circumstances the receipt of a partnership profits interest for services is a taxable event under section 83 of the Internal Revenue Code. See, e.g., *Campbell v. Commissioner,* T.C.M. 1990–236, *rev'd,* 943 F.2d 815 (8th Cir.1991); *St. John v. United States,* No. 82–1134 (C.D.Ill. Nov. 16, 1983). The courts have also found that typically the profits interest received has speculative or no determinable value at the time of receipt. See *Campbell,* 943 F.2d at 823; *St. John.* In *Diamond v. Commissioner,* 56 T.C. 530 (1971), *aff'd,* 492 F.2d 286 (7th Cir.1974), however, the court assumed that the interest received by the taxpayer was a partnership profits interest and found the value of the interest was readily determinable. In that case, the interest was sold soon after receipt.

Section 4. Application

.01   Other than as provided below, if a person receives a profits interest for the provision of services to or for the benefit of a partnership in a partner capacity or in anticipation of being a partner, the Internal Revenue Service will not treat the receipt of such an interest as a taxable event for the partner or the partnership.

.02   This revenue procedure does not apply:

(1) If the profits interest relates to a substantially certain and predictable stream of income from partnership assets, such as income from high-quality debt securities or a high-quality net lease;

(2) If within two years of receipt, the partner disposes of the profits interest; or

(3) If the profits interest is a limited partnership interest in a "publicly traded partnership" within the meaning of section 7704(b) of the Internal Revenue Code.

Problem 6–2

What are the tax consequences in Problem 6–1 if Joan receives a one-third interest in all future profits and losses of the partnership, but no interest in partnership capital as of the date of her admission?

Chapter 7

BASIS OF A PARTNER'S
PARTNERSHIP INTEREST;
LOSS LIMITATIONS

Code References: §§ 702(a); 703(a); 704(d); 705(a); 733; 752(a)–(b). **See briefly:** §§ 264(a)(1); 465(a)–(b); 469(a)–(c), (h)(2); 1031(a).

Regulations: §§ 1.704–1(d); 1.731–1(a)(1)(ii); 1.752–2(a), (b), and (f) example (1), 1.752–3; Prop.Reg. §§ 1.465–7, –22(a), –24(a).

A. INTRODUCTION; FLOW THROUGH OF TAX CONSEQUENCES

One of the primary reasons that small business entities seek to be taxed as partnerships, rather than corporations, is the "flow through" concept which applies to partnerships. Gains of the enterprise flow through to the individual partners, with no tax at the entity level. Similarly, losses of the business are passed through to the individual owners for use on their personal returns rather than being "trapped" in the entity. The flow through of these tax attributes affects, and is affected by, the basis of an individual partner in his partnership interest.

The basis for a partner's partnership interest initially is determined under § 722 which provides that the basis is the amount of money contributed to the partnership and the adjusted basis to the contributing partner of any property contributed. The basis mechanism for a partnership employs an entity concept since income is computed at the partnership level. It is taxed, however, at the partner level (i.e., the conduit or flow through approach). Those earnings upon which the partner is taxed may not have been distributed to the partner. Consequently, adjustments to the basis for the partner's partnership interest are required to avoid double taxation upon the sale or liquidation of the interest.

Section 705 adjusts the partner's basis in his or her partnership interest to reflect the operations of the partnership. The basis is *increased* by the partner's distributive share for the year of (1) taxable income of the partnership, (2) partnership income exempt from income tax, and (3) other miscellaneous adjustments. Similarly, the basis is *decreased,* but not below zero, by (1) distributions by the partnership, (2) the partner's distributive share of partnership losses, (3) expenditures of the partnership not deductible in computing its taxable income and not properly chargeable to capital account, and (4) other miscellaneous adjustments. Thus, the concept of the basis of a partner's partnership interest in large part reflects his or her economic rights therein. For example, if a partner contributes $200 cash for a partnership interest and the share of *undistributed* partnership earnings for the year upon which the partner is taxed is $300, the basis in the partnership interest is increased to $500. Upon a sale or liquidation of the interest (presumably for its $500 value in this example), these adjustments ensure that the partner is not taxed again on the $300 of undistributed partnership income.

Problem 7–1

April and Beverly are equal partners in a general law firm which operates as a partnership. April has a basis of $30,000 in her partnership interest. Beverly has a basis of $10,000 in her partnership interest. What is the effect of each of the following events on the basis of each partner's partnership interest? When is the effect taken into account?

   a. The partnership makes a charitable contribution of $5,000.

   b. Each partner's distributive share of partnership taxable income is $10,000.

   c. The partnership has $8,000 in interest income from an investment in tax exempt municipal bonds.

   d. The partnership makes a cash distribution of $10,000 to each partner.

   e. The partnership exchanged rental real estate with a fair market value of $100,000 and an adjusted basis of $30,000 for other real estate worth $100,000 in a qualifying § 1031 exchange.

   f. The partnership paid $2,000 in life insurance premiums to insure the lives of key employees with the partnership named as beneficiary.

B. § 704(d) LIMITATION

An aspect of the basis concept of a partnership interest which is important in the small business context is the § 704(d) limitation which restricts the deduction of a partner's share of partnership losses to the amount of the basis for the partnership interest. Thus, for example, a partner with a $1,000 share of losses, but only a $400 basis, will not be entitled to claim the full amount of the loss deduction on his or her personal tax return for the year. Instead, $600 of the loss deduction will be suspended. In such a case, the first step in loss utilization (compliance with the § 704(d) loss limitation in order to move the loss *out* of the partnership to the partner) is not met. As evidenced by the *Sennett* decision, reproduced below, failure to extract the loss from the partnership due to the § 704(d) limitation may have significant consequences.

SENNETT v. COMMISSIONER

752 F.2d 428 (9th Cir.1985).

PER CURIAM: Taxpayers William and Sandra Sennett claimed an ordinary loss deduction of $109,061 on their 1969 tax return. This loss represented William Sennett's share of the ordinary losses incurred in 1968 by Professional Properties Partnership ("PPP") when it repurchased his interest in the partnership. The Commissioner of Internal Revenue disallowed the deduction asserting inter alia that in 1969 Sennett had no basis in an interest in PPP since he had left the partnership in 1968 and is precluded by § 704(d) and Treas.Reg. § 1.704–1(d) from claiming any loss. The Tax Court, *80 T.C. 825,* ruled against petitioners. It held that a former partner may not invoke the loss carryover provisions of section 704(d) in the tax year after the withdrawal from the partnership of that partner. We agree and affirm.

FACTS

Sennett entered PPP as a limited partner in December 1967. PPP's total capital at that time was approximately $402,000. Sennett contributed $135,000 and received a 33.5% interest in the partnership. In 1967 PPP reported an ordinary loss of $405,329, and Sennett reported his allowable distributive share of $135,000.

Sennett sold his interest in PPP on November 26, 1968, with an effective date of December 1, 1968. The contract provided that PPP would pay Sennett $250,000, in annual installments with interest. Sennett agreed to pay PPP within one year the total loss allocated to Sennett's surrendered interest. PPP then sold twenty percent of Sennett's interest to a third party. PPP's return in 1968 reported a negative capital account of $109,061, corresponding to the eighty percent portion of the partnership interest PPP bought from Sennett and retained.

On May 15, 1969, Sennett and PPP executed an amended agreement which reduced PPP's obligation to $240,000, without interest if paid in full by December 31, 1969, or if paid one-half in 1969 and the rest in 1970, at seven percent interest. PPP executed a promissory note to Sennett for $240,000, which Sennett signed as paid in full. Sennett meanwhile paid PPP $109,061, which was eighty percent of his share of PPP's losses. On his 1969 return Sennett reported $240,000 long-term capital gain and $109,061 as his distributive share of PPP's ordinary loss. The Commissioner disallowed the ordinary loss and maintained that, instead, there should be a long-term capital gain reported of

$130,939 ($240,000 − $109,061).   The Tax Court agreed and the Sennetts took this appeal.

ANALYSIS

... In deciding whether Sennett can deduct a $109,061 loss, we must look to 26 U.S.C. § 704(d).   The statute provides:

> Limitation on Allowance of Losses.—A partner's distributive share of partnership loss (including capital loss) shall be allowed only to the extent of the adjusted basis of such partner's interest in the partnership at the end of the partnership year in which such loss occurred.   Any excess of such loss over such basis shall be allowed as a deduction at the end of the partnership year in which such excess is repaid to the partnership.   (Emphasis added.)

Treas.Reg. § 1.704–1(d)—in force in 1969 and having substantively the same effect now—interprets the statute as allowing only a partner to benefit from the carryover allowed by subsection 704(d).   The Commissioner relies upon this regulation in disallowing the deduction, since Sennett was not a partner in the year he repaid the excess.   Sennett does not deny this.   Nor does he deny that his basis was zero when PPP purchased his interest and incurred the loss in 1968.   Sennett argues instead that the regulation is merely an "interpretive regulation," and entitled to little or no weight.   Sennett points to statutory language which allows the taxpayer to claim a deduction in the amount of the excess of basis in the partnership.   He claims he repaid the loss in 1969 and is entitled to the deduction regardless of his lack of partner status.

This circuit has held that an interpretive regulation will be given effect if "it is a reasonable interpretation of the statute's plain language, its origin, and its purpose."   "A Treasury regulation 'is not invalid simply because the statutory language will support a contrary interpretation.'"   As will be explained below, restricting carryover to partners is a reasonable interpretation in light of the wording of the statute and the legislative history.

Statutory language supports the Treasury Regulation.   For example, the presence of the word "partner" at the beginning of subsection 704(d) strongly implies that a taxpayer must be a partner to take advantage of the carryover.

The Treasury Regulation's interpretation is also supported by a review of the legislative history of the statute.   Section 704(d), as initially adopted by the House, allowed for deduction of the distributive share to the extent of adjusted basis.   There was no provision for a carryover of the excess loss until the excess was repaid.   The bill the Senate passed, which was the version Congress enacted, provided for carryover.   The accompanying Senate Report sums up both sentences of subsection 704(d) in a fashion that demonstrates the committee felt the subsection limited carryover to partners.   It states:

> Your committee has revised subsection (d) of the House bill to provide that any loss in excess of the basis of a partner's partnership

interest may be allowed as a deduction only at the end of the partnership year in which the loss is repaid, either directly, or out of future profits.

Subsection (d), as amended, may be illustrated as follows. Assume that a partner has a basis of $50 for his interest, and his distributive share of partnership loss is $100. Under the subsection, the partner's distributive share of the loss would be limited to $50, thereby decreasing the basis of his interest to zero. The remaining $50 loss would not be recognized, unless the partner makes a further contribution of $50. If, however, the partner repays the $50 loss to the partnership out of his share of partnership income for the following year, then the additional $50 loss will be recognized at the end of the year in which such repayment is made.

Limiting carryover to those who are partners at the time of repayment, as Treas.Reg. § 1.704–1(d) does, effectuates congressional intent to allow deductions only to the extent of adjusted basis. When a partner repays the excess loss, it is, as the Senate Report notes, "a further contribution" to the partnership. The partner thereby increases his basis by an amount equal to the loss and reduces it to zero by taking the loss. Nor is the partnership element merely a formal distinction, since the partner repaying the excess loss increases his interest in the partnership and his exposure to loss. Sennett's position, in contrast, was that of a debtor with rights superior to those of partners.

Conclusion

Since Sennett was not a member of the partnership at the time he attempted to invoke the loss carryover provisions of section 704(d) by repaying his claimed share of the loss; he was not entitled to deduct a portion of PPP's 1967 and 1968 losses. The decision of the Tax Court rejecting the $109,061 deduction and setting taxpayer's long-term capital gain for the 1969 taxable year at $130,939 is affirmed.

Problem 7–2

Same as Problem 7–1, except that item b is a distributive share of partnership loss (instead of gain) in the amount of $10,000 to each partner. If all of the loss is not allowed to a partner, what is the character of the disallowed loss?

Problem 7–3

Using the facts of Problem 7–2, assume that on January 1 of the next year, Beverly sold her partnership interest to Charles for $10,000. Assume that the resulting AC partnership has no income or deductions for that year. Does Charles succeed to Beverly's "suspended" carryover loss?

C. BASIS GENERATION THROUGH PARTNERSHIP LIABILITIES

A small business incurs various types of liabilities in the course of its business operations such as trade payables, bank debt, and loans payable to its owners. If the business entity is taxed as a partnership, these debts affect basis. The basis of a partnership interest is adjusted to reflect partnership liabilities. Under § 752(a), liabilities incurred by a partnership may increase a partner's basis. To the extent of a partner's share of any partnership liabilities, § 752(a) provides that such amount is treated as a contribution of money by the partner to the partnership which increases (just as a cash contribution would) the adjusted basis of his or her interest. Likewise, under § 752(b), when partnership liabilities are reduced or a partner is relieved of a share of partnership liabilities, that amount is treated as a distribution from the partnership to the partner which reduces the basis of the partnership interest.

In many ways, § 752 merely codifies the *Crane* doctrine in the partnership context. In essence, § 752(a) reflects the typical increased basis adjustment when a taxpayer incurs a liability in the acquisition of an asset. Section 752(b) is similarly modeled to reflect the principle that a third party's assumption of a taxpayer's liability generates economic benefits which in the individual context gives rise to income realization. The constructive cash contributions and distributions dictated by § 752 provide for similar consequences. If the amount distributed is greater than the partner's basis, the excess is recognized as gain under § 731 which further instructs that such gain is to be treated as though it were from the sale or exchange of the interest.

In order to determine a partner's share of the partnership's liabilities, both the nature of the partnership (general or limited) and the nature of the liability (recourse or nonrecourse) must be considered. Regulation § 1.752–1 establishes the boundaries of the liability allocation rules. Different sharing rules apply depending on the nature of the liability. Under the Regulations, recourse liabilities are allocated according to the partner's economic risk of loss on such an obligation—in large part because such a focus evidences the funding agreement between the partners for the liability in the case of default and an inadequacy of partnership assets. Reg. § 1.752–2.

However, personal liability does not exist for nonrecourse liabilities in the event of default. Consequently, nonrecourse liabilities will be funded with partnership capital and earnings and therefore are allocated among the partners generally according to their profit ratios. The profits ratio specified for such a liability generally is determinative. There are, however, priority allocation provisions for any portion of the liability attributable to minimum gain arising under § 704(b) or § 704(c). Reg. § 1.752–3. Thus, a partner with a 10% interest in profits and a 15% interest in losses could have a $10,000 share in a $100,000 nonrecourse liability while having a $15,000 share in a $100,-000 recourse liability.

While the above-discussed sharing rules are fully applicable in the general partnership context, for policy reasons, the rules are altered in the limited partnership or limited liability company context. With regard to recourse liabilities, limited partners are protected under state law (except to the extent they are obligated to make additional contributions to the partnership) against liability to the creditors of the partnership. Thus, where a limited partner has fully met his or her contribution, he or she will not share in recourse liabilities as he or she bears no risk of loss therefor. Instead, the liability will be allocated exclusively to the general partners in accordance with their risk of loss under state law or under the partnership agreement. If the limited partner is obligated to the partnership for additional contributions, he or she is entitled to a portion of the liability if the partner bears the economic risk of loss. However, with respect to nonrecourse liabilities, as no partner (not even a general partner) is liable upon default, the Regulations in keeping with the policy described above allocate such liabilities generally to all partners, including limited partners, generally pursuant to their profit ratios.

Notwithstanding the above-described rules, over the years partners have attempted to utilize "hybrid" instruments to effectuate their desired allocation formula. For example, limited partners may seek increased basis for loss pass-through purposes by obtaining nonrecourse financing. A partnership unable to procure pure nonrecourse financing might instead enter into a nonrecourse agreement at the partnership level while simultaneously having its general partners execute a guaranty agreement. However, the courts, the Service, and Congress attacked such financing devices by identifying the party who bore the ultimate risk of loss and determined the partners' shares of the liability accordingly. Consequently, in cases of hybrid financing, the traditional recourse and nonrecourse rules are inapplicable and such liabilities are allocated according to the risk of loss standard. Reg. § 1.752–2.

REVENUE RULING 88–77
1988–2 C.B. 128.

ISSUE

For purposes of computing the adjusted basis of a partner's interest in a cash basis partnership, are accrued but unpaid expenses and accounts payable "liabilities of a partnership" or "partnership liabilities" within the meaning of section 752 of the Internal Revenue Code?

FACTS

A is a partner in *P* partnership. *P* files returns on a calendar year basis and uses the cash receipts and disbursements method of accounting. At the close of the taxable year at issue, *P*'s accrued expenses and accounts payable consisted of 100*x* dollars for interest expense and accounts payable of 200*x* dollars for services received.

LAW AND ANALYSIS

Section 722 of the Code provides that a partner's basis is increased by the amount of money the partner contributes to the partnership.

Section 752(a) of the Code provides that any increase in a partner's share of the liabilities of a partnership, or any increase in a partner's individual liabilities by reason of the assumption by the partner of partnership liabilities, is treated as a contribution of money by the partner to the partnership.

Rev.Rul. 60–345, 1960–2 C.B. 211, holds that, for purposes of section 752 of the Code, the term "liabilities" includes a cash basis partnership's obligations for the payment of outstanding trade accounts, notes, and accrued expenses.

The present issue is similar to that arising under section 357(c) of the Code when property and liabilities are contributed to a controlled corporation in exchange for stock. For purposes of determining the basis of the stock received in the exchange under section 358 and any gain that must be recognized on the exchange under section 357(c), section 357(c)(3) provides that the term "liabilities" shall not include obligations the payment of which would give rise to a deduction or that would constitute a guaranteed payment under section 736(a). This rule is subject to an exception found in section 357(c)(3)(B) for liabilities the incurrence of which resulted in the creation of, or an increase in, the basis of any property. Section 357(c)(3) was added by the Revenue Act of 1978.

The legislative history accompanying the amendment to section 704(c) made by the Tax Reform Act of 1984 explicitly rejected the conclusion reached in Revenue Ruling 60–345 in favor of an interpretation of section 752 that is consistent with section 357(c). See H.R.Rep. No. 861, 98th Cong., 2d Sess. 856–857 (1984), 1984–3 (Vol. 2) C.B. 110, 111.

Under P's method of accounting, P's obligations to pay amounts incurred for interest and services are not deductible until paid. For purposes of section 752 of the Code, the terms "liabilities of a partnership" and "partnership liabilities" include an obligation only if and to the extent that incurring the liability creates or increases the basis to the partnership of any of the partnership's assets (including cash attributable to borrowings), gives rise to an immediate deduction to the partnership, or, under section 705(a)(2)(B), currently decreases a partner's basis in the partner's partnership interest. The preceding sentence uses the term "assets" to include capitalized items that are properly allocable to future periods, such as organizational expenses and construction period expenses.

The liabilities incurred by P for interest expense and services do not create or increase the basis of a partnership asset or give rise to a deduction when incurred. Therefore, for purposes of computing A's adjusted basis in P, A may not treat P's accrued expenses and accounts payable as a liability of the partnership.

HOLDING

For purposes of computing the adjusted basis of a partner's interest in a cash basis partnership, accrued but unpaid expenses and accounts payable are not "liabilities of a partnership" or "partnership liabilities" within the meaning of section 752 of the Code.

REVENUE RULING 94–4

1994–1 C.B. 195.

ISSUE

If a deemed distribution of money under § 752(b) of the Internal Revenue Code occurs as a result of a decrease in a partner's share of the liabilities of a partnership, is the deemed distribution taken into account at the time of the distribution or at the end of the partnership taxable year?

LAW

Under § 752(b), a decrease in a partner's share of partnership liabilities is considered a distribution of money to the partner by the partnership. The partner will recognize gain under § 731(a)(1) if the distribution of money exceeds the adjusted basis of the partner's interest immediately before the distribution.

Section 1.731–1(a)(1)(ii) of the Income Tax Regulations provides that for purposes of §§ 731 and 705, advances or drawings of money or property against a partner's distributive share of income are treated as current distributions made on the last day of the partnership taxable year with respect to that partner.

Rev.Rul. 92–97, 1992–2 C.B. 124, treats a deemed distribution of money to a partner resulting from a cancellation of debt as an advance or drawing under § 1.731–1(a)(1)(ii) against that partner's distributive share of cancellation of indebtedness income.

HOLDING

A deemed distribution of money under § 752(b) resulting from a decrease in a partner's share of the liabilities of a partnership is treated as an advance or drawing of money under § 1.731–1(a)(1)(ii) to the extent of the partner's distributive share of income for the partnership taxable year. An amount treated as an advance or drawing of money is taken into account at the end of the partnership taxable year. A deemed distribution of money resulting from a cancellation of debt may qualify for advance or drawing treatment under this revenue ruling and under Rev.Rul. 92–97.

Problem 7–4

Alan and Booth operate a computer leasing business as equal partners through their partnership which has no realty activities. Each contributed $10,000 to the capital of the partnership. The partnership purchased $100,000 worth of computers for $20,000 cash, subject to an $80,000 recourse mortgage which is a general obligation of the partnership. The partnership broke even from a cash flow standpoint, but incurred a $30,000 tax loss attributable exclusively to depreciation on the personal property in its first year of operation.

    a. What are the partners' bases for their partnership interests? How much of the partnership loss may each partner deduct?

    b. What if the partnership liability is nonrecourse? What if Alan personally guaranteed the loan, but Booth did not?

    c. What if the partnership liability is recourse and Alan and Booth share profits 40%–60% and losses 70%–30%?

    d. Same as c except the liability is nonrecourse.

    e. Same as b except the partnership is a limited partnership with Booth as the limited partner, and Alan does *not* personally guarantee the loan.

    f. Same as e except the liability is recourse. Assume the limited partner has no further obligation to make capital contributions and the partnership agreement provides that all loss will be allocated to the general partner once the limited partner's capital account is reduced to zero.

D.   AT RISK LIMITATION

As is evident from the prior discussion, basis may be generated through various types of partnership obligations thereby avoiding the § 704(d) limitation on loss availability. However, as regards partnership losses, two other limitations on loss availability must be confronted, namely, the at risk rules and the passive loss rules. (See E below).

The at risk rules of § 465 deny the deduction of losses in excess of the amount a partner is at risk. A partner is at risk to the extent of any money contributed to the partnership, the adjusted basis of any property contributed thereto, and the share of partnership recourse liabilities. Generally, nonrecourse liabilities do not constitute amounts at risk. Thus, a limited partner may have basis under § 752 and § 704(d) through nonrecourse financing but not be at risk for such amounts. Consequently, the loss would not be available for use on his or her personal return.

An exception to the general policy of the at risk rules exists for "qualified nonrecourse financing" with regard to real estate activities. For example, limited partners participating in a limited partnership investing in an apartment complex with qualified nonrecourse financing would have an equivalent total of basis and at risk amounts.

PRITCHETT v. COMMISSIONER
827 F.2d 644 (9th Cir.1987).

SKOPIL, CIRCUIT JUDGE.

We must decide in this case whether taxpayers, limited partners in five similar partnerships engaged in oil and gas drilling operations, were

"at risk" pursuant to 26 U.S.C. § 465 on certain recourse notes and thus entitled to deduct distributive shares of noncash partnership losses. The Tax Court in a reviewed, split decision held that each taxpayer was at risk only to the extent of actual cash contribution. We reject the Tax Court's rationale in holding that taxpayers were not at risk on the recourse debt. We remand to allow the Tax Court to consider the Commissioner's alternative theory that taxpayers were not at risk because the creditor had an impermissible role in the activity at issue.
* * *

FACTS AND PROCEEDINGS BELOW

Taxpayers are each members in similar limited partnerships formed to conduct oil and gas operations. All five partnerships entered into agreements with Fairfield Drilling Corporation ("Fairfield") whereby Fairfield agreed to drill, develop, and exploit any productive wells. Fairfield provided all necessary equipment and expertise. Pursuant to a "turnkey" agreement, each partnership paid cash and executed a recourse note to Fairfield. Each note was non-interest-bearing and matured in fifteen years. Each was secured by virtually all of the maker-partnership's assets. The principal for each note was to be paid from net income available to each partnership if the drilling operations proved successful. Only the general partners were personally liable under the notes. Nevertheless, each partnership agreement provided that if the notes were not paid off at maturity, the limited partners would be personally obligated to make additional capital contributions to cover the deficiency when called upon to do so by the general partners.

Each partnership elected to use accrual accounting and to deduct intangible drilling costs as an expense. The partnership agreements provided that all losses were to be allocated among limited partners in proportion to their respective capital contributions. Because there was no income in the tax year in question, each limited partner deducted from taxable income a distributive share of partnership loss. The Commissioner disallowed that portion of the deduction based on the note.

The Tax Court affirmed by a 9–7 vote the Commissioner's action. The majority held that under the partnership agreements the limited partners had no personal liability on the notes for the tax year in question and therefore they were at risk under section 465 only for the actual cash contribution made to the partnerships. Any potential liability was "merely a contingency" since in the first year of the partnership it was not known whether income would be sufficient to pay off the note or even whether the general partners would in fact exercise their discretion to make a cash call on an unpaid balance fifteen years later.

Seven judges dissented in three separate opinions. One judge reasoned that for federal tax purposes, "both general and limited partners are personally liable for a pro rata portion of the partnership's recourse obligation to Fairfield." Another found nothing in the agreements to indicate the general partners had unilateral discretion to waive the cash call. A majority of the dissenting judges apparently believed, however, that the Commissioner's actions might be affirmed on the alternative ground that section 465(b)(3)(A) provides that amounts borrowed are not at risk if the money is borrowed from someone with an interest in the activity at issue. The majority notes this alternative ground but expressly does not adopt it.

These timely appeals followed.

DISCUSSION

In 1976 Congress added section 465 to the Internal Revenue Code to combat abuse of tax shelters caused by nonrecourse financing. *See Commissioner v. Tufts,* 461 U.S. 300, 309 n. 7 (1983). Section 465 forbids a taxpayer from taking a loss in excess of amounts at risk in the investment. The statute provides in relevant part that:

> (1) * * * a taxpayer shall be considered at risk for . . .

> (A) the amount of money * * * contributed by the taxpayer to the activity, and

> (B) amounts borrowed with respect to such activity * * *.

> (2) * * * a taxpayer shall be considered at risk with respect to amounts borrowed * * * to the extent that he—

> (A) is personally liable for the repayment of such amounts * * *.

The limited partners argue that the notes create at risk debt because each limited partner is personally liable. The contract provisions provide that if the notes are not paid off by the successful drilling operations, "the General Partners *will* by written notice call for additional capital contributions in an amount sufficient to pay the outstanding balance" and that "[e]ach Limited Partner *shall* be obligated to pay in cash to the Partnership" the amount called. (Emphasis added). It is clear, however, as the majority opinion notes, that the limited partners are not directly and personally liable to Fairfield. Even assuming a third party beneficiary right, Fairfield had no recourse against the limited partners until the end of the note's fifteen year term.

Whether the Tax Court's decision is correct hinges on its characterization of taxpayers' obligation as indirect and secondary. In a decision rendered shortly after *Pritchett,* the Tax Court sought to distinguish between direct and indirect liability. *Abramson v. Commissioner,* 86 T.C. 360, 375–76 (1986). In that reviewed decision the Tax Court, by a 15–1 vote, held that limited partners' pro rata shares of partnership debt that was to be repaid in whole or in part out of partnership revenues was at risk. The limited partners had a direct contractual liability to a third party seller of goods. *Abramson* distinguished *Pritchett* by noting:

> In *Pritchett* the limited partners were not directly liable to the lender on the partnership obligation. Rather, the general partner was personally liable to the lender on the recourse obligation, and the limited partners were, if anything, potential indemnitors of the

general partner. The limited partners were not obligated on any debt for purposes of section 465 until the general partner called for contributions to the partnership. Consequently, in *Pritchett* the limited partners had not borrowed any amount within the meaning of section 465(b)(2). In this case, to the contrary, each partner is personally and directly liable for a pro rata part of the amount owed to the seller * * *. Because each partner's liability for the partnership debt (in the words of the statute, for the "amounts borrowed") ran directly to the seller and each partner's liability was personal each partner is at risk for his proportionate share of amount owed to the seller.

We agree that Congress intended to condition section 465's exclusion of deductions in part on whether the liability for borrowing is primary or secondary. The statute expressly requires that the taxpayer be "personally liable for the repayment." 26 U.S.C. § 465(b)(2)(A). In debate on the Deficit Reduction Act of 1984, a House Report explained that section 465 limits an at-risk loss to, *inter alia,* "amounts borrowed for use in the activity with respect to which the taxpayer has *personal* liability." H.R.Rep. No. 98–432, Part II, 98th Cong., 2d Sess. 1506, *reprinted in* 1984 U.S.Code Cong. & Admin.News 697, 1146 (emphasis added). If the limited partnership agreements here create only contingent liability, we will affirm the Tax Court's decision to disallow taxpayers' deductions.

We conclude, however, that the liability of the limited partners was unavoidable and hence not contingent. In *Melvin v. Commissioner,* 88 T.C. 63 (1987), the Tax Court appeared to answer the question posed here by concluding that

> the fact that the partnership or other partners remain in the "chain of liability" should not detract from the at-risk amount of the parties who do have the ultimate liability. The critical inquiry should be who is the obligor of last resort, and in determining who has the ultimate economic responsibility for the loan, the substance of the transaction controls.

Melvin, 88 T.C. at 75 (citing *Raphan v. United States,* 759 F.2d 879, 885 (Fed.Cir.1985)). Applying that standard we have no reservation in concluding that taxpayers, by virtue of their contractual obligations, have ultimate responsibility for the debt. *See Bennion v. Commissioner,* 88 T.C. 684, 695 (1987) (applying the *Melvin* standard to taxpayer's "Guarantee Agreement" to determine that taxpayer was ultimately liable on a debt obligation even though the obligation flowed through others). Furthermore, we are not dissuaded by the Tax Court's reasoning that the debt is contingent because the general partners may elect to not make the cash calls. The contracts made the call mandatory and "economic reality" dictates that the partners would do so. *See Durkin v. Commissioner,* 87 T.C. 1329, 1379 (1986) (concluding that economic reality assured that promissory notes of limited partners to the partnership would be enforced).

The Tax Court also reasoned that the debt was contingent since it was not known in the tax year in question whether sufficient partnership revenues would satisfy the notes prior to or on maturity. We find the Tax Court's reasoning on this point faulty. If the notes required balloon payments upon maturity, the limited partners' obligation to contribute additional funds would be "certain." The acceleration of payments should not be a factor in the taxation analysis. In *Abramson,* like this case, early payment was tied to the success of the operation. No mention was made in *Abramson* that the debt was contingent. Furthermore, the fact that the obligation may not become due for several years in the future is of no significance to the allocation of a pro rata share of the taxpayers' debt in the tax year in question. *See Taube v. Commissioner,* 88 T.C. 464, 487 (1987) (debt due years in future is nevertheless genuine indebtedness fully includable in basis); *Melvin,* 88 T.C. at 73 ("debt obligations of a partnership that are payable in later years generally are to be included in the at-risk amounts").

The Commissioner argued below and on appeal that taxpayers' deductions are alternatively barred by section 465(b)(3). That subsection provides that "amounts borrowed shall not be considered to be at risk with respect to an activity if such amounts are borrowed from any person who * * * has an interest (other than an interest as a creditor) in such activity." § 465(b)(3)(A). The legislative history suggests that "*any type of financial interest* in the activity (other than as a creditor) would constitute a prohibited 'other interest' under section 465." *Bennion,* 88 T.C. at 696 (citing to Staff of Joint Committee on Taxation, General Explanation of Tax Reform Act of 1976 at 39, 1976–3 C.B. (Vol. 2) 51) (emphasis in original). Furthermore, proposed Treasury regulations provide that a lender will be deemed to have a prohibited interest if it has either a capital interest or an interest in the net profits of the activity. *See id.* (citing Sec. 1.465–8(b), Proposed Income Tax Regs., 44 Fed.Reg. 32239 (June 5, 1979)).

The agreements here provided that Fairfield would receive twenty percent of the gross sales of oil and gas, payable if the partnerships achieved certain profit levels. Judge Simpson concluded that these arrangements gave Fairfield a "substantial interest" in the partnership. Judge Cohen stated that he shared Judge Simpson's impression that Fairfield appears to be a person having an interest in the activity, but that "[t]his should be explored further by the finder of facts." We agree with Judge Cohen's suggestion that this possibility should be explored further. Although we may affirm a correct decision on any basis supported by the record, remand is appropriate when a lower court's "application of an incorrect legal standard leaves * * * an inadequate factual record on which to affirm."

Finally, the Commissioner argues that even if the debts are at risk and thus deductible, the amounts should nevertheless be limited to the present value of the notes. Section 465(b)(4) provides that "a taxpayer shall not be considered at risk with respect to amounts protected against loss through nonrecourse financing, guarantees, stop loss agreements, *or other similar arrangements.*" § 465(b)(4) (emphasis added). The Commissioner argues that interest-free notes should be regarded as a "similar arrangement."

Our review of the record indicates that this issue was not raised below. "As a general rule, we will not consider an issue raised for the first time on appeal." Although there are exceptions to the rule, the better practice is to remand to allow the Tax Court to address such an issue first. See id. (trial tactics and legal arguments may have been different if the Commissioner had argued the issue below). Accordingly, we also remand this issue for the Tax Court's consideration.

Reversed and Remanded.

E.   PASSIVE LOSS LIMITATION

The final limitation with regard to the deductibility of partnership losses generated by an operating business is the passive loss limitation of § 469. Prior to the disposition of a passive activity, losses derived from a passive activity may be deducted only against passive income and may not offset income from salaries, etc. Subject to regulatory exceptions, a limited partnership interest is deemed under § 469(i)(6)(C) to be a passive activity. Accordingly, the availability of losses relating to such an interest is seriously curtailed. As noted in the legislative history of § 469:

> In the case of a limited partnership interest, except to the extent provided by regulations [500 hours of participation], it is conclusively presumed that the taxpayer has not materially participated in the activity. In general, under relevant State laws, a limited partnership interest is characterized by limited liability, and in order to maintain limited liability status, a limited partner, as such, cannot be active in the partnership's business. The presumption that a limited partnership interest is passive applies even when the taxpayer possesses the limited partnership interest indirectly through a tiered entity arrangement (e.g., the taxpayer owns a general partnership interest, or stock in an S corporation, and the partnership or corporation in which the taxpayer owns such interest itself owns a limited partnership interest in another entity).

> When a taxpayer possesses both a limited partnership interest and another type of interest, such as a general partnership interest, with respect to an activity, except as otherwise provided in regulations, lack of material participation is conclusively presumed with respect to the limited partnership interest (thus limiting the use of deductions and credits allocable thereto). The presence of material participation for purposes of any other interests in the activity owned by the taxpayer is determined with reference to the relevant facts and circumstances.

> Under the Act, the Secretary of the Treasury is empowered to provide through regulations that limited partnership interests in

certain circumstances will not be treated (other than through the application of the general facts and circumstances test regarding material participation) as interests in passive activities. It is intended that this grant of authority be used to prevent taxpayers from manipulating the rule that limited partnerships generally are passive, in attempting to evade the passive loss provision.

Problem 7–5

Assuming the same facts as Problem 7–4(a) and (b), does § 465 have any effect on the partners or the partnership? What effect does § 469 have?

Chapter 8

TAXING PARTNERSHIP OPERATIONS—CHARACTERIZATION AND COMPUTATION OF PARTNERSHIP INCOME

Code References: §§ 702(a) and (b); 703(a); 704(a); 724.

Regulations: §§ 1.701–2(a)–(d) example (1); 1.702–1(a) and (b).

A. INTRODUCTION

One factor which must be considered by small business owners in deciding to form a partnership or an entity taxed as a partnership is the additional complexity and expense in the creation of a new entity. Partnership agreements must be drafted, tax identification numbers applied for, assets transferred, and separate books set up for the new entity. Attorneys and accountants must be paid to do these things. In addition, an additional tax return must be filed each year. The required reporting and calculations on that return can be quite complex, again requiring accounting assistance.

Although a partnership is not a taxable entity, it is required to compute its taxable income as though it were a taxpayer. Under § 703(a), a partnership calculates taxable income in the same manner as an individual taxpayer. However, § 703(a)(2) denies certain deductions in computing partnership income because these deductions are allowed to the individual partners on their separate tax returns. To afford the partnership a deduction of such items would result in a double benefit. For example, personal exemptions provided by § 151 are not deductible by the partnership, but instead are taken by the partners individually.

In order to determine personal tax liability, each partner takes into account separately his or her distributive share of the partnership's income, gain, loss, deduction, or credit. Section 702(a) enumerates six specific items (e.g., capital gains and losses, § 1231 gains and losses, charitable contributions, etc.) which must be separately stated by the partnership, a seventh category of those items requiring separate statement by specific reference in the Regulations, and a final catchall category of all other items, often referred to as "bottom-line profit or loss."

Separate statement is required for the categories of § 702(a)(1)–(7) because the ultimate tax effects of those items are dependent upon the factual particulars of each partner. For example, a capital loss of $10,000 per partner will be of limited utility to a partner with no capital gain but will be fully available to a partner with $10,000 or more of capital gain. Separate statement prevents distortion of a partner's tax setting. Each item of partnership income, gain, loss, deduction, or credit is separately reported on schedule K to the partnership tax return (Form 1065) and on schedule K–1 which is distributed to each partner.

Problem 8–1

Lost Galleons Company is a partnership which hunts for sunken Spanish ships. It is composed of individual limited partners, Simon and Warren, who provide capital, and a corporate general partner, Acme Shipping, Inc. Each partner has a one-third interest in each item of income and deduction, unless specified to the contrary. Simon also operates a sole proprietorship, pawn brokerage business. Determine each partner's distributive share of income and deductions, assuming the following receipts and expenditures.

   a. $10,000 in long-term capital gain.

   b. $3,000 in dividends from a domestic corporation.

   c. $15,000 expenditure for property qualifying for § 179. Simon also purchased $20,000 in qualifying property for use in his sole proprietorship pawn business.

   d. $40,000 in depreciation expense, the first $10,000 of which is specially allocated to the limited partners by the partnership agreement.

   e. $200,000 treasure trove (under Regulation § 1.61–14).

   f. $43,000 of § 162 expense.

B. CHARACTERIZATION AT PARTNERSHIP LEVEL

The entity characteristic of a partnership is emphasized by § 702(b) which provides that the tax character of items constituting each partner's distributive share is determined at the partnership level, without regard to the trade or business of each partner. Thus, for example, a disposition of property by a partnership will be characterized by the nature of the partnership's activities with respect to that property—holding period, capital asset status, etc. On the whole, the professions and individual activities of the member partners are irrelevant to such a determination. However, it must be remembered that a partnership acts through its partners. Therefore, the actions of a partner may prove relevant to the characterization issue if taken on behalf of the partnership.

PODELL v. COMMISSIONER

55 T.C. 429 (1970).

QUEALY, JUDGE.

The only question presented for decision is whether amounts received by petitioner on the sale of certain real estate are taxable as ordinary income under section 61 or as capital gain. * * *

During each of the years 1964 and 1965, Hyman Podell (hereinafter referred to as petitioner) entered into an oral agreement with Mr. Cain Young (hereinafter referred to as Young), a real estate operator located in Brooklyn, New York, whereby petitioner advanced various amounts of money to Young to be used for the purchase and renovation of certain residential real estate. Young was to provide the actual management for the project. Petitioner entered into the agreement with Young in each of the years in the hope that the renovation of the buildings purchased pursuant to the agreement would help in the rehabilitation of certain slum areas in Brooklyn.

Pursuant to the aforesaid agreement, Young purchased various buildings in the Bedford–Stuyvesant, Crown Heights, and other areas of Brooklyn, New York. Young renovated the buildings, refinanced them, and sold them at the best possible price obtainable. In 1964, petitioner and Young purchased, renovated, and sold nine buildings. In 1965, petitioner and Young purchased, renovated, and sold five buildings. In other years, the number was less. The aforesaid activities constituted only a portion of the total activities carried on by Young.

Young held the aforementioned buildings for sale in the ordinary course of business. In addition, petitioner and Young shared equally in the profit or loss on the sale of each of the buildings. In 1964 petitioner's share of the net gain realized from his agreement with Young was $4,198.03. In 1965, petitioner's share of the net gain realized from his agreement with Young was $2,903.41.

Petitioner is engaged in the full-time practice of law, and he has paid regular taxes on his earnings as an attorney. He did not actively participate in the purchase, the renovation, or the sale of the real estate.

ULTIMATE FINDING OF FACT

The oral agreements entered into between petitioner and Young in 1964 and 1965 established a joint venture for the purpose of purchasing, renovating, and selling certain residential real estate in the ordinary course of trade or business.

OPINION

In this case, during each of the years 1964 and 1965, petitioner entered into an oral agreement with Young for the purchase, renovation, and sale of certain residential real estate. Profit and loss realized on the sale of such property was shared equally by petitioner and Young.

Section 1221, which defines "capital asset," provides in pertinent part:

> For purposes of this subtitle, the term "capital asset" means property held by the taxpayer (whether or not connected with his trade or business), but does not include—
>
> (1) stock in trade of the taxpayer or other property of a kind which would properly be included in the inventory of the taxpayer if on hand at the close of the taxable year, *or property held by the taxpayer primarily for sale to customers in the ordinary course of his trade or business;* [Emphasis supplied.]

Petitioner maintains that the properties sold were capital assets and that any gains on those sales should be taxed as capital gains.

Respondent argues that the oral agreements between petitioner and Young established a partnership or joint venture for the purposes of purchasing, renovating, and selling real estate in the ordinary course of business, and that consequently, the gains arose from the sale of noncapital assets and are to be treated as ordinary income.

We have found as an ultimate fact that the agreement between petitioner and Young gave rise to a joint venture. Under section 761(a), a joint venture is included within the definition of a "partnership" for purposes of the internal revenue laws (henceforth in this opinion, the terms are used interchangeably). Section 761(a) provides:

> (a) PARTNERSHIP.—For purposes of this subtitle, the term "partnership" *includes* a syndicate, group, pool, *joint venture* or other unincorporated organization through or by means of which any business, financial operation, or venture is carried on, and which is not, within the meaning of this title [subtitle], a corporation or a trust or estate * * *. [Emphasis supplied.]

A joint venture has been defined as a "special combination of two or more persons, where in some specific venture a profit is jointly sought without any actual partnership or corporate designation."

The elements of a joint venture are: (a) A contract (express or implied) showing that it was the intent of the parties that a business venture be established; (b) an agreement for joint control and proprietorship; (c) a contribution of money, property, and/or services by the prospective joint venturers; and (d) a sharing of profits, but not necessarily of losses (although some jurisdictions require that there be a sharing of losses).

In many respects, the concept of joint venture is similar to the concept of partnership, and many of the principles of partnership law are applicable to joint ventures. A primary distinction between the two concepts is that a joint venture is generally established for a single business venture (even though the business of managing the venture to a successful conclusion may continue for a number of years) while a partnership is formed to carry on a business for profit over a long period of time.

It is undisputed that petitioner and Young joined in an agreement establishing a joint business venture to acquire, improve, and resell residential property at a profit, and it is immaterial that the petitioner was motivated, in part, by social objectives. There was a contribution to the business of property, services, or money by each of the parties involved. Petitioner and Young also agreed to share equally in any resulting gain or loss.

The fact that petitioner did not exercise as much managerial control over the day-to-day activities relating to the purchase, renovation, and sale of the real estate as Young is not sufficient reason for this Court to find against the existence of a joint venture. While petitioner gave Young discretion with respect to all aspects of the purchase, renovation, and sale of the real estate in question, petitioner retained the power to approve of the steps undertaken by Young to execute their agreement through his control over his continued contributions of funds to the venture.

The real estate acquired by the joint venture is to be considered partnership property for purposes of taxation. Section 702(a) provides, in part:

> (a) GENERAL RULE.—In determining his income tax, each partner shall take into account separately *his distributive share of the partnership's*—
>
> (1) gains and losses from sales or exchanges of capital assets held for not more than 6 months,
>
> (2) gains and losses from sales or exchanges of capital assets held for more than 6 months,
>
> [Emphasis supplied.]

Section 702(a) establishes the "conduit rule" for the income taxation of partnerships and provides:

> (b) CHARACTER OF ITEMS CONSTITUTING DISTRIBUTIVE SHARE.—The character of any item of income, gain, loss, deduction, or credit included in a partner's distributive share * * * shall be determined as if such item were realized directly from the source from which realized by the partnership, or incurred in the same manner as incurred by the partnership.

In essence, the "conduit rule" requires that for the purpose of determining the nature of an item of income, gain, loss, deduction, or credit in the hands of the partnership before distribution or a partner (joint venturer—henceforth in this opinion the terms "partner" and "joint venturer" are used interchangeably) after distribution, the partnership is to be viewed as an entity and such items are to be characterized from the viewpoint of the partnership rather than from the viewpoint of an individual partner. Thus, the phrase "his trade or business" in section 1221(1) clearly refers to the trade or business of the partner-ship, despite the fact that under section 701 partnerships are not subject to income tax. It is the intent of the partnership and not that of any specific partner which is determinative in characterizing the income for purposes of taxation.

The trade or business of the joint venture or partnership in this case during the years in question was the purchase, renovation, and sale of certain residential real estate irrespective of and separately from the various businesses or professions of the individual joint venturers. The real estate sold by the joint venture was held for sale to the customers of the joint venture in the ordinary course of the joint venture's business with the consequence that the residential real estate parcels were not capital assets in the hands of the joint venture. Consequently, the income realized by the joint venture on the sale of the real estate was ordinary income. Therefore, applying the "conduit rule" of section 702(b), this income remained ordinary income in the hands of the joint venturers.

The cases of *United States v. Rosebrook,* 318 F.2d 316 (C.A.9, 1963), and *Riddell v. Scales,* 406 F.2d 210 (C.A.9, 1969), which look to the purposes of the joint venturers in determining the character of the income, are readily distinguishable from the case before us. In *Rose-brook,* there was direct ownership of the property in question by the taxpayer even though her interest had been committed to a joint venture. Furthermore, the taxpayer had succeeded involuntarily to ownership of the property and participation in the joint venture through her father. In the case before us, these factors are not present. In *Riddell v. Scales, supra,* the joint venture as an entity was not engaged in the real estate business.

Petitioner relies heavily on *Austin v. Commissioner,* 263 F.2d 460 (C.A.9, 1959), to support his position. His reliance is without foundation. The facts of *Austin* are entirely distinguishable from the case at hand. In *Austin,* the taxpayer was an attorney who individually sold vacant lots over a period of years. He was not a participant in a joint venture that had as its primary purpose the purchase, renovation, and sale of residential real estate to its customers in the ordinary course of its business. In the case before us, petitioner was engaged in such a joint venture, and the character of the income in his hands is determined by the character it would have had if it had remained with the joint venture. Since it would be ordinary income to the joint venture, it is ordinary income to petitioner. In short, *Austin* is irrelevant in terms of the facts of this case.

Decision will be entered for the respondent.

UNITED STATES v. BASYE

410 U.S. 441 (1973).

MR. JUSTICE POWELL delivered the opinion of the Court:

This is a partnership income tax case brought here by the United States on a petition for writ of certiorari from the Court of Appeals for the Ninth Circuit. * * * Because we find that the decision is incompatible with basic principles of income taxation as developed in our prior cases, we reverse.

I.

Respondents, each of whom is a physician, are partners in a limited partnership known as Permanente Medical Group, which was organized in California in 1949. Associated with the partnership are over 200 partner physicians, as well as numerous nonpartner physicians and other employees. In 1959, Permanente entered into an agreement with Kaiser Foundation Health Plan, Inc., a nonprofit corporation providing prepaid medical care and hospital services to its dues-paying members.

Pursuant to the terms of the agreement, Permanente agreed to supply medical services for the 390,000 member-families, or about 900,-000 individuals, in Kaiser's Northern California Region which covers primarily the San Francisco Bay area. In exchange for those services, Kaiser agreed to pay the partnership a "base compensation" composed of two elements. First, Kaiser undertook to pay directly to the partnership a sum each month computed on the basis of the total number of members enrolled in the health program. That number was multiplied by a stated fee, which originally was set at a little over $2.60. The second item of compensation—and the one that has occasioned the present dispute—called for the creation of a program, funded entirely by Kaiser, to pay retirement benefits to Permanente's partner and nonpartner physicians.

The pertinent compensation provision of the agreement did not itself establish the details of the retirement program; it simply obligated Kaiser to make contributions to such a program in the event that the parties might thereafter agree to adopt one. As might be expected, a separate trust agreement establishing the contemplated plan soon was executed by Permanente, Kaiser, and the Bank of America Trust and Savings Association, acting as trustee. Under this agreement Kaiser agreed to make payments to the trust at a predetermined rate, initially pegged at 12 cents per health plan member per month. Additionally, Kaiser made a flat payment of $200,000 to start the fund and agreed that its pro rata payment obligation would be retroactive to the date of the signing of the medical service agreement.

The beneficiaries of the trust were all partner and nonpartner physicians who, had completed at least two years of continuous service with the partnership and who elected to participate. The trust maintained a separate tentative account for each beneficiary. As periodic payments were received from Kaiser, the funds were allocated among these accounts pursuant to a complicated formula designed to take into consideration on a relative basis each participant's compensation level, length of service, and age. No physician was eligible to receive the amounts in his tentative account prior to retirement, and retirement established entitlement only if the participant had rendered at least 15 years of continuous service or 10 years of continuous service and had attained age 65. Prior to such time, however, the trust agreement explicitly provided that no interest in any tentative account was to be regarded as having vested in any particular beneficiary. The agreement also provided for the forfeiture of any physician's interest and its redistribution among the remaining participants if he were to terminate his relationship with Permanente prior to retirement. A similar forfeiture and redistribution also would occur if, after retirement, a physician were to render professional services for any hospital or health plan other than one operated by Kaiser. The trust agreement further stipulated that a retired physician's right to receive benefits would cease if he were to refuse any reasonable request to render consultative services to any Kaiser-operated health plan.

The agreement provided that the plan would continue irrespective either of changes in the partnership's personnel or of alterations in its organizational structure. The plan would survive any reorganization of the partnership so long as at least 50% of the plan's participants remained associated with the reorganized entity. In the event of dissolution or of a nonqualifying reorganization, all of the amounts in the trust were to be divided among the participants entitled thereto in amounts governed by each participant's tentative account. Under no circumstances, however, could payments from Kaiser to the trust be recouped by Kaiser: once compensation was paid into the trust it was thereafter committed exclusively to the benefit of Permanente's participating physicians.

Upon the retirement of any partner or eligible nonpartner physician, if he had satisfied each of the requirements for participation, the amount that had accumulated in his tentative account over the years would be applied to the purchase of a retirement income contract. While the program thus provided obvious benefits to Permanente's physicians, it also served Kaiser's interests. By providing attractive deferred benefits for Permanente's staff of professionals, the retirement plan was designed to "create an incentive" for physicians to remain with Permanente and thus "insure" that Kaiser would have a "stable and reliable group of physicians."

During the years from the plan's inception until its discontinuance in 1963, Kaiser paid a total of more than $2,000,000 into the trust. Permanente, however, did not report these payments as income in its partnership returns. Nor did the individual partners include these payments in the computations of their distributive shares of the partnership's taxable income. The Commissioner assessed deficiencies against each partner-respondent for his distributive share of the amount paid by Kaiser. Respondents, after paying the assessments under protest, filed these consolidated suits for refund.

The Commissioner premised his assessment on the conclusion that Kaiser's payments to the trust constituted a form of compensation to the partnership for the services it rendered and therefore was income to the partnership. And, notwithstanding the deflection of those payments to the retirement trust and their current unavailability to the partners, the partners were still taxable on their distributive shares of that compensation. Both the District Court and the Court of Appeals disagreed. They held that the payments to the fund were not income to the partnership because it did not receive them and never had a "right to receive" them. They reasoned that the partnership, as an entity, should be disregarded and that each partner should be treated simply as a potential beneficiary of his tentative share of the retirement fund. Viewed in this light, no presently taxable income could be attributed to these cash basis' taxpayers because of the contingent and forfeitable nature of the fund allocations.

We hold that the courts below erred and that respondents were properly taxable on the partnership's retirement fund income. This conclusion rests on two familiar principles of income taxation, first, that income is taxed to the party who earns it and that liability may not be avoided through an anticipatory assignment of that income, and, second, that partners are taxable on their distributive or proportionate shares of current partnership income irrespective of whether that income is actually distributed to them. The ensuing discussion is simply an application of those principles to the facts of the present case.

II.

Section 703 of the Internal Revenue Code of 1954, insofar as pertinent here, prescribes that "[t]he taxable income of a partnership shall be computed in the same manner as in the case of an individual." § 703(a). Thus, while the partnership itself pays no taxes, § 701, it must report the income it generates and such income must be calculated in largely the same manner as an individual computes his personal income. For this purpose, then, the partnership is regarded as an independently recognizable entity apart from the aggregate of its partners. Once its income is ascertained and reported, its existence may be disregarded since each partner must pay a tax on a portion of the total income as if the partnership were merely an agent or conduit through which the income passed.[8]

---

8. There has been a great deal of discussion in the briefs and in the lower court opinions with respect to whether a partnership is to be viewed as an "entity" or as a "conduit." We find ourselves in agreement with the Solicitor General's remark during oral argument when he suggested that "[i]t seems odd that we should still be discussing such things in 1972." The legislative history indicates, and the commentators agree, that partnerships are entities for purposes of calculating and filling informational returns but that they are conduits through which the taxpaying obligation passes to the individual partners in accord with their distributive shares.

In determining any partner's income, it is first necessary to compute the gross income of the partnership. One of the major sources of gross income, as defined in § 61(a)(1) of the Code, is "compensation for services, including fees, commissions, and similar items." There can be no question that Kaiser's payments to the retirement trust were compensation for services rendered by the partnership under the medical service agreement. These payments constituted an integral part of the employment arrangement. The agreement itself called for two forms of "base compensation" to be paid in exchange for services rendered— direct per-member, per-month payments to the partnership and other, similarly computed, payments to the trust. Nor was the receipt of these payments contingent upon any condition other than continuation of the contractual relationship and the performance of the prescribed medical services. Payments to the trust, much like the direct payments to the partnership, were not forfeitable by the partnership or recoverable by Kaiser upon the happening of any contingency.

Yet the courts below, focusing on the fact that the retirement fund payments were never actually received by the partnership but were contributed directly to the trust, found that the payments were not includable as income in the partnership's returns. The view of tax accountability upon which this conclusion rests is incompatible with a foundational rule, which this Court has described as "the first principle of income taxation: that income must be taxed to him who earns it." The entity earning the income—whether a partnership or an individual taxpayer—cannot avoid taxation by entering into a contractual arrangement whereby that income is diverted to some other person or entity. Such arrangements, known to the tax law as "anticipatory assignments of income," have frequently been held ineffective as means of avoiding tax liability. The seminal precedent, written over 40 years ago, is Mr. Justice Holmes' opinion for a unanimous Court in *Lucas v. Earl,* 281 U.S. 111 (1930). There the taxpayer entered into a contract with his wife whereby she became entitled to one-half of any income he might earn in the future. On the belief that a taxpayer was accountable only for income actually received by him, the husband thereafter reported only half of his income. The Court, unwilling to accept that a reasonable construction of the tax laws permitted such easy deflection of income tax liability, held that the taxpayer was responsible for the entire amount of his income.

* * * The principle of *Lucas v. Earl,* that he who earns income may not avoid taxation through anticipatory arrangements no matter how clever or subtle, has been repeatedly invoked by this Court and stands today as a cornerstone of our graduated income tax system. And, of course, that principle applies with equal force in assessing partnership income.

Permanente's agreement with Kaiser, whereby a portion of the partnership compensation was deflected to the retirement fund, is certainly within the ambit of *Lucas v. Earl.* The partnership earned the income and, as a result of arm's-length bargaining with Kaiser, was responsible for its diversion into the trust fund. The Court of Appeals found the *Lucas* principle inapplicable because Permanente "never had the right itself to receive the payments made into the trust as current income." In support of this assertion, the court relied on language in the agreed statement of facts stipulating that "the payments * * * were paid solely to fund the retirement plan, and were not otherwise available to [Permanente] * * *." Emphasizing that the fund was created to serve Kaiser's interest in a stable source of qualified, experienced physicians, the court found that Permanente could not have received that income except in the form in which it was received.

The court's reasoning seems to be that, before the partnership could be found to have received income, there must be proof that "Permanente agreed to accept less direct compensation from Kaiser in exchange for the retirement plan payments." Apart from the inherent difficulty of adducing such evidence, we know of no authority imposing this burden upon the Government. Nor do we believe that the guiding principle of *Lucas v. Earl* may be so easily circumvented. Kaiser's motives for making payments are irrelevant to the determination whether those amounts may fairly be viewed as compensation for services rendered. Neither does Kaiser's apparent insistence upon payment to the trust deprive the agreed contributions of their character as compensation. The Government need not prove that the taxpayer had complete and unrestricted power to designate the manner and form in which his income is received. We may assume, especially in view of the relatively unfavorable tax status of self-employed persons with respect to the tax treatment of retirement plans, that many partnerships would eagerly accept conditions similar to those prescribed by this trust in consideration for tax-deferral benefits of the sort suggested here. We think it clear, however, that the tax laws permit no such easy road to tax avoidance or deferment. Despite the novelty and ingenuity of this arrangement, Permanente's "base compensation" in the form of payments to a retirement fund was income to the partnership and should have been reported as such.

III.

Since the retirement fund payments should have been reported as income to the partnership, along with other income received from Kaiser, the individual partners should have included their shares of that income in their individual returns. §§ 61(a)(13), 702, 704. For it is axiomatic that each partner must pay taxes on his distributive share of the partnership's income without regard to whether that amount is actually distributed to him. *Heiner v. Mellon,* 304 U.S. 271 (1938), decided under a predecessor to the current partnership provisions of the Code, articulates the salient proposition. After concluding that "distributive" share means the "proportionate" share as determined by the partnership agreement, the Court stated:

"The tax is thus imposed upon the partner's proportionate share of the net income of the partnership, and the fact that it may not be currently distributable, whether by agreement of the parties or by operation of law, is not material."

Few principles of partnership taxation are more firmly established than that no matter the reason for nondistribution each partner must pay taxes on his distributive share. Treas.Reg. § 1.702–1.

The courts below reasoned to the contrary, holding that the partners here were not properly taxable on the amounts contributed to the retirement fund. This view, apparently, was based on the assumption that each partner's distributive share prior to retirement was too contingent and unascertainable to constitute presently recognizable income. It is true that no partner knew with certainty exactly how much he would ultimately receive or whether he would in fact be entitled to receive anything. But the existence of conditions upon the actual receipt by a partner of income fully earned by the partnership is irrelevant in determining the amount of tax due from him. The fact that the courts below placed such emphasis on this factor suggests the basic misapprehension under which they labored in this case. Rather than being viewed as responsible contributors to the partnership's total income, respondent-partners were seen only as contingent beneficiaries of the trust. In some measure, this misplaced focus on the considerations of uncertainty and forfeitability may be a consequence of the erroneous manner in which the Commissioner originally assessed the partners' deficiencies. The Commissioner divided Kaiser's trust fund payments into two categories: (1) payments earmarked for the tentative accounts of *nonpartner* physicians; and (2) those allotted to *partner* physicians. The payments to the trust for the former category of nonpartner physicians were correctly counted as income to the partners in accord with the distributive-share formula as established in the partnership agreement. The latter payments to the tentative accounts of the individual partners, however, were improperly allocated to each partner pursuant to the complex formula in the retirement plan itself, just as if that agreement operated as an amendment to the partnership agreement.

The Solicitor General, alluding to this miscomputation during oral argument, suggested that this error "may be what threw the court below off the track." It should be clear that the contingent and unascertainable nature of each partner's share under the retirement trust is irrelevant to the computation of his distributive share. The partnership had received as income a definite sum which was not subject to diminution or forfeiture. Only its ultimate disposition among the employees and partners remained uncertain. For purposes of income tax computation it made no difference that some partners might have elected not to participate in the retirement program or that, for any number of reasons, they might not ultimately receive any of the trust's benefits. Indeed, as the Government suggests, the result would be quite the same if the "potential beneficiaries included no partners at all, but were children, relatives, or other objects of the partnership's largesse." The sole operative consideration is that the income had been received by the partnership, not what disposition might have been effected once the funds were received.

IV.

In summary, we find this case controlled by familiar and long-settled principles of income and partnership taxation. There being no doubt about the character of the payments as compensation, or about their actual receipt, the partnership was obligated to report them as income presently received. Likewise, each partner was responsible for his distributive share of that income. We, therefore, reverse the judgments and remand the case with directions that judgments be entered for the United States.

It is so ordered.

Problem 8–2

Jack is a chemist who never has owned real estate. Barney subdivides real estate as his primary business activity. They form a partnership. Two years later, the partnership sells one of its real properties at a gain after extensive marketing efforts. What are the tax consequences to the partners?

C. THE ANTI–ABUSE REGULATION

The Service recently published Regulation § 1.701–2 titled "Anti–Abuse Rule." The Regulation is intended to safeguard against the use of Subchapter K for tax avoidance purposes. As issued, the Regulation provides that if a partnership is formed, a principal purpose of which is to reduce substantially the present value of the partners' "aggregate federal tax liability," the Commissioner can recast the transaction.

The Regulation begins with a broad statement of the intent behind Subchapter K, echoing the familiar refrain that Subchapter K is intended to maximize flexibility for those parties wishing to conduct a joint business without incurring tax at the entity level. However, the Regulation is quick to note that implicit behind this congressional purpose are three requirements: (1) the partnership must be bona fide and its activities must possess a "substantial" business purpose; (2) the selected form of its activities must pass muster under the substance over form doctrine; and (3), subject to specified exceptions, the activities of the partnership and its members must reflect the parties' economic agreement and properly reflect income.

The Regulation provides that Subchapter K must be applied consistent with these broad principles. While some would conclude that such warnings are firmly embedded in the judicially conceived doctrines of substance over form and business purpose, the Regulation proceeds to codify these standards by providing that "if a partnership is formed or availed of in connection with a transaction a principal purpose of which is to reduce substantially the present value of the partners' aggregate federal tax liability in a manner that is inconsistent with the intent of

Subchapter K, the Commissioner can recast the transaction for federal tax purposes, as appropriate to achieve tax results that are consistent with the intent of Subchapter K, in light of the applicable statutory and regulatory provisions and the pertinent facts and circumstances." Even though the selected structure of a transaction complies with the literal provisions of Subchapter K, the Service is authorized by the Regulations to determine that:

1. The purported partnership should be disregarded in whole or in part in determining the tax effects of the transaction;

2. One or more of the purported partners should not be treated as a partner;

3. The methods of accounting used by the partnership or a partner should be adjusted to reflect clearly the partnership's or the partner's income;

4. The allocations of the partnership's items of income, gain, loss, deduction, or credit should be disregarded and reallocated; or

5. The intended tax treatment should otherwise be precluded.

The Regulation mandates that the determination of a principal purpose to reduce the partners' overall aggregate tax liability is based on "all the facts and circumstances." It provides the following list of seven factors which, although not exhaustive, are "illustrative" of the factors to be considered:

1. The present value of the partner's aggregate tax liability utilizing a partnership structure is less than it would be if the parties had owned the assets directly and operated in an individual capacity.

2. A similar focus as factor 1, but integrating various steps as a single transaction.

3. A partner necessary to achieve the desired tax results has a nominal interest in the partnership, is insulated from meaningful liability, or has little profit participation other than a preferred return on capital.

4. Substantially all of the partners are related either directly or indirectly.

5. Partnership items which comply literally with provisions of Regulations § 1.704–1 and § 1.704–2 produce results which are inconsistent with their purpose, particularly in light of any partner's tax exempt status or significant tax attributes such as net operating loss carryovers.

6. The benefits and burdens of property nominally contributed to the partnership are substantially retained by the contributor or a related party.

7. The benefits and burdens of property are shifted to a distributee partner before or after the property is distributed.

The Regulations present numerous examples attempting to establish the contours of the anti-abuse doctrine. Reg. § 1.701–2(d) examples (1)–(11). Of the 11 income tax examples in § 1.701–2(d) of the Regulations, eight illustrate situations that are consistent with the purpose of Subchapter K. The three examples which are inconsistent with the mandated proper intention are: example (7) involving a partner with a nominal interest for a temporary period; example (8) involving a plan to duplicate losses through an absence of a § 754 election; and example (11) involving a plan to distort basis allocations artificially under § 732.

The Regulation specifically provides that, in addition to the anti-abuse rule, the Service can continue to apply the familiar judicial principles of substance over form, step transactions, and sham transactions to attack abusive transactions. There are some who believe that the basic purpose of the Regulation is to "codify by Regulation" these doctrines, that the anti-abuse rule adds nothing that could not be accomplished by these principles, and is simply a notification, with its attendant in terrorem effect, of an intent to more aggressively pursue these approaches. However, the clear implication of the Regulation is that it is an additional weapon for the Commissioner to use.

Problem 8–3

Douglas, a wealthy individual, and Houser, Inc. form a limited partnership sharing profits, losses, and capital in a 99%–1% ratio. The primary purpose for selecting the limited partnership vehicle is to maximize protection from personal liability, while avoiding an additional tax at the entity level. Does such an arrangement violate the anti-abuse Regulation?

D. LIMITATION ON CONVERSION OF INCOME CHARACTERIZATION

Given the focus of § 702(b) on the *partnership's* activities with respect to partnership property, the entity could be utilized for conversion of character purposes. Assume that a partner contributes property, characterized as inventory as regards his holding, to a partnership which is not a dealer in such property as determined by the partnership's activities as regards such property. If respected, the partner, by use of the partnership, would have converted ordinary income into § 1231 or capital gain. To safeguard against such abuse, § 724 mandates a continuation of the property's status to the partnership.

Chapter 9

TAXING PARTNERSHIP OPERATIONS—PARTNERSHIP TAXABLE YEAR

Code References: § 706(b).

Regulations: § 1.706–1T(a), (b), and (d).

A. INTRODUCTION

Each business entity taxed as a partnership must have a taxable year. In the past, many such businesses, particularly law firm partnerships, used the selection of their taxable year as a strategic tool for deferring the income of the individual partners. Under current rules and Regulations, little opportunity for deferral remains.

According to § 706(a), a partner's distributive share of partnership income, gain, loss, deduction, or credit shall be included in his gross income "for any taxable year of the partnership ending within or with the taxable year of the partner." As a consequence, if the partnership's taxable year were different from that of its partners, potential tax savings could arise from the benefits of deferring income into a subsequent year. For example, if Steve and Marty, calendar-year taxpayers, were equal partners in a new partnership that selected a fiscal year ending January 31, deferral benefits would arise when they started their operations on February 1 since the income from the first 11 months of their first year would not pass through as income until January 31 of the second year and, therefore, not be taxable to the partners until the end of the second year.

Historically, such a procedural election for the partnership was available. Congress began limiting such possibilities through the enactment of § 706 in the 1954 Code which sought in many cases to bring the tax reporting periods for partners and their partnership into harmony. The Tax Reform Act of 1986 further amended § 706(b)(1) to reduce the deferral of partners' income taxes through the use of a partnership taxable year different from that of the partners. Estimated tax requirements applicable to the individual partners also limit the usefulness of this technique.

B. SELECTION OF TAXABLE YEAR

Section 706(b)(1)(B) establishes priority rules for determining the taxable year of the partnership. First, a partnership must have the same taxable year as the common taxable year (if any) of the partner or partners who have an aggregate interest in the partnership profits and capital greater than 50 percent. Thus, in the typical setting of a partnership with five equal individual members, each of whom has a calendar year, the partnership must select a calendar year. Very few individuals are permitted to use a taxable year other than the calendar year.

Corporations, however, may often have taxable years other than a calendar year. A small business entity taxed as a partnership may have one or more corporations as partners or members. If there is no one partner or combination of partners with the same taxable year who own a majority-in-interest of the partnership, the partnership must adopt the common taxable year of all of the principal partners of the partnership. A principal partner is a person owning an interest of five percent or greater in partnership capital or profits. Like the majority-in-interest requirement, the intent of the principal partner requirement is to conform the partnership taxable year to the same taxable year as that of the partners who own the greatest interest in the partnership and have a common taxable year. For example, if a partnership were formed with a corporate general partner with a fiscal year ending May 31 owning 60 percent of the partnership and 10 calendar-year limited partners owning 4 percent each, the partnership would be required to adopt a taxable year ending May 31 under the majority-in-interest rule. In this situation, deferral of income could occur for the individual partners.

Finally, if the partnership is unable to determine its taxable year by reference to either the majority-in-interest requirement or the principal partner requirement, it must adopt a calendar year or other period as prescribed in Regulations. In this case, the adoption of a calendar year may not be effective in reducing the deferral of the partners' income taxes. Consequently, Regulation § 1.706–1T provides that the partnership taxable year shall be the taxable year of the partner that results in the least aggregate deferral of income to the partners. The Regulations provide detailed guidelines as to how this determination is made. In general, the aggregate deferral for a particular year is the sum of the amounts determined for each partner by multiplying the months of deferral for each partner generated by that year times his interest in profits. The year of the partner which produces the smallest sum will be controlling.

As a practical matter, most small business partnerships will use a calendar year for tax purposes because most are comprised of individual partners who are required to employ a calendar year rather than a fiscal year. The rules of § 706 generally come into play when a partnership is formed which has non-individual partners, e.g. corporations, trusts, or other partnerships, which are more likely to operate on non-calendar years.

Problem 9–1

Fred owns Management, Inc. (MI), a C Corporation, which manages real estate. Its fiscal year ends October 31. Heidi owns Brokerage, Inc. (BI), a C Corporation, which sells commercial real estate. BI's fiscal year ends June 30. Carl manages the parking lots of several buildings which are in turn managed by MI. Carl is a key employee of MI and is a calendar year taxpayer. MI, BI, and Carl form the Realty Services partnership with the following interests in capital and profits: MI and BI each have 48%, Carl has 4%.

    a.   What is the partnership's taxable year?

    b.   Same as a except that BI has a fiscal year ending October 31.

C. BUSINESS PURPOSE EXCEPTION

Notwithstanding the taxable year dictated by § 706(b)(1)(B), under § 706(b)(1)(C) the partnership may use any other taxable year if an acceptable business purpose is established. Many small businesses, particularly retail businesses with a large amount of seasonal sales revenue, may be able to establish that such business purposes exist. Revenue Ruling 87–57, reproduced below, contains examples of circumstances that may or may not constitute valid business purposes. For example, maintaining record-keeping consistency (e.g., fiscal year partnership forced by § 706 onto a calendar year) is not an acceptable purpose, while the adoption of a year reflecting the enterprise's business cycle is a valid business purpose. Because of the deferral benefits of such a period, a business purpose is established only if the nontax reasons for the use of the requested year are compelling.

REVENUE RULING 87–57

1987–2 C.B. 117.

Issue

In the situations described below, has a partnership, an S Corporation, or a personal service corporation established, to the satisfaction of the Secretary, a business purpose for adopting, retaining, or changing its tax year?

Facts

In each of these situations, the taxpayer is a partnership, an S corporation, or a personal service corporation. In addition, in each instance the owners of the taxpayer have tax years that differ from the tax year requested by the taxpayer. The requested tax year is not a "grandfathered fiscal year" within the meaning of section 5.01(2) of Rev.Proc. 87–32, * * *.

Situation 1. The taxpayer desires to use a January 31 tax year. The taxpayer's reason for the requested tax year is that that year corresponds to the natural business year for the taxpayer's type of business as suggested by the Natural Business Year Committee of the American Institute of Certified Public Accountants (AICPA) in an official release published in 100 *Journal of Accountancy* 59 (December 1955). In addition, the taxpayer is using a January 31 fiscal year for financial reporting purposes.

Situation 2. The taxpayer desires to use a September 30 tax year. The taxpayer's reasons for the requested tax year are that the taxpayer's accountant is extremely busy during the first six months of the year and that, if the taxpayer were to have a September 30 tax year, the taxpayer would receive a reduced charge for the accountant's services.

Situation 3. The taxpayer desires to retain its November 30 tax year. The taxpayer's reasons for the requested tax year are that the taxpayer has used a November 30 tax year since the inception of its business 15 years ago and that, if the taxpayer is required to change its tax year, it would lose its recordkeeping consistency and thus would suffer a financial hardship in changing the records to another year.

Situation 4. The taxpayer desires to use a tax year ending September 30. The taxpayer's reason for the requested tax year is that the taxpayer desires to issue timely tax information (for example, Schedules K–1, Form 1065 Partner's Share of Income, Credits, Deductions, Etc.) to its owners to facilitate the filing of timely returns by its owners.

Situation 5. The taxpayer desires to use a November 30 tax year. The taxpayer can establish a natural business year ending on January 31 under section 4.01(1) of Rev.Proc. 87–32. If the taxpayer had not satisfied the natural business year test for January 31, it would have met the natural business year test for November 30.

Situation 6. The taxpayer desires to use a June 30 tax year. The taxpayer's reason for the requested tax year is that it coincides with the taxpayer's natural business year. For this taxpayer, June 30 is not a "natural business year," within the meaning of section 4.01(1) of Rev. Proc. 87–32. This failure to satisfy section 4.01(1) of Rev.Proc. 87–32 is caused by unusual gross receipts figures for several months during the 47–month period (36–month period for requested tax year plus additional 11–month period for comparing requested tax year with other potential tax years) covered by the test. The figures for those months were unusual because a labor strike closed the taxpayer's business during a period that included its normal peak season. The taxpayer has data for the most recent five years demonstrating that the requested tax year would have satisfied the definition of a natural business year within the meaning of section 4.01(1) of Rev.Proc. 87–32, if the strike had not occurred.

Situation 7. The taxpayer desires to use a May 31 tax year. The taxpayer's reason for the requested tax year is that due to weather conditions the business is operational only during the period of September 1 through May 31. For the 10 years it has been in business, the taxpayer has had insignificant gross receipts for the period June 1 through August 31. The facility used by the taxpayer is not used for any other purpose during the three months of insignificant gross receipts. This taxpayer does not have a "natural business year," within the meaning of section 4.01(1) of Rev.Proc. 87–32.

Situation 8. The taxpayer desires to continue to use a March 31 tax year. The taxpayer changed its method of accounting to the accrual method for the tax year ended March 31, 1987. The taxpayer's reason for the requested tax year is that it coincides with the taxpayer's natural business year. For this taxpayer, March 31 is not a "natural business year," within the meaning of section 4.01(1) of Rev.Proc. 87–32. The 25–percent test in section 4.01(1) of Rev.Proc. 87–32 requires the taxpayer to compute the gross receipts on the basis of the method of accounting used to file its return for each year of the test. Therefore, the taxpayer must compute gross receipts on the cash method of accounting for tax years prior to the tax year ended March 31, 1987. The taxpayer has audited financial statements that were prepared on the basis of an accrual method that is acceptable for tax purposes. The taxpayer's gross receipts based on the accrual method would satisfy the 25–percent test for a tax year ending March 31.

Law and Analysis

Section 441(b)(1) of the Internal Revenue Code provides that the term "taxable year" generally means the taxpayer's annual accounting period, if it is a calendar year or a fiscal year. Section 441(c) provides that the term "annual accounting period" means the annual period on the basis of which the taxpayer regularly computes its income in keeping its books. Section 441(d) defines the term "calendar year" as a period of 12 months ending on December 31. Section 441(e) defines the term "fiscal year" as a period of 12 months ending on the last day of any month other than December or a 52–53 week period as described in section 441(f). See also sections 1.441–1 and 1.441–2 of the Income Tax Regulations. * * *

Prior to the Act, Rev.Proc. 74–33, 1974–2 C.B. 489, set forth the factors considered in determining if a "natural business year" existed for purposes of granting a request for a change in accounting period. The Conference Report for the Act, 2 H.R.Rep. No. 99–841 (Conf.Rep.), 99th Cong., 2d Sess. II–319 (1986), states that the conferees intend that any partnership that received permission under the provisions of Rev.Proc. 74–33 to use a fiscal tax year (other than a tax year that resulted in a three-month-or-less deferral of income) will be allowed to continue to use such tax year without obtaining the approval of the Secretary. Similarly, any S corporation that received permission to use a fiscal tax year (other than a tax year that resulted in a three-month-or-less deferral of income) which permission was granted on or after the effective date of Rev.Proc. 74–33 will be allowed to continue to use such tax year without obtaining the approval of the Secretary. *See* Rev.Proc. 87–32, which defines the term "grandfathered fiscal year" to include tax years for which a taxpayer received the permission described in the Conference Report. None of the taxpayers in the factual situations here is requesting to retain a grandfathered fiscal year.

With respect to the establishment of a business purpose for the use of a tax year, the Conference Report states that the Secretary may prescribe tests to be used to establish the existence of a business purpose if, in the discretion of the Secretary, such tests are desirable and expedient towards the efficient administration of the tax laws. Rev. Proc. 87–32 sets forth a mechanical natural business year test and an ownership tax year test that, if either is satisfied, establish, to the satisfaction of the Secretary, a business purpose (as described in sections 441(i), 706(b)(1)(C), and 1378(b)(2)) for a taxpayer to retain, and in limited situations, adopt or change to a tax year.

A taxpayer that cannot satisfy any of the tests set forth in Rev.Proc. 87–32 must establish a business purpose based on consideration of all the facts and circumstances, including the tax consequences. The tax consequences to be considered include: (1) deferring a substantial portion of a taxpayer's income or shifting a substantial portion of a taxpayer's deductions from one year to another to reduce substantially a taxpayer's tax liability; (2) causing a similar deferral or shift in the case of any other person, such as a partner, a beneficiary, or a shareholder in an S corporation; and (3) creating a short period in which there is a substantial net operating loss.

The Conference Report lists various nontax factors that will ordinarily not be sufficient to establish that the business purpose requirement for a particular tax year has been met. These factors are: (1) the use of a particular year for regulatory or financial accounting purposes; (2) the hiring patterns of a particular business—for example, the fact that a firm typically hires staff during certain times of the year; (3) the use of a particular year for administrative purposes, such as the admission or retirement of partners or shareholders, promotion of staff, and compensation or retirement arrangements with staff, partners, or shareholders; and (4) the fact that a particular business involves the use of price lists, a model year, or other items that change on an annual basis.

Both tax factors and nontax factors must be considered for purposes of determining whether a taxpayer has established a business purpose for the requested tax year. In this context, the Conference Report demonstrates the significant weight that must be assigned to tax factors. The four nontax factors that the report identifies as ordinarily insufficient all involve issues of convenience for the taxpayer. Accordingly, if a requested tax year creates deferral or distortion, the taxpayer's nontax factors must demonstrate compelling reasons for the requested tax year.

The taxpayer in each of the eight situations must establish, to the satisfaction of the Secretary, a business purpose for the use of the requested tax year. Each taxpayer has nontax, business reasons for the use of the requested tax year. However, because the requested tax year is different from the tax year of the taxpayer's owners, the taxpayer's use of the requested tax year would inherently create deferral or distortion. Under these circumstances, the taxpayer can establish, to the satisfaction of the Secretary, a business purpose for the requested tax year only if the nontax reasons for the use of that year are compelling.

The taxpayer's reason for the requested tax year in *Situation 1* is that the requested tax year is the natural business year suggested by the Natural Business Year Committee of the AICPA and the taxpayer uses the requested tax year for financial statement purposes. As stated in the Conference Report, the use of a particular year for financial accounting purposes is not sufficient to establish that the business purpose requirement for that year has been met. In addition, the natural business year suggested by the AICPA is not based upon the taxpayer's own facts and circumstances.

In *Situations 2–4,* the taxpayers' reasons for the requested tax years are to take advantage of an accountant's reduced rate (*Situation 2*), to have recordkeeping consistency (*Situation 3*), and to issue timely tax information forms to partners (*Situation 4*). The reasons given in these three situations are ones of convenience to the taxpayers. Although the reasons are not among those specifically enumerated in the Conference Report, they are very similar to the convenience reasons listed there as being insufficient to establish that the business purpose requirement for a requested tax year has been met.

The taxpayer's reason in *Situation 5* is that the requested November 30 tax year would be a natural business year but for the fact that the January 31 year produces a higher percentage under the 25–percent test of Rev.Proc. 87–32. Because a November 30 fiscal year satisfies the 25–percent test and results in less deferral to the shareholders than January 31, the Commissioner, in his discretion, considers it desirable and expedient for the efficient administration of the tax laws for this taxpayer to use November 30 as its tax year. Accordingly, the taxpayer has established a business purpose for using the requested tax year. *See* 2 H.R.Rep. No. 99–841 at II–319.

The taxpayer's reasons in *Situation 6* are that the requested tax year coincides with the taxpayer's natural business year and that, if the strike had not occurred, the requested year would have been a natural business year according to the test set forth in Rev.Proc. 87–32. The taxpayer's failure to establish a natural business year under the 25–percent test is due to unusual circumstances that occurred during the test period and that were beyond the taxpayer's control. The historical data support the taxpayer's contention that, in the absence of these unusual circumstances, the requested year would have qualified as the taxpayer's natural business year. Thus, the Commissioner is satisfied that the taxpayer has established a business purpose for the requested tax year.

The taxpayer's reason in *Situation 7* is that the requested May 31 tax year coincides with the time the taxpayer has closed down operations for the past 10 years. That closing is not within the taxpayer's control. Accordingly, the taxpayer has established a business purpose for using the requested tax year.

The taxpayer's reason in *Situation 8* is that the requested March 31 tax year coincides with the taxpayer's natural business year and that, if the taxpayer had used the accrual method of accounting, the requested year would have been a natural business year according to the test set forth in Rev.Proc. 87–32. The taxpayer has changed its method of accounting to the accrual method. Therefore, it is reasonable for the Commissioner, to allow the taxpayer to use a March 31 tax year if the accrual method, which will be used for all future tax years, would establish a natural business year ending on March 31.

HOLDING

Each taxpayer in *Situations 1–4* has failed to establish, to the satisfaction of the Secretary, a business purpose for the use of its requested tax year. Each taxpayer in *Situations 5–8* has established, to the satisfaction of the Secretary, a business purpose for the use of its requested tax year.

Problem 9–2

The Cannery, a calendar year partnership, desires to change from a calendar year to a fiscal year ending April 30th. The partnership has a canning season which extends from September 1st to April 1st. All partners are calendar year partners. Is the Service likely to grant approval?

Chapter 10

TAXING PARTNERSHIP OPERATIONS—DETERMINING THE PARTNERS' DISTRIBUTIVE SHARES

Code References: §§ 704(b) and (c)(1)(A); 761(c).

Regulations: §§ 1.704–1(a), (b)(1)(i) and (vi), (b)(2)(i)–(iii), (b)(3)(i) and (ii), 1.704–2(b)–(d)(1), (e), (f)(1), (g)(2), (m) example (1)(i)–(iii), 1.704–3(a)(1)–(3), (b)(1)–(2) example (1), (c)(1)–(4) example (1); 1.1245–1(e)(2).

A. INTRODUCTION

One significant advantage of selecting a partnership over a proprietorship, S Corporation, or C Corporation for the operation of a small business is the ability of partners to legally shift among themselves the business income or loss or the items making up such income or loss. While such flexibility generally results only in timing differences which must subsequently be accounted for, it remains an important feature to many small businesses and their owners.

As discussed previously in Chapter 8, a partner's distributive share of partnership operations under § 702 is reported on the partner's personal tax return. Under § 704(a), a partner's distributive share for any taxable year is determined by the partnership agreement which under § 761 includes amendments thereto up to the date required for the filing of the partnership return (usually three and one-half months following the close of the taxable year). This rule allows changes to be made to partner-sharing arrangements after the tax year is complete. If the partnership agreement does not address a particular item or if the allocation provided for in the agreement does not have substantial economic effect, under § 704(b), a partner's distributive share is determined "in accordance with the partner's interest in the partnership" (a facts and circumstances analysis).

As noted, one of the hallmarks of the use of the partnership entity as a small business vehicle is the emphasis on flexibility which is permitted in Subchapter K. Section 704(b) possibly is the provision which most illustrates such treatment. Thereunder, any specific item (income, gain, loss deduction, or credit) can be allocated for a particular year in a fashion different from the other items. Additionally, the item allocation as well as an allocation of overall results (bottom-line profit or loss) can vary on a yearly basis.

B. ASSIGNMENT OF INCOME

A familiar doctrine in the tax area is that statutory enactments are frequently circumscribed by judicial policies. While § 704 affords great latitude to the parties, an overriding consideration is whether allocations made between the partners pursuant to the statute and Regulations are bounded by the assignment of income doctrine. In the case of *Schneer v. Commissioner,* which follows, the Tax Court addresses this issue.

SCHNEER v. COMMISSIONER

97 T.C. 643 (1991).

GERBER, JUDGE.

FINDINGS OF FACT

* * * Petitioners resided at Croton–On–Hudson, New York, at the time the petition was filed in this case. Stephen B. Schneer * * * was a practicing attorney during the years 1983, 1984, and 1985. Until February 25, 1983, petitioner was an associate with the law firm of Ballon, Stoll & Itzler (BSI). BSI was a partnership. Petitioner was not a partner in BSI and he did not share in general partnership profits. Petitioner's financial arrangement with BSI consisted of a fixed or set salary and a percentage of any fees which arose from clients petitioner brought or referred to the firm.

BSI did not have a written partnership agreement, and no written agreement existed in connection with petitioner's relationship as an associate with BSI. When petitioner left BSI he had an understanding that he would continue to receive his percentage of fees which arose from clients he had referred when he was an associate with BSI. Petitioner was expected to consult regarding clients he referred to BSI and whose fees were to be shared by petitioner. Petitioner would have become entitled to his percentage of the fees even if he had not been called upon to consult.

After petitioner left BSI and while he was a partner of two other law partnerships (other than BSI) he consulted on numerous occasions concerning BSI clients. Most of the 1984 and 1985 fees received under this agreement were attributable to Terri Girl and Prince, clients that petitioner had brought to BSI. Neither the remaining BSI attorneys nor petitioner had contemplated whether petitioner would receive the fees if he refused to consult concerning the clients referred by petitioner. For the years under consideration, petitioner consulted with BSI attorneys on each occasion his services were requested. The services provided by petitioner to BSI consisted of legal advice and consultation on legal matters.

Late in February 1983, petitioner became a partner in the law firm of Bandler & Kass (B & K), and on August 1, 1985, petitioner became a partner in the law firm of Sylvor, Schneer, Gold & Morelli (SSG & M). BSI, B & K, SSG & M, and petitioner, at all pertinent times, kept their books and reported their income on the cash method of accounting. Neither B & K nor SSG & M had written partnership agreements. The agreement between the partners of B & K was that each partner would receive a percentage of the partnership profits derived from all fees received beginning the date the partner joined the partnership. In addition, petitioner agreed to turn over to the partnership all legal fees received after joining the partnership, regardless of whether the fees were earned in the partnership's name or from the partnership's contractual relationship with the client. The same agreement existed between the partners of SSG & M, including petitioner.

During 1984 and 1985, BSI remitted $21,329 and $10,585 to petitioner. The amounts represented petitioner's percentage of fees from BSI clients that he had referred to BSI at a time when he was an associate with BSI. With the exception of $1,250 for the 1984 taxable year, all of the fees received during 1984 and 1985 were for work performed after petitioner left BSI. Petitioner, pursuant to his agreements with B & K and SSG & M, turned those accounts over to the appropriate partnership. B & K and SSG & M, in turn, treated the amounts as partnership income which was distributed to each partner (including petitioner) according to the partner's percentage share of partnership profits.

BSI's 1984 records reflect that of the $21,329 total, $944 was attributable to Prince and $17,060 was attributable to Terri Girl. The remainder of the $21,329 remitted for 1984 ($3,325) was attributable to BSI clients for which petitioner had not consulted since leaving BSI during February 1983. The 1985 records of BSI reflect that the entire amount ($10,585) was attributable to Prince. BSI records reflect that billings and fees were made and received from BSI clients at various times during the year, but that petitioner received one annual aggregate payment.

Opinion

We consider here basic principles of income taxation. There is agreement that the amounts paid to petitioner by his former employer-law firm are income in the year of receipt. The question is whether petitioner (individually) or the partners of petitioner's partnerships (including petitioner) should report the income in their respective shares.

The parties have couched the issue in terms of the anticipatory assignment-of-income principles. Equally important to this case, however, is the viability of the principle that partners may pool their earnings and report partnership income in amounts different from their contribution to the pool. See sec. 704(a) and (b). The parties' arguments bring into focus potential conflict between these two principles and compel us to address both.

First, we examine the parties' arguments with respect to the assignment-of-income doctrine. Respondent argues that petitioner earned the income in question before leaving BSI, despite the fact that petitioner did not receive that income until he was a partner in B & K and, later, SSG & M. According to respondent, by entering into partnership agreements requiring payment of all legal fees to his new partnerships, petitioner anticipatorily assigned to those partnerships the income earned but not yet received from BSI. * * *

Petitioner contends that the income in question was not earned until after he left BSI and joined B & K and SSG & M. He argues that the income received from BSI is reportable by the partners of the B & K and SSG & M partnerships (including petitioner) in their respective shares. Petitioner also points out that partnership agreements, which like the ones in issue allocate and redistribute partners' income, have received the approval of respondent in Rev.Rul. 64–90, 1964–1 C.B. (Part 1) 226. Petitioner argues that he was obligated to consult with BSI in order to be entitled to the BSI fees. Petitioner concedes that, for some of the income in question, no consultation was performed or requested. He emphasizes, however, that a substantial amount (about 90 percent) of the fees involved clients of BSI for whom consultation was performed. Finally, petitioner believes that his failure to consult would have resulted in loss of the fees.

The principle of assignment of income, in the context of Federal taxation, first arose in *Lucas v. Earl,* where the Supreme Court, interpreting the Revenue Act of 1918, held that income from a husband-taxpayer's legal practice was taxable to him, even though he and his wife had entered into a valid contract under State law to split all income earned by each of them. In so holding, Justice Holmes, speaking for the Court, stated:

> There is no doubt that the statute could tax salaries to those who earned them and provide that the tax could not be escaped by anticipatory arrangements and contracts however skillfully devised to prevent the salary when paid from vesting even for a second in the man who earned it.

From that pervasive and simply stated interpretation, a plethora of cases and learned studies have sprung forth. * * *

In this case, petitioner was not entitled to the referral fees unless the work for the referred clients had been successfully completed. On the other hand, petitioner would be entitled to the fees if the work was completed or if at the time of the assignment there was nothing contingent in petitioner's right to collect his percentage of the fees. Additionally, the majority of the services had not been performed prior to petitioner's leaving BSI. In this regard services had been performed with respect to $1,250 prior to 1984. With respect to $3,325 of the $21,329 of fees received in 1984, petitioner did not consult and was not required to do anything subsequent to leaving BSI to be entitled to those fees. With respect to the remainder of the $21,329 for 1984 and all of the 1985 fees, petitioner was called upon to and did consult while he was a partner of B & K or SSG & M.

We must decide whether petitioner had earned the fees in question prior to assigning them to the B & K or the SSG & M partnerships. Although petitioner was on the cash method, the principles that control use of the cash method are not suited to this inquiry. For purposes of the assignment-of-income doctrine, it must be determined whether the income was earned prior to an assignment. The principles underlying the cash method do not focus upon when income is earned, the focus is upon when income is actually or constructively received. The accrual method, however, involves a question of when income is earned, rather than when it is received. We accordingly consider the principles underlying the accrual method for the purpose of determining whether petitioner had "earned" the income in question prior to the time he agreed to turn it over to the B & K or SSG & M partnerships * * *.

The transaction under consideration is one where petitioner had an agreement under which he would receive a percentage of fees received by BSI from clients who were referred by petitioner while he was an employee of BSI. Inherent in petitioner's unconditional right to payment is the condition precedent that billable services have been performed for the referred client. Additionally, petitioner's right to payment may also be subject to a second condition precedent that he may be required to consult and be involved in performing the services to be billed. Finally, there is the conditional aspect of payment. If the referred client does not pay for services rendered, then petitioner will not receive his percentage.

The possibility that the client might not pay his obligation once services are performed is insufficient to cause the deferral of income for an accrual method taxpayer. On the other hand, the prerequisite of performance of the services prior to any liability on the part of the obligor is an essential to satisfying the all-events test. The right to receive income cannot become fixed before the obligor has an obligation to pay. Recognition of liability by the obligor is the essence of accrual.

The record in this case reflects that, with the exception of $1,250 of services performed in prior years, the billings and payments in question were performed and collected subsequent to the time of assignment of the income. The requirement that petitioner may have been called upon to consult is part of the contingency relating to the performance of the work prior to liability being established or fixed. The absence of consulting by petitioner is not decisive in the setting of this case.

Additionally, as a corollary to the income principles, under section 461(h) a taxpayer is not entitled to a deduction under the accrual method unless there has been economic performance, i.e., the services have been performed or the property delivered.

With these principles as our guide, we hold that petitioner had not earned the fees in question prior to leaving BSI, with the exception of the $1,250 received for services performed in an earlier year. More specifically, we hold that petitioner earned the income in question while a partner of a partnership to which he had agreed to pay such income. With respect to substantially all of the fees in issue, BSI records reflect that clients were billed and payment received during the years in issue. Moreover, if petitioner had refused a request for his consultation, it was, at very least, questionable whether he would have received his share of the fee if the work had been successfully completed without him. Petitioner was requested to and did provide further services with regard to clients from which about 90 percent of the fees were generated. We note that BSI did not request consultation with respect to $3,325 remitted during 1984. However, that amount was not earned as of the time of the assignment because the work had not yet been performed for the BSI clients (irrespective of whether or not petitioner would be called upon to consult). Accordingly, with the exception of $1,250 for petitioner's 1984 taxable year, we hold that petitioner had not earned the income in question prior to leaving BSI and did not make an anticipatory assignment of income which had been earned.

Two additional related questions remain for our consideration. First, respondent argues that irrespective of when petitioner earned the income from BSI, "there was no relationship * * * [between] the past activity of introducing a client to * * * [BSI], and the petitioner's work as a partner with * * * [B & K or SSG & M]." According to respondent, petitioner should not be allowed to characterize as partnership income fees that did not have a requisite or direct relationship to a partnership's business. In making this argument, respondent attempts to limit and modify his longstanding and judicially approved position in Rev.Rul. 64–90, 1964–1 C.B. (Part 1) 226. Second, while we generally hold that petitioner did not make an assignment of income already earned, the possibility that this was an assignment of unearned income was not foreclosed.

These final two questions bring into focus the true nature of the potential conflict in this case—between respondent's revenue ruling and the assignment-of-income doctrine. Both questions, in their own way, ask whether any partnership agreement—under which partners agree in advance to turn over to the partnership all income from their individual efforts—can survive scrutiny under the assignment-of-income principles.

Rev.Rul. 64–90, 1964–1 C.B. (Part 1) at 226–227, in pertinent part, contains the following:

> Federal income tax treatment of compensation received by a partner and paid over to a partnership where the partner, who uses

the cash receipts and disbursements method of accounting, files his returns on a calendar year basis and the partnership, which also uses the cash method, files its returns on a fiscal year basis.

Advice has been requested regarding the Federal income tax consequences of a change in the terms of a partnership agreement to provide that all compensation received by the partners will be paid over to the partnership immediately upon receipt.

In the instant case, several individuals formed a partnership for the purpose of engaging in the general practice of law. Aside from the partnership business, each of the partners has performed services from time to time in his individual capacity and not as a partner. The several partners have always regarded the fees received for such services as compensation to the recipient as an individual * * *.

In the instant case, the general practice of the partnership consists of rendering legal advice and services. Consequently, fees received by a partner for similar services performed in his individual capacity will be considered as partnership income if paid to the partnership in accordance with the agreement. Those fees need not be reported separately by the partner on his individual return. However, the partner's distributive share of the partnership's taxable income which he must report on his individual return will include a portion of such fees. [Emphasis supplied.]

A key requirement of this ruling is that the services for which fees are received by individual partners must be *similar* to those normally performed by the partnership. Cases dealing with similar partnership agreement situations have also enforced this requirement. Respondent now attempts to add to this requirement by arguing that the fees here in question were earned through activity, which was admittedly legal work, but was not sufficiently related to the work of petitioner's new partnerships. In other words, respondent argues that the income here was earned in BSI's business activity and not B & K's or SSG & M's business activity * * *.

There is no need for us to adopt a broader view of petitioner's partnership in this case. His referral fee income was clearly earned through activities "within the ambit" of the business of his new partnerships. Their business was the practice of law as was petitioner's consulting activity for BSI. His work was incident to the conduct of the business of his partnerships. We decline to adopt respondent's more narrow characterization of the business of petitioner's new partnerships. Neither the case law nor respondent's rulings support such a characterization.

Thus, we arrive at the final question in this case. We have already held that petitioner had not yet earned the majority of the income in question when he joined his new partnerships. Additionally, petitioner's fee income from his BSI clients qualifies, under the case law and respondent's rulings, as income generated by services sufficiently related to the business conducted by petitioner's new partnerships. If we decide that petitioner's partnerships should report the income in question, petitioner would be taxable only to the extent of his respective partnership share. This would allow petitioner, through his partnership agreements with B & K and SSG & M, to assign income not yet earned from BSI. Thus, the case law and respondent's rulings permit (without explanation), in a partnership setting, the type of assignment addressed by *Lucas v. Earl*. We must reconcile the principle behind Rev.Rul. 64–90, 1964–1 C.B. (Part 1) 226, with *Lucas v. Earl*. The question is whether income not yet earned and anticipatorily assigned under certain partnership agreements are without the reach of the assignment-of-income principle.

The Internal Revenue Code of 1954 provided the first comprehensive statutory scheme for the tax treatment of partners and partnerships. No section of the 1954 Code, successive amendments or acts, nor the legislative history specifically addresses the treatment of income earned by partners in their individual capacity but which is pooled with other partnership income. It is implicit in subchapter K, however, that the pooling of income and losses of partners was intended by Congress. This question is more easily answered where the partnership contracts with the client for services which are then performed by the partner. The question becomes more complex where the partner contracts and performs the services when he is a partner.

Moreover, no opinion contains a satisfactory rationale as to why partnership pooling agreements do not come within the holding of *Lucas v. Earl*. Even in *Mayes* and *Hamm* (where the attempted pooling of income was treated as a prohibited assignment of income) it is suggested that in the appropriate circumstances, a partnership agreement that effectuates anticipatory assignments of income should be respected for tax purposes. Indeed, other opinions contain similar holdings.

The fundamental theme penned by Justice Holmes provides that the individual who earns income is liable for the tax. It is obvious that the partnership, as an abstract entity, does not provide the physical and mental activity that facilitates the process of "earning" income. Only a partner can do so. The income earned is turned over to the partnership due solely to a contractual agreement, i.e., an assignment, in advance, of income.

The pooling of income is essential to the meaningful existence of subchapter K. If partners were not able to share profits in an amount disproportionate to the ratio in which they earned the underlying income, the partnership provisions of the Code would, to some extent, be rendered unnecessary.

The provisions of subchapter K tacitly imply that the pooling of income is permissible. Said implication may provide sufficient reason to conclude that a partnership should be treated as an entity for the purpose of pooling the income of its partners. Under an entity approach, the income would be considered that of the partnership rather than the partner, even though the partner's individual efforts may have earned the income. If the partnership is treated as an entity earning the income, then assignment-of-income concepts would not come into play. * * *

The theory concerning partnerships as entities is not easily defined. It is well established that the partnership form is a hybrid—part separate entity, part aggregate. The difficulty lies in deciding whether a particular set of circumstances relate to one end or the other of the partnership hybrid spectrum. The Supreme Court in *Basye* stated that "partnerships are entities for purposes of calculating and filing informational returns but * * * they are conduits through which the taxpaying obligation passes to the individual partners in accord with their distributive shares." This analysis provides some foundation for the idea that partners should report their distributive share, rather than the fruits of their personal labors. But it does not provide any guidance concerning the type of income or service that should be brought within the entity concept as it relates to partnerships.

The principle we must analyze in this case involves the role of the partnership with respect to the function of earning income. A general partnership is "an association of two or more persons to carry on as co-owners a business for profit." Uniform Partnership Act sec. 6(1). Either a partnership or a corporation may enter into a contract with clients to perform services. In a partnership, however, either the entity or the individual may enter into contracts. The question we seek to answer is whether this distinction should be treated differently.

For purposes of an entity concept approach to partnerships, we must consider the type and source of income which should be included. Because we have already determined that the type of activity generating the income is relevant to an assignment-of-income analysis in the partnership setting, we focus our analysis of partnerships as entities on situations where the income is of a type normally earned by the partnership. Only in such situations has a partner acted as part of the partnership entity.

The entity concept as it relates to partnerships is based, in part, on the concept that a partner may further the business of the partnership by performing services in the name of the partnership or individually. The name and reputation of a professional partnership plays a role in the financial success of the partnership business. If the partners perform services in the name of the partnership or individually they are, nonetheless, associated with the partnership as a partner. This is the very essence of a professional service partnership, because each partner, although acting individually, is furthering the business of the partnership. * * *

The lack of structure inherent in the partnership form does not lend itself to easy resolution of the assignment-of-income question. A partnership's characteristics do, however, militate in favor of treating a partner's income from services performed in an individual capacity, which are contractually obligated to the partnership for allocation in accord with the preestablished distributive shares, in the same manner as income earned through partnership engagement.

Accordingly, in circumstances where individuals are not joining in a venture merely to avoid the effect of *Lucas v. Earl,* it is appropriate to treat income earned by partners individually, as income earned by the partnership entity, i.e., partnership income, to be allocated to partners in their respective shares. To provide the essential continuity necessary for the use of an entity concept in the partnership setting, the income should be earned from an activity which can reasonably be associated with the partnership's business activity. In the setting of this case, with the exception of $1,250 in 1984, petitioner was a partner of B & K or SSG & M when the fees were earned. Additionally, about 90 percent of the fees were, in part, earned through petitioner's efforts while he was a partner of B & K or SSG & M.

There is no apparent attempt to avoid the incidence of tax by the formation or operation of the partnerships in this case. Petitioner, in performing legal work for clients of another firm, was a partner with the law firms of B & K and SSG & M. In view of the foregoing, we hold that, with the exception of $1,250 for 1984, the fee income from BSI was correctly returned by the two partnerships in accord with the respective partnership agreements. * * *

Decision will be entered under Rule 155.

C. SPECIAL ALLOCATIONS

The flexibility of § 704 in shifting partnership items between the partners is subject to the limitation that the allocation must possess substantial economic effect. In essence, the statutory standard seeks to match tax effects with economic effects and thus requires economic benefit in return for the allocation of a tax gain and economic burden in return for the allocation of a tax loss. The Regulations stipulate in detailed fashion various requirements for meeting the economic effect test *and* the substantiality test.

For the economic effect test, the Regulations mandate that the partnership maintain capital accounts which reflect the allocations, that liquidation rights be governed by the capital accounts, and that, if any capital account has a deficit balance, the partner is obligated to return that amount to the partnership. Through these accounting and legal requirements, the partner receiving a tax allocation also will bear its financial benefit or burden.

For example, assume that Alan and Beverly form a partnership with a $10 cash contribution by each. Accordingly, each has a beginning capital account balance of $10. If the partnership experiences a $10 loss for the year and the partners agree that it is to be allocated exclusively to Beverly, the allocation should possess economic effect if it is reflected in the capital accounts because Beverly's capital account will be reduced to $0. If there is a liquidation of the partnership and the partnership agreement mandates liquidation in accordance with capital accounts, as it must if the initial allocation is to be recognized, then Alan will take the $10 and Beverly will receive nothing since only $10 is left in the partnership after the loss. Beverly's entitlement to the extra $5 of deductions costs her $5 in liquidation proceeds and this offset is the essence of "economic effect."

If the partnership is not liquidated and in the second year of partnership operations incurs another $10 loss which is allocated to Beverly, Beverly will have a $10 deficit capital account while Alan will have a $10 positive account. The partnership would now have no assets and upon liquidation would have nothing to distribute. However, provided a deficit payback agreement exists, as it must in order for the allocation to be recognized, Beverly will be required to contribute an additional $10 to the partnership as part of its liquidation, thereby bringing her capital account to $0. The contributed funds will then be distributed to Alan on liquidation in satisfaction of his positive capital account balance. Again, Beverly will have paid a net amount of $10 for the extra $10 of deductions. If a deficit payback provision were missing, such would not be the case, and the original special allocation would not be respected by the Service. It should be noted that a $1 tax deduction is never worth $1, since it yields only a cash saving equal to the deducting partner's tax rate. Thus, disregarding the time value of money, the economic effect requirement often means that the payback for the special allocation is greater than the original benefit received.

Even if an allocation possesses economic effect, it will not be respected for § 704(b) purposes unless it meets the substantiality requirement as well. The allocation must affect "substantially" the dollar amounts to be received by the partners from the partnership. An allocation will not meet this test if it is a shifting allocation (offsetting allocations within a single year), a transitory allocation (offsetting allocations over a number of years), or one under which all parties benefit.

With regard to shifting and transitory allocations, the focus of the Regulations is on whether the effects on the capital accounts are similar but the overall tax liabilities of the partners are reduced. For example, assume a partnership had a $100 § 1231 loss and a $100 ordinary loss. Alice in her personal capacity had a $100 § 1231 gain and Bates did not. An allocation of the § 1231 loss to Bates and the ordinary loss to Alice would be shifting allocations. The decreases in the capital accounts of both partners would be similar (i.e., $100) but the overall tax results of the parties would be reduced compared to the results that would arise if the partnership items were allocated on an equal basis. This is so because Alice could report the entire § 1231 gain as capital gain whereas, if there were no special allocation, she would have to offset it with her share of the § 1231 loss.

With regard to the more general overriding facts and circumstances test, if the allocation is of disparate amounts to the capital accounts but the overall tax liabilities of the partners are reduced (e.g., an allocation of tax exempt income to one partner and a disparate amount of ordinary income to the other partner who has expiring net operating losses), the allocation also fails the substantiality test.

Should an allocation fail either test (economic effect or substantiality), the allocation will be reallocated according to the partners' "interests in the partnership." While the standard for defining that term employs a facts and circumstances analysis, the Regulations emphasize as relevant to such a determination the partners' shares of partnership contributions, rights to cash flow, liquidation rights, and *economic* profit and loss allocations. In some small business partnerships, this might be an easy task. However, in those where the sharing of capital, profits, and losses is in disparate proportions, it is not.

ORRISCH v. COMMISSIONER

55 T.C. 395 (1970).

FEATHERSTONE, JUDGE.

* * * The principal purpose of the special allocation to petitioners of all of the deductions for depreciation taken by the Orrisch–Crisafi partnership for 1966 and 1967 was the avoidance of income tax.

OPINION

The only issue presented for decision is whether tax effect can be given the agreement between petitioners and the Crisafis that, beginning with 1966, all the partnership's depreciation deductions were to be allocated to petitioners for their use in computing their individual income tax liabilities. In our view, the answer must be in the negative, and the amounts of each of the partners' deductions for the depreciation of partnership property must be determined in accordance with the ratio used generally in computing their distributive shares of the partnership's profits and losses.

Among the important innovations of the 1954 Code are limited provisions for flexibility in arrangements for the sharing of income, losses, and deductions arising from business activities conducted through partnerships. The authority for special allocations of such items appears in section 704(a), which provides that a partner's share of any item of income, gain, loss, deduction, or credit shall be determined by the partnership agreement. That rule is coupled with a limitation in section 704(b), however, which states that a special allocation of an item will be disregarded if its "principal purpose" is the avoidance or evasion of Federal income tax. In case a special allocation is disregarded, the partner's share of the item is to be determined in accordance with the ratio by which the partners divide the general profits or losses of the partnership.

The report of the Senate Committee on Finance accompanying the bill finally enacted as the 1954 Code (S.Rept. No. 1622, to accompany

H.R. 8300 (Pub.L. No. 591), 83d Cong., 2d Sess., p. 379 (1954)) explained the tax-avoidance restriction prescribed by section 704(b) as follows:

> Subsection (b) * * * provides that if the principal purpose of any provision in the partnership agreement dealing with a partner's distributive share of a particular item is to avoid or evade the Federal income tax, the partner's distributive share of that item shall be redetermined in accordance with his distributive share of partnership income or loss described in section 702(a)(9) [i.e., the ratio used by the partners for dividing general profits or losses] * * *.

> Where, however, a provision in a partnership agreement for a special allocation of certain items has substantial economic effect and is not merely a device for reducing the taxes of certain partners without actually affecting their shares of partnership income, then such a provision will be recognized for tax purposes * * *.

This reference to "substantial economic effect" did not appear in the House Ways and Means Committee report (H.Rept. No. 1337, to accompany H.R. 8300 (Pub.L. No. 591), 83d Cong., 2d Sess., p. A223 (1954)) discussing section 704(b), and was apparently added in the Senate Finance Committee to allay fears that special allocations of income or deductions would be denied effect in every case where the allocation resulted in a reduction in the income tax liabilities of one or more of the partners. The statement is an affirmation that special allocations are ordinarily to be recognized if they have business validity apart from their tax consequences.

In resolving the question whether the principal purpose of a provision in a partnership agreement is the avoidance or evasion of Federal income tax, all the facts and circumstances in relation to the provision must be taken into account. Section 1.704–1(b)(2), Income Tax Regs., lists the following as relevant circumstances to be considered:

> Whether the partnership or a partner individually has a business purpose for the allocation; whether the allocation has "substantial economic effect", that is, whether the allocation may actually affect the dollar amount of the partners' shares of the total partnership income or loss independently of tax consequences; whether related items of income, gain, loss, deduction, or credit from the same source are subject to the same allocation; whether the allocation was made without recognition of normal business factors and only after the amount of the specially allocated item could reasonably be estimated; the duration of the allocation; and the overall tax consequences of the allocation * * *.

Applying these standards, we do not think the special allocation of depreciation in the present case can be given effect.

The evidence is persuasive that the special allocation of depreciation was adopted for a tax-avoidance rather than a business purpose. Depreciation was the only item which was adjusted by the parties; both the income from the buildings and the expenses incurred in their operation, maintenance, and repair were allocated to the partners equally. Since the deduction for depreciation does not vary from year to year with the fortunes of the business, the parties obviously knew what the tax effect of the special allocation would be at the time they adopted it. Furthermore, as shown by our Findings, petitioners had large amounts of income which would be offset by the additional deduction for depreciation; the Crisafis, in contrast, had no taxable income from which to subtract the partnership depreciation deductions, and, due to depreciation deductions which they were obtaining with respect to other housing projects, could expect to have no taxable income in the near future. On the other hand, the insulation of the Crisafis from at least part of a potential capital gains tax was an obvious tax advantage. The inference is unmistakably clear that the agreement did not reflect normal business considerations but was designed primarily to minimize the overall tax liabilities of the partners.

Petitioners urge that the special allocation of the depreciation deduction was adopted in order to equalize the capital accounts of the partners, correcting a disparity ($14,000) in the amounts initially contributed to the partnership by them ($26,500) and the Crisafis ($12,500). But the evidence does not support this contention. Under the special allocation agreement, petitioners were to be entitled, in computing their individual income tax liabilities, to deduct the full amount of the depreciation realized on the partnership property. For 1966, as an example, petitioners were allocated a sum ($18,904) equal to the depreciation on the partnership property ($18,412) plus one-half of the net loss computed without regard to depreciation ($492). The other one-half of the net loss was, of course, allocated to the Crisafis. Petitioners' allocation ($18,904) was then applied to reduce their capital account. The depreciation specially allocated to petitioners ($18,412) in 1966 alone exceeded the amount of the disparity in the contributions. Indeed, at the end of 1967, petitioners' capital account showed a deficit of $25,187.11 compared with a positive balance of $105.65 in the Crisafis' account. By the time the partnership's properties are fully depreciated, the amount of the reduction in petitioners' capital account will approximate the remaining basis for the buildings as of the end of 1967. The Crisafis' capital account will be adjusted only for contributions, withdrawals, gain or loss, without regard to depreciation, and similar adjustments for these factors will also be made in petitioners' capital account. Thus, rather than correcting an imbalance in the capital accounts of the partners, the special allocation of depreciation will create a vastly greater imbalance than existed at the end of 1966. In the light of these facts, we find it incredible that equalization of the capital accounts was the objective of the special allocation.

Petitioners rely primarily on the argument that the allocation has "substantial economic effect" in that it is reflected in the capital accounts of the partners. Referring to the material quoted above from the report of the Senate Committee on Finance, they contend that this alone is sufficient to show that the special allocation served a business rather than a tax-avoidance purpose.

According to the regulations, an allocation has economic effect if it "may actually affect the dollar amount of the partners' shares of the total partnership income or loss independently of tax consequences." The agreement in this case provided not only for the allocation of depreciation to petitioners but also for gain on the sale of the partnership property to be "charged back" to them. The charge back would cause the gain, for tax purposes, to be allocated on the books entirely to petitioners to the extent of the special allocation of depreciation, and their capital account would be correspondingly increased. The remainder of the gain, if any, would be shared equally by the partners. If the gain on the sale were to equal or exceed the depreciation specially allocated to petitioners, the increase in their capital account caused by the charge back would exactly equal the depreciation deductions previously allowed to them and the proceeds of the sale of the property would be divided equally. In such circumstances, the only effect of the allocation would be a trade of tax consequences, i.e., the Crisafis would relinquish a current depreciation deduction in exchange for exoneration from all or part of the capital gains tax when the property is sold, and petitioners would enjoy a larger current depreciation deduction but would assume a larger ultimate capital gains tax liability. Quite clearly, if the property is sold at a gain, the special allocation will affect only the tax liabilities of the partners and will have no other economic effect.

To find any economic effect of the special allocation agreement aside from its tax consequences, we must, therefore, look to see who is to bear the economic burden of the depreciation if the buildings should be sold for a sum less than their original cost. There is not one syllable of evidence bearing directly on this crucial point. We have noted, however, that when the buildings are fully depreciated, petitioners' capital account will have a deficit, or there will be a disparity in the capital accounts, approximately equal to the undepreciated basis of the buildings as of the beginning of 1966. Under normal accounting procedures, if the building were sold at a gain less than the amount of such disparity petitioners would either be required to contribute to the partnership a sum equal to the remaining deficit in their capital account after the gain on the sale had been added back or would be entitled to receive a proportionately smaller share of the partnership assets on liquidation. Based on the record as a whole, we do not think the partners ever agreed to such an arrangement. On dissolution, we think the partners contemplated an equal division of the partnership assets which would be adjusted only for disparities in cash contributions or withdrawals. Certainly there is no evidence to show otherwise. That being true, the special allocation does not "actually affect the dollar amount of the partners' share of the total partnership income or loss independently of tax consequences" within the meaning of the regulation referred to above.

Our interpretation of the partnership agreement is supported by an analysis of a somewhat similar agreement, quoted in material part in our

Findings, which petitioners made as part of a marital property settlement agreement in 1968. Under this agreement, Orrisch was entitled to deduct all the depreciation for 1968 in computing his income tax liability, and his wife was to deduct none; but on the sale of the property they were to first reimburse Orrisch for "such moneys as he may have advanced," and then divide the balance of the "profits or proceeds" of the sale equally, each party to report one-half of the capital gain or loss on his income tax return. In the 1969 amendment to this agreement the unequal allocation of the depreciation deduction was discontinued, and a provision similar to the partnership "charge back" was added, i.e., while the proceeds of the sale were to be divided equally, only Orrisch's basis was to be reduced by the depreciation allowed for 1968 so that he would pay taxes on a larger portion of the gain realized on the sale. Significantly, in both this agreement and the partnership agreement, as we interpret it, each party's share of the sales proceeds was determined independently from his share of the depreciation deduction.

In the light of all the evidence we have found as an ultimate fact that the "principal purpose" of the special allocation agreement was tax avoidance within the meaning of section 704(b). Accordingly, the deduction for depreciation for 1966 and 1967 must be allocated between the parties in the same manner as other deductions.

Decision will be entered for the respondent.

GOLDFINE v. COMMISSIONER

80 T.C. 843 (1983).

PARKER, JUDGE.

* * * Blackard and Goldfine entered into a joint venture to own and operate an apartment complex. Each contributed one-half of the initial capital. Under the terms of their agreement, each was to share equally the proceeds of the sale of the joint venture assets, and any net proceeds on liquidation. Each actually shared equally certain cash distributions representing proceeds from refinanced loans. Each was equally liable for cash losses (i.e., any losses computed without depreciation). However, the joint venture agreement allocated to Goldfine all of the depreciation deductions, and allocated to Blackard all of the net income computed without depreciation. We must decide whether the principal purpose of these allocations was the avoidance or evasion of income taxes.

Partners must report as income their distributive shares of partnership income. Sec. 702(a). Section 704 grants partners great latitude in determining themselves by their partnership agreement what their distributive shares will be. Normally, a partner's distributive share of income, gain, loss, deduction, or credit will be determined by the terms of the partnership agreement. Sec. 704(a). However, section 704(b) imposes certain limitations upon the partners' right to fix their distributive share. For pre–1976 taxable years, those limitations were phrased in terms of a tax-avoidance test, namely, that allocations of an "item" of income, gain, loss, deduction, or credit would be disregarded if the principal purpose of the allocation was avoidance or evasion of tax (sec. 704(b)(2)). That tax-avoidance test did not differ significantly from the "substantial economic effect" test that was adopted in 1976. And both before and after 1976, an allocation of bottom line income or loss (sec. 704(a)(9) before 1976) must likewise have economic substance in the sense that it reflects the *actual* division of income or loss among the partners when viewed from the standpoint of economic, rather than tax, consequences.

In a pre–1976 situation, as here, under the express language of section 704(b) "a partner's distributive share of any item of income is determined in accordance with his distributive share of taxable income or loss unless the partnership agreement provides special allocations, in which case the allocations are effective for Federal tax purposes unless the principal purpose of the allocation is the avoidance or evasion of income tax." If the special allocation is disregarded, the partners' shares of the item are determined in accordance with the ratio by which the partners, themselves, divide the general profits and losses of the partnership.

* * * The most important of these tests, and the sole test after 1976 is "substantial economic effect," by which we look to see that the partner to whom the item is specially allocated for tax purposes also bears the economic burdens and benefits of that specially allocated item. If a partner's allocation of an item of income or deduction is reflected in his capital account and if the liquidation proceeds of the entity are distributed in accordance with the capital account balances, the allocation has substantial economic effect. Moreover, where a partner's capital account registers a deficit, he must have the obligation upon liquidation to restore that deficit. Absent such an obligation, the other partner or partners would have to bear part of the economic cost of the special allocations that resulted in the deficit capital account. We will apply the above "capital accounts analysis" to the facts of the instant case.

It is apparent that the allocation of depreciation to Goldfine lacks substantial economic effect. While the special allocation is reflected in Goldfine's capital account, the partnership agreement does not provide that the partners are liable to restore deficits in their capital accounts. Petitioners argue that the Illinois Uniform Partnership Act imposes such an obligation upon the partners. We do not believe that the Uniform Partnership Act makes any express provision for such restoration, but we need not address petitioners' argument. Even assuming that Goldfine must restore his deficit, it is clear from the partnership agreement that the assets on dissolution are not to be distributed on the basis of the balances in the partners' capital accounts. Rather, upon liquidation, the partnership agreement plainly calls for an equal division of the net proceeds. The agreement, drafted by Goldfine himself, expressly provided that upon sale of the assets "the gain shall be divided equally between the parties hereto, meaning sales price less mortgage balance due, taxes, and costs of the sale and then equally sharing the net proceeds of the sale." Similarly, the agreement expressly provided for equal division of the net proceeds in the event of termination, defining net proceeds as "the sales or agreed appraised price, less the mortgage indebtedness and taxes." Thus, under the "capital accounts analysis," Goldfine does not bear the economic burden of the depreciation deductions allocated to him.

However, petitioners argue that the allocation nonetheless has substantial economic effect because in fact Goldfine would actually have borne any losses that might have resulted. Petitioners argue that since Blackard was insolvent at the time of the agreement, Goldfine's guarantee of Blackard's indebtedness upon Yorkshire made certain that Goldfine, alone, would actually pay any loss. We disagree. The record is inadequate to support a finding that Blackard was in fact insolvent at the time the parties executed their agreement. Moreover, petitioners' argument ignores Richard's guarantee of one of the five promissory notes. We conclude that the special allocation of depreciation to Goldfine lacked substantial economic effect. * * *

In light of the lack of substantial economic effect, the lack of business purpose or business validity apart from the tax consequences, the fact of Goldfine's actual knowledge of the amounts of depreciation deductions that would be allocated to him over the 10–year period, and the fact of Goldfine's express admission that without the allocation of depreciation deductions he would not have entered into the agreement, we conclude that the principal purpose of the special allocation of depreciation deductions to Goldfine was the avoidance or evasion of income taxes.

The joint venture agreement also allocated to Blackard all of Black–Gold's net income computed without depreciation. * * *

Accordingly, we are free to apply the factors in section 1.704–1(b), Income Tax Regs., quoted above, to determine whether the special allocations to Blackard were made principally for tax-avoidance purposes. These allocations were made subject to normal business risks and their amounts were not subject to reasonable estimation. The allocations to Blackard of net cash flow, and net income without depreciation, were dependent solely upon Black–Gold's success. The fluctuations in net income without depreciation reported by Blackard, and cash distributions (including management fees) to Blackard between 1971 and 1979, demonstrate that these amounts could not be reasonably estimated at the outset of the venture. Blackard apparently wanted the positive cash flow to service its other debts, and this factor could perhaps indicate a business purpose on the part of one of the partners, independent of that partner's tax concerns. However, these are only three of the several factors we must consider in determining whether the principal purpose of the allocations was tax avoidance.

As indicated above, however, the crucial factor is whether allocations have "substantial economic effect." It is here that the allocations to

Blackard must fail. Although the allocations and distributions to Blackard are reflected in its capital account, the partnership agreement expressly provides that the net proceeds on liquidation are to be divided equally between Blackard and Goldfine, not on the basis of their capital account balances. During Black–Gold's 1972 tax year, Blackard withdrew funds representing Black–Gold's cash flow in the amount of $6,502, while it was charged with $22,150 in net income. During Black–Gold's 1973 tax year, Blackard withdrew $8,092 representing Black–Gold's cash flow while being charged with net income of $11,881. Thus, in both years, the amount of Black–Gold's cash flow distributed to Blackard did not equal the total amount of income that was charged to and reported by Blackard. Equal distributions to Blackard and Goldfine of net liquidation proceeds would result in Goldfine's receiving profits charged and taxed to Blackard. Likewise, after reallocating back to Blackard its distributive share of the partnership depreciation deductions improperly allocated to Goldfine, an equal distribution of the net liquidation proceeds to Blackard and Goldfine might not restore to Blackard all of the items charged to its capital account. In either case, the special allocations do not affect the partners' actual division of profits and losses, and therefore lack substantial economic effect.

Finally, the overall tax consequences to Blackard and Goldfine also indicate a tax-avoidance purpose. Blackard was allocated "net income" upon which Blackard paid no taxes because it was offset against Blackard's net operating losses from its other operations. Goldfine reported large depreciation losses which offset large portions of his income from his law practice otherwise subject to tax at a 50–percent marginal rate. Thus, the actual tax effect of the allocations, if permitted, would be to minimize the parties' overall tax burdens. After weighing all the facts, we conclude that the principal purpose of the allocations to Blackard, as with the special allocation to Goldfine, was the avoidance or evasion of income taxes.

* * * As discussed above, the allocations to Blackard have no real effect on the actual manner in which the partners divided Black–Gold's profits and losses. Accordingly, we conclude that the allocation to Blackard was not bona fide because it did not affect the actual economic rights and obligations of the partners and did not reflect the *actual* division of income or loss between the partners when viewed from the standpoint of economic, rather than tax, consequences.

Finally, having invalidated for tax purposes the special allocation of depreciation to petitioner and the allocations to Blackard, we should consider the proper distributive share upon which Goldfine is taxable. Each partner contributed an equal amount of capital and, under the agreement, each was to share equally in net proceeds from the sale of partnership assets and in the net proceeds from liquidation of the partnership. Moreover, each shared equally any "real" cash losses (i.e., losses computed without depreciation). In his notice of deficiency, respondent determined that Goldfine's distributive share of each partnership item was 50 percent, and the record is insufficient to establish that Goldfine's distributive share is other than 50 percent. However, the partnership agreement entitled Blackard to all of the cash flow distributions and Blackard actually received those cash distributions. And it is not clear whether or not respondent took this factor into account in determining Goldfine's distributive share.[18] The parties may wish to consider this matter and may be able to attend to it in the computation under Rule 155 if that can be done without the necessity of reopening the record.

To reflect the parties' concessions and the foregoing,

Decision will be entered under Rule 155.

Problem 10–1

Quentin and Ralph form a partnership which will operate a bicycle shop. Each partner contributes $30,000. During its first year of operation, the partnership loses $10,000. The partners agree that the loss should be allocated to Ralph. What requirements must be met for the allocation to have substantial economic effect? What are the tax and capital account effects of the allocation? What "cost" does Ralph pay for receiving the special allocation?

18. The treatment of cash flow special allocations is unsettled, and we express no view on the matter. We have found no cases directly dealing with the question, and the commentators are divided. Willis suggests that distributions of cash flow, even as a special allocation, should be governed by sec. 731, so that such cash flow distributions are taxable only to the extent they exceed the distributee partner's basis. 2 A. Willis, J. Pennell & P. Postlewaite, Partnership Taxation, sec. 82.16, at 82–40 to 82–43 (3d ed. 1982). Others suggest that where the cash flow allocations are not reflected in partner capital accounts upon which liquidation proceeds are to be distributed, the cash flow distributions may be— (1) taxable to the distributee partner under sec. 707(a) or 707(c); (2) a special allocation of gross receipts taxable as part of the distributive share under sec. 702 (with a commensurate reduction in basis under sec. 731 for the cash distribution); or (3) taxable as a "capital shift from the other partners." W. McKee, W. Nelson & R. Whitmire, Federal Taxation of Partnerships and Partners, pars. 10.07[2], 10.07[3], at 10–51 to 10–53; Solomon, "Current Planning for Partnership Start-up, Including Special Allocations, Retroactive Allocations and Guaranteed Payments," 37 N.Y.U.Tax.Inst., sec. 13.03[4], at 13–37 to 13–38 (1979).

Blackard is not a party to this litigation, but the tax treatment to it of the cash flow allocation and distributions would logically and consistently affect the manner in which those distributions should be considered in determining Goldfine's distributive share. If the cash flow distributions are treated solely under sec. 731, and thus not independently taxable, determining Goldfine's distributive share at 50 percent may result in unequal treatment for so-called equal partners—Blackard and Goldfine will have shared equally (1) bottom line taxable income and loss, (2) loan refinancing distributions, (3) asset sale distributions, and (4) liquidation distributions, but Blackard will have received all of the cash flow distributions while Goldfine will have received nothing in return. One way to equalize their positions might be to give Goldfine an additional amount of Black–Gold's bottom line losses in an amount equal to Blackard's cash flow distributions, and then to divide the remaining taxable loss equally between Blackard and Goldfine. Thus, their hypothetical capital accounts would be reduced by equal amounts, maintaining their equal partnership. On the other hand, if the cash flow distributions are independently taxable to Blackard, as McKee and Solomon suggest, then there is no need to give Goldfine an additional amount of Black–Gold's bottom line loss since a determination of 50–percent distributive shares will maintain equality between the equal partners. The record does not indicate whether the cash flow distributions were taxed to Blackard independently of secs. 702 and 731. The record is singularly devoid of any information as to the tax treatment of Blackard.

Problem 10–2

Jerry and Sarah form the Realty Co. partnership with cash contributions of $50,000 each. Each partner has a one-half interest in the capital, profits, and losses. The partnership purchases an apartment building and attendant personal property for $100,000 on January 1, 1997. Jerry wishes to shelter income from nonpartnership activities, so the partnership agreement allocates to him the entire depreciation deduction of $5,000 per year. The partners agree to reflect the depreciation allocation by appropriately adjusting capital accounts and to distribute proceeds on liquidation in accordance with capital account balances. Assume that expenses other than depreciation exactly equal income. What cash would be distributed to the partners on January 1, 2000 if the property is sold alternatively for $85,000, $100,000, and $70,000 and the partnership subsequently liquidated? Does the allocation possess substantial economic effect?

Problem 10–3

What result if Tom and David form an equal general partnership each contributing $5,000? The partnership borrows $90,000 on a recourse basis and purchases a building for $100,000 in 1997. Assuming the depreciation expense is $5,000 per year and the parties agree that all depreciation will be allocated to Tom, what are their capital accounts in 2000? What are their tax bases? What results if the building is sold alternatively for $85,000, $100,000, and $70,000 to a purchaser and thereafter the partnership satisfies the liability?

Problem 10–4

John and Beth enter into a partnership agreement on January 1, 1997. John contributes $25,000 cash and agrees to devote his full-time services to the partnership. Beth contributes $500,000 cash. The partnership agreement possesses economic effect, i.e., capital accounts, liquidation rights, and deficit payback. The agreement also provides that all deductions and taxable loss will be allocated to Beth until there is net taxable income and then Beth will be allocated an amount of income equal to her prior allocated losses. Thereafter, all taxable income or loss will be allocated equally. Determine the substantiality of the partnership allocation agreement under the following circumstances:

a. The partnership is formed for wildcat oil drilling of a particular piece of property.

b. The partnership is formed to acquire and lease machinery. Because of the nature of the machinery and its depreciable life, there is a strong likelihood at the time of formation that Beth's allocations will be completely offset by December 31, 2001.

c. In b, assume that the allocations are not expected to be completely offset until December 31, 2007.

Problem 10–5

What result in Problem 10–2 where the property is sold alternatively for $85,000, $100,000, and $70,000, if Jerry and Sarah agree that any gain (to the extent of prior depreciation allocations) arising on the disposition of the property will be charged to Jerry? Does the original allocation and charge-back allocation have economic effect? Are they substantial?

D. ALLOCATIONS OF ITEMS LACKING ECONOMIC EFFECT

While most tax allocations are susceptible of compliance with the § 704(b) requirements, some items are pure tax items—credits, depreciation recapture, tax preference items, and deductions attributable to nonrecourse financing—incapable of possessing economic effect. For example, if Ruth and Philip contribute $10 each to a partnership which purchases an asset for $20 and thereby generates a $2 credit (such as a low income housing credit), the partner's capital accounts will remain at $10 each regardless of how the credit is allocated. Credits are government subsidies that do not affect capital accounts. Nevertheless, the § 704(b) Regulations will deem allocations of such items to be in compliance with a partner's interest in the partnership if specified standards of the Regulations for such an allocation are met. Often the controlling standard employs a "piggyback" approach permitting an allocation of that item if it follows an underlying allocation which is itself susceptible of, and possesses, economic effect.

An important example of this concept involves nonrecourse deductions. Nonrecourse deductions are those deductions or expenditures that are attributable to nonrecourse liabilities of the partnership. Nonrecourse liabilities of a partnership are those for which neither the partnership nor any partner is liable beyond the value of the property securing the liability and thus for which no partner bears the economic risk of loss. Nonrecourse deductions may arise in the small business context, particularly in connection with real estate owned by the business. The allocation of nonrecourse deductions among the partners cannot have economic effect because any economic burden in connection with them will not fall on the partners but will be borne exclusively by the creditor.

Under the Regulations, nonrecourse deductions, therefore, *must* be allocated among the partners in accordance with their interests in the partnership. As noted, the determination of a particular partner's interest in the partnership can sometimes be complex. However, the Regulations provide that an allocation of nonrecourse deductions that meets the "safe harbor" test will be deemed to be in accordance with the partners' interests in the partnership.

The "safe harbor" standard is met upon compliance with the following four-factor test:

1. At all times, the partnership agreement must require that the capital accounts be maintained in compliance with the Regulations and liquidating distributions will be made in accordance with the capital accounts.

2.   Allocations of nonrecourse deductions must be reasonably consistent with allocations, which have substantial economic effect, of some other significant partnership item attributable to the property securing the nonrecourse debt.

3.   The partnership agreement must provide for a minimum gain chargeback.

4.   All other material allocations and capital account adjustments must be recognized under Regulations § 1.704–1(b).

Allocations of deductions attributable to nonrecourse debt cannot have economic effect. The partner receiving the benefit of the tax deduction will not have a commensurate economic burden through the payment of actual dollars or the relinquishment of rights thereto. The minimum gain chargeback provision requires the partner who benefited from deductions which reduced the basis of the asset subject to the nonrecourse debt (such as real property depreciation deductions on a building financed with nonrecourse debt) to report such gain, at least, to the extent the nonrecourse debt exceeds the basis of the property. Consequently, the Regulations construct a standard under which the allocation will be upheld if it "piggybacks" a relevant allocation attributable to the nonrecourse property that meets the § 704(b) standard and if a process (the minimum gain chargeback) exists which ensures that the recipient of the deductions will bear at least a tax, although not a full economic, burden.

REVENUE RULING 92–97
1992–2 C.B. 124.

Issue

If a partner is allocated a share of the partnership's cancellation of indebtedness (COD) income that differs from the partner's share of the cancelled debt under section 752(b) of the Internal Revenue Code, does the allocation of COD income have substantial economic effect under section 704(b)?

Facts

Situation 1. In year 1, *A* contributes $10x and *B* contributes $90x to form *AB,* a general partnership. *A* and *B* share the partnership's losses 10 percent and 90 percent, respectively, and share the partnership's income 50 percent each (*i.e.,* income allocations do not first restore previous losses). The partnership maintains capital accounts under the rules of section 1.704–1(b)(2)(iv) of the Income Tax Regulations, and the partners agree to liquidate according to positive capital account balances under the rules of section 1.704–1(b)(2)(ii)(*b*)(2).

Under applicable state law, *A* and *B* are jointly and severally liable to creditors for all partnership recourse liabilities. However, *A* and *B* do not agree to unconditional deficit restoration obligations as described in section 1.704–1(b)(2)(ii)(*b*)(*3*) of the regulations; they are obligated to restore deficit capital accounts only to the extent necessary to pay creditors. Thus, if *AB* were to liquidate after paying all creditors, and one partner had a positive capital account balance, the other partner would not be required to restore a deficit capital account to permit a liquidating distribution to the partner with a positive capital account balance.

Because the partners do not have unconditional deficit restoration obligations, the economic effect test of section 1.704–1(b)(2)(ii)(*b*) of the regulations is not met. However, *A* and *B* agree to a qualified income offset and are treated under section 1.704–1(b)(2)(ii)(*c*) as having a limited obligation to restore deficit capital accounts by reason of their liability to *AB* 's creditors. Accordingly, the requirements of the alternate test for economic effect of section 1.704–1(b)(2)(ii)(*d*) are met.

AB purchases property for $1000*x* from an unrelated seller, paying $100*x* in cash and borrowing the $900*x* balance from an unrelated bank that is not the seller of the property. The note is a general obligation of the partnership, and no partner has been relieved from personal liability. The principal of the loan is due in 6 years; interest is payable semi-annually at the applicable federal rate.

A and *B* bear an economic risk of loss equal to $90*x* and $810*x*, respectively, for the partnership's $900*x* recourse liability and each increases basis in the partnership interest (outside basis) accordingly. See section 1.752–2 of the regulations.

The property generates $200*x* of depreciation each year for 5 years. All other partnership deductions and losses exactly equal the partnership's income, so that in each of its first 5 taxable years *AB* has a net loss of $200*x*. Under the partnership agreement, these losses are allocated 10 percent to *A* and 90 percent to *B*. The losses reduce *A* 's capital account to negative $90*x* and *B* 's capital account to negative $810*x*. At the beginning of year 6, after the fair market value of *AB* 's property has substantially declined, the creditor cancels the debt as part of a work-out arrangement. Because of the cancellation of the debt, *A* and *B* are no longer treated as obligated to restore their deficit capital accounts.

Situation 2. The facts are the same as *Situation 1,* except that *A* and *B* agree to unconditional deficit restoration obligations as described in section 1.704–1(b)(2)(ii)(*b*)(*3*) of the regulations. *A* and *B* thus have an obligation to restore deficit capital accounts not only to pay creditors, but to satisfy the other partner's positive capital account balance on liquidation.

Law and Analysis

Section 61(a)(12) of the Code requires the amount of a taxpayer's discharged debt to be included in gross income.

Under section 108(a) of the Code, COD income is excluded from gross income if the debt is discharged in a title 11 case, if the taxpayer is insolvent, or if the debt discharged is qualified farm indebtedness. If a partnership's liability is discharged, the partnership recognizes income equal to the amount of debt cancelled and must allocate that income to the partners as a separately stated item under section 702(a). Under section 108(d)(6), the section 108(a) exclusions are applied at the partner level to the COD income.

If an allocation of a share of a partnership's COD income is made to a partner, and the allocation has substantial economic effect, the partner increases outside basis under section 705(a)(1)(A) of the Code, receives a capital account increase under section 1.704–1(b)(2)(iv)(b)(3) of the regulations, and must determine, based on the partner's own circumstances, if all or part of the distributive share may be excluded from gross income under section 108(a).

Under section 722 of the Code, a partner's outside basis is increased by the amount of money and the adjusted basis of property contributed to the partnership. Under section 731(a), a partner recognizes gain from the sale or exchange of a partnership interest to the extent the partner receives a distribution of money from the partnership that exceeds the partner's outside basis immediately before the distribution. Under section 733, a partner's outside basis is decreased (but not below zero) by the amount of any distribution of money from the partnership. Under section 752(a), an increase in a partner's share of partnership liabilities is treated as a contribution of money by the partner to the partnership. Under section 752(a), an increase in a partner's share of partnership liabilities is treated as a contribution of money by the partner to the partnership. Under section 752(b), a decrease in a partner's share of partnership liabilities is treated as a distribution of money by the partnership to the partner.

Although section 731(a) of the Code requires gain recognition if a distribution of money exceeds the distributee partner's outside basis immediately before the distribution, section 1.731–1(a)(1)(ii) of the regulations treats certain distributions as occurring at the end of the partnership's taxable year. Under section 1.731–1(a)(1)(ii), advances or drawings of money or property against a partner's distributive share of income are treated as current distributions made on the last day of the partnership taxable year.

Under section 704(b) of the Code and the regulations thereunder, allocations of a partnership's items of income, gain, loss, deduction, or credit provided for in the partnership agreement will be respected if the allocations have substantial economic effect. Allocations that fail to have substantial economic effect will be reallocated according to the partners' economic interests in the partnership. The fundamental principles for establishing economic effect require an allocation to be consistent with the partners' underlying economic arrangement. A partner allocated a share of income should enjoy any corresponding economic benefit, and a partner allocated a share of losses or deductions should bear any corresponding economic burden. *See* section 1.704–1(b)(2)(ii)(a) of the regulations.

To come within the safe harbor for establishing economic effect in section 1.704–1(b)(2)(ii) of the regulations, partners must agree to maintain capital accounts under the rules of section 1.704–1(b)(2)(iv) and liquidate according to positive capital account balances; in addition, any partner with a deficit capital account must either agree to an unconditional deficit restoration obligation as described in section 1.704–1(b)(2)(ii)(*b*)(*3*) (as in *Situation 2*) or satisfy the requirements of the alternate test for economic effect provided in section 1.704–1(b)(2)(ii)(*d*) (as in *Situation 1*).

In *Situations 1 and 2,* the allocations of losses to A and B in years 1 through 5 meet the economic effect requirements under sections 1.704–1(b)(2)(ii)(*d*) and 1.704–1(b)(2)(ii)(*b*) of the regulations. These allocations are thus within the economic effect safe harbor provided by the regulations under section 704 of the Code.

In year 6, when the $900x$ recourse liability is cancelled, the partnership recognizes $900x$ of COD income that must be allocated to A and B as a separately stated item under section 702(a) of the Code. In both *Situations 1 and 2,* A and B receive a deemed distribution of money equal to $90x$ and $810x$, respectively, because of the decrease in their shares of the liability when the debt is cancelled. *See* section 752(b) and section 1.752–1(c) of the regulations. Under section 733, A and B reduce outside bases (but not below zero) by $90x$ and $180x$, respectively, and under section 731(a), A and B recognize gain to the extent their respective distributions exceed their outside bases at the end of year 6.

Situation 1 Analysis

The *AB* partnership agreement provides for income to be allocated equally between A and B. However, in *situation 1,* the allocation of the partnership's COD income $450x$ to A and $450x$ to B, which would cause A 's capital account to equal $360x$ (negative $90x$ plus $450x$) and B 's capital account to equal negative $360x$ (negative $810x$ plus $450x$), cannot have economic effect even though the partners maintain capital accounts and liquidate according to positive capital accounts. The cancellation of the debt eliminates both partners' obligations to restore a deficit capital account, and neither partner has an independent deficit restoration obligation that could be invoked to satisfy the other partner's positive capital account. Because the partners' deficit restoration obligations were dependent on the cancelled debt, A can neither enjoy the economic benefit of an allocation of COD income exceeding $90x$ nor bear the economic burden of an allocation of COD income of less than $90x$. Similarly, B can neither enjoy the economic benefit of an allocation of COD income exceeding $810x$ nor bear the economic burden of an allocation of COD income of less than $810x$. *See* section 1.704–1(b)(5), *Example 15(iii),* of the regulations. Thus, for the partnership's allocations of the COD income to have economic effect, the COD income must be allocated $90x$ to A and $810x$ to B, which is the same ratio as the decrease in A 's and B 's shares of partnership liability.

When the COD income is properly allocated, the outside bases of A and B are increased under section 705(a)(1)(A) of the Code by $90x$ and $810x$, respectively, for their distributive shares of the partnership's COD income. Under section 108(d)(6), A and B individually determine if any portion of their distributive shares is excluded from gross income. Under section 705(a)(2), the outside bases of A and B are decreased by $90x$ and $810x$, respectively, for their distributions of money under section 752(b) resulting from the cancellation of the debt. A and B recognize no gain under section 731 in year 6 because the distributive shares of COD income provide an outside basis increase for each partner sufficient to cover the distribution of money to that partner. Because of the integral relationship between the COD income and the section 752(b) distribution of money from the cancelled debt, section 1.731–1(a)(1)(ii) of the regulations treats the distribution of money to each partner from the cancellation of the debt as occurring at the end of AB's taxable year as an advance or drawing against that partner's distributive share of COD income.

Situation 2 Analysis

In *Situation 2,* the allocation of the partnership's COD income $450x$ to A and $450x$ to B, which causes A's capital account to equal $360x$ and B's capital account to equal negative $360x$, has economic effect and, therefore, meets the substantial economic effect safe harbor if substantiality is independently established. Because B's deficit restoration obligation is not dependent on the cancelled debt and can be invoked to satisfy A's positive capital account, the allocation of COD income results in B incurring an obligation to contribute $360x$ to satisfy A's $360x$ positive capital account. Similarly, if the COD income were allocated so that A had a deficit capital account balance, A would incur an obligation to contribute the amount of the deficit to satisfy B's positive capital account.

Under section 705(a)(1)(A) of the Code, the outside bases of A and B are increased by $450x$ each, for their distributive shares of the partnership's COD income. Under section 103(d)(6). A and B individually determine if any portion of their distributive shares is excluded from gross income. This allocation, which is not in proportion to the partners' shares of the cancelled debt under section 752(b), causes B to recognize a $360x$ capital gain under sections 752(b), and 731(a). Although B's outside basis is increased under section 705(a)(1)(A) for B's $450x$ distributive share of COD income, the $310x$ distribution of money resulting from the decrease in B's share of the partnership liability exceeds B's outside basis by $360x$.

B recognizes gain even though the distribution of money from the cancellation of the debt is treated under section 1.731–1(a)(1)(ii) of the regulations as occurring at the end of AB's taxable year. Because of the application of section 1.731–1(a)(1)(ii), however, A does not recognize gain in *Situation 2*. A's outside basis is increased by the allocation to A of $450x$ of the partnership's COD income, so the $90x$ distribution of money resulting from the decrease in *A* 's share of the partnership liability does not exceed *A* 's outside basis. After adjustment for the $90*x* distribution, *A* has an outside basis of $360*x*.

HOLDING

An allocation to a partner of a share of the partnership's cancellation of indebtedness income that differs from the partner's share of the cancelled debt under section 752(b) of the Code has substantial economic effect under section 704(b) if (1) the deficit restoration obligations covering any negative capital account balances resulting from the COD income allocations can be invoked to satisfy other partners' positive capital account balances. (2) the requirements of the economic effect test are otherwise met, and (3) substantiality is independently established.

* * *

Problem 10–6

Steve and Marsha own equal interests in a limited liability company which is taxed as a partnership. The company is in the business of renting party equipment and supplies. Determine the validity of the allocations set forth in the company's operating agreement.

   a.   All depreciation deductions related to § 1245 property are allocated to Steve and all gain on disposition up to the aggregate depreciation is charged back to Steve. At a time when a party tent (cost basis $10,000) has a depreciated basis of $3,600, it is sold for $12,000. What are the results to the partners of the allocation? How could adverse consequences to Marsha on the disposition have been avoided?

   b.   Assume in Problem 10–3 that the partnership borrows on a nonrecourse basis, and the building declines in value to $85,000 at which time the partnership forfeits the ownership rights.

E.   ALLOCATIONS REGARDING CONTRIBUTED PROPERTY

Another tax allocation which cannot have economic effect is precontribution gain or loss extant in property contributed to the partnership since typically it is valued for capital account purposes at its value (i.e., book value) rather than its tax basis. For example, if Jean and Grace form a partnership and Jean contributes cash of $30 and Grace contributes an asset with a basis of $10 and a value of $30, each will have a capital account of $30. Grace's asset, however, holds a potential tax liability on gain of $20 when it is sold by the partnership. Such settings are addressed by § 704(c) which generally mandates that precontribution gain or loss be allocated to the contributor of the property. Thus, income or loss shifting through the use of the partnership vehicle is not permitted. Similarly, if the contributed property is depreciable and if its transferred basis does not produce tax depreciation equal to book depreciation, § 704(c) suggests a remedial allocation under which the contributor's share of depreciation is allocated to the other partners to offset the tax system's denial of their economic set of expectations.

Furthermore, § 724 ensures that the contributor cannot employ a partnership for character conversion through the contribution of assets. For example, if a partner who was a dealer with respect to certain property could contribute it to a nondealer partnership, then the ordinary income taint could be removed upon the partnership's subsequent sale of the property. Section 724 safeguards against these potential abuses by forcing a character retention for the contributed property.

Problem 10–7

Stan, Gary, and Doris decide to form a pizza delivery partnership on January 1, 1997. Each partner has a one-third interest in capital, profits, and losses.

Stan contributed a personal automobile with a holding period of over one year, value of $20,000, and a basis of $10,000. (Assume that the partnership elects to depreciate it on a straight-line basis with a five-year recovery period for tax purposes and a five-year useful life for book purposes.) Gary contributed $20,000 cash. Doris contributed $10,000 in cash plus land with a value of $10,000, basis of $4,000, and a holding period in excess of one year, held by Doris and the partnership as an investment. The following are alternative situations.

a. Assume the partnership sells the land contributed by Doris at its fair market value of $10,000. What is the effect on the income, basis, and capital accounts of each partner?

b. The automobile contributed by Stan is depreciated for two years on a straight-line basis. How much depreciation must be allocated under § 704(c), and to which partners, in order to take into account the variation between basis and fair market value on contribution? What is the effect on the income, basis, and capital account of each partner?

c. In a, assume that the partnership sold the land for $7,000. Stan and Gary want to take into account for tax purposes their economic loss on the transaction. What result?

d. Assume in a that the land was inventory property within the meaning of § 751(d)(2) as to Doris but was investment property as regards the partnership. What result to the parties if the land is sold for $13,000 in 1998? What result if it is sold for $13,000 in 2003?

e. Assume that Gary contributed a capital asset with a basis of $35,000 and fair market value of $20,000 instead of a cash contribution of $20,000 and that the partnership is a dealer as regards that property. What result if the property is sold for $22,000 in 1998? What result if the property is sold for $18,000 in 1998?

Chapter 11

TAXING PARTNERSHIP OPERATIONS—TRANSACTIONS BETWEEN RELATED PARTIES

Code References: §§ 267(a)(1), (2), (d)(1)–(4), (e); 704(a); 707; 263(a).

Regulations: §§ 1.707–1; 1.267(b)–1(b).

A. INTRODUCTION

While a partnership is treated as an entity for certain tax purposes, it functions as a business only through the efforts of its partners or employees. Particularly in the small business context, the partners of the partnership may also serve as its employees, lenders, suppliers, or customers. When property or money is transferred between the partnership and its partners, special tax issues arise.

Payments made by a partnership to a partner can be divided into three categories: (1) the partner's distributive share as determined under § 704 of partnership income, (2) payments to a partner engaged in a transaction with the partnership other than in the capacity of a member of the partnership (§ 707(a)), and (3) a guaranteed payment—one determined without regard to the income of the partnership and made to a partner as compensation for services or the use of capital (§ 707(c)). Thus, when a partner deals with the partnership, the schizophrenia so frequently encountered in the partnership area (the entity/aggregate approach) is squarely confronted.

B. § 707(a) TRANSACTIONS; § 707(c) GUARANTEED PAYMENTS

Section 707(a) and (c) adopt an entity approach with respect to transactions between a partner and the partnership. Under § 707(a), if a partner engages in a transaction with a partnership, other than in the capacity of a member of the partnership, the transaction is treated as one between the partnership and a nonpartner. Similarly, a § 707(c) guaranteed payment, made to a partner in the capacity of a partner and determined without regard to the income of the partnership, is afforded entity treatment. Thus, the recipient derives income under § 61, typically ordinary, except in the setting of a sale of property to the partnership. The partnership is entitled to a deduction unless the payment is a capital expenditure under § 263.

Any other allocation and payment to a partner is a portion of the partner's distributive share as determined under § 704, which applies the aggregate approach. The character of the income to the partner when earned by the partnership is dependent upon its characterization at the partnership level. This treatment holds even if the distribution of the subject income is not forthcoming until a later year. When the distribution is made, it is tested under § 731 and produces gain to the partner only if it exceeds the basis for the partner's partnership interest.

In differentiating between the three categories of payments, it should be noted that the tax distinctions between a § 707(a) payment and a § 707(c) payment are minimal. The distinguishing factor between the two is whether the services were rendered in a capacity of being a partner (a facts and circumstances test), yet in either case the recipient typically receives ordinary income while the partnership receives an attendant deduction unless the payment constitutes a capital expenditure.

The distinguishing feature between § 704(a), on the one hand, and § 707(a) and § 707(c), on the other, is that the former is determined with respect to the income of the partnership. The Regulations highlight this fact by noting that an agreement among the partners that one will receive a 30 percent share of partnership income but not less than $10,000 would not give rise to a guaranteed payment when the partnership income for the year is greater than $33,333, for example $60,000 (i.e., the total payment of $18,000 constitutes the partner's distributive share). Reg. § 1.707–1(c) example (2). Payments through partnership allocations may give rise to characterizations as other than ordinary income (i.e., tax-exempt, capital gain, etc.). In addition, such payments may be "sheltered" from tax by partnership deductions or losses not otherwise available to a partner in his individual capacity.

REVENUE RULING 81–300
1981–2 C.B. 143.

ISSUE

Are the management fees paid to partners under the circumstances described below distributive shares of partnership income or guaranteed payments under section 707(c) of the Internal Revenue Code?

FACTS

The taxpayers are the general partners in a limited partnership formed to purchase, develop and operate a shopping center. The partnership agreement specifies the taxpayers' shares of the profit and loss of the partnership. The general partners have a ten percent interest in each item of partnership income, gain, loss, deduction, or credit. In addition, the partnership agreement provides that the general partners must contribute their time, managerial abilities and best efforts to the partnership and that in return for their managerial services each will receive a fee of five percent of the gross rentals received by the partnership. These amounts will be paid to the general partners in all events.

Pursuant to the partnership agreement, the taxpayers carried out their duties as general partners and provided the management services required in the operation of the shopping centers. The management fee of five percent of gross rentals were reasonable in amount for the services rendered.

LAW AND ANALYSIS

Section 707(a) of the Code provides that if a partner engages in a transaction with a partnership other than in the capacity of a member of such partnership, the transaction shall, except as otherwise provided in this section, be considered as occurring between the partnership and one who is not a partner.

Section 1.707–1(a) of the Income Tax Regulations provides that a partner who engages in a transaction with a partnership other than in the capacity of a partner shall be treated as if the partner were not a member of the partnership with respect to such transaction. The regulation's section further states that such transactions include the rendering of services by the partner to the partnership and that the substance of the transaction will govern rather than its form.

Section 707(c) of the Code provides that to the extent determined without regard to the income of the partnership, payments to a partner for services, termed "guaranteed payments", shall be considered as made to one who is not a member of the partnership, but only for purposes of section 61(a) and, subject to section 263, for purposes of section 162(a).

In *Pratt v. Commissioner,* 64 T.C. 203 (1975), *aff'd in part, rev'd in part,* 550 F.2d 1023 (5th Cir.1977), under substantially similar facts to those in this case, both the United States Tax Court and the United States Court of Appeals for the Fifth Circuit held that management fees based on a percentage of gross rentals were not payments described in section 707(a) of the Code. The courts found that the terms of the partnership agreement and the actions of the parties indicated that the taxpayers were performing the management services in their capacities as general partners. *Compare* Rev.Rul. 81–301, this page, this Bulletin.

When a determination is made that a partner is performing services in the capacity of a partner, a question arises whether the compensation for the services is a guaranteed payment under section 707(c) of the Code or a distributive share of partnership income under section 704. In *Pratt,* the Tax Court held that the management fees were not guaranteed payments because they were computed as a percentage of gross rental income received by the partnership. The court reasoned that the gross rental income was "income" of the partnerships and, thus, the statutory test for a guaranteed payment, that it be "determined without regard to the income of the partnership", was not satisfied. On appeal, the taxpayer's argument was limited to the section 707(a) issue and the Fifth Circuit found it unnecessary to consider the application of section 707(c).

The legislative history of the Internal Revenue Code of 1954 indicates the intent of Congress to treat partnerships as entities in the case of certain transactions between partners and their partnerships. See S.Rep. No. 1622, 83d Cong., 2d Sess. 92 (1954). The Internal Revenue Code of 1939 and prior Revenue Acts contain no comparable provision and the courts had split on the question of whether a partner could deal with the partnership as an outsider. *Compare Lloyd v. Commissioner,* 15 B.T.A. 82 (1929) and *Wegener v. Commissioner,* 119 F.2d 49 (5th Cir.1941), *aff'g* 41 B.T.A. 857 (1940), *cert. denied* 314 U.S. 643 (1941). This resulted both in uncertainty and in substantial computational problems when an aggregate theory was applied and the payment to a partner exceeded the partnership income. In such situations, the fixed salary was treated as a withdrawal of capital, taxable to the salaried partner to the extent that the withdrawal was made from the capital of other partners. *See,* for example, Rev.Rul. 55–30, 1955–1 C.B. 430. Terming such treatment as unrealistic and unnecessarily complicated, Congress enacted section 707(a) and (c) of the Code of 1954. Under section 707(a) the partnership is considered an unrelated entity for all purposes. Under section 707(c), the partnership is considered an unrelated entity for purposes of sections 61 and 162 to the extent that it makes a guaranteed payment for services or for the use of capital.

Although a fixed amount is the most obvious form of guaranteed payment, there are situations in which compensation for services is determined by reference to an item of gross income. For example, it is not unusual to compensate a manager of real property by reference to the gross rental income that the property produces. Such compensation arrangements do not give the provider of the service a share in the profits of the enterprise, but are designed to accurately measure the value of the services that are provided.

Thus, in view of the legislative history and the purpose underlying section 707 of the Code, the term "guaranteed payment" should not be limited to fixed amounts. A payment for services determined by reference to an item of gross income will be a guaranteed payment if, on the basis of all of the facts and circumstances, the payment is compensation rather than a share of partnership profits. Relevant facts would include the reasonableness of the payment for the services provided and whether the method used to determine the amount of the payment would have been used to compensate an unrelated party for the services.

It is the position of the Internal Revenue Service that in *Pratt* the management fees were guaranteed payments under section 707(c) of the Code. On the facts presented, the payments were not disguised distributions of partnership net income, but were compensation for services payable without regard to partnership income.

HOLDING

The management fees are guaranteed payments under section 707(c) of the Code.

REVENUE RULING 81–301

1981–2 C.B. 144.

ISSUE

Is an allocation based on a percentage of gross income paid to an advisor general partner subject to section 707(a) of the Internal Revenue Code, under the circumstances described below?

FACTS

ABC is a partnership formed in accordance with the Uniform Limited Partnership Act of a state and is registered with the Securities and Exchange Commission as an open-end diversified management company pursuant to the Investment Company Act of 1940, as amended. Under the partnership agreement, *ABC*'s assets must consist only of municipal bonds, certain readily-marketable temporary investments, and cash. The agreement provides for two classes of general partners: (1) "director general partners" (directors) who are individuals and (2) one "adviser general partner" (adviser) that is a corporate investment adviser registered as such in accordance with the Investment Advisers Act of 1940, 15 U.S.C.A., section 80b–5 (1971).

Under the partnership agreement, the directors are compensated and have complete and exclusive control over the management, conduct, and operation of *ABC*'s activities. The directors are authorized to appoint agents and employees to perform duties on behalf of *ABC* and these agents may be, but need not be, general partners. Under the partnership agreement, the adviser has no rights, powers, or authority as a general partner, except that, subject to the supervision of the directors, the adviser is authorized to manage the investment and reinvestment of *ABC*'s assets. The adviser is responsible for payment of any expenses incurred in the performance of its investment advisory duties, including those for office space and facilities, equipment, and any of its personnel used to service and administer *ABC*'s investments. The adviser is not personally liable to the other partners for any losses incurred in the investment and reinvestment of *ABC*'s assets.

The nature of the adviser's services are substantially the same as those it renders as an independent contractor or agent for persons other than *ABC* and, under the agreement, the adviser is not precluded from engaging in such transactions with others.

Each general partner, including the adviser general partner, is required to contribute sufficient cash to *ABC* to acquire at least a one percent interest in the partnership. The agreement requires an allocation of 10 percent of *ABC*'s daily gross income to the adviser. After reduction by the compensation allocable to the directors and the adviser, *ABC*'s items of income, gain, loss, deduction, and credit are divided according to the percentage interests held by each partner.

The adviser's right to 10 percent of *ABC*'s daily gross income for managing *ABC*'s investment must be approved at least annually by a majority vote of the directors or a majority vote of all the partnership interests. Furthermore, the directors may remove the adviser as investment manager at any time on 60 days written notice to the adviser. The adviser can terminate its investment manager status by giving 60 days written notice to the directors. The agreement provides that the adviser will no longer be a general partner after removal or withdrawal as investment manager, but will continue to participate as a limited partner in the income, gains, losses, deductions, and credits attributable to the percentage interest that it holds.

LAW AND ANALYSIS

Section 61(a)(1) of the Code provides that, except as otherwise provided by law, gross income means all income from whatever source derived, including compensation for services, including fees, commissions, and similar items.

Section 702(a) of the Code provides that in determining the income tax of a partner each partner must take into account separately such partner's distributive share of the partnership's items of income, gain, loss, deduction, or credit.

Section 707(a) of the Code provides that if a partner engages in a transaction with a partnership other than as a member of such partnership, the transaction shall, except as otherwise provided in section 707, be considered as occurring between the partnership and one who is not a partner.

Section 1.707–1(a) of the Income Tax Regulations provides that a partner who engages in a transaction with a partnership other than in the capacity as a partner shall be treated as if not a member of the partnership with respect to such transaction. Such transactions include the rendering of services by the partner to the partnership. In all cases, the substance of the transaction will govern rather than its form.

Section 707(c) of the Code provides that to the extent determined without regard to the income of the partnership, payments to a partner for services shall be considered as made to one who is not a member of the partnership, but only for purposes of section 61(a) and, subject to section 263, for purposes of section 162(a).

Although the adviser is identified in the agreement as an "adviser general partner," the adviser provides similar services to others as part of its regular trade or business, and its management of the investment and reinvestment of *ABC*'s assets is supervised by the directors. Also it can be relieved of its duties and right to compensation at any time (with 60 days notice) by a majority vote of the directors. Further, the adviser pays its own expenses and is not personally liable to the other partners for any losses incurred in the investment and reinvestment of *ABC*'s assets. The services performed by the adviser are, in substance, not performed in the capacity of a general partner, but are performed in the capacity of a person who is not a partner.

The 10 percent daily gross income allocation paid to the adviser is paid to the adviser in its capacity other than as a partner. Therefore, the gross income allocation is not a part of the adviser's distributive share of partnership income under section 702(a) of the Code or a guaranteed payment under section 707(c).

HOLDING

The 10 percent daily gross income allocation paid to the adviser is subject to section 707(a) of the Code and taxable to the adviser under section 61 as compensation for services rendered. The amount paid is deductible by the partnership under section 162, subject to the provisions of section 263.

REVENUE RULING 81–150
1981–1 C.B. 119.

ISSUE

Is a management fee deductible in the year paid under the circumstances described below?

FACTS

P is a limited partnership organized to acquire an offshore drilling rig and to engage in contract drilling of oil and gas wells for major oil companies. The drilling rig will be constructed by a shipbuilding company, and will have a useful life of 10 years. The drilling rig is expected to be completed in July, 1981, at which time it will be placed in operation.

In 1980, *P* paid the managing partner a management fee of 325*x* dollars. The management fee is to compensate the managing partner for supervising construction and financing of the drilling rig and for managing the partnership during construction of the drilling rig.

P uses the cash method of accounting for receipts and expenditures and reports income on a calendar year basis. *P* proposes to deduct the management fee in the year paid.

LAW AND ANALYSIS

Section 162 of the Internal Revenue Code provides for a deduction of all ordinary and necessary expenses paid or incurred during the taxable year in carrying on a trade or business.

Section 263(a) of the Code provides, generally, that no deduction shall be allowed for capital expenditures.

Section 1.263(a)–2(a) of the Income Tax Regulations provides that the term capital expenditures includes the cost of acquisition, construction, or erection of buildings, machinery and equipment, furniture and fixtures, and similar property having a useful life substantially beyond the taxable year.

Section 195(a) of the Code provides that start-up expenditures paid or incurred after July 29, 1980, in taxable years ending after such date, may, at the election of the taxpayer, be treated as deferred expenses to be deducted over a period of not less than 60 months as may be selected by the taxpayer (beginning with the month in which the business begins).

Section 195(b) defines "start-up expenditure" to mean any amount paid or incurred in connection with investigating the creation or acquisition of an active trade or business, or creating an active trade or business, and which, if paid in connection with the expansion of an existing trade or business, would be allowable as a deduction for the taxable year in which paid or incurred.

Section 195(c)(1) requires that an election under this section be made not later than the time prescribed by law for filing the return for the taxable year in which the business begins (including extensions thereof).

In *Woodward v. Commissioner,* 397 U.S. 572 (1970), 1970–1 C.B. 56, the Supreme Court of the United States distinguished costs that are deductible under section 162 of the Code from costs that are capital expenditures. The court stated that: "It has long been recognized, as a general matter, that costs incurred in the acquisition or disposition of a capital asset are to be treated as capital expenditures."

In the present case, the management fee is to compensate the managing partner for supervising construction and financing of the drilling rig and for managing the partnership during construction of the drilling rig. The portion of the fee attributable to the supervision of construction and financing of the drilling rig is a cost incurred in the acquisition of a capital asset; as such, it is a capital expenditure, to be treated as part of the cost of the drilling rig. Such portion of the management fee is not a start-up expenditure within the meaning of section 195(b) of the Code.

With regard to the deductibility of the remaining portion of the management fee, it should be noted that in order to qualify as a deductible business expense under section 162 of the Code, an expense must be (a) incurred in carrying on a trade or business, (b) ordinary and necessary, and (c) paid or incurred during the taxable year. See *Commissioner v. Lincoln Savings and Loan Ass'n,* 403 U.S. 345 (1971), 1971–2 C.B. 116.

In *Richmond Television Corporation v. United States,* 345 F.2d 901 (4th Cir.1965), the taxpayer, a corporation organized to operate a television station, applied for a broadcasting license in 1952. Prior to receipt of its broadcasting license and commencement of its broadcasting activities in 1956, the taxpayer incurred expenses in training prospective employees. The taxpayer deducted these expenses as business expenses under section 162 of the Code in taxable years 1952 through 1956.

In addressing the issue of the deductibility of business expenses, the court, in *Richmond Television,* stated that a taxpayer "has not 'engaged in carrying on a trade or business' within the intendment of section 162(a) until such time as the business has begun to function as a going concern and performed those activities for which it was organized." The court held that the taxpayer was not "engaged in carrying on a trade or business" until the broadcasting license was issued and broadcasting commenced. Because the expenditures for training prospective employees were made before the license was issued and before broadcasting commenced, the court held that they were capital expenditures and not deductible under section 162(a) of the Code.

In the present case, *P* will not be engaged in carrying on a trade or business until July, 1981, when the drilling rig will be completed and placed in operation. Because the management fee will be paid to the managing partner prior to July, 1981, the portion of the fee that is attributable to the management of the partnership during construction of the drilling rig will not be deductible as a business expense under section 162 of the Code. To the extent that such fee or portion thereof will be paid or incurred after July 29, 1980, however, it is a start-up expenditure within the meaning of section 195 of the Code because it was paid in creating an active trade or business and would have been currently deductible had the business already commenced operation. Should *P* make an election, in accordance with the provisions of section 195(c) of the Code, to treat the start-up expenditure as a deferred expense, it shall be allowed as a ratable deduction over such period of not less than 60 months as may be selected by *P* beginning with July, 1981.

Holding

The portion of the management fee that is attributable to the supervision of construction and financing of the drilling rig is a capital expenditure, as defined in section 263 of the Code, and is treated as part of the cost of the drilling rig. The portion of the management fee that is attributable to the management of the partnership during construction of the drilling rig is not deductible in the year paid, under section 162 of the Code, but must be capitalized; that part of this amount paid or incurred after July 29, 1980, is a start-up expenditure which *P* may elect to deduct under section 195 of the Code.

Problem 11–1

Andrea is a partner with two other equal partners in a partnership which operates an ice cream store. The partnership leased its building from Andrea at an annual rent of $20,000 (its fair rental value). Andrea continued to depreciate the building. How should the transaction be characterized?

Problem 11–2

Assume in Problem 11–1 that the partnership is on the accrual method of accounting, Andrea is a cash method taxpayer, Andrea and the partnership are calendar year taxpayers, and the payment is a § 707(a) payment. The partnership accrued the payment in 1997 but did not make payment until April 1, 1998. What result?

Problem 11–3

Susan, Matthew, and Jennifer are law partners. The partnership agreement provides that Susan will receive a salary of $21,000 per year for her services as a lawyer without regard to the partnership income, plus one-third of the taxable income or loss of the partnership after the deduction for her salary. At the end of 1997, before deducting Susan's salary, the partnership had ordinary income of $12,000. The partnership also holds certain securities which are sold during the year, yielding long-term capital gain of $30,000 and short-term capital gain of $9,000. Before the end of 1997, the partnership paid $21,000 to Susan. The partnership and its partners are cash method, calendar year taxpayers. What are the results to Susan and to the partnership?

Problem 11–4

Assume alternatively in Problem 11–3 that Susan is to receive one-third of the ordinary income of the partnership, as determined before any guaranteed payment is taken into account, but not less than $21,000. In addition, she is to receive one-third of the losses. Capital gains and losses are to be shared equally.

a. What result if the ordinary income of the partnership is $90,000?

b. What result if the ordinary income of the partnership is $30,000?

C. GROSS INCOME ALLOCATIONS

Income allocations at times have been used in an attempt to avoid the capitalization requirements of § 263 by disguising the sale of property to a partnership as a contribution in exchange for an allocation and subsequent distribution of income from the partnership. Similar efforts were employed in the service arena by transferring a partnership interest in return for the rendition of services which otherwise would have been nondeductible due to § 263.

Section 707(a)(2)(A) provides for the treatment of both the partner who transfers property or services in exchange for a related allocation and distribution and the partnership when the transaction properly is characterized as one in which the partner is not acting in the capacity of a partner. The goal is to prevent the partnership from in effect obtaining a deduction for acquiring an asset or services which should be capitalized.

For example, if the partnership purchases a capital asset, its costs must be capitalized and, at best, amortized over the life of the asset. If, instead, the partnership makes the transferor a "partner," allocating and distributing to him or her a portion of partnership income, in effect the partnership has achieved a deduction for the property because the allocation to the transferor reduces the amount of income taxable to the other partners.

Section 707(a)(2)(A) is aimed at preventing a partnership from obtaining this "deduction" for services or property received which should be capitalized by treating the provider as a partner and allocating to that partner a share of partnership income. The effect of the provision is to deny the transferor status as a partner, thus denying the partnership the advantage sought.

There are a variety of situations intended to be remedied by this provision. Some of them are as follows:

1. The organizer or syndicator of a partnership is one of the partners and is given a special allocation and related distribution of income (gross or net) to pay for his or her services. The effect is to give the partnership a current deduction (as income is paid to the syndicator) for organizational and syndication fees (not deductible under § 709) by reducing the taxable income allocable to other partners.

2. The partnership, engaged in real estate development, makes its architect a partner instead of employing the architect in a nonpartner capacity and allocates and distributes to the architect a portion of partnership income instead of paying a fee. This, too, gives the partnership the effect of a current deduction for an item which should otherwise be capitalized.

3. A consultant to the partnership is made a partner and is allocated a portion of the partnership's capital gain or tax-exempt income in lieu of a fee, thus converting into a preferred class of income what would have been ordinary income had the consultant simply been hired by the partnership.

Problem 11–5

A commercial office building constructed by a partnership is projected to generate gross income of at least $100,000 per year indefinitely. Its architect, Thomas, whose normal fee for such services is $40,000, contributes cash for a 25–percent interest in the partnership and receives both a 25–percent distributive share of net income for the life of the partnership, and an allocation of $20,000 of partnership gross income for each of the first two years of partnership operations after lease-up. The partnership is expected to have sufficient cash available to distribute $20,000 to the architect in each of the first two years, and the agreement requires such a distribution. What result to the partnership and Thomas?

D. LOSS DISALLOWANCE AND CHARACTER CONVERSION

With respect to one type of § 707(a) transaction, i.e., the sale of property between a partner and a partnership, the tax treatment of the parties differs significantly from the typical § 707(a) or § 707(c) payment. In these cases, the purchaser (e.g., the partnership) must capitalize the sales price under § 263 and § 1012 and recoup the purchase price, if at all, through depreciation or amortization deductions under § 167, § 168, or § 197. The seller of the property (e.g., the partner) will determine gain or loss characterized by the seller's personal factual particulars respecting holding period and capital asset status.

However, in some potentially abusive settings, the Code imposes rules for loss disallowance or character conversion. Section 707(b) addresses transactions between a partner or a related person and a controlled partnership (greater than 50% ownership). In the case of losses, § 707(b) disallows the deduction and, in the case of certain gains, it transmutes potential capital gain into ordinary income. Furthermore, in cases where the partnership is not controlled and the sale takes place between the partnership and a person related to a partner, Regulation § 1.267(b)–1(b) employs an aggregate approach and disallows the loss attributable to that portion of the sale attributable to the related partner.

Problem 11–6

Al and Barbara are brother and sister. They operate a painting contracting business with Charles, who is unrelated, as a partnership. Al sells a computer, with an adjusted basis of $10,000, to the partnership for $4,000. The partners have equal interests in the capital, profits, and losses of the partnership. What are the results to Al and the partnership?

Problem 11–7

Assume in Problem 11–6 that the partnership subsequently sold the computer to an unrelated party. What are the results to Al and the partnership if the sales price was:

a. $5,000?

b. $15,000?

Problem 11–8

Assume alternatively in Problem 11–6 that Dan, the father of Charles, sold the computer to the partnership. What is the result to Dan? What result to the partnership?

Problem 11–9

Phil is a 90% partner in a real estate investment partnership. Phil sold vacant land with an adjusted basis of $50,000 to the partnership for

$200,000. The partnership originally planned to hold the land for investment but one year later began subdividing the property into lots for sale. What are the tax consequences to Phil? What if he had held the property primarily for sale?

Chapter 12

PARTNERSHIP DISTRIBUTIONS— CURRENT DISTRIBUTIONS

Code References: §§ 707(a)(2)(B); 731(a) and (b); 732(a)–(c); 733; 735; 737(a)–(c).

Regulations: §§ 1.705–1(a)(1); 1.707–3(a)–(d); 1.731–1(a) and (b); 1.732–1(a)–(c); 1.735–1; 1.737–1(a)–(d).

A. INTRODUCTION; GAIN RECOGNITION

In the course of its operations, a small business operating as a partnership will make various distributions to its owners during a year. The most typical form of current (as opposed to liquidating) distribution is that of money. As the partners are in need of funds with which to support themselves, at various times during the year the partnership will distribute cash. Under § 731, a partner does not recognize gain unless the amount of the distributed money exceeds the basis for his or her partnership interest. This treatment reflects sound tax policy since the partner in many cases has been previously taxed on the earnings of the partnership which gave rise to a basis adjustment for his partnership interest, regardless of whether any of such funds were distributed.

Thus, in contrast to the corporate tax treatment, the distribution of cash is viewed first as a return of the partner's capital contributions and income which has been previously taxed to him or her. Only after these amounts have been disgorged by the partnership do additional distributions generate income. The excess of the amount distributed over the partner's basis for his or her partnership interest is treated as gain arising from the sale or exchange of a partnership interest and is therefore generally characterized as capital. Under no circumstances will loss be recognized on a current distribution. In order to ease the administrative difficulties in determining whether gain arose on actual or constructive (through liability relief under § 752(b)) cash distributions made during the year, Regulation § 1.731–1(b) provides that cash distributions which are advances or draws are to be aggregated and tested at year end. Section 1.705–1(a) of the Regulations provides that basis typically is determined at year end unless all or a part of the partnership interest is sold or a complete liquidation thereof occurs. Thus, by implication, the Regulation suggests that all current distributions (even in a partial, as opposed to a complete, liquidation) are tested against basis under § 731 at year end.

Problem 12–1

Sam and Dave each contribute $5,000 to start a record store. Sam works in the store. On January 1, 1997, when the store opens, the basis for Sam's interest in the partnership is $5,000. Sam draws $1,000 each month from the partnership during 1997. The partnership is on a calendar year. All distributions are in cash. The partnership has no profits from January to November, i.e., income equaling expenses (excluding Sam's draw). With strong Christmas sales, the partnership has profits of $15,000 for December. Sam's share of the profits is 50%. Does Sam have taxable income because of the withdrawals during the first 11 months of the partnership's taxable year?

B.   NONRECOGNITION; CARRYOVER OF BASIS ON CURRENT PROPERTY DISTRIBUTIONS

In a nonliquidating distribution of property, rather than cash, no gain or loss is recognized. The Code permits nonrecognition of gain in such settings because the taxpayer has not "liquidated" his investment. Instead, the distributee partner retains a proprietary investment in the distributed property. Additionally, the tax basis of the distributed property to the distributee partner is that which the property possessed at the partnership level prior to distribution. As one has come to expect on nonrecognition treatment, deferral, not exemption, is conferred and the carryover of basis treatment preserves the predistribution gain or loss to be recognized when the distributed asset is subsequently sold. Such a rule applies under § 732(a)(1), unless the basis for the partnership interest of the distributee partner is less than the partnership's basis for the distributed asset, in which case the lesser amount will be the distributed asset's basis. Thus, for example, if the basis for a partner's partnership interest is $20 and the partnership distributes currently property with a basis of $10 and fair market value of $15, the property will have a basis of $10 to the distributee partner. If, however, the distributee's basis for his partnership interest were $6, the distributed property would take a basis of $6. Furthermore, the basis for a partner's *partnership interest* is reduced under § 733 by the amount of money distributed or the basis assumed for the distributed property under § 732.

Should both cash and property be distributed currently by a partnership, the Code and the Regulations adopt a pro-taxpayer interpretation under which the cash is tested first for gain recognition under § 731 and thereafter the property is tested under § 732. Thus, if cash of $20 and property with a basis to the partnership of $25 is distributed currently to a partner with a basis for the partnership interest of $30, no gain will be recognized under § 731 and the distributed property will take a basis of $10 (i.e., the remaining basis after the $20 basis reduction of the partnership interest for the distributed cash).

Two other rules affecting current distributions should be observed. First, under § 732(c), if unrealized receivables or inventory are distributed in conjunction with other property, a priority rule accords a transferred basis to those items. Generally, such an approach is intended to safeguard the ordinary income component of the partnership assets because under § 735 such items will generate ordinary income upon their subsequent disposition and under the basis preservation rules of § 732(c) they will retain the full amount of the ordinary income potential. Additionally, if multiple assets in either class (receivables and inventory or other assets) are distributed and the remaining basis for the partner's partnership interest is less than the collective bases therefor, that basis is allocated among those assets in a ratio of *their* respective bases. The basis is still first allocated to the receivables and inventory, however.

Problem 12–2

Norma, Jane, Becky, and Todger own a card and novelty shop which is operated as a limited liability company. The limited liability company is taxed as a partnership. The partnership has the following assets:

Assets	Adjusted Basis	Fair Market Value
Cash	$ 80	$ 80
Accounts Receivable (cash method)	0	40
Inventory	80	120
Land (investment)	40	120
Total	$200	$360

Basis in Partnership Interest	
Norma	$ 40
Jane	30
Becky	20
Todger	10
Total	$100

The partners have equal partnership interests. The bases of their interests are different because they purchased them from former partners at varying points in time. The partnership has never elected under § 754. Each partnership interest has been held for more than one year. In the following questions, determine each partner's taxable gain or loss, basis in each distributed asset, basis in the partnership interest, and the results to the partnership.

a. The partnership distributes $20 in cash and a one-fourth undivided interest in the land to each partner.

b. The partnership distributes $10 in cash, one-fourth of the accounts receivable, and a one-fourth undivided interest in the land to each partner.

c. The partnership distributes one-fourth of the inventory and a one-fourth undivided interest in the land to each partner.

Problem 12–3

A partnership has many assets, one of which is land with an adjusted basis of $18 and a fair market value of $20. The partnership purchased the land on September 30, 1996. Cal, a one-third partner, receives this land as a current distribution on January 1, 1997. Prior to the distribution, Cal's basis in his partnership interest, which he purchased on December 29, 1995, was $100.

a. On February 1, 1997, Cal sells the land at a gain. Assuming the land is a capital asset to Cal, will the capital gain be long-term or short-term?

b. What would be the answer in a if Cal sold the land on October 2, 1997?

c. Assume that, instead of land, the asset distributed to Cal on January 1, 1997, was inventory. If the inventory is sold by Cal on June 1, 1997, for $20, Cal's gain is $2. What is the character of this gain?

C. LIMITATIONS ON DEFERRAL OF TAX ON APPRECIATED CONTRIBUTED PROPERTY

Congress enacted § 737 in 1994 to provide for gain recognition upon the distribution of partnership property (other than cash) possessing unrecognized precontribution gain to any partner. The purpose of § 737 is to complement the safeguard provision of § 704(c)(1)(B). Thereunder, if property contributed by a partner to the partnership is distributed to another partner within five years, the precontribution gain or loss is recognized and allocated to the contributor. Section 737 is intended to address the method of avoiding § 704(c) gain recognition through the distribution of other property to the contributor of appreciated property.

Section 737 provides for gain recognition by the original contributor on any distribution (current or liquidating) to him or her to the extent of the lesser of (1) the excess of the fair market value of the property distributed (other than cash) over the partner's basis for his partnership interest reduced by any money distributed or (2) the net precontribution gain of the partner. The concept of net precontribution gain tracks with § 704(c)(1)(B) and includes the net gain attributable to any property held by the partnership on the date of the distribution which was contributed to the partnership within the preceding five-year period. The statutory phrase "net gain" ensures that contributions of loss property are taken into account and reduce the potential gain to be recognized under § 737, but a net loss is not recognized. Furthermore, if any such property had previously been distributed to another partner,

§ 737 is inapplicable to that gain since recognition would have previously arisen under § 704(c)(1)(B).

Problem 12–4

Al, Betty, and Charlie form an equal partnership. Al contributes land worth $30,000 with an adjusted basis of $10,000, while Betty contributes artwork with a value and basis of $30,000 and Charlie contributes $30,000 cash. Three years later, the land is worth $210,000 and the artwork is worth $20,000. The partnership makes a current distribution to Al of the artwork at a time when his basis for his partnership interest is $15,000. At that time, the land was still held by the partnership. What result if the artwork had been worth $45,000?

D. DISGUISED SALE

If a partnership is to be formed with some of the partners furnishing property and others supplying cash, the transaction can be accomplished in a number of ways with different economic and tax effects. For example, assume that Al and Beth decide to form an equal partnership. Al will provide property with a basis of $10,000 and a value of $20,000. Beth will supply $20,000 cash. The following choices are available:

1. If Al contributes the property and Beth contributes $20,000 in cash, their *economic* capital accounts will be equal. There will be no tax effects on the contribution. The partnership will have a basis of $10,000 for the property. § 723.

2. Al can sell one-half of the property to Beth for $10,000. Each then can contribute his or her one-half interest in the property to the partnership plus one-half the amount of money that will be needed (presumably $10,000 each). Economic capital accounts will be equal. Al will have recognized $5,000 gain ($10,000 received for one-half of the property minus one-half of Al's basis in the property) on the sale to Beth. The basis of the property to the partnership will be $15,000 (Al's $5,000 basis for the remaining one-half interest he contributes, plus Beth's $10,-000 basis for the interest which she bought from Al and contributed).

3. Beth can contribute $20,000 cash to the partnership. Al can *sell* the property to the partnership for its value of $20,000. Al then will be required to contribute the $20,000 to the partnership for the partners to have equal economic capital accounts. His sale to the partnership would yield no capital account in and of itself. Al will have recognized $10,000 of gain on the sale. The basis of the property to the partnership will be its purchase price of $20,000.

4. Beth can contribute $10,000 cash to the partnership. Al can contribute a one-half interest in the property to the partnership and sell the other one-half interest in the property to the

partnership for $10,000. Al will recognize gain of $5,000. The partnership will have a basis for the property of $15,000 ($10,-000 for the one-half purchased, plus $5,000 for the one half contributed by Al). The partners' economic capital accounts will be equal.

The tax results of each of these choices are clear and straightforward.

Another method of accomplishing the transaction would be for Al to contribute the property to the partnership, and Beth to contribute $10,000 cash. Al's economic capital account would be $20,000, the value of the property, and Beth's would be $10,000, the money contributed. The partnership agreement would provide that Al is entitled to receive the first $10,000 of cash distributions to equalize the partners' economic capital accounts. Beth's $10,000 contribution would be distributed immediately to Al, reducing Al's economic capital account to $10,000. Prior to the Tax Reform Act of 1984, the tax results of this transaction would have been unclear.

Based solely on the form of the transaction, a contribution to the partnership by Al under § 721 and a subsequent distribution by the partnership to Al under § 731, no gain would be recognized by Al, since the cash distribution did not exceed the basis of his partnership interest. Under § 722, the basis for Al's partnership interest immediately after the contribution would be $10,000, the basis of the property contributed, and the $10,000 distribution to him would be applied under § 731 against that entire basis. However, economically all of the parties are in the same position as though either choice 2 or 4 above had been used, in either of which Al would have recognized gain because the transaction was structured as a sale. The issue, therefore, is whether what in form is a contribution under § 721 and a distribution under § 731 is in substance a sale either from Al to Beth (choice 2) or from Al to the partnership (choice 4) of one-half of the property.

Section 707(a)(2)(B) provides that if money or property is transferred directly or indirectly to a partnership by a partner, and there is a related direct or indirect transfer of money or other property to that, or another, partner by the partnership, and "the transfers ... when viewed together, are properly characterized as a sale or exchange of property," they will be treated either as a transaction between the partnership and a partner not acting in the capacity of a partner, or as a transaction between partners acting other than as members of the partnership. Extensive Regulations under § 1.707–3 through § 1.707–9 have been promulgated to delineate bona fide distributions from disguised sales. Section 707(a)(2)(B) was specifically designed to avoid the uncertainty created by the *Otey* decision which follows.

OTEY v. COMMISSIONER

70 T.C. 312 (1978), *affirmed per curiam* 634 F.2d 1046 (6th Cir.1980).

HALL, JUDGE.

* * * Petitioner made a contribution of property worth $65,000 to a partnership of which he was a partner. Within a short period after such contribution the partnership borrowed funds on which petitioner was jointly and severally liable, and pursuant to agreement distributed $64,750 of such borrowed funds to petitioner, retaining petitioner's property. The distribution of $64,750 did not exceed petitioner's basis in the partnership. The question presented is whether petitioner in reality "sold" his property to the partnership. Respondent, relying on section 707, contends that he did.

Section 707 provides that "If a partner engages in a transaction with a partnership other than in his capacity as a member of such partnership, the transaction shall ... be considered as occurring between the partnership and one who is not a partner," and section 1.707–1(a), Income Tax Regs., provides that "In all cases, the substance of the transaction will govern rather than its form."

Petitioner relies on section 721—"No gain or loss shall be recognized to a partnership or to any of its partners in the case of a contribution of property to the partnership in exchange for an interest in the partnership"—and section 731—"In the case of a distribution by a partnership to a partner * * * gain shall not be recognized to such partner, except to the extent any money distributed exceeds the adjusted basis of such partner's interest in the partnership immediately before the distribution."

We are cautioned, however, by section 1.731–1(c)(3), Income Tax Regs., as follows:

> (3) If there is a contribution of property to a partnership and within a short period:

> (i) Before or after such contribution other property is distributed to the contributing partner and the contributed property is retained by the partnership, or

> (ii) After such contribution the contributed property is distributed to another partner,

such distribution may not fall within the scope of section 731. Section 731 does not apply to a distribution of property, if, in fact, the distribution was made in order to effect an exchange of property between two or more of the partners or between the partnership and a partner. Such a transaction shall be treated as an exchange of property.

Thus we are faced with the question whether this transaction, which was in form a contribution of property to a partnership followed by a distribution of loan proceeds to the contributing partner, was in substance a sale of the property to the partnership by the partner.

Respondent relies on certain facts which he deems crucial. First, the property, which petitioner inherited from his uncle, was taken by petitioner in joint tenancy with his wife. To convey the property to the partnership, the wife had to join in the conveyance. Since she was not a partner, respondent concludes that at least as to half the real property there must have been a sale. However, since the wife apparently had only a legal title as joint tenant in the property, having contributed nothing to the acquisition, we find this argument unpersuasive. There is no indication in the record that petitioner intended to make a gift of half of the property to his wife and it appears the use of joint tenancy was merely intended as a convenient and customary means of reducing probate costs in the event of petitioner's death prior to his wife's death.

Second, respondent contends that because neither partner contributed any cash to the partnership, and all available cash had to come from borrowing, "it is unconvincing that a partner would withdraw funds for his personal use when these funds were needed for the project." Respondent also points out that on the Department of Housing and Urban Development Mortgagor's Certificate of Actual Cost, the cost of the land was stated to be $64,750. Respondent then concludes that "considered as a whole, the facts portray a sale of property to the partnership." We disagree.

Subchapter K provides two possible methods of analyzing the transfer by petitioner of his Heiman Street property to the partnership, with sharply divergent tax consequences depending upon which analysis applies. Using the contribution approach, sections 721 and 731 treat a partner's contribution of property to his partnership as a nonrecognizing transaction, producing neither gain nor loss, and withdrawals from the partnership are treated as reductions in basis rather than as taxable events. If these sections are applicable, we must sustain petitioner, because the immediate recourse borrowing by the partnership would (like most other borrowing) be a nontaxable event, increasing the basis of the parties in their partnership interest under sections 752(a) and 722. The distribution to a partner (petitioner) of part of the borrowed funds would not generate gain but would simply reduce pro tanta the distributee's basis under sections 731(a)(1) and 733. This approach treats petitioner in a manner rather similar to a proprietor. Had petitioner simply decided to use his Heiman Street property as a proprietor for an FHA housing project and had he been able to obtain an FHA construction loan in an amount exceeding the cost of building the proposed structure, and diverted to his personal use $64,750 of the loan, no gain or loss would have been realized. This would be the case even had he been able to borrow the money only by agreeing to pay half his profits over to Thurman for acting as the cosigner on the loan. Sections 721 and 731 parallel this treatment.

But the Code also recognizes that in some cases partners do not deal with a partnership in their capacity as partners. Even though they are personally on both sides of a transaction with the partnership to the extent of their partnership interest, partners may on occasion deal with the partnership in a capacity other than as a partner and must treat such dealings with the partnership accordingly under section 707. This section, among other things, prevents use of the partnership provisions to render nontaxable what would in substance have been a taxable exchange if it had not been "run through" the partnership. For example, respondent has ruled that if two parties contribute to their partnership their equal interest in stock of two corporations and then liquidate the partnership with each taking all of the stock of one corporation, a taxable exchange has occurred. Rev.Rul. 57–200, 1957–1 C.B. 205. The partnership form may not be employed to evade the limitations in section 1031, and section 707 is the mechanism for guarding this gate.

Neither the Code and regulations nor the case law offers a great deal of guidance for distinguishing whether transactions such as those before us are to be characterized as a contribution (nontaxable) under section 721, as petitioner contends, or as a sale to the partnership other than in the capacity of a partner (taxable) under section 707, as respondent urges. It is at least clear from the above-quoted regulation under section 731 that application or not of section 707 is not always merely elective with a taxpayer. Occasions exist on which he must be thrust unwillingly within it in order for it to serve its above-described prophylactic function. And the regulations provide that "In all cases, the substance of the transaction will govern rather than its form."

The Code and regulations make more explicit the "ground rules" for the application of section 707 where performance of services by a partner for the partnership is involved as distinguished from a transfer of property. In the case of personal services, the characteristic which distinguishes ordinary distributions taxed under section 731 from "guaranteed payments" taxed under section 707 is the extent to which such payments are determined without regard to the income of the partnership. Section 707 provides no explicit assistance analogous to section 707(c) where transfers of property are involved, but the guaranteed payments provision may provide useful indications of the drafters' intent. However, section 1.721–1(a), Income Tax Regs., does shed some light on the applicable rule. "Thus, if the transfer of property by the partner to the partnership results in the receipt by the partner of money or other consideration, including a promissory obligation fixed in amount and time for payment, the transaction will be treated as a sale or exchange under section 707 rather than as a contribution under section 721."

A few cases have considered whether transfers of property by partners to partnerships were or were not taxable under section 707. In *Davis v. Commissioner,* a Memorandum Opinion of this Court, 29 T.C.M. 749, 39 P–H Memo.T.C. par. 70,170 (1970), the taxpayer transferred land to a joint venture in which he was held to have been a partner. It was agreed that he would be paid for the property with the first available funds and in all events whether the project was a success or failure. In form the transaction was a sale. His 50–percent partner would have been required to put up half the purchase price if the venture could not pay. We there held the transaction was governed by section 707 and not by section 721. The taxpayer recognized long-term capital gain on the sale.

In *Oliver v. Commissioner,* a Memorandum Opinion of this Court, 13 T.C.M. 67, 23 P–H Memo.T.C. par. 54,034 (1954), the taxpayer transferred 40 lots to a partnership in which he owned a 50–percent interest. In form, the transaction was a sale to the partnership, and the taxpayer claimed long-term capital gain treatment. However, the other partner contributed no capital, and the 40 lots constituted the sole capital of the partnership at its inception. We held that in substance the "sale" amounted to a capital contribution to the partnership. The taxpayer's capital account was credited with the taxpayer's cost of the lots and later with the excess of the FHA appraisal over that cost. There was no other partnership capital and had the taxpayer not contributed the lots there would have been no partnership business. While *Oliver* dealt with years preceding the 1954 Code, the issue decided therein of whether the transfer was in substance a sale or a capital contribution is essentially the same as whether section 707 or section 721 should apply under the law applicable to our case.

Willis argues that partners in effect may choose between coming within section 707 or section 721 by the choice they make between substantively identical methods of capitalizing their partnership. He does not construe the "substance of the transaction" language of regulation section 1.707–1(a) as authorizing respondent to recharacterize a transaction which is formally a sale, even if it is merely a method chosen for capitalizing the partnership, in the absence of an attempted end run around section 1031's limitations. 1 A. Willis, Partnership Taxation, secs. 14.08 and 33.07 (2d ed. 1976).

Turning to the facts before us, a number of circumstances militate in favor of a conclusion that section 721 rather than section 707 should govern. In the first place, the form of the transaction was a contribution to capital rather than a sale, and there are no elements of artificiality in the form selected which should induce us to be particularly astute to look behind it. Without deciding here (because we need not decide) the extent to which Willis is correct in his view that partners may elect to capitalize their partnership under section 707 by employing the necessary formal steps, this partnership clearly did not so elect. Second, and most importantly, the capital in question (borrowed funds aside) was emplaced in the partnership at its inception and as a part of the very raison d'etre of the partnership. Without this transfer, the partnership would have had no assets and no business. It is therefore most difficult for us to agree with respondent that the transaction was between petitioner and the partnership *other than in petitioner's capacity as a partner.* See *Oliver v. Commissioner, supra.* Third, the capital in question was the *only* contributed capital of the partnership. To treat this as an outside transaction would require us to hold in effect that no nonborrowed capital was contributed at all. While such partnerships can of course exist, they are unusual and it would seem very strained to contend that this is such a case. The property had to be in the partnership to make the borrowing possible. Fourth, petitioner enjoyed here no guarantee by the partnership that he would be paid (and get to keep) the $65,000 in all events. Compare *Davis v. Commissioner, supra.* True, most of that sum was distributed to him almost at once out of borrowed funds, but he remained personally liable for the entire borrowing. Accordingly, we do not consider the transaction to be one described in section 1.721–1(a), Income Tax Regs., resulting "in the receipt by the partner of money or other consideration, including a promissory obligation fixed in amount and time for payment," and causing applicability of section 707. Provisions for preferential distributions out of borrowed funds to restore capital accounts to equality after non-pro rata partnership contributions do not necessarily demonstrate that the contributions were really sales. An important feature distinguishing transfers in the capacity of a partner from section 707 transactions is whether payment by the partnership to the partner is at the risk of the economic fortunes of the partnership. In the present case, whether partnership cash flow would ever suffice to repay the distributed $64,750 to the bank would depend on the partnership's subsequent economic fortunes. If they were adverse, petitioner could be called on to repay the loan himself. Fifth, the pattern here is a usual and customary partnership capitalization arrangement, under which the partner who put up a greater share of the capital than his share of partnership profits is to receive preferential distributions to equalize capital accounts. The only unusual feature here is the immediate availability of the equalizing distribution out of excess borrowed funds. The normality of this general pattern would make it most unsettling were we to accept respondent's invitation to recharacterize the capitalization of the partnership on account thereof. Finally, although respondent relies briefly on the early cash distribution to petitioner of the excess borrowed funds, this payment does not constitute the kind of attempted end run around the limitations of section 1031 which the regulations properly seek to block. Were there no partnership at all, a taxpayer could borrow funds on the security of appreciated property and apply them to his personal use without triggering gain. Had the distributed funds come directly from the other partner, respondent's case would be stronger. While it may be argued that the funds have come indirectly from Thurman because his credit facilitated the loan, the fact is that the loan was a partnership loan on which the partnership was primarily liable, and both partners were jointly and severally liable for the full loan if the partnership defaulted. We do not view the factual pattern here as constituting a disguised sale of the land to Thurman or the partnership. For all the above reasons, we cannot sustain respondent in his attempted recharacterization of the transfer as a sale.

Respondent also places reliance upon the fact that the cost of the land transfer was stated to be $64,750 in cash in documents filed with the FHA. We do not view this as particularly significant since we do not believe that the implied "sale" label so affixed is determinative. To the extent labels are important, the label used in the partnership agreement itself is far more significant as an indication of the parties' true intent as between themselves.

We hold that the transfer constituted in substance what it was in form—the initial capitalization of the partnership. The early withdrawal of borrowed cash in an amount substantially equivalent to the agreed value of the contributed property reduced petitioner's basis in the partnership but did not create income to him. Secs. 731(a)(1) and 733.

Decision will be entered under Rule 155.

Problem 12–5

Abigail transfers real property with a basis of $1,000,000 and a fair market value of $5,000,000 to an existing partnership for an interest therein. Shortly thereafter, the partnership distributes $1,500,000 to Abigail.

    a.   What result?

    b.   What if the distribution occurred one year after the contribution?

    c.   What if the distribution occurred three years after the contribution?

Chapter 13

TRANSFERS OF PARTNERSHIP INTERESTS—SALE OF PARTNERSHIP INTEREST UNAFFECTED BY § 751(a)

Cross References: §§ 741; 742; 705(a); 706(a), (c); 752(d).

Regulations: §§ 1.705–1(a); 1.706–1(a), (c)(2), (4); 1.741–1; 1.742–1; 1.752–1(h).

A. INTRODUCTION

When a partner decides to "cash in his chips" with regard to all or a part of his or her small business partnership, there are several options. He or she could convince his partners to use partnership assets for the payoff. Alternatively, the partnership interest could be sold to the other partners or to an unrelated third party for cash or property derived from sources outside the partnership. Because of the interplay of the entity and aggregate concepts within the partnership tax structure, the sale of a partnership interest is generally more complicated than the sale of stock by a shareholder of a small business operated as a corporation. This chapter examines the sale of an interest in a partnership which has no "hot assets" under § 751.

Upon the disposition of a partnership interest by sale or exchange, the amount realized is offset against the partner's adjusted basis for the interest, with the differential recognized as gain or loss. In determining the amount realized on the sale, § 752(d), taking an aggregate rather than entity approach, commands that liabilities of the partnership be taken into account in a fashion similar to the treatment of liabilities in a sole proprietorship context. Thus, under the principles enunciated by the Supreme Court in *Crane v. Commissioner,* 331 U.S. 1 (1947), and *Commissioner v. Tufts,* 461 U.S. 300 (1983), which follows in this chapter, a partner's share of the partnership liabilities as determined under § 752 will constitute an amount realized when he transfers his partnership interest.

B. CHARACTERIZATION OF GAIN OR LOSS

After a determination of the amount of the gain or loss realized, recognized, and allowable, characterization issues must be confronted. Except as provided in § 751(a), § 741 stipulates that the gain or loss on the sale of a partnership interest is considered to be from the sale or exchange of a capital asset. Given the Supreme Court's narrow construction of the *Corn Products* doctrine in *Arkansas Best Corp. v. Commissioner,* 485 U.S. 212 (1988), short-term or long-term capital characterization (subject to § 751) invariably will arise on the sale or exchange of an interest in a partnership. See Chapter 2.

A sale of the partnership interest on any day other than the first day of the year requires a preliminary income or loss calculation and partnership interest basis adjustment to reflect the selling partner's share of the partnership's pre-sale operations for the year. Without such adjustment, the selling partner could convert ordinary income into capital gain as the portion of the sales proceeds attributable to normal business operations (usually ordinary income) would be transmuted into income derived for the disposition of the partnership interest (capital gain). However, § 706(c) closes the selling partner's taxable year for the purposes of that partnership on the date of sale if the partner disposes of the entire interest. Thus, under § 706(a) and § 702, the partner would report his or her distributive share of the partnership's gain or loss for such period and adjust the basis for his or her partnership interest accordingly under § 705(a)(1)(A). The distributive share portion of the amount realized will be characterized by the nature of the partnership's operations as ordinary income or loss, short-term or long-term capital gain or loss, and § 1231 gain or loss, while the remainder of the transaction will be addressed exclusively by § 741 (subject to § 751).

The Regulations permit a determination of the distributive share either by an interim closing of the books (an actual tracing of precise results up to the date of sale) or by a proration of the results for the *entire* year between the seller and the purchaser of the interest based on the time period of ownership. For a calendar year taxpayer in a calendar year partnership, this decision may be made with hindsight at the beginning of the following year. In other taxable year situations, returns may have to be filed reflecting the sale before the yearly results of the partnership are known.

A similar proration is employed on the disposition of less than a partner's entire interest. Although the partnership year does not close for the selling partner in such a case, the varying interest rule of § 706(c)(2)(B) and (d) applies, producing similar results. Furthermore, § 706(d)(2) and (3) provides allocation rules for assigning various deductions to particular time periods.

C. TREATMENT OF LIABILITIES

The Supreme Court in *Commissioner v. Tufts,* which follows, upheld the *Crane* doctrine and treated nonrecourse debt as a "true loan." The fact that the amount of the loan exceeded the property's fair market value was "irrelevant." The full amount of the liability must be taken into account in computing the amount realized. The Court further held that the fair market value limitation of § 752(c) was limited to transactions between a partner and the partnership and could not be incorporated into § 752(d) governing the treatment of liabilities on the sale of a partnership interest.

In 1984, Congress added subsection (g) to § 7701 which provides that for all of the income tax provisions, in determining gain or loss with respect to any property, the fair market value of the property shall be deemed to be not less than any nonrecourse debt to which the property is subject. This provision codifies the *Tufts* decision, but should be imposed only if the nonrecourse debt had been included in the basis of the property.

Although a share of partnership liabilities in the same amount is included both in the basis of a partner's partnership interest and in the amount the partner is considered to have received on a transfer of that interest, the liabilities of which the partner is relieved on the transfer can exceed the tax basis of that partner's partnership interest. That partner's basis may have been reduced, for instance, by partnership losses or by the partner's withdrawals from the partnership without a comparable reduction in partnership liabilities.

COMMISSIONER v. TUFTS

461 U.S. 300 (1983).

Justice Blackmun delivered the opinion of the Court.

Over 35 years ago, in *Crane v. Commissioner,* 331 U.S. 1 (1947), this Court ruled that a taxpayer, who sold property encumbered by a nonrecourse mortgage (the amount of the mortgage being less than the property's value), must include the unpaid balance of the mortgage in the computation of the amount the taxpayer realized on the sale. The case now before us presents the question whether the same rule applies when the unpaid amount of the nonrecourse mortgage exceeds the fair market value of the property sold.

I

On August 1, 1970, respondent Clark Pelt, a builder, and his wholly owned corporation, respondent Clark, Inc., formed a general partnership. The purpose of the partnership was to construct a 120–unit apartment complex in Duncanville, Tex., a Dallas suburb. Neither Pelt nor Clark, Inc., made any capital contribution to the partnership. Six days later, the partnership entered into a mortgage loan agreement with the Farm

& Home Savings Association (F & H). Under the agreement, F & H was committed for a $1,851,500 loan for the complex. In return, the partnership executed a note and a deed of trust in favor of F & H. The partnership obtained the loan on a nonrecourse basis: neither the partnership nor its partners assumed any personal liability for repayment of the loan. Pelt later admitted four friends and relatives, respondents Tufts, Steger, Stephens, and Austin, as general partners. None of them contributed capital upon entering the partnership.

The construction of the complex was completed in August 1971. During 1971, each partner made small capital contributions to the partnership; in 1972, however, only Pelt made a contribution. The total of the partners' capital contributions was $44,212. In each tax year, all partners claimed as income tax deductions their allocable shares of ordinary losses and depreciation. The deductions taken by the partners in 1971 and 1972 totalled $439,972. Due to these contributions and deductions, the partnership's adjusted basis in the property in August 1972 was $1,455,740.

In 1971 and 1972, major employers in the Duncanville area laid off significant numbers of workers. As a result, the partnership's rental income was less than expected, and it was unable to make the payments due on the mortgage. Each partner, on August 28, 1972, sold his partnership interest to an unrelated third party, Fred Bayles. As consideration, Bayles agreed to reimburse each partner's sale expenses up to $250; he also assumed the nonrecourse mortgage.

On the date of transfer, the fair market value of the property did not exceed $1,400,000. Each partner reported the sale on his federal income tax return and indicated that a partnership loss of $55,740 had been sustained. The Commissioner of Internal Revenue, on audit, determined that the sale resulted in a partnership capital gain of approximately $400,000. His theory was that the partnership had realized the full amount of the nonrecourse obligation.

Relying on *Millar v. Commissioner,* 577 F.2d 212, 215 (CA3), cert. denied, 439 U.S. 1046 (1978), the United States Tax Court, in an unreviewed decision, upheld the asserted deficiencies. 70 T.C. 756 (1978). The United States Court of Appeals for the Fifth Circuit reversed. 651 F.2d 1058 (1981). That court expressly disagreed with the *Millar* analysis, and, in limiting *Crane v. Commissioner, supra,* to its facts, questioned the theoretical underpinnings of the *Crane* decision. We granted certiorari to resolve the conflict.

II

Section 752(d) of the Internal Revenue Code of 1954, 26 U.S.C. § 752(d), specifically provides that liabilities involved in the sale or exchange of a partnership interest are to "be treated in the same manner as liabilities in connection with the sale or exchange of property not associated with partnerships." Section 1001 governs the determination of gains and losses on the disposition of property. Under § 1001(a), the gain or loss from a sale or other disposition of property is defined as the difference between "the amount realized" on the disposition and the property's adjusted basis. Subsection (b) of § 1001 defines "amount realized": "The amount realized from the sale or other disposition of property shall be the sum of any money received plus the fair market value of the property (other than money) received." At issue is the application of the latter provision to the disposition of property encumbered by a nonrecourse mortgage of an amount in excess of the property's fair market value.

A

In *Crane v. Commissioner, supra,* this Court took the first and controlling step toward the resolution of this issue. Beulah B. Crane was the sole beneficiary under the will of her deceased husband. At his death in January 1932, he owned an apartment building that was then mortgaged for an amount which proved to be equal to its fair market value, as determined for federal estate tax purposes. The widow, of course, was not personally liable on the mortgage. She operated the building for nearly seven years, hoping to turn it into a profitable venture; during that period, she claimed income tax deductions for depreciation, property taxes, interest, and operating expenses, but did not make payments upon the mortgage principal. In computing her basis for the depreciation deductions, she included the full amount of the mortgage debt. In November 1938, with her hopes unfulfilled and the mortgagee threatening foreclosure, Mrs. Crane sold the building. The purchaser took the property subject to the mortgage and paid Crane $3,000; of that amount, $500 went for the expenses of the sale.

Crane reported a gain of $2,500 on the transaction. She reasoned that her basis in the property was zero (despite her earlier depreciation deductions based on including the amount of the mortgage) and that the amount she realized from the sale was simply the cash she received. The Commissioner disputed this claim. He asserted that Crane's basis in the property, under § 113(a)(5) of the Revenue Act of 1938, 52 Stat. 490 (the current version is § 1014 of the 1954 Code, as amended, 26 U.S.C. § 1014 (1976 ed. and Supp. V)), was the property's fair market value at the time of her husband's death, adjusted for depreciation in the interim, and that the amount realized was the net cash received plus the amount of the outstanding mortgage assumed by the purchaser.

In upholding the Commissioner's interpretation of § 113(a)(5) of the 1938 Act, the Court observed that to regard merely the taxpayer's equity in the property as her basis would lead to depreciation deductions less than the actual physical deterioration of the property, and would require the basis to be recomputed with each payment on the mortgage. The Court rejected Crane's claim that any loss due to depreciation belonged to the mortgagee. The effect of the Court's ruling was that the taxpayer's basis was the value of the property undiminished by the mortgage.

The Court next proceeded to determine the amount realized under § 111(b) of the 1938 Act, 52 Stat. 484 (the current version is § 1001(b) of the 1954 Code, 26 U.S.C. § 1001(b)). In order to avoid the "absurdity," see 331 U.S., at 13, of Crane's realizing only $2,500 on the sale of property worth over a quarter of a million dollars, the Court treated the amount realized as it had treated basis, that is, by including the outstanding value of the mortgage. To do otherwise would have permitted Crane to recognize a tax loss unconnected with any actual economic loss. The Court refused to construe one section of the Revenue Act so as "to frustrate the Act as a whole."

Crane, however, insisted that the nonrecourse nature of the mortgage required different treatment. The Court, for two reasons, disagreed. First, excluding the nonrecourse debt from the amount realized would result in the same absurdity and frustration of the Code. Second, the Court concluded that Crane obtained an economic benefit from the purchaser's assumption of the mortgage identical to the benefit conferred by the cancellation of personal debt. Because the value of the property in that case exceeded the amount of the mortgage, it was in Crane's economic interest to treat the mortgage as a personal obligation; only by so doing could she realize upon sale the appreciation in her equity represented by the $2,500 boot. The purchaser's assumption of the liability thus resulted in a taxable economic benefit to her, just as if she had been given, in addition to the boot, a sum of cash sufficient to satisfy the mortgage.

In a footnote, pertinent to the present case, the Court observed:

"Obviously, if the value of the property is less than the amount of the mortgage, a mortgagor who is not personally liable cannot realize a benefit equal to the mortgage. Consequently, a different problem might be encountered where a mortgagor abandoned the property or transferred it subject to the mortgage without receiving boot. That is not this case."

B

This case presents that unresolved issue. We are disinclined to overrule *Crane,* and we conclude that the same rule applies when the unpaid amount of the nonrecourse mortgage exceeds the value of the property transferred. *Crane* ultimately does not rest on its limited theory of economic benefit; instead, we read *Crane* to have approved the Commissioner's decision to treat a nonrecourse mortgage in this context as a true loan. This approval underlies *Crane's* holdings that the amount of the nonrecourse liability is to be included in calculating both the basis and the amount realized on disposition. That the amount of the loan exceeds the fair market value of the property thus becomes irrelevant.

When a taxpayer receives a loan, he incurs an obligation to repay that loan at some future date. Because of this obligation, the loan proceeds do not qualify as income to the taxpayer. When he fulfills the obligation, the repayment of the loan likewise has no effect on his tax liability.

Another consequence to the taxpayer from this obligation occurs when the taxpayer applies the loan proceeds to the purchase price of property used to secure the loan. Because of the obligation to repay, the taxpayer is entitled to include the amount of the loan in computing his basis in the property; the loan, under § 1012, is part of the taxpayer's cost of the property. Although a different approach might have been taken with respect to a nonrecourse mortgage loan,[5] the Commissioner has chosen to accord it the same treatment he gives to a recourse mortgage loan. The Court approved that choice in *Crane,* and the respondents do not challenge it here. The choice and its resultant benefits to the taxpayer are predicated on the assumption that the mortgage will be repaid in full.

When encumbered property is sold or otherwise disposed of and the purchaser assumes the mortgage, the associated extinguishment of the mortgagor's obligation to repay is accounted for in the computation of the amount realized. Because no difference between recourse and nonrecourse obligations is recognized in calculating basis, *Crane* teaches that the Commissioner may ignore the nonrecourse nature of the obligation in determining the amount realized upon disposition of the encumbered property. He thus may include in the amount realized the amount of the nonrecourse mortgage assumed by the purchaser. The rationale for this treatment is that the original inclusion of the amount of the mortgage in basis rested on the assumption that the mortgagor incurred an obligation to repay. Moreover, this treatment balances the fact that the mortgagor originally received the proceeds of the nonrecourse loan tax-free on the same assumption. Unless the outstanding amount of the mortgage is deemed to be realized, the mortgagor effectively will have received untaxed income at the time the loan was extended and will have received an unwarranted increase in the basis of his property. The Commissioner's interpretation of § 1001(b) in this fashion cannot be said to be unreasonable.

C

The Commissioner in fact has applied this rule even when the fair market value of the property falls below the amount of the nonrecourse obligation. Treas.Reg. § 1.1001–2(b), 26 CFR § 1.1001–2(b) (1982);

---

5. The Commissioner might have adopted the theory, implicit in Crane's contentions, that a nonrecourse mortgage is not true debt, but, instead, is a form of joint investment by the mortgagor and the mortgagee. On this approach, nonrecourse debt would be considered a contingent liability, under which the mortgagor's payments on the debt gradually increase his interest in the property while decreasing that of the mortgagee. Because the taxpayer's investment in the property would not include the nonrecourse debt, the taxpayer would not be permitted to include that debt in basis.

We express no view as to whether such an approach would be consistent with the statutory structure and, if so, and *Crane* were not on the books, whether that approach would be preferred over *Crane's* analysis. We note only that the *Crane* Court's resolution of the basis issue presumed that when property is purchased with proceeds from a nonrecourse mortgage, the purchaser becomes the sole owner of the property. Under the *Crane* approach, the mortgagee is entitled to no portion of the basis. The nonrecourse mortgage is part of the mortgagor's investment in the property, and does not constitute a coinvestment by the mortgagee.

Rev.Rul. 76–111, 1976–1 Cum.Bull. 214. Because the theory on which the rule is based applies equally in this situation, we have no reason, after *Crane,* to question this treatment.[11]

Respondents received a mortgage loan with the concomitant obligation to repay by the year 2012. The only difference between that mortgage and one on which the borrower is personally liable is that the mortgagee's remedy is limited to foreclosing on the securing property. This difference does not alter the nature of the obligation; its only effect is to shift from the borrower to the lender any potential loss caused by devaluation of the property. If the fair market value of the property falls below the amount of the outstanding obligation, the mortgagee's ability to protect its interests is impaired, for the mortgagor is free to abandon the property to the mortgagee and be relieved of his obligation.

This, however, does not erase the fact that the mortgagor received the loan proceeds tax-free and included them in his basis on the understanding that he had an obligation to repay the full amount. When the obligation is canceled, the mortgagor is relieved of his responsibility to repay the sum he originally received and thus realizes value to that extent within the meaning of § 1001(b). From the mortgagor's point of view, when his obligation is assumed by a third party who purchases the encumbered property, it is as if the mortgagor first had

---

11. Professor Wayne G. Barnett, as *amicus* in the present case, argues that the liability and property portions of the transaction should be accounted for separately. Under his view, there was a transfer of the property for $1.4 million, and there was a cancellation of the $1.85 million obligation for a payment of $1.4 million. The former resulted in a capital loss of $50,000, and the latter in the realization of $450,000 of ordinary income. Taxation of the ordinary income might be deferred under § 108 by a reduction of respondents' bases in their partnership interests.

Although this indeed could be a justifiable mode of analysis, it has not been adopted by the Commissioner. Nor is there anything to indicate that the Code requires the Commissioner to adopt it. We note that Professor Barnett's approach does assume that recourse and nonrecourse debt may be treated identically.

The Commissioner also has chosen not to characterize the transaction as cancellation of indebtedness. We are not presented with and do not decide the contours of the cancellation-of-indebtedness doctrine. We note only that our approach does not fall within certain prior interpretations of that doctrine. In one view, the doctrine rests on the same initial premise as our analysis here—an obligation to repay—but the doctrine relies on a freeing-of-assets theory to attribute ordinary income to the debtor upon cancellation. According to that view, when nonrecourse debt is forgiven, the debtor's basis in the securing property is reduced by the amount of debt canceled, and realization of income is deferred until the sale of the property. Because that interpretation attributes income only when assets are freed, however, an insolvent debtor realizes income just to the extent his assets exceed his liabilities after the cancellation. Similarly, if the nonrecourse indebtedness exceeds the value of the securing property, the taxpayer never realizes the full amount of the obligation canceled because the tax law has not recognized negative basis.

Although the economic benefit prong of *Crane* also relies on a freeing-of-assets theory, that theory is irrelevant to our broader approach. In the context of a sale or disposition of property under § 1001, the extinguishment of the obligation to repay is not ordinary income; instead, the amount of the canceled debt is included in the amount realized, and enters into the computation of gain or loss on the disposition of property. According to *Crane,* this treatment is no different when the obligation is nonrecourse: the basis is not reduced as in the cancellation-of-indebtedness context, and the full value of the outstanding liability is included in the amount realized. Thus, the problem of negative basis is avoided.

been paid with cash borrowed by the third party from the mortgagee on a nonrecourse basis, and then had used the cash to satisfy his obligation to the mortgagee.

Moreover, this approach avoids the absurdity the Court recognized in *Crane*. Because of the remedy accompanying the mortgage in the nonrecourse situation, the depreciation in the fair market value of the property is relevant economically only to the mortgagee, who by lending on a nonrecourse basis remains at risk. To permit the taxpayer to limit his realization to the fair market value of the property would be to recognize a tax loss for which he has suffered no corresponding economic loss. Such a result would be to construe "one section of the Act * * * so as * * * to defeat the intention of another or to frustrate the Act as a whole."

In the specific circumstances of *Crane,* the economic benefit theory did support the Commissioner's treatment of the nonrecourse mortgage as a personal obligation. The footnote in *Crane* acknowledged the limitations of that theory when applied to a different set of facts. *Crane* also stands for the broader proposition, however, that a nonrecourse loan should be treated as a true loan. We therefore hold that a taxpayer must account for the proceeds of obligations he has received tax-free and included in basis. Nothing in either § 1001(b) or in the Court's prior decisions requires the Commissioner to permit a taxpayer to treat a sale of encumbered property asymmetrically, by including the proceeds of the nonrecourse obligation in basis but not accounting for the proceeds upon transfer of the encumbered property.

III

Relying on the Code's § 752(c), 26 U.S.C. § 752(c), however, respondents argue that Congress has provided for precisely this type of asymmetrical treatment in the sale or disposition of partnership property. Section 752 prescribes the tax treatment of certain partnership transactions, and § 752(c) provides that "[f]or purposes of this section, a liability to which property is subject shall, to the extent of the fair market value of such property, be considered as a liability of the owner of the property." Section 752(c) could be read to apply to a sale or disposition of partnership property, and thus to limit the amount realized to the fair market value of the property transferred. Inconsistent with this interpretation, however, is the language of § 752(d), which specifically mandates that partnership liabilities be treated "in the same manner as liabilities in connection with the sale or exchange of property not associated with partnerships." The apparent conflict of these subsections renders the facial meaning of the statute ambiguous, and therefore we must look to the statute's structure and legislative history.

Subsections (a) and (b) of § 752 prescribe rules for the treatment of liabilities in transactions between a partner and his partnership, and thus for determining the partner's adjusted basis in his partnership interest. Under § 704(d), a partner's distributive share of partnership losses is limited to the adjusted basis of his partnership interest. When partnership liabilities are increased or when a partner takes on the liabilities of the partnership, § 752(a) treats the amount of the increase or the amount assumed as a contribution by the partner to the partnership. This treatment results in an increase in the adjusted basis of the partner's interest and a concomitant increase in the § 704(d) limit on his distributive share of any partnership loss. Conversely, under § 752(b), a decrease in partnership liabilities or the assumption of a partner's liabilities by the partnership has the effect of a distribution, thereby reducing the limit on the partner's distributive share of the partnership's losses. When property encumbered by liabilities is contributed to or distributed from the partnership, § 752(c) prescribes that the liability shall be considered to be assumed by the transferee only to the extent of the property's fair market value.

The legislative history indicates that Congress contemplated this application of § 752(c). Mention of the fair market value limitation occurs only in the context of transactions under subsections (a) and (b). The sole reference to subsection (d) does not discuss the limitation. While the legislative history is certainly not conclusive, it indicates that the fair market value limitation of § 752(c) was directed to transactions between a partner and his partnership. 1 A. Willis, J. Pennell, & P. Postlewaite, Partnership Taxation § 44.03, p. 44–3 (3d ed. 1981); Simmons, *Tufts v. Commissioner:* Amount Realized Limited to Fair Market Value, 15 U.C.D.L.Rev. 577, 611–613 (1982).

By placing a fair market value limitation on liabilities connected with property contributions to and distributions from partnerships under subsections (a) and (b), Congress apparently intended § 752(c) to prevent a partner from inflating the basis of his partnership interest. Otherwise, a partner with no additional capital at risk in the partnership could raise the § 704(d) limit on his distributive share of partnership losses or could reduce his taxable gain upon disposition of his partnership interest. There is no potential for similar abuse in the context of § 752(d) sales of partnership interests to unrelated third parties. In light of the above, we interpret subsection (c) to apply only to § 752(a) and (b) transactions, and not to limit the amount realized in a sale or exchange of a partnership interest under § 752(d).

IV

When a taxpayer sells or disposes of property encumbered by a nonrecourse obligation, the Commissioner properly requires him to include among the assets realized the outstanding amount of the obligation. The fair market value of the property is irrelevant to this calculation. We find this interpretation to be consistent with *Crane v. Commissioner,* 331 U.S. 1 (1947), and to implement the statutory mandate in a reasonable manner.

The judgment of the Court of Appeals is therefore reversed.

It is so ordered.

REVENUE RULING 75-194

1975–1 C.B. 80.

Advice has been requested concerning the Federal income tax consequences of the contribution of an interest in a limited partnership to a charitable organization in the situation described below.

L became a limited partner in a partnership on its formation in 1971. In 1974, *L* contributed his entire limited partnership interest to a charitable organization described in section 170(c) of the Internal Revenue Code of 1954. On that date all of the partnership liabilities were liabilities on which neither *L*, the other partners, nor the partnership had assumed any personal liability. Also on that date, *L*'s proportionate share of the value of the partnership assets was greater than his proportionate share of the partnership liabilities and because of partnership losses *L*'s adjusted basis for his partnership interest was less than his proportionate share of the partnership liabilities. At the time of the contribution the partnership had no unrealized receivables or inventory items described in section 751.

Section 170(a) of the Code provides the general rule that there shall be allowed as a deduction any "charitable contribution" (as defined in section 170(c)) payment of which is made within the taxable year.

Section 1.170A–1(c) of the Income Tax Regulations provides, in part, that if a contribution is made in property other than money, the amount of the contribution is the fair market value of the property at the time of the contribution reduced as provided in section 170(e)(1) of the Code.

Section 741 of the Code provides, in pertinent part, that in the case of a sale or exchange of an interest in a partnership, gain or loss shall be recognized to the transferor partner and shall be considered gain or loss from the sale or exchange of a capital asset, except as otherwise provided in section 751.

Section 752(c) of the Code provides that for purposes of section 752, a liability to which property is subject shall, to the extent of the fair market value of such property, be considered as a liability of the owner of the property.

Section 1.752–1(e) of the regulations provides, in part, that where none of the partners have any personal liability with respect to a partnership liability (as in the case of a mortgage on real estate acquired by the partnership without assumption by the partnership or any of the partners of any liability on the mortgage), then all partners, included limited partners, shall be considered as sharing such liability under section 752(c) of the Code in the same proportion as they share the profits.

Section 752(d) of the Code and section 1.752–1(d) of the regulations provide that where there is a sale or exchange of an interest in a partnership, liabilities shall be treated in the same manner as liabilities in connection with the sale or exchange of property not associated with partnerships. For example, if a partner sells his interest in a partnership for $750 cash and at the same time transfers to the purchaser his share of partnership liabilities amounting to $250, the amount realized by the seller on the transaction is $1,000. See also Rev.Rul. 74–40, 1974–1 C.B. 159.

Section 1011(b) of the Code provides the rules for allocating adjusted basis in the case of a "bargain sale" to a charitable organization where a deduction is allowable under section 170 by reason of such sale. Section 1.170A–4(c)(2)(iii) of the regulations defines a "bargain sale" as a transfer of property which is in part a sale or exchange of the property and in part a charitable contribution, as defined in section 170(c), of the property. Sections 1.170A–4(c) and 1.1011–2 contain rules and examples with respect to the computation of gain and the amount of the charitable contribution in the case of a "bargain sale."

Section 1.1011–2(a)(3) of the regulations provides that if property is transferred subject to an indebtedness, the amount of the indebtedness must be treated as an amount realized for purposes of determining whether there is a sale or exchange to which section 1011(b) of the Code and section 1.1011–2 apply, even though the transferee does not agree to assume or pay the indebtedness.

Since the value of L's share of the partnership assets at the time he transferred his partnership interest exceeded his share of partnership liabilities at that time, a charitable contribution deduction is allowable under section 170 of the Code, subject to the reductions and limitations set forth therein. At the same time, pursuant to sections 752(d) and 1011(b), the amount of L's share of partnership liabilities at the time of the transfer constitutes an amount realized by L. Based on the foregoing, a bargain sale within the meaning of sections 170 and 1011(b) has occurred.

Accordingly, in the instant case, L has a recognized gain on the transfer equal to the excess of the amount realized by L over that portion of the adjusted basis of L's partnership interest (at the time of the transfer) allocable to the sale under section 1011(b) of the Code. Since the partnership had no unrealized receivables or appreciated inventory items described in section 751, the gain is considered a gain from the sale of a capital asset under section 741.

Problem 13–1

Jenny, Jessie, and Ruth are equal partners in a partnership which holds various rental properties. The partnership is a cash method, January 31 fiscal year, general partnership known as JJR Enterprises. Each partner has a one-third interest in the capital, profits, and losses of JJR Enterprises. Each contributed $10 in cash to the partnership. The partners have refurbished the properties but the partnership has had no income to date.

ABC Balance Sheet
(1/31/97)

Assets	Book Value and Adjusted Basis	Fair Market Value
1	$20	$20
2	10	25
3	30	45
Total	$60	$90

Liabilities & Capital Per Financial Accounting Records		
Liabilities		
Mortgage	$30	$30
Capital		
Jenny	10	20
Jessie	10	20
Ruth	10	20
Total Liabilities & Capital	$60	$90

1. On February 1, 1997, Sarah offers to purchase Jenny's interest in JJR Enterprises for $20 cash. Assume that JJR Enterprises has no § 751(c) or § 751(d) assets. If Jenny accepts the offer, what is the amount and character of her gain or loss?

2. Assume that asset number 2 on the balance sheet consisted of five separate units which were not inventory items within the meaning of § 751(d)(2), each with a fair market value of $5 and an adjusted basis of $2. JJR Enterprises's only transactions during its fiscal year ending in 1998 were the sales of these units. These sales resulted in income for the fiscal year ending in 1998 of $15. They took place on February 1, April 1, June 1, September 1, and October 1.

   a. On August 1, 1997, Jenny sells her interest to Sarah for $20 cash. What is Jenny's share of income of JJR Enterprises for its fiscal year ending in 1998? When must she report this income? What is the amount and character of Jenny's gain or loss from the sale of her partnership interest?

   b. What would be the answer in a if some of the records of JJR Enterprises had been destroyed in a fire and it were impossible to determine the dates on which the items had been sold other than that they were sold sometime during the year 1997? What if it were merely inconvenient to close the books at the time of Jenny's sale?

   c. What would be the answers to a and b if Jenny had sold one-half of her interest in JJR Enterprises to Sarah on August 1, 1997 for $10 cash?

D. LIKE–KIND EXCHANGES

Prior to 1984, a tax free exchange by a partner of his or her general partnership interest for a general partnership interest in another partnership was possible, providing the underlying assets of both partnerships were of a kind that would qualify under § 1031. The courts refused to accept the position of the Service that a partnership interest came within the category of items excluded from § 1031(a) protection by the provision "(not including ... stocks, bonds, notes, choses in action, certificates of trust or beneficial interests, or other securities or evidences of indebtedness or interest)." However, the Tax Court denied nontaxable treatment to an exchange of a general partnership interest for a limited partnership interest, presumably because the interests were not like kind or because the limited partnership interest was a "chose in action" or a "security," which is excluded from the § 1031(a) exchange provisions.

The Tax Reform Act of 1984 amended § 1031 to clearly provide that the section does not permit an exchange of partnership interests as like-kind property without recognition of gain or loss. The amendment effectively overrules the case law permitting such exchanges. The reason for the limitation seems to be the belief that partnership interests are investments similar to those that traditionally have been excluded from § 1031, the position taken, and lost, in the courts by the Service. Also given as a reason for the provision is the concern that investors in tax shelters could use § 1031 to avoid the taxation of gain inherent in a "burned out" tax shelter. The Senate Report states that the rule is not intended to apply to an exchange of interests in the same partnership.

Chapter 14

TRANSFER OF PARTNERSHIP INTERESTS—TRANSFERS OF COLLAPSIBLE PARTNERSHIP INTERESTS

———————

Code References: §§ 64; 751(a), (c), (d); 1245(a)(1); 1250(a)(1)(A).

Regulations: § 1.751–1(a)(1) and (2), (c)(1)–(3) and (4)(iii), (d), (g) example (1).

A. INTRODUCTION

The sale of a partnership interest is even more complicated when the partnership in which the interest is sold possesses "hot assets." With the exception of pure investment partnerships, almost all small businesses will have such assets since, even if they do not hold inventory as such, they are likely to have unrealized receivables. It should be noted that this latter term includes many items which are beyond the accounting definition of "receivables" but which would generate ordinary income if realized at the partnership level. The small business tax adviser must be aware of whether such items exist before advising a partner on the tax effects of the sale of his interest.

As discussed in Chapter 13, a partner characterizes his gain or loss on the sale or exchange of a partnership interest under § 741 which generally provides for capital asset status. This is an entity approach. It does not assess the results which would have arisen had the partner sold his share of each partnership asset directly. When the partnership does not possess significant ordinary income assets, the entity approach makes little difference. For example, if a partnership owns two appreciated assets which would produce a short-term capital gain and a § 1231 gain if sold by the partnership, the characterization of a partner's gain on the sale of that interest under § 741 as long-term capital is not particularly offensive from a policy standpoint. However, if the sale of the partnership assets would have produced ordinary income, the conver-

278

sion potential of § 741 would be excessive. As a consequence, Congress enacted § 751 which overrides § 741 and ensures in the appropriate setting that the ordinary income component of the partnership interest is preserved. Thus, the price of the "pass through" nature of the tax aspects of the partnership business operations is a similar "pass through" treatment when a partnership interest is sold in a partnership which owns significant ordinary income assets.

B. LIMITATION ON CAPITAL CHARACTERIZATION

Section 751 focuses on the "tainted" assets of the partnership. These are also sometimes referred to as the partnership's "hot assets." Under § 751(c) and (d), the partnership's unrealized receivables (which, under the expanded definition, includes rights to payments which would produce ordinary income and which have not been taken into account previously as well as most recapture items such as § 1245, etc.) and inventory items (partnership assets which would produce ordinary income if sold by the partnership *or* the transferor partner) are isolated. Thus, the statutory definition covers far more than mere receivables. In the case of such "receivables," their classification as such taints their status and mandates the application of § 751. Regarding inventory items, the section is brought into play only if they are substantially appreciated—i.e., their collective value must exceed 120% of their collective basis. However, the value of inventory items of most businesses will easily exceed their cost by 20 percent.

Once classified as unrealized receivables or substantially appreciated inventory, these assets are isolated and the selling partner's share of their values and their bases to the partnership are compared in order to determine the ordinary income component of the sale of a partnership interest. Thus, for example, if a 25 percent partner sold his or her partnership interest and the partnership's § 751 assets possessed a total value of $200 and a total basis (as determined under § 732 for a *current* distribution) of $80, the partner would have $30 ordinary income ($50–$20) under § 751(a). The remainder of the partner's sale transaction would be characterized under § 741 after reducing the total amount realized and the selling partner's adjusted basis for the partnership interest by the amount of the consideration and partnership asset basis attributable to the § 751 assets.

Problem 14–1

Sandy, Mel, Rodney, and Joe formed a calendar year partnership which, among other things, produces and sells bingo cards. Each holds a one-fourth interest in the capital, profits, and losses of the partnership. The original contributions to the partnership were $10 in cash from each partner. The partnership has neither earned any income nor received additional contributions. The partnership uses an accrual method for the purchase and sale of inventory and the cash method for all other purposes. In addition to producing bingo cards for sale, the partnership renders consulting services to some of its bingo parlor customers. The partners derive their income exclusively from the partnership.

Partnership Balance Sheet
(12/31/96)

Assets	Book Value and Adjusted Basis	Fair Market Value
Cash	$ 20	$ 20
Accounts Receivable (from services)	-0-	25
Inventory	20	25
Stock (investment)	160	160
Land (investment)	20	50
Total Assets	$220	$280

Liabilities & Capital Per Financial Accounting Records		
Liabilities		
Mortgages	$180	$180
Capital		
Sandy	10	25
Mel	10	25
Rodney	10	25
Joe	10	25
Total Liabilities & Capital	$220	$280

a. What would be Sandy's share of the partnership's potential ordinary income if she does not sell her partnership interest?

b. On January 1, 1997, Michelle offers Sandy $25 cash for her interest in the partnership. If Sandy accepts Michelle's offer, what is the amount and character of Sandy's gain or loss?

c. What would be the difference in your answer in a if the partnership had been an accrual method taxpayer for all items?

C. DEFINITION OF UNREALIZED RECEIV-ABLES AND SUBSTANTIALLY APPRE-CIATED INVENTORY

As discussed in Chapter 13, capital characterization will apply on the sale or exchange of a partnership interest except to the extent § 751 applies. In essence, § 751 employs a modified aggregate approach and attempts, albeit imperfectly, to preclude the conversion of ordinary income into capital gain. The statutory focus of § 751 is on two classes of assets—unrealized receivables and substantially appreciated inventory.

1. UNREALIZED RECEIVABLES

Section 751(c) defines "unrealized receivables" to include the traditional receivable concept of a right to payment for "goods delivered, or to be delivered" to the extent not previously includable in income under the method of accounting used by the partnership. This provision, by its definition, only applies to those goods with respect to which the proceeds from a sale or exchange "would be treated as amounts received from the sale or exchange of property other than a capital asset," i.e., ordinary income assets. For example, if a partnership makes a credit sale of inventory (not a capital asset) which will produce $100 of income, it has an unrealized receivable of $100 if it reports on the cash receipts method, but it does not have an unrealized receivable if it reports on the accrual method. It should be noted that, in the case of many small businesses, accounts receivable for the sale of goods will not constitute unrealized receivables under § 751(c) because the Regulations provide that when inventories are used, the accrual method of accounting generally is required. The accrual method of accounting for inventories also diminishes the possibility that the inventory will be "substantially appreciated."

"Unrealized receivables" also include the right to payment for "services rendered or to be rendered" to the extent not previously includable in income under the method of accounting used by the partnership, a concept encompassing the cash method of accounting. By definition, under the cash method, an unpaid statement for *services* has not been included in gross income. The right to receive such payment is an unrealized receivable.

The concept of unrealized receivables, however, includes far more than traditional business receivables. It has expanded over the years with the addition to the Code of the recapture provisions. Defining unrealized receivables to include recapture amounts ensures that tax planning efforts do not convert ordinary income into capital gain through the use of the partnership form for doing business. The most familiar, and broadest in application, of these recapture provisions are those regarding depreciation. The depreciation recapture provision of § 1245 requires that, when certain depreciable personal property is sold or exchanged, a portion of the gain representing a specified amount of depreciation previously deducted be reported as ordinary income.

2. SUBSTANTIALLY APPRECIATED INVENTORY

Substantially appreciated inventory items of a partnership are also subject to the aggregate approach of § 751. The term "inventory items" is defined broadly and employs a focus on the character of the partnership's assets at *both* the partnership level and the level of the selling partner. The most common components of the term include:

1.   Property of the partnership described in § 1221(1);

2.   Any other property of the partnership which, on sale or exchange by the partnership, would be considered as property other than a capital asset and other than property described in § 1231; and

3. Any other property held by the partnership which, *if held by the selling or distributee partner,* would be considered property of the type described in subparagraph 1 or 2.

LEDOUX v. COMMISSIONER

77 T.C. 293 (1981), *affirmed per curiam,* 695 F.2d 1320 (11th Cir.1983).

STERRETT, JUDGE.

* * * The sole issue presented is whether a portion of the amount received by petitioner on the sale of his 25–percent partnership interest is taxable as ordinary income and not as capital gain. More specifically, we must decide whether any portion of the sales price is attributable to "unrealized receivables" of the partnership.

Generally, gain or loss on the sale or exchange of a partnership interest is treated as capital gain or loss. Sec. 741. Prior to 1954, a partner could escape ordinary income tax treatment on his portion of the partnership's unrealized receivables by selling or exchanging his interest in the partnership and treating the gain or loss therefrom as capital gain or loss. To curb such abuses, section 751 was enacted to deal with the problem of the so-called "collapsible partnership." Section 751 provides, in part, as follows:

SEC. 751. UNREALIZED RECEIVABLES AND INVENTORY ITEMS

(a) SALE OR EXCHANGE OF INTEREST IN PARTNERSHIP.—The amount of any money, or the fair market value of any property, received by a transferor partner in exchange for all or a part of his interest in the partnership attributable to—

(1) unrealized receivables of the partnership . . .

(c) UNREALIZED RECEIVABLES.—For purposes of this subchapter, the term "unrealized receivables" includes, to the extent not previously includible in income under the method of accounting used by the partnership, any rights (contractual or otherwise) to payment for— * * *

(2) services rendered, or to be rendered * * *

Petitioner contends that the dog track agreement gave the Collins–Ledoux partnership the right to manage and operate the dog track. According to petitioner, the agreement did not give the partnership any contractual rights to receive future payments and did not impose any obligation on the partnership to perform services. Rather, the agreement merely gave the partnership the right to occupy and use all of the corporation's properties (including the racetrack facilities and the racing permit) in operating its dog track business; if the partnership exercised such right, it would be obligated to make annual payments to the corporation based upon specified percentages of the annual mutuel handle. Thus, because the dog track agreement was in the nature of a leasehold agreement rather than an employment contract, it did not create the type of "unrealized receivables" referred to in section 751.

Respondent, on the other hand, contends that the partnership operated the racetrack for the corporation and was paid a portion of the profits for its efforts.   As such, the agreement was in the nature of a management employment contract.   When petitioner sold his partnership interest to the Collinses in 1972, the main right that he sold was a contract right to receive income in the future for yet-to-be-rendered personal services.   This, respondent asserts, is supported by the fact that petitioner determined the sales price for his partnership interest by capitalizing his 1972 annual income (approximately $160,000) by a factor of 5.   Therefore, respondent contends that the portion of the gain realized by petitioner that is attributable to the management contract should be characterized as an amount received for unrealized receivables of the partnership.   Consequently, such gain should be characterized as ordinary income under section 751.

The legislative history is not wholly clear with respect to the types of assets that Congress intended to place under the umbrella of "unrealized receivables."   The House report states:

> The term "unrealized receivables or fees" is used to apply to any rights to income which have not been included in gross income under the method of accounting employed by the partnership.   The provision is applicable mainly to cash basis partnerships which have acquired a contractual or other legal right to income for goods or services * * *.

Essentially the same language appears in the report of the Senate committee.   In addition, the regulations elaborate on the meaning of "unrealized receivables" as used in section 751.   Section 1.751–1(c), Income Tax Regs., provides:

> Sec. 1.751–1(c) *Unrealized receivables.*   (1) The term "unrealized receivables", * * * means any rights (contractual or otherwise) to payment for—
>
> (i) Goods delivered or to be delivered (to the extent that such payment would be treated as received for property other than a capital asset), or
>
> (ii) Services rendered or to be rendered, to the extent that income arising from such rights to payment was not previously includible in income under the method of accounting employed by the partnership.   Such rights must have arisen under contracts or agreements in existence at the time of sale or distribution, although the partnership may not be able to enforce payment until a later time.   For example, the term includes trade accounts receivable of a cash method taxpayer, and rights to payment for work or goods begun but incomplete at the time of the sale or distribution * * *.
>
> (3) In determining the amount of the sale price attributable to such unrealized receivables, or their value in a distribution treated as a sale or exchange, any arm's length agreement between the buyer and the seller, or between the partnership and the distributee

partner, will generally establish the amount or value. In the absence of such an agreement, full account shall be taken not only of the estimated cost of completing performance of the contract or agreement, but also of the time between the sale or distribution and the time of payment.

The language of the legislative history and the regulations indicates that the term "unrealized receivables" includes any contractual or other right to payment for goods delivered or to be delivered or services rendered or to be rendered. Therefore, an analysis of the nature of the rights under the dog track agreement, in the context of the aforementioned legal framework, becomes appropriate. A number of cases have dealt with the meaning of "unrealized receivables" and thereby have helped to define the scope of the term. Courts that have considered the term "unrealized receivables" generally have said that it should be given a broad interpretation. For instance, in *Logan v. Commissioner,* 51 T.C. 482, 486 (1968), we held that a partnership's right in quantum meruit to payment for work in progress constituted an unrealized receivable even though there was no express agreement between the partnership and its clients requiring payment.

In *Roth v. Commissioner,* 321 F.2d 607 (9th Cir.1963), affg. 38 T.C. 171 (1962), the Ninth Circuit dealt with the sale of an interest in a partnership which produced a movie and then gave a 10–year distribution right to Paramount Pictures Corp. in return for a percentage of the gross receipts. The selling partner claimed that his right to a portion of the payments expected under the partnership's contract with Paramount did not constitute an unrealized receivable. The court rejected this view, however, reasoning that Congress "meant to exclude from capital gains treatment any receipts which would have been treated as ordinary income to the partner if no transfer of the partnership interest had occurred." Therefore, the partnership's right to payments under the distribution contract was in the nature of an unrealized receivable.

A third example of the broad interpretation given to the term "unrealized receivable" is *United States v. Eidson,* 310 F.2d 111 (5th Cir.1962), revg. an unreported opinion (W.D.Tex.1961). The court there considered the nature of a management contract which was similar to the one at issue in the instant case. The case arose in the context of a sale by a partnership of all of its rights to operate and manage a mutual insurance company. The selling partnership received $170,000 for the rights it held under the management contract, and the Government asserted that the total amount should be treated as ordinary income. The Court of Appeals agreed with the Government's view on the ground that what was being assigned was not a capital asset whose value had accrued over a period of years; rather, the right to operate the company and receive profits therefrom during the remaining life of the contract was the real subject of the assignment. 310 F.2d at 116. The Fifth Circuit found the Supreme Court's holding in *Commissioner v. P.G. Lake, Inc.,* 356 U.S. 260 (1958), to be conclusive:

The substance of what was assigned was the right to receive future income. The substance of what was received was the present value of income which the recipient would otherwise obtain in the future. In short, consideration was paid for the right to receive future income, not for an increase in the value of the income-producing property. [356 U.S. at 266, cited in 310 F.2d at 115.]

In *United States v. Woolsey,* 326 F.2d 287 (5th Cir.1963), revg. 208 F.Supp. 325 (S.D.Tex.1962), the Fifth Circuit again faced a situation similar to the one that we face herein. The Fifth Circuit considered whether proceeds received by taxpayers on the sale of their partnership interests were to be treated as ordinary income or capital gain. There, the court was faced with the sale of interests in a partnership which held, as one of its assets, a 25–year contract to manage a mutual insurance company. As in the instant case, the contract gave the partners the right to render services for the term of the contract and to earn ordinary income in the future. In holding that the partnership's management contract constituted an unrealized receivable, the court stated:

> When we look at the underlying right assigned in this case, we cannot escape the conclusion that so much of the consideration which relates to the right to earn ordinary income in the future under the "management contract," taxable to the assignee as ordinary income, is likewise taxable to the assignor as ordinary income although such income must be earned. Section 751 has defined "unrealized receivables" to include any rights, contractual or otherwise, to ordinary income from "services rendered, *or to be rendered,*" (emphasis added) to the extent that the same were not previously includable in income by the partnership, with the result that capital gains rates cannot be applied to the rights to income under the facts of this case, which would constitute ordinary income had the same been received in due course by the partnership * * *. It is our conclusion that such portion of the consideration received by the taxpayers in this case as properly should be allocated to the present value of their right to earn ordinary income in the future under the "management contract" is subject to taxation as ordinary income * * *.

Petitioner attempts to distinguish *United States v. Woolsey, supra,* and *United States v. Eidson,* supra, from the instant case by arguing that those cases involved a sale or termination of contracts to manage mutual insurance companies in Texas and that the management contracts therein were in the nature of employment agreements. After closely scrutinizing the facts in those cases, we conclude that petitioner's position has no merit. The fact that the *Woolsey* case involved sale of 100 percent of the partnership interests, as opposed to a sale of only a 25–percent partnership interest herein, is of no consequence. In addition, the fact that *Eidson* involved the surrender of the partnership's contract right to manage the insurance company, as opposed to the continued partnership operation in the instant case, also is not a material factual distinction.

The dog track agreement at issue in the instant case is similar to the management contract considered by the Fifth Circuit in *Woolsey.* Each gives the respective partnership the right to operate a business for a period of years and to earn ordinary income in return for payments of specified amounts to the corporation that holds the State charter. Therefore, based on our analysis of the statutory language, the legislative history, and the regulations and relevant case law, we are compelled to find that the dog track agreement gave the petitioner an interest that amounted to an "unrealized receivable" within the meaning of section 751(c).

Petitioner further contends that the dog track agreement does not represent an unrealized receivable because it does not require or obligate the partnership to perform personal services in the future. The agreement only gives, the argument continues, the Collins–Ledoux partnership the right to engage in a business.

We find this argument to be unpersuasive. The words of section 751(c), providing that the term "unrealized receivable" includes the right to payment for "services rendered, or to be rendered," do not preclude that section's application to a situation where, as here, the performance of services is not required by the agreement. As the Fifth Circuit said in *United States v. Eidson,* supra:

> The fact that * * * income would not be received by the [partnership] unless they performed the services which the contract required of them, that is, actively managed the affairs of the insurance company in a manner that would produce a profit after all of the necessary expenditures, does not, it seems clear, affect the nature of this payment. It affects only the amount. That is, the fact that the taxpayers would have to spend their time and energies in performing services for which the compensation would be received merely affects the price at which they would be willing to assign or transfer the contract * * *.

Consequently, a portion of the consideration received by Ledoux on the sale of his partnership interest is subject to taxation as ordinary income.

Having established that the dog track agreement qualifies as an unrealized receivable, we next consider whether all or only part of petitioner's gain in excess of the amount attributable to his share of tangible partnership assets should be treated as ordinary income. Petitioner argues that this excess gain was attributable to goodwill or the value of a going concern.

With respect to goodwill, we note that petitioner's attorney drafted, and petitioner signed, the agreement for sale of partnership interest, dated October 17, 1972, which contains the following statement in paragraph 7:

7. In the determination of the purchase price set forth in this agreement, the parties acknowledge no consideration has been given to any item of goodwill.

The meaning of the words "no consideration" is not entirely free from doubt. They could mean that no thought was given to an allocation of any of the sales price to goodwill, or they could indicate that the parties agreed that no part of the purchase price was allocated to goodwill. The testimony of the attorney who prepared the document indicates, however, that he did consider the implications of the sale of goodwill and even did research on the subject. He testified that he believed, albeit incorrectly, that, if goodwill were part of the purchase price, his client would not be entitled to capital gains treatment.

* * * We find as a fact that petitioner agreed at arm's length with the purchasers of his partnership interest that no part of the purchase price should be attributable to goodwill. * * *

We next turn to petitioner's contention that part or all of the purchase price received in excess of the value of tangible assets is attributable to value of a going concern. In *VGS Corp. v. Commissioner*, 68 T.C. 563 (1977), we stated that—

Going-concern value is, in essence, the additional element of value which attaches to property by reason of its existence as an integral part of a going concern * * *. [T]he ability of a business to continue to function and generate income without interruption as a consequence of the change in ownership, is a vital part of the value of a going concern * * *. [68 T.C. at 591–592; citations omitted.]

However, in the instant case, the ability of the dogracing track to continue to function after the sale of Ledoux's partnership interest was due to the remaining partners' retention of rights to operate under the dog track agreement. Without such agreement, there would have been no continuing right to operate a business and no right to continue to earn income. Thus, the amount paid in excess of the value of Ledoux's share of the tangible assets was not for the intangible value of the business as a going concern but rather for Ledoux's rights under the dog track agreement.

Finally, we turn to petitioner's claim that a determination of the value of rights arising from the dog track agreement has never been made and no evidence of the value of such rights was submitted in this case. We note that the $800,000 purchase price was proposed by petitioner and was accepted by Jack Collins and Jerry Collins in an arm's-length agreement of sale evidenced in the memorandum of agreement of July 19, 1972, and the agreement for sale of partnership interest of October 17, 1972. In addition, the October 17, 1972, sales agreement, written by petitioner's attorney, provided in paragraph 1 that the "Seller [Ledoux] sells to buyer [Jerry Collins and Jack Collins] all of his interest in [the partnership] * * * including but not limited to, *the seller's right to income* and to acquire the capital stock of The Sanford–Orlando Kennel Club, Inc." (Emphasis added.) Section 1.751–1(c)(3), Income

Tax Regs., provides that an arm's-length agreement between the buyer and the seller generally will establish the value attributable to unrealized receivables.

Based on the provision in the agreement that no part of the consideration was attributable to goodwill, it is clear to us that the parties were aware that they could, if they so desired, have provided that no part of the consideration was attributable to the dog track agreement. No such provision was made. Furthermore, the agreement clearly stated that one of the assets purchased was Ledoux's rights to future income. Considering that petitioner calculated the purchase price by capitalizing future earnings expected under the dog track agreement, we conclude that the portion of Ledoux's gain in excess of the amount attributable to tangible assets was attributable to an unrealized receivable as reflected by the dog track agreement.

Decision will be entered for the respondent.

Problem 14–2

Sitzmark Co. is a partnership which runs a ski shop. The partnership business is renting and selling ski equipment and providing ski lessons. The partnership owns the lot and building where the shop is located. The building was built by the partnership at a cost of $186 and was first ready for use on January 1, 1994. As of December 31, 1996, the partnership has taken depreciation on a straight-line basis of $5.50.

The ski equipment that Sitzmark holds for sale to its customers has been purchased as needed. The ski equipment that it uses for rental purposes was purchased for $65 on January 1, 1995, and the depreciation taken as of December 31, 1996 was $42.

Sue, Picabo, Billy, and Pepi each own a one-fourth interest in capital, profits, and losses of the partnership. Independently, Sue sells unimproved real estate as a full-time career. Other than her personal residence, Sue does not own any real estate for purposes of investment. In order to devote more time to her real estate business, Sue decides to sell her partnership interest in Sitzmark to Hans for $155 on January 1, 1997. Sue's basis in her partnership interest is $110 resulting from her contributions, distributive share of partnership income, and partnership distributions to her. The partnership had no liabilities at the time of the sale of Sue's interest.

All parties agree that Sue's interest in each asset is one-fourth of the fair market value of that asset. The purchase price of the partnership interest is allocated in that manner. Sitzmark has a calendar year and uses the cash method of accounting.

The assets of the partnership as of December 31, 1996 are as follows:

	Adjusted Basis	Fair Market Value	Face Amount
1. Accounts Receivable			
a. Sale of skis and other equipment prior to December 31, 1996.	$ –0–	$ 20.00	$50.00

		Adjusted Basis	Fair Market Value	Face Amount
b.	Ski lessons given prior to December 31, 1996.	–0–	20.00	50.00
c.	Signed contracts for lessons to be given in January, 1998 (one-half of the lessons are terminable at will). Estimated cost to complete the contracts is $10 which was taken into account in arriving at the fair market value.	–0–	30.00	50.00
d.	Sale of common stock of XYW, Inc. which has been held for less than one year and was a capital asset, payable in 1997. The basis is equal to the stock's basis prior to sale.	4.00	8.00	
2.	Skis for sale	20.00	26.00	
3.	Boots for sale	15.00	12.00	
4.	Bindings for sale	10.00	16.00	
5.	Poles for sale	5.00	14.00	
6.	Ski jackets, sweaters, goggles, and other equipment for sale	30.00	40.00	
7.	Skis, boots, bindings, poles, and other equipment held only for rental purposes	23.00	32.00	
8.	Land			
	a. Investment lots	36.00	40.00	
	b. Lot where the shop is located	20.00	17.50	
9.	Building where the shop is located	180.50	194.50	
10.	Investment stock	96.50	150.00	
		$440.00	$620.00	

a.   Which assets constitute § 751(c) property?

b.   Which assets constitute § 751(d) property?

Chapter 15

PARTNERSHIP DISTRIBUTIONS— DISTRIBUTIONS IN LIQUIDATION OF THE PARTNERSHIP

Code References: §§ 731(a); 732(b) and (c); 733; 735(a).

Regulations: §§ 1.731–1(a) and (b); 1.732–1(b) and (c).

A. INTRODUCTION: GAIN OR LOSS RECOGNITION

One "exit vehicle" for the owners of a small business who no longer wish to operate it is to simply divide up its assets and distribute them to the owners. In the partnership context (unlike the corporate context), this can generally be accomplished without any immediate risk of taxable income to the partners.

While the focus previously was on *current* distributions (including *partial* liquidations) where § 751(b) is inapplicable, this material considers *liquidating* distributions not involving § 751(b). Distributions where § 751 is relevant are discussed in Chapter 16. The gain recognition rules of § 731 applicable to distributions of cash apply to a complete liquidation of the partnership. In mixed distributions of cash and property, the cash distribution is applied to basis first and any remaining basis which the partner has in the partnership interest is applied to the distributed property. In contrast to the rules for current distributions which preclude loss recognition, loss may be recognized on the complete liquidation of a partner's interest if *only* cash, unrealized receivables, and/or inventory is distributed. The amount of the loss is the excess of the basis of the distributee's partnership interest over (1) the amount of money distributed and (2) the § 732 basis for the distributed property.

SPECTOR v. COMMISSIONER

641 F.2d 376 (5th Cir.1981).

JOHNSON, CIRCUIT JUDGE.

In this suit brought against the Commissioner of Internal Revenue for redetermination of tax deficiencies for the years 1972 and 1973, the principal issue is whether a transaction in which taxpayer surrendered his partnership interest in an accounting firm in exchange for a specified sum constitutes a "sale" of his partnership interest, thus creating long term capital gain under section 741 of the Internal Revenue Code of 1954, or whether the transaction was a "liquidation" of taxpayer's interest under section 707(c), thus producing ordinary income gain under section 736(a)(2). The Commissioner determined on audit that taxpayer was bound to the transaction as structured by the parties, and that it therefore was a liquidation of taxpayer's interest, producing ordinary income gain. The Tax Court, 71 T.C. 1017, reversed the Commissioner's determination, and held that the transaction was a sale, although it was structured and consummated by all of the parties as a liquidation. For reasons that follow, the decision of the Tax Court is reversed, and the case remanded for further proceedings.

I.

Prior to 1969, taxpayer was a partner in the accounting firm of Spector, Wilson & Co. (Spector partnership). Taxpayer decided to divest himself of his practice with that firm, and to work exclusively for a single client. Consequently, in the early part of 1969 he approached a business acquaintance, who was a partner in another accounting firm, Bielstein, LaHourcade & Lewis (Bielstein partnership), in an effort to dispose of his practice. Negotiations proceeded over a six week period, and culminated in a written agreement dated February 24, 1969, which provided for the sale of the Spector partnership's accounts receivable to the Bielstein partnership, for the merger of the Spector and Bielstein partnerships, and for the withdrawal of taxpayer from the merged partnership, with payments to him by the merged partnership of amounts designated as "guaranteed payments to a retiring partner." Taxpayer negotiated the details of the agreement with Lewis, the tax partner of the Bielstein partnership. Paragraph 7 of the agreement provided:

> 7. In the agreement for withdrawal, Bielstein agrees to pay the $96,000 as guaranteed payments to a retiring partner with one-half explicitly allocated to an agreement not to compete for the term of the payout.

On May 2, 1969, two agreements were signed to implement the plan outlined in the February 24 agreement. The first agreement, called the "Merger Agreement," provided that the Bielstein firm would merge with the Spector firm on May 3, 1969. The second agreement, called the "Withdrawal Agreement," provided that taxpayer would withdraw from the merged partnership on May 5, 1969, and would receive the agreed-upon consideration from the new firm:

> In consideration of for [sic] Spector's withdrawal, Spector will be entitled to receive from the partnership for services or for the use of capital a "guaranteed payment" of $96,000 * * *.

> Furthermore, none of the guaranteed payments provided for in this agreement are for partnership property within the meaning of Section 736 IRC of 1954 * * *.

> The meaning attributed to the words "guaranteed payments" provided for in this contract is the definition provided for such term in Section 707 of the Internal Revenue Code of 1954 and Regulation Section 1.707–1(c).

The amount of $96,000 to be paid to taxpayer was determined by valuing his practice at one hundred percent of its average gross annual fees.

Before the bargain was struck, the tax consequences flowing from the transaction to taxpayer and to the continuing partners was a point of intense negotiation. As practicing public accountants, all of the parties to the transaction were fully aware that the tax consequences to each would depend upon how the transaction was structured. The Tax Court found that the parties structured the transaction as a merger of the two partnerships followed by taxpayer's withdrawal from the merged firm for the sole purpose of allowing the continuing partners a deduction for income tax purposes, under section 736(a)(2) of the Code, of the amounts paid to taxpayer. Indeed, the record clearly reflects that the transaction would not have been consummated absent taxpayer's written agreement on this issue; the Tax Court found that the continuing partners would not have agreed to pay to taxpayer the total compensation of $96,000 unless the transaction were structured as a deductible "liquidation" of taxpayer's interest pursuant to section 736(a)(2).

Under the agreement, taxpayer was nominally a partner in the Bielstein–Spector partnership for only three days. He never actually performed any services for the partnership. He had no desk or office. He contributed no additional capital to the merged firm. At no time did any party to the transaction intend or expect taxpayer to actually engage in the practice of accounting with the members of the Bielstein–Spector partnership. Simply stated, the transaction was carefully structured as a merger followed by a liquidation of taxpayer's interest for the express purpose of assuming a bargained-for tax posture, and thereby of allocating the tax consequences flowing therefrom in an agreed-upon manner.

Pursuant to the agreement, taxpayer received installments of $23,-500 from the Bielstein–Spector partnership in 1972 and 1973. He did not, however, report either sum as a "guaranteed payment" in liquidation of his partnership interest. On audit, the Commissioner determined that the entire amount received by taxpayer in each year should have been reported as a "guaranteed payment" to a retiring partner under section 736(a)(2) and, therefore, as ordinary income. Taxpayer thereupon brought this action in the Tax Court, seeking review of the Commissioner's deficiency determination.

In attempting to avoid the tax consequences flowing from the agreement as structured by the parties, taxpayer argued before the Tax Court that the form of the transaction should be disregarded, and that the true substance of the transaction was a sale, rather than a liquidation, of taxpayer's interest. The Tax Court found that taxpayer had presented "strong proof that the agreements which he signed did not reflect reality insofar as his status as a partner in the Bielstein partnership is concerned." Because taxpayer never became a real partner in the merged firm, the court concluded that "in essence the Bielstein partnership purchased [taxpayer's] share of the goodwill of Spector, Wilson & Company," and that the payments were not a "liquidation" of taxpayer's interest in the new partnership. The Tax Court therefore concluded that except to the extent the payments to taxpayer were allocated to the covenant not to compete, the transaction created long term capital gain pursuant to section 741 of the Code rather than ordinary income gain pursuant to section 736(a)(2), as the Commissioner had determined, and set aside the Commissioner's deficiency determination to that extent. In so holding, the Tax Court found it unnecessary to address taxpayer's alternative argument, i.e., that the payments made to taxpayer were for goodwill as provided in section 736(b)(2)(B) of the Code.

On appeal, the Commissioner argues that the Tax Court erred in allowing taxpayer to disavow the form of the transaction as agreed to by the parties on the mere showing that it did not comport with "economic reality." The Commissioner further argues that the Tax Court's holding is inconsistent with the policy underlying sections 736 and 741 of the Code. As an alternative to the Tax Court's approach, the Commissioner urges this Court to adopt the rule set forth in *Commissioner of Internal Revenue v. Danielson,* 378 F.2d 771 (3d Cir.1967).

II.

Prior to the enactment of the 1954 Code, there existed no comprehensive guidelines concerning the tax consequences resulting from a partner's withdrawal from a partnership. Subchapter K of the 1954 Code, of which sections 736 and 741 are a part, attempted to set forth the "first comprehensive statutory treatment of partners and partnerships in the history of the income tax laws." The principal objectives of the 1954 changes were "simplicity, flexibility, and equity as between the partners."

Under Subchapter K, there are at least two ways in which withdrawing partners may characterize the disposition of their partnership interests: the transaction may be structured either as a "sale" of the partnership interest pursuant to section 741 of the Code, or as a "liquidation" of that interest pursuant to section 736. The net economic result is the same under either approach: The withdrawing partner relinquishes his or her interest in exchange for a specified payment or payments. Depending upon which approach is selected, however, the tax consequences to the withdrawing and continuing partners vary greatly. If characterized as a section 741 "sale," any tax benefits flow to the withdrawing partner, who may be permitted to report any gain that results therefrom as capital, rather than ordinary income gain. Under this selection, the payments are not deductible by the continuing partners, but simply are capitalized as the purchase price of the withdrawing partner's interest and, as such, become the cost basis of the interest so acquired. By comparison, if the transaction is structured as a section 736 "liquidation" of the withdrawing partner's interest, with the payments denominated as "guaranteed payments," the tax benefit flows to the continuing partners, who are able to deduct from partnership income the payments so made. Under this selection the withdrawing partner must report the payments as ordinary income.

From the foregoing, it is readily apparent that the withdrawing and continuing partners will have adverse tax interests. Because a partner's withdrawal generally can be structured either as a section 741 sale or as a section 736 liquidation, the form of the transaction may become a major negotiating point between the parties. Indeed, in *David A. Foxman,* 41 T.C. 535 (1964), *aff'd,* 352 F.2d 466 (3d Cir.1965), the Tax Court, after examining the legislative history underlying Subchapter K, noted that

> one of the underlying philosophic objectives of the 1954 Code was to permit partners themselves to determine their tax burdens *inter sese* to a certain extent, and this is what the committee reports meant when they referred to "flexibility." The theory was that the partners would take their prospective tax liabilities into account in bargaining with one another.

Relying upon these principles, the Tax Court in *Foxman* concluded:

> [T]his policy of "flexibility" is particularly pertinent in determining the tax consequences of the withdrawal of a partner. Where the practical differences between a "sale" and a "liquidation" are, at most, slight, if they exist at all, and where the tax consequences to the partners can vary greatly, it is in accord with the purpose of the statutory provisions to allow the partners themselves, through arm's length negotiations, to determine whether to take the "sale" route or the "liquidation" route, thereby allocating the tax burdens among themselves.

Unlike the section 741 "sale," the section 736 "liquidation" may occur only in transactions between a partner and his or her own partnership. In the case *sub judice* the Tax Court, after reviewing the evidence, and applying the test set forth in *Commissioner v. Culbertson,* 337 U.S. 733, 742 (1949), for determining the existence of a partnership, held that:

> [t]he merger of partnerships, followed by [taxpayer's] withdrawal from a "merged" partnership, as described in the agreements, never actually occurred. What did occur was a sale by [taxpayer] of his

share of the goodwill of [the Spector partnership], not to his partnership or to continuing partners, but to outsiders, the Bielstein partnership. Section 736 is, therefore, inapplicable because it applies to payments made by a partnership to one of its own partners.

The Commissioner does not challenge the Tax Court's finding of fact that taxpayer was not a "bona fide" partner in the Bielstein–Spector partnership. Rather, the Commissioner argues that the Tax Court erred in allowing taxpayer to avoid the tax consequences of the form of the transaction as bargained for and agreed to by the parties merely by adducing "strong proof" that it did not comport with "economic reality," and that taxpayer, having knowingly and voluntarily agreed to structure the transaction as a section 736 liquidation, should be bound by his bargain.

III.

Just as the Commissioner in determining income tax liabilities may look through the form of a transaction to its substance, so, as a general rule, may he bind a taxpayer to the form in which the taxpayer has cast a transaction. * * *

Courts have recognized an exception to the foregoing principle, however, and will allow a taxpayer to challenge the form of a transaction when necessary to avoid unjust results. * * *

As the foregoing cases indicate, when determining whether a taxpayer has adduced strong proof that a contractual allocation to a covenant not to compete in reality was in payment for something else, a major inquiry is whether the covenant bears "economic reality" to the circumstances surrounding the transaction, i.e., whether the allocation to the covenant bears some relationship to its actual value. In the case *sub judice* the Tax Court limited its inquiry to this single factor and concluded that because taxpayer could not have liquidated his interest in a partnership of which he never became a member, the form of the transaction as agreed to by the parties lacked economic reality.

One difficulty with the Tax Court's approach is the aforementioned absence of any substantial difference in terms of "economic reality" between a section 736 liquidation and a section 741 sale of a partnership interest. In a particular case, a covenant not to compete indeed may be so without value as to be devoid of "economic reality." As noted in *Foxman,* however, the fundamental theory underlying Subchapter K is that, given the substantial, if not total, identity in terms of economic net result between a sale and liquidation, the withdrawing and continuing partners should be allowed to allocate the resulting tax benefits and burdens as they see fit. Notwithstanding the fact that a section 736 liquidation may occur only in transactions between a partner and his or her own partnership, once the parties have agreed to structure the transaction in such a way as to comply with that requirement, "economic reality" does not provide a ground upon which that form can be set aside.

Moreover, in contrast to the Tax Court's application of the "strong proof" rule in the present case, the prior decisions of this Court reveal a concern for the type of equitable considerations that traditionally have been invoked when determining whether a party to a transaction may, in fairness, be held to its obligations arising thereunder. Whereas *Balthrope* refers to the situation in which one party, at the expense of the other, tax-ignorant, party slips a covenant into the contract, 356 F.2d at 31, 33–34, *Dixie Finance,* 474 F.2d at 504–05 and *Sonnleitner,* 598 F.2d at 467–68, place emphasis upon whether the covenants involved therein were given for value and were bargained for at arm's length. Although, under the approach adopted in the foregoing cases, the absence of any relationship between "economic reality" and the agreement indeed may be strong evidence of mistake, fraud, overreaching, duress, or perhaps some other ground for equitable recission, such as inadequacy of consideration, those decisions simply do not elevate the "economic reality" inquiry to that of a talisman, and require the Commissioner to blind himself to other relevant factors. In none of those decisions did this Court allow a taxpayer, having voluntarily and at arms length bargained for a particular form of transaction, with complete foreknowledge of the tax consequences flowing therefrom, and having represented to the Commissioner that the chosen form reflected the true nature of the transaction, to disavow that form as a sham designed for the sole purpose of misleading the Commissioner, and, having already received substantial nontax benefits therefrom, adopt one with more favorable present tax consequences.

Indeed, this Court in an analogous factual situation has strongly rejected the notion that a taxpayer may bind the Commissioner to a secret understanding as to the effect of an agreement. In *Winn–Dixie Montgomery, Inc. v. United States,* 444 F.2d 677 (5th Cir.1971), taxpayer argued that because it did not intend to allocate any portion of the purchase price to goodwill, the Commissioner should be bound by that determination, absent a contrary expression in the agreement. This Court responded:

> No decision holds or suggests that such a one-sided, uncommunicated apportionment of a sales price is conclusive on the taxing authorities, and it is obvious that it would be dangerous and unfair to lay down that categorical rule. The whole trend of the law in this area is against binding the Revenue Service by such a secret, unilateral, subjective allocation which is not carried over into the agreement.

The above-quoted admonition is particularly appropriate in the present case, and we adhere to the principle expressed therein. * * *

B. BASIS OF DISTRIBUTED PROPERTY

With respect to property distributions which completely liquidate a departing partner's interest, the basis for the distributed property in the hands of the distributee partner is determined under § 732(b) and

§ 732(c). Instead of assuming a *carryover* basis from the partnership (as with current distributions), the general rule of § 732(b) accords the distributed property a *substituted* basis derived from the basis of the distributee partner's partnership interest. Thus, for example, if the partnership distributes an asset other than an unrealized receivable or inventory asset to a partner with a basis of $100 for his or her partnership interest, the asset will take a $100 basis regardless of whether its basis in the hands of the partnership was $200 or $50.

However, if an unrealized receivable or inventory item is distributed in a complete liquidation of a partnership interest, the § 732(c) allocation rule mandates that its basis be determined first. The distributee partner's basis in these designated types of assets is the same as their adjusted basis to the partnership. If such assets are the subject of multiple in-kind distributions and their collective bases in the hands of the partnership exceed the partner's basis for his or her partnership interest, that partner's basis is allocated among the assets in proportion to their bases to the partnership (not fair market value). If assets which are not such designated assets are then distributed, the remaining basis for the partner's partnership interest, after the application of § 732(c)(1), is allocated to them in proportion to their adjusted bases to the partnership.

REVENUE RULING 74–40

1974–1 C.B. 159.

Advice has been requested concerning the Federal income tax consequences to a limited partner in the situations described below.

Situation 1: *L* is a limited partner in partnership *GL* to which he contributed $10,000 in cash on its formation. His distributive share of partnership items of income and loss is 10 percent and he is not entitled to receive any guaranteed payments. The adjusted basis of his partnership interest at the end of the current year is $20,000. His proportionate share of partnership liabilities, on which neither he, the other partners nor the partnership have assumed any personal liability, is $15,000. The partnership has no other liabilities. *L* sells his interest in the partnership to *M*, an unrelated taxpayer, for $10,000 in cash. At the time of the transaction the partnership had no unrealized receivables or inventory items described in section 751 of the Internal Revenue Code of 1954 nor any goodwill and *L* had been paid his distributive share of partnership income.

Section 752(c) of the Internal Revenue Code of 1954 provides that for purposes of section 752, a liability to which property is subject shall, to the extent of the fair market value of such property, be considered as a liability of the owner of the property.

Section 1.752–1(e) of the Income Tax Regulations provides, in part, that where none of the partners have any personal liability with respect to a partnership liability (as in the case of a mortgage on real estate acquired by the partnership without the assumption by the partnership or any of the partners of any liability on the mortgage), then all partners, including limited partners, shall be considered as sharing such liability under section 752(c) of the Code in the same proportion as they share the profits.

Section 1.752–1(d) of the regulations provides that where there is a sale or exchange of an interest in a partnership, liabilities shall be treated in the same manner as liabilities in connection with the sale or exchange of property not associated with partnerships. For example, if a partner sells his interest in a partnership for $750 cash and at the same time transfers to the purchaser his share of partnership liabilities amounting to $250, the amount realized by the seller on the transaction is $1,000.

Section 741 of the Code provides, in pertinent part, that in the case of a sale or exchange of an interest in a partnership, gain or loss shall be recognized to the transferor partner and shall be considered gain or loss from the sale or exchange of a capital asset, except as otherwise provided in section 751 of the Code (relating to unrealized receivables and inventory items which have appreciated substantially in value).

Accordingly, in the instant situation, the amount realized by *L* from the sale of his partnership interest is $25,000, consisting of cash in the amount of $10,000 and release from his share of partnership liabilities in the amount of $15,000. Since the adjusted basis of *L*'s interest in the partnership is $20,000, he realized a gain of $5,000 determined under the provisions of section 741 of the Code.

Situation 2: The facts are the same as in situation 1, except that *L* withdraws from the partnership and the partnership distributes $10,000 to him in cash in complete liquidation of his interest in the partnership.

Section 752(b) of the Code provides that any decrease in a partner's share of the liabilities of a partnership, or any decrease in a partner's individual liabilities by reason of the assumption by the partnership of such individual liabilities, shall be considered as a distribution of money to the partner by the partnership.

Section 731(a) of the Code provides, in pertinent part, that in the case of a distribution by a partnership to a partner gain shall not be recognized to such partner, except to the extent that any money distributed exceeds the adjusted basis of such partner's interest in the partnership immediately before the distribution. Any gain recognized under section 731(a) shall be considered as a gain from the sale or exchange of the partnership interest of the distributee partner.

Section 731(c) of the Code provides, in part, that section 731 shall not apply to the extent otherwise provided by section 736 (relating to payments to a retiring partner or a deceased partner's successor in interest) and section 751 of the Code (relating to unrealized receivables and inventory items).

Section 736(b) of the Code provides, in pertinent part, that payments made in liquidation of the interest of a retiring partner or a deceased partner shall, to the extent such payments are determined to be made in exchange for the interest of such partner in partnership property, be considered as a distribution by the partnership and not as a distributive share of partnership income or guaranteed payment.

Section 1.736–1(b)(1) of the Income Tax Regulations provides, in pertinent part, that gain or loss with respect to distributions under section 736(b) of the Code will be recognized to the distributee to the extent provided in section 731 of the Code.

Accordingly, in the instant situation, distributions to L with respect to his partnership interest total $25,000 and consist of cash in the amount of $10,000 and a decrease in his share of the partnership liabilities in the amount of $15,000 that is considered under section 752(b) of the Code as a distribution of money to L by the partnership.

Furthermore, since the money distributed ($25,000) exceeds the adjusted basis of L 's interest in the partnership immediately before the distribution ($20,000), he realizes a gain of $5,000 determined under the provisions of section 731(a) of the Code.

Situation 3: Instead of selling his interest L withdraws from the partnership at a time when the adjusted basis of his interest in the partnership is zero and his proportionate share of partnership liabilities, all of which consist of liabilities on which neither he, the other partners nor the partnership have assumed any personal liability, is $15,000.

Accordingly, L is considered to have received a distribution of money from the partnership of $15,000 and realizes a gain of $15,000 determined under the provisions of section 731(a) of the Code.

Problem 15–1

Dagmar and Ingrid are equal partners in a shoe repair shop. The partnership has the following assets:

	Book Value and Adjusted Basis	Fair Market Value
Cash	$ 60	$ 60
Accounts Receivable	–0–	30
Inventory	30	30
Land (investment)	120	60
Total	$210	$180

Dagmar's basis in her partnership interest is $100. Ingrid's basis is $75. Dagmar and Ingrid purchased their interests from Steve and Ted in separate transactions spanning a three-year period without precipitating a termination of the partnership. The partnership never has elected under § 754. What is each partner's gain or loss and basis in the distributed assets if the partnership is totally liquidated as follows?

    a. Dagmar and Ingrid each receive one-half of the cash, accounts receivable, inventory, and land.

b. Dagmar receives the land, one-half of the inventory, and one-half of the accounts receivable, and Ingrid receives the cash, one-half of the inventory, and one-half of the accounts receivable.

c. Dagmar receives the cash, one-half of the inventory, and one-half of the accounts receivable, and Ingrid receives the land, one-half of the inventory, and one-half of the accounts receivable.

d. Dagmar receives the land and the accounts receivable, and Ingrid receives the cash and inventory.

e. Dagmar receives the cash and accounts receivable, and Ingrid receives the land and the inventory.

C. LIQUIDATION OF TWO–PERSON PARTNERSHIP

As discussed in the *Spector* decision, a definitional issue arises as to whether a partner's exit should be treated for tax purposes as a sale of a partnership interest or instead as a liquidation of that interest. However, where a two-person partnership is involved, as evidenced by *McCauslen v. Commissioner,* which follows, the issue is more complicated.

McCAUSLEN v. COMMISSIONER
45 T.C. 588 (1966).

MULRONEY, JUDGE.

Respondent determined a deficiency in petitioners' income tax for 1959 in the amount of $20,738.86. The only issue is whether the gain realized by petitioners from a sale of certain partnership properties acquired by them under a buy-sell agreement is taxable as a long-term or short-term capital gain, which turns upon whether petitioners are entitled to use the partnership's holding period with respect to such properties.

All of the facts were stipulated and they are so found.

Edwin E. and Frances E. McCauslen, husband and wife, are residents of Steubenville, Ohio. They filed their joint Federal income tax return for 1959 with the district director of internal revenue at Cleveland, Ohio.

In 1946 petitioner Edwin E. McCauslen and his brother, William T. McCauslen, formed a two-man partnership to engage in the nursery, greenhouse, wholesale, and retail flower business. Both men were equal, active partners in the business until William died on March 7, 1959, and after William's death the floral business was continued by the petitioner. The partnership had a fiscal year ending May 31 for tax and accounting purposes.

On October 17, 1956, petitioner and William (together with their wives) executed an agreement which provided, in part, as follows:

WHEREAS, Edwin E. McCauslen and William T. McCauslen are partners operating at Steubenville, Ohio, under the firm name of McCauslen Florists;

WHEREAS, the parties mutually desire to enter into an agreement by which, on the event of the death of one of them, the survivor shall purchase and the decedent's estate shall sell the share of the latter in the partnership at a price determinable by such agreement;

WHEREAS, the parties mutually desire that life insurance be used as a means of providing all or a portion of the funds with which to finance the obligations arising under such sale and purchase agreement;

Now, THEREFORE, IT IS MUTUALLY AGREED by and between the parties hereto, and on behalf of their eventual heirs and personal representatives, as follows:

1. On the death of a partner, the surviving partner shall purchase and the decedent's estate shall sell the share of the latter in the partnership for a consideration equal to 80% of the book value of each share as shown by the books of the partnership as of the close of the fiscal year next preceding the date of death, after the books have been closed and adjusted by a certified public accountant in accordance with good accounting practice to include all known assets and liabilities of the partnership but before any provision for income tax liability of the individual partners and with no valuation recorded for good will or other intangibles, whether or not same exists * * *.

4. The surviving partner shall be under obligation to save and protect the decedent's estate from all legitimate claims and demands on account of the obligations and debts of the partnership. As a means of assuring the fulfillment of this obligation, the decedent's estate may condition the conveyance of its share in the partnership upon the procurement and submission by the surviving partner of releases or agreements by the partnership creditors effectively exonerating the decedent's estate from such debts or claims. Any such claims or demands may, however, if satisfied by the surviving partners, be used to recompute the book value of the shares and the consideration provided in paragraph No. 2 above, in accordance with the partnership participation existing just prior to the death of a partner * * *.

10. This agreement does not purport to be an agreement of partnership, its purpose being merely to establish a basis and means as between the partners of effecting a sale and purchase of the share of a partner on his death. Any partnership agreement existing between the partners shall continue in effect unchanged as it may relate to the subject matter of this agreement, in which respect it shall be regarded as amended or superseded.

William died on March 7, 1959, and pursuant to the agreement of October 17, 1956, petitioner acquired William's partnership interest. On May 28, 1959, petitioner sold for $200,000 a greenhouse and greenhouse equipment which had previously been owned by the partnership for a period of longer than 6 months.

Petitioner and his wife reported the sale on their 1959 return as follows:

SALE OF GREENHOUSE BUSINESS

Sold to Dieckmann Bros., May 28, 1959		$200,000.00
Less commission to broker		8,000.00
Net sale price		192,000.00
Less cost of assets sold:		
Land	$35,172.75	
Greenhouse and equipment $185,388.32		
Less depreciation to date 155,316.16	30,072.16	65,244.91
Long-term capital gain		126,755.00

Respondent in his statutory notice of deficiency increased petitioners' taxable income for 1959 and explained the adjustment as follows:

During the taxable year ended December 31, 1959 you sold a greenhouse and equipment for $200,000.00. You reported the gain realized of $126,755.00 as a long-term capital gain on Schedule D of your income tax return. Since one-half of your interest in these assets was acquired by you within 6 months before their sale, it is held that under Section 1222 of the Internal Revenue Code, the gain on this portion is a short-term capital gain * * *. Section 741 of the Internal Revenue Code of 1954 recognizes a partnership interest as a capital asset which may be sold or exchanged with capital gain or loss treatment. When petitioner purchased the decedent's interest in the partnership from the estate pursuant to the October 17, 1956, agreement, the partnership was terminated. Sec. 708(b). At that point petitioner owned all of the partnership assets, i.e., the assets attributable to his own one-half partnership interest since 1946 in the two-man partnership, as well as the assets attributable to the decedent's partnership interest acquired by petitioner in 1959.

There does not now appear to be any dispute between the parties as to the proper bases to be applied to the partnership assets in petitioner's hands after the termination of the partnership. Moreover, as to the proper holding period of these assets, respondent recognizes that petitioner acquired by distribution that portion of the partnership assets relating to his own partnership interest and that with respect to such assets the petitioner is entitled to include the partnership's holding period. Therefore, when petitioner in May 1959 (less than 6 months after decedent's death) sold some of the former partnership assets which had previously been held by the partnership for more than 6 months, the partnership's holding period could be tacked on to petitioner's holding period for that portion of the assets attributable to his own partnership interest, entitling him to long-term capital gains treatment of a portion of the gain realized.

Petitioner argues that he is also entitled to tack on the holding period of the partnership to the portion of the partnership assets he acquired when he purchased the partnership interest of the decedent partner from the estate. Petitioner relies upon section 735, the pertinent portions of which we have set forth in a footnote, and which in section 735(b) provides that in determining the period for which a partner has held property received in a distribution from a partnership (excluding certain inventory items), there shall be included the holding period of the partnership with respect to such property.

We believe that petitioner's reliance upon section 735(b) is misplaced. Sections 731 through 735 represent an attempt to deal comprehensively with the whole problem of partnership distributions of property. Generally, the statutory sections allow tax-free distributions of property by a partnership, with provisions for a carryover basis or a substituted basis, depending upon the type of distribution, and for adjustments to the basis of a distributee partner's interest in the partnership. Section 735 merely follows the distributed partnership property into the hands of the partner and describes the character of the gain or loss when the partner disposes of such distributed property, and in section 735(b) provides that the holding period of the partnership for the distributed property may be tacked on to the holding period in the hands of the partner. The emphasis throughout these sections is upon distributions to a partner in connection with an existing partnership interest.

Much of the complexity of the partnership provisions in the 1954 Code arises because they are based upon conflicting concepts of the nature of a partnership, i.e., the entity approach and the aggregate approach, as well as from Congress' desire to introduce a certain amount of flexibility in this area of partnership taxation. Thus, as we indicated in the *Foxman* case, drastic tax differences can result depending upon the categorization of a transaction (for example, as a "sale" of a partnership interest rather than a "liquidation" of such interest), even though the ultimate economic effect is much the same. Therefore, it would seem that concepts which might be meaningful under one section might prove misleading under another section.

The provision for tacking on the partnership's holding period is entirely consistent with the general statutory scheme of postponing recognition of gain or loss until the distributee partner finally disposes of the distributed partnership property. But where, as here, a partner acquires another partner's share by purchase and, as a consequence of the termination of the partnership resulting from such purchase, acquires the partnership assets relating to such purchased interest, the statute has no application. The statute cannot be construed as permitting the purchaser to tack on the partnership's holding period of such assets. In effect, petitioner is contending that he purchased assets belonging to another with a built-in holding period. Neither logic nor necessity supports such an argument and we do not believe that section 735(b) calls for such a result.

Since petitioner's purchase of the decedent's partnership interest resulted in a termination of the partnership under section 708(b), it is our view that petitioner acquired the partnership assets relating to such interest by purchase, rather than by any distribution from the partnership, and that petitioner's holding period for such assets begins from the date of such purchase. Consequently, we agree with respondent's determination that petitioner's holding period for the assets attributable to the purchased interest was less than 6 months at the time of their sale by petitioner on May 28, 1959, with the result that the portion of the gain attributable to such assets is taxable as short-term capital gain.

Reviewed by the Court.

Decision will be entered under Rule 50.

Chapter 16

PARTNERSHIP DISTRIBUTIONS— DISTRIBUTIONS FROM A COLLAPSIBLE PARTNERSHIP

Code References: §§ 751(b); 702(a)(7).

Regulations: §§ 1.751–1(b), (g) example (2).

A. INTRODUCTION

When Subchapter K was added to the Code in 1954, it was intended to provide a relatively simple framework for the taxation of partners and partnerships which did not previously exist. Since then, the rules have been added to and interpreted by Regulation, judicial decision, and administrative Ruling in such a way as to make partnerships one of the more complex areas of the tax law. The "collapsible partnership" rules are a good example of a statutory safeguard which often creates unexpected results for small businesses which are taxed as partnerships. The owners of these businesses are unlikely to pay for sophisticated tax advice each time they make a distribution from a partnership or sell a partnership interest. In this setting, operating as a partnership can be a negative for a small business enterprise.

Section 751(a) serves to prevent, in the context of the sale of a partnership interest, the conversion potential of ordinary income into capital gain through the use of § 741. While at first glance a similar safeguard would appear unnecessary in the distribution context (§ 735 generally ensures ordinary income characterization on the subsequent sale of unrealized receivables or inventory), § 751(b) prevents a trading of such income potential with another party. For example, in a two person partnership, if an inventory asset were distributed to one partner in a low tax bracket or with net operating loss carryovers, while a capital asset of equal value were distributed to the other, high bracket partner, a shifting of net tax benefits between the partners would be possible. Consequently, § 751(b) is designed to act as a safeguard and applies in the distribution context if a partner receives a disproportionate amount (more or less than his share) of the partnership's collective value of "unrealized receivables" or "substantially appreciated inventory." As seen in Chapter 14, the definition of these two terms is more complex than one would expect.

B. LIMITATION ON CAPITAL CHARACTERIZATION

In determining the applicability of § 751(b), initially the amount of the partner's share of the § 751 assets (generally ordinary income producing assets of the partnership and sometimes known as "hot assets") is determined. This amount is then compared to the amount of the assets such partner actually receives in a distribution plus his or her remaining share of those assets still owned by the partnership. Thus, if a partner's partnership interest were worth $100 of which $30 was attributable to the partnership's § 751 assets and the partner was liquidated for $100 in cash, the distributee would be considered to have relinquished his $30 worth of § 751 assets for $30 of the cash received. The other partners would be viewed as paying $30 cash to acquire the departing partner's "hot assets."

To the extent that the distribution is disproportionate as to § 751 assets, a fictional exchange is created by § 751(b) and its Regulations. The distributee is treated as receiving his or her proportionate interest of the § 751 property as a current distribution by the partnership which is thereafter exchanged in a taxable transaction for the actual consideration received. For example, in the above hypothetical, if the basis for the § 751 property constructively distributed were $10 (and the distributee's basis for his or her entire partnership interest were a greater amount), then the distributee would be deemed to have sold those assets for $30 cash to the other partners. This would generate a $20 gain ($30–$10) characterized by the nature of the relinquished property, in this case ordinary.

A converse setting could arise if the distributee *actually* received a greater amount of § 751 property than his or her proportionate share, in which case the gain if any would be characterized accordingly as capital gain or § 1231 gain. That is, the distributee partner would be treated as exchanging non–§ 751 assets in order to obtain his or her excess share of the § 751 assets. This constructive exchange rule overrides §§ 731 and 732 and will often turn an apparently non-taxable partnership distribution into an unexpected taxable one.

In the constructive sale or exchange treatment of § 751(b), it is also possible for the partnership (i.e., the other partners) to recognize tax consequences as well. No gain or loss is recognized in the above hypothetical because the partnership is viewed as having purchased the $30 of tainted assets for $30 cash. A basis adjustment to the partnership for the inventory from $10 to $30 would occur. However, if the partnership is deemed to relinquish any asset other than cash in the constructive exchange, it will recognize gain or loss as well as adjust the basis of the partnership assets. This will be reflected in the tax returns of the non-distributee partners.

The remainder of the distribution to the distributee partner (in the above example $70) is tested under the traditional rules of § 731 and § 732 against the distributee's basis for the partnership interest after reduction by the basis of the constructively distributed property.

REVENUE RULING 77–412
1977–2 C.B. 223.

Advice has been requested concerning the Federal income tax consequences upon the complete liquidation of a two person partnership involving the non-pro rata distribution of "section 751 property" to the partners.

Section 751 of the Internal Revenue Code of 1954 governs the treatment of unrealized receivables of the partnership (as defined in section 751(c)) and inventory items of the partnership that have appreciated substantially in value (as defined in section 751(d)), insofar as they affect sales or exchanges of partnership interests and certain distributions by a partnership. Unrealized receivables and substantially appreciated inventory items are referred to as "section 751 property."

Under section 751(a) of the Code, the amount of any money, or the fair market value of any property, received by a transferor partner in exchange for all or a part of such partner's interest in the partnership attributable to section 751 property, is considered an amount realized from the sale or exchange of property other than a capital asset. Thus, any gain or loss attributable to the sale or exchange of section 751 property would be ordinary income or loss.

Section 751(b)(1) of the Code provides that where a partner receives, in a distribution, partnership section 751 property in exchange for all or a part of such partner's interest in other partnership property (including money), or receives other partnership property (including money) in exchange for all or a part of an interest in partnership section 751 property, such transaction shall be considered as a sale or exchange of such property between the distributee and the partnership (as constituted after the distribution). Consequently, section 751(b) of the Code applies to that part of the distribution to a partner that consists of the non-pro rata distribution of the partnership section 751 property in exchange for other property, or the non-pro rata distribution of other partnership property in exchange for section 751 property.

In *Yourman v. United States,* 277 F.Supp. 818 (S.D.Calif.1967), the court held that section 751 of the Code applied to a non-pro rata distribution of section 751 property of a partnership even though the partnership did not continue in existence after the distribution.

Accordingly in the case of a two person partnership, to the extent that a partner either receives section 751 property in exchange for relinquishing any part of such partner's interest in other property, or receives other property in exchange for relinquishing any part of the interest in section 751 property, the distribution is treated as a sale or exchange of such properties between the distributee partner and the partnership (as constituted after the distribution), even though after the distribution the partnership consists of a single individual.

For example, the non-pro rata distribution by a two person partnership of section 751 property to its partners, *A* and *B,* as part of a distribution resulting in a complete liquidation of the partnership, can be viewed in two ways, both of which result in the same tax consequences to each party to the transaction. In the non-pro rata distribution, partner *A* receives more partnership section 751 property than *A*'s underlying interest in such property, while partner *B* receives more partnership other property than *B*'s interest in such property. Partner *A* may be treated as the distributee partner who has exchanged part of an interest in partnership property other than section 751 property with the partnership as constituted after the distribution (partner *B*) for section 751 property. Partner *A* would be treated as realizing gain or loss on a sale or exchange of the property other than section 751 property, and the partnership as constituted after the distribution would realize ordinary income or loss on the exchange of the section 751 property.

Partner *B* may be treated as the distributee partner who has exchanged part of an interest in the partnership section 751 property with the partnership as constituted after the distribution (partner *A*) for other property. Partner *B* would be treated as realizing ordinary income or loss on the exchange of the section 751 property, and the partnership as constituted after the distribution would realize gain or loss on a sale or exchange of the other property. However, regardless of which partner is considered to be the distributee and which is considered to be the remaining partner, the Federal income tax consequences are the same to each partner.

Problem 16–1

1. Ed, Rich, Shelly, and Linda own and operate their health food store as a partnership. The partnership has the following balance sheet:

Assets	Book Value and Adjusted Basis	Fair Market Value
Cash	$240	$240
Inventory	60	100
Capital Asset X	100	260
	$400	$600

Capital	Book Value and Adjusted Basis	Fair Market Value
Ed	$100	$150
Rich	100	150
Shelly	100	150
Linda	100	150
	$400	$600

Ed's interest is terminated when the partnership distributes $150 cash to him.

    a. What is Ed's taxable gain on the distribution? What is the character of this gain?

    b. What is the gain to the partnership on this distribution? What is the character of this gain?

    c. What is the partnership's adjusted basis in the inventory following the distribution?

    d. What is the reconstructed tax balance sheet of the partnership following the distribution?

C. ROLE OF LIABILITIES

It must be remembered that most partnerships have liabilities which may come into play in a § 751(b) transaction. Under § 752(b), a decrease in a partner's share of partnership liabilities is considered a cash distribution. Thus, if part of the consideration for a partner's retirement or reduction in interest is a reduction in a share of partnership liabilities, for § 751(b) purposes he has received a distribution of cash which is a non–§ 751 asset. To the extent that the actual distributed cash plus the deemed cash distribution, or the deemed cash distribution alone, exceeds his pro rata share of non–§ 751 assets, § 751(b) must be considered. Such considerations also may arise in "flips" of a partner's profits or loss interest which change liability ratios. These types of situations are particular traps for the unsuspecting small business operators who have appreciated inventory or receivables.

The issue of a § 751(b) distribution through the relief from liabilities can arise even on the admission of a partner. In Revenue Ruling 84–102, which follows, the Service ruled that § 751(b) was applicable upon the entry of a new partner into a partnership which had liabilities and unrealized receivables. The new partner's entry resulted in a constructive cash distribution under § 752(b) to the existing partners because the new partner shared in the partnership liabilities, thereby reducing the shares of the existing partners in those liabilities. A similar decrease in the existing partners' interests in unrealized receivables (and substantially appreciated inventory) was held to occur. Section 751(b) applied to the existing partners as a portion of the constructive cash distribution was made in return for a decrease in their interest in the hot assets which precipitated gain recognition under § 751(b). However, the Service held that the entering partner was immune from § 751(b) because there was no actual or deemed distribution of property to him.

REVENUE RULING 84–102

1984–2 C.B. 119.

ISSUE

What are the consequences to the partners under section 751(b) of the Internal Revenue Code when a new partner joins the partnership under the circumstances described below?

FACTS

A, B, and C were equal partners in partnership P. At the time of the transaction described below, the value of each partner's interest was $25x$ dollars. *D* acquired a 25 percent interest in P by contributing $25x$ dollars to P. Prior to D's contribution, the liabilities of P totaled $100x$ dollars, and each partner's share of the liabilities was approximately $33.3x$ dollars. In addition, the unrealized receivables of P (as defined in section 751(c) of the Code) were $40x$ dollars, and each partner's share of the unrealized receivables was approximately $13.3x$ dollars. After the contribution by D, each partner's share of the liabilities of P was $25x$ dollars; A, B, and C's share of P's liabilities each decreased by approximately $8.3x$ dollars. Furthermore, each partner's share of P's unrealized receivables was $10x$ dollars; A, B, and C's share of the unrealized receivables each decreased by approximately $3.3x$ dollars.

LAW AND ANALYSIS

Section 721(a) of the Internal Revenue Code provides that no gain or loss shall be recognized to a partnership or to any of its partners in the case of a contribution of property to the partnership in exchange for an interest in the partnership.

Section 722 of the Code provides that the basis of an interest in a partnership acquired by a contribution of property, including money, to the partnership shall be the amount of such money and the adjusted basis of such property to the contributing partner.

Section 752(a) of the Code provides that any increase in a partner's share of the liabilities of a partnership shall be considered as a contribution of money by such partner to the partnership.

Section 752(b) of the Code provides that any decrease in a partner's share of the liabilities of a partnership shall be considered as a distribution of money to the partner by the partnership.

Pursuant to sections 733 and 731(a)(1) of the Code, a distribution of money by a partnership to a partner results in a reduction of the partner's basis in the partnership interest and, to the extent the distribution exceeds basis, capital gain to the partner. However, section 731(c) provides that section 731 shall not apply to the extent otherwise provided by section 751. See also sections 1.731–1(a)(1) and 1.751–1(b) of the Income Tax Regulations.

Section 751(b)(1)(B) of the Code provides that, to the extent a partner receives a distribution of partnership property (including money) other than property described in section 751(a)(1) or (2) in exchange for all or part of the partner's interest in partnership property described in section 751(a)(1) or (2), such transaction shall be considered a sale or exchange of such property between the distributee partner and the partnership. Section 751(a)(1) of the Code refers to the "unrealized receivables" of a partnership as defined in section 751(c) of the Code.

In the instant case, A, B, and C are each treated as having received a cash distribution from P of 8.3x dollars in accordance with section 752(b) of the Code. Of this amount, 3.3x dollars is treated under sections 731(c) and 751(b)(1)(B) as being received by each partner in exchange for the interest in unrealized receivables given up. The remaining 5x dollars is treated in accordance with section 731(a) of the Code.

Although D has a 10x dollar interest in the unrealized receivables of P upon becoming a partner, section 751(b) of the Code has no application with respect to D. There is no actual or deemed distribution of property from P to D as required by 751(b). Further, D has an "increased" interest in the unrealized receivables of P as a result of becoming a partner. Any distribution of property (other than property described in section 751(a)(1) or (2)) from P to D would have to result in a decreased interest in the unrealized receivables for 751(b)(1)(B) to apply.

HOLDING

The tax consequences to D of becoming a partner are determined under sections 721, 722 and 752(a) of the Code. D is treated as having contributed 50x dollars, the actual contribution of 25x dollars plus the deemed contribution of 25x dollars under section 752(a), in exchange for the partnership interest. D's basis in the partnership interest is 50x dollars in accordance with section 722 of the Code. Section 751(b) does not apply to new partner D because there is no actual or deemed distribution of property from P to D.

Partners A, B, and C are each treated as having received a distribution of 8.3x dollars under section 752(b) of the Code. Of this amount, 3.3x dollars is treated under section 751(b)(1)(B) as being received by each partner in exchange for the interest in unrealized receivables given up.

Chapter 17

DEATH OR RETIREMENT OF A PARTNER—PAYMENTS IN LIQUIDATION OF THE INTEREST OF A RETIRED PARTNER

Code References: § 736.

Regulations: § 1.736–1.

A. INTRODUCTION

When a partner in a small business partnership dies or retires, the partnership may, either by obligation under a previously executed buy/sell agreement or by contemporaneous negotiations, purchase the interest of the departing partner. This is to be distinguished from the situation in which the remaining partners (rather than the partnership) purchase the interest. In the partnership context, the complete acquisition of a partner's interest by the partnership is known as a liquidation of the partner's interest (even though the partnership itself is not liquidated). In the corporate context, such a purchase would be called a redemption. See discussion at Chapter 34.

When the interest of a retired partner, or of his or her successor in the case of death, is completely liquidated by partnership distributions, § 736 dictates the tax consequences to the recipient and to the partnership, albeit in some cases with reference to other sections of the Code previously considered. Section 736 is not applicable to a sale or exchange of a partnership interest to other partners or third parties, to a partial liquidation of a partner's interest by the partnership, or to a current distribution of partnership property to an existing partner. These situations have been examined in prior chapters.

B. § 736(a) AND (b) PAYMENTS

When it applies, § 736 forces a bifurcation of the partnership distribution to a partner into two categories—§ 736(b) payments (those made in exchange for a partner's interest in partnership property) and, if any, § 736(a) payments (all other payments by the partnership to the retiring partner or the successors of the deceased partner). Payments for a partner's interest in partnership property encompass payments for most of the departing partner's rights in partnership property. However, in the case of a partnership for which capital is not a material income producing factor, i.e., a service partnership, payments to a withdrawing general partner for unrealized receivables as defined at § 751(c) and unspecified goodwill *will not* constitute § 736(b) payments. Thus, the distribution to be received by the withdrawing partner is allocated first to the category of § 736(b) payments (if any) and then to § 736(a) payments (if any). The fact that unspecified goodwill for some partnerships constitutes a § 736(a) interest while specified goodwill falls within § 736(b) permits some significant latitude in structuring the transaction—it is the partnership and distributee partner who will "specify" whether goodwill exists or merely ignore it as "unspecified" goodwill. Buy/sell agreements between partners frequently designate, in advance, what the partnership is buying when it pays for the partnership interest, thereby dictating the tax results.

The tax treatment of § 736(b) payments has been discussed previously since such payments are subject to the general rules of § 731 and § 751(b). Section 736(a) payments fall into either of two categories—a guaranteed payment or a distributive share of partnership income—depending on whether they are computed without regard to partnership income or, in the alternative, as a share of the partnership's net income. Once classified, the § 736(a) payments are taxed and characterized according to the general rules governing guaranteed payments and distributive shares. Thus, both the distributee and the partnership may be affected by the classification of the payments: with regard to the recipient, § 736(a) treatment frequently generates ordinary income while § 736(b) results often in capital characterization; with regard to the partnership, § 736(a) treatment often results in a deduction (or its equivalent) in contrast to the nondeductibility of § 736(b) payments.

As § 736 payments frequently span a number of years, the Regulations provide numerous timing and allocation rules for determining the taxable year in which the § 736(a) or § 736(b) payments are deemed received by the distributee partner.

FOXMAN v. COMMISSIONER

352 F.2d 466 (3d Cir.1965).

Smith, Circuit Judge

This matter is before the Court on petitions to review decisions of the Tax Court, 41 T.C. 535, in three related cases consolidated for the purpose of hearing. The petitions of Foxman and Grenell challenge the decision as erroneous only as it relates to them. The petition of the Commissioner seeks a review of the decision as it relates to Jacobowitz only if it is determined by us that the Tax Court erred in the other two cases.

The cases came before the Tax Court on stipulations of fact, numerous written exhibits and the conflicting testimony of several witnesses, including the taxpayers. The relevant and material facts found by the Tax Court are fully detailed in its opinion. We repeat only those which may contribute to an understanding of the narrow issue before us.

As the result of agreements reached in February of 1955, and January of 1956, Foxman, Grenell and Jacobowitz became equal partners in a commercial enterprise which was then trading under the name of Abbey Record Manufacturing Company, hereinafter identified as the Company. They also became equal shareholders in a corporation known as Sound Plastics, Inc. When differences of opinion arose in the spring of 1956, efforts were made to persuade Jacobowitz to withdraw from the partnership. These efforts failed at that time but were resumed in March of 1957. Thereafter the parties entered into negotiations which, on May 21, 1957, culminated in a contract for the acquisition of Jacobowitz's interest in the partnership of Foxman and Grenell. The terms and conditions, except one not here material, were substantially in accord with an option to purchase offered earlier to Foxman and Grenell. The relevant portions of the final contract are set forth in the Tax Court's opinion.

The contract, prepared by an attorney representing Foxman and Grenell, referred to them as the "Second Party," and to Jacobowitz as the "First Party." We regard as particularly pertinent to the issue before us the following clauses:

"WHEREAS, the parties hereto are equal owners and the sole partners of Abbey Record Mfg. Co., a partnership, * * *, and are also the sole stockholders, officers and directors of Sound Plastics, Inc., a corporation organized under the laws of the State of New York; and

"WHEREAS, the first party is desirous of selling, conveying, transferring and assigning all of his right, title and interest in and to his one-third share and interest in the said Abbey to the second parties; and

"WHEREAS, the second parties are desirous of conveying, transferring and assigning all of their right, title and interest in and to their combined two-thirds shares and interest in Sound Plastics, Inc., to the first party;

"Now, THEREFORE, IT IS MUTUALLY AGREED AS FOLLOWS:

"*First:* The second parties hereby purchase all the right, title, share and interest of the first party in Abbey and the first party does hereby sell, transfer, convey and assign all of his right, title, interest and share in Abbey and in the moneys in banks, trade names, accounts due, or to become due, and in all other assets of any kind whatsoever, belonging to said Abbey, for and in consideration of the following * * *"

The stated consideration was cash in the sum of $242,500; the assignment by Foxman and Grenell of their stock in Sound Plastics; and the transfer of an automobile, title to which was held by the Company. The agreement provided for the payment of $67,500 upon consummation of the contract and payment of the balance as follows: $67,500 on January 2, 1958, and $90,000 in equal monthly installments, payable on the first of each month after January 30, 1958. This balance was evidenced by a series of promissory notes, payment of which was secured by a chattel mortgage on the assets of the Company. This mortgage, like the contract, referred to a sale by Jacobowitz of his partnership interest to Foxman and Grenell. The notes were executed in the name of the Company as the purported maker and were signed by Foxman and Grenell, who also endorsed them under a guarantee of payment.

The down payment of $67,500 was by a cashier's check which was issued in exchange for a check drawn on the account of the Company. The first note, in the amount of $67,500, which became due on January 2, 1958, was timely paid by a check drawn on the Company's account. Pursuant to the terms of an option reserved to Foxman and Grenell, they elected to prepay the balance of $90,000 on January 28, 1958, thereby relieving themselves of an obligation to pay Jacobowitz a further $17,550, designated in the contract as a consultant's fee. They delivered to Jacobowitz a cashier's check which was charged against the account of the Company.

In its partnership return for the fiscal year ending February 28, 1958, the Company treated the sum of $159,656.09, the consideration received by Jacobowitz less the value of his interest in partnership property, as a guaranteed payment made in liquidation of a retiring partner's interest under § 736(a)(2) of the Internal Revenue Code of 1954, Title 26 U.S.C.A. This treatment resulted in a substantial reduction of the distributive shares of Foxman and Grenell and consequently a proportionate decrease in their possible tax liability. In his income tax return Jacobowitz treated the sum of $164,356.09, the consideration less the value of his partnership interest, as a long term capital gain realized upon the sale of his interest. This, of course, resulted in a tax advantage favorable to him. The Commissioner determined deficiencies against each of the taxpayers in amounts not relevant to the issue before us and each filed separate petitions for redetermination.

The critical issue before the Tax Court was raised by the antithetical positions maintained by Foxman and Grenell on one side and Jacobowitz on the other. The former, relying on § 736(a)(2), contended that the transaction, evidenced by the contract, constituted a liquidation of a retiring partner's interest and that the consideration paid was accorded correct treatment in the partnership return. The latter contended that the transaction constituted a sale of his partnership interest and, under § 741 of the Code, 26 U.S.C.A., the profit realized was correctly treated in his return as a capital gain. The Tax Court rejected the position of Foxman and Grenell and held that the deficiency determinations as to them were not erroneous; it sustained the position of Jacobowitz and held that the deficiency determination as to him was erroneous. The petitioners Foxman and Grenell challenge that decision as erroneous and not in accord with the law.

It appears from the evidence, which the Tax Court apparently found credible, that the negotiations which led to the consummation of the contract of May 21, 1957, related to a contemplated sale of Jacobowitz's partnership interest to Foxman and Grenell. The option offered to Foxman and Grenell early in May of 1957, referred to a sale and the execution of "a bill of sale" upon completion of the agreement. The relevant provisions of the contract were couched in terms of "purchase" and "sale." The contract was signed by Foxman and Grenell, individually, and by them on behalf of the Company, although the Company assumed no liability thereunder. The obligation to purchase Jacobowitz's interest was solely that of Foxman and Grenell. The chattel mortgage on the partnership assets was given to secure payment.

Notwithstanding these facts and the lack of any ambiguity in the contract, Foxman and Grenell argue that the factors unequivocally determinative of the substance of the transaction were: the initial payment of $67,500 by a cashier's check issued in exchange for a check drawn on the account of the Company; the second payment in a similar amount by check drawn on the Company's account; the execution of notes in the name of the Company as maker; and, the prepayment of the notes by cashier's check charged against the Company's account.

This argument unduly emphasizes form in preference to substance. While form may be relevant "[t]he incidence of taxation depends upon the substance of a transaction." The "transaction must be viewed as a whole, and each step, from the commencement of negotiations" to consummation, is relevant. Ibid. Where, as here, there has been a transfer and an acquisition of property pursuant to a contract, the nature of the transaction does not depend solely on the means employed to effect payment. Ibid.

It is apparent from the opinion of the Tax Court that careful consideration was given to the factors relied upon by Foxman and Grenell. It is therein stated:

> "These notes were endorsed by Foxman and Grenell individually, and the liability of [the Company] thereon was merely in the nature of security for their primary obligation under the agreement of May 21, 1957. The fact that they utilized partnership resources to discharge their own individual liability in such manner can hardly convert into a section 736 'liquidation' what would otherwise qualify as a section 741 'sale'." * * *

> "* * * the payments received by Jacobowitz were in discharge of their [Foxman's and Grenell's] obligation under the agreement, and not that of [the Company.] It was they who procured those payments in their own behalf from the assets of the partnership which they controlled. The use of [the Company] to make payment was wholly within their discretion and of no concern to Jacobowitz; his only interest was payment."

We are of the opinion that the quoted statements represent a fair appraisal of the true significance of the notes and the means employed to effect payment.

When the members of the partnership decided that Jacobowitz would withdraw in the interest of harmony they had a choice of means by which his withdrawal could be effected. They could have agreed inter se on either liquidation or sale. On a consideration of the plain language of the contract, the negotiations which preceded its consummation, the intent of the parties as reflected by their conduct, and the circumstances surrounding the transaction, the Tax Court found that the transaction was in substance a sale and not a liquidation of a retiring partner's interest. This finding is amply supported by the evidence in the record. The partners having employed the sale method to achieve their objective, Foxman and Grenell cannot avoid the tax consequences by a hindsight application of principles they now find advantageous to them and disadvantageous to Jacobowitz.

The issue before the Tax Court was essentially one of fact and its decision thereon may not be reversed in the absence of a showing that its findings were not supported by substantial evidence or that its decision was not in accord with the law. There has been no such showing in this case.

The decisions of the Tax Court will be affirmed.

WOODHALL v. COMMISSIONER

454 F.2d 226 (9th Cir.1972).

Choy, Circuit Judge.

W. Lyle Woodhall died on January 20, 1964, leaving Mrs. Woodhall as his sole heir and executrix. For 1964, Mrs. Woodhall filed a joint income tax return as surviving spouse. She also filed a fiduciary income tax return for the estate for part of 1964. For 1965, she filed an individual tax return and a fiduciary return.

The Commissioner of Internal Revenue determined deficiencies against Mrs. Woodhall for the years 1964 and 1965. The ground was that she had not declared as income certain amounts which came to her from the sale of her husband's interest in a partnership. Mrs. Woodhall petitioned the Tax Court for a declaration that she did not owe the deficiencies. The Tax Court upheld the Commissioner's determination and Mrs. Woodhall appeals. We affirm.

From January 1958 until his death, Woodhall was equal partner with his brother, Eldon Woodhall, in a lath and plaster contracting business known as Woodhall Brothers.

In December 1961, the brothers executed a written buy-sell agreement, which provided that "upon the death of either partner the partnership shall terminate and the survivor shall purchase the decedent's interest in the partnership." The price was to be determined according to a formula set out in the agreement. The formula defined accounts payable and included certain valuations for fixed assets, inventory, accounts receivable and other assets. It is the accounts receivable item that generates this controversy over Mrs. Woodhall's income for 1964 and 1965.

Because the partnership reported income on a cash basis, Woodhall had not paid taxes on his share of the accounts receivable which were outstanding at the time of his death. Mrs. Woodhall, in filing her tax returns as an individual and as executrix of her husband's estate, did not report as income the amounts allocated to the accounts receivable. Instead Mrs. Woodhall's tax returns stated that no gain had been realized by the sale of her husband's partnership interest because the tax basis of the interest was the fair market value at the time of death and this was the same as the sale price.

The issue presented is whether portions of payments received by Mrs. Woodhall, as executrix of the estate and as surviving spouse, constitute income in respect of a decedent under § 691(a)(1) of the Internal Revenue Code and are therefore subject to income taxes to the extent that such portions are allocable to unrealized receivables.

Generally, the sale of a partnership interest is an occasion for determining the character of gain or loss "to the transferor partner" as provided by § 741. In the case at bar, however, there was technically no "transferor partner" to accomplish the sale. The Woodhall Brothers partnership terminated automatically upon the death of Woodhall by operation of the buy-sell agreement, as well as under common law. Mrs. Woodhall, as executrix of the estate and as holder of a community property interest, was the transferor.

A tax regulation recognizes that § 741 applies when the sale of the partnership interest results in a termination of the partnership. The question arises whether a termination of the partnership by operation of a written agreement of the parties upon the death of one partner has the same effect.

The legislative history of § 741 explicitly deals with this question. The House report reads as follows:

"Transfer of an interest in a partnership (§§ 741–743, 751)

(1) General rules.—Under present decisions the sale of a partnership interest is generally considered to be a sale of a capital asset, and any gain or loss realized is treated as capital gain or loss. It is not clear whether the sale of an interest whose value is attributable to uncollected rights to income gives rise to capital gain or ordinary income * * *

* * *

(2) Unrealized receivables or fees ... In order to prevent the conversion of potential ordinary income into capital gain by virtue of

transfers of partnership interests, certain rules have been adopted * * * which will apply to *all* dispositions of partnership interests

* * *

A decedent partner's share of unrealized receivables and fees will be treated as income in respect of a decedent. Such rights to income will be taxed to the estate or heirs when collected ...

* * *

The term 'unrealized receivables or fees' is used to apply to any rights to income which have not been included in gross income under the method of accounting employed by the partnership. The provision is applicable mainly to cash basis partnerships which have acquired a contractual or other legal right to income for goods or services." House Report No. 1337, to accompany H.R. 8300 (Pub.L. 591), 83rd Cong., 2d Sess., pp. 70–71 (1954) (emphasis added).

The Senate report is similar, with only technical amendments which do not alter the basic statement of purpose in the House report. Senate Report No. 1622, to accompany H.R. 8300 (Pub.L. 591), 83rd Cong., 2d Sess., pp. 396 (1954).

Mrs. Woodhall's approach to the issue was much different. On the sale of her husband's partnership interest, she attempted to elect to establish the tax basis as the fair market value on the date of her husband's death. By this means, the sale price would be the same as the fair market value; there would be no gain and so no income to be taxed.

Mrs. Woodhall contends that the payments she received for the accounts receivable do not come within § 691(a), pertaining to income in respect of a decedent. Section 691(f), she points out, makes cross-reference to § 753, for application of § 691 to income in respect of a deceased partner. Section 753, in turn, refers to § 736 which provides that payments by a partnership for a deceased partner's interest in unrealized receivables shall be considered income in respect of a decedent under § 691. Mrs. Woodhall argues that a payment by a surviving partner is distinct from a payment by a partnership. Thus, she would have us interpret § 753, in conjunction with § 736, exclusively. In effect, this means that no payment other than one by a partnership which continues after one partner's death could constitute income in respect of a deceased partner. We reject this reading of the statutes.

The approach suggested by Mrs. Woodhall is not an appropriate characterization of the transfer of funds to her. Reading § 691 in the light of § 741, it is clear that Congress intended that the money Mrs. Woodhall received as an allocation from the unrealized accounts receivable be treated as income in respect of a decedent.

The Court of Appeals for the Eighth Circuit has just recently ruled that accounts receivable of a partnership shared in by a successor in interest of a deceased partner constituted income in respect of a decedent. *Quick's Trust v. Commissioner of Internal Revenue,* 444 F.2d 90 (8th Cir.1971). The instant case is substantially the same.

We hold that the Commissioner rightly determined deficiencies against Mrs. Woodhall in the tax years 1964 and 1965 * * *

Problem 17–1

Mildred, Jake, Wilma, and Sean operate an accounting practice as a calendar year, cash method, general partnership. It is a service partnership for which capital is not a material income producing factor. Each partner has a one-fourth interest in capital, profits, and losses, which they received on an initial contribution of $20,000 each to the partnership.

Partnership Balance Sheet
(12/31/97)

Assets	Adjusted Basis	Fair Market Value
Cash	$48,000	$ 48,000
Accounts Receivable	-0-	20,000
Real Property	40,000	44,000
	$88,000	$112,000

Liabilities & Capital		
Liabilities		
Mortgage (recourse)	$ 8,000	$ 8,000
Capital Accounts		
Mildred	20,000	26,000
Jake	20,000	26,000
Wilma	20,000	26,000
Sean	20,000	26,000
	$88,000	$112,000

a. Mildred retires December 31, 1997, and pursuant to the partnership agreement receives a lump sum distribution of $30,000 in complete liquidation of her interest. What are the consequences to Mildred and to the partnership?

b. Same as in a, except that the partnership agreement provides that all payments in excess of the fair market value of the retiring partner's share of partnership assets are a *premium*.

c. Same as in a, except that the partnership agreement provides that all payments in excess of the fair market value of the retiring partner's share of partnership assets are either a guaranteed payment or goodwill.

d. Same as in a, except that the partnership agreement provides that all payments in excess of the fair market value of the retiring partner's share of partnership assets are considered received in exchange for goodwill.

e. Same as in a, except that the partnership agreement provides that Mildred will receive a lump sum distribution of $25,000 on December 31, 1997, plus 20% of the net income of the partnership for the year 1997. The partnership's net income for 1997 is $80,000.

Chapter 18

ADJUSTMENT TO THE BASIS OF PARTNERSHIP ASSETS—OPTIONAL ADJUSTMENTS TO BASIS OF PARTNERSHIP ASSETS WHEN PARTNERSHIP INTERESTS ARE TRANSFERRED

Code References: §§ 742; 743; 754; 755.

Regulations: § 1.743–1(a)–(b)(2) example (1); 1.754–1(a) and (b); 1.755–1(a)(1), (b)(2), and (c) examples (1) and (2).

A. INTRODUCTION

It is possible that a person buying into a business by acquiring a partnership interest from an existing partner may not "get what he paid for." From a tax standpoint, the new owner may expect to have the share of the assets he purchased treated as reflecting that purchase price. While such a result is possible, it may depend upon the incoming partner (or his tax advisor) being aware of the concept of the § 754 election.

As previously discussed, for the purposes of many Code provisions, the partnership is treated as an entity separate and distinct from its members. Additionally, for recordation and computation purposes, the partnership determines its tax results based upon its business or investment operations, including the determination of any gain or loss arising upon the sale or exchange of its assets.

Upon formation of a partnership, the aggregate of the partners' bases for their partnership interests ("outside basis") will equal the partnership's bases for its assets ("inside basis") due to the interaction of § 722, § 723, and § 752. During the operational phase of the partnership, the aggregate outside bases of the original partners will generally track the partnership's inside bases in its assets. However, upon the sale or exchange of a partnership interest, inside basis of partnership assets and outside aggregate bases of the partners in their partnership interests will often no longer run in tandem because the incoming purchaser of the partnership interest is paying fair market value for the interest rather than its historical basis.

The fair market value paid becomes the purchaser's outside basis under § 742. The general rule is that his or her share of the partnership's inside asset basis is not adjusted accordingly due to the prohibition on such adjustments by § 743(a). Therefore, upon the subsequent disposition by the partnership of an asset, the purchaser would be required to recognize his or her share of partnership preacquisition gain or loss even though the partner is really receiving a return of capital because full fair market value for the interest, which value is based upon the acquisition date value of the partnership assets, was paid. While ultimately (assuming no further fluctuation in the value of the partnership's assets) any gain or loss will be offset by an equivalent amount of gain or loss upon sale or liquidation of the incoming partner's partnership interest, inequities arise because of timing and characterization considerations.

In order to remedy (albeit in some cases only in part) such disparities, § 743(b) provides for an adjustment (for the benefit of *only* the purchaser of the partnership interest) to the basis of the assets of the partnership to reflect the disparity between asset basis and value at the time of purchase of the interest. A prerequisite to such treatment is a *partnership* election under § 754 which is binding for all subsequent transfers of partnership interests and distributions of partnership assets. The election may be revoked with the consent of the Service. It should be noted that the § 754 election must be made by the partnership, of which the purchaser is not yet a partner.

As part of the negotiations to acquire a partnership interest, a purchaser may require that the partnership make the election as a condition precedent to his or her obligation to purchase. The selling partner would then have to convince the existing partners to go along with the election if it was not already in place.

B. § 743(b) ADJUSTMENT

The amount of § 743(b) adjustment is the difference between the purchase price and the purchaser's share of the bases of the partnership's assets at the time of purchase. Under § 743(c), the allocation rules of § 755 control the determination of the adjustment for each particular asset. Section 755 provides that the overall adjustment is allocated between two classes of assets: (1) § 1221/§ 1231 assets and (2) all other assets, based on relative appreciation or depreciation. Thereafter, a similar allocation is made within each particular class. While the theory of the § 743(b) adjustment is sound and its operation in some cases is perfect by yielding an adjustment for an asset which, when coupled with the purchaser's share of the asset's common basis to the partnership, equals fair market value, technical flaws in the allocation rules preclude such results in all cases.

The § 743(b) adjustment not only comes into play on the everyday operations of the partnership (limiting gain or loss on the disposition of partnership assets), but also affects basis determination of the assets upon their distribution to the partners. Thus, depending upon whether the asset is distributed to the purchaser or another partner, the basis of the asset distributed or other assets of the partnership may be affected.

REVENUE RULING 87–115

1987–2 C.B. 163.

Issues

Under section 743(b) of the Internal Revenue Code, does a sale of an interest in an upper-tier partnership (*UTP*) result in an adjustment to the basis of the property of a lower-tier partnership (*LTP*) in which *UTP* has an interest if:

(1) both *UTP* and *LTP* have made an election under section 754?

(2) only *UTP* has made the election under section 754?

(3) only *LTP* has made the election under section 754?

Facts

UTP is a partnership in which *A, B, C,* and *D* are equal partners. *UTP* is a partnership in which *A, B, C,* and *D* each contributed 30x dollars of cash to *UTP* upon its formation, and they each have a 30x interest in partnership capital and surplus. *A*'s share of the adjusted basis of partnership property is 30x dollars, the sum of *A*'s interest as a partner in partnership capital and surplus, plus *A*'s share of partnership liabilities (neither *UTP* nor *LTP* have any liabilities). *UTP* is an equal partner in *LTP,* along with *X* and *Y. LTP* was formed by *X, Y,* and *Z,* who each contributed 110x dollars of cash to *LTP* upon its formation. *UTP* purchased its interest in *LTP* from *Z* for 80x dollars in a taxable year for which *LTP* did not have an election under section 754 in effect. *UTP, X,* and *Y* each have a 110x dollar interest in partnership capital and surplus.

UTP has an adjusted basis of 120x dollars in its property as follows: an adjusted basis of 80x dollars in its partnership interest in *LTP* and an adjusted basis of 40x dollars in inventory. *UTP*'s partnership interest in *LTP* has a fair market value of 120x dollars, and *UTP*'s inventory has a fair market value of 80x dollars. *LTP* has only one asset, a capital asset that is not a section 751 asset. *LTP*'s asset has an adjusted basis of 330x dollars and a fair market value of 360x dollars.

In 1985, *A* sold *A*'s entire interest in *UTP* to *E* for 50x dollars.

Situation 1

Both *UTP* and *LTP* have valid section 754 elections in effect.

Situation 2

UTP has a section 754 election in effect, but *LTP* does not.

Situation 3

UTP does not have a section 754 election in effect, but *LTP* does.

LAW AND ANALYSIS

Section 742 of the Code provides that the basis of an interest in a partnership acquired other than by contribution shall be determined under part II of subchapter O of chapter 1 (sections 1011 through 1015).

Section 1012 of the Code provides, with certain exceptions, that the basis of property shall be the cost of such property.

Section 754 of the Code provides that if a partnership files an election, in accordance with regulations prescribed by the Secretary, the basis of partnership property shall be adjusted, in the case of a transfer of a partnership interest, in the manner provided in section 743(b). Such election shall apply with respect to all transfers of interests in the partnership during the taxable year with respect to which such election was filed and all subsequent years.

Section 743(a) of the Code provides the general rule that the basis of partnership property shall not be adjusted as the result of a transfer of an interest in a partnership by sale or exchange or on the death of a partner unless the election provided by section 754 is in effect with respect to such partnership.

Section 743(b) of the Code provides that, in the case of a transfer of an interest in a partnership by sale or exchange or upon the death of a partner, a partnership with respect to which the election provided in section 754 is in effect shall (1) increase the adjusted basis of partnership property by the excess of the basis to the transferee partner of such partner's interest in the partnership over the partner's proportionate share of the adjusted basis of partnership property; or (2) decrease the adjusted basis of partnership property by the excess of the transferee partner's proportionate share of the adjusted basis of partnership property over the basis of such partner's interest in the partnership. Section 743(b) further provides that the increase or decrease shall be an adjustment to the basis of partnership property with respect to the transferee partner only.

Section 1.743–1(b)(1) of the Income Tax Regulations provides that, in general, a partner's share of the adjusted basis of partnership property is equal to the sum of that partner's interest as a partner in partnership capital and surplus, plus that partner's share of partnership liabilities.

Section 755(a) of the Code requires that, in general, the amount of the basis adjustment be allocated among partnership assets in a manner which has the effect of reducing the difference between the fair market value and the adjusted basis of those assets, or in any other manner permitted by the regulations prescribed by the Secretary.

Section 755(b) of the Code provides that in applying the allocation rules provided in section 755(a), increases or decreases in the adjusted basis of partnership property arising from the transfer of an interest attributable to (1) capital assets and property described in section 1231(b) ("capital assets"), or (2) any other property of the partnership, shall in general be allocated to partnership property of like character.

Section 1.755–1(b)(2) of the Income Tax Regulations provides that to the extent an amount paid by a purchaser of a partnership interest is attributable to the value of capital assets, any difference between the amount so attributable and the transferee partner's share of the partnership basis of such property shall constitute a special basis adjustment with respect to partnership capital assets. Similarly, any such difference attributable to any other property of the partnership shall constitute a special basis adjustment with respect to such property.

Section 741 of the Code provides that, except as provided in section 751, the gain or loss on the exchange of an interest in a partnership shall be considered as a gain or loss from the sale of a capital asset.

Rev.Rul. 78–2, 1978–1 C.B. 202, concerns the transfer of an interest in an investment partnership, X, which is a partner of an operating partnership, Y. The ruling concludes that if elections under section 754 of the Code are in effect for X and Y, the adjustment to the basis of partnership property under section 743(b) includes (a) an adjustment to X's partnership interest in Y and (b) a corresponding basis adjustment to Y's property with respect to X and the transferee partner of X only.

In essence, if an election under section 754 is not in effect, the partnership is treated as an independent entity, separate from its partners. Thus, absent a section 754 election, even though the transferee receives a cost basis for the acquired partnership interest, the partnership does not adjust the transferee's share of the adjusted basis of partnership property. If, however, an election under section 754 is in effect, the partnership is treated more like an aggregate of its partners, and the transferee's overall basis in the assets of the partnership is generally the same as it would have been had the transferee acquired a direct interest in its share of those assets. Nevertheless, the transferee's adjusted basis for specific partnership assets will not necessarily equal the basis the assets would have had if the transferee had acquired a direct interest in the assets. The difference is due to the fact that the transferee's basis in specific partnership assets is controlled by section 755, which does not adopt a pure aggregate approach. *See* section 1.755–1(c) of the regulations.

Situation 1

E purchased *A*'s interest for 50x dollars. Thus, under section 742, *E*'s basis in *E*'s partnership interest is 50x dollars. Because *UTP* made a valid section 754 election, under section 743(b) *UTP* must increase the adjusted basis of its property by 20x dollars, the excess of the transferee partner's basis in the partnership interest (50x dollars) over that partner's share of the adjusted basis of such property. Under section 1.743–1(b)(1), *E* 's share of the adjusted basis of partnership property is 30x dollars, because *E* succeeds to *A* 's interest in partnership capital and surplus. *See, e.g.,* section 1.743–1(b)(1) Example (2). The 20x dollar special basis adjustment raises *UTP* 's adjusted basis in its partnership property to 140x dollars, but the additional 20x dollars must be segregated and allocated solely to *E*. Under section 755, the 20x dollars must be allocated between capital assets (*UTP* 's interest in *LTP*) and other assets (*UTP* 's inventory).

Under section 1.755–1(b)(2) of the regulations, to the extent that an amount paid by a purchaser of a partnership interest (here, 50x dollars) is attributable to the value of capital assets (here, 120x dollars, the value of *UTP* 's interest in *LTP*), any difference between the amount so attributable and the transferee partner's share of the partnership basis of such property constitutes a special basis adjustment with respect to such capital assets. In the instant case, 30x dollars (60 percent of 50x dollars) of *E* 's purchase price is attributable to the value of *UTP* 's interest in *LTP,* because 120x dollars, the value of *UTP* 's interest in *LTP,* is 60 percent of 200x dollars, the total value of *UTP* 's property. Thus, 10x dollars, the difference between the 30x dollars attributable to the value of *UTP* 's interest in *LTP* and 20x dollars, *E* 's proportionate share of *UTP* 's basis in *LTP,* is a special basis adjustment to *UTP* 's interest in *LTP*. This adjustment gives *E* an adjusted basis of 30x dollars in *UTP* 's interest in *LTP*. The remaining 10x dollars of the 20x dollar special basis adjustment is allocated to the adjusted basis of *UTP* 's inventory. This gives *E* a 20x dollar adjusted basis in *UTP* 's inventory.

Because *UTP* made a section 754 election manifesting an intent to be treated as an aggregate for purposes of sections 754 and 743, it is appropriate, for purposes of section 743 and 754, to treat the sale of *A* 's partnership interest in *UTP* as a deemed sale of an interest in *LTP*. The selling price of *E* 's share of *UTP* 's interest in *LTP* is deemed to equal *E* 's share of *UTP* 's adjusted basis in *LTP,* 30x dollars (¼ of 80x dollars plus 10x dollars, *E* 's special basis adjustment). Further, this deemed sale of an interest in *LTP* triggers the application of section 743(b) to *LTP*. Because *LTP* made a valid section 754 election, under section 743(b) *LTP* must increase the adjusted basis of its partnership property by 2.5x dollars, the excess of *E* 's share of *UTP* 's adjusted basis in *LTP* (30x dollars) over *E* 's share of the adjusted basis of *LTP* 's property (¼ of 110x dollars, or 27.5x dollars). Section 755 applies to *LTP* to allocate this basis adjustment, but because *LTP* has only one asset, no allocation is necessary. The 2.5x dollar adjustment must be segregated and allocated solely to *UTP* and *E,* the transferee partner of *UTP*.

Situation 2

UTP has made a valid section 754 election. Thus, as in *Situation 1*, E gets an adjusted basis of 30x dollars in UTP's interest in LTP and an adjusted basis of 20x dollars in UTP's inventory. Also, as in *Situation 1*, because UTP made a section 754 election, it is appropriate, for purposes of sections 754 and 743, to treat the sale of A's interest in UTP as the sale of an interest in LTP. However, in this situation, LTP does not have a section 754 election in effect. That is, under section 743(a), LTP chose not to have the basis of its property adjusted as the result of the transfer of an interest in it. Thus, E's purchase of a partnership interest in UTP has no affect on LTP's adjusted basis in its property.

Situation 3

LTP has made a valid election under section 754, but UTP does not make a section 754 election. On the sale by A of an interest in UTP, E succeeds to A's 20x dollar adjusted basis in UTP's interest in LTP and to A's 10x dollar adjusted basis in UTP's inventory. E succeeds to these bases because, by not making a section 754 election, UTP chose not to have the basis of its property adjusted as the result of the transfer of an interest in UTP.

In addition, by not making a section 754 election, UTP manifested an intent to be treated as an entity for purposes of sections 754 and 743. Thus, it is inappropriate, for purposes of sections 754 and 743, to treat A's sale of an interest in UTP as the sale of an interest in LTP. Consequently, UTP cannot increase E's share of the basis of LTP's property. Nevertheless, LTP's section 754 election is not meaningless. If UTP were to sell its partnership interest in LTP, the purchaser's share of the adjusted basis of LTP's assets would be adjusted.

HOLDINGS

Situation 1

Upon the sale of A's partnership interest in UTP, the transferee's (E's) share of UTP's adjusted basis in its assets is adjusted by the amount by which the basis in E's partnership interest differs from E's share of UTP's adjusted basis in its assets. In addition, E's share of LTP's adjusted basis in its assets is adjusted by the amount by which E's share of UTP's adjusted basis in LTP differs from E's share of the adjusted basis of LTP's property.

Situation 2

Upon the sale of A's partnership interest in UTP, E's share of UTP's adjusted basis in its assets is adjusted by the amount by which the basis in E's partnership interest differs from E's share of UTP's adjusted basis in its assets. However, because LTP did not make a section 754 election, the transfer does not affect LTP's adjusted basis in its property.

Situation 3

The sale of *A*'s partnership interest in *UTP* does not affect either *UTP*'s adjusted basis in its property or *LTP*'s adjusted basis in its property.

Problem 18–1

Meade, Gerald, and Jim own the Novelty Factory Company which is a calendar year, accrual method partnership. Each partner has a one-third interest in capital and profits. The basis of each partnership interest is $73,333 (one-third of the aggregate bases of the partnership assets).

Meade sells his partnership interest to Walt for $95,000 cash. Immediately prior to the sale, the balance sheet of the partnership was as follows:

Assets	Book Value and Adjusted Basis	Fair Market Value
Cash	$ 75,000	$ 75,000
Accounts Receivable	30,000	30,000
Inventory	10,000	15,000
Building (assume no § 1250 recapture potential)	55,000	70,000
Investment Land—Parcel X	40,000	90,000
Investment Land—Parcel Y	10,000	45,000
	$220,000	$325,000

Liabilities & Capital Per Financial Accounting Records		
Liabilities	$ 40,000	$ 40,000
Capital: Meade	60,000	95,000
Gerald	60,000	95,000
Jim	60,000	95,000
	$220,000	$325,000

a. What are the tax consequences to Walt and the remaining partners if the partnership does not make a § 754 election?

b. Same as a, except that the partnership elected under § 754. What is Walt's total basis adjustment?

c. Allocate the basis adjustment determined in b to the various partnership assets.

Problem 18–2

Same as Problem 18–1, except assume that the building had a fair market value of $30,000 and that Parcel X had a fair market value of $130,000. Assume alternatively that the fair market value of Parcel X remained at $90,000 and the building had a fair market value of $30,000, but the purchaser, Walt, still paid $95,000 for the partnership interest in an arm's-length transaction.

Chapter 19

ADJUSTMENT TO THE BASIS OF PARTNERSHIP ASSETS—OPTIONAL ADJUSTMENTS TO BASIS OF PARTNERSHIP ASSETS IN CONNECTION WITH DISTRIBUTION OF PARTNERSHIP ASSETS

Code References: §§ 734; 732(d).
Regulations: §§ 1.734–1; 1.732–1(d).

A. INTRODUCTION

Another of the complexities involved in utilizing the partnership vehicle relates to basis adjustments to partnership assets upon certain distributions of partnership assets to one of the partners. While these adjustments can be advantageous to the non-distributee partners, the partnership's tax advisors must remain alert to their availability in a given situation and must ensure that the § 754 election is made where appropriate.

As discussed in Chapter 18, the § 743(b) basis adjustment rules attempt to ensure that inside partnership asset bases and outside partnership interests bases run in tandem and that a purchaser or other successor in interest of a partnership interest does not realize gain or loss accruing prior to the acquisition of the partnership interest. A companion adjustment to § 743(b), that of § 734(b), attempts to effectuate the same policy in the context of partnership distributions. In contrast to the § 743(b) adjustment, however, which is personal to the new partner who acquires an interest by purchase, bequest, or devise, the § 734(b) adjustment is available to the partnership as a whole and, therefore, all of its partners.

B.   § 734(b) ADJUSTMENT

As seen in the § 751(b) analysis in Chapter 16, a distribution of partnership assets, unless pro rata among the members, may be treated under partnership tax law principles as an exchange (or purchase) of some share of the nondistributed assets by the nondistributee partners for the relinquishment of their share of the assets distributed to the distributee partner.   The § 734(b) adjustment so treats such a transaction.

For example, as evidenced by the Regulations, if a three-person partnership possesses two assets, cash of $11,000 and a § 1221 asset with a basis of $19,000 and value of $22,000, a complete liquidation for cash of a partner with basis in his partnership interest of $10,000 and a value of $11,000 will produce a $1,000 gain to the distributee.   A partnership with a § 754 election in effect would be entitled to a § 734(b) basis adjustment increase of $1,000 to the § 1221 asset.   The asset would consequently take a $20,000 basis for a subsequent sale by the partnership.   Only $2,000 of gain would be recognized by the partnership if it sold the asset for its fair value.   In essence, the adjustment compensates for the fact that the partnership did not distribute to the distributee his pro rata share of each asset ($3,667 cash and one-third of the § 1221 asset with a basis of $6,333 and value of $7,333) which would preserve the $1,000 gain potential for the distributee and retain for the partnership only a $2,000 gain (basis for the remaining two-thirds interest in the § 1221 asset of $12,666 and a value of $14,666) in the undistributed assets.   Because the distributee has reported $1,000 gain on the distribution and the partnership retains the gain potential of $2,000, all partnership gain has been either reported or preserved.

Similar adjustments are available in the case of loss distributions arising under § 731 and for basis increases or decreases arising for distributed assets over their predistribution basis to the partnership. The § 734(b) adjustment is allocated to the same category of retained assets as the type of distributed assets generating the increase or decrease in basis.   The Regulations dictate that gain or loss arising from the distribution of cash constitutes an adjustment attributable to § 1221/§ 1231 assets.   Allocations of the adjustment in the case of multiple undistributed assets of the partnership are governed by § 755. See Chapter 18.

REVENUE RULING 92–15

1992–1 C.B. 215.

Issues

(1) An upper-tier partnership (*UTP*), has an interest in a lower-tier partnership (*LTP*), and both partnerships have elections in effect under section 754 of the Internal Revenue Code. If *UTP* distributes property to a partner and, as a consequence of the distribution, adjusts the basis

of its interest in *LTP* under section 734(b), does *LTP* also adjust the basis of its property under section 734(b)?

(2) An upper-tier partnership (*UTP*) distributes its interest in a lower-tier partnership (*LTP*) to a partner of *UTP*, while both partnerships have elections in effect under section 754 of the Code. If section 732(a)(2) applies to limit the distributee partner's basis in the distributed partnership interest, does *UTP* increase the basis of its undistributed property to the extent provided in section 734(b)(1)(B)?

FACTS

A and *B* are partners in partnership *UTP*, each with a 50 percent interest in the capital, profits and losses of the partnership. *A*'s partnership interest in *UTP* has an adjusted basis of zero and a fair market value of 160*x* dollars. *UTP* has no liabilities and only two properties, capital asset *X* and a 10 percent interest in the capital, profits and losses of partnership *LTP*. Asset *X* has an adjusted basis to *UTP* of 140*x* dollars and a fair market value of 240*x* dollars. *UTP*'s interest in *LTP* has an adjusted basis to *UTP* of 30*x* dollars and a fair market value of 80*x* dollars.

LTP has no liabilities and only two properties, capital asset *Y* and noncapital asset *Z*. Asset *Y* has an adjusted basis of 200*x* dollars and a fair market value of 700*x* dollars. Asset *Z* has an adjusted basis of zero and a fair market value of 100*x* dollars. *UTP*'s share of the adjusted basis of *LTP*'s properties is 20*x* dollars.

For the taxable year in which the events described in Situations 1 and 2 occur, *UTP* and *LTP* make valid elections under section 754 of the Code. Capital assets *X* and *Y*, and noncapital asset *Z*, are not assets described in section 751. Section 732(d) does not apply to *A*.

Situation 1

UTP distributes one-half of capital asset *X* to partner *A*, in order to reduce *A*'s 50 percent interest in *UTP* to 20 percent, and increase *B*'s interest to 80 percent. The distribution reduces the value of *A*'s partnership interest in *UTP* to 40*x* dollars.

Situation 2

UTP distributes its partnership interest in *LTP* to partner *A*, in order to reduce *A*'s 50 percent interest in *UTP* to 33 percent. The distribution reduces the value of *A*'s partnership interest in *UTP* to 80*x* dollars.

LAW AND ANALYSIS

Section 734(a) of the Code provides that the basis of partnership property is not adjusted as the result of a distribution of property to a partner unless the partnership has an election in effect under section 754 of the Code.

Section 743(a) of the Code provides that the basis of partnership property is not adjusted as the result of a transfer of an interest in a partnership unless the partnership has an election in effect under section 754 of the Code.

Section 754 of the Code provides that if a partnership files an election in accordance with regulations prescribed by the Secretary, the basis of partnership property is adjusted, in the case of a distribution of property, in the manner provided in section 734(b), and, in the case of a transfer of a partnership interest, in the manner provided in section 743(b).

Section 734(b) of the Code provides that, in the case of a distribution of property to a partner, a partnership that has a section 754 election in effect increases or decreases the adjusted basis of partnership property under specified circumstances. Under section 734(b)(1)(A), the amount of increase is the amount of any gain recognized to the distributee partner with respect to the distribution. Under section 734(b)(1)(B), in the case of distributed property to which section 732(a)(2) applies, the amount of increase also includes the excess of the adjusted basis of the distributed property immediately before the distribution over the basis of the distributed property to the distributee. The partnership does not make the adjustment described in the preceding sentence if the distributed property is an interest in another partnership that does not have an election in effect under section 754 of the Code.

Section 732(a)(1) of the Code provides that the basis of property (other than money) distributed by a partnership to a partner other than in liquidation of the partner's interest is generally equal to the property's adjusted basis to the partnership immediately before the distribution. Section 732(a)(2), however, limits the basis of the property to the distributee partner to the adjusted basis of the partner's interest in the partnership reduced by any money distributed in the same transaction.

Section 734(c) of the Code requires the allocation of any basis adjustment among partnership properties in accordance with section 755 of the Code.

Section 743(b) of the Code provides that, in the case of a transfer of an interest in a partnership by sale or exchange or upon the death of a partner, a partnership that has a section 754 election in effect increases or decreases the adjusted basis of partnership property under specified circumstances.

Section 743(c) of the Code requires the allocation of any basis adjustment among partnership properties in accordance with section 755 of the Code.

Section 755(a)(1) of the Code provides that the basis adjustment is allocated among partnership properties in a manner that reduces the difference between the fair market value and the adjusted bases of those properties. Section 755(b) provides that in applying the allocation rules of section 755(a), increases or decreases in the adjusted basis of partnership property arising from a distribution of, or a transfer of an interest attributable to, (1) capital assets and property described in section

1231(b) ("capital assets"), or (2) any other property of the partnership, are allocated to partnership property of like character.

Section 1.755–1(b)(1) of the Income Tax Regulations provides that where there is an adjustment to the basis of undistributed partnership property under section 734(b)(1)(B) of the Code, the adjustment is allocated to remaining partnership property of a character similar to that of the distributed property.

Section 1.755–1(a)(1)(ii) of the regulations provides that if there is an increase in basis to be allocated to partnership assets, such increase must be allocated only to assets whose values exceed their bases and in proportion to the difference between the value and basis of each. No increase may be made, however, to the basis of any asset the adjusted basis of which equals or exceeds its fair market value.

Section 741 of the Code provides that, except as provided in section 751, the gain or loss from the sale or exchange of an interest in a partnership is considered to be a gain or loss from the sale or exchange of a capital asset.

Section 708(b)(1)(B) of the Code provides that a partnership is considered terminated if, within a 12 month period, there is a sale or exchange of 50 percent or more of the total interest in partnership capital and profits. Section 1.708–1(b)(1)(ii) of the regulations provides that the liquidation of a partnership interest is not a sale or exchange for purposes of section 708(b)(1). Section 761(e) provides that, for purposes of sections 708 and 743, any distribution of an interest in a partnership (not otherwise treated as an exchange) is treated as an exchange.

Situation 1

UTP distributes one-half of capital asset X to partner A, reducing the value of A's partnership interest to 40x dollars. Under section 732(a)(1) of the Code, A's basis in the distributed half of asset X would be equal to the basis of the distributed half of asset X to UTP immediately before the distribution, or 70x dollars. Section 732(a)(2), however, limits A's basis in the distributed half of asset X to A's basis in its UTP partnership interest, or zero. Because UTP has a section 754 election in effect, under section 734(b)(1)(B), UTP increases the adjusted basis of its remaining property by 70x dollars, the excess of the adjusted basis of the distributed property to UTP immediately before the distribution (70x dollars) over the basis of the distributed property to A (zero).

Section 755(b) of the Code and section 1.755–1(b)(1) of the regulations provide that the basis adjustment to undistributed partnership property under section 734(b)(1)(B) is allocated to remaining partnership property of a character similar to that of the distributed property. UTP's remaining property is the undistributed half of asset X and its interest in LTP, both of which, like asset X, are capital assets. Section 755(a) generally requires a reduction of the difference between the fair market value and the adjusted basis of undistributed property. In this case, the undistributed half of asset X and UTP's partnership interest in

LTP each have a difference of $50x$ dollars between fair market value and adjusted basis. Section 1.755–1(a)(1)(ii) requires that a section 734(b) basis increase be allocated among partnership assets in proportion to the difference between the value and the basis of each. Accordingly, the $70x$ dollar basis adjustment is allocated equally among *UTP*'s two assets, so that *UTP* increases its basis in the undistributed half of asset X from $70x$ dollars to $105x$ dollars, and increases its basis in *LTP* from $30x$ dollars to $65x$ dollars.

Because both *UTP* and *LTP* have made elections under section 754 of the Code, it is appropriate to treat *UTP*'s distribution of one-half of asset X to A and the subsequent $35x$ dollar increase to *UTP*'s basis in *LTP* as an event that triggers a section 734(b) basis increase of $35x$ dollars to *UTP*'s share of *LTP*'s assets. Under section 755(b) of the Code and section 1.755–1(b)(1) of the regulations, the basis adjustment to undistributed partnership property under section 734(b)(1)(B) is allocated to remaining partnership property of a character similar to that of the distributed property. Accordingly, *LTP* increases its basis in *UTP*'s share of asset Y from $20x$ dollars to $55x$ dollars. This adjustment to basis is for *UTP* only and does not affect the basis in *LTP* property of other partners of *LTP*. No adjustment is made to *UTP*'s share of *LTP*'s basis in noncapital asset Z.

Although A's interest in *UTP* is reduced from 50 percent to 20 percent, the reduction of A's interest in *UTP* is effected by a distribution, which is not considered a sale or exchange of a *UTP* interest for purposes of section 708 of the Code. *Cf.* section 1.708–1(b)(1)(ii) of the regulations.

Under the facts addressed by this ruling, *UTP* and *LTP* were allowed to increase the basis of undistributed property. Under other circumstances, upper- and lower-tier partnerships might be required to decrease the basis of undistributed property in accordance with the principles described above. For example, if a partner in an upper-tier partnership (with a section 754 election in effect) is distributed property in liquidation of the partner's interest, and the partner has a higher basis in its partnership interest than in the distributed partnership property, the upper-tier partnership must decrease its adjusted basis in its remaining partnership property under section 734(b)(2) of the Code. If this adjustment results in a reduction in the upper-tier partnership's basis in its partnership interest in a lower-tier partnership (which also has a section 754 election in effect), the lower-tier partnership must decrease its adjusted basis in the upper-tier partnership's proportionate share of the lower-tier partnership's assets under section 734(b)(2) as well.

Situation 2

UTP distributes its partnership interest in *LTP* to partner A, reducing A's 50 percent interest in *UTP* to 33 percent. Under section 732(a)(2) of the Code, A's basis in the distributed *LTP* interest is equal to A's basis in its *UTP* partnership interest, or zero. Because both *UTP* and *LTP* have section 754 elections in effect, under section 734(b)(1)(B), *UTP* increases the adjusted basis of its remaining property (asset *X*) by 30*x* dollars, the excess of the adjusted basis of the distributed property to *UTP* immediately before the distribution (30*x* dollars) over the basis of the distributed property to *A* (zero).

UTP makes the above basis adjustment only because both *UTP* and *LTP* have elections in effect under section 754 of the Code. See the last sentence of section 734(b), which limits the applicability of section 734(b)(1)(B).

Under section 761(e) of the Code, *UTP*'s distribution of its interest in *LTP* is treated as an exchange of the interest in *LTP* for purposes of section 743. Because *LTP* has a section 754 election in effect, under section 743(b)(2) *LTP* would decrease the adjusted basis of its property by 20*x* dollars, the excess of *A*'s proportionate share of the adjusted basis of *LTP*'s property (20*x* dollars) over the basis of *A*'s interest in *LTP* (zero). However, section 1.755–1(a)(1)–(iii) of the regulations prevents *LTP* from decreasing the basis of either of its assets because both asset *Y* and asset *Z* have fair market values which equal or exceed their bases.

Under section 761(e) of the Code, *UTP*'s distribution of its interest in *LTP* is treated as an exchange of a 10 percent interest in *LTP* for purposes of the partnership termination provisions in section 708. *See* Rev.Rul. 87–50, 1987–1 C.B. 157. The reduction of *A*'s interest in *UTP* is not considered a sale or exchange for purposes of section 708. *Cf.* section 1.708–1(b)(1)(ii) of the regulations.

HOLDINGS

(1) If partnership *UTP* and partnership *LTP* have elections in effect under section 754 of the Code, if *UTP* distributes property to a partner and one of *UTP*'s undistributed properties is an interest in partnership *LTP,* and if *UTP* adjusts the basis of its interest in *LTP* under section 734(b), then this adjustment is an event that is deemed to require *LTP* to adjust the basis of its property under section 734(b) by the same amount. This adjustment to basis is for *UTP* only and does not affect the basis in *LTP* property of other partners of *LTP*.

(2) If partnership *UTP* distributes its interest in partnership *LTP* to a partner of *UTP* while both partnerships have elections in effect under section 754 of the Code, and if section 732(a)(2) applies to the distributed partnership interest, *UTP* increases the basis of its undistributed property to the extent provided in section 734(b)(1)(B).

Problem 19–1

Rental Real Estate Co. is a partnership formed by Stu, Henry, and Hal to purchase and hold property for appreciation. Each partner has a basis of $10,000 for his one-third interest in the partnership which has a § 754 election in effect. Calculate the basis adjustment under § 754 to the partnership property if the partnership liquidates Stu's entire partnership interest in each of the following circumstances.

a. The partnership has assets consisting of cash of $11,000 and property with a partnership basis of $19,000 and a value of $22,000 and no liabilities. Stu receives $11,000 in cash for his interest.

b. The partnership has assets consisting of cash of $9,000 and property with a partnership basis of $21,000 and a value of $18,000 and no liabilities. Stu receives $9,000 in cash for his interest.

c. The partnership has cash of $4,000 and two pieces of property with bases of $11,000 and $15,000 and values of $11,000 and $18,000, respectively. Stu receives the property valued at $11,000 in return for his interest.

d. The partnership has cash of $4,000 and two pieces of property with bases of $9,000 and $17,000 and values of $9,000 and $14,000, respectively. Stu receives the property valued at $9,000 in return for his interest.

C. § 732(d) ADJUSTMENT

The use of § 732(d) is elective with the transferee partner, although in some circumstances its application may be *required*. Perhaps no other provision of Subchapter K is less understood and more overlooked.

The purpose of § 732(d) is to give, to the extent possible, the same result to the distributee partner who acquired an interest by transfer that would have arisen if the § 754 election had been in effect at the time of the transfer and the § 743(b) adjustment had been made. However, the basis of the distributed property under a § 732(d) adjustment will not necessarily be the same as if there had been a § 743(b) adjustment.

Section 732(d) is available to a partner who: (1) acquires his partnership interest by purchase or inheritance from another partner when the partnership did not have a § 754 election in effect for the year of the transfer, and (2) receives a distribution of property other than money within two years after the transfer of the partnership interest. In those circumstances, the partner may elect to treat as the adjusted partnership basis of the distributed property the adjusted basis the property would have had to the partnership if the § 743(b) adjustment were made when the partner acquired his interest.

However, in certain settings, § 732(d) is mandatory in its application. If a partner acquired the partnership interest by a transfer to which the § 754 election was *not* in effect, he or she may be required to apply the § 732(d) adjustment to a distribution made at *any time* (not only within two years). The treatment is required if at the time the interest was acquired (1) the fair market value of all partnership property (other than money) exceeds 110% of its adjusted basis to the partnership; (2) an allocation of basis under § 732(c), if the interest had been liquidated immediately after the transfer, would have shifted basis from property not subject to an allowance for depreciation, depletion, or amortization to property subject to such allowance; and (3) a special basis adjustment under § 743(b) would change the basis to the distribu-tee of the property actually distributed.

RUDD v. COMMISSIONER

79 T.C. 225 (1982).

* * *

OPINION

The parties agree that goodwill was an asset of the partnership and that petitioner and four other partners acquired the rights to the partnership's name upon dissolution of the partnership. The parties disagree, however, as to the composition of the partnership's goodwill and the tax consequences of abandoning the use of the partnership's name.

Petitioner contends that the partnership's goodwill was embodied entirely in the partnership's name and therefore, when the use of the partnership's name was abandoned in 1971, a loss of goodwill occurred for which petitioner (having obtained a portion of the partnership's goodwill as a liquidating distribution) is entitled to a deduction under section 165(a) for his entire basis in the goodwill.[13] Respondent main-tains that the partnership's goodwill consisted of its clients and, since the business of the partnership was continued after its dissolution without the loss of clients, there was no abandonment of goodwill. In the alternative, respondent asserts that not all of the partnership's goodwill was abandoned, and petitioner has failed to establish what portion of the goodwill was abandoned. Respondent further contends that, if we find that goodwill was abandoned in any amount, then (1) section 731(a)(2) operates to deny recognition in 1971 of the loss from such abandonment, or (2) any abandonment loss recognizable by peti-tioner is a capital loss pursuant to section 731(a), rather than an ordinary loss.

We agree with petitioner that he is entitled to a loss deduction in 1971 for the abandonment of his interest in the partnership's name, but we do not agree that the partnership's goodwill was embodied entirely in

---

13. The partnership claimed a deduc-tion of $111,900 for loss of goodwill on its 1971 tax return. As a result, the distribu-tive share of the partnership's income re-ported by petitioner on his 1971 income tax return included a portion of this deduction for loss of goodwill. The partnership was not entitled to such a deduction, however, since it had no tax basis in goodwill (in the absence of a sec. 754 election and basis adjustment under sec. 743(b)). Petitioner conceded at trial that the manner in which the loss of goodwill was originally reported was improper, and relies solely on the posi-tion stated in the text, *supra*. Respondent does not contend he was surprised by peti-tioner's shift. Petitioner, of course, retains the burden of proof. We proceed to consid-er petitioner's new position. *Estate of Stark v. Commissioner,* 45 B.T.A. 882, 891 (1941).

In view of the stipulation of the parties that the partners abandoned the partner-ship's name, we are not called upon to decide whether the partnership or the part-ners (including petitioner) abandoned the use of the partnership's name.

the partnership's name. Accordingly, the amount of petitioner's loss deduction is determined herein.

Goodwill may be defined as an intangible (or group of intangibles) associated with the going-concern value of a business. The abandonment of a component of goodwill which is a clearly identifiable and severable asset entitles the taxpayer to a loss deduction under section 165(a).

The facts and circumstances of the instant case convince us that the partnership's name was a clearly identifiable and severable asset of the partnership which contributed to the partnership's goodwill.

When it was dissolved in 1971, the partnership had been in business in the Muskegon area for almost 40 years, and it was the largest accounting firm in the area. The partnership attracted clients from all along the Lake Michigan shoreline. The partnership's name was well recognized in the area and the partners feared that business might be hurt if the partnership's name was changed in any way. In some instances, the partnership's name attracted new clients. When an effort was made by one partner to add his name to the partnership's name, the other partners refused. A certified public accountant in Holland, Mich., 35 miles south of Muskegon, shared the net profits of his accounting firm for longer than 20 years solely for the use of the partnership's name. Petitioner also adduced testimony as to the importance of a firm name in the public accounting industry, at least in Michigan. This testimony indicated that, in general, firms with well-established names become less successful if they change their names; and in some instances, firms with well-established names can continue to be successful despite turnover of personnel or even despite a lower quality of services rendered.

The foregoing factors collectively lead us to conclude that the partnership's name was a clearly identifiable and valuable intangible asset of the partnership which was responsible, to some extent, for client attraction and retention.

Petitioner is entitled to a deduction in the amount of his basis in the partnership's name for 1971, the year in which the name was abandoned. However, as more fully discussed, *infra,* the partnership's name was not the only intangible accounting for the partnership's goodwill.

Before examining how the amount of the deductible abandonment loss is to be determined, we will consider respondent's alternative arguments.

Respondent states that he "does not here contest that some of the goodwill of [the partnership] was tied directly to the name of the firm." Nevertheless, he asserts that "petitioner has failed to establish what portion of the goodwill was abandoned" and so is entitled to no deduction at all. In so arguing, respondent has overlooked the fact that value of abandoned property at the time of abandonment has little if any effect on deductibility. Deductibility depends on the fact of abandonment of the partnership's name (not the goodwill) and a determination of petitioner's basis in the partnership's name. The partnership's name was abandoned in 1971, and we are obligated to determine the amount of the name's deductible basis. We reject respondent's argument that no deduction whatsoever is allowable merely because petitioner has failed to establish the precise amount that is allowable.

Respondent argues that section 731(a)(2) precludes recognition of any loss by petitioner. Section 731(a)(2) provides the rule for recognition of loss *on a distribution* by a partnership to a partner. As petitioner correctly points out, petitioner's claim is for a loss arising from the abandonment of the partnership's name by petitioner *after* he received an interest in the name as a distribution from the partnership—petitioner does not claim a loss on the distribution. Accordingly, we conclude that section 731 does not apply, and so this provision does not preclude recognition of petitioner's loss.

Respondent further argues that goodwill "constituted an integral and indivisible part of the petitioner's partnership interest" and therefore the partnership "could not separately distribute the goodwill to the various partners." We disagree. Goodwill, though an intangible, may be sold, exchanged, disposed of, and even abandoned, like any other asset. In any event, we have found the partnership's name to be a clearly identifiable and severable asset, and we reject respondent's assertion that it was not capable of being distributed to the partners.

Petitioner maintains that his entire basis in the partnership's goodwill is embodied in the partnership's name, and all of it was abandoned in 1971, and, so, all of it is deductible for 1971. Respondent asserts that no deduction is to be allowed. We believe the correct answer lies between the parties' positions.

The goodwill of a public accounting firm can generally be described as the intangibles that attract new clients and induce existing clients to continue using the firm. These intangibles may include an established firm name, a general or specific location of the firm, client files and workpapers (including correspondence, audit information, financial statements, tax returns, etc.), a reputation for general or specialized services, an ongoing working relationship between the firm's personnel and clients, or accounting, auditing, and tax systems used by the firm.

We are convinced that there were other transferable intangibles associated with the partnership's business which contributed to client patronage. These intangibles included the following: a base of clients requiring ongoing or recurring services by the partnership, client files and workpapers, a working relationship between the partnership's personnel and clients, and a long-standing reputation for accounting services in the Muskegon area. Moreover, we do not believe that these intangibles were abandoned when the partnership was dissolved.

The partnership was terminated as of October 1, 1971, and dissolved in 1971, except for the winding up of its affairs. On that same date, the partnership's five most active partners and all of its staff accountants began working for Alexander Grant. The remaining three partners (the name partners) had agreed not to engage in the practice of public accounting in the Muskegon area for specified periods of time. Also on October 1, 1971, the partnership's fixed assets were transferred to Alexander Grant. The record does not indicate who had the right to contact the partnership's clients or to use client files and workpapers. We doubt that Alexander Grant would employ the entire accounting staff of the partnership (except for the name partners) and obtain all of its fixed assets unless a substantial portion of the partnership's business was to be continued by Alexander Grant. It is highly unlikely that Alexander Grant's Muskegon office was growing so rapidly that it could absorb in its own practice a two-to-threefold increase in its partners and staff of accountants. Neither do we think that petitioner would turn his back on a client base developed over a 39–year period, including 19 years of his own efforts, for which he paid a large premium. Integral to the continuation of the partnership's business, we think, were the partnership's other intangibles, discussed *supra*. In any event, petitioner, who bears the burden of proving how much of the basis for goodwill should be allocated to the partnership's name, has not convinced us that these intangibles were abandoned or otherwise lost their usefulness on the dissolution of the partnership.

As detailed *infra*, petitioner's adjusted basis in the partnership's goodwill (and derivatively, in the partnership's name) must be determined under the special basis rule provided in section 732(d). This rule requires that we look at the assets of a partnership at the time a partnership interest is purchased by the transferee partner who is to receive the special basis adjustment or allocation under section 732(d). Sec. 1.732–1(d)(1)(vi), Income Tax Regs. See sec. 743(b) and the regulations thereunder. Accordingly, in determining the portion of goodwill associated with the partnership's name, we must examine the partnership's goodwill as of the date petitioner purchased each of his interests in the partnership.

We are convinced that the partnership's name was a significant component of its goodwill. When petitioner purchased his first interest (10 percent) in the partnership, it had been in existence for almost 26 years. About that time, the partnership became the largest public accounting firm in the Muskegon area and maintained that position until its dissolution. Its reputation was well established in the area throughout the years when petitioner was purchasing his interests. Also throughout this period, a certified public accountant in Holland, Mich., shared his net profits with the name partners solely for the use of the partnership's name.

On the other hand, we believe a substantial portion of the partnership's goodwill was embodied in its client relationships. Under the written partnership agreement of 1967, the voluntary withdrawal of a partner would result in a forfeiture of 50 to 100 percent of the goodwill attributable to the partner's interest, depending on whether or not the withdrawing partner intended to accept employment with a client or former client. The partnership agreement prohibited any partner from practicing public accounting within a 75–mile radius of Muskegon for 5 years after the partner voluntarily withdrew or retired, and also forbade any partner from being employed by a client after retirement. In our view, these provisions of the partnership agreement were intended to protect the partnership's client base and business relationship with clients, which we have concluded were intangibles contributing to the partnership's goodwill. On dissolution of the partnership, the name partners remained subject to the restrictions on competition in the Muskegon area and employment by clients. This, too, was a measure taken to protect the partnership's client base. It is evident that the partners set a high value on those components of goodwill other than the partnership's name.

"In a case such as this, 'an accurate allocation of value among the several classes of intangibles is impossible, and we must make the broadest kind of estimate.' " Using our best judgment and taking into consideration the foregoing factors, we have found that, overall, the portion of the partnership's goodwill that was embodied in the partnership's name was 20 percent when petitioner purchased his interests in the partnership.

We conclude that the partnership's name was a clearly identifiable and severable asset. Since petitioner and four other partners received this asset in 1971 as a distribution from the partnership under the terms of the dissolution agreement and abandoned it in that year, we hold that petitioner is entitled to an abandonment loss deduction under section 165(a) for 1971.

Under section 165(b), the amount of petitioner's loss deduction is measured by his adjusted basis in the partnership's name. The following recounts our journey through subchapter K of the Internal Revenue Code of 1954 in search of petitioner's adjusted basis in the partnership's name.

Petitioner received accounts receivable, furniture and fixtures, intangible assets (the partnership's name and other elements encompassed in goodwill), and money in liquidation of his interest in the partnership. Under section 732(b), the basis of this distributed property (other than the money) is an amount equal to the adjusted basis of petitioner's interest in the partnership, reduced by the money distributed. The basis is allocated among the distributed properties pursuant to section 732(c). Section 732(c)(1) requires that the basis be allocated first to any unrealized receivables and inventory items in an amount equal to the adjusted basis of each such property to the partnership. No unrealized receivables were distributed to petitioner; basis is to be allocated to the accounts receivable in an amount equal to the adjusted basis of the accounts receivable to the partnership, since they represent inventory items. Section 732(c)(2) provides that the remaining basis is to be allocated to any other distributed properties in proportion to their adjusted bases to the partnership. Therefore, petitioner's basis in his partnership interest, reduced by money distributed to him and amounts allocated to the accounts receivable, is to be allocated to the furniture and fixtures and the goodwill distributed to him in proportion to their adjusted bases to the partnership.

The parties agree that the partnership's adjusted basis in the goodwill was zero. The partnership did not make an election under section 754 which would have increased the partnership's basis in goodwill to reflect amounts paid by petitioner (and others) for goodwill. Therefore, at first glance, it appears that petitioner's remaining basis in his partnership interest would be allocated entirely to the furniture and fixtures. Since petitioner's basis in his partnership interest includes the premiums he paid for goodwill (see table 1 *supra*), the result of this allocation would be to allocate the amount he paid for goodwill to the furniture and fixtures, thereby assigning bases to the latter assets in excess of their fair market values. Section 732(d) prevents this odd result by treating the partnership's adjusted basis in distributed property, to the extent possible, as though (1) a section 754 election had been in effect when the distributee partner acquired his partnership interest by transfer, and (2) a section 743(b) adjustment had been made.

As authorized by the last sentence of section 732(d), section 1.732–1(d)(4), Income Tax Regs., requires a partner, who acquired any part of his partnership interest in a transfer to which the election provided in section 754 was not in effect, to apply the special basis rule contained in section 732(d) to a distribution to him, whether or not made within 2 years after the transfer, if the three conditions of the regulation are met. At the time of each of petitioner's purchases of an interest in the partnership, the fair market value of all partnership property (other than money) exceeded 110 percent of its adjusted basis to the partnership. Thus, the first condition of the regulation is met.

The second condition of the regulation is also met. Petitioner purchased various interests in the partnership, as shown in table 1 *supra.* As to each purchase, he paid an amount in excess of the respective interest's proportionate share of the partnership's adjusted basis in its property. It is agreed that the excess was paid for goodwill. If there had been a liquidation of the partnership immediately after each of petitioner's purchases, petitioner's basis in his partnership interest (reduced by money distributable to him and amounts allocable to accounts receivable under section 732(c)(1)) would have been allocated entirely to furniture and fixtures under section 732(c)(2) because the partnership had no basis in its goodwill. Thus, an allocation of basis under section 732(c) would have resulted in a shift of basis from property not subject to an allowance for depreciation, depletion, or amortization (goodwill) to property subject to such an allowance (furniture and fixtures).

The final condition of the regulation is that a special basis adjustment under section 743(b) would change the basis of the transferee partner in the property actually distributed. Under section 743(b), a partnership's adjusted basis in its property is increased by the excess of the transferee partner's basis in his partnership interest over his proportionate share of the adjusted basis of all the partnership property. This excess is then allocated among partnership properties in accordance with section 755. Sec. 743(c). The regulations under section 755 provide that, if there is an increase in basis to be allocated to partnership assets, then the increase must be allocated only to assets whose values exceed their bases. Sec. 1.755–1(a)(1)(ii), Income Tax Regs. Further, a portion of the adjustment must be allocated to partnership goodwill to the extent that goodwill exists and is reflected in the price at which the partnership interest is sold. Sec. 1.755–1(a)(1)(iv), Income Tax Regs. Since the parties agree that goodwill was the only asset of the partnership whose fair market value exceeded its basis to the partnership when petitioner purchased each of his interests, a special basis adjustment under section 743(b) would increase the partnership's adjusted basis in goodwill with respect to each premium paid by petitioner. This, in turn, would result in the allocation of a portion of petitioner's basis in his partnership interest (reduced by money distributed to him and amounts allocated to accounts receivable under section 732(c)(1)) to goodwill under section 732(c)(2). Thus, a special basis adjustment under section 743(b) would change petitioner's basis in property actually distributed (furniture and fixtures and goodwill), the third condition of the regulation.

We conclude that petitioner's basis in goodwill must be computed using the special basis rule provided in section 732(d). Sec. 1.732–1(d)(4), Income Tax Regs. Consequently, for purposes of allocating petitioner's basis under section 732(c), the partnership's adjusted basis in goodwill is treated as though the above-described section 743(b) adjustments with respect to petitioner's purchases of partnership interests had been made. Therefore, a portion of petitioner's basis in his partnership interest is allocable to goodwill on its distribution by the partnership.

Petitioner calculates the amount of his basis allocable to goodwill to be $32,733. However, this amount appears to be the partnership's adjusted basis (determined under sec. 732(d)) in petitioner's proportionate share of goodwill. See table 1 *supra*. From the information in the record, we are unable to determine the precise computation of petitioner's basis in goodwill and so we leave this determination to the computation under Rule 155, Tax Court Rules of Practice and Procedure. Petitioner is entitled to a loss deduction equal to 20 percent of his adjusted basis in goodwill.

As a final matter, respondent contends that any loss recognizable by petitioner is a capital loss. In support thereof, respondent relies on section 731(a) and derivatively on section 741. We have already concluded that petitioner's loss is not governed by section 731(a). For the same reason, we also reject this argument. Notwithstanding the fact that goodwill is a capital asset, petitioner's loss is an ordinary loss since an abandonment involves no sale or exchange.

To reflect the conclusions reached herein,

Decision will be entered under Rule 155.

Problem 19–2

The partnership described in Problem 19–1 has invested in several parcels of investment realty. The balance sheet of the partnership (equal profits, losses, and capital account) at the time of Stu's sale of his one-third interest to Paul, an unrelated third party, is:

Assets	Adjusted Basis	Fair Market Value
Land	$ 15,000	$165,000
Depreciable Property (net of reserve for depreciation)	150,000	150,000
Total	$165,000	$315,000

Capital		
Stu	$ 55,000	$105,000
Henry	55,000	105,000
Hal	55,000	105,000
Total	$165,000	$315,000

Assume a § 754 election is not in effect. Paul purchases Stu's partnership interest for $105,000. Four years later (with no change in values and no net income or loss other than depreciation), the partnership is dissolved. Paul receives an undivided one-third interest in the land and an undivided one-third interest in the depreciable property. At the time of distribution, the partnership's adjusted basis for the depreciable property has been reduced to $135,000 by the allowance of $15,000 of depreciation deductions. Paul's one-third share of the depreciation deduction reduced the adjusted basis of his partnership interest from the $105,000 purchase price to $100,000 at the date of distribution. What are the tax consequences to Paul?

Chapter 20

TERMINATION OF A PARTNERSHIP

Code References: §§ 706(c); 708; 761(e); 168(i)(7).

Regulations: §§ 1.706–1(c)(3)(vi) example (3); 1.708–1; 1.736–1(a)(6); 1.741–1(b); 1.1245–4(c).

A. INTRODUCTION: EVENTS PRECIPITATING

The partnership status of a small business entity may terminate, for tax purposes, in several different ways. Some are obvious and some are not. When partnership tax status is ended, various tax ramifications flow to the partners. A partnership may terminate for state law purposes and remain alive for tax purposes. Similarly, a tax termination can occur even though the partnership is fully operational and extant for state partnership law purposes.

Earlier materials have discussed the tax consequences to particular partners of the disposition (sale, exchange, or liquidation) of partnership interests, but the effects on the partnership and its other members generally have not been covered. This topic is addressed by § 708 which prescribes the governing rules as to when a partnership terminates. The two most obvious circumstances precipitating a termination are when an enterprise completely ceases to conduct operations or continues to conduct operations but not in a partnership mode (e.g., as a sole proprietorship with only one remaining "partner"). In either case, § 708 mandates a termination of the partnership and a determination of the tax consequences based on the assumption of distributions in complete liquidation of the members' interests. In such a case, gain or loss may be recognized and basis must be determined for any assets distributed to the former partners. As is discussed in Part B of this chapter, however, a partnership can terminate for tax purposes even though its business continues.

Problem 20–1

Millie and Rhonda are equal law partners in the family law partnership and are calendar year taxpayers. The family law partnership is on a June

30th fiscal year. Determine the tax consequences, if any, in the following alternative circumstances.

    a. Millie sold her partnership interest to Rhonda on September 30, 1997.

    b. Millie and Rhonda agreed on December 31, 1996, to terminate the partnership and on that date sold the partnership's operating assets for cash. The proceeds of sale were placed in a certificate of deposit in the name of the partnership. When the account matured on July 1, 1997, the proceeds were distributed to Millie and Rhonda.

    c. Harry joined the partnership on June 30, 1997 in return for a significant cash contribution which resulted in his having a 55% interest in partnership capital, profits, and losses.

    d. Millie gave her partnership interest to her daughter, Beth, on July 15, 1997.

    e. Millie sold one-half of her partnership interest (25%) to Beth on June 30, 1996. Beth sold this interest to Max on May 30, 1997. Rhonda sold one-half of her partnership interest to Frank on October 31, 1997.

B. CONSTRUCTIVE TERMINATION

The other event under § 708 precipitating a termination is the sale or exchange during a 12–month period of 50% or more of the partnership interests. While the policy behind this aspect of § 708 is to force a tax termination upon a significant alteration of the ownership interests in the partnership, it should be noted that not all ownership changes are subject to § 708. For example, transfers of interests by gift or bequest are exempted by the Regulations, as well as ownership shifts through the admission of a new partner or the withdrawal of an old partner. Thus, a definitional issue is confronted as to what constitutes a requisite sale or exchange of a partnership interest for § 708 purposes. The resolution of this issue has been facilitated through the passage of § 761(e).

Once such a shift (causing a "constructive termination") has occurred, the Regulations dictate that the transaction be viewed as the distribution of all of the partnership's assets and liabilities to its members (including the member who acquired the interest which precipitated the termination), followed immediately by a recontribution of such items to the new partnership. This fictional distribution/recontribution treatment can produce numerous tax consequences ranging from gain or loss recognition, reallocation of basis, new § 704(c) allocations, etc. These consequences may prove particularly onerous, as the partnership throughout the requisite time period conducts normal business operations and does not *actually* distribute funds or property to its members. As this casebook went to press, the Service issued Proposed Regulations which, if finalized, will minimize the tax consequences of such an event. See Prop.Reg. § 1.708–1(b)(1)(iv).

REVENUE RULING 86–73
1986–1 C.B. 282.

ISSUE

If a 50 percent interest in a partnership is sold causing the partnership to terminate under section 708(b)(1)(B) of the Internal Revenue Code and a section 754 election is in effect for the taxable year in which the sale occurs, does the election apply with respect to the incoming partner so that the bases of any partnership assets are adjusted prior to their deemed distribution to the partner?

FACTS

T, a 50 percent partner in *PT*, a partnership, sold *T*'s interest to *A*. For the taxable year in which the sale occurred, *PT* had an election in effect under section 754 of the Code, and the fair market value of *PT*'s property exceeded its adjusted basis.

LAW AND ANALYSIS

Section 708(b)(1)(B) of the Code provides that a partnership shall be considered as terminated if within a twelve month period there is a sale or exchange of 50 percent or more of the total interest in partnership capital and profits.

Section 1.708–1(b)(1)(iv) of the Income Tax Regulations provides that if a partnership is terminated by a sale or exchange of an interest, the partnership is deemed to distribute its properties to the purchaser and to the other remaining partners in proportion to their respective interests in the partnership properties. Immediately thereafter, the purchaser and the other remaining partners are deemed to contribute the properties to a new partnership. The last sentence of that provision states that, for an election of basis adjustments by the purchaser and other remaining partners, see sections 732(d) and 743(b) of the Code and the regulations thereunder.

Section 732(b) of the Code provides that the basis of property (other than money) distributed by a partnership to a partner in liquidation of the partner's interest shall be an amount equal to the adjusted basis of such partner's interest in the partnership reduced by any money distributed in the same transaction.

Section 732(c) of the Code provides that the basis of distributed properties to which section 732(b) is applicable generally shall be allocated first to any unrealized receivables and inventory items in an amount equal to the adjusted basis of each such property to the partnership and, to the extent of any remaining basis, to any other distributed properties in proportion to their adjusted bases to the partnership.

Section 1.732–2(b) of the regulations provides that in the case of a distribution of property to a partner who acquired any part of an interest in a transfer as to which an election under section 754 of the Code was in effect, then, for the purposes of section 732, the adjusted partnership basis of the distributed property shall take into account the transferee's special basis adjustment for the distributed property under section 743(b).

Section 743(b) of the Code provides that in the case of a transfer of an interest in a partnership by sale or exchange, a partnership as to which the election provided in section 754 is in effect shall (1) increase the adjusted basis of the partnership property by the excess of the basis to the transferee partner of the partner's interest in the partnership over the partner's proportionate share of the adjusted basis of the partnership property, or (2) decrease the adjusted basis of the partnership property by the excess of the transferee partner's proportionate share of the adjusted basis of the partnership property over the basis of the partner's interest in the partnership. Such increase or decrease generally constitutes an adjustment to the basis of partnership property with respect to the transferee partner only.

Section 754 of the Code provides the manner in which a partnership shall file an election to adjust the basis of partnership property under section 743.

Section 755(a) of the Code provides that any increase or decrease in the adjusted basis of partnership property under section 743(b) shall be allocated in a manner which has the effect of reducing the difference between the fair market value and the adjusted basis of partnership properties.

The issue here is whether the section 754 election applies to adjust the basis of partnership assets with respect to the incoming 50 percent partner before the constructive liquidation of the partnership that occurs under section 1.708–1(b)(1)(iv) of the regulations, or whether the sale of the 50 percent interest to the incoming partner extinguishes the section 754 election before it can be applied.

The language of section 1.708–1(b)(1)(iv) of the regulations treats the partnership property as constructively distributed to the incoming purchaser and the remaining partners. This indicates that the purchaser is a partner for the instant before the constructive liquidating distribution is deemed to occur; thus, the purchaser is a partner at least for the purpose of the termination. Since the purchaser is a partner in the instant before termination, the section 754 election applies in that instant, and the incoming partner's basis in the partnership assets is correspondingly adjusted. Upon the deemed distribution-recontribution under section 1.708–1(b)(1)(iv), the special basis adjustment under section 743(b) of the Code is taken into account in applying sections 732(b) and (c). If the new partnership, *PA,* wants to make a section 754 election, it will have to file a new election.

The legislative history of section 743 buttresses the conclusion that the adjustment of basis of partnership assets is made before the deemed liquidating distribution occurs. The report of the Senate Finance Committee, S.Rep. No. 1622, 83d Cong., 2d Sess. 399 (1954), contains an example in which a section 754 election is applied to adjust the basis of partnership assets when a fifty percent interest in a partnership is sold.

HOLDING

If a 50 percent interest in a partnership is sold causing the partnership to terminate under section 708(b)(1)(B) of the Code, a section 754 election that is in effect for the taxable year in which the sale occurs applies with respect to the incoming partner. Therefore, the bases of any partnership assets are adjusted pursuant to sections 743 and 755 prior to their deemed distribution to the incoming partner.

REVENUE RULING 87–50

1987–1 C.B. 157.

ISSUE

In a multi-tier partnership arrangement, if a partner's interest in a parent partnership is sold—with a resulting termination of the parent under section 708(b)(1)(B) of the Internal Revenue Code—then, for purposes of section 708(b), does that sale also cause an exchange of the parent partnership's interest in the capital and profits of the subsidiary partnership?

FACTS

A had owned a 60 percent interest in partnership *PAB*. *PAB* in turn was a parent partnership that owned an 80 percent partnership interest in the capital and profits of *PRS*, a subsidiary partnership. *A* sold to *C A*'s entire 60 percent interest in *PAB*.

LAW AND ANALYSIS

Section 708(b)(1)(B) of the Code provides that a partnership will be considered terminated if within a 12–month period there is a sale or exchange of 50 percent or more of the total interest in partnership capital and profits.

Section 1.708–1(b)(1)(iv) of the Income Tax Regulations provides that if a partnership is terminated by a sale or exchange of a partner's interest, the partnership is deemed to have distributed all of its properties to the purchaser and other remaining partners in proportion to their respective interests in the partnership properties. Immediately thereafter, the purchaser and the other remaining partners are deemed to have contributed the properties to a new partnership, either for the continuation of the business or for its dissolution and winding up.

Section 761(e) of the Code provides that, for purposes of section 708, any distribution (not otherwise treated as an exchange) shall be treated as an exchange.

The sale of *A*'s 60 percent partnership interest in the parent partnership, *PAB,* results in a termination of *PAB* under section 708(b)(1)(B) of the Code. Pursuant to section 1.708–1(b)(1)(iv) of the regulations, the termination causes *PAB* to liquidate for federal tax purposes, and *PAB* is deemed to have distributed all of its assets to its partners. Among the assets that *PAB* is deemed to have distributed is *PAB*'s 80 percent interest in the capital and profits of the subsidiary partnership, *PRS*. Under section 761(e), the distribution of *PAB*'s partnership interest in *PRS* is treated as an exchange for purposes of section 708. Therefore, the sale of *A*'s 60 percent interest in the capital and profits of *PAB* causes an exchange of *PAB*'s 80 percent interest in the capital and profits of *PRS*. Since *PAB* owns more than 50 percent of the capital and profits interest in *PRS,* the subsidiary partnership *PRS* terminates under section 708(b)(1)(B) upon *PAB*'s deemed distribution of its interest in *PRS*.

HOLDING

In a multi-tier partnership arrangement, if the sale or exchange of an interest in the capital and profits of a parent partnership causes the termination of the parent under section 708(b)(1)(B) of the Code, then, for purposes of applying section 708 to the subsidiary partnership, the parent partnership is treated as exchanging its entire partnership interest in the subsidiary partnership.

REVENUE RULING 87–51

1987–1 C.B. 158.

ISSUE

In a multi-tiered partnership arrangement, if a partner of an upper-tier partnership sells a partnership interest of less than 50 percent of the capital and profits of the upper-tier partnership, then, for purposes of section 708(b)(1)(B) of the Internal Revenue Code, is that sale also considered a sale of the partner's proportionate share of the upper-tier partnership's interest in a lower-tier partnership?

FACTS

AB is a partnership that holds a 50 percent interest in the capital and profits of *XYZ,* another partnership. *A,* a partner in *AB,* sold *A* 's 40 percent interest in the capital and profits of *AB,* and, within twelve months of the sale by *A, X,* a partner in *XYZ,* sold all of *X* 's 30 percent interest in the capital and profits of *XYZ.* There were no other sales of interests in either *AB* or *XYZ* during the same twelve month period.

LAW AND ANALYSIS

Section 708(b)(1)(B) of the Code provides that a partnership will be considered terminated if within a 12–month period there is a sale or exchange of 50 percent or more of the total interest in partnership capital and profits.

Section 741 of the Code provides that, in the case of a sale or exchange of an interest in a partnership, gain or loss shall be recognized to the transferor partner. Such gain or loss shall be considered as gain or loss from the sale or exchange of a capital asset, except as otherwise provided in section 751 (relating to unrealized receivables and inventory items which have appreciated substantially in value).

In the present situation, *A* sold a 40 percent partnership interest in *AB,* which held a 50 percent partnership interest in the partnership *XYZ.* In addition, within twelve months of the sale by *A, X* sold a 30 percent interest in *XYZ.* If *A*'s sale of a 40 percent partnership interest in *AB* is also considered a sale of a 20 percent (40 percent of 50 percent) interest in *XYZ,* then *A*'s sale of the 20 percent interest combined with *X*'s sale of a 30 percent interest in *XYZ* within twelve months would result in the termination of *XYZ* under section 708(b)(1)(B) of the Code.

Under the provisions of subchapter K of the Code, a partnership is considered for various purposes to be either an aggregate of its partners or an entity, transactionally independent of its partners. Generally, subchapter K adopts an entity approach with respect to transactions involving partnership interests. *See* Rev.Rul. 75–62, 1975–1 C.B. 188. Whether an aggregate or entity theory of partnerships should be applied to a particular Code section depends upon which theory is more appropriate to such section. *See* S.Rep. No. 1622, 83d Cong., 2d Sess. 89 (1954), and H.R.Rep. No. 2543, 83d Cong., 2d Sess. 59 (1954); *Casel v. Commissioner,* 79 T.C. 424 (1982). The termination of a partnership under section 708(b)(1)(B) depends on whether there was a sale or exchange of a partnership interest and on whether there was a transfer of at least 50 percent of the total interest in partnership capital and profits. Because section 708(b)(1)(B) is an entity-oriented provision, an entity approach is more appropriate for that section.

Thus, in a multi-tiered partnership arrangement, the sale of a partner's interest in the capital and profits of an upper-tier partnership that is itself a partner in a lower-tier partnership is not a sale of the partner's proportionate share of the underlying assets of the upper-tier partnership for purposes of section 708(b)(1)(B). Rather, under section 741, the sale of *A*'s interest in *AB* is considered the sale of a single capital asset, the interest in *AB.* Accordingly, only *A*'s sale of a 30 percent partnership interest in *XYZ* qualifies for the determination of whether there has been a sale or exchange of 50 percent or more of the total interest in the partnership capital and profits of *XYZ.*

HOLDING

In a multi-tiered partnership arrangement, the sale of a partner's interest in an upper-tier partnership that does not trigger a termination of the upper tier partnership is not considered a sale of that partner's proportionate share of the upper-tier partnership's interest in a lower-tier partnership for purposes of the termination provisions of section 708(b)(1)(B) of the Code * * *.

Problem 20–2

Acme Loan Company is owned 50% by Kathy, 25% by Steve, and 25% by Basil. Kathy sold her 50% interest in the partnership to Milt on July 1, 1997, resulting in a termination of the partnership under § 708(b)(1)(B).

One of the operating assets of the partnership was a computer. The partnership has been depreciating the machine, which has several more years of life, at an accelerated rate. Additionally, the partnership possessed significant amounts of cash. Furthermore, the partnership terminated at a time when Basil had a zero basis in his partnership interest and $5,000 in suspended losses as a result of § 704(d). What are the tax consequences to the partnership and its partners?

C. MERGERS AND DIVISIONS

In addition to the above-described terminating events, § 708 prescribes termination rules for partnership mergers and divisions. Under the merger rules, it is possible for the new partnership to be a continuation of none or one of the merging partnerships. In the division setting, the number of continuing partnerships ranges from none to all of the surviving partnerships.

REVENUE RULING 77–458

1977–2 C.B. 220.

Advice has been requested as to the Federal income tax consequences of a merger of several partnerships under the circumstances described below.

A and B, individual taxpayers, are general partners in ten partnerships (P1–P10) that are engaged in retail merchandising businesses. A and B each have a 50 percent interest in the capital and profits of each of the partnerships.

In order to eliminate multiple information returns required by section 6031 of the Internal Revenue Code of 1954 and to achieve other operating economies, A and B plan the following transaction. The smaller partnerships P2–10 will transfer all of their assets and liabilities to P1 (the largest partnership by dollar value of assets) in exchange for partnership interests in P1. P2–10 will then distribute their interests in P1 to A and B. A and B will receive no other property as a result of the transaction and each will continue to own 50 percent of the capital and profits of P1. P1 will retain and continue to use in its business all property received in the merger.

Section 708(b)(2)(A) of the Code provides that in the case of a merger or consolidation of two or more partnerships, the resulting partnership shall, for purposes of this section, be considered the continuation of any merging or consolidating partnership whose members own an interest of more than 50 percent in the capital and profits of the resulting partnership.

Section 1.708–1(b)(2)(i) of the Income Tax Regulations provides, in part, that if the resulting partnership can be considered a continuation of more than one of the merging or consolidating partnerships it shall, unless the Commissioner permits otherwise, be considered the continuation of that partnership that is credited with the contribution of the greatest dollar value of assets to the resulting partnership. Any other merging or consolidating partnership shall be considered as terminated.

Section 721(a) of the Code provides the general rule that no gain or loss shall be recognized to a partnership or to any of its partners in the case of a contribution of property to the partnership in exchange for an interest in the partnership.

Section 723 of the Code provides, in part, that the basis of property contributed to a partnership by a partner shall be the adjusted basis of such property to the contributing partner at the time of the contribution.

Section 731(a)(1) of the Code provides that in a distribution by a partnership to a partner, gain shall not be recognized to such partner, except to the extent that any money distributed exceeds the adjusted basis of such partner's interest in the partnership immediately before the distribution. Under section 731(a)(2), loss shall not be recognized except when a distribution in liquidation of a partner's interest consists solely of money, unrealized receivables, or substantially appreciated inventory.

Section 731(b) of the Code provides that no gain or loss shall be recognized to a partnership on a distribution to a partner of property, including money.

Section 731(c) of the Code provides that section 731 shall not apply to the extent otherwise provided by sections 736 and 751.

Section 732(b) of the Code provides that the basis of property (other than money) distributed by a partnership to a partner in liquidation of the partner's interest shall be an amount equal to the adjusted basis of such partner's interest in the partnership reduced by any money distributed in the same transaction.

Section 751(a) of the Code provides that the amount of money, or the fair market value of any property, received by a transferor partner in exchange for all or a part of such partner's interest in the partnership attributable to (1) unrealized receivables of the partnership, or (2) inventory items of the partnership that have appreciated substantially in value, shall be considered an amount realized from the sale or exchange of property other than a capital asset.

Section 751(b) of the Code provides, in part, that to the extent a partner receives in a distribution either partnership property described in section 751(a)(1) or 751(a)(2) (section 751 property) in exchange for all or a part of such partner's interest in other partnership property (including money), or partnership property (including money) other than section 751 property in exchange for all or a part of such partner's interest in partnership section 751 property, such transaction shall, under regulations prescribed by the Secretary of the Treasury, be considered as a sale or exchange of such property between the distributee and the partnership (as constituted after the distribution).

Rev.Rul. 68–289, 1968–1 C.B. 314, which deals with the merger of three commonly owned limited partnerships, holds that the partnership that contributes the greatest dollar value of assets is the continuing partnership and the other partnerships are treated as having contributed all of their assets and transferred their liabilities to the resulting partnership in exchange for a partnership interest. Thereafter, the smaller partnerships are considered terminated and their partners are considered to have received in liquidation partnership interests in the resulting partnership with a basis to them as determined under section 732(b) of the Code * * *.

Section 47(a) of the Code and section 1.47–1(a) of the regulations provide for the recomputation of the investment credit claimed on section 38 property if that property is disposed of, or otherwise ceases to be section 38 property with respect to the taxpayer, before the close of the useful life that was taken into account in computing that investment credit.

Section 47(b) of the Code, however, provides that, for purposes of section 47(a), property shall not be treated as ceasing to be section 38 property with respect to the taxpayer by reason of a mere change in the form of conducting the trade or business so long as the property is retained in such trade or business as section 38 property and the taxpayer retains a substantial interest in such trade or business. Sections 1.47–3(f)(1)(i) and (ii) of the regulations amplify this portion of section 47(b) by stating that the recomputation provisions will not apply provided that: (1) the section 38 property is retained as section 38 property in the same trade or business; (2) the transferor of such section 38 property (or in a case in which the transferor is a partnership, the partner) retains a substantial interest in such trade or business; (3) substantially all the assets necessary to operate such trade or business are transferred to the transferee to whom such section 38 property is transferred; and (4) the basis of such section 38 property in the hands of the transferee is determined in whole or in part by reference to the basis of such section 38 property in the hands of the transferor.

Accordingly, the Federal income tax consequences of the above described merger of *P2–10* into *P1* are as follows:

1) In accordance with section 1.708–1(b)(2)(i) of the regulations, *P1* will be considered the surviving partnership since it will contribute the greatest dollar value of assets to the resulting partnership.

2) After the merger of *P1* and *P2–10,* the latter partnerships will be considered terminated and their taxable years shall be closed in accordance with the provisions of section 706(c) and *P2–10* will file their final information returns for the taxable year ending upon the date of the merger.

3) Since in the liquidation of *P2–10, A* and *B* will not receive a distribution either of section 751 property in exchange for all or a part of an interest in other partnership property or partnership property other than section 751 property in exchange for all or part of an interest in

section 751 property, that transaction will not be considered a sale or exchange under section 751(b) of the Code.

4) Under section 721(a) of the Code, no gain or loss will be recognized to any of the partnerships on the contribution of the assets and transfer of the liabilities of *P2–10* to *P1* in exchange for a partnership interest in *P1*.

5) Under section 731(b) of the Code, no gain or loss will be recognized to *P2–10* on the distribution of their partnership interests in *P1* to their respective partners, *A* and *B*.

6) Since neither *A* nor *B* will receive money, unrealized receivables, or inventory as a result of the distributions in liquidation by *P2–10*, no gain or loss will be recognized by *A* or *B* under section 731(a) of the Code, on account of such distributions.

7) Under section 723 of the Code, the basis to *P1* of the property to be contributed to it by *P2–10* will be the adjusted basis of such property to *P2–10* at the time of its contribution.

8) Under section 732(b) of the Code, the basis to *A* and *B* of a partnership interest in *P1* distributed to them by *P2–10* in liquidation will be the adjusted basis to *A* and *B* of their partnership interest in each of the terminating partnerships * * *.

11) Pursuant to section 47(b) of the Code and section 1.47–3(f) of the regulations the recomputation provisions of section 47(a) and section 1.47–1(a) will not apply.

Problem 20–3

Mary and John are equal law partners, as are Marcel and Dave. The two firms agree to merge as of September 30, 1997. What are the tax consequences under the following alternative circumstances?

a. After the merger, each partner owns a 25% capital and profits interest.

b. After the merger, Mary and John each own a 15% capital and profits interest and Marcel and Dave, because of higher revenues in their old firm, each own a 35% interest.

Problem 20–4

Tom, Dick, and Sherry are equal partners in the Candy partnership. The partnership had elected under § 754, which it belatedly realized was a mistake. On January 1, 1997, the partnership decided to split the organization into the Acme partnership, comprised of Tom and Dick, and the Dairy partnership, comprised of Dick and Sherry. Each of the two resulting partnerships are equal as to profits, losses, and capital. Discuss the tax consequences of the division.

Chapter 21

SELECTION OF THE CORPORATE ENTITY

Code References: §§ 1(a)–(d), 11, 1014(a), 1363(a), 1366(a).

Regulations: §§ 1.162–7, –8, –9; 301.7701–2(a)(1)–(3).

A. CHOICE OF ENTITY

As discussed in Chapter 1, the individual or individuals who begin a new business or who review the structure of an ongoing business have traditionally faced three entity choices: sole proprietorship, partnership, and corporation. The entity choice decision became more complicated in 1958 with the introduction of the "Subchapter S" election. The Subchapter S election was hailed as a means of allowing a corporation to maintain its liability protection for state law purposes but, at the same time, to be "taxed as a partnership" (an oversimplification at best).

In the 1960's and 1970's, the spectrum of choices was again expanded by the advent of the limited partnership as a business entity, facilitated through various Rulings and cases which allowed the limited partnership to be taxed as a partnership despite various corporation-like characteristics. Beginning in the 1980's and continuing into the 1990's, led by the unlikely jurisdiction of Wyoming, the limited liability company has become a sixth entity choice for conducting business operations. Limited liability company statutes now exist in almost all states, their growth fueled by national accounting firms seeking multi-state limited liability entities after the savings and loan debacle of the late 1980's during which many partners of such firms were held liable for the acts of their partners in other jurisdictions. The success of the limited liability company as a business entity has prompted some legislatures to authorize the use of limited liability partnerships, limited liability limited partnerships, and limited partnership associations, all of which are taxed as partnerships but have the characteristic of limited liability for the entity owners.

Since the Service first publicly acquiesced in the treatment of the limited liability company as a partnership for tax purposes in 1988, nearly all of the states have adopted legislation recognizing the limited liability company as a sanctioned business entity. See Rev.Rul. 88–76, 1988–2 C.B. 360 and discussion at Chapter 4. Given the growing number of choices, and the particular complexities of each, it is easy to see why a small business owner may need the advice of corporate or tax counsel in making the decision of which entity to employ.

The first 20 chapters have focused on businesses taxed as a sole proprietorship or a partnership as a form of doing business. In connection with partnership taxation, they have reviewed the potential choices of a limited partnership, limited liability company, or other "hybrid" entity. The remaining 15 chapters will focus upon the corporation, which has historically been the most popular small business entity. This review will include an analysis of the "S election" which allows a corporation to be taxed as an "S corporation." As will be seen, the S election is strictly a federal tax convention and in no way changes the entity's limited liability status from a state corporate law point of view. However, its use has been seriously impacted and eroded through the emergence of the limited liability company.

The entrepreneur who selects a corporation as his or her form of business entity needs tax advice. The corporation is a separate entity for tax purposes. It is, itself, a taxpayer subject to a graduated set of tax rates on its net income under § 11. The corporation is subject to its own elaborate set of tax rules and its own body of tax law which has interpreted those rules since the genesis of the corporate income tax in 1909 (although it was then treated as an excise tax since it pre-dated the enactment of the Sixteenth Amendment). The corporate tax rules apply to Ma and Pa Grocery, Inc. as well as General Motors, Inc. A corporation must file its own tax return (separate and apart from those of its individual owners) and, if it has taxable income, must pay its own tax. The S election may allow what would otherwise be corporate income to be passed through to the business owners and taxed to them individually rather than at the corporate level. As will be seen, however, the rules relating to S corporations are extremely complex and such pass-through is a far cry from allowing the corporation to be taxed as a partnership.

The remainder of this chapter focuses upon the basic non-tax and tax considerations which an entrepreneur must review before electing to operate his or her business as a corporation.

B. NON–TAX CONSIDERATIONS

The simple reason that most business owners have historically utilized the corporation as their operating entity is the state law concept of limited liability. The corporate entity, if properly formed and maintained, insulates its owners from liability for certain corporate obligations. The potential liabilities which arise in the operation of a typical small business include tort liability, contract liability, and creditor liability. The protection from tort liability is extremely important in the event that the entity has more than one owner and/or employee. While an entrepreneur is always personally responsible for his or her own negligent acts, the corporate shield can protect against the acts of co-owners or employees. Contracts with suppliers and customers are normally made through the corporate business entity. Liabilities for failure to perform on such contracts would normally be limited to the assets of the corporation and would not subject the owners to individual liability. In addition, liability to lenders and other creditors may be limited if incurred by the corporate entity. Finally, shareholders of a corporation are not subject to a right of contribution from fellow share-holders as partners in a partnership generally are. In practical terms, however, most traditional commercial lenders require personal guaran-ties by the business owners, thereby subjecting their personal assets to the liability for repayment. Nevertheless, many loans made to corpora-tions are not guaranteed by the shareholders, particularly loans made to the corporation by co-owners or other insiders. Minority interest own-ers of a corporate business are often not required to personally guaran-tee corporate debt.

While each state has its own corporate statutes, the basic concept of each is limited liability protection to the owners of the entity. Such limited liability is not available in a sole proprietorship or a general partnership. While it may be available in a limited partnership, such an entity requires a relatively complex structure and the protection extends only to the limited, not the general, partners. Finally, while limited liability protection is available in a limited liability company and other hybrid partnership entities, not all states recognize these entities and their relative novelty and the lack of a body of interpretive law may deter the conservative businessman or his or her counsel. Conversely, a one-man entrepreneur who remains responsible for his or her own torts and who must personally guarantee all obligations of the business achieves little or no liability insulation by incorporating.

The choice of a limited liability company or other limited liability partnership entity over a corporation as an operating entity may be less clear than it initially would seem. Although the limited liability compa-ny gives state law liability protection and avoids the entity-level corpo-rate tax, the mechanics of operating the corporation and the rights of its owners, vis-a-vis other owners and the entity, are well-established. Moreover, as will be seen in later chapters, the entity-level tax of the corporation is often illusory since it may be avoided through various planning techniques.

In terms of state law rights and obligations, there are time-tested principles in most state corporate statutes. For instance, a minority interest holder in a corporation normally has certain rights under most corporate statutes to dissent from drastic corporate action, while no such right or obligation exists in the typical hybrid entity statute.

Secondly, a limited liability company or other partnership limited liability entity, even though it may be recognized in the state of its organization, may have difficulty enforcing its limited liability feature if it "does business" in a state with no similar statute. A corporation, on the other hand, can normally qualify to do business as a limited liability entity in a foreign state through a simple time-tested registration process.

Thirdly, virtually all state corporate statutes have relatively flexible and simple provisions relating to the expansion or sale of an existing business through mergers and consolidations with other corporations. As will be seen, compliance with these state law provisions is often coordinated with federal tax rules granting tax-advantaged treatment to such mergers. The requirements and results of the fusion of a limited liability company with a corporation are not well-settled. In fact, an entity operating its business as a corporation may find it simply impossible, either because of adverse tax consequences or lack of a state law mechanism, to merge the corporation into a limited liability company. Thus, businesses existing as corporate entities may not be able to convert to limited liability company status and a business operated as a limited liability company may be an unlikely acquisition target for other expanding corporations.

Finally, in most states, the limited liability company and limited liability partnership entities require two or more owners. In those states where one "member" is permitted, the tax treatment of the entity is unclear. A single individual, however, can clearly form a corporation and be its sole shareholder.

C. TAX CONSIDERATIONS

A corporation is a separate taxable entity with its own tax rates, tax rules, tax returns, and tax Regulations. In addition to the basic concept of associates (although a corporation may have only one "associate") and an objective to carry on a business for profit, for classification purposes the Regulations deem the primary remaining corporate characteristics to be continuity of life, centralized management, limited liability, and free transferability of interests. See Reg. § 301.7701–2. As noted in Chapter 4, the law of partnership/association classification gradually degenerated into a derby of determining how many of these characteristics a partnership (or a limited liability company) might have. Possession of two or less of the four "swing" characteristics leads to taxation as a partnership. It is clear, however, that an entity formed as a state law corporation almost invariably will be taxed as a corporation and not a partnership.

Thus, when a businessperson forms a corporation, he or she must be prepared to maintain the state law formalities which protect the limited liability of the entity (thereby preventing a piercing of the "corporate veil"). Additionally, he or she must be prepared to file a separate tax return (and possibly pay tax) on the income of the corporation.

Putting aside graduated rates which tax certain low and high levels of income at different percentages, the basic corporate tax rate for most small business corporations is currently 34%. While § 11 has graduated rates with the highest bracket of 35%, it does not come into play until the entity's taxable income exceeds $10,000,000. Similarly, the basic individual marginal tax rate for most mid-income individuals is 31%. The highest brackets for individuals under § 1 are 36% and 39.6%. However, the 36% bracket is applicable only to taxable income in excess of $140,000 for married individuals filing jointly and $115,000 for single individuals. The 39.6% bracket is applicable only to income in excess of $250,000. Thus, if a corporation has taxable income of $100,000, it would theoretically (putting aside the graduated rates) pay tax of $34,-000 to the federal government. If the remaining $66,000 were distributed to the corporation's sole shareholder, he or she would pay tax of 31%, or $20,460. Thus, the combined tax rate would be 54.46%.

In practice, however, small businesses are often able to avoid tax at the corporate level through various techniques. The most obvious of these is reducing or eliminating the corporate tax through the use of allowable corporate tax deductions. This method is examined in detail in Chapter 30. If an individual entrepreneur is actively involved in the business, the corporation is permitted a deduction under § 162 for reasonable compensation paid for services rendered. The payment of such compensation, and its deduction from corporate-level income, is the most obvious and frequently utilized method of eliminating tax at the corporate entity level. There are, however, many other corporate tax avoidance techniques.

Another frequently utilized method of avoiding tax at the corporate level is the S election. In an S corporation, the income of the corporation is, in most cases, not taxed at the corporate level but is passed through proportionately as income to the individual owners of the business. However, as will be seen in Chapter 29: (1) the S election cannot be used by all corporations; (2) in certain rather complex situations, there *is* a corporate tax (if the corporation was previously operated as a C corporation); and (3) an S corporation shareholder, like a partner, is taxed on the income even though the cash relating to that taxable income remains in the corporation and is not made available by distribution to the individual owner.

As noted, the marginal individual tax rate after 1996 for most small businesspersons is 31%. If, however, an individual is particularly successful, the combined federal tax rate (including taxes for Medicare based on percentage of income, etc.) could exceed 40%. In that situation, the maximum corporate tax rate is *less* than the individual tax rate and makes it at least temporarily advantageous for an entrepreneur to retain profits in the corporation, paying the lower corporate tax rate of 34%. This would be attractive if the funds were not distributed to the shareholders because the corporation was expanding or otherwise had uses for the funds at the corporate level. Such a retention of funds at lower corporate rates (rather than distributing them to the higher-bracket individual owners) may also be advantageous in situations where the individual owner of the corporation holds the stock until death, thereby obtaining for it a "stepped-up" tax basis for his or her heirs or beneficiaries, under § 1014(a), thereby avoiding income tax on the appreciation of his stock due to the increase in the value of the corporation. As will be seen in Chapter 33, however, the corporation may be subject to penalty taxes in such situations if the build-up of cash in the corporation is excessive and for the purpose of avoiding the higher individual tax rates and not for a bona fide business purpose.

Finally, in viewing the corporation as a potential business entity, the entrepreneur must focus on the tax consequences if he or she ultimately sells or liquidates the operations. The tax rules are very different for corporations than for proprietorships and entities taxed as partnerships. A major change in the tax law in 1986, generally known as the "repeal of the *General Utilities* doctrine," has made the corporate vehicle less attractive due to the imposition of a corporate tax on any appreciated corporate assets at the end of the business cycle regardless of whether they are sold to third parties or distributed to the shareholders. This treatment will be more thoroughly discussed in Chapter 35.

Problem 21–1

Macey is the sole shareholder of Hardware Corporation which operates a hardware store. She works each day in the business but pays herself no current salary. The corporation's gross receipts are $200,000 and its deductible expenses and cost of goods sold total $140,000. What tax result occurs to Macey and/or the corporation if:

1. Prior to the end of the taxable year, Macey pays herself accrued salary and/or bonus of $60,000?

2. Prior to the end of the taxable year, Macey pays herself accrued salary and/or bonus of $20,000?

3. In order to expand her business, Macey pays herself nothing but retains the funds in the corporation for future inventory expansion?

Problem 21–2

What result in problem 21–1 assuming that Macey had made a valid S election for Hardware Corporation at the beginning of the taxable year.

Chapter 22

CORPORATE FORMATION—§ 351

Code References: §§ 351(a) and (d)(1), 368(c), 1032.

Regulations: § 1.351–1(a).

A. INTRODUCTION

In order for a corporation to begin business, it must acquire the assets required for its business operations. Such acquisition may take place either (1) by the shareholder(s) of the corporation contributing cash to the corporation which, in turn, uses it to acquire business assets, or (2) by the shareholder group transferring its own previously held or newly acquired assets to the corporation. From a tax standpoint, attention must be paid to both the corporation and the shareholder group since the corporation is an independent taxpayer.

Under § 1032, a corporation generally does not recognize gain on the issuance of its stock to shareholders. Thus, if a corporation issues 100 shares of its stock to its sole shareholder in exchange for $1,000, it does not recognize taxable income even though it has *realized* gain of $1,000 since its stock had a basis of zero at the time of issuance. Section 1032 prevents such gain from being recognized by the corporation. To the shareholder transferring cash, no gain is realized (since the stock value equals the amount of cash contributed) and, in the above example, the shareholder would have a $1,000 tax basis in the stock received. See discussion at Chapter 24.

If, however, the shareholder transfers appreciated or depreciated property in exchange for the stock, gain or loss would be *realized*. Section 1032 does not prevent recognition to the shareholder since it applies only to the corporation. Rather, the shareholder must rely upon § 351 to avoid recognition of the gain (or loss) which would otherwise be equal to the difference between the adjusted basis of the property transferred and the value of the stock received. A transferor shareholder recognizes no gain on the transfer of property to a corporation if (1) the transfer is solely in exchange for stock of the transferee corporation; (2) the transferor is in "control" of the transferee corporation immediately after the exchange; and (3) certain other requirements of § 351 are satisfied. Thus, the tax treatment of the transferor shareholder is more complicated than that of the transferee corporation. If the requirements of § 351 are not met, the transferor shareholder will recognize gain to the extent that the value of the stock (which presumably equals the net fair market value of the property transferred) exceeds the adjusted basis of the property transferred. Such gain may well generate taxable income in a situation where the transferor shareholder receives no cash with which to pay the resulting income tax.

If the requirements of § 351 are met, however, the entrepreneur may begin operating business in corporate form without the imposition of a tax upon the transfer of the business assets into the corporation. The basic premise of § 351 is that a transfer of appreciated or depreciated property to a corporation controlled by the transferor works a change of form only and should not be an occasion for recognizing gain or loss on the transferred property. The taxpayer has not actually "cashed in" on the gain inherent in the appreciated property. Rather, he or she has merely received stock in exchange for the business assets, thereby continuing the venture in corporate form. See *Portland Oil Co. v. Commissioner,* 109 F.2d 479 (1st Cir.1940).

Because of the underlying rationale that the transfer of property to a controlled corporation is merely a change of form and therefore should not generate tax, the Service has taken the stance that the protection of § 351 should not apply in certain situations even though the technical requirements of the statute are met. As evidenced by the following cases, the Service has asserted, with some success, that § 351 will provide protection to the transferor/shareholder only if the transfer has a bona fide business purpose and the transfer is not made purely for a tax avoidance motive.

CARUTH v. UNITED STATES

688 F.Supp. 1129 (N.D.Tex.1987).

Memorandum Opinion

Buchmeyer, District Judge.

This is an income tax case. It involves such exotic tax concepts as the "assignment of income" doctrine, the "economic realities" test, the "step-transaction" analysis, the business purpose requirement, and even an overworked horticultural metaphor. * * *

I. The Facts

In April of 1978, W.W. and Mabel Caruth ("Caruth") owned the following shares of stock of North Park Inn, Inc. ("North Park"), a Texas corporation:

Class of Stock	Number of Shares Owned	Percentage of Ownership To Total Shares
Common Stock Class A Voting	87.5	75%
Common Stock Class B Non–Voting	337.5	75%
Preferred Stock Non–Voting (Callable at $100)	1,000	100%

The remaining shares of Class A and Class B common stock of North Park were owned by Caruth's nephews, Harold Byrd and Caruth Byrd.

In 1978, Caruth also owned 100% of the shares of the Caruth Corporation—which he had started almost 40 years before (his "first corporation") and which was an active business, with assets that included the Inwood Village Shopping Center in Dallas, a lumber company, a steel company, and two Florida hotels (Plantation Inn and Happy Dolphin Inn).

For some time before April of 1978, Caruth had been thinking about having North Park declare dividends "in order to get money out of" this company. He planned to "wind down" the activities of North Park because the manager of the North Park Inn hotel was "about to die." Caruth also wanted to buy the North Park shares held by his two nephews, but they had refused—and he hoped he might reach agreement with the nephews after they received a substantial dividend. And, *on April 14, 1978,* Caruth advised the Dallas Community Chest Trust Fund ("Community Chest") that he was "contemplating the gift of a substantial amount" of North Park stock.

At the same time (April of 1978), Caruth was considering a "capital contribution" to the Caruth Corporation, which was having "more and more operations in Florida." Since the North Park operations were being "wound down," that company did not need cash reserves so Caruth knew he could make this "capital contribution" by giving North Park stock to the Caruth Corporation and having North Park declare a dividend.

Caruth did not get any legal advice from a tax specialist about these contemplated transactions. However, Caruth was knowledgeable about their tax consequences—he had an undergraduate degree in accounting and a masters degree from Harvard—and he was also aware of the possible, unfavorable impact of the "accumulated earnings tax" upon the capital reserves of North Park.

This, then, was the basic factual background in which the following events took place:

(i) On May 5, 1978, Caruth transferred his 337.5 shares of North Park Class B common stock (non-voting) to the Caruth Corporation.

(ii) On May 8, 1978, North Park declared a dividend of $1,500 per share, payable on May 17, 1978 to those who were shareholders of record on May 15, 1978.

(iii) On May 9, 1978, Caruth donated his 1000 shares of North Park preferred (non-voting) to the Community Chest.

(iv) On the dividend record date, May 15, 1978, the Community Chest was the shareholder of record of the 1000 shares of preferred stock of North Park; the Caruth Corporation was the shareholder of record of the 337.5 shares of Class B common stock; and Caruth remained the shareholder of record of the 37.5 shares of Class A common stock (voting) of North Park.

On May 17, 1978, the dividend payment date, North Park paid the dividends—which had been declared on May 8, 1978—to the shareholders of record on May 15, 1978. Consequently, the Community Chest received a total dividend of $1,500,000 ($1500 per share for its 1000 shares of North Park stock) * * * the Caruth Corporation received a total dividend of $506,250 ($1500 per share for its 337.5 shares) * * * and W.W. Caruth received $56,250 ($1500 per share for his 37.5 shares).

Some two months later, on July 26, 1978, the Community Chest sent a letter to Caruth asking if he knew of someone who might buy the 1000 shares of non-voting preferred of North Park stock for the call price, $100 per share. *Caruth had not made any agreement to repurchase this stock when it was donated to the Community Chest.* However, on April 11, 1979, almost nine months after the Community Chest inquiry, Caruth wrote the Community Chest that, since he "didn't know of anyone else who is in the market for this stock and since the company is under my management," Caruth would repurchase the stock himself for $100,000. The 1000 shares of North Park were transferred back to Caruth for this amount.

In the Caruth tax return for 1978, the 1000 shares of North Park stock donated to the Community Chest were valued at $1,600,000 ($1,600 per share). The Internal Revenue Service objected, claiming that the dividend income on this stock should be attributed to Caruth because of the "assignment of income" doctrine. The IRS also took the position that the dividend income on the 337.5 shares of stock transferred to the Caruth Corporation should be attributed to Caruth, not to the corporation. * * *

III. The Transfer of Stock to Caruth Corporation

The second issue involves the 337.5 shares of common stock transferred to the Caruth Corporation, the taxpayer's wholly-owned corporation, on May 5, 1978—four days *before* North Park declared a dividend of $1,500 per share payable on May 17 to the record shareholders on May 15, 1978.

The parties agree that section 351 of the Code should determine this dispute concerning the transfer of property to a controlled corporation. However, the IRS—relying, by analogy, upon *Gregory v. Helvering,* 293

U.S. 465 (1935), argues that all transactions undertaken pursuant to section 351—the organization of or the transfer of property to a controlled corporation—like transactions involving the reorganization of a controlled corporation under section 368, must have a "business purpose." In response, Caruth argues that section 351 protects all transactions which fit within its *express* requirements; and—since section 351 does not expressly require a business purpose—a taxpayer may therefore transfer property to his controlled corporation, without adverse tax consequences, pursuant to section 351 "for good reason, bad reason, or no reason at all".

The "business purpose" doctrine originated in *Gregory v. Helvering.* Under it, a transaction is not to be given effect for tax purposes unless it serves a legitimate business purpose other than tax avoidance. Thus, *Gregory* established the general principle that, in order to fit within a particular provision of the tax code, a transaction must satisfy not only the language of the statute, but also must have a purpose that lies within the spirit of the statute.

For the following reasons, this Court holds that there must be a business purpose for a transaction under section 351 (just as there must be a business purpose for section 368 transactions under *Gregory v. Helvering*)—but that, at trial, Caruth did in fact establish that there was a business purpose for the transfer of the North Park stock to the wholly-owned company, the Caruth Corporation.

Section 351 Requires a Business Purpose

The starting point for any statutory analysis is the plain language of the provision in question. Section 351 provides that a taxpayer may transfer property to a corporation solely in exchange for stock or securities of that corporation—and recognize no gain or loss on the disposition of that property—so long as he controls the corporation after the transfer. However, like the provisions concerning the reorganization of controlled corporations in section 368, section 351 does not *explicitly* require that transfers to controlled corporations have a business purpose.

Nevertheless, the IRS urges that the purpose of section 351 will be frustrated unless the transactions it covers are required to have a business purpose. This appears to be a case of first impression, and "the duty of this Court is to give effect to the intent of Congress.... Consequently, a thorough consideration of the relevant legislative history is required."

The long history of section 351, which begins in 1918, is summarized in Appendix A to this opinion. It reveals that the various corporate "organization" provisions (which preceded section 351) were closely bound to the corporate "reorganization" provisions (like section 368). In promulgating these sections, Congress recognized the economic reality that corporate readjustments do not meaningfully change the identity of the person controlling the transferred property. Indeed, corporate "organization" and "reorganization" transactions were always considered simultaneously by Congress; and for 33 years they occupied the same sections in the code. This legislative history indicates that the principles governing corporate reorganizations under section 368 should also be relevant to transactions involving controlled corporations under section 351.

The current statutory framework supports this conclusion. Part III of the Internal Revenue Code of 1954 addresses only corporate organizations and reorganizations. Both the organization transactions pursued under section 351 and those involving a plan of reorganization under section 368 rely upon the same basis provisions for the transferor and for the corporation. Where a party to the exchange assumes a liability of the transferor—whether the transferor is an individual or a corporation—or where the transferee acquires property subject to a liability, both sections 351 and 361 require reference to section 357 for determination of the tax consequences of the transaction. This scheme of interdependence clearly identifies the nearly uniform economic natures of the organization or transfer provisions under section 351 and the reorganization provisions of section 368.

The overlap between section 351 and section 368 appears evident. Indeed, the potential for simultaneous application of section 351 and the other reorganization definitions to a single exchange has been well documented. In addition, both sections have been subject to two judicially created doctrines the "step-transaction" analysis and the "continuity of interest" test. * * *

For these reasons, it seems clear that section 351 and the reorganization provisions (of section 368) are cumulative, and not mutually exclusive. Therefore, the business purpose requirement should be applied to section 351, just as it has been applied to section 368.

This conclusion is supported by several cases which *imply* that a business purpose is required for a section 351 transfer. For example, in *Hempt Bros., Inc. v. United States,* 490 F.2d 1172 (3d Cir.1974), the question was whether the assignment of income doctrine might supercede the non-recognition provision of section 351. In concluding that the doctrine did not apply, the court was "influenced by the fact that the subject of the assignment was accounts receivable for partnership's goods and services sold in the regular course of business, that *the change of business form from partnership to corporation [pursuant to section 351] had a basic business purpose and was not designed for the purpose of deliberate tax avoidance....*" Although the *Hempt Bros.* court did not directly hold that an exchange under section 351 requires a business purpose, it clearly indicated that these types of corporate readjustments are governed by the same principles that apply to reorganizations.

Therefore, the transfer of property to a controlled corporation must, under section 351, have a business purpose. Indeed, the opposite conclusion "would result in permitting the § [351] exemption to be used as a device for evading taxes Congress intended to impose on many gains actually realized...." Accordingly, in this case, Caruth was required to prove that there was a business purpose for the transfer of the North Park common stock to the Caruth Corporation.

There Was a Business Purpose for the Transfer

Whether or not Caruth did have a business purpose in transferring the North Park stock to a wholly-owned Company, the Caruth Corporation, is a question of fact. The trial evidence presented by the plaintiffs on this issue was simple, but convincing.

The Caruth Corporation had been in business for over 40 years. In 1978, its assets included the Inwood Shopping Center, a lumber company, a steel business, and two hotels in Florida. In contrast, Caruth testified that the activities of North Park were being "wound down." Since North Park did not need capital reserves—and since the Caruth corporation was having "more and more operations in Florida"—Caruth wanted to make a "capital contribution" to the Caruth Corporation by the transfer of the North Park stock.

Accordingly, on May 5, 1978, the 337.5 shares of North Park common were transferred to the Caruth Corporation as a "capital contribution"—and that corporation received the $506,250 in dividends on May 17, 1978. Caruth testified that this provided the Caruth Corporation with additional funds for its business operations, and that it also increased the assets of the Caruth Corporation and its ability to borrow money should the need arise.

The Caruth Corporation continued in business, and continued to own the North Park stock, until it was liquidated in 1984. And, there was no evidence that the Caruth Corporation was a meaningless, shell corporation which was merely being used for tax avoidance purposes.

It is true, as the IRS contends, that the evidence *did not* show that the Caruth Corporation was on the brink of financial disaster or that a significant capital contribution was essential to the corporation's survival. However, Caruth did not need to prove either of these circumstances in order to establish that there was a business purpose for the transfer of the North Park stock to the Caruth Corporation. Indeed, if this were the test, then the only shareholders who would be able to demonstrate a business purpose under section 351 for capital contributions to controlled corporations would be those whose corporations were unsuccessful or were near bankruptcy.

Therefore, Caruth did establish—as required by section 351—that there was a business purpose for the transfer of the North Park stock to the wholly-owned company, the Caruth Corporation. * * *

B. APPLICATION OF § 351 TO A NEW ENTERPRISE

As noted previously, an entrepreneur starting a business in corporate form may either transfer cash to the corporation or, in the alternative, transfer his or her existing or acquired individual property to the corporation in exchange for its stock. In either case, there must be a transfer of "property" to the corporation in order for § 351 to protect the transfer from gain recognition. The term property is not defined in the statute. Revenue Ruling 69–357, 1969–1 C.B. 101, indicates that the term clearly includes cash. This may be a moot point since the transferor would not *realize* gain on the transfer of cash in exchange for stock and therefore would not be concerned about its recognition. The transfer by the shareholder of appreciated inventory, equipment, machinery, or other similar business property will be protected by the provisions of § 351 so long as all of its requirements are met. As will be seen in Chapter 24, any gain inherent in such transferred assets will not be lost but will remain subject to future tax through the mechanism of a carryover of the tax basis of such property in the hands of the corporation.

1. DEFINITION OF "PROPERTY" FOR PURPOSES OF § 351

While the transfer of cash, furniture, fixtures, equipment, machinery, and inventory may obviously qualify as property for the purposes of § 351 protection, the classification of other types of assets may be less clear. The transfer of rights to intangible property which was created by personal services, such as patents or secret formulas, is an example. Even more problematic would be the transfer of assets not evidenced by any documentation such as know-how, manufacturing techniques, and other similar business intangible assets. When an intangible asset has been created by the services of the contributing shareholder, the issue of whether such intangible asset is property for the purposes of § 351 is raised. As will be seen later in this Chapter, personal services are not property protected by § 351 and stock received for services is generally taxable to the recipient shareholder. Nevertheless, it appears clear that the Service has acquiesced in the concept that intangible assets constitute property for the purposes of § 351 protection. Additionally, the enactment of § 197 regarding the amortization of intangible assets further supports a classification of such assets as property. Revenue Ruling 64–56, reproduced below, provides that, in order to ascertain whether property has been transferred for the purposes of § 351, services that are ancillary and subsidiary to the transfer of property may be disregarded and will not cause the transfer to be taxable. More substantial services, however, will make the transaction wholly or partially taxable.

REVENUE RULING 64–56
1964–1 C.B. 133.

The Internal Revenue Service has received inquiries whether technical "know-how" constitutes property which can be transferred, without recognition of gain or loss, in exchange for stock * * * under section 351 of the Internal Revenue Code of 1954.

The issue has been drawn to the attention of the Service, particularly in cases in which a manufacturer agrees to assist a newly organized foreign corporation to enter upon a business abroad of making and selling the same kind of product as it makes. The transferor typically grants to the transferee rights to use manufacturing processes in which the transferor has exclusive rights by virtue of process patents or the protection otherwise extended by law to the owner of a process. The transferor also often agrees to furnish technical assistance in the construction and operation of the plant and to provide on a continuing basis technical information as to new developments in the field.

Some of this consideration is commonly called "know-how." In exchange, the transferee typically issues to the transferor all or part of its stock.

Section 351 of the Code provides, in part, as follows:

(a) GENERAL RULE.—No gain or loss shall be recognized *if property is transferred* to a corporation by one or more persons solely *in exchange for stock* ... in such corporation and immediately after the exchange such person or persons are in control (as defined in section 368(c)) of the corporation. For purposes of this section, *stock or securities issued for services shall not be considered as issued in return for property.* (Emphasis added.)

Since the term "know-how" does not appear in section 351 of the Code, its meaning is immaterial in applying this section, and the Service will look behind the term in each case to determine to what extent, if any, the items so called constitute "property * * * transferred to a corporation * * * in exchange for stock."

The term "property" for purposes of section 351 of the Code will be held to include anything qualifying as "secret processes and formulas" within the meaning of sections 861(a)(4) and 862(a)(4) of the Code and any other secret information as to a device, process, etc., in the general nature of a patentable invention without regard to whether a patent has been applied for, and without regard to whether it is patentable in the patent law sense. Other information which is secret will be given consideration as "property" on a case-by-case basis.

The fact that information is recorded on paper or some other physical material is not itself an indication that the information is property.

It is assumed for the purpose of this Revenue Ruling that the country in which the transferee is to operate affords to the transferor substantial legal protection against the unauthorized disclosure and use of the process, formula, or other secret information involved.

Once it is established that "property" has been transferred, the transfer will be tax-free under section 351 even though services were used to produce the property. Such is generally the case where the transferor developed the property primarily for use in its own manufacturing business. However, where the information transferred has been developed specially for the transferee, the stock received in exchange for it may be treated as payment for services rendered.

Where the transferor agrees to perform services in connection with a transfer of property, tax-free treatment will be accorded if the services are merely ancillary and subsidiary to the property transfer. Whether or not services are merely ancillary and subsidiary to a property transfer is a question of fact. Ancillary and subsidiary services could be performed, for example, in promoting the transaction by demonstrating and explaining the use of the property, or by assisting in the effective "starting-up" of the property transferred, or by performing under a guarantee relating to such effective starting-up.

Where both property and services are furnished as consideration, and the services are not merely ancillary and subsidiary to the property transfer, a reasonable allocation is to be made.

Training the transferee's employees in skills of any grade through expertness, for example, in a recognized profession, craft, or trade is to be distinguished as essentially educational and, like any other teaching services, is taxable when compensated in stock or otherwise, without being affected by section 351 of the Code. However, where the transferee's employees concerned already have the particular skills in question, it will ordinarily follow as a matter of fact that other consideration alone and not training in those skills is being furnished for the transferor's stock.

Continuing technical assistance after the starting-up phase will not be regarded as performance under a guarantee, and the consideration therefor will ordinarily be treated as compensation for professional services, taxable without regard to section 351 of the Code.

Assistance in the construction of a plant building to house machinery transferred, or to house machinery to be used in applying a patented or other process or formula which qualifies as property transferred, will ordinarily be considered to be in the nature of an architect's or construction engineer's services rendered to the transferee and not merely rendered on behalf of the transferor in producing, or promoting the sale or exchange of, the things transferred. Similarly, advice as to the layout of plant machinery and equipment may be so unrelated to the particular property transferred as to constitute no more than a rendering of advisory services to the transferee.

The transferee of all substantial rights in property of the kind hereinbefore specified will be treated as a transfer of property for purposes of section 351 of the Code. The transfer will also qualify under section 351 of the Code if the transferred rights extend to all of the territory of one or more countries and consist of all substantial rights therein, the transfer being clearly limited to such territory, notwithstanding that rights are retained as to some other country's territory.

The property right in a formula may consist of the method of making a composition and the composition itself, namely the proportions of its ingredients, or it may consist of only the method of making the composition. Where the property right in the secret formula consists of both the composition and the method of making it, the unqualified transfer in perpetuity of the exclusive right to use the formula, including the right to use and sell the products made from and representing the formula, within all the territory of the country will be treated as the transfer of all substantial rights in the property in that country.

The unqualified transfer in perpetuity of the exclusive right to use a secret process or other similar secret information qualifying as property within all the territory of a country, or the unqualified transfer in perpetuity of the exclusive right to make, use and sell an unpatented but secret product within all the territory of a country, will be treated as the transfer of all substantial rights in the property in that country.

2. STOCK ISSUED FOR SERVICES

In the case of the entrepreneur beginning a new business, it is unlikely that stock would be issued in exchange for past services to such business. It is possible, however, that stock would be issued for services which the contributing shareholder rendered in producing or acquiring the assets which are being transferred to the new business. If these are more than incidental services, the issues raised in Revenue Ruling 64–56 would apply. The situation may be different, however, if the stock were issued to the shareholder in exchange for *future* services to be performed on behalf of the corporation. The Regulations under § 351 disqualify stock issued for services "rendered or to be rendered to or for the benefit of the issuing corporation." Reg. § 1.351–1(a)(1)(i). In such a case, the stock received by the transferring shareholder would constitute immediate income taxable as compensation for services rendered. The gain would be ordinary, not capital. The recognition provisions of the Code are unconcerned that the recipient shareholder receives no cash with which to pay the tax generated by this income recognition.

In practice, it is not always certain whether stock is received by a transferring shareholder in exchange for the property he transfers or, rather, in exchange for some past or future services. Oftentimes, the stock is in fact issued in exchange for both property and services. In such a case, the correct tax result would be to tax the shareholder only on that portion of the stock received for services. The careful practitioner, however, will attempt to arrange the transaction so that the stock is being received for property and not for services.

UNITED STATES v. FRAZELL

335 F.2d 487 (5th Cir.1964).

Tuttle, Chief Judge.

This is an appeal by the Government from a judgment in favor of the taxpayer. As the largely undisputed facts are set out at length in the opinion of the district court, only a summary will be presented here. On February 9, 1951, William Frazell, a geologist, entered into a contract with the N.H. Wheless Oil Company, a partnership, and W.C. Woolf, under which Frazell was to check certain areas to determine whether potentially productive oil and gas properties might be procured there. He was to recommend those properties he found suitable to Wheless and Woolf, and upon their joint approval he was to attempt to acquire such properties, taking title thereto in the names of Wheless and Woolf in equal shares. In return for these services, Frazell was to receive "a monthly salary or drawing account," plus expenses, and specified interests in the property acquired. It was agreed, however, "that Frazell shall not be entitled to, nor shall he be considered as owning, any interest in said properties until such time as Wheless and Woolf shall have recovered their full costs and expenses of said properties including the amounts paid out to Frazell."

The arrangement proved successful, and it was evident in the early part of 1955 that Wheless and Woolf would fully recover their costs and expenses by the end of November of that year. In April 1955, the 1951 contract was terminated, and by contract dated April 20, 1955, all the properties acquired under the earlier arrangement were transferred to the W.W.F. Corporation, a Delaware corporation formed specifically to acquire these properties in return for the issuance of debentures to Wheless and Woolf and of stock to Wheless, Woolf, and Frazell. Frazell received 6,500 shares of W.W.F. stock (13% of the total issued), having a fair market value of $91,000.00, but he included no part of this amount in his 1955 income tax return. The Commissioner ruled that the $91,000.00 should have been included in income and assessed a deficiency, which Frazell paid under protest and seeks to recover here.

Frazell contends that he received the W.W.F. stock in a tax-free exchange within the terms of section 351(a), Internal Revenue Code of 1954. The district court agreed that section 351(a) is applicable in this case. This was said to follow from that court's finding that the 1951 contract created a "joint venture" among the three participants. We take no issue with the trial court's finding of fact in this matter, but it does not follow from the categorization of the 1951 arrangement as a "joint venture" that the April 1955 transactions resulted in no taxable income to Frazell.

It is fundamental that "compensation for services" is taxable as ordinary income under the Internal Revenue Code of 1954. This principle applies whether the one compensated for his services is an employee receiving a salary, fees, or commission, one receiving corporate securities, or a "service partner" receiving an interest in the partnership.

The regulation pertaining to partnerships provides that

"the value of an interest in such partnership capital so transferred to a partner as compensation for services constitutes income to the partner under section 61. The amount of such income is the fair market value of the interest in capital so transferred * * * at the time the transfer is made for past services. * * * The time when such income is realized depends on all the facts and circumstances, including any substantial restrictions or conditions on the compensated partner's right to withdraw or otherwise dispose of such interest."

This rule would have been directly applicable had the 1951 contract continued in effect through November 1955, the date on which Wheless and Woolf would have fully recovered their costs in the venture. The contract made it clear that Frazell would "not have the right to dispose of any rights which may accrue to him" before those costs were recovered. But after November, he would have received a largely unrestricted interest in about 13% of the partnership properties. That this interest was primarily, if not entirely, in return for Frazell's services to the enterprise is undisputed. Thus, so much of the interest Frazell was to receive in November 1955 as could be attributed to his services for the oil venture would have been ordinary income to him in the year of receipt.

The applicable rule is in no way changed by Frazell's contention that his interest in the enterprise was a "carried interest." There are three recognized varieties of "carried interest," and each "may be created under varied circumstances, e.g., * * * as compensation for services rendered, e.g., by a geologist. * * *" The interest created by the 1951 contract most nearly fits into the "Menahan" category of "carried interests;" that is, "a springing executory interest * * * conveyed by the carrying party [Wheless and Woolf] to the carried party [Frazell], such interest to become possessory upon the satisfaction of * * * [the carrying party's] costs." Even if Frazell is taken to have had some sort of interest in the properties in question from their first acquisition, his interest would not have become possessory until November 1955. Under Treasury Regulation § 1.721–1(b)(1), the value of that interest would have been taxable to him at that time.

The fact that the contract was terminated prior to November 1955 should have no effect on the tax consequences of Frazell's arrangements. The transactions of April 1955 may be viewed in either of two ways: (1) If Frazell's partnership interest became possessory immediately upon the termination of the 1951 contract, so much of that interest received as compensation for services was taxable to him under the rule of Treasury Regulation § 1.721(b)(1). Thereafter, the transfer of his interest for W.W.F. stock was tax-free under section 351(a). (2) If the $91,000.00 of W.W.F. stock was given in substitution for the partnership interest originally contemplated, so much of that stock received in compensation for services was taxable to Frazell under section 351(a). As either view of the 1955 transactions results in ordinary income to Frazell there is no reason for us to split hairs and choose between them.

This is not to say that the full $91,000.00 is ordinary income. The trial court found that, just as Wheless and Woolf contributed large amounts of capital, "Frazell supplied to the venture a very valuable oil map which was his private property." Indeed the record shows that prior to entering into the 1951 contract Frazell had acquired several maps which apparently proved very helpful to the work of the venture.

Among the reasons given by Mr. Wheless for desiring to employ Frazell was that "he had accumulated maps, geological data and various information that was valuable to the arrangement that it would have taken a long time for someone else just moving into the territory to accumulate." And Frazell himself testified that he "had contributed considerable information and maps which resulted in the discovery and production of oil. * * * " Although it is clear that the greater part of the 13% interest received by Frazell was received as compensation for services, the court's finding and the cited testimony suggest that some part of that interest might have been received in return for "property;" namely, the maps. That part of the property Frazell received in 1955 attributable to his contribution of maps is not taxable in 1955 no matter whether we view the interest received as a partnership interest vesting on the termination of the 1951 contract (I.R.C.1954 § 721) or as shares of W.W.F. stock given in substitution therefor. (I.R.C.1954 § 315(a)).

Before the nonrecognition rule can be applied to the maps in this case, however, two factual determinations must be made: (1) Did Frazell contribute the maps in question to the oil venture or did he keep them as his own personal property? (2) If he contributed them to the venture, what was their value at the time they were contributed? As the burden of proof on both of these issues lies with the taxpayer, it might be argued that he is foreclosed in these issues because of the silence of the record on these points. However, we prefer to remand the case to the district court to permit it to make findings on these two issues. * * *

Reversed and remanded.

3. TRANSFERS BY MORE THAN ONE SHAREHOLDER

The prior discussion has focused on the formation of a new business by one shareholder contributing property to the corporation in exchange for its stock. The provisions of § 351 also protect a transfer of property by two or more shareholders to a corporation so long as those shareholders control the corporation following the transfer. The definition of "control" and the effect of the timing of contributions by different shareholders is discussed later in this Chapter. Under the Regulations, it is clear, however, that if one shareholder transfers office furniture and equipment to a corporation in exchange for 50% of its stock and another shareholder simultaneously transfers inventory to the corporation in exchange for the remaining 50% of the stock, both transfers are protected by § 351. Neither shareholder would recognize gain on the transfer of the property even though the value of such properties exceeded their tax bases.

Problem 22–1

Alice and Earl decide to start a retail badge and trophy business. Alice contributes $50,000 cash necessary for inventory acquisition, lease deposit, and other start-up costs. Earl contributes certain engraving and sewing equipment which he owns. Earl's property has a tax basis of $30,000 and a value of $50,000. Each is issued 100 shares of A & E Badge & Trophy, Inc.

1. Do either Alice or Earl recognize gain?

2. Does the corporation recognize gain?

3. What if Earl, in exchange for agreeing to act as general manager of the business, receives 100 additional shares?

4. What if Earl receives an additional 100 shares for contributing a patented engraving process in which he has no tax basis?

5. What if Earl starts the business by himself, transferring his assets for 100 shares of stock. One year later, realizing he needs funds, he solicits Alice to contribute $50,000 in cash for 100 shares?

C. INCORPORATION OF AN ONGOING BUSINESS

The prior portion of this Chapter focused on the entrepreneur who decides to *begin* his or her business as a corporation. This section focuses on the incorporation of an ongoing business, i.e., one that has been operating as a proprietorship, partnership, or other entity prior to the time its owners decide to transfer the assets of the business to a corporation. Once again, the transferor owners must rely on § 351 to protect them from the potential recognition of gain if the assets transferred have value in excess of their tax basis. In the case of an ongoing business, however, the issues surrounding the transfer of the business assets are often more complex than those in the start-up situation. In addition to the basic business assets such as inventory, furniture, fixtures, supplies, and other similar items, an ongoing business will have other assets such as receivables, reserves, prepaid expenses, as well as less tangible assets such as reputation, goodwill, know-how, customer lists, contracts, and other similar items. Each of these assets must be examined in the context of § 351 to ensure that there are no adverse tax consequences when the ongoing business is incorporated.

D. ASSETS WHICH MIGHT BE TRANSFERRED BY A GOING CONCERN

1. INVENTORY

Inventory qualifies as property for the purposes of § 351. Thus, the basic protection of § 351 is clearly afforded to the transfer of inventory to the corporation. Once the inventory is owned by the corporation, however, rules for inventory accounting may be different than those allowed in a proprietorship or partnership. See *Las Cruces Oil Co. v. Commissioner,* 62 T.C. 764 (1974).

2. FURNITURE, FIXTURES AND EQUIPMENT

Like inventory, furniture, fixtures, supplies, and equipment transferred by an ongoing business to a corporation will be protected from gain or loss recognition so long as the control and other requirements of

§ 351 are met. Such property is perhaps the category which most clearly falls within the "change of business form" rationale for which § 351 was adopted. As discussed in Chapter 24, any gain inherent in such transferred property will be preserved by the carryover of the transferor's tax basis to the corporation. Similarly, that basis is used by the corporation for depreciating or amortizing any of the transferred assets which are subject to such treatment.

3. RECEIVABLES

The transfer of receivables is more complex. A receivable represents potential income resulting from the sale of a product or the rendition of services by the proprietorship or predecessor entity prior to the transfer to the corporation. Thus, the tax effect of the contribution of accounts receivable to the transferee corporation may depend upon the accounting method used by the transferor. If the transferor business used a cash method of accounting, it would have a zero basis in its receivables and therefore (under the basis rules discussed in Chapter 24) the transferee corporation would take a zero basis for them and recognize income as the receivables are paid. If the transferor used an accrual method of accounting, the transferor would have already included the face amount of the receivables in income prior to the transfer. Therefore, the transferor would have a basis in the receivables equal to the amount previously included in income and the transferee corporation would inherit that basis. Upon the collection of the receivables, the corporation would not recognize any additional income.

In either event, the transfer of the receivables themselves will generally not generate income to the transferor shareholders. Transfer by a cash-method taxpayer of accounts receivable or other income rights which have not previously been reported as income could provide a vehicle for the shifting of income from a higher-bracket taxpayer (the transferor) to a lower one (the transferee corporation). While the Service has occasionally attacked particularly abusive situations under the "assignment of income doctrine," the general rule is that no inclusion is required in the transferor shareholder's gross income either at the time of the § 351 exchange or at the time that the transferee corporation receives the cash represented by the transferred item of income. See *Weinberg v. Commissioner,* 44 T.C. 233 (1965), *affirmed sub. nom., Commissioner v. Sugar Daddy, Inc.,* 386 F.2d 836 (9th Cir. 1967).

REVENUE RULING 80–198

1980–2 C.B. 113.

Issue

Under the circumstances described below, do the nonrecognition of gain or loss provisions of section 351 of the Internal Revenue Code apply to a transfer of the operating assets of an ongoing sole proprietorship (including unrealized accounts receivable) to a corporation in exchange solely for the common stock of a corporation and the assumption by the corporation of the proprietorship liabilities?

FACTS

Individual *A* conducted a medical practice as a sole proprietorship, the income of which was reported on the cash receipts and disbursements method of accounting. *A* transferred to a newly organized corporation all of the operating assets of the sole proprietorship in exchange for all of the stock of the corporation, plus the assumption by the corporation of all of the liabilities of the sole proprietorship. The purpose of the incorporation was to provide a form of business organization that would be more conducive to the planned expansion of the medical services to be made available by the business enterprise.

The assets transferred were tangible assets having a fair market value of $40,000 and an adjusted basis of $30,000 and unrealized trade accounts receivable having a face amount of $20,000 and an adjusted basis of zero. The liabilities assumed by the corporation consisted of trade accounts payable in the face amount of $10,000. The liabilities assumed by the corporation also included a mortgage liability, related to the tangible property transferred, of $10,000. *A* had neither accumulated the accounts receivable nor prepaid any of the liabilities of the sole proprietorship in a manner inconsistent with normal business practices in anticipation of the incorporation. If *A* had paid the trade accounts payable liabilities, the amounts paid would have been deductible by *A* as ordinary and necessary business expenses under section 162 of the Code. The new corporation continued to utilize the cash receipts and disbursements method of accounting.

LAW AND ANALYSIS

The applicable section of the Code is section 351(a), which provides that no gain or loss shall be recognized when property is transferred to a corporation in exchange solely for stock and securities and the transferor is in control (as defined by section 368(c)) of the transferee corporation immediately after the transfer.

In *Hempt Bros., Inc. v. United States,* 490 F.2d 1172 (3d Cir.1974), the United States Court of Appeals for the Third Circuit held, as the Internal Revenue Service contended, that a cash basis transferee corporation was taxable on the monies it collected on accounts receivable that had been transferred to it by a cash basis partnership in a transaction described in section 351(a) of the Code. The corporate taxpayer contended that it was not obligated to include the accounts receivable in income; rather the transferor partnership should have been taxed on the stock the partnership received under the assignment of income doctrine which is predicated on the well established general principle that income be taxed to the party that earned it.

The court in *Hempt Bros.* solved the conflict between the assignment of income doctrine and the statutory nonrecognition provisions of section 351 of the Code by reasoning that if the cash basis transferor were taxed on the transfer of the accounts receivable, the specific congressional intent reflected in section 351(a) that the incorporation of an ongoing business should be facilitated by making the incorporation tax free would be frustrated.

The facts of the instant case are similar to those in *Hempt Bros.* in that there was a valid business purpose for the transfer of the accounts receivable along with all of the assets and liabilities of *A* 's proprietorship to a corporate transferee that would continue the business of the transferor. Further, *A* had neither accumulated the accounts receivable nor prepaid any of the account payable liabilities of the sole proprietorship in anticipation of the incorporation, which is an indication that, under the facts and circumstances of the case, the transaction was not designed for tax avoidance.

HOLDING

The transfer by *A* of the operating assets of the sole proprietorship (including unrealized accounts receivable) to the corporation in exchange solely for the common stock of the corporation and the assumption by the corporation of the proprietorship liabilities (including accounts payable) is an exchange within the meaning of section 351(a) of the Code. Therefore, no gain or loss is recognized to *A* with respect to the property transferred, including the accounts receivable. * * * The corporation, under the cash receipts and disbursements method of accounting, will report in its income the account receivables as collected, and will be allowed deductions under section 162 for the payments it makes to satisfy the assumed trade accounts payable when such payments are made. * * *

LIMITATIONS

Section 351 of the Code does not apply to a transfer of accounts receivable which constitute an assignment of an income right in a case such as *Brown v. Commissioner,* 40 B.T.A. 565 (1939), *aff'd* 115 F.2d 337 (2d Cir.1940). In *Brown,* an attorney transferred to a corporation, in which he was the sole owner, a one-half interest in a claim for legal services performed by the attorney and his law partner. In exchange, the attorney received additional stock of the corporation. The claim represented the corporation's only asset. Subsequent to the receipt by the corporation of the proceeds of the claim, the attorney gave all of the stock of the corporation to his wife. The United States Court of Appeals for the Second Circuit found that the transfer of the claim for the fee to the corporation had no purpose other than to avoid taxes and held that in such a case the intervention of the corporation would not prevent the attorney from being liable for the tax on the income which resulted from services under the assignment of income rule of *Lucas v. Earl,* 281 U.S. 111 (1930). Accordingly, in a case of a transfer to a controlled corporation of an account receivable in respect of services rendered where there is a tax avoidance purpose for the transaction (which might be evidenced by the corporation not conducting an ongoing business), the Internal

Revenue Service will continue to apply assignment of income principles and require that the transferor of such a receivable include it in income when received by the transferee corporation.

4. INTANGIBLE ASSETS

In the start-up context, intangible business assets such as contracts, customer lists, employee base, licenses, and other similar intangible property will generally qualify for nonrecognition under § 351 so long as they do not constitute a subterfuge for personal services rendered. See also § 197.

Problem 22–2

Joy and Ruth have operated, as equal partners, a successful novelty and gift shop for several years. They have accounted for the business operations on the cash method. Their balance sheet is as follows:

Assets		Liabilities And Equity	
Inventory	$25,000	Trade Payables	$ 5,000
Furniture, Fixtures		Bank Debt	10,000
& Equipment	10,000	Back Salary Owed Ruth	3,000
Cash	10,000	Equity and Accumulated	
Receivables	15,000	Earnings	47,000
Mail Order			$65,000
Customer Lists	5,000		
	$65,000		

The owners transfer all of their assets and liabilities to a new corporation, each receiving 100 shares of its stock.

1. Does § 351 apply?

2. What if Ruth forgives the obligation to pay her back salary in exchange for additional stock?

3. If the corporation subsequently collects *all* of the receivables, what tax result to it?

4. Is the result different if the business had been accounted for on an accrual basis prior to the transfer?

5. What if, prior to the transfer, a customer sent a check for $5,000 (which would reduce receivables by $5,000 and increase cash by $5,000) and Joy returns the check, asking the customer to pay after the date of incorporation, so that the funds will be taxed at the lower corporate tax rate?

E.   TIMING OF CONTRIBUTIONS

The mere fact that a person transfers property to a newly formed or existing corporation solely in exchange for its stock does not ensure that the transfer will avoid gain recognition. Rather, the transfer must be examined in more detail to confirm that other technical requirements of the Code are met. Section 351(a) provides that the persons transferring the property to the corporation in exchange for its stock must be "in control" of the corporation immediately after the transfer. The same section recognizes that there may be "one or more persons" transferring property to the corporation in a § 351 contribution scenario. It is these one or more persons who must control the corporation "immediately after the transfer."

These statutory requirements raise three separate issues, each of which has, over the years, spawned considerable litigation. These are: (1) What is the definition of control?; (2) What is the meaning of the phrase immediately after the transfer in the context of the timing of the control?; and (3) If there is more than one transferor, when may their contributions be aggregated for the purposes of determining the control group and when must they be separated?

The next three subsections of this Chapter deal with these issues. The final subsection deals with the intentional avoidance of § 351 in situations where a taxpayer desires a taxable transaction.

1. THE CONTROL REQUIREMENT

The Code requires that, in order to qualify under § 351, the persons transferring property to a corporation must be in control of such corporation immediately after the exchange. The definition of control is set forth in § 368(c). Here, the trail becomes (unnecessarily?) complex. Section 368(c) requires that, in order to be in control of a corporation, the person or persons seeking to establish such control must have the ownership of stock possessing (1) at least 80% of the total combined voting power of all classes of stock entitled to vote, and (2) at least 80% of the total number of shares of all other classes of stock of the corporation. In those corporations which have only one class of stock, the test is relatively simple.

For corporations with multiple classes of shares, however, the taxpayer or tax attorney seeking to establish control must be more careful. It is clear that the 80% rules apply to issued (not authorized) shares of the corporation's stock and they apply only to stock, not warrants, options, or other rights to receive stock in the future. See Reg. § 1.351–1(a)(1). The guidance of the statute and Regulations beyond these relatively simple concepts is not great. Small business corporations may often have a second class of common or a class of preferred stock designed to separate investors from active business operators. The investor stock may allow voting only on certain major corporate actions. The basic concept of the statute is that the transferor group must control 80% of the voting stock and 80% of the nonvoting stock of each class of the subject corporation. The definition of "voting stock" is, however, unclear. Further, while different classes of stock may have different values, the test in the statute is purely quantitative. Thus, even in the small business context, the entrepreneur and his or her counsel must pay attention to whether the stock issued meets the control requirement.

REVENUE RULING 59–259

1959–2 C.B. 115.

Advice has been requested whether "control" as defined in section 368(c) of the Internal Revenue Code of 1954 requires ownership of at least 80 percent of the total number of shares of each class of non-voting stock for the purposes of section 351 of the Code.

Certain persons transferred property to a corporation in exchange for voting and non-voting stock, i.e., 83 percent of the Class A voting common stock, 83 percent of the Class A non-voting common stock, and 22 percent of the non-voting preferred stock. However, due to the relative number of non-voting common and preferred shares outstanding, these persons owned more than 80 percent of the total number of shares of the outstanding non-voting stock.

Section 351 of the Code provides, in effect, that no gain or loss shall be recognized to the transferors of property to a corporation if immediately after the transfer, the transferors are in "control" of the corporation as defined by section 368(c) of the Code.

Section 368(c) of such Code in defining "control" states, in part, as follows:

> * * * the term "control" means the ownership of stock possessing at least 80 percent of the total combined voting power of all classes of stock entitled to vote and *at least 80 percent of the total number of shares of all other classes of stock of the corporation.* [Italics supplied.]

The legislative history of section 368(c) of the Code indicates a congressional intent that ownership of *each* class of non-voting stock is required. The provisions of what is now section 368(c) of the Code were first enacted into law as section 202(c)(3) of the Revenue Act of 1921. That section as originally passed by the House of Representatives (H.R. 8245, 67th Cong.,* (1921)), defined "control" as the ownership of:

> * * * at least 80 per centum of the voting stock and 80 per centum of all other classes of stock of the corporation * * *.

The section was reported out of the Senate and enacted into law in a form substantially identical to its present form, retaining the reference to classes of non-voting stock. It is apparent, therefore, that the words "classes of stock" as used in section 368(c) of the Code refers to ownership of 80 percent of the total number of shares of each class of non-voting stock, as there is no other logical reason for retaining the words "classes of stock" in section 202(c)(3) of the Revenue Act of 1921.

Moreover, percentage ownership of the number of non-voting shares outstanding, as contrasted to percentage ownership of each class of non-voting shares, is ordinarily of no significance and can lead to results which are inconsistent with the statutory scheme and clear congressional purpose. Ownership of large numbers of non-voting shares in a multiclass stock structure would not necessarily assure, in itself, the continuation of substantial proprietory interests in modified corporate forms as contemplated by the statute. See section 1.368–1 of the Income Tax Regulations.

In view of the foregoing, it is held that "control" as defined by section 368(c) requires ownership of stock possessing at least 80 percent of the total combined voting power of all classes of voting stock and the ownership of at least 80 percent of the total number of shares of each class of outstanding non-voting stock. Therefore, a transfer of property under the above circumstances does not constitute a transfer to a controlled corporation within the purview of section 351 of the Code.

Problem 22–3

Ted owns all 100 shares of the voting common stock of Ted's Pizza, Inc., which operates a restaurant. When the corporation was formed two years ago, Ted's father-in-law, Boris, was issued 100 shares of nonvoting preferred stock in the corporation in exchange for $10,000 in initial seed money. Ted now contributes a delivery van to the corporation which has a value of $15,000 and a basis of $5,000. In exchange, he receives an additional 10 shares of voting common stock of the corporation.

1. Is the transaction taxable to Ted?

2. If so, how much gain does he recognize?

3. Does the corporation recognize gain?

4. What if Boris simultaneously contributed $15,000 for another 10 shares of nonvoting preferred?

5. What if Boris simultaneously contributed $1,500 for 1 share of voting common?

2. THE IMMEDIATELY AFTER THE EXCHANGE REQUIRE-MENT

Not only must the transferors control the corporation to qualify for § 351 treatment, they must control it immediately after the exchange. This requirement has given rise to considerable litigation in situations where the transferor shareholder receives the corporate stock and then immediately transfers it (or enough of it to forfeit control) to a third party who is not one of the transferors. Even though the immediately thereafter requirement would, by its own definition, seem to be a fleeting temporal notion, it will not be met if the recipient shareholder is, when he or she receives the shares, under a binding obligation to transfer them. The underlying issue is the application of the "step transaction doctrine." If applied, that doctrine treats the stock as flowing directly to the third party, disregarding the intermediate transfer. Thus, the transferor never achieves control.

INTERMOUNTAIN LUMBER COMPANY
v. COMMISSIONER

65 T.C. 1025 (1976).

From 1948 until March of 1964, Mr. Dee Shook (hereinafter Shook) individually owned a sawmill at Conner, Mont. During that time Mr. Milo Wilson (hereinafter Wilson) had logs processed there into rough lumber for a fee. Shook owned the remaining logs processed at the sawmill, which constituted about half of all the logs processed there.

From 1954 until March of 1964, rough lumber from the sawmill was processed into finished lumber at a separate finishing plant which Shook and Wilson owned as equal shareholders.

In March of 1964, fire damaged the sawmill. Shook and Wilson wanted to replace it with a larger one so that the finishing plant could operate at full capacity. Shook was financially unable, however, to do so. He accordingly induced Wilson to personally coguarantee a $200,000 loan to provide financing. In return, Wilson insisted upon an equal voice in rebuilding the sawmill and upon an opportunity to become an equal shareholder with Shook in the new sawmill.

On May 28, 1964, Shook, Wilson, and two other individuals, all acting as incorporators, executed articles of incorporation for S & W Sawmill, Inc. (hereinafter S & W). The corporate name, S & W, was derived from the names Shook and Wilson.

Minutes of the first stockholders meeting on July 7, 1964, stated in part that "Mr. Shook informed the meeting that a separate agreement was being prepared between he and Mr. Wilson providing for the sale of one-half of his stock to Mr. Wilson." Also on that date 1 share was issued to each of the other two incorporators.

Shook executed a bill of sale for his sawmill equipment and deeded his sawmill site to S & W on July 15 and 16, 1964, respectively. In exchange, Shook received 364 S & W shares on July 15, 1964. Shook and Wilson also received 1 share each as incorporators. The 364 shares and the 4 incorporation shares constituted all outstanding capital stock of S & W on July 15, 1964.

Also on that date, minutes of a special meeting stated in part that "The President, Dee Shook, announced that he and Milo E. Wilson had entered into an agreement whereby Mr. Wilson was to purchase 182 shares of Mr. Shook's stock." * * *

On July 15, 1964, Shook also executed an irrevocable proxy granting to Wilson voting rights in 182 shares until September 10, 1965. Two other documents also executed on that date related to share ownership between Shook and Wilson. One, entitled "S & W Sawmill, Inc. Stockholders' Restrictive Agreement," provided in part as follows:

such provisions [against stock transferability] do not apply to the presently existing Agreement for Sale and Purchase of Stock entered into between Dee Shook and Milo E. Wilson, dated the 15th day of July, 1964, and providing for the purchase by Milo E. Wilson of 182 shares of stock in the company.

IT IS THE INTENTION AND PURPOSE of the incorporators that the majority of the ownership of the corporation is to be held by Dee Shook and Milo E. Wilson on an equal share basis when Milo E. Wilson completes the purchase of the stock certificates which are the subject of said purchase agreement.

The other, entitled "Option To Buy Stock Forming Part Of Stockholders' Restrictive Agreement," provided in part that "the ownership of shares in S & W Sawmill, Inc., as the same now stands, to-wit: Dee Shook 365 shares, Milo E. Wilson 1 shares [sic] * * * shall continue."

In connection with the agreement for sale, Shook deposited stock certificates representing 182 shares with an escrow agent on July 17, 1964.

On August 19, 1964, S & W borrowed $200,000, in part upon the personal guarantees of Shook, Wilson, and their wives. The loan agreement referred to Shook and Wilson as "the principal officers and stockholders" of S & W. S & W agreed therein to insure the lives of Shook and Wilson for $100,000 each.

On March 19, 1965, Shook and Wilson agreed to purchase additional shares from S & W. * * *

Wilson made all payments in 1965 and 1966 specified in the agreement for sale and accordingly claimed interest deductions on his Federal income tax returns for those years.

On July 1, 1967, before principal payments were required by the agreement for sale, petitioner purchased all outstanding S & W stock. * * *

OPINION

Section 351 provides, in part, that no gain shall be recognized if property is transferred to a corporation by one or more persons solely in exchange for stock or securities in such corporation and immediately after the exchange such person or persons are in control of the corporation. "Control" is defined for this purpose in section 368(c) as ownership of stock possessing at least 80 percent of the total combined voting power of all classes of stock entitled to vote and at least 80 percent of the total number of shares of all other classes of stock of the corporation.

In this case, respondent is in the unusual posture of arguing that a transfer to a corporation in return for stock was nontaxable under section 351, and Intermountain is in the equally unusual posture of arguing that the transfer was taxable because section 351 was inapplicable. * * *

Petitioner * * * maintains that the transfer to S & W of all of S & W's property at the time of incorporation by the primary incorporator, one Dee Shook, was a taxable sale. It asserts that section 351 was inapplicable because an agreement for sale required Shook, as part of the incorporation transaction, to sell almost half of the S & W shares outstanding to one Milo Wilson over a period of time, thereby depriving Shook of the requisite percentage of stock necessary for "control" of S & W immediately after the exchange.

Respondent, on the other hand, maintains that the agreement between Shook and Wilson did not deprive Shook of ownership of the shares immediately after the exchange, as the stock purchase agreement merely gave Wilson an option to purchase the shares. Shook accordingly was in "control" of the corporation and the exchange was thus nontaxable under section 351.

Respondent has abandoned on brief his contention that Wilson was a transferor of property and therefore a person to also be counted for purposes of control under section 351. Respondent is correct in doing so, since Wilson did not transfer any property to S & W upon its initial formation in July of 1964. Wilson's agreement to transfer cash for corporate stock in March of 1965 cannot be considered part of the same transaction.

Since Wilson was not a transferor of property and therefore cannot be counted for control under section 351, we must determine if Shook alone owned the requisite percentage of shares for control. This determination depends upon whether, under all facts and circumstances surrounding the agreement for sale of 182 shares between Shook and Wilson, ownership of those shares was in Shook or Wilson.

A determination of "ownership," as that term is used in section 368(c) and for purposes of control under section 351, depends upon the obligations and freedom of action of the transferee with respect to the stock when he acquired it from the corporation. Such traditional ownership attributes as legal title, voting rights, and possession of stock certificates are not conclusive. If the transferee, as part of the transaction by which the shares were acquired, has irrevocably foregone or relinquished at that time the legal right to determine whether to keep the shares, ownership in such shares is lacking for purposes of section 351. By contrast, if there are no restrictions upon freedom of action at the time he acquired the shares, it is immaterial how soon thereafter the transferee elects to dispose of his stock or whether such disposition is in accord with a preconceived plan not amounting to a binding obligation.

After considering the entire record, we have concluded that Shook and Wilson intended to consummate a sale of the S & W stock, that they never doubted that the sale would be completed, that the sale was an integral part of the incorporation transaction, and that they considered themselves to be coowners of S & W upon execution of the stock purchase agreement in 1964. These conclusions are supported by minutes of the first stockholders meeting on July 7, 1964, at which Shook characterized the agreement for sale as a "sale"; minutes of a special meeting on July 15, 1964, at which Shook stated Wilson was to "purchase" half of Shook's stock; the "Agreement for Sale and Purchase of Stock" itself, dated July 15, 1964, which is drawn as an installment sale and which provides for payment of interest on unpaid principal; Wilson's deduction of interest expenses in connection with the agreement for sale, which would be inconsistent with an option; the S & W loan agreement, in which Shook and Wilson held themselves out as the "principal stockholders" of S & W and in which S & W covenanted to equally insure Shook and Wilson for $100,000; the March 1965 stock purchase agreement with S & W, which indicated that Shook and Wilson *"are* to remain *equal"* (emphasis added) shareholders in S & W; the letter of May 1967 from Shook and Wilson to Intermountain, which indicated that Wilson owed Shook the principal balance due on the shares as an unpaid obligation; and all surrounding facts and circumstances leading to corporate formation and execution of the above documents. Inconsistent and self-serving testimony of Shook and Wilson regarding their intent and understanding of the documents in evidence is unpersuasive in view of the record as a whole to alter interpretation of the transaction as a sale of stock by Shook to Wilson.

We accordingly cannot accept respondent's contention that the substance varied from the form of this transaction, which was, of course, labeled a "sale." The parties executed an "option" agreement on the same day that the "agreement for sale" was executed, and we have no doubt that they could and indeed did correctly distinguish between a sale and an option.

The agreement for sale's forfeiture clause, which provided that Wilson forfeited the right to purchase a proportionate number of shares for which timely principal payments were not made, did not convert it into an option agreement. Furthermore, the agreement for sale made no provision for forgiving interest payments on the remaining principal due should principal payments not be made on earlier dates; indeed, it specifically provided that "Interest payment must always be kept current before any delivery of stock is to be made resulting from a payment of principal."

We thus believe that Shook, as part of the same transaction by which the shares were acquired (indeed, the agreement for sale was executed before the sawmill was deeded to S & W), had relinquished when he acquired those shares the legal right to determine whether to keep them. Shook was under an obligation, upon receipt of the shares, to transfer the stock as he received Wilson's principal payments. We note also that the agreement for sale gave Wilson the right to prepay principal and receive all 182 shares at any time in advance. Shook therefore did not own, within the meaning of section 368(c), the requisite percentage of stock immediately after the exchange to control the corporation as required for nontaxable treatment under section 351.

We note also that the basic premise of section 351 is to avoid recognition of gain or loss resulting from transfer of property to a corporation which works a change of form only. Accordingly, if the transferor sells his stock as part of the same transaction, the transaction is taxable because there has been more than a mere change in form. In this case, the transferor agreed to sell and did sell 50 percent of the stock to be received, placed the certificates in the possession of an escrow agent, and granted a binding proxy to the purchaser to vote the stock being sold. Far more than a mere change in form was effected.

We accordingly hold for petitioner. * * *

Decisions will be entered under Rule 155.

Problem 22–4

Ike's Used Cars is a sole proprietorship. Mogul Motors, Inc. wants to acquire Ike's business, but does not want to assume Ike's numerous contingent liabilities. Mogul enters into an agreement whereby Ike will transfer his business' assets (but not liabilities) to a newly formed corporation (Ike, Inc.) in exchange for all its stock. Once incorporated, Mogul will acquire all of the shares of Ike, Inc. in exchange for Mogul stock. Ike, Inc. would then be a subsidiary of Mogul, Inc. and Ike would be a minority shareholder of Mogul.

1. Does Ike's transfer of assets for all of Ike, Inc.'s shares qualify under § 351?

2. What if Mogul had an *option* to acquire the shares of Ike, Inc.?

3. What if the contract called for Mogul to acquire the Ike, Inc. shares for cash?

4. What if there were no contract, but Mogul acquired the Ike, Inc. shares for its stock one week following the Ike, Inc. incorporation?

3. ONE OR MORE TRANSFERORS REQUIREMENT

When a sole proprietor transfers all of his business assets to a corporation in exchange for its stock which he then holds while the business operates as a corporation, the application of § 351 is clear. When there are two or more transferors who receive stock in exchange for transferred assets, however, more planning is required. A particular problem arises where multiple transferors do not transfer their property to the corporation simultaneously. If the transfers are viewed separately, then the individual transferors may not control the corporation after their particular transfer. If the transfers are viewed together, however, then the stockholdings of the two transferors may be amalgamated for the purposes of determining whether the control requirement is met.

The Regulations indicate that the statute "does not necessarily require simultaneous exchanges by two or more persons, but comprehends a situation where the rights of the parties have been previously defined and the execution of the agreement proceeds with an expedition consistent with orderly procedure." See Reg. § 1.351–1(a)(1). While this Regulation provides comfort to multiple transfers made pursuant to a single integrated plan, there remain many questions in the practical context of whether transfers by more than one transferor may be amalgamated for the purposes of determining control requirement. If they are not, the separate transfers will most often not fall within the purview of § 351 and will be taxable transactions. Once again, the application of § 351 in this situation may turn on the judicial application (this time to the taxpayer's benefit) of the step transaction doctrine which, if applied, would view the various transfers as simply separate steps in one integrated transaction.

Problem 22–5

Basil transfers $100,000 to a newly formed corporation in exchange for 100 shares of its common stock. Three months later, Cyril transfers to the corporation an unencumbered rental condominium unit with a basis of $50,000 and a value of $100,000. He is issued 100 shares of the corporation's common stock in exchange for his contribution.

1. What is the tax result of Basil's contribution?

2. Is Cyril's contribution tax-free under § 351?

3. What if Basil and Cyril had entered into a pre-existing written contract obligating them to make their respective contributions?

4. What if the contract between them was oral?

5. What if Basil and Cyril had intended to make the contributions simultaneously, but Cyril was delayed as a result of having to remove an unexpected cloud on the title of the condominium?

4.   INTENTIONAL AVOIDANCE OF § 351

There are some situations in which a taxpayer prefers to treat the transfer of property to his controlled corporation as a taxable event rather than a nonrecognition event. Among such circumstances are: (1) the taxpayer's recognized gain may be subject to offset by existing operating losses of the taxpayer; (2) the taxpayer may wish to recognize capital gain if he has otherwise nondeductible capital losses; and (3) if the property being transferred to the corporation has a value less than its basis, the transferor shareholder may wish to recognize the loss inherent in the exchange. The most common method of avoiding the application of § 351 is to structure the transaction so that the control requirements of § 351 are intentionally not satisfied. Another technique is to simply characterize the transaction as a sale to the corporation by its controlling shareholder in exchange for debt obligations of the corporation. Neither of these techniques, however, is foolproof. The Service or a court may use the step transaction doctrine (against the taxpayer) to disregard the intentional avoidance of the control requirement. Similarly, the transaction may be recharacterized so that the debt instrument of the corporation is treated as equity (i.e., stock), thereby, bringing § 351 into play.

SIX SEAM COMPANY, INC. v. UNITED STATES

524 F.2d 347 (6th Cir.1975).

ENGEL, CIRCUIT JUDGE. * * *

Six Seam was incorporated in 1959 and until April, 1961, its business consisted solely of operating a tipple used in the preparation of coal for commercial sale. The tipple crushed, sorted and washed coal. At no time during this period did Six Seam itself engage in the business of actually mining coal. Rather, it purchased raw coal from various local mines and merely processed the coal through its tipple. The coal tipple itself was leased by Six Seam from a third party, the Kington family. Taxpayer incurred net operating losses of $73,017 and $24,437 during fiscal years of 1960 and 1961 respectively. In March, 1961, Six Seam, heavily in debt, ceased operating the tipple. In April, 1961 it sub-leased the use of the tipple to one of its suppliers, Walnut Grove Mining. Initially, Six Seam had attempted to sell the tipple rights to Walnut Grove, but the latter was not in a position to purchase the facility. The sub-lease to Walnut Grove was not exclusive since Six Seam reserved the opportunity to process any of its coal through the tipple. The record indicates that Six Seam never subsequently availed itself of this reserved right. When Six Seam executed the lease, it notified various governmental agencies that it was terminating its business.

The Board of Directors of Six Seam on March 20, 1961, authorized the acceptance for surrender and cancellation of the stock of any shareholder who desired to tender his shares to the corporation. The resolution provided no consideration for the surrendered shares, but relieved the shareholder of his personal guarantee on a $75,000 note executed by Six Seam to a Kentucky bank. In May, 1961, the shareholders of Six Seam agreed to sell their stock to Coiltown Mining Company, Inc. for a total of $100 plus the full assumption by the latter of Six Seam's corporate liabilities. Coiltown was a coal mining company which for many years had been engaged in extracting coal from the Klondike Mine in Kentucky under contracts for the sale of coal to the Tennessee Valley Authority. During the remainder of 1961 and throughout 1962, Six Seam, now a wholly owned subsidiary of Coiltown, did not engage in any active business except to receive rental income from the lease of the tipple to Walnut Grove.

In 1961 and prior years Coiltown had encountered increasing difficulty in completing a coal supply contract with the Tennessee Valley Authority. The shareholders were concerned that potential liabilities in contractual damages would be incurred by the corporation if Coiltown defaulted on its contract with TVA. Since Coiltown had been accumulating liquid reserves in preparation for liquidation of the corporation and distribution to the shareholders, the specific fear was that a large contractual liability would deplete the "nest egg" of over $1,000,000 in cash and marketable securities. Therefore, to insulate the liquid assets of Coiltown from potentially ruinous liability on the TVA contract, the shareholders of Coiltown decided, as found by the district court,

> "... to reactivate Six Seam, a wholly-owned, but dormant, subsidiary of Coiltown, and endeavor to persuade TVA to substitute it for Coiltown on the T–4 Contract and to release Coiltown and the surety on its $325,000.00 performance bond from that contract...."

Pursuant to the plan, Six Seam on April 1, 1963, issued and Coiltown purchased an additional 3,030 shares of Six Seam stock for $303,000. On the same date Six Seam purchased all of Coiltown's mining equipment for $145,000 and all of its mining supplies for $41,-291. Out of the remaining cash, Six Seam paid all of its outstanding debts and obligations, including an account payable to Coiltown of $66,000. When these transactions were completed, Six Seam owned all of Coiltown's mining assets and in addition had approximately $50,000 working capital to begin mining operations. Concerning this transaction, the district court found that

> "The sole purpose and intent underlying the transfer by Coiltown of its mining and other operating assets to Six Seam on April 1, 1963, was to enable Coiltown's shareholders to get out of the coal mining business at the minimum possible risk of loss. And that those assets were not transferred to Six Seam pursuant to any plan to reorganize Coiltown so that its shareholders could continue in the coal mining business in modified corporate form to Six Seam...."

By September 1964, the earlier production difficulties had been resolved and Six Seam was able successfully to complete performance under the TVA contract. Six Seam subsequently leased the mining equipment it had obtained from Coiltown to Pyro Mining Company. Pyro exercised the option under the lease and in January, 1965, purchased the mining equipment for $320,000. * * *

The intent of Section 351 is to allow a taxpayer or group of taxpayers to rearrange the structure of a business without incurring tax costs. Without Section 351, if a proprietor of a business decided to incorporate, the paper transfer of the business assets from the ownership of the proprietor to the new corporation would result in taxation of the difference of the fair market value of the assets over the adjusted basis. Congress believed that a mere change of form of ownership without the relinquishment of control of the property was insignificant to justify taxation.

> "There is, in short, a transfer in form only, a technical transfer not one of substance. The section is designed to give present tax relief for internal rearrangements of the taxpayer's own assets, accompanied by no sacrifice of control and no real generation of income for the owner—and to defer taxation until a true outside disposition is made."

E.I. DuPont de Nemours & Co. v. United States, 471 F.2d 1211, 1214 (Ct.Cl.1973).

The operation of Section 351 is mandatory when a transfer of property to a controlled corporation occurs. "No gain or loss *shall* be recognized ..." Thus if a transaction is within the scope of Section 351, taxable gain is postponed and the basis remains the same.

If Coiltown had contributed the mining assets to Six Seam's capital structure in exchange for 3,030 shares the literal provisions of Section 351 would have been invoked, since there would be a transfer of property to a corporation solely in exchange for stock in such corporation. Since Coiltown controlled Six Seam as a wholly owned subsidiary, the only question is whether the transfer of cash to Six Seam for stock and its return on the same day to Coiltown for the mining equipment should have a different tax consequence. Without the cash infusion by Coiltown, Six Seam would have been unable to "purchase" the mining equipment. The capital contribution to Six Seam and the "sale" occurred on the same day. In short, the two steps constituted an integrated plan. In apparent agreement are the district court's own findings. Under such circumstances we are compelled to hold that even "though the form of the subject transaction was that of a sale, it is clear that substance, not form, controls in determining the effect of the transaction for federal income tax purposes."

The district court did not address itself to the question of whether Section 351 was applicable, but rather made a finding that the price paid for the mining assets was reasonable and consequently the sale was bona fide. However, the reasonableness of the price paid for property transferred to a controlled corporation is irrelevant. If a transaction is within the scope of Section 351, Section 362 mandates that the basis shall remain the same without regard to the fair price of the property. Nor do we consider ourselves bound by the district court determination since "this case hinges * * * on the legal characterization, for federal income tax purposes, of the transactions between the parties. That characterization is not a question of fact, but rather one of law." * * *

Problem 22–6

Shirley contributes property to Newco, Inc. which has a value of $100 and a basis of $50. LaVerne contributes property with a value of $100 and a basis of $150. In exchange, Shirley receives all 100 shares of the common stock of Newco. LaVerne receives a note of the corporation with a face amount of $100. The terms of the note indicate that it is unsecured, subordinate to other corporate debt, and the "interest" is not a fixed rate but rather an amount equal to 50% of Newco's annual cash flow. The principal of the note is payable only upon the liquidation of the corporation.

1. What result to LaVerne if the note is recharacterized as stock?

2. What if it is treated as a note?

3. Does the characterization make a difference to Shirley?

Chapter 23

PROPERTY RECEIVED BY THE TRANSFERRING SHAREHOLDER IN A § 351 TRANSACTION

Code References: §§ 351(b); 357(a)–(c); 1239(a)–(c).
Regulations: §§ 1.351–2; 1.357–1, & –2; 1.368–1(b).

A. INTRODUCTION

This Chapter focuses on the tax effects to the entrepreneur/shareholder when he or she receives stock, securities, or other property from a controlled corporation in exchange for the transfer of property to it. Section 351(a) permits the transfer by the shareholder of property to the corporation on a tax-free basis only if the transfer is "solely in exchange for stock" of the transferee corporation. As discussed below, this is somewhat of a statutory overstatement, since it is tempered by other Code provisions. Nevertheless, the tax planner must clearly ensure that there is an exchange (that is, the shareholder receives *something* from the corporation) and must ensure that at least a portion of what is received is "stock."

Prior to the amendment of § 351 in 1989, a transferor could also receive "securities" of the transferee corporation and fall within the protective umbrella of § 351. The elimination of securities as acceptable corporate currency made irrelevant an entire body of law which had arisen in the § 351 arena as to what constitutes a security. The primary exercise in those days was distinguishing short-term debt, which was clearly not a security, from longer-term obligations of the corporation, which might qualify as a security. See *Camp Wolters Enterprises, Inc. v. Commissioner*, 22 T.C. 737 (1954), *affirmed*, 230 F.2d 555 (5th Cir.1956). Under current law, the adviser's task is simpler. He or she must ensure that the shareholder receives stock from the transferee corporation. Any other form of corporate consideration, including securities, is unprotected by § 351. The underlying rationale is that the receipt of any debt instrument, including those which might qualify as securities, provides, through the eventual payment of the corporate debt, a vehicle for the transferring shareholder to "cash in" the investment rather than maintain a continuity of interest in the ongoing business. The drafters of the Code decided that the receipt of such an interest was not a mere change in the form of doing business worthy of nonrecognition treatment for tax purposes. The Regulations, at § 1.368–1(b), embrace such a rationale for most tax-free corporate transactions.

B. DEFINITION OF "STOCK"

Until the statute was changed in 1989, there was little reason to distinguish between "stock" and "securities" received in a corporate transfer since both were qualifying "paper" for the purposes of § 351. Consequently, most of the litigation and interpretation revolved around whether the transferring shareholder received at least a security as opposed to something less, such as a short-term note. The latter type of consideration was deemed, under then applicable case law, not to be "continuity-carrying" paper. Under current law, the distinction between a short-term debt and a long-term security is unimportant, since only stock constitutes qualifying consideration.

The term stock is not clearly defined in the Code, the Regulations, or any Ruling or pronouncement. Through analyzing cases in analogous areas (such as the area of corporate reorganizations where the term stock has been held to have the same meaning that it is to have for purposes of § 351), however, certain conclusions can be drawn. It appears clear that stock includes both common and preferred stock of the transferee corporation, whether that stock is voting or nonvoting. See *Marsan Realty Corp. v. Commissioner,* 22 T.C.M. (CCH) 1513 (1963). More difficult issues arise, however, when the shareholder receives more sophisticated instruments, such as stock rights or warrants or contingent stock interests. In the small business context, where more than one owner of the business is involved, there may be a business reason, such as uncertainty as to the value of the property being transferred to the corporation, to use future stock rights. The right to receive (or not receive) the future shares might, for instance, be contingent upon how that transferred property performs in the new business. In other situations, stock may be issued only if the business survives to a designated future date or upon the occurrence of a subsequent event indicating the true value of a shareholder contribution. This is commonly known as an "earn out." Where the future right is strictly a contingent stock right, which can yield only additional shares of the corporation and which requires no additional consideration from the shareholder, the courts have held that right to be stock. See *Carlberg v. United States,* 281 F.2d 507 (8th Cir.1960). Where the future right is an option or warrant, requiring additional consideration of the shareholder, it is not stock for purposes of § 351.

HAMRICK v. COMMISSIONER

43 T.C. 21 (1964).

FINDINGS OF FACT

The stipulation of facts and the exhibits thereto are incorporated herein by this reference. * * *

Jet Line Products, Inc., hereinafter referred to as Jet, is a corporation organized under the laws of North Carolina in October 1957, originally as Jet Line Gun Co., Inc. The present name was adopted in December 1959. The stock of this corporation was originally of the par value of $100 per share. This was revised by amendment in August 1959 to the par value of $1 per share.

Prior to April 1957, James C. Hamrick, hereinafter sometimes referred to as the petitioner, was employed as an electrician by an electrical contractor and was also engaged part time in the business of selling and installing radios, intercom equipment, and related products. Owen L. Hensley, who had some experience in electrical work and engineering, worked with Hamrick to develop an idea using a gas-propelled cartridge to carry a lead line through various types of conduits. By April 22, 1957, they had designed and reduced to practice a device to produce this result. They desired to patent and market this invention. They secured the services of William B. Webb and Charles F. Coira, Jr., attorneys, and Arthur R. Newcombe, a financial advisor. An application for a patent was filed July 29, 1957, and a patent for the device was issued in March 1960.

In planning to market the invention, Newcombe located cash investors willing to supply $35,000 for this purpose. Hamrick and Hensley wanted two-thirds of the stock of the proposed corporation while the investors wanted Hamrick's and Hensley's shares limited to 51 percent. A compromise was reached to allow Hamrick and Hensley each to receive initially slightly more than 25 percent of the issued stock and to allow the issue to them of additional shares up to a total of two-thirds if warranted by earnings and according to an agreed formula. * * *

On November 6, 1957, Hamrick and Hensley executed an assignment of their invention to the corporation: * * *

[P]ursuant to the foregoing assignment, Jet issued 190 shares of its capital stock to Hamrick and 190 shares to Hensley, and pursuant to the subscription agreement issued 350 shares to the cash investors for cash in the amount of $35,000, and, for services rendered, 5 shares to Carpenter and Webb, 5 shares to Charles F. Coira, Jr., and 10 shares to Newcombe. * * *

As of September 30, 1960, Jet issued to Hamrick, pursuant to the foregoing agreements, 14,910 shares of its capital stock. * * *

As of September 30, 1960, Hamrick had received all the shares to which he was entitled under the assignment of November 6, 1957, and the agreement of November 24, 1958.

On November 5, 1958, the petitioner sold three shares of Jet stock ($100 par value) for $300. In September 1959 he sold 600 shares ($1 par value) for $4 per share and 2,000 shares for $3.89 per share. In April 1960 he sold 275 shares for $12.41 per share. In September 1960 he sold 5,000 shares for $14.65 per share to Shuford Mills Co., Inc., a corporation, of Hickory, N.C. * * *

OPINION

The principal issue involves the taxable status of shares of capital stock issued by Jet to Hamrick in 1958, 1959, and 1960 pursuant to the assignment of November 6, 1957, and the memorandum of agreement of November 24, 1958. The petitioner contends that the provisions of section 351(a) of the Internal Revenue Code of 1954 apply, that all the stock he received was received in exchange for property, and that no gain or loss is to be recognized upon such receipt.

It will facilitate discussion if we treat all the stock involved as of the par value of $1. On this basis, Hamrick received the following amounts at the time stated:

Year	Shares
1957	19,000
1958	4,070
1959	9,824
1960	14,249

Of the stock received in 1960, 8,106 shares brought the total issued to Hamrick up to one-third of the total issued by Jet, and the additional 6,143 brought his total up to 44 percent of the issued stock. * * *

The respondent concedes that the shares petitioner received in 1957 were received in a nontaxable exchange, but takes the position that the next 22,000 shares, received in 1958, 1959, and 1960, bringing the petitioner's total to one-third of the issued stock, represented long-term capital gains under section 1235 of the Internal Revenue Code of 1954, to the extent of the fair market value of the stock, and that the last 6,143 shares received in 1960 are taxable as ordinary income.

The respondent contends that section 351(a) is not applicable because (1) the right to receive the additional shares was [not] "stock". * * *

The respondent's first argument is that the right of the petitioner to receive additional stock in Jet was [not] stock * * * within the meaning of section 351(a) but was "other property," which is to be recognized as gain to the extent of its fair market value. Respondent cites *Helvering v. Southwest Consol. Corp.*, 315 U.S. 194 (1942), in which assets were acquired in a reorganization for voting stock and warrants which allowed the holder to acquire shares of stock upon payment of specified sums. The issue was whether the assets were acquired in a reorganization * * * solely for voting stock. The Court said that "solely" leaves no leeway and that voting stock plus some other consideration does not meet the requirements, and held that the warrants were not voting stock nor did they carry the rights of a shareholder. The respondent says that the petitioner's contract right to acquire Jet stock was not the equivalent of stock but had more of the characteristics of the warrants in the cited case.

The petitioner cites *Carlberg v. United States,* 281 F.2d 507 (C.A.8, 1960), which involved an exchange of stock for stock and certificates of contingent interest. The issue was whether such certificates were "stock" within the meaning of section 354(a)(1) of the 1954 Code or "other property," within the meaning of section 356(a)(1). The case arose from the merger of two lumber companies, referred to as Maryland and Missouri, into International Paper Co. At the time, Missouri had pending substantial unsettled liabilities. To protect International, certain shares were reserved and certificates of contingent interest issued with respect to them. The stockholders of Maryland and Missouri received shares of International plus certificates. When the liabilities were settled, the reserved shares would be distributed in accordance with the certificates if settlement were made within 10 years. The purpose of the device was to place the ultimate burden of the liabilities on the Missouri stockholders. The court referred to the *Southwest* case, and observed that there were obvious differences between the warrants in that case and the certificates in *Carlberg,* as the warrants provided rights to purchase at stated prices during a stated time, the holders having only an option to purchase, while the certificate holders were immediately entitled to all the reserved shares to be distributed and need take no positive action nor provide further consideration. The court said that the certificates could produce nothing but stock, that the arrangement for reserved shares seemed an ideal and logical solution of the problem of the contingent liabilities, and that what the holder possessed was either stock or nothing. The court held that the property interest represented by the certificates was "stock" within the meaning of section 354(a)(1) rather than "other property" or "boot."

The contract here was a solution of a problem, as in *Carlberg.* The cash investors were willing to allow Hamrick and Hensley voting control of the corporation to be formed but were unwilling to put up $35,000 for only one-third of the shares in an untried invention. The inventors wanted one-third of the stock each. The arrangement for additional shares to be issued to them in the event the invention proved salable was a compromise and a good faith solution of their differences. There was a valid business purpose in the arrangement. If earnings were meager, the investors would receive in dividends nearly half of them. If the business was successful, they would be content with one-third of satisfactory earnings. The inventors were willing to take the hazard of the salability of their invention which, if successful, would result in their receiving eventually the interests they wanted.

The respondent concedes that the stock issued in 1957 was received in exchange for the transfer of property. The contract right to receive additional stock was also a part of the consideration for the transfer.

The right, as in *Carlberg,* can produce nothing other than stock to the petitioner. While the exact number of shares is not specified, what the petitioner can receive is nothing other than stock. Applying the rule of substance over form, we must conclude that the substance of the contract provides for only a stockholder's interest. It does not represent current gain, but additional equity ownership.

In *Carlberg,* the certificates authorized the issue of additional stock if certain conditions were met within 10 years. Here the contract authorized the issue of additional stock if certain conditions were met within 7 years. The stock was authorized and available for issuance if the conditions were met. The principle of the *Carlberg* case is applicable here, and Hamrick's right under the agreement was the equivalent of stock. * * *

Problem 23–1

Walt and John operate separate real estate management companies. They decide to merge their operations by forming a corporation. Walt is unsure whether all of John's management contracts will be renewed. Consequently, Walt is initially issued 100 shares and John 80. If John's contracts are renewed within one year, he will be issued an additional 20 shares.

1. What is the tax result to John and Walt at the time of formation?

2. What result if the contracts are renewed and John receives his additional 20 shares?

3. What if, at the time of formation, John receives a note of the corporation, payable in one year, which can be converted into 20 shares of stock if the contracts are renewed?

4. What if John, at the time of formation, receives the right to purchase 20 additional shares of stock if the contracts are renewed? The purchase price is the value of the stock on the formation date of the corporation, even though the shares may have appreciated at the time such right is exercised.

C. RECEIPT OF SECURITIES, CASH, OR OTHER PROPERTY

The statutory concept that the transferor must receive only stock of the transferee corporation in exchange for his transferred assets in order to qualify for tax-free treatment under § 351 is somewhat misleading. If other property is received (including securities, cash, or any property other than stock of the transferee corporation), § 351(b) requires gain recognition, but *only* to the extent of (1) the amount of the money received, plus (2) the fair market value of other property received. It also prohibits loss recognition in any event. While there may be gain to the extent of the cash or value of other property received, any additional gain to the transferor shareholder which remains inherent in the stock received is not required to be recognized. Thus, the transfer may be partially taxable and partially tax-deferred under § 351.

Any nonqualifying property received by the shareholder, whether it be cash, securities, or other property, is known in tax parlance as "boot." To the extent that such boot is received in exchange for transferred property, there is a taxable exchange between the transferring shareholder and the corporation. Such gain gives rise to a whole separate set of problems for the tax adviser, including the determination of whether the character of the gain is ordinary or capital and, in the latter case, whether it is long-term or short-term. Since the transfer may be with a related party, the answers to these questions are often complex. See § 1239. In addition, if the consideration received from the corporation is a security or other form of corporate debt, the issue arises as to whether the recipient shareholder can report his income on the installment method, thereby deferring the reporting of a portion of the gain to subsequent years when the payments on the corporate note of debenture are received. There are also problems of allocating the basis of the property transferred to the corporation between the qualifying stock received by the transferring shareholder and the boot received in the transaction.

REVENUE RULING 68–55
1968–1 C.B. 140.

Advice has been requested as to the correct method of determining the amount and character of the gain to be recognized by Corporation X under section 351(b) of the Internal Revenue Code of 1954 under the circumstances described below.

Corporation Y was organized by X and A, an individual who owned no stock in X. A transferred $20x$ dollars to Y in exchange for stock of Y having a fair market value of $20x$ dollars and X transferred to Y three separate assets and received in exchange stock of Y having a fair market value of $100x$ dollars plus cash of $10x$ dollars.

In accordance with the facts set forth in the table below if X had sold at fair market value each of the three assets if transferred to Y, the result would have been as follows:

	Asset I	Asset II	Asset III
Character of asset	Capital asset held more than 6 months.	Capital asset held not more than 6 months.	Section 1245 property.
Fair market value	$22x	$33x	$55x
Adjusted basis	40x	20x	25x
Gain (loss)	($18x)	$13x	$30x
Character of Gain or loss	Long-term capital loss.	Short-term capital gain.	Ordinary income.

The facts in the instant case disclose that with respect to the section 1245 property the depreciation subject to recapture exceeds the amount of gain that would be recognized on a sale at fair market value. Therefore, all of such gain would be treated as ordinary income under section 1245(a)(1) of the Code.

Under section 351(a) of the Code, no gain or loss is recognized if property is transferred to a corporation solely in exchange for its stock and immediately after the exchange the transferor is in control of the corporation. If section 351(a) of the Code would apply to an exchange but for the fact that there is received, in addition to the property permitted to be received without recognition of gain, other property or money, then under section 351(b) of the Code gain (if any) to the recipient will be recognized, but in an amount not in excess of the sum of such money and the fair market value of such other property received, and no loss to the recipient will be recognized.

The first question presented is how to determine the amount of gain to be recognized under section 351(b) of the Code. The general rule is that each asset transferred must be considered to have been separately exchanged. Thus, for purposes of making computations under section 351(b) of the Code, it is not proper to total the bases of the various assets transferred and to subtract this total from the fair market value of the total consideration received in the exchange. Moreover, any treatment other than an asset-by-asset approach would have the effect of allowing losses that are specifically disallowed by section 351(b)(2) of the Code.

The second question presented is how, for purposes of making computations under section 351(b) of the Code, to allocate the cash and stock received to the amount realized as to each asset transferred in the exchange. The asset-by-asset approach for computing the amount of gain realized in the exchange requires that for this purpose the fair market value of each category of consideration received must be separately allocated to the transferred assets in proportion to the relative fair market values of the transferred assets. See section 1.1245–4(c)(1) of the Income Tax Regulations which, for the same reasons, requires that for purposes of computing the amount of gain to which section 1245 of the Code applies each category of consideration received must be allocated to the properties transferred in proportion to their relative fair market values.

Accordingly, the amount and character of the gain recognized in the exchange should be computed as follows:

	Total	*Asset I*	*Asset II*	*Asset III*
Fair market value of asset transferred	$110x	$22x	$33x	$55x
Percent of total fair market value	....	20%	30%	50%
Fair market value of Y stock received in exchange	$100x	$20x	$30x	$50x
Cash received in exchange	10x	2x	3x	5x
Amount realized	$110x	$22x	$33x	$55x
Adjusted basis	....	40x	20x	25x
Gain (loss) realized	....	($18x)	$13x	$30x

Under section 351(b)(2) of the Code the loss of 18x dollars realized on the exchange of Asset Number I is not recognized. Such loss may not be used to offset the gains realized on the exchanges of the other assets.

Under section 351(b)(1) of the Code, the gain of 13x dollars realized on the exchange of Asset Number II will be recognized as short-term capital gain in the amount of 3x dollars, the amount of cash received. Under sections 351(b)(1) and 1245(b)(3) of the Code, the gain of 30x dollars realized on the exchange of Asset Number III will be recognized as ordinary income in the amount of 5x dollars, the amount of cash received.

Problem 23–2

Sven owns all of the shares of Alpine, Inc. which operates a luge sled rental concession. Lars agrees to invest in the company. Lars transfers $50,000 in exchange for 100 shares of stock. Sven, who already has 50 shares of Alpine, Inc., contributes 50 additional luge sleds to the corporation in exchange for 50 more shares, a note from Alpine in the amount of $10,000 due in one year, and a used snow-making machine with a value of $4,000. Sven's basis for the contributed luge sleds was $5,000.

1. What tax result to Lars?

2. Does Sven have income? If so, how much?

3. When does Sven report his income?

D. ASSUMPTION OF SHAREHOLDER LIABILITIES

Particularly in those situations where owners are incorporating an ongoing business, the incorporating transfer will often involve not only the transfer of assets to, but also the assumption of liabilities by, the corporation. Such an assumption could be viewed under the tax law as constituting additional consideration to such shareholder, thereby being a form of boot which triggers the gain inherent in the appreciated transferred assets. Such would be the proper result except for § 357(a) which dictates that the transferee corporation's assumption of a liability (or acquisition of property *subject to* a liability) is not treated as boot and does not prevent an exchange from qualifying under § 351. While the basic rule of § 357(a) is straightforward, it has certain specified exceptions.

1. TAX AVOIDANCE MOTIVES

If the principal purpose of the debt assumption (or creation of the debt by the transferor just prior to its assumption) is tax avoidance, § 357(a) will not apply and gain may be recognized under § 357(b). The most obvious example of such efforts is the unnecessary attachment of debt to the business assets immediately prior to their transfer to the corporation, thereby allowing the shareholder to "cash in" on a portion of his investment without tax, since loan proceeds are not income. Such a procedure may be deemed to be the equivalent of receiving cash "boot" from the corporation. If bona fide debt *is* incurred shortly before a § 351 transfer, the corporate minutes should be replete with independent business reasons for the loan. It would also be beneficial to the taxpayer's position if the loan proceeds were contributed to the corporation as part of the § 351 transfer.

2. LIABILITIES IN EXCESS OF THE BASIS OF THE TRANSFERRED ASSETS

A second exception to § 357(a) is set forth in § 357(c). This provision treats liabilities encumbering the transferred property or liabilities assumed by the transferee corporation as boot to the extent that they exceed the aggregate adjusted basis of the properties transferred. Under prior law, this could pose an unexpected problem for cash-method taxpayers who transferred receivables (with a zero basis) in exchange for stock and an assumption of the transferor's accounts payable. If the accounts payable were deemed to be a liability, a taxable transaction would often occur. This gave rise to some interesting litigation which was ultimately resolved by the enactment of § 357(c)(3) which excludes from the definition of liabilities those obligations which would give rise to a deduction if they have been paid by the transferor/shareholder. Trade payables obviously fall within this exception and therefore may be assumed by the transferor corporation without tax effect.

Trade payables aside, there are other types of liabilities, such as mortgage debt and bank debt, which might well be transferred in the incorporation of a going business. The tax adviser must know the tax basis of such properties. If liabilities exceed the basis of the assets transferred, gain will result. The excess debt is treated as being received in exchange for the property transferred. The character of the gain as capital or ordinary will depend on the character, holding period, and appreciation levels of the assets transferred. The gain on depreciable property may also be converted from capital to ordinary by the related party rules of § 1239. Where there is only one transferor, these rules may be relatively easy to apply. Where there is more than one transferor, § 357(c) is applied on a transferor-by-transferor basis. Each transferor with liabilities in excess of the basis of the transferred assets must report gain. Such persons may not "utilize" the excess basis of a fellow transferor.

DRYBROUGH v. COMMISSIONER

42 T.C. 1029 (1964), affirmed in part, reversed
in part, 376 F.2d 350 (6th Cir.1967).

TRAIN, JUDGE: * * *

The issues which remain for decision are:

(1) Whether respondent erred in determining that the assumption of existing mortgages by five controlled corporations to which F.W. Drybrough transferred improved real estate in 1957 was for the principal purpose of avoiding Federal income tax on the exchange, or was not for a bona fide business purpose, so that the entire amount of the liability

assumed on the exchange is to be considered as money received by F.W. Drybrough on the exchange under section 357(b), I.R.C. 1954; * * *

FINDINGS OF FACT

Some of the facts have been stipulated and the stipulation of facts, together with the exhibits attached thereto, is incorporated herein by this reference.

F.W. Drybrough (hereinafter sometimes referred to as Drybrough) and Marion S. Drybrough (hereinafter sometimes referred to as Marion) filed timely joint individual Federal income tax returns with the district director of internal revenue for the district of Kentucky for the years 1956, 1957, and 1958. * * *

Drybrough became a resident of Louisville, Ky., in 1913. From that time until 1917, he and Marion worked for a collection agency in that city. In July 1917, they left that agency and, together with Marion's sister, started United Mercantile Agencies (hereinafter sometimes referred to as UMA), a Kentucky corporation operating a commercial wholesale collection agency. Drybrough and Marion were married in August 1919.

Drybrough became interested in investing in Louisville real estate about 1920, and between 1920 and 1940 acquired at least 20 or 30 different parcels, principally in the downtown business district. Frequently, he borrowed money to purchase these parcels, and mortgaged the properties as security for the loans.

In 1940, Drybrough owned five parcels of realty, all of which were encumbered by mortgages or vendor's liens. In 1945 he purchased two more parcels; in 1946 he purchased an additional two parcels. In 1940, 1945, and 1946 he borrowed money from the National Life & Accident Insurance Co. of Nashville, Tenn. (sometimes hereinafter referred to as National Life), in the respective amounts of $200,000, $200,000, and $500,000, secured in each case by mortgages on his real estate. Drybrough used the proceeds of the first two loans to pay off a portion of existing loans. Except for $9,028.90 which was to paid to Drybrough, the proceeds of the 1946 loan were used by Drybrough to pay off the balance of the 1945 loan and several smaller loans.

On April 30, 1953, Drybrough borrowed $700,000 from National Life. This loan is hereinafter sometimes referred to as the 1953 loan. Drybrough and Marion signed a $700,000 note payable to the order of Lowry Watkins Co., Inc. (sometimes hereinafter referred to as Watkins Co.), brokers, and executed a mortgage covering six properties owned by Drybrough. On the same day Watkins Co. assigned the note and mortgage to National Life. The proceeds of the loan were intended to be, and were, the property of Drybrough. * * *

In June 1957, Drybrough caused to be formed five new corporations. In exchange for all of their stock, Drybrough (together with Drybrough, Jr., in the case of the 620 South Fifth Street property) transferred the real estate which had been encumbered by the 1953 and 1957 loans.

The following tabulation shows the names of newly formed corporations; the date of incorporation and transfer of property to the various corporations; the total fair market value of the property transferred to the various corporations for all purposes of this case other than computation under Rule 50; Drybrough and Drybrough, Jr.'s total adjusted basis in the property transferred to the corporations, at the date of the transfer; the fair market value of the depreciable improvements at the time of the transfer and incorporation; the liability assumed by 620 South Fifth Street, Inc., on the 1957 loan and the portion of the balance due on the 1953 loan assumed by the other corporations; and the unamortized capitalized loan expense applicable to the loan assumed:

Name of corporation	Date of incorporation and transfer of property	Total fair market value of property	Drybrough's total basis	Fair market value of depreciable improvements	Drybrough's basis in depreciable improvements	Liabilities assumed	Unamortized capitalized loan expense
620 South Fifth Street, Inc.	6/28/57	$238,750	$103,840.12	$179,200	$41,875.50	$149,000	$ 557.75
655 South Fifth Street, Inc.	6/1/57	397,250	161,076.16	30,000	157.03	250,000	1,543.29
800 South Fourth Street, Inc.	6/1/57	200,000	83,682.17	49,210	8,831.41	100,000	617.32
720 South Fifth Street, Inc.	6/1/57	212,750	83,293.28	29,975	3,280.42	75,000	462.98
725 South Fourth Street, Inc.	6/1/57	234,400	79,955.94	20,560	635.32	175,000	1,080.28

All of the shares of stock of the new corporations were issued to Drybrough except in the case of 620 South Fifth Street, Inc.; he received 60 percent of the stock thereof and Drybrough, Jr., received 40 percent. 620 South Fifth Street, Inc., assumed the $149,000 balance of the $150,000 1957 loan; the other four corporations each assumed the stated portions of the $600,000 balance of the 1953 loan.

In their 1957 joint Federal income tax return, Drybrough and Marion reported a long-term capital gain of $223,806.12 from the transfers of property to the newly created controlled corporations. This amount represented the amount of mortgage debt assumed by the corporations which was in excess of Drybrough's basis, excluding the 40–percent undivided interest in the 620 South Fifth Street, Inc., property which was owned by Drybrough, Jr., at the date of the transfer. * * *

OPINION

Issue 1

The first issue for decision is whether Drybrough has sustained the burden of proof imposed upon him by section 357(b) and has shown that his principal purpose in certain transfers was a bona fide business purpose and was not the avoidance of Federal income taxes. A short historical sketch of the origin of section 357(b) is helpful in deciding this question.

In 1938 the Supreme Court decided *United States v. Hendler,* 303 U.S. 564 (1938), which held that liabilities assumed in section 351–type transfers were taxable to the transferor. In the aftermath of *Hendler,*

Congress enacted section 112(k) of the 1939 Code, to accord nonrecognition treatment to certain corporate adjustments. In order to differentiate between those transactions which justified nonrecognition and those which did not, section 112(k) placed the burden on the taxpayer of proving by the clear preponderance of the evidence that his principal purpose with respect to the assumption of liability was not to avoid Federal income tax on the exchange and was a bona fide business purpose. If the taxpayer failed of this burden, the liability assumed was to be treated as money received by the taxpayer upon the exchange. Since the assumption of the liability by the corporation in a section 351 tax-free transfer released funds to the transferor taxpayer there was inherent the possibility that this transfer could be used by taxpayers to avoid taxes. The exception in section 112(k) was passed to deal with this situation.

Section 357(b) of the 1954 Code is a reenactment of the above-mentioned exception clause of section 112(k). Section 357(c) adds to what was section 112(k) a provision whereby the excess of the liabilities assumed over the transferor's basis is treated as a gain on the exchange. Drybrough reported gain on the exchange under section 357(c); respondent contends that such gain comes within the purview of section 357(b) and that Drybrough has failed to sustain the burden imposed upon him by such section. We agree with respondent.

Drybrough asserts that his purposes for the transactions herein involved were: Decreasing the amount of his gross estate for death tax purposes, the making of gifts to his son, the perpetuation of family holdings and the flexible management thereof, the avoidance of personal liability on future loans, and the facilitation of improvements that might be added to individual properties. Assuming, *arguendo,* that the above motives constituted bona fide business purposes, Drybrough still has failed to establish that his principal purpose was not that of tax avoidance.

It is always difficult to determine subjective intent, but "taking into consideration the nature of the liability and the circumstances in the light of which the arrangement for the assumption * * * was made," we find that Drybrough has fallen far short of sustaining his burden of proof. While the reasons he has given are not implausible, when they are considered in conjunction with all his activities regarding the properties here involved we are not persuaded that the reasons he has given constituted his principal purpose in this situation. We believe that these reasons were in large part afterthoughts on the part of Drybrough and his tax advisers, assembled to provide an economic justification for a tax-motivated transaction.

In 1953 when Drybrough placed the $700,000 blanket mortgage on his properties, he received approximately $342,000 in cash, which he deposited in his personal checking account. With these proceeds he paid off amounts advanced by UMA and Marion and transferred $208,602 to the Public Garage checking account. The bulk of this latter amount went toward purchasing tax-exempt securities in Marion's name, and none of the proceeds in the 1953 loan were used in connection with the encumbered real estate. Drybrough urges that the focal point of our inquiry should be his purpose with respect to the assumption on the exchange and contends that Congress was concerned with the "taxpayer's specific purpose in having a liability assumed and not with taxpayer's reason for entering into the tax-free exchange." In view of the introductory language of section 357(b), i.e., "taking into consideration the nature of the liability and the circumstances in the light of which the arrangement for the assumption * * * was made," we cannot read this section in the restrictive manner urged by Drybrough. We believe that it is relevant to the 1957 assumption of Drybrough's liabilities by the newly formed corporations to consider the nature of the liability assumed. When the 1953 loan was made to Drybrough, he received more than half of the mortgage proceeds; when the corporations assumed the $600,000 outstanding balance, Drybrough was relieved for all practical purposes of the liability to pay back any of the mortgage indebtedness. The mortgages assumed by the corporations were secured by the properties owned by the corporations, the values of which were well in excess of the amount of the outstanding loan balance. Thus, although Drybrough stood as surety for the corporate indebtedness, he would not, as a practical matter, have been called upon to satisfy the liabilities, except in the most unusual circumstances. Thus, when the entire set of transactions is viewed as a whole, what has occurred is that Drybrough has received a substantial amount of cash which, under his theory, he is not obligated to repay and upon which he will not be required to pay Federal income tax. It is precisely this situation with which Congress intended to deal when it passed section 112(k) of the 1939 Code.

Drybrough's testimony that his business purposes outweighed the tax considerations inherent in this set of transactions has not persuaded us. He appeared to us to be a man of considerable business experience and quite aware of the tax consequences which would result from these transactions. He maintains the largest collection agency in the country, and has many other business interests, especially in the real estate field. He was quite conscious of taxes, having discussed his tax affairs with his accountants, attorneys, and banker. While normally tax planning and reduction of tax liability by legitimate means will not adversely affect a taxpayer, section 357(b) is to be applied if the taxpayer fails to show that tax avoidance was not his principal purpose, regardless of whether such avoidance comes within any other provision of the Code. Drybrough's correspondence with Lowry Watkins and National Life reflect his tax-consciousness. On August 22, 1956, Drybrough stated in a letter to Watkins that he was "eager to mortgage them [the 620 South Fifth Street and another property] to the limit before combining these two properties in a corporation." On February 27, 1957, in a letter to National Life requesting that the 1953 loan be broken into four mortgages, Drybrough stated that he had been "wanting to incorporate some of my properties and interests for quite a long time"; that he would give his son a substantial interest in the equity and pay a gift tax thereon; and that "After clearing up the gift tax situation, we would incorporate the property * * *. *This will bring about a very substantial income tax saving* and there would be no need or purpose in withdrawing the earnings from these corporations. Hence, they would soon be extremely well heeled against adverse conditions or they could retire the mortgage ahead of time, a very good annuity in each instance for my son." (Emphasis supplied.) We are unpersuaded by Drybrough's contention that these letters were merely "salesmanship" on his part in order to be able to obtain the loans he desired.

By having the corporations assume his liabilities, Drybrough was relieved of making the mortgage payments, which could thereafter be made from the earnings of the corporations while his net equity in the properties remained unchanged by the transfer. Further, the corporations received deductions for interest paid and took depreciation on the new, higher bases of the properties.

In August 1956 the property at 620 South Fifth Street was released from the 1953 blanket mortgage. On March 15, 1957, Drybrough remortgaged this property as security for a new $150,000 loan from the Liberty Bank. The proceeds of this loan were not used in connection with the property at 620 South Fifth Street. In May 1957 Drybrough made a gift to his son of an undivided 40–percent interest in the above property. In June 1957 Drybrough and his son transferred their respective interests in the property to a newly formed corporation which assumed the $149,000 outstanding balance on the March 15, 1957, loan. It is Drybrough's contention that the assumption of this mortgage, like the assumption by the four parking lot corporations of portions of the 1953 mortgage, was not done principally to avoid Federal income taxes but was done for a bona fide business purpose. We cannot accept this contention. We accord but little weight to any of Drybrough's contentions as to the substantiality of the business purposes which he contends motivated him to encumber the 620 South Fifth Street property with a new $150,000 loan just 2 months before the incorporation of 620 South Fifth Street, Inc., and its assumption of the loan. The instant situation is very similar to the situation in *W.H. Weaver,* 32 T.C. 411 (1959), affirmed sub nom. *Bryan v. Commissioner,* 281 F.2d 238 (C.A.4, 1960). In that case the petitioner used personal funds and proceeds of loans upon which he was personally liable to acquire land and construct houses thereon. After construction was completed he transferred the property to four corporations in exchange for their stock and assumption of all of his liabilities. The liabilities were approximately $158,000 greater than petitioner's basis in the properties. The corporations obtained FHA loans and paid off the assumed indebtedness immediately. We held that petitioner's principal purpose was the avoidance of Federal income tax and that under section 112(k) of the 1939 Code gain was to be recognized to the extent of the indebtedness assumed.

In the instant case, 620 South Fifth Street, Inc., assumed the $149,000 balance on the $150,000 loan which Drybrough had obtained 2 months prior to its incorporation. Similarly, the four parking lot corporations assumed portions of the 1953 blanket mortgage loan, releasing Drybrough from his primary obligation on this debt. While we are aware of no requirement that Drybrough have paid off the 1953 loan before transferring the properties to the corporations, Drybrough has presented us with no substantial bona fide business purpose for placing the new $150,000 loan on the 620 South Fifth Street property, and, except insofar as it further increased his financial liquidity, no business purpose which was served by the release of the mortgage proceeds for his use. Drybrough contends that he had other business ventures in mind for which he wished to have liquid capital available, but during 1956 and 1957 Drybrough had sizable amounts of tax-exempt securities which were readily marketable and could have been used for his other investments. * * *

Another indication of Drybrough's tax-consciousness in the formation of the corporations and their assumption of the outstanding mortgages is the manner in which Drybrough structured these transactions. His gifts to his son of 40–percent interests in the properties were made in two different fashions. The four parking lot corporations received the properties from Drybrough and *then* he made a gift of 40 percent of their stock to his son, whereas, in the case of the 620 South Fifth Street property, Drybrough first made a gift of a 40–percent undivided interest in the property to his son and then they *both* transferred the property to the newly formed corporation. In this manner, the latter transaction did not come within the literal language of section 1239 and Drybrough expected to receive capital gains thereon. Drybrough has suggested no reason why he handled this transaction differently from those involving the parking lot properties, and since it involved the largest amount of gain attributable to depreciable property, we conclude that it was done primarily because of the tax considerations.

Based upon the above indicia of Drybrough's concern with the tax consequences of the transactions here involved, several other less significant instances of his tax planning, plus the lack of credence which we give to Drybrough's contentions that he was motivated principally by bona fide business purposes, we find that Drybrough has failed to sustain the burden imposed upon him by section 357(b)(2). Because he has failed to sustain this burden, the assumption of Drybrough's liabilities shall be considered as money received by him on the exchange, for purposes of section 351. As stated in the legislative history of section 357(b)(1):

> Where such a tax avoidance purpose exists, the total amount of the liabilities assumed will be considered as money received by the taxpayer and not merely a particular liability with respect to which the tax avoidance purpose existed. * * * [S.Rept. No. 1622, 83d Cong., 2d Sess., p. 270 (1954).]

Drybrough contends that the 620 South Fifth Street transaction should be treated differently than those involving the four parking lot properties, in that the latter group involved the assumption of mortgages which were expanded over the years rather than newly created. We believe that Drybrough had the same purpose with regard to all the properties: the avoidance of tax on the proceeds which he would have after the existing mortgages were retired. We believe that the transfers to each of the five newly formed corporations runs afoul of 357(b), whether we view them as separate, unrelated transfers, or as part of an overall plan. * * *

Problem 23–3

Jane has owned and operated an ice cream store for ten years. All of her equipment and machinery has been depreciated to a tax basis of zero. Jane has bank debt (not a trade payable) of $10,000. Dave wants to invest $25,000 to be used to expand the store. A new corporation, Diary Prince, Inc., is formed. Dave contributes $25,000 for 100 shares. Jane contributes assets with a basis of zero and value of $35,000 for 100 shares. The corporation also assumes Jane's $10,000 debt to the local bank.

1. Does Dave have gain? If so, how much?

2. Does Jane have gain? If so, how much?

3. How is the character of Jane's gain, if any, determined?

4. What if the $10,000 liability constituted payables to suppliers instead of bank debt?

5. What if Jane borrowed the $10,000 from the bank immediately before the incorporation, and either (i) spent the loan proceeds on a new car; (ii) purchased a new cooler which was contributed to the business; or (iii) paid off $10,000 in trade payables?

Chapter 24

TAX BASIS CONSIDERATIONS UPON FORMATION OF A CORPORATION

Code References: §§ 358(a), (b), and (d); 362(a).

Regulations: §§ 1.358–1(a), –2(a)(1)–(3) and (c) –3; 1.362–1(a).

A. INTRODUCTION

When an entrepreneur transfers appreciated property to a corporation in exchange for its stock, both the individual and the corporation have *realized* gain. The appreciation inherent in the shareholder's contributed property has been converted into other property (the shares of corporate stock). Similarly, the corporation's shares, which normally have no basis since they did not cost the corporation anything to issue, are converted into property with a specific market value. As seen in prior chapters, the effect of §§ 351 and 1032, when they apply, is to defer the *recognition* of the realized gain.

The tariff for nonrecognition in the tax law is generally a preservation of the tax basis of the property transferred and received. This is accomplished by either "carrying over" the basis of the transferred property in the hands of the transferee (the corporation) or "substituting" the basis of the property transferred into the property received by the transferor (the shareholder). The effect of such basis preservation is to make the "nonrecognition" of taxable income somewhat of an overstatement. Rather, the gain inherent in the appreciated property is preserved so that on any subsequent realization event, which is not protected by a nonrecognition provision of the Code, the inherent gain will be recognized by the then transferor.

In the case of the organization of a corporation, where two distinct taxpayers are involved, any gain inherent in the property which a shareholder transfers to the corporation is normally preserved both in the newly acquired corporate assets and in the stock received by the transferring shareholder. Thus, if either the corporation (assets) or the

411

shareholder (stock) were to dispose of such property at a price higher than the carried over basis (in the case of the corporation) or substituted basis (in the case of the shareholder's stock), gain would be recognized. In a sense, the transferring shareholder has thereby created the possibility of double taxation by the mere organizational transfer to a C corporation.

A basic corollary rule is that if a taxpayer recognizes income at the time of the transfer, the property received will be entitled to the "benefit" of increasing its tax basis by the amount of gain recognized. In the corporate organization context, such gain normally arises from the receipt of boot, i.e., any property received other than corporate stock. When boot is recognized by the shareholder, it will generally result in an increase in the basis of the property received by the corporation.

B. THE CORPORATION'S BASIS

Section 362(a) provides that the basis of the property received by the transferee corporation in a § 351 transfer will be carried over from the transferring shareholder. As noted, such basis will be increased by the amount of any gain recognized by the transferring shareholder. The assumption of the contributor's liabilities by the corporation does not increase its basis in the assets received unless such assumption results in gain to the transferring shareholder under § 357(b) or (c). However, there are minor exceptions to the basic rule. For instance, if a shareholder transfers property which was personal use property (and therefore not subject to depreciation) in his or her own hands but is business property in the hands of the corporation (such as a personal use vehicle transferred by the shareholder to be used for business purposes by the corporation), the basis of the property in the hands of the corporation for loss and depreciation purposes will be the lower of the shareholder's cost (basis) or value at the time of transfer. See Reg. § 1.167(g)–1. However, for purposes of gain determination, the basis to the corporation is the carryover basis from the shareholder.

Although it is not entirely clear from the Regulations, the corporation will take the shareholder's basis in each asset received in exchange for stock, even though the assets have different levels of appreciation. That is, basis is not shifted from a nonappreciated asset to an appreciated asset based upon their relative values. Rather, the corporation stands in the shoes of the transferor shareholder as to his or her basis in each of the assets transferred. See *P.A. Birren & Son v. Commissioner,* 116 F.2d 718 (7th Cir.1940). The effect of this is generally favorable to the corporation since it does not require that basis be shifted to goodwill or going concern value which will ordinarily have some value but no basis and which is generally depreciated or amortized over a longer period than other assets.

As noted, § 362 permits the transferee corporation to increase the basis of the assets received when the transferor shareholder recognizes boot income. While not entirely clear, it appears that such additional basis bonus to the corporation should be allocated to the transferred assets in proportion of the respective appreciation of the contributed assets, thereby increasing the basis of the assets which gave rise to the gain in the hands of the transferring shareholder.

C. TAX BASIS TO THE TRANSFEROR SHAREHOLDER

In the simplest situation, the stock received by the transferor shareholder obtains its tax basis by substituting the aggregate basis of the assets transferred to the corporation. Section 358(a)(1) states that the basis of the stock received by the shareholder is the same as the basis of the property transferred. The Regulations provide that if more than one class of stock is received by the shareholder, the basis is allocated among the classes in proportion to the fair market values of such classes. See Reg. § 1.358–2(b).

Things become somewhat more complicated in a situation where the transferring shareholder receives boot from the corporation. Boot may be either in the form of cash or other property received by the shareholder from the corporation or it may result from the corporation assuming (or taking property subject to) liabilities of the contributing shareholder. If the boot received is money, basis in the stock received is increased by the amount of gain recognized under § 351(b)(1), but decreased by the amount of cash received. Thus, if the amount of cash received does not exceed the overall gain realized, it would have the effect of a "wash" and the transferor shareholder's basis in the stock would be the adjusted basis of the property transferred to the corporation. The shareholder would, however, have a tax bill to pay on the cash received. If the boot received from the corporation is property other than money, that *property* (not the stock received) takes a basis in the hands of the transferor shareholder equal to its fair market value. Such fair market value will also be the measure of the gain which must be recognized by the transferor shareholder in the event that the aggregate property transferred by such shareholder to the corporation is appreciated by at least the amount of the value of the boot. Once again, this has the net effect similar to the receipt of cash boot since the basis of the stock received by the shareholder continues to be that of the assets transferred. The boot property, however, generally receives a step-up in basis to fair market value at the cost of constituting income to the transferor shareholder.

REVENUE RULING 85–164
1985–2 CB 117

ISSUE

May a transferor determine the bases and holding periods of stock and securities received in a transfer under section 351 of the Internal Revenue Code by designating the specific property to be exchanged for particular stock or securities?

FACTS

A, an individual, was engaged in a business as a sole proprietor. The assets of the sole proprietorship consisted of trade accounts receivable with an adjusted basis of zero and a fair market value of 60*x* dollars, machinery with an adjusted basis of 5*x* dollars and a fair market value of 10*x* dollars, and real estate (land and building) with an adjusted basis of 25*x* dollars and a fair market value of 30*x* dollars. *A* had held the real estate and machinery for over one year. Both the real estate and machinery were property described in section 1231 of the Code.

In order to limit personal liability, *A* transferred all of the assets associated with the sole proprietorship to a new corporation, *Y*, in exchange for all of *Y*'s stock and securities. *A* transferred the accounts receivable to *Y* in exchange for 100 shares of common stock, the fair market value of which was 60*x* dollars. *A* transferred the machinery and real estate to *Y* in exchange for [preferred stock], which had a * * * fair market value of 40*x* dollars. The selection of specific items for exchange was made to allocate assets with a high basis and long-term holding period to the securities.

LAW AND ANALYSIS

Section 351(a) of the Code provides that no gain or loss will be recognized if property is transferred to a corporation by a person solely in exchange for stock * * * in such corporation and immediately after the exchange such person is in control (as defined in section 368(c)) of the corporation.

Section 358(a)(1) of the Code and section 1.358–1 of the Income Tax Regulations provide that in the case of an exchange to which section 351 applies in which only non-recognition property is received, the basis of all of the stock * * * received in the exchange shall be the same as the basis of all property exchanged therefor. Section 358(b)(1) directs that, under regulations prescribed by the Secretary, the basis determined under subsection (a)(1) shall be allocated among the properties permitted to be received without the recognition of gain or loss.

Section 1.358–2(a) of the regulations prescribes rules for the allocation of basis among nonrecognition property received in corporate reorganization exchanges governed by sections 354, 355, 356 and 371(b). In all other cases, including exchanges under section 351, section 1.358–2(b)(2) provides that the basis of property transferred shall be allocated among all the stock * * * received in proportion to the fair market values of the stock of each class * * *.

Section 1223(1) and section 1.1223–1(a) of the regulations require that, in determining the period for which a taxpayer has held property received in an exchange, there shall be included the period for which he held the property exchanged if (i) in the taxpayer's hands the property received has the same basis in whole or in part as the property exchanged and (ii) for exchanges after March 1, 1954, the property exchanges were at the time of exchange a capital asset as defined in section

1221 or property used in a trade or business as described in section 1231.
* * *

Rev.Rul. 68–55, 1968–1 C.B. 140, holds that when property is transferred to a corporation under section 351(a) of the Code each asset must be considered transferred separately in exchange for a proportionate share of each of the various categories of the total consideration received.

In the instant case, A formed Y by transferring all of the business assets of the sole proprietorship to Y in exchange solely for all of Y's stock * * *. Y will continue to carry on the business that A conducted, and A will remain in control of Y. The transfer, therefore, is subject to section 351 of the Code, with the bases and holding periods of the Y stock * * * in the hands of A determined under sections 358 and 1223 of the Code respectively.

Holding

A may not determine the bases and holding periods of the Y stock * * * received by designating specific property to be exchanged for particular stock or securities. Under sections 1.358–1 and 1.358–2(b)(2) of the regulations, the aggregate basis of the property transferred is allocated among the stock * * * in proportion to the fair market values of each class. The holding period of the Y stock * * * received by A is determined by referring to the assets deemed exchanged for each portion of the stock * * *. The aggregate basis of the property transferred was $30x$ dollars. Since the stock * * * A received had fair market values of $60x$ dollars and $40x$ dollars, respectively, a basis of $18x$ dollars ($60x/100x \times 30x$) is allocated to the [preferred stock] received. In addition, each share of Y stock * * * received by A has a split holding period and a split basis for purposes of determining long-term or short-term capital gain or loss. That fraction of each share of Y stock * * * attributable to the real estate and machinery ($40x/100x$) is traded as including the period (over one year) for which A held the real estate and machinery and has a basis solely attributable to the real estate and machinery (*e.g.*, the $40x/100x$ of each share of stock attributable to the real estate and machinery will have a basis of $.18x$ dollars ($18x/100$ shares)). The fraction of each share of Y stock * * * attributable to the accounts receivable ($60x/100x$) has a holding period beginning on the day after the exchange and has a zero basis. If part or all of the stock * * * received in the exchange is disposed of at a time when the split holding period is relevant in determining tax liability, the same fractions will be applied to apportion the amount realized among the above components of the stock * * *.

D. LIABILITY ASSUMPTION

If the transferee corporation assumes the liability of the transferor, § 358(d) provides that the amount of the liability is treated for basis purposes as money received by the transferor shareholder. Unless there is a tax avoidance motive, this does not necessarily mean that it is recognized as income to the transferor. Rather, to the extent of such liability assumption, it merely reduces the basis of the shareholder in the stock received. If the liability assumption exceeds the basis of the property transferred by the shareholder, gain to the extent of the excess will result to the shareholder under § 357(c) at the time of transfer. If the liability is less than the aggregate basis of the properties transferred to the corporation, the effect is merely to reduce the basis in the transferor's stock and defer the gain recognition until the shareholder subsequently disposes of his or her stock in a taxable transaction.

Problem 24–1

Sue and Tom, sole law practitioners, decide to join forces by forming Whiplash, P.C., a professional corporation. Sue transfers all of her furniture and equipment with a basis of $5,000 and a value of $10,000. Tom contributes $5,000 cash and computer equipment, which has a basis of $4,000 and a value of $20,000, but which is encumbered by a debt of $15,000. The debt is assumed by the P.C. Tom and Sue each receive 100 shares of the stock of the P.C.

1. Do either Sue or Tom recognize gain?

2. What is the basis of Sue and Tom in their stock?

3. What is P.C.'s basis for Sue's furniture and equipment?

4. What is the basis of Tom's computer in the hands of Whiplash, P.C.?

5. Does P.C. recognize gain?

Problem 24–2

Bob and Ted own equal shares in Jalopy Rentals, Inc., an operating used car rental agency. Bob contributes $20,000 cash to the ongoing business and receives an additional 100 shares of common stock and 100 shares of 8% cumulative preferred stock with a face value of $10,000. Ted contributes three vehicles, a truck with basis of $6,000 and a value of $10,000, a van with basis of $2,000 and a value of $7,000, and a car with basis of $7,000 and a value of $4,000. In exchange, Ted receives 200 additional shares of common stock and a "junker" car with a basis and a value of $1,000.

1. What is Bob's basis in his stock?

2. What is Ted's basis in his stock?

3. What is Ted's basis in the junker car?

4. What is the basis to the corporation for the three vehicles contributed by Ted?

5. Does the corporation have gain on the transfer of the junker car?

Chapter 25

CORPORATE DEBT *VERSUS* EQUITY

Code References: §§ 165(g); 166; 385; and 1361(a), (b).
Regulations: §§ 1.1361–1(1)(1)–(2)(iv), (4)(i)–(ii), (5).

A. INTRODUCTION

When an investor advances funds or other property to a corporation, he or she receives, in return, a financial stake in the corporation which constitutes either debt or equity. The corporate books and records will generally reflect the advance as one or the other, and corporate officers will normally make appropriate distributions of stock (if the contribution is equity) or a note or other debt instrument (if the contribution is a debt). State law allows a corporation to accept contributions as either equity or debt, or a combination of the two. Such advances may be made by new investors or by those who already have a stake in the corporate business. From a non-tax standpoint, the investor may wish to have the contribution characterized as debt, rather than equity, so that creditor remedies, including a forced bankruptcy, are available to enforce repayment. The holder of an equity position generally has no such remedies to enforce repayment of the contribution unless and until the corporation is liquidated.

1. ORGANIZATION

From a tax standpoint, the characterization of an advance to a corporation as either debt or equity is important to both the investor and the corporation. Its significance surfaces at various points in the life of the entity. At the time of a corporation's organization, a transfer of property under § 351 will be tax-deferred only if the transferring shareholder receives the *stock* of the corporation in exchange for the contribution. To the extent that corporate debt is received for appreciated property instead of stock, the protection of § 351 will not be afforded and the transaction will be taxable with the debt being treated as moot.

2. OPERATION

During its operating life, a corporation may make distributions to its investors. Distributions on equity are treated, under §§ 301 and 302, differently than distributions on debt. From the corporation's tax standpoint, none of the equity-based distributions, including (1) a dividend, (2) a return of investor capital, or (3) a redemption or liquidation of outstanding shares, are expenditures which yield tax deductions. The payment of interest to a corporate creditor, however, generally constitutes a deductible corporate expense, even if the creditor is also a shareholder. On the investor side, a dividend or interest received from a corporation will generally be taxable as ordinary income.

Payments made by a corporation in redemption of stock may be a return of capital, capital gain, or a dividend under the rules of §§ 301 and 302. In a closely held corporation, the dividend possibility is particularly strong since the safe harbors of § 302(b) are more difficult to meet than in a widely held entity. The recipient of a debt repayment, on the other hand, will be taxable only to the extent that the payment constitutes interest. If it represents a repayment of debt principal, it is not taxable. Depending upon the characteristics of the distributing corporation and the structure of its shareholder group, it may be advantageous for either the corporation or the distributee investor to seek debt-based characterization for certain corporate distributions and equity-based characterization for others.

3. LIQUIDATION OR DISSOLUTION

When a corporation terminates and dissolves, the status of a shareholder's investment as either debt or equity can cause disparate tax results. Distributions in liquidation of a corporation may be a return of stock basis or a capital gain under § 331. Repayment of debt in a corporate liquidation is taxable only to the extent it represents interest, in which case it is ordinary income. A shareholder's basis in stock of a worthless corporation generally generates a long-term capital loss to its holder pursuant to § 165(g). When corporate debt, on the other hand, becomes worthless, it may, under § 166, generate a short-term capital loss or even ordinary loss to its holder depending upon the circumstances under which the advance was made.

Because of the different treatment described above, considerable tax litigation has arisen over the years as to the proper characterization of a corporate investment as debt or equity. Because of the variables involved, the Service and the taxpayer may exchange positions and arguments depending upon the facts of the particular case involved. Due to the complexity of the problem and the variety of hybrid corporate financing instruments which have developed, attempts to resolve the debt/equity dilemma through legislation and Treasury Regulations have essentially failed. While certain "bright line" tests have arisen, the determination of whether the advance of an investor constitutes debt on one hand, or equity on the other, has been reduced in the tax law to a "facts and circumstances" test. The original documentation and characterization of the investment by the corporation and its advisers is often a key factor.

The ensuing sections of this chapter analyze the other factors which have been developed by the judiciary in an effort to distinguish debt from equity. They also examine the meager statutory and regulatory guidance given by Congress and the Treasury Department. Finally, there is an examination of certain planning techniques available in structuring a corporate investment between debt and equity.

B. FACTORS DEVELOPED BY THE COURTS IN DISTINGUISHING DEBT FROM EQUITY

Frequent tax litigation has not resulted in a clear division between debt and equity. Instead, the courts, over time, have developed a catalogue of factors, some or all of which are applied to reach a solution in a given factual situation. The facts and circumstances test factors often lead to structural contortions by taxpayers seeking to bring themselves within one category or the other. In such cases as *Fin Hay Realty Co. v. United States*, 398 F.2d 694 (3d Cir.1968), and *Hardman v. United States*, 827 F.2d 1409 (9th Cir.1987), courts have identified approximately a dozen factors to be examined in distinguishing a debt from an equity investment. These factors include subjective considerations, such as the intent of the parties and the amount of relative risk involved in the investment, as well as objective factors, such as the debt/equity ratio of the corporation and the proportionality of the debt holdings in comparison to the shareholdings of the corporation. Additional factors that have been utilized are:

(1) The designation of the certificates evidencing the investment as either stock on the one hand, or a note or bond on the other;

(2) The presence or absence of a fixed maturity or due date;

(3) Whether the repayment is contingent upon the success of the corporate business;

(4) The right of the holder to enforce the payment as a debt;

(5) The interest holder's participation in management;

(6) The status of the instrument as it relates to other corporate creditors (i.e., is the investment subordinate to other debt and therefore dependent upon the success of the corporate business for repayment?);

(7) The payment of "interest" being required only out of the earnings of the corporation; and

(8) The ability of the corporation to obtain debt from outside financing sources.

At bottom, the analysis reverts to a "smell" test, focusing upon whether the investor looks like a creditor or looks like an equity investor.

A creditor generally has the right to receive the repayment of the debt at a given time with a fixed rate of return. A creditor's investment is often secured and its repayment is not necessarily contingent upon the overall success of the business of the entity. A creditor generally does not participate in the management of a corporation.

An equity investor, on the other hand, generally has no right to receive a return of the investment at a specific time or at any specific rate. He or she generally has a greater "upside" profit potential than would a creditor in the event that the business is successful. The shareholder generally has the right to participate, at least through the election of directors, in the management and operation of the corporation. An equity investor generally receives, upon the sale or liquidation of the corporation, a return of the investment only after all creditors of the corporation have been paid. While these distinctions appear to be relatively straightforward, they have, in application, proven not to be so.

HARDMAN v. UNITED STATES

827 F.2d 1409 (9th Cir.1987).

TANG, CIRCUIT JUDGE:

Rudolph A. and Frances N. Hardman and Hardman, Inc. appeal district court decisions upholding tax deficiencies assessed by the Internal Revenue Service. The taxpayers characterized a $109,568 payment by Hardman, Inc. as part consideration for the purchase of property from Mrs. Hardman. The Hardmans treated the payment as capital gain and Hardman, Inc. added the payment to its basis in the property. The IRS characterized the payment as a dividend from Hardman, Inc. to Frances Hardman taxable as ordinary income to Mrs. Hardman and improperly added to the corporation's basis on resale.

I.

Frances Hardman owns twenty-five percent of Hardman, Inc. Together, Mr. and Mrs. Hardman own eighty-nine percent. In February, 1968, Frances Hardman purchased Hale Field, a 100 acre tract of undeveloped land, for $225,000. She made a downpayment and executed a secured promissory note for the remainder of the purchase price. Unable to keep up with the payments, she conveyed the property to Hardman, Inc. in 1972. By this time, Mrs. Hardman had made three annual payments on the promissory note. Hardman, Inc. reimbursed Mrs. Hardman for the three annual payments and the down payment; assumed the promissory note; and executed the following contract:

> In consideration of Frances N. Hardman selling her one hundred (100) acres of Hale Field property to Hardman, Inc. at her cost, Hardman, Inc. hereby agrees to pay Frances N. Hardman one-third of any net profit that Hardman, Inc. may derive from said property.

The contract appeared on corporate stationery, and was signed by Rudolph Hardman as president.

Hardman, Inc. later purchased twenty acres of land adjoining Hale Field. In 1977, the corporation resold the property, including the additional twenty acres, for $600,000. It paid Mrs. Hardman $109,568, one third of the net profit attributable to the 100 acres of Hale Field. The Hardmans reported the payment as gain from the sale of real property and took a corresponding capital gains deduction. Hardman, Inc. added the payment to its basis in the property and calculated its capital gains accordingly.

The IRS assessed deficiencies against the Hardmans and Hardman, Inc. * * *

The district court concluded that the 1972 transaction between Mrs. Hardman and Hardman, Inc. was an equity investment by Mrs. Hardman in the corporation and that the 1977 payment was a dividend taxable as ordinary income. The court reasoned that the difference between a stockholder and a creditor is that the stockholder accepts the corporate risk of loss in return for possible profit participation. The creditor does not undertake such risk. The court concluded that the 1972 transaction more closely resembled a contribution to capital because the instrument executed by Hardman, Inc. did not contain the traditional indicia of a debt instrument: "an unconditional obligation to pay a principal sum certain, with interest, on or before a fixed maturity date not ambiguously remote in the future." The court held that "Mrs. Hardman and Corporation are essentially participants in a joint venture with Mrs. Hardman contributing the capital...." The Hardmans and Hardman, Inc. timely appeal.

II.

Substance, not form, controls the characterization of a taxable transaction. Courts will not tolerate the use of mere formalisms solely to alter tax liabilities. On the other hand, we recognize that tax consequences are an important consideration in many commercial transactions and the mere fact that a bona fide transaction is arranged in such a way that it confers tax benefits does not invalidate the transaction.

Whether the $109,568 payment in 1977 was in satisfaction of an obligation arising from a sale or a dividend cannot be viewed in isolation but must be considered in the context of the overall transaction. The parties agree that the payment correlates to the 1972 property transfer. In this context, characterization of the payment turns on the nature of the property transfer. The Hardmans have characterized this transaction as a sale of property financed in part by a loan to the corporation. Mrs. Hardman's inability to keep up with the payments serves as a valid business reason for transferring the land in exchange for uncertain future profits. Courts closely scrutinize the economic reality of such transactions to determine whether the taxpayer's characterization is genuine or whether the transaction was, as the IRS contends here, a sale in name only. If a transfer by a shareholder to her corporation is found to be an equity investment, payments of "interest" or "principal" by the corporation will be treated as constructive dividends or redemptions. This is because Congress has chosen to tax distributions to shareholders of corporate earnings and profits at ordinary income tax rates. We cannot condone taxpayer attempts to bleed off corporate profits at capital gains rates. On the other hand, Congress has chosen to tax gains from the sale of property at lower capital gains rates. We will not permit the IRS to characterize genuine gains from the sale of property as ordinary income.

This court has identified eleven factors which, to varying degrees, influence resolution of the question of whether a transfer to a corporation by a shareholder is a sale (debt) or a contribution to capital (equity).[1]

(1) the names given to the certificates evidencing the indebtedness;

(2) the presence or absence of a maturity date;

(3) the source of the payments;

(4) the right to enforce payment of principal and interest;

(5) participation and management;

(6) a status equal to or inferior to that of regular corporate creditors;

(7) the intent of the parties;

(8) "thin" or adequate capitalization;

(9) identity of interest between creditor and stockholder;

(10) payment of interest only out of "dividend" money;

(11) the ability of the corporation to obtain loans from outside lending institutions.

No one factor is decisive. The court must examine the particular circumstances of each case. "The object of the inquiry is not to count factors, but to evaluate them."

---

1. In 1969, Congress authorized the Secretary of the Treasury to prescribe regulations setting forth the factors to be considered in determining whether an advance is debt or equity. 26 U.S.C. § 385 (1982). In the statute, Congress set forth five factors which the Secretary could, but was not required, to include in the regulations:

(1) whether there is a written unconditional promise to pay on demand or on a specified date a sum certain in money in return for an adequate consideration in money or monies worth, and to pay a fixed rate of interest,

(2) whether there is subordination to or preference over any indebtedness of the corporation,

(3) the ratio of debt to equity of the corporation,

(4) whether there is convertibility into the stock of the corporation, and

(5) the relationship between holdings of stock in the corporation and holdings of the interest in question.

26 U.S.C. § 385(b) (1982). Thirteen years later, in 1982, the Secretary promulgated regulations. However, the Secretary withdrew those regulations on July 6, 1983, and now it appears likely that the Treasury Department will recommend repeal of § 385. *See* B. Bittker & J. Eustice ¶ 4.05 (1986 Cumm.Supp. No. 3).

In upholding the determination of the Commissioner, the district court cited only one of the eleven factors, the absence of a maturity date and other indicia of bona fide indebtedness. The court also emphasized the fact that this was not a traditional arms length transaction but one between related parties. Although a transaction between a stockholder and her corporation invites close scrutiny, a transaction must not be disregarded simply because it was not at arms length. It is true that "[t]he typical indicia of a debt are a sum certain payable over a specific period of time at a stipulated rate of interest." However, there is "no general requirement that transactions be entered into in a conventional way for them to be recognized as having the usual tax result."

We review for clear error a district court's determination of whether a transaction between a shareholder and her company constitutes a sale or a contribution to capital. When a lower court has overemphasized one of the eleven debt-equity factors, "this court has consistently been disposed to reverse." However, we will reverse only if, in considering all of the factors, we find that the court clearly erred.

1. *Names Given to the Certificates Evidencing the Indebtedness.* The issuance of a stock certificate indicates an equity contribution and the issuance of a bond, debenture or note indicates a bona fide indebtedness. The document executed by Hardman, Inc. lacks a name, but it contains language typical of a promissory note: "[I]n consideration of ...," "Hardman, Inc. hereby agrees to pay...." The document contains no language typical of a stock certificate such as reference to dividend, voting or redemption rights. This factor weighs in favor of a finding that the transaction was a sale.

2. *The Presence or Absence of a Maturity Date.* The absence of a fixed maturity date indicates that repayment is tied to the fortunes of the business. The contract contains no fixed maturity date. Furthermore, as the district court pointed out, repayment is not unconditional, nor is the amount of principal and interest stated in a sum certain. These are important factors and the district court concluded that they compelled a finding that the property transfer was a contribution to capital. Although we find merit in the court's finding, we note that the document contains more of the traditional indicia of a debt instrument than that of an equity instrument. Although there is no fixed maturity date, repayment is tied to a fairly certain event—sale of the property—and guarantees payment of an amount relative to the value of the property. An equity instrument, on the other hand, contains no guarantee of dividend payments in any amount at any time.

3. *The Source of Payments.* If repayment is not dependent upon earnings, the transaction more resembles a sale. On its face, this factor seems to weigh in favor of a finding of equity because the payment came from corporate profits. However, the payment did not come from the general earnings and profits of the corporation but rather profits from the resale of this particular tract of land. The contract entitled Mrs. Hardman to receive one-third of the profits from resale even if the

company suffered a loss in its overall operations. A distribution is a dividend only to the extent of the corporation's accumulated earnings and profits. That this payment is tied to the sale of the property, and not the overall fortunes of the corporation, makes it logically distinct from a payment out of earnings and profits. Accordingly, this factor supports a finding that the transaction was in satisfaction of the obligation arising from the original sale rather than a dividend distribution.

4. *The Right to Enforce the Payment of Principal and Interest.* The presence of an enforceable obligation to pay a share of the profits on resale of the property supports a finding that the transfer was a sale. Mrs. Hardman had an absolute right to enforce the terms of the contract. This feature distinguishes the contract from a stock instrument in which there is no right to enforce payment of dividends. The fact that payment was contingent upon the resale of the property does not make the contract unenforceable.

5. *Participation in Management.* If a stockholder's percentage interest in the corporation or voting rights increase as a result of the transfer, it will contribute to a finding that the transfer was a contribution to capital rather than a sale. Mrs. Hardman's percentage of ownership and control did not change as a result of the transfer.

6. *A Status Equal to or Inferior to that of Regular Corporate Creditors.* Equity participants take a subordinate position to creditors regarding right to payment upon liquidation. There is no evidence that the parties subordinated Mrs. Hardman's position to those of non-stockholder creditors. Presumably she had an equal right to enforce payment, indicating that the transfer was a sale.

7. *The Intent of the Parties.* All of the objective evidence points to a conclusion that the parties intended the transaction to be a sale rather than a contribution to capital. The document executed by Hardman, Inc. contains language typical of a promissory note. The written argument and deposition submitted by the Hardmans and Hardman, Inc. indicate that the parties intended the transaction to be a sale. The government argues that the transaction "clearly was designed to improperly convert a subsequent dividend distribution into capital gain" but offers nothing to support this assertion. We note that the purpose of this entire inquiry is to decipher the true intent of the parties. All eleven factors contribute to this evaluation. However, the objective evidence of intent one-sidedly favors the interpretation given by the Hardmans.

8. *"Thin" or Adequate Capitalization.* Thin capitalization evidences a capital contribution. A high ratio of debt to equity tends to show that the obligation is unrealistic or beyond the corporation's ability to perform. The district court found that the "[c]orporation did not appear to be 'thinly' capitalized but, rather, appeared to be an on-going, viable corporation with assets other than the property acquired from Mrs. Hardman." This finding supports a conclusion that the transfer was a sale.

9. *Identity of Interest Between Creditor and Stockholder.* If the property or funds advanced is in proportion to the stockholder's capital interest, it will lend to a finding that the transfer was a contribution to capital. Here, only Mrs. Hardman transferred property to the corporation and the corporation distributed money only to her in connection with the sale of Hale Field. There was no correlation whatsoever between her percentage interest in the corporation and the amount of money distributed to her.

10. *Payment of Interest Only Out of "Dividend" Money.* This factor is essentially the same as the third factor, "the source of the payments." As we noted earlier, the payment related to profits from the sale of the land not overall earnings and profits. The company was obligated to pay regardless of whether it had accumulated earnings and profits. Therefore, the payment was not from "dividend" money.

11. *The Ability of the Corporation to Obtain Loans from Outside Lending Institutions.* If a corporation is able to borrow funds from outside sources, the transaction has the appearance of a bona fide indebtedness and indicates that the shareholder acted in the same manner toward the corporation as "ordinary reasonable creditors would have acted." If no reasonable creditor would have sold property to the corporation with payments to be made in the future, an inference arises that a reasonable shareholder would not do so either. The district court found that Hardman, Inc. was an ongoing, viable corporation with assets other than the property acquired from Mrs. Hardman. Presumably Hardman, Inc. could easily obtain financing from other sources and the government makes no assertion to the contrary. This factor weighs in favor of a finding that the obligation accompanying the transfer of the property to Hardman, Inc. was a bona fide indebtedness.

III.

Our analysis of this transaction in light of these eleven factors leads us to conclude that Mrs. Hardman's transfer of the Hale Field property to Hardman, Inc. was a sale rather than a contribution to capital. We recognize that the lack of formalities in the instrument executed by Hardman, Inc., raises the suspicion that the transaction was a disguised attempt to extract earnings and profits from the corporation at favorable capital gains tax rates. However, we find that the trial court erred in relying on this sole factor and neglecting to consider fully the several other factors, all of which point to the opposite conclusion. Accordingly, the decision of the district court is reversed and this case is remanded for a determination of the amount of excess taxes paid by the Hardmans and Hardman, Inc.

C.   SECTION 385 AND PROPOSED REGULATIONS

The uncertainty created by the complex analytical formula developed by the judiciary and the inability of the Service to resolve definitional problems through administrative pronouncements were both motivating factors behind the enactment of § 385 in 1969. Section 385(a) authorizes the Treasury Department to clarify the law in this area through the issuance of Regulations. Section 385(b) gives the Treasury Department certain basic guidelines to follow in developing its Regulations. The § 385(b) five factors are apparently those of the previously developed judicial factors which Congress felt were most important to be inserted into the defining Regulations. The theory of the enactment was that the precise distinctions between debt and equity were incapable of definition by statute but, with proper guidance and regulatory authority, the Treasury Department could utilize the legislative mandate to develop rules which would put litigation in this area largely to rest.

In March of 1980, nearly eleven years after the enactment of § 385, Regulations were proposed. The Regulations adopted a relatively revolutionary approach which provoked a deluge of commentary and testimony from tax practitioners and taxpayers. On December 29, 1980, in the eleventh hour of the Carter administration, the final Regulations were adopted. Although considerably more narrow in scope than the Proposed Regulations, they incorporated the same general objectives by adding certainty to the law and abandoning the "all-or-nothing" approach to classifying an advance as debt or equity in favor of a "valuation approach" wherever possible. The valuation approach called for instruments issued by corporations to be generally accepted as debt or equity in the form issued by the corporation but to be valued by discounting or increasing their face value. That is, a debt instrument issued by a corporation to a shareholder worth less than its face value was treated as debt to the extent of its value but, to the extent of such excess, was treated as a contribution of the capital of the corporation. If, on the other hand, a debt instrument had a fair market value greater than its face, the contributor, if also a shareholder, would receive a § 301 distribution as a result of the premium.

Although the Regulations were adopted in final form at the end of 1980, their effective date was delayed several times in order to provide time for additional comment. During the extension period, new Proposed Regulations were issued and finally the entire project was withdrawn in 1983. No new Regulations have been issued since that date, thereby essentially rendering § 385 nugatory and returning to the judiciary the issue of distinguishing debt from equity.

D. DEBT v. EQUITY IN S CORPORATIONS

The categorization of corporate instruments as either debt or equity may be particularly important in S corporations. Only small business corporations can be S corporations under § 1361(a)(1). A corporation which has more than one class of stock often cannot qualify as a small business corporation under § 1361(b)(1)(D). Only differences in voting rights are permitted among different classes of S corporation stock. If there are differences in dividend, liquidation, or other rights, an S election is not available and a corporation which has made an S election is disqualified for any year in which disqualifying classes of stock are deemed to be outstanding.

If an obligation of the corporation, even though denominated as debt, is ultimately determined to be equity, it may constitute a second class of stock which will disqualify an apparent S election. The Regulations under § 1.1361–1(1) specifically address this issue. The Regulations provide safe harbor debt treatment for certain obligations which are (1) clearly traditional debt, (2) short-term unwritten advances from a shareholder to an S corporation which do not exceed $10,000 in the aggregate, and (3) any debt instruments which are held by the owners of the S corporation in the same proportion as their outstanding stock even if that debt would be treated as equity under general tax principles. That is, even though the advance appears to be equity, it will not be treated as a second class of stock so long as it is made proportionally by the S corporation shareholders.

If the above safe harbors are not met; if the debt instrument constitutes equity under the judicial principles described in the prior sections of this chapter; and if a principal purpose of the corporate financial arrangement is to avoid the one class of stock rules under § 1361, then the purported debt instrument will be treated as a second class of stock and disqualify the S election. As a matter of practice, such disqualifications take place after a tax audit or litigation, resulting in retroactive disqualification, thereby converting the corporation from an S corporation to a C corporation for prior years. On the other hand, the Service has been singularly unsuccessful in having purported corporate debt treated as a second class of stock under § 1361.

E. DEBT/EQUITY PLANNING POSSIBILITIES

Many tax advisers, in organizing a new corporation, deliberately divide investor contributions between debt and equity. By staying within the established judicial rules to ensure that the debt is not subsequently recharacterized as a form of equity, the tax planner may provide a vehicle for tax-advantaged corporate distributions to investors in the event that the corporation's business is successful. The splitting of the investment may also create a more advantageous tax deduction to the investor in the event that the corporation is not successful.

Assuming that judicial rules relating to debt creation are complied with and assuming no state law restrictions on the issuance of such debt, the combination of debt and equity is often a wise planning tool. The distribution of money from an operating corporation in repayment of debt principal is not taxable income to the recipient, even though he or she may also be a shareholder of the corporation. The payment of interest on such debt is deductible to the corporation, whereas a dividend payment on the stock would not be. Thus, for instance, if the corporation issued stock and debt in equal proportions at the time of its creation, so that the debt/equity ratio of the corporation is one-to-one, and if the debt bore all of the other badges of a bona fide debt, such as a reasonable rate of interest, security, a fixed due date, etc., the debt instrument would provide an otherwise unavailable vehicle for the distribution of accumulated corporate funds to shareholders from an operating C corporation.

In addition, the existence of debt at the outset of the corporation's existence may, if the corporation ultimately proves successful, be a vehicle to postpone liability to the corporation for penalty taxes on accumulated earnings under § 531. *See* discussion at Chapter 33. The necessity of retaining cash or working capital to pay debts, including shareholder debts, may constitute a valid reason for the nonpayment of dividends to shareholders, such retention being a "reasonable need of the business."

Problem 25–1

George and Rich form a new corporation, Ground Investors, Inc., to invest in speculative, undeveloped real estate. George and Rich each contribute $100 at the time of the incorporation. Ten dollars of the contribution is reflected on the corporate books as equity and George and Rich are each issued 10 shares of the corporation's common stock. The remaining $90 contribution is evidenced by the corporation's promissory note. The note is unsecured and payable only when the property to be purchased by the corporation is sold. The interest payable on the note is one-half of any net profits realized by the corporation on the sale of the property to be purchased. The corporation utilizes the $200 contributed by Rich and George to purchase undeveloped real estate. The property is held by the corporation for a period of two years when it is sold for $400. Following the sale, $180 of the sale proceeds are utilized to repay the principal debt of $90 to each George and Rich. They each also receive $50 as interest on their debt payment. The remaining $120 of the sale proceeds is distributed $60 each to Rich and George as a corporate operating distribution.

1. Should the debt portion of the contribution by Rich and George be treated as equity?

2. What is the tax result to the corporation if the debt characterization of the $90 contributed by each of George and Rich is upheld?

3. What if the entire contribution of $100 by each shareholder is treated as equity?

4. What if Rich and George had made an S election for the corporation?

5. What if, in the initial organization, the debt/equity contributions were $50 each, the debt bore interest at a rate of 10% with an incentive "kicker" of one-third of the corporate profits, and the note was due three years following its date of issuance, regardless of whether the property was sold?

Chapter 26

PLANNING FOR BUSINESS LOSSES OR BUSINESS FAILURE

Code References: §§ 1211; 1244; 1366(a) and (d); 1367(a)(2)(B).

Regulation: §§ 1.1244(a)–1, (b)–1, and (c)–1.

A. INTRODUCTION

An entrepreneur commencing a new business or incorporating an existing business will generally be optimistic about its success. It is the often unpleasant task of the tax adviser to point out that many small businesses are unsuccessful. Consequently, initial tax planning includes putting into place the proper assurances that financial losses which might occur in the business will result in all available tax savings to the corporation or its owners. Many of the tax advantages flowing from corporate business losses are elective. The business attorney must therefore be particularly alert to ensure that the appropriate choices are made when the corporation is initially formed.

If the corporate form of business operation is selected and no initial tax planning is done, adverse tax consequences can result if the business fails. For instance, if a businessman contributes money or property to a corporation for its stock and the business is economically unsuccessful, the resulting tax losses will accrue only to the corporation itself and, unless certain of the planning techniques discussed below are employed, will not be available to benefit the entrepreneur himself. Such losses are "trapped" in the corporation and may never be usable for the benefit of any taxpayer if the corporation never generates taxable income. If the business becomes so unsuccessful that the corporate stock held by the owner must be sold at less than its tax basis or, worse, abandoned as worthless, the resulting loss to the shareholder typically will be treated as a capital loss. Under § 1211(b), net capital losses (capital losses in excess of capital gains for the year) may be offset against the ordinary income of an individual only to the extent of $3,000 per year. Thus, an entrepreneur who suffers an actual economic loss of $100,000 through the failure of his or her business corporation can, unless proper planning is in place, deduct only $3,000 per year of such loss against any ordinary income.

The adverse results described above were, in fact, the general rule until Congress enacted certain curative provisions relating to the use of small business corporations. Since the utilization of a sole proprietorship or a partnership in the above-described scenario would result in deductible operating losses to the entrepreneur, Congress attempted to make available the same ordinary loss possibility to small businesses operating in the corporate form. Two of the concepts introduced into the Code by the Small Business Tax Revision Act of 1958 were "Section 1244 stock" and the "Subchapter S corporation." If small business stock qualifies as § 1244 stock, an entrepreneur incurring a loss on such stock can, within certain limits, deduct it as an ordinary (rather than capital) loss against other income. If a small business corporation elects to be taxed as an S corporation, the operating losses it incurs may be deducted by its owners (rather than by the corporate entity itself) on an annual basis as they are incurred. Eliminating the corporate entity as a taxpayer allows the qualifying S corporation to be taxed as a partnership for the purpose of passing losses through to its owners. Like the proprietorship or partnership, such losses may be subject to other limitations including the passive loss rules and at risk limitations which are discussed at Chapter 7.

In a less dramatic gesture, Congress has also allowed the corporate taxpayer to make an election to amortize the expenses incurred in its organization over a period of five years. Section 248 allows such amortization only if a written election is made. If the election is not made, the expenses are capitalized at the corporate level. At the shareholder level, the amount invested by the corporate owner in such expenses would be added to the basis for the stock and would be deductible only if the stock became worthless or was sold, and then limited to a capital loss unless § 1244 were applicable. If the election is made, however, the organizational expenses (such as legal fees, incorporation fees, and other costs incurred in organizing the corporate entity) may be amortized over 60 months and, if the corporation dissolves before the end of the five-year period, the remaining balance of the unamortized organizational expenses are deductible. While these deductions are allowed at the corporate level, they may be passed through to the individual owners if an S election has been made.

B. SECTION 1244 STOCK

Section 1244 allows ordinary loss treatment to (1) individuals (or a partnership); (2) who recognize a loss on § 1244 stock; (3) which was originally issued to them; (4) for money or property; (5) by a domestic small business corporation. The total annual loss permitted from all § 1244 stock losses is $50,000 per taxable year ($100,000 if a joint return is filed). Any excess over the annual limitation is treated as a capital loss. To qualify as a small business corporation, the total investment in the corporation may not exceed $1,000,000 and the corporation must generally have an active business rather than merely operating as an investment entity. The ordinary loss treatment is available only to an individual (or partnership) who owns stock in the small business corporation. Trusts, corporations, or other unqualified shareholders may not take advantage of its provisions. The shareholder claiming the loss must be the person to whom the shares were originally issued. The provision is not applicable to stock originally belonging to another. The provisions of § 1244 can also apply to stock which is issued by an ongoing (rather than start-up) business so long as the other requirements of the statute are met. If the stock is issued, however, when the business of the corporation has already failed and the funds contributed to the corporation are to be used merely to pay creditors, the rationale behind § 1244 does not apply and the losses incurred on such stock will not be treated as ordinary loss.

Section 1244 stock may be either common or preferred stock so long as the issuing corporation is a domestic (rather than foreign) corporation. The stock must be issued for money or other property and it must be issued by a small business corporation. Small business corporation status is met generally if the corporation operates an active business and its capitalization does not exceed $1,000,000.

Unlike the rules under prior law, there are no requirements regarding the adoption of a plan or making a formal election to be treated as § 1244 stock. If the other requirements of § 1244 are satisfied, its provisions apply to any loss on stock which, but for § 1244, would be treated as a loss from the sale or exchange of a capital asset. However, good practice dictates a recognition in the corporation's organizational minutes that the issued shares are "§ 1244 stock." In addition, any person claiming a deduction for ordinary loss under § 1244 must file with the tax return a statement setting forth the facts which allow the stock to qualify for § 1244 treatment.

The loss on § 1244 stock will generally be the amount of the shareholder's initial investment in the qualifying stock. In an S corporation, such loss will be reduced by interim losses taken by the shareholder as passed through from the S corporation. If a shareholder makes additional contributions to the capital of the corporation, they will not qualify for § 1244 treatment unless additional shares are issued. Thus, shares *should* be issued in such situations, even if they do not change the corporation's proportionate share ownership.

It should also be noted that there are special situations which override the § 1244 ordinary loss treatment, such as § 267, which disallows any loss (capital or ordinary) on certain sales between related parties. For instance, if a shareholder of an unsuccessful (but still operating) corporation sold the shares to his or her child in an effort to recognize loss upon the decline in the value of the shares, § 267 would disallow the loss altogether, making its characterization under § 1244 irrelevant.

HILL v. COMMISSIONER

51 T.C. 621 (1969).

The principal issue is whether the petitioners are entitled to deductions as ordinary losses for amounts purportedly paid for stock issued as "Section 1244 stock" by the corporation. * * *

OPINION

The petitioners made investments in DeVere, a small business corporation, in April 1962. Each invested $1,000 in stock and loaned $11,000 more on the corporation's note. In addition, Hill and Coats each cosigned the corporation's notes given in borrowing money from the bank. The venture proved unsuccessful and in December 1962 Hill and Coats, who were among the directors of DeVere, met with other directors to consider what might be done. At that time DeVere was insolvent and owed accounts payable in excess of $9,000, owed the bank approximately $38,000 in principal and interest, and had assets of approximately $5,000. It also owed $11,000 to each of five stockholders, including these three petitioners. Hill and Coats were each fully liable for the debt to the bank. If each paid one-half of this it would cost him about $19,000 in addition to any losses resulting from the $1,000 stock investment and the $11,000 loan which DeVere could not repay. Each of the petitioners would be entitled to claim a deduction of some $7,400 as his share of DeVere's net operating loss. Sec. 1374, I.R.C.1954. The remainder of his loss on the original investment and loan and the loss of Hill and Coats on the guaranty would be available only as nonbusiness bad debt deductions under section 166(d)(2), I.R.C.1954.

In this situation, the directors of DeVere, including Hill and Coats, who were obligated for the largest amounts, took steps to avail the stockholders of the benefits which they believed were afforded under the provisions of section 1244 of the Internal Revenue Code of 1954. The directors canceled all previous stock offerings and authorized a new stock offering pursuant to section 1244. Hill and Coats each acquired 12,604 shares of this stock for $31,510, and received back $11,000 on account of his loan made in April, leaving $20,510 from each with DeVere. The corporation paid the principal and interest owing to the bank, $38,266.24, thus relieving Hill and Coats of further liability on their guaranty. Hill and Coats disposed of this stock a week or so later to B & C Investment Co., a partnership formed by some of their attorneys. Shervey paid $11,000 to DeVere and acquired 4,400 shares and received back $11,000 on account of his loan. He likewise disposed of the 4,400 shares to B & C. All the petitioners disposed of their original stockholdings to B & C.

* * * The petitioners claimed deductions as ordinary losses on account of the purchase and sale of the DeVere stock they received in December as section 1244 stock.

The petitioners contend that the action taken by the directors of DeVere in authorizing sale of section 1244 stock and the petitioners' subsequent transactions in such stock complied in all respects with the requirements of section 1244 and entitle them to treat the losses thereon as ordinary losses. They say that section 1244 was availed of to achieve the result for which it was enacted by the Congress, namely to save taxes with respect to investments in small business corporations.

The congressional intent is stated in H.Rept. No. 2198, 85th Cong., 1st Sess., 1959–2 C.B. 710, as follows:

> This is a bill to aid and encourage small business. It is not, however, an attempt to settle all of the small businesses' problems, even in the area of Federal taxation. Instead, it constitutes a step, undertaken within the limits of the present fiscal requirements, to deal with a few of the more important tax problems of small business. The goals of the bill are summarized below.

> (1) The bill is designed to increase the volume of outside funds which will be made available for the financing of small business. Encouragement for external financing is provided by the ordinary loss treatment accorded investments in small business which do not prove to be successful. In this manner the risk element in small-business investments will be decreased for all such investments, including the enterprises which ultimately succeed, as well as those which fail.

Respondent does not suggest that the action of the directors and the petitioners failed to comply with the technical requirements of section 1244. We assume for the purpose of this case that the procedures adopted and the transactions carried out by the parties met these requirements in the literal sense. Nevertheless, we hold that section 1244 is not applicable to authorize treatment as ordinary losses of the losses claimed by petitioners upon disposition of the stock they acquired in December 1962.

Section 1244, as explained above, was intended to encourage investments in small business enterprises. The petitioners' payments to DeVere for this stock were not investments. Shervey paid in $11,000 and received it back immediately, purportedly in payment of the earlier loan of that amount. This could not properly be termed an investment. The same applies to $11,000 of the amounts paid in by Hill and by Coats which they received back in the same guise. Of the additional amount of $20,510 paid in by each of them, $19,133.12 went to pay the principal and interest due the bank and thus to relieve them of liability on their guaranty. They were to this extent paying their personal debts, not investing in the business of the corporation. The record does not show the disposition of the small amount left over, but it would not cover the other debts of the corporation.

In *Wesley H. Morgan,* 46 T.C. 878 (1966), the taxpayers were members of a partnership which invested in a small business corporation. The corporation was unsuccessful and the directors voted to liquidate. The partnership purportedly purchased section 1244 stock in an amount sufficient to pay the corporation's debts. The partners claimed ordinary losses from their shares of this stock. This Court, in denying the taxpayers' contention, stated:

> However laudable the motives behind this payment, it certainly does not fall within the spirit of section 1244 nor does it accomplish the purpose for which Congress enacted that section. According to the committee report, *supra,* section 1244 was designed to encourage investments in small businesses presumably to permit them to carry on their business, not to provide an ordinary loss deduction for bailing out the corporation's creditors after it had ceased doing business.

The Court said further:

> But we will not accept the argument that it was paid for stock which was admittedly worthless at the time of issuance and which would represent an additional interest in a corporation which was insolvent and was already in the process of dissolution. The only reason this would be done would be to create a tax deduction. We cannot agree that this payment resulted in a loss on section 1244 stock, whether or not the stock purportedly issued technically qualified as section 1244 stock; and we so hold.   * * *

The petitioners argue that DeVere had not ceased to do business and was not in liquidation, therefore the decision in *Morgan* is not applicable. It appears from the evidence that DeVere had ceased doing business. Its records show no rental receipts after September 1962. It filed a "final return" of excise tax with the State tax commission on February 14, 1963, for the quarter ended September 30, 1962. One of the original incorporators, Arnie Bergh, testified that he knew of no plan to carry on business by DeVere beyond the period of the fair, which ended in October 1962. None of the petitioners testified at the hearing and no evidence was produced indicating an intention on the part of any of the stockholders to continue the corporation's activities. The corporation had disposed of its trailers and had no facilities or equipment for continuing the motel business. Its income tax return for the following year showed no business activity.   * * *

Problem 26–1

In 1996, Allan contributes $20,000 to a newly formed C corporation in exchange for all of its shares. The funds are used to acquire a sporting goods store. In 1997, Allan contributes another $10,000 to the corporation to cover operational losses. No additional stock is issued at this time. In 1998, creditors foreclose on the business, seizing its assets. Allan voluntarily contributes an additional $15,000 to satisfy their claims against the corporation. In exchange for the $15,000, he receives an additional 100 shares of the corporation's stock. The business closes its doors in late 1998 and Allan's shares are worthless.

1.   How much § 1244 loss can Allan claim in 1998?

2.   Would it have made a difference if Allan had been issued additional shares for his 1997 contribution?

3.   What if, as a result of the 1997 contribution, the corporation was revived, surviving until its subsequent demise in 2000?

C.   INITIAL TAX LOSS PLANNING— THE S ELECTION

The advantages of the S election as an overall tax planning tool for a small business are discussed in detail in Chapter 29.   Initial consideration of the S election as a tax planning vehicle for the utilization of potential losses of a new enterprise is briefly reviewed in this section. The same corporation may make both an S election and have its stock qualify as § 1244.   The S election, if available, is often more important because: (1) an S election allows business loss deductions to be taken as they are sustained by a corporation rather than only when the stock of the corporation is sold or exchanged or becomes worthless; (2) S corporation losses may be taken by shareholders who were not the original shareholders of the corporation, unlike § 1244 losses; (3) there is no maximum dollar limitation for the capitalization of an S corporation; and (4) there is no $100,000 ($50,000 for single taxpayers or separate returns) annual loss limitation on the pass-through of losses from an S corporation.

The requirements for qualification as an S corporation, however, are significantly more stringent than those relating to § 1244 stock.   As discussed in Chapter 29, S corporation requirements limit the number of shareholders, their nationality, and the characteristics of the stock issued by the corporation.   Furthermore, they provide that a partnership and certain other entities may not be an S corporation shareholder.   In many cases, however, these limitations will not be relevant and the S corporation election will be proper for a starting small business.   Even if the corporation intends to terminate the S election in the future, it is often wise to operate as an S corporation at the outset, so that start-up losses of the new enterprise may be passed through to the individual shareholders and deducted against their other income (subject to the at risk and passive loss rules discussed in Chapter 7).

It is important to note that the election procedures for S corporation status are formal.   Moreover, it is particularly important at the start of a business operation to focus on the tax basis rules for S corporation stock as they relate to the limitation on the deduction by shareholders of S corporation losses.   An S corporation shareholder may deduct losses only to the extent of the tax basis in his or her shares.   Such basis is initially comprised of the capital contributed to the corporation and any loans which he or she makes to the corporation.   Loans which are made by a third party directly to the corporate entity itself, however, do not (unlike a partnership) add to the basis of the shareholder in the shares.   Consequently, if losses are anticipated in the early going of the enterprise, it is frequently wise for the individual shareholder to borrow directly from the lender and then, in turn, loan the funds to the corporation. This procedure would allow losses in the case where a loan directly to the corporation (even if guaranteed by the corporate shareholder) would not give the shareholder basis against which to take losses of the corporation.

As noted previously, the tax adviser must also be familiar with the at-risk rules of § 465 and passive loss limitations imposed by § 469. Even if the S corporation shareholder's basis is properly structured to allow losses, the losses may be disallowed or deferred by the at risk rules or by the passive loss rules if the shareholder does not take a sufficiently active role in the corporate business.

ESTATE OF DANIEL LEAVITT v. COMMISSIONER

90 T.C. 206 (1988).

NIMS, Judge: * * *

The only issue for decision is whether a shareholder's guarantee of the debt of an electing small business corporation under subchapter S of the Internal Revenue Code increases the shareholder's basis in his stock in the corporation. * * *

VAFLA Corp. (hereinafter referred to as the corporation), was an electing small business corporation under subchapter S during the years in issue and was incorporated in February 1979, to acquire and operate the Six–Gun Territory Amusement Park near Tampa, Florida. The initial issue of the corporation's capital stock took place in March 1979, and consisted of 100,000 shares. Daniel Leavitt and Anthony D. Cuzzocrea each paid $10,000 cash for their shares on or before September 30, 1979.

The first taxable year of the corporation consisted of 7 months and ended on September 30, 1979. As of September 30, 1979, the corporation had suffered a net operating loss of $265,566.47 and had a retained earnings deficit of $345,370.20. During its second taxable year ending September 30, 1980, the corporation suffered a net operating loss of $482,181.22 and had a retained earnings deficit of $1,093,383.56. During its third taxable year ending September 30, 1981, the corporation suffered a net operating loss of $475,175.70 and had a retained earnings deficit of $1,908,680.22.

From August 2, 1979, through August 27, 1979, Anthony D. Cuzzocrea and Daniel Leavitt, as well as other shareholders, signed guarantee agreements whereby each agreed to be jointly and severally liable for all indebtedness of the corporation to the Bank of Virginia. All the guarantees to the Bank of Virginia were unlimited except the guarantee of Anthony D. Cuzzocrea which was limited to $300,000.

The corporation borrowed $300,000 from the Bank of Virginia for which it issued a promissory note to the bank dated September 12, 1979.

The purpose of the loan was to fund VAFLA's existing and anticipated operating deficits.

At the time the loan was made, the corporation's liabilities exceeded its assets, and the corporation had so little available cash that it could not meet its cash-flow requirements. Virtually all of the corporation's assets were encumbered as collateral for a purchase money indebtedness of approximately $1 million to National Service Industries, Inc. In processing the loan, the Bank of Virginia was provided a statement of income for the corporation for its first 3 months of operation during which the corporation experienced a loss of $142,410.16, resulting in a negative net worth of $82,410.16 as of May 31, 1979.

Seven of the corporation's shareholders agreed to guarantee the $300,000 loan personally. According to the financial statements submitted to the bank, these shareholders had an aggregate net worth of $3,407,286 and immediate liquidity (cash and securities) of $382,542. The loan was approved only because of the financial strength of the guarantors. * * *

Daniel and Evelyn M. Leavitt deducted a loss of $13,808 attributable to the corporation on their 1979 joint Federal income tax return. Respondent disallowed $3,808 of this deduction. Anthony D. and Marjorie F. Cuzzocrea deducted losses of $13,808, $29,921, and $22,746 attributable to the corporation on their 1979, 1980, and 1981 joint Federal income tax returns, respectively. Respondent disallowed all of these deductions in excess of $10,000.

Respondent takes the position that shareholders Daniel Leavitt and Anthony D. Cuzzocrea may not deduct losses attributable to the corporation in excess of their initial basis in their shares of the corporation. Petitioners maintain that their guarantees of the $300,000 loan to the corporation from the Bank of Virginia increased their basis in their stock sufficiently to allow deductions for their proportionate shares of losses attributable to the corporation during the years in issue. * * *

We must determine whether petitioners' guarantee of the $300,000 loan from the Bank of Virginia to the corporation increased the basis in petitioners' stock in the corporation.

It is well settled that:

the fact that shareholders may be primarily liable on indebtedness of a corporation to a third party does not mean that this indebtedness is "indebtedness of the corporation to the shareholder" within the meaning of section 1374(c)(2)(B). No form of indirect borrowing, be it guaranty, surety, accommodation, comaking or otherwise, gives rise to indebtedness from the corporation to the shareholders until and unless the shareholders pay part or all of the obligation. * * *

In the instant case, petitioners have never been called upon to pay any of the loan that they guaranteed. Accordingly, the guarantees that petitioners executed do not increase any indebtedness of the corporation to them.

Nevertheless, petitioners ask us to view the guarantee transactions as constructive loans from the banks to petitioners and, in turn, contributions of those same funds by petitioners to the capital of the corporation. In other words, petitioners contend that their guarantees of the $300,000 loan from the Bank of Virginia to the corporation should increase their basis in the stock of the corporation. We disagree.

Under former section 1374(c)(2) corporate debts to third parties guaranteed by the shareholder, whether collateralized or not, do not lead to an increase in the shareholder's basis in his subchapter S corporation stock. To increase the basis in the stock of a subchapter S corporation, there must be an economic outlay or a realization of income on the part of the shareholder.

The term "basis," for purposes of section 1374(c), is defined in section 1012. Section 1012 provides the general rule that the "basis of property shall be the cost of such property." Section 1.1012–1(a), Income Tax Regs., defines "cost" to mean the "amount paid" for property "in cash or other property." Because petitioners' guarantees in this case do not constitute cash or other property, they cannot be included in the basis of petitioners' stock in the corporation.

In *Borg v. Commissioner,* an electing small business corporation owed one of its shareholders unpaid salary for his performance of services as evidenced by notes from the corporation to the shareholder. The shareholder did not report any part of the unpaid salary as income in his returns. The shareholder in *Borg* argued that the notes for the unpaid salary increased his basis in the indebtedness of the corporation to him. We held that because the shareholder had incurred no cost in connection with the notes, he had no basis in the notes and therefore there was no addition to the adjusted basis of the indebtedness of the corporation to the shareholder. We explained:

> cost for the purposes of the Code ordinarily means cost to the taxpayer. Where a taxpayer has not previously reported, recognized, or even *realized* income, it cannot be said that he has a basis for a note evidencing his right to receive such income at some time in the future. That petitioner Joe E. Borg performed valuable services for Borg Steel is undeniable; however, the performance of services, involving neither the realization of taxable income nor a capital outlay, is not the kind of cost that would be shown in a cash receipts and disbursements system of income accounting. Since the services performed by petitioner Joe E. Borg had no cost within the meaning of section 1012, his notes for unpaid salary had a basis of zero and, therefore, added nothing to the adjusted basis for indebtedness for the purpose of computing the section 1374(c)(2) limitation on net operating loss deductions.

In this case, petitioners' guarantees did not require any capital outlay on their part during the years in issue. Without capital outlay or a realization of income, as required by *Borg,* petitioners cannot increase their adjusted basis in their stock in the corporation. Nor can it of course be said that the guarantees in question were corporate debt obligations to petitioners which acquired a basis resulting from any capital outlays by petitioners. Petitioners ask, however, that we ignore the form of the transaction, i.e., a loan from the Bank of Virginia to the corporation that was guaranteed by its shareholders, and find that the bank actually loaned the money to the shareholder-guarantors who then advanced the proceeds of the loan as a contribution to the capital of the corporation. We decline to adopt petitioners' view of the transaction.

The Bank of Virginia loaned the money to the corporation and not to petitioners. The proceeds of the loan were to be used in the operation of the corporation's business. Petitioners submitted no evidence that they were free to dispose of the proceeds of the loan as they wished. Nor were the payments on the loan reported as constructive dividends on the corporation's Federal income tax returns or on petitioners' Federal income tax returns during the years in issue. Accordingly, we find that the transaction was in fact a loan by the bank to the corporation guaranteed by the shareholders.

Nevertheless, petitioners ask that we apply traditional debt-equity principles in determining the nature of the transaction in this case. Petitioners maintain that because the corporation was insolvent at the time the loan was made and because the bank would not have advanced the funds to the corporation without the shareholders' guarantees, the loan was in fact a loan from the bank to the shareholders who then advanced the proceeds of the loan as a contribution to the capital of the corporation. We decline to adopt traditional debt-equity principles in this case. * * *

In *Selfe v. United States,* 778 F.2d 769 (11th Cir.1985), the 11th Circuit applied a debt-equity analysis and held that a shareholder's guarantee of a loan made to a subchapter S corporation may be treated for tax purposes as an equity investment in the corporation where the lender looks to the shareholder as the primary obligor. We respectfully disagree with the 11th Circuit and hold that a shareholder's guarantee of a loan to a subchapter S corporation may not be treated as an equity investment in the corporation absent an economic outlay by the shareholder.

The *Selfe* opinion was based primarily on *Plantation Patterns, Inc. v. Commissioner,* 462 F.2d 712 (5th Cir.1972), affg. T.C.Memo. 1970–182, in which the Fifth Circuit affirmed as not clearly erroneous a finding by this Court that a transaction structured as a loan by an independent third party to a corporation, and guaranteed by a shareholder, was in substance a loan to the shareholder followed by his contribution of the loan proceeds to the corporation, and that as a result the corporation's payments of principal and interest on the debt constituted constructive dividends to the shareholder.

However, the corporation in *Plantation Patterns* was a subchapter C corporation. We decline to apply the debt-equity analysis used in *Plantation Patterns* to the guarantee of a loan to a subchapter S corporation. Congress has promulgated a set of rules designed to limit the amount of deductions allowable to a shareholder of a subchapter S corporation to the amount he has actually invested in the corporation and the amounts of income from the corporation included in the shareholder's gross income. The report of the Committee on Finance of the Senate underscores Congress' purpose as follows:

> The amount of the net operating loss apportioned to any shareholder pursuant to the above rule is limited under section 1374(c)(2) to the adjusted basis of the shareholder's *investment* in the corporation; that is, to the adjusted basis of the stock in the corporation owned by the shareholder and the adjusted basis of any indebtedness of the corporation to the shareholder. * * *

As we construed this language in *Perry v. Commissioner,* 54 T.C. 1293, 1296 (1970), the use of the word "investment" reveals an intent, on the part of the committees, to limit the applicability of section 1374(c)(2) to the actual economic outlay of the shareholder in question. To allow petitioners to increase the basis of their stock without a capital outlay or a realization of income would provide them a means of avoiding these limitations.

> In *Selfe,* the court also relied on *In re Lane,* 742 F.2d 1311 (11th Cir.1984), in which the 11th Circuit applied a debt-equity analysis and held that funds advanced to a subchapter S corporation by a shareholder and payments made by the shareholder as guarantor of corporate obligations to institutional lenders were capital contributions rather than loans from the shareholder to the corporation. In *Lane,* the shareholder had actually paid the amounts he had guaranteed and, therefore, the amounts he paid could be considered a contribution to capital. In this case, petitioners have not paid any of the loans they guaranteed and, therefore, have contributed nothing to the capital of the corporation. * * *

Problem 26–2

Ted and his wife, Alice, have developed a frozen yogurt recipe. They contribute $100,000 to Yogurt, Inc. They receive, in exchange, 100 shares of Yogurt, Inc. stock which they hold as joint tenants. They make an S election. The contributed funds are used to purchase a manufacturing plant. The corporation borrows an additional $100,000 from Colonial Bank to refurbish the plant. The debt is personally guaranteed by Ted and Alice. Sales are poor and the business loses $75,000 in its first year and $50,000 in its second. Ted and Alice work full-time in the business.

1. How much loss is deductible to Ted and Alice in the first year?
2. How much loss is deductible in the second year?
3. What if they had personally borrowed from Colonial and, in turn, loaned or contributed those funds to the corporation?
4. What if they had not elected S corporation status?
5. If they close the business, will § 1244 help?

Chapter 27

SELECTION OF THE CORPORATION'S TAXABLE YEAR

Code References: §§ 280(H)(a), (c); 441(a)–(e); 442; 444; 1366(a)(1); 1378; 7519(a)–(b).

Regulation: §§ 1.441–1T(a)–(b)(3).

A. INTRODUCTION

One of the final considerations to be contemplated by the entrepreneur and his or her tax advisers when forming a corporation is the selection of its taxable year. Although this may seem a relatively insignificant accounting matter, the utilization of a particular corporate taxable year as a means of deferring taxable income by the entity's owners has a significant history.

Historically, the basic deferral concept was to adopt a taxable year ending early in the calendar year. For example, an incorporated attorney with an individual calendar year might adopt a corporate fiscal year ending on January 31st. He or she would then use one of two techniques to defer individual income: (1) in January of each year, he or she would declare a bonus of all remaining corporate profit, thereby creating a § 162 deduction at the corporate level which would eliminate all of the corporation's taxable income yet postpone his or her payment of tax since the income arose in the year of its receipt; or (2) he or she would, at the outset, make an "S election" for the corporation. Under S corporation rules, the annual taxable income of a corporation is reportable by its individual shareholders, in proportion to their shareholdings, at the end of the corporation's taxable year. Once again, the net income would be reportable by the individual in the beginning of the subsequent year.

Under either of these techniques, there would be no corporate income reported. The individual income flowing to the owner as a result of the bonus or S corporate operations would flow to the shareholder in

441

January. As such, it would not require the payment of tax until April 15th of the following year, thereby creating as much as a 15–month deferral on the reporting of the income earned through the attorney's efforts.

Perceiving the abuse connected with the utilization of such deferral techniques, Congress has taken several actions. First, the strengthening of the corporate withholding and individual estimated tax requirements often forces the individual taxpayer to make his or her tax payments simultaneously with the receipt of the bonus or at least in quarterly estimated payments on income earned in any given year, rather than waiting until the following April. At the corporate level, §§ 441 and 444 now make it extremely difficult for an S corporation to operate on a year other than the calendar year. Similarly, the same sections generally prevent a C corporation which meets the definition of a "personal service corporation" (which includes most professional corporations) from utilizing a year other than the calendar year. The requirement to utilize the calendar year largely eliminates the potential for deferral. C corporations which are not a personal service corporation can generally utilize a fiscal year of their choice, although the choices are also limited and there are still certain anti-deferral provisions applicable to such corporations which elect fiscal years.

B. S CORPORATIONS

No corporation may make the S election unless it adopts a "permitted taxable year." A permitted year is a taxable year that ends on December 31 unless a corporation establishes to the satisfaction of the Service that it has a valid business purpose for adopting a different year. An S corporation may, however, make an election under § 444 to adopt a taxable year with a deferral period of three months or less. This generally means that such a fiscal year would end on either September 30, October 31, or November 30. As such, the S corporation shareholder's individual taxable years (which are almost always the calendar year) will end within three months of that of the corporation itself, minimizing deferral possibilities.

If the § 444 election is made, however, the Code extracts a price. Section 7519 effectively requires S corporations to pay approximately the same amount as the shareholders would have paid in actual tax payments for the short period had the corporation adopted a calendar year. However, because the S corporation is ultimately entitled to a refund of the required payments when it terminates its election or adopts a calendar year, the payments are, in effect, an interest-free loan to the Service of the deferral benefits. The calculation of the required corporate payments is extremely complex and, in a small business, the complexities of complying with § 7519 may outweigh any perceived benefit of making the § 444 election in order to utilize a non-calendar year.

The other method available to an S corporation which desires a fiscal year is to make a request to the Service for such a year, provided it is based upon a valid business purpose. What constitutes a valid business purpose is described with some specificity in the Regulations. See Reg. § 1.442–1(b)(1). An S corporation will receive automatic approval of its request for a fiscal year if the taxable year coincides with the corporation's natural business year. This occurs if at least 25% of the corporation's annual gross receipts, measured as of the year end, are received within the last two months of the requested tax year. This rule was designed to accommodate seasonal businesses and applies only if the test is met for three consecutive years. See Rev.Proc. 87–32, 1987–2 C.B. 396.

If the mathematical test relating to the natural business year cannot be met, the taxpayer may appeal to the Service under a facts and circumstances test, but he or she must establish both a valid business purpose and that no substantial deferral of income accrues to the S corporation shareholders. These provisions have been strictly applied by the Service to essentially deny fiscal year utilization by S corporations unless they can meet the natural business year test.

C. PERSONAL SERVICE CORPORATIONS

A personal service corporation is a C corporation engaged primarily in the business of performing personal services when such services are substantially performed by employee-owners who own more than 10% of the fair market value of the stock of the corporation during the year. The performance of services in the fields of health, law, engineering, architecture, accounting, actuarial science, performing arts, and consulting are personal service activities. To preclude deferral possibilities, the Tax Reform Act of 1986 placed severe limitations on the use of fiscal years by personal service corporations. It is now extremely difficult for a personal service corporation to utilize a year other than a calendar year. Like S corporations, the personal service corporation may make a § 444 election to utilize a taxable year other than a calendar year if the deferral period is three months or less. Once again, however, a price is extracted for the election. Section 280(H), which applies to any taxable year in which a personal service corporation has a § 444 election in effect, provides a limitation on the deduction of amounts paid to employee-owners. If the personal service corporation does not satisfy minimum distribution requirements, employee compensation paid by the personal service corporation may not be deductible. The purpose of this provision is to prevent the corporation from loading a disproportionate amount of the employee compensation into the deferral period.

Like an S corporation, a personal service corporation *may* use a fiscal year if it meets the natural business year test described in the prior section. A fiscal year is also available in the unlikely event that it can establish facts and circumstances setting forth a non-tax motivated business purpose for adopting a non-calendar year.

REVENUE RULING 87–57

1987–2 C.B. 117.

ISSUE

In the situations described below, has * * * an S Corporation, or a personal service corporation established, to the satisfaction of the Secretary, a business purpose for adopting, retaining, or changing its tax year?

FACTS

In each of these situations, the taxpayer is * * * an S corporation, or a personal service corporation. In addition, in each instance the owners of the taxpayer have tax years that differ from the tax year requested by the taxpayer. * * *

Situation 1. The taxpayer desires to use a January 31 tax year. The taxpayer's reason for the requested tax year is that that year corresponds to the natural business year for the taxpayer's type of business as suggested by the Natural Business Year Committee of the American Institute of Certified Public Accountants (AICPA) in an official release published in 100 *Journal of Accountancy* 59 (December 1955). In addition, the taxpayer is using a January 31 fiscal year for financial reporting purposes.

Situation 2. The taxpayer desires to use a September 30 tax year. The taxpayer's reasons for the requested tax year are that the taxpayer's accountant is extremely busy during the first six months of the year and that, if the taxpayer were to have a September 30 tax year, the taxpayer would receive a reduced charge for the accountant's services.

Situation 3. The taxpayer desires to retain its November 30 tax year. The taxpayer's reasons for the requested tax year are that the taxpayer has used a November 30 tax year since the inception of its business 15 years ago and that, if the taxpayer is required to change its tax year, it would lose its recordkeeping consistency and thus would suffer a financial hardship in changing the records to another year.

Situation 4. The taxpayer desires to use a tax year ending September 30. The taxpayer's reason for the requested tax year is that the taxpayer desires to issue timely tax information * * * to its owners to facilitate the filing of timely returns by its owners.

Situation 5. The taxpayer desires to use a November 30 tax year. The taxpayer can establish a natural business year ending on January 31 under section 4.01(1) of Rev.Proc. 87–32. If the taxpayer had not satisfied the natural business year test for January 31, it would have met the natural business year test for November 30.

Situation 6. The taxpayer desires to use a June 30 tax year. The taxpayer's reason for the requested tax year is that it coincides with the taxpayer's natural business year. For this taxpayer, June 30 is not a "natural business year," within the meaning of section 4.01(1) of Rev.

Proc. 87–32. This failure to satisfy section 4.01(1) of Rev.Proc. 87–32 is caused by unusual gross receipts figures for several months during the 47–month period (36–month period for requested tax year plus additional 11–month period for comparing requested tax year with other potential tax years) covered by the test. The figures for those months were unusual because a labor strike closed the taxpayer's business during a period that included its normal peak season. The taxpayer has data for the most recent five years demonstrating that the requested tax year would have satisfied the definition of a natural business year within the meaning of section 4.01(1) of Rev.Proc. 87–32, if the strike had not occurred.

Situation 7. The taxpayer desires to use a May 31 tax year. The taxpayer's reason for the requested tax year is that due to weather conditions the business is operational only during the period of September 1 through May 31. For the 10 years it has been in business, the taxpayer has had insignificant gross receipts for the period June 1 through August 31. The facility used by the taxpayer is not used for any other purpose during the three months of insignificant gross receipts. This taxpayer does not have a "natural business year," within the meaning of section 4.01(1) of Rev.Proc. 87–32.

Situation 8. The taxpayer desires to continue to use a March 31 tax year. The taxpayer changed its method of accounting to the accrual method for the tax year ended March 31, 1987. The taxpayer's reason for the requested tax year is that it coincides with the taxpayer's natural business year. For this taxpayer, March 31 is not a "natural business year," within the meaning of section 4.01(1) of Rev.Proc. 87–32. The 25–percent test in section 4.01(1) of Rev.Proc. 87–32 requires the taxpayer to compute the gross receipts on the basis of the method of accounting used to file its return for each year of the test. Therefore, the taxpayer must compute gross receipts on the cash method of accounting for tax years prior to the tax year ended March 31, 1987. The taxpayer has audited financial statements that were prepared on the basis of an accrual method that is acceptable for tax purposes. The taxpayer's gross receipts based on the accrual method would satisfy the 25–percent test for a tax year ending March 31.

Law and Analysis

Section 441(b)(1) of the Internal Revenue Code provides that the term "taxable year" generally means the taxpayer's annual accounting period, if it is a calendar year or a fiscal year. Section 441(c) provides that the term "annual accounting period" means the annual period on the basis of which the taxpayer regularly computes its income in keeping its books. Section 441(d) defines the term "calendar year" as a period of 12 months ending on December 31. * * *

Section 441(i) of the Code, * * * provides that the tax year of any personal service corporation shall be the calendar year unless the corporation establishes, to the satisfaction of the Secretary, a business purpose for having a different period for its tax year. Any deferral of income to shareholders is not to be treated as a business purpose. * * *

Section 1378(a) of the Code, * * * provides that the tax year of an S corporation shall be a "permitted year." Section 1378(b) defines the term "permitted year" as a tax year which (1) is a year ending December 31, or (2) is any other accounting period for which the corporation establishes a business purpose to the satisfaction of the Secretary. Any deferral of income to shareholders is not to be treated as a business purpose. * * *

A taxpayer that cannot satisfy any of the tests set forth in Rev.Proc. 87–32 must establish a business purpose based on consideration of all the facts and circumstances, including the tax consequences. The tax consequences to be considered include: (1) deferring a substantial portion of a taxpayer's income or shifting a substantial portion of a taxpayer's deductions from one year to another to reduce substantially a taxpayer's tax liability; (2) causing a similar deferral or shift in the case of any other person, such as * * * a beneficiary, or a shareholder in an S corporation; and (3) creating a short period in which there is a substantial net operating loss.

The Conference Report lists various nontax factors that will ordinarily not be sufficient to establish that the business purpose requirement for a particular tax year has been met. These factors are: (1) the use of a particular year for regulatory or financial accounting purposes; (2) the hiring patterns of a particular business—for example, the fact that a firm typically hires staff during certain times of the year; (3) the use of a particular year for administrative purposes, such as the admission or retirement of * * * shareholders, promotion of staff, and compensation or retirement arrangements with staff, * * * or shareholders; and (4) the fact that a particular business involves the use of price lists, a model year, or other items that change on an annual basis.

Both tax factors and nontax factors must be considered for purposes of determining whether a taxpayer has established a business purpose for the requested tax year. In this context, the Conference Report demonstrates the significant weight that must be assigned to tax factors. The four nontax factors that the report identifies as ordinarily insufficient all involve issues of convenience for the taxpayer. Accordingly, if a requested tax year creates deferral or distortion, the taxpayer's nontax factors must demonstrate compelling reasons for the requested tax year.

The taxpayer in each of the eight situations must establish, to the satisfaction of the Secretary, a business purpose for the use of the requested tax year. Each taxpayer has nontax, business reasons for the use of the requested tax year. However, because the requested tax year is different from the tax year of the taxpayer's owners, the taxpayer's use of the requested tax year would inherently create deferral or distortion. Under these circumstances, the taxpayer can establish, to the satisfaction of the Secretary, a business purpose for the requested tax year only if the nontax reasons for the use of that year are compelling.

The taxpayer's reason for the requested tax year in *Situation 1* is that the requested tax year is the natural business year suggested by the Natural Business Year Committee of the AICPA and the taxpayer uses the requested tax year for financial statement purposes. As stated in the Conference Report, the use of a particular year for financial accounting purposes is not sufficient to establish that the business purpose requirement for that year has been met. In addition, the natural business year suggested by the AICPA is not based upon the taxpayer's own facts and circumstances.

In *Situations 2–4,* the taxpayers' reasons for the requested tax years are to take advantage of an accountant's reduced rate (*Situation 2*), to have recordkeeping consistency (*Situation 3*), and to issue timely tax information * * * (*Situation 4*). The reasons given in these three situations are ones of convenience to the taxpayers. Although the reasons are not among those specifically enumerated in the Conference Report, they are very similar to the convenience reasons listed there as being insufficient to establish that the business purpose requirement for a requested tax year has been met.

The taxpayer's reason in *Situation 5* is that the requested November 30 tax year would be a natural business year but for the fact that the January 31 year produces a higher percentage under the 25–percent test of Rev.Proc. 87–32. Because a November 30 fiscal year satisfies the 25–percent test and results in less deferral to the shareholders than January 31, the Commissioner, in his discretion, considers it desirable and expedient for the efficient administration of the tax laws for this taxpayer to use November 30 as its tax year. Accordingly, the taxpayer has established a business purpose for using the requested tax year.

The taxpayer's reasons in *Situation 6* are that the requested tax year coincides with the taxpayer's natural business year and that, if the strike had not occurred, the requested year would have been a natural business year according to the test set forth in Rev.Proc. 87–32. The taxpayer's failure to establish a natural business year under the 25–percent test is due to unusual circumstances that occurred during the test period and that were beyond the taxpayer's control. The historical data support the taxpayer's contention that, in the absence of these unusual circumstances, the requested year would have qualified as the taxpayer's natural business year. Thus, the Commissioner is satisfied that the taxpayer has established a business purpose for the requested tax year.

The taxpayer's reason in *Situation 7* is that the requested May 31 tax year coincides with the time the taxpayer has closed down operations for the past 10 years. That closing is not within the taxpayer's control. Accordingly, the taxpayer has established a business purpose for using the requested tax year.

The taxpayer's reason in *Situation 8* is that the requested March 31 tax year coincides with the taxpayer's natural business year and that, if the taxpayer had used the accrual method of accounting, the requested year would have been a natural business year according to the test set forth in Rev.Proc. 87–32. The taxpayer has changed its method of accounting to the accrual method. Therefore, it is reasonable for the Commissioner, to allow the taxpayer to use a March 31 tax year if the accrual method, which will be used for all future tax years, would establish a natural business year ending on March 31.

HOLDING

Each taxpayer in *Situations 1–4* has failed to establish, to the satisfaction of the Secretary, a business purpose for the use of its requested tax year. Each taxpayer in *Situations 5–8* has established, to the satisfaction of the Secretary, a business purpose for the use of its requested tax year.

Problem 27–1

Clayton and Bill are calendar-year CPAs who have incorporated their practice as Tax, Inc. They each own 50% of the corporation's shares and an S election has been made. Their business has operated for five years and its primary activity is tax return preparation for businesses and business owners. Because of changes in the tax Code, all of their clients (corporate, partnership, and individual) are on a calendar tax year. The corporation has, for the past three years, received 30% of its annual receipts in March and 30% in April of each year.

1. Can Tax, Inc. adopt a fiscal year?

2. If so, in what month(s) may the year end?

3. What if no S election had been filed?

4. Could Tax, Inc. select a calendar year?

5. If Tax, Inc. has $150,000 of income at the end of its April 30 tax year, $75,000 each will be passed through as income to Clayton and Bill under the S corporation rules. When will they pay their individual tax on this amount?

    a. What if, on April 29, the corporation distributed a bonus of $100,000 to Clayton, who had produced the lion's share of the accounting work?

    b. What if the $100,000 was distributed as a bonus to Clayton because he had incurred a $100,000 § 1244 loss earlier in the year and could therefore shelter the income?

D.   C CORPORATIONS

C corporations which are not personal service corporations have more flexibility in the adoption of their taxable year. For such corporations, § 441 merely requires that (1) the taxable year be the same as the entity's accounting period; (2) the taxable year not exceed 12 calendar months (with minor exceptions); (3) the corporation's books of account be kept in accordance with such period; and (4) the taxable year be adopted by the corporation no later than the time prescribed for the filing of the return for such taxable year (2½ months following the end of such year).

While these requirements are relatively straightforward, problems can arise in connection with the formation of new business corporations. Often, a corporation is legally formed but is not activated because of a delay in the transfer of the business property to the entity or a delay in the acquisition of a going business by the entity. Technically, the corporation still must file tax returns. It may be important to file a return, even though the corporation has no income, in order to obtain the appropriate taxable year under the statutory requirements. Otherwise, a calendar year may be mandated.

A corporation which is immediately operating has flexibility in connection with the election of its initial year. Since the first year of the corporation will generally always be a short year (less than 12 months), the corporation has up to an 11-month "free look" to determine its year. That is, if the corporation were to incur losses in the initial month but gradually become profitable, the owners could wait until the "break-even" month occurred and select that month as the first fiscal year of the corporation. The corporation would pay no tax for that initial year, but would be "stuck" with such year since subsequent changes of year are generally subject to the approval of the Service.

REVENUE RULING 92–13

1992–1 C.B. 665.

Section 1. Purpose

The purpose of this revenue procedure is to provide a procedure for certain corporations to obtain expeditious approval of a change of their annual accounting period. * * *

Section 2. Background

.01 Section 1.442–1(a)(1) of the Income Tax Regulations provides that a taxpayer must obtain prior approval from the Commissioner for a change of its annual accounting period or the change must be authorized under the regulations.

.02 Section 1.442–1(b)(1) of the regulations provides that in order to secure prior approval of a change of its annual accounting period, the taxpayer must file an application on a Form 1128 (Application to Adopt, Change or Retain a Tax Year) with the Commissioner of Internal Revenue, on or before the 15th day of the second calendar month following the close of the taxpayer's short taxable year. Section 1.442–1(b)(1) also provides that approval will not be granted unless the taxpayer and the Commissioner agree to the terms, conditions, and adjustments under which the change will be effected.

.03 Section 1.442–1(c)(1) of the regulations provides a special rule for certain corporations whereby a corporation may change its annual accounting period without the prior approval of the Commissioner if all the conditions in section 1.442–1(c)(2) are satisfied, certain filing requirements are met, and the corporation is not of the type described in sections 1.442–1(c)(4) and (5), or subject to section 859 of the Internal Revenue Code.

.04   Section 1.442–1(c)(2) of the regulations provides that a corporation may change its annual accounting period without the prior approval of the Commissioner if the following conditions are satisfied:

(1) The corporation has not changed its annual accounting period within the 10 calendar year period ending with the calendar year that includes the beginning of the short period required to effect the change;

(2) The short period required to effect the change of annual accounting period is not a taxable year in which the corporation has a net operating loss as described in section 172 of the Code;

(3) The taxable income of the corporation for the short period required to effect the change of annual accounting period is, if placed on an annual basis, 80 percent or more of the taxable income of the corporation for the taxable year immediately preceding the short period;

(4) The corporation, if it had a special status (as defined in section 1.442–1(c)(2)(iv) of the regulations) either for the short period or for the taxable year immediately preceding the short period, must have the same special status for both the short period and the preceding taxable year; and

(5) The corporation does not attempt to make an S corporation election (under section 1362 of the Code) that purports to become effective for the taxable year immediately following the short period.

.05   Section 1.443–1(b)(1)(i) of the regulations provides that if a return is made for a short period resulting from a change of an annual accounting period, the taxable income for the short period shall be placed on an annual basis by multiplying the income by 12 and dividing the result by the number of months in the short period. Unless section 443(b)(2) of the Code and section 1.443–1(b)(2) apply, the tax for the short period shall be the same part of the tax computed on an annual basis as the number of months in the short period is of 12 months.
* * *

Section 4. Scope

.01   This revenue procedure applies to a corporation that:

(1) cannot satisfy all the conditions of section 1.442–1(c)(2) of the regulations regarding a change of an annual accounting period without the prior approval of the Commissioner;

(2) has not changed its annual accounting period at any time within the last 6 calendar years (or within any of the calendar years the taxpayer has been in existence if less than 6 years) ending with the calendar year that includes the beginning of the short period required to effect the change of annual accounting period; * * *

(5) is not an S corporation (as defined in section 1361 of the Code) and does not attempt to make an S corporation election effective for the taxable year immediately following the short period. *See* Rev.Proc. 87–32, 1987–2 C.B. 396, for procedures to follow in changing an annual accounting period for an S corporation;

(6) is not a personal service corporation (as defined in section 441(i) of the Code). *See* Rev.Proc. 87–32 for procedures to follow in changing an annual accounting period for a personal service corporation; * * *

.03 Corporations which are unable to use the automatic provisions of this revenue procedure or section 1.442–1(c) of the regulations must secure prior approval from the Commissioner for a change in an accounting period pursuant to section 1.442–1(b)(1).

SECTION 5. APPLICATION

.01 In accordance with sections 1.442–1(a)(1) and 1.442–1(b)(1) of the regulations, approval is hereby granted under the specific circumstances described below to any corporation or consolidated group eligible under this revenue procedure to change its annual accounting period. Approval is granted beginning with the short period required to effect the change. A corporation (including the common parent of a consolidated group) must complete and file a current Form 1128 in the manner described in section 7 of this revenue procedure and otherwise comply with the provisions of this revenue procedure. The common parent corporation must clearly indicate that the Form 1128 is filed on behalf of the common parent corporation and all its subsidiaries, and the common parent corporation must answer all relevant questions on the Form 1128 for each member of the consolidated group. * * *

SECTION 6. COMPLIANCE WITH CONDITIONS

.01 In accordance with section 1.442–1(b)(1) of the regulations, approval of a change of a taxpayer's annual accounting period will not be granted unless the taxpayer and the Commissioner agree to the terms, conditions, and adjustments under which the change will be effected. In connection with the change of a corporation's annual accounting period pursuant to this revenue procedure, all the terms, conditions, and adjustments are set forth herein.

.02 Corporations changing their annual accounting period pursuant to this revenue procedure without complying with or satisfying all the conditions of this revenue procedure will be deemed to have initiated the change in annual accounting period without the consent of the Commissioner. * * *

Problem 27–2

In February, Ursula opens an ice cream franchise utilizing a C corporation of which she is the sole shareholder. In the first three months of operations, the corporation loses $10,000, $5,000, and $3,000, respectively. In May, it finally makes $1,000 and in the summer months (June, July, and August) it makes $8,000 per month.

1. May Ursula elect to file a tax return for the corporation with a July 31 year-end?

2. May Ursula elect an August 31 year-end?

3. If she selects July 31, what will the corporate income be for the year?

4. What will her corporation's income be if she elects August 31?

5. What if the corporation declares a bonus of $7,000 to Ursula (for her extraordinary employee efforts) on August 30 and then elects an August 31 year?

6. Can Ursula wait and see how the corporation performs during the autumn months before selecting the corporate year?

7. What is the latest fiscal year she can select for the corporation?

Chapter 28

TAX RATE AND ACCOUNTING STRATEGIES FOR PROFIT- ABLE CORPORATIONS

Code References: §§ 1(a); 11; 446(a)–(c); 448(a)–(b); 461(a), (g), (h).

Regulation: §§ 1.461–1(a), –4(a)–(e).

A. INTRODUCTION

The prior seven chapters have focused upon the tax aspects of the organization and start-up planning for a new business operating in corporate form. This chapter and the two following chapters focus on the tax considerations involved in a corporate business which is past the start-up stage and operating profitably.

The primary focus of corporate tax planning in this context is the avoidance of double taxation. The C corporation is a separate taxable entity which files its own return and pays its own tax to the federal government. Any profits remaining after the payment of that tax which are distributed to the shareholders as dividends are once again subject to federal tax at the shareholder level. See discussion at Chapter 31. Chapter 29 focuses on avoiding the corporate level of tax by electing out of C corporation status to become either an S corporation or some other type of "pass through" entity. Chapter 30 deals with the utilization of allowable deductions to reduce or eliminate the corporate income, thereby avoiding the first level of federal tax. This chapter, however, focuses on corporate tax planning through utilization of various tax rate differentials and certain accounting conventions.

By way of example, assume that a small business operating as a C corporation generates annual operating income of $250,000. The corporation must file an income tax return (Form 1120) with the federal government. Under current rate structures of § 11, taxable income of $250,000 would require the corporation to pay tax of $80,750 (15% × the first $50,000 of profit; 25% × the next $25,000 of profit; 34% × the next $175,000 of profit; and 5% × income in excess of $100,000). If the corporation then elected to distribute the remaining $169,250 of profit as a dividend to its shareholders and if those shareholders were in the 31% marginal tax bracket, the individual shareholders would pay an additional tax of $52,468 to the federal government on their individual tax returns. The combined bill of $133,218 yields a federal tax bite of 53.29%. The tariff is even higher in situations where the individual tax rate is in the 36% or 39.6% bracket and when state corporate and personal income taxes and federal Medicare taxes are included.

A large portion of corporate tax planning for small corporate businesses revolves around avoiding this adverse double tax. This chapter focuses on three aspects of that planning. The first deals with the disparity between individual and corporate rates and focuses on situations in which the entrepreneur operating as a C corporation can actually take advantage of taxation at the corporate level, particularly where the profits being taxed are retained for use in the business. The second addresses the utilization of different accounting methods which may affect the computation of corporate income. The final section considers methods of accelerating or deferring the timing of income or deductions to affect the amount of taxable income at the corporate level.

B. TAKING ADVANTAGE OF CORPORATE TAX RATES

After ten years to the contrary, as a result of the Revenue Reconciliation Act of 1993, marginal tax rates for individuals became higher than those for corporations. Beginning in 1993, high-income individuals face a maximum marginal individual tax bracket of 39.6%. In addition, the income "cap" was removed from the Medicare assessment, effectively adding another 1.45% tax, thereby bringing the effective individual federal tax rate to over 41% for high-income taxpayers. As noted previously, the tax rate for corporate income in excess of $75,000 is 34%. Only when the corporation has income of $10 million or more does the rate become 35%. The corporate entity must also match the 1.45% Medicare tax paid by the employee on his or her wages. As a result of the increase in the individual tax rate, the traditional planning strategy of avoiding corporate tax through either making an S election or eliminating corporate profits through deductible salary or bonus payments to a shareholder/employee has become less attractive for small business corporations. Before, even where the funds were needed in the corporate business, the profits would often be distributed to the individual owner at his or her lower tax rate. After paying the lower tax, he or she would loan or contribute the remaining funds back to the corporation for its use. Such techniques are no longer economically viable under the existing rate structure.

Even in situations where the funds are not immediately needed in the corporate business, consideration should be given to retaining the profits in the small business corporation even though a corporate tax must be paid. Because of the graduated corporate rate structure, $50,000 in profit can remain in the corporation at a corporate tax cost of $7,500 (15%). $75,000 may be retained at a cost of $13,750 (18.3%), and $100,000 for $22,500 (22.5%) in taxes. If these funds were distributed by the corporation to the shareholder/employees, they would typically incur a higher rate of tax. One planning technique for small business corporations is to distribute corporate profit as bonuses or compensation to the shareholder/employees *except for* the last $75,000 or $100,000 of corporate profit, upon which the corporate tax is paid. This technique has three advantages: (1) the retained corporate income is not taxed at the 34% maximum corporate rate because of the graduated rate system; (2) the funds distributed to the shareholder/employees *may* be taxed at less than 34%; and (3) the distribution of *all* corporate earnings to shareholder/employees may, as will be seen in Chapter 30, draw the scrutiny of the Service.

When all corporate income is distributed to shareholder/employees, particularly in year-end bonuses, the Service may take the position that the compensation paid is unreasonable and actually constitutes a disguised dividend to the shareholders (especially if made in proportion to shareholdings). A disguised dividend is not deductible by the corporation and the distribution would therefore result in payment of tax by both the corporation and the individual. Obviously, bonuses to the sole shareholder of a small business corporation are always in proportion to his or her shareholdings.

Problem 28–1

Kathy and Susan are attorneys practicing as a professional C corporation. Each has received salary income of $150,000 during the year. The corporation, just prior to year end, projects $200,000 of taxable income (over and above salaries paid) if no distributions are made.

1. What tax result to the corporation if Kathy and Susan each receive a bonus of $100,000 on the last day of the year?

2. What tax result would the bonus distribution have for Kathy and Susan, assuming no unusual personal losses or deductions for either?

3. What result if $100,000 is retained in the corporation and a $50,000 bonus is distributed to each of Kathy and Susan?

4. What if the corporation, at year-end, pays $25,000 to cover a malpractice insurance premium coming due the next month, declares and distributes a bonus of $50,000 each to Kathy and Susan, and retains $75,000 for working capital?

5. What if the entire $200,000 is retained by the corporation?

C. ACCOUNTING METHODS

Another election to be made by a small business corporation which may affect the timing and/or amount of its income and losses for tax purposes is the choice of an accounting method. This decision is often made through a combination of advice from the entrepreneur's attorney and accountant. While book income for accounting purposes is often different than taxable income, the general rule of § 446(a) is that taxable income "shall be computed under the method of accounting on the basis of which the taxpayer regularly computes his income in keeping his books." For a new business, this means that the corporation has a choice of accounting methods. This choice generally is between the cash method or the accrual method, although certain hybrid methods or other more exotic methods may be utilized in certain peculiar situations. Regardless of the method of choice, § 446(b) imposes an overall requirement that, for tax purposes, the method selected must "clearly reflect income." Taxpayers electing a particular accounting method solely on the basis that it will provide a tax advantage may run afoul of the clear reflection of income test.

The most common choice of a small business taxpayer is between the cash and accrual method. Because Congress has perceived potential abuses if the cash method is used, § 448 now limits the use of cash method accounting for certain types of entities. C corporations, for instance, may not use the cash method of accounting unless they are engaged in a farming business, are qualified personal service corporations, or have gross receipts under $5 million.

In general, a taxpayer using the cash method of accounting recognizes income upon the receipt of cash, property, or services. Rights to receive future payments are not included in income. A cash method taxpayer normally becomes entitled to a deduction for tax purposes upon the payment of an obligation. Payments for items which have a useful life substantially beyond the close of the taxable year and other prepayments may, however, be subject to restrictions and not currently deductible. Reg. § 1.446–1(c)(1)(i).

An accrual method taxpayer generally recognizes income when all events have occurred which fix the right to receive the income and the amount of the receipt is determinable with reasonable accuracy (the "all events test"). Accrual method taxpayers are entitled to deductions in the year in which all events have occurred which establish the fact of the liability and the amount of the deduction can be determined with reasonable accuracy. The deduction side of the all events test prohibits current deduction of reserves for anticipated future expenditures in most cases. Reg. § 1.446–1(c)(1)(ii).

As will be seen in the next section of this chapter, selection of the accounting method by the corporation will have an effect on certain techniques used by corporate taxpayers to regulate the timing of certain income and deductions.

D. TIMING OF INCOME AND DEDUCTIONS

There are many reasons why a small business corporation might desire to have control over the timing of its taxable income and its deductible loss. In the case of a C corporation, such reasons might be: (1) to maintain corporate income at a level of $75,000 or below to avoid the higher corporate tax bracket; (2) to accelerate income into a given year in order to utilize an expiring net operating loss carryforward; (3) to defer income and accelerate deductions in a current year if an S election is to be made for the next year (thereby eliminating the corporate-level tax); and (4) to defer income into a subsequent year if the current year has produced so much income that the payment of such amounts to shareholder/employees are in jeopardy of being treated as excessive compensation.

In the case of an S corporation, the entity may desire to control the amount of its income or deductions in a given year in order to interface the income it passes through with the tax situations of its individual shareholders who may wish to have either additional income or loss in given situations. A particular problem for the shareholders of an S corporation occurs when the corporation passes taxable income to its shareholders but does not have cash available for distribution with which to pay the resulting tax. In most planning, the corporation seeks to defer income beyond the end of its taxable year and accelerate deductions into the current taxable year in order to reduce current-year income or create a loss.

1. CASH METHOD

As noted in the prior section of this chapter, not all small businesses may elect the cash method of accounting. For those which may, however, the cash method provides considerable latitude in controlling the timing of income and deductions. A cash method taxpayer recognizes income on the receipt (or constructive receipt) of all items of income, including cash, property, and services. Reg. § 1.446–1(c)(1)(i). Thus, a corporate service business such as a law firm or accounting firm desiring to minimize its income could simply elect, at year end, not to send out bills for services performed. There are, however, some exceptions and limitations to the income upon receipt rule of a cash method taxpayer. For instance, if a taxpayer receives, in lieu of payment, a note or other obligation which is secured and immediately transferrable, the obligation might rise to the level of a cash equivalent and, if so, will be includable in income to a cash method taxpayer at its current fair market value. Similarly, if a payment is deferred by being placed in an escrow or trust account with the interest payable to the recipient corporation and the sole obstacle to the receipt of the funds is the passage of time (to a point beyond the end of the corporation's taxable year), income again may result under the economic benefit rule. Finally, if a payment is tendered to the corporation and the corporation "turns its back" on the payment, requesting that it be paid at a later time, the corporation will be deemed to have constructively received the payment. Despite these provisions, it is clear that a taxpayer may *contract* for the receipt of payment at a future time even though the paying party has the ability to pay currently and even though the deferral is tax-motivated.

On the deduction side, a cash method taxpayer has a large degree of control over the timing of deductions simply by controlling the time at which the checks are written to pay its bills. Again, however, there are limitations. In order to generate a deduction, the payment must be for a current expense and not for a capital item. Under § 263, payments for "permanent improvements or betterments" or expenditures which "result in the creation of an asset having a useful life which extends substantially beyond the close of the taxable year" must be capitalized. Furthermore, there are limitations on amounts which a cash method taxpayer may prepay. The creation of deductions at year-end by prepayment of recurring expenses has been a traditional method of reducing corporate income for a given year. The Service has challenged such prepayments, with varying success, on the basis that they either (1) lack a business purpose and are therefore nondeductible; or (2) that allowing their deduction would not clearly reflect the income of the taxpayer. Cash method taxpayers have been somewhat successful in sustaining deductions for prepaid period costs (such as insurance, taxes, and rent) so long as the payment is not more than one year in advance.

2. ACCRUAL METHOD

For accrual method taxpayers, the rules are different. On the income side, the all events test is generally met when the taxpayer has performed the services required to generate the income resulting from those services. Although it is less clear than under the cash method, a service-providing taxpayer could probably avoid accrual income by not sending out bills. See *Decision, Inc. v. Commissioner*, 47 T.C. 58 (1966). Once billed in a specific amount, however, the income is earned and reportable by the corporate taxpayer even though not yet paid. Interestingly, if an accrual method taxpayer is in *receipt* of a prepayment for services not yet performed (as from a corporate client seeking to obtain a year-end deduction for prepaid services), the income may have to be reported by the accrual method taxpayer even though the income has not yet technically been earned.

Accrual method taxpayers become entitled to deductions when "all events have occurred which determine the fact of liability and the amount of such liability can be determined with reasonable accuracy." This generally means that the payment is deductible when it is due or when performance on the part of the other party has occurred. In the case of prepayments, § 461 provides special rules for accrual method taxpayers. Section 461(h)(1) specifically provides that "the all events test shall not be treated as met any earlier than when economic performance with respect to the item occurs." As to services and property provided to a taxpayer, economic performance occurs as the service and property are provided or as the use occurs. Under a special regulatory rule, however, an accrual method taxpayer may treat economic performance as occurring upon payment if the taxpayer reasonably expects the property or services to be provided within three and one-half months after the date of payment. Reg. § 1.461–4(d)(6)(ii). In essence, this allows an accrual method corporation to make a year-end prepayment to regular trade creditors for up to three and one-half months of services or goods to be provided in the subsequent year.

REVENUE PROCEDURE 71–21
1971–2 C.B. 549.

Section 1. Purpose

The purpose of this Revenue Procedure is to implement an administrative decision, made by the Commissioner in the exercise of his discretion under section 446 of the Internal Revenue Code of 1954, to allow accrual method taxpayers in certain specified and limited circumstances to defer the inclusion in gross income for Federal income tax purposes of payments received (or amounts due and payable) in one taxable year for services to be performed by the end of the next succeeding taxable year. Amounts due and payable are, for purposes of this Revenue Procedure, treated as payments received.

Section 2. Background

In general, tax accounting requires that payments received for services to be performed in the future must be included in gross income in the taxable year of receipt. However, this treatment varies from financial accounting conventions consistently used by many accrual method taxpayers in the treatment of payments received in one taxable year for services to be performed by them in the next succeeding taxable year. The purpose of this Revenue Procedure is to reconcile the tax and financial accounting treatment of such payments in a large proportion of these cases without permitting extended deferral in the time of including such payments in gross income for Federal income tax purposes. Such reconciliation will facilitate reporting and verification of such items from the standpoint of both the taxpayers affected and the Internal Revenue Service.

Section 3. Permissible Methods

.01 An accrual method taxpayer who receives a payment for services to be performed by him in the future and who includes such payment in gross income in the year of receipt is using a proper method of accounting.

.02 An accrual method taxpayer who, pursuant to an agreement (written or otherwise), receives a payment in one taxable year for services, where all of the services under such agreement are required by the agreement as it exists at the end of the taxable year of receipt to be performed by him before the end of the next succeeding taxable year, may include such payment in gross income as earned through the performance of the services, subject to the limitations provided in sections 3.07, 3.08, and 3.11. However, if the inclusion in gross income of payments received is properly deferred under the preceding sentence and for any reason a portion of such services is not performed by the end of the next succeeding taxable year, the amount allocable to the services not so performed must be included in gross income in such next succeeding year, regardless of when (if ever) such services are performed.

.03 Except as provided in sections 3.04 and 3.05, a payment received by an accrual method taxpayer pursuant to an agreement for the performance by him of services must be included in his gross income in the taxable year of receipt if under the terms of the agreement as it exists at the end of such year:

(a) Any portion of the services is to be performed by him after the end of the taxable year immediately succeeding the year of receipt; or

(b) Any portion of the services is to be performed by him at an unspecified future date which may be after the end of the taxable year immediately succeeding the year of receipt. * * *

.06 In any case in which an advance payment is received pursuant to an agreement which requires the taxpayer to perform contingent services, the amount of an advance payment which is earned in a taxable year through the performance of such services may be determined (a) on a statistical basis if adequate data are available to the taxpayer; (b) on a straight-line ratable basis over the time period of the agreement if it is not unreasonable to anticipate at the end of the taxable year of receipt that a substantially ratable portion of the services will be performed in the next succeeding taxable year; or (c) by the use of any other basis that in the opinion of the Commissioner, results in a clear reflection of income.

.07 Where an agreement requires that a taxpayer perform contingent services (including for this purpose the replacement of parts or materials where the obligation to replace is incidental to an agreement providing for the performance of personal services) with respect to property which is sold, leased, built, installed, or constructed by such taxpayer (or a related person as defined in section 3.10), advance payments received with respect to such agreement may be included in gross income under the method prescribed in section 3.02 only if in the normal course of his business the taxpayer offers to sell, lease, build, install, or construct the property without such a contingent service agreement.

.08 This Revenue Procedure has no application to amounts received under guaranty or warranty contracts or to prepaid rent or prepaid interest. However, for purposes of this Revenue Procedure and section 1.61–8(b) of the Income Tax Regulations (requiring "advance rentals" to be included in income in the year of receipt), the term "rent" does not include payments for the use or occupancy of rooms or other space where significant services are also rendered to the occupant, such as for the use or occupancy of rooms or other quarters in hotels, boarding houses, or apartment houses furnishing hotel services or in tourist homes, motor courts, or motels. * * *

.11 The amount of any advance payment includible as gross receipts in gross income in the taxable year of receipt by a taxpayer under the foregoing rules shall be no less than the amount of such payment included as gross receipts in gross income for purposes of his books and records and all reports (including consolidated financial statements) to shareholders, partners, other proprietors or beneficiaries and for credit purposes.

.12 The above rules may be illustrated in part as follows:

(1) On November 1, 1970, *A,* a calendar year accrual method taxpayer in the business of giving dancing lessons, receives a payment for a one-year contract commencing on that date which provides for 48 individual, one-hour lessons. Eight lessons are provided in 1970. Under the method prescribed in section 3.02, *A* must include $\frac{1}{6}$ of the payment in income for 1970, and $\frac{5}{6}$ of such payment in 1971, regardless of whether *A* is for any reason unable to give all the lessons under the contract by the end of 1971.

(2) Assume the same facts as in Example 1 except that the payment is received for a two-year contract commencing on November 1, 1970, under which 96 lessons are provided. The taxpayer must include the entire payment in his gross income in 1970 since a portion of the services may be performed in 1972.

(3) On June 1, 1970, *B,* a calendar year accrual method taxpayer who is a landscape architect, receives a payment for services which, under the terms of the agreement, must be completed by December, 1971. On December 31, 1970, *B* estimates that $\frac{3}{4}$ of the work under the agreement has been completed. Under the method prescribed in section 3.02, *B* must include $\frac{3}{4}$ of the payment in 1970. The remaining $\frac{1}{4}$ of such payment must be included in 1971, regardless of whether *B* is for any reason unable to complete the job in 1971.

(4) In 1970, *C,* a calendar year accrual method taxpayer in the television repair business, receives payments for one-year contracts under which *C* agrees to repair (or, incidental to providing such repair service, to replace) certain parts in the customer's television set if such parts fail to function properly. The television sets to be serviced under *C*'s contracts were not sold, leased, built, installed, or constructed by *C* or by a person related to *C* within the meaning of section 3.10. Therefore, section 3.07 does not apply, and *C* may adopt the method prescribed in section 3.02. Under such method *C* must include such payments in income over the period earned in accordance with one of the bases prescribed in section 3.06, provided that any portion of the payments not included in income in 1970 must be included in income in 1971.

(5) In 1971, *D,* a calendar year accrual method taxpayer in the business of manufacturing, selling and servicing television sets, receives

payments for one-year contingent service contracts with respect to television sets sold by *D* in 1971. *D* offers television sets for sale without contingent service contracts. Under these circumstances, the requirement of section 3.07 is satisfied, and *D* may adopt the method prescribed in section 3.02. Under such method *D* must include such payments in income over the period earned in accordance with one of the bases prescribed in section 3.06, provided that any portion of the payments not included in income in 1971 must be included in income in 1972. * * *

Problem 28–2

Indemnity Title Insurance Company has operated as a C corporation with great success. It is the sales agent for a Title Insurance Underwriting Company. Indemnity's tax advisers have rearranged its ownership so that it will be eligible to elect S corporation status on the first day of its next tax year. Indemnity is forecasting $2 million of corporate profit, after all salary and bonus payments, on sales of just over $20,000,000. Advisers are seeking to defer some of the income into the next year when no income tax will be payable at the corporate level.

1. May Indemnity use the cash method of accounting?

2. Assuming an accrual method, what if, on the last day of its C corporation year, Indemnity prepays 3½ months of insurance premiums and accounting fees?

3. What if the company prepays 3½ months of management wages?

   a. What if a manager quits one month later?

   b. What if it prepays one year of management wages?

4. Prior to real estate closings, Indemnity issues customers a "commitment" to issue the title insurance in the future. At the closing, Indemnity collects its premium for the insurance. The title policy itself is issued approximately 60 days following closing, after all documents have been recorded (by Indemnity) in appropriate real property records.

   a. What if Indemnity delays the actual closings of transactions requiring the issuance of title policies with the effect of deferring $1,000,-000 in premiums into the next year?

   b. What if the closings take place and the premiums are paid during the current year, but the policies are issued the following year?

Chapter 29

USE OF THE S ELECTION BY A PROFITABLE SMALL BUSINESS

Code References: §§ 469(c)(2), (7); 1361(b), (c), 1362(a), (b), 1363(a), (b); 1366(a), (b); 1367(a); 1368; 1374.

Regulation: §§ 1.1361–1(1); 1.1362–1; 1.1367–1; 1.1368–1(a)–(e), –2(a), (b); 1.1374–1.

A. INTRODUCTION

Chapter 26 introduced the concept of utilizing the S corporation election as a planning vehicle for passing tax losses of a start-up or unprofitable businesses through to the business owners. This chapter deals with the reverse situation in which a profitable business, operating in corporate form, utilizes the S election to avoid double taxation. When the Subchapter S corporation concept was introduced by Congress in 1958, its basic purpose was to allow a small business to operate with the state law protection of a corporation without paying federal tax at the corporate level. The original provisions governing Subchapter S corporations, however, were extremely complex and, in operation, created a tax scheme which was much more complicated than simply "taxing the business as a partnership." Many of the complexities of the early Subchapter S corporations were eliminated in the Subchapter S Revision Act of 1982, which changed the designation of electing corporations from "Subchapter S corporations" to "S corporations." The Tax Reform Act of 1986 indirectly made the utilization of S corporations more popular by making it more difficult to avoid double taxation in C corporations and by continuing a rate structure in which the individual rates were lower than the C corporation rates. The recent changes in the rate structure whereby the individual rates exceed those of C corporations and the emergence of the limited liability company and similar entities as alternative business forms which provide liability protection and taxation as a partnership have diminished the popularity of the S corporation in recent years.

Despite the changes in the federal rate structure making maximum individual rates higher than corporate rates, the attractiveness of the S corporation over the C corporation remains simply because of the single level of tax. A C corporation with $100,000 of taxable income would pay a federal corporate tax of $22,500. Upon distribution of the remaining $77,500 to its individual shareholder/employee in the 31% tax bracket, the individual would pay an additional $24,025, for a total tax bill of $46,525. If the same corporation made the S election, there would be no tax at the corporate level and the entire $100,000 would be subject to tax at the individual shareholder's rate of 31%, yielding a tax bite of only $31,000. As will be seen in Chapter 30, there may be ways of avoiding the C corporation tax in the prior example. S corporation status, however, removes the necessity for avoiding such tax and that luxury is the *sine qua non* of electing S corporation status.

Not all corporations are eligible to make the S election. S corporations are limited as to number and type of shareholders. With minor exceptions, they may have only one class of stock. There are sometimes limitations upon the type of business an S corporation may operate. An S corporation may not own a subsidiary (i.e., 80% or greater ownership of another corporation's stock).

Operating a profitable business as an S corporation will not produce the same result, even after the Subchapter S Revision Act, as operating in partnership form. Differences remain in (1) the ability to pass through gains in all cases with a single tax to the shareholders; (2) the ability to specially allocate gains or losses to specific shareholders; and (3) the determination of tax basis with regard to liabilities.

Particular complications arise when a corporation which has been operating its business as a C corporation elects to become an S corporation. The conversion from C corporation to S corporation status brings into play a distinct set of rules which places the electing corporation in a hybrid status for a period of at least ten years. The various considerations involved in making such a conversion are discussed in detail later in this chapter.

In summary, while the S corporation remains a viable entity choice for a small business operation, its various restrictions and complications, combined with the emergence of the limited liability company and similar hybrid entities, make it a less frequent choice of small business operators.

B. QUALIFICATION FOR AN ELECTION OF S CORPORATION STATUS

Not all corporations may be S corporations. There are numerous requirements at both the entity and shareholder level. The rationale behind the various rules is not always clear.

1. CORPORATION REQUIREMENTS

In order to qualify as an S corporation, the corporation itself must be a domestic, rather than foreign, corporation. In addition, it must be a "small business corporation." This definition excludes insurance companies, financial institutions, and members of any affiliated group. Because an S corporation may not be a member of an affiliated group, it may not have subsidiaries (a corporation of which it holds 80% or more of the stock). Generally, it may have only one class of stock. This means that the shareholders must have identical liquidation and distribution rights from the corporation. In this context, the Service may, and often does, take the position that shareholder debt is actually equity and, as such, constitutes a disqualifying second class of stock. The Regulations provide an exception to this rule allowing differences in voting rights (e.g., one class voting and one class nonvoting) so long as the other characteristics of the shares are identical.

2. SHAREHOLDER REQUIREMENTS

An S corporation may not have more than 35 shareholders. No shareholder may be a nonresident alien. Finally, all shareholders must be either individuals, estates, or certain specified types of trusts. Corporations (whether S or C), partnerships, limited liability companies, and most trusts may not be S corporation shareholders.

Historically, no trust could be a shareholder in an S corporation. Gradually, however, because of the limitations placed upon the flexibility of shareholders seeking to use trusts as estate planning or creditor protection vehicles, Regulations and legislation eased the trust restrictions. Now, there are several types of trusts which may be qualified S corporation shareholders: (1) trusts which are treated as "grantor" trusts under §§ 671–79; (2) trusts which hold shares as a result of the death of a former individual shareholder; (3) voting trusts; and, most importantly, (4) qualified Subchapter S trusts ("Qualified Trusts").

In an effort to liberalize the restrictive shareholder requirements relating to S corporations, the Qualified Trust was introduced into the Code in 1989. While the Qualified Trust concept allows more trusts to be S corporation shareholders, the Qualified Trust rules themselves are extremely complex and can be a trap for the unwary. In general, a Qualified Trust is a trust requiring that (1) during the life of the current income beneficiary, there can be only one income beneficiary (no "spray" powers); (2) corpus distributions during the current income beneficiary's life can be made only to that beneficiary; (3) the current income beneficiary's interest must terminate on the earlier of his or her death or the termination of the trust; and (4) if the trust terminates during the current income beneficiary's life, the trust assets are to be distributed to the current income beneficiary. The interpretation of these rules has given rise to an enormous amount of litigation and ruling activity. In situations where S corporation shares are transferred to a trust which does not qualify as a Qualified Trust, the trust may be reformed to remove the disqualifying features.

The use of the Qualified Trust is important in many planning situations. It is generally used to shift current income and appreciation without vesting control in junior shareholders. Because of the creditor protection and lack of control by the beneficiary, it is often a more useful planning vehicle than an outright gift of stock. The vehicle is often used by small businesses to gradually transfer equity in an appreciating business to the next generation. It is less effective in transferring current income to lower-bracket shareholders since the income will be taxed at the higher bracket of other family members if the trust beneficiary is under 14 years of age.

3. EFFECTS OF NONQUALIFICATION

Generally, if at any time during the S corporation's taxable year, it does not meet all of the corporate and shareholder-level requirements, the S corporation election and status will be terminated. The termination normally takes place on the date of its cessation to qualify and is prospective only. A revocation of S corporation status, however, can be retroactive if made within the first 2½ months of the taxable year. Generally, when S corporation status is terminated, it cannot be re-elected for five years after the taxable year of termination. However, in the case of inadvertent terminations, the Service has become increasingly sympathetic to waivers of the termination or waiver of the five-year waiting period. Even with the liberalization of the Service's position, however, the failure of a small business corporation to monitor its shareholders and corporate structure, each of which may lead to an inadvertent S termination, remains a potential for extremely adverse tax results.

PAIGE v. UNITED STATES

580 F.2d 960 (9th Cir.1978).

SKOPIL, DISTRICT JUDGE:

Plaintiff-taxpayers appeal from the denial of their claim for a tax refund. The issue involved is whether taxpayers' corporation qualified for the subchapter S election provided in 26 U.S.C. § 1371 (1954). We hold that it did not. We affirm.

Tackmer made the subchapter S election in 1965. The government now contends that Tackmer Corporation had more than one class of stock.

Tackmer is a small California company that was first incorporated in 1965. When Tackmer first issued stock, it received two different kinds of consideration. Plaintiffs and another party assigned their rights to an exclusive license agreement in exchange for Tackmer stock ("property shareholders"). Eight other parties paid cash ("cash shareholders").

The Articles of Incorporation state that "No distinction shall exist between the shares of the corporation [or] the holders thereof." The applicable California Corporation Code, § 304 (West 1949), stated that there could be no distinction between shares unless specified in the Articles.

Before Tackmer could issue any stock, it was required to obtain a permit from the California Department of Corporations. The California Corporation Code gave the Department authority to impose conditions on corporations for the protection of the public. Pursuant to this authority the Department had a policy of imposing certain conditions on small corporations such as Tackmer which were capitalized with both cash and property that had an indeterminate value. The purpose of the conditions was to protect the shareholders who paid with cash from having their interests diluted by overissue of stock to the shareholders who paid with property.

The conditions imposed by the Department of Corporations were as follows:

(a) The stock had to be deposited in escrow and could not be sold without the Department's consent;

(b) If the company defaulted on dividend payments for two years, the cash shareholders would have irrevocable power of attorney to vote the property shareholders' shares for the board of directors;

(c) On dissolution, the property shareholders had to waive their rights to the distribution of assets until the cash shareholders had received the full amount of their purchase price plus any unpaid accumulated dividends at 5% per year;

(d) The property shareholders had to waive their rights to any dividends until the cash shareholders annually received cumulative dividends equal to 5% of the purchase price per share;

(e) The conditions were to remain in effect until the shares were released from escrow. The conditions were in effect from 1965 to 1970.

The property shareholders signed an agreement with the company stating that they would abide by the conditions. The taxpayers admit that the conditions could have been waived by the cash shareholders. Notwithstanding the conditions, the differences between the two kinds of shareholders were never taken into account and all dividends were distributed on a pro rata basis.

A corporation must meet six requirements in order to qualify for subchapter S tax treatment. The applicable statute reads:

"For purposes of ... subchapter [S, a qualifying corporation is] a domestic corporation which is not a member of an affiliated group ... and which does not—

"(1) have more than 10 shareholders;

"(2) have as a shareholder a person (other than an estate) who is not an individual;

"(3) have a nonresident alien as a shareholder; and

"(4) *have more than one class of stock.*" * * *

The taxpayers contend that because the Articles and state law authorized only one class of stock, there can be only one class for subchapter S purposes. We hold, however, that the interpretation of subchapter S qualifications is a federal question.

Treas.Reg. § 1.1371–1(g) provides that "If the outstanding shares of stock of the corporation are not identical with respect to the *rights* and interests which they convey in the control, profits, and assets of the corporation, then the corporation is considered to have more than one class of stock" [emphasis added]. The cash shareholders had preferred rights over property shareholders, notwithstanding that the cash shareholders chose not to exercise those rights. The possibility of the exercise of differing rights is enough to disqualify a corporation for subchapter S tax treatment.

Taxpayers' assertion that Tackmer in fact made all distributions on a pro rata basis is irrelevant. A corporation's qualifications for subchapter S status is judged at the date of election. The court may not consider Tackmer's actual distributions after its election. The language in the statute is clear. Tax planners must be able to assume that the court will give it its plain meaning. * * *

There is a strong policy behind the requirement that subchapter S corporations have only one class of stock. The corporations themselves pay no corporate income tax. The shareholders pay individual income tax on a pro rata share of all corporate income, regardless of whether any money or property has actually been distributed to the shareholder. If the statute allowed more than one class of stock, complicated allocation problems could arise.

The example given in the government's brief illustrates the potential problems. Assume that during its first taxable year Tackmer had earnings and profits of $5,500 and had declared and paid a preference dividend to the cash shareholders only. Pursuant to Condition (d) of the California Department of Corporations requirements, the minimum dividend would be $2,575. This would leave the corporation with an undistributed taxable income of $2,925. This sum would be taxed pro rata to all the shareholders:

To the cash shareholders $1,043
    (who have 5,100 of the 14,300 shares)
To the property shareholders $1,882
    (who have 9,200 of 14,300 shares)
                                                              $2,925

If Tackmer had no earnings and profits its second year, it would still be obligated to pay $2,575 under Condition (d). It would pay the distribution out of funds generated during its first year. That is, it would pay to the cash shareholders money that had been taxed to, but not received by, both cash and property shareholders. In computing the proper liability of cash shareholders with respect to this distribution, it would be necessary to attribute in an equitable manner to cash shareholders taxes paid by property shareholders. This would introduce substantial complexity in the administration of subchapter S. It was this type of *potential* difficulty which Congress sought to avoid by limiting subchapter S corporations to one class of stock.

We agree with the taxpayers that the purpose of subchapter S is to benefit small corporations such as the one here. It is unfortunate that a requirement of state law has caused a result that no one intended. However, the taxpayers' subjective intent to create one class of stock cannot be allowed to override statutory requirements. Congress has set forth specific objective requirements for subchapter S qualification, and we must follow the mandate of the statute.

We Affirm.

C. TAXATION OF AN OPERATING S CORPORATION

1. GENERAL

When a corporation and its shareholders qualify to be taxed as an S corporation, a relatively complex set of rules apply. The primary feature of the S corporation is that there will be no taxation at the corporate level, with gains and losses of the corporation being passed through to its shareholders in proportion to their shareholdings. As will be seen, however, even this basic concept is not entirely true since there are certain corporate-level taxes which must be paid by certain S corporations. The other basic idea of the S corporation election is that it will allow the entity to be "taxed as a partnership." While there are similarities in certain aspects of the taxation of partnerships and S corporations, there are also significant differences. In particular, the rules relating to partnerships, as discussed in Chapter 10, allow partnerships some flexibility in allocating gains and losses among the various partners, so long as such allocations ultimately prove to have "substantial economic effect." Such special allocations are not available to S corporations.

Although the S corporation is designed to pass through its gains and losses to its shareholders in proportion to their shareholdings, certain calculations and elections are made at the corporate, rather than individual shareholder, level. The corporation files its own tax return, reporting the income and deductions generated by its business or investments. Its overall income or loss is calculated and reported on Form 1120S which is filed on behalf of the S corporation itself. Many of the tax elections which affect the S corporation's computation of income are made at the corporate level. For example, accounting method, depreciation methods, inventory methods, and various other elections which significantly affect the entity's taxable income or losses are made at the corporate level, not subject to variation among the shareholder/owners.

The Form 1120S which must be filed on behalf of the corporation is generally due, for a calendar year corporation, on March 15th. Since the S corporation normally pays no tax, its income and losses are passed through to the individual owners by reporting their share on a K–1 schedule attached to the 1120S and sent to each shareholder. If the return is timely filed, the individual shareholders will have their K–1 forms in time for reporting their share of the S corporation income on their individual tax returns, generally due on April 15th.

The 1120S return contains all of the income and deductions of the corporation. As with partnerships, however, those items are divided into two categories: separately stated items and non-separately stated items. Separately stated items are those which retain their individual tax character as they are passed through to the shareholders. The non-separately stated items are part of a lump sum amount of the residual items flowing from the S corporation. The separately stated items are not included in the S corporation's calculation of taxable income or loss. Separately stated items are those with a special tax character that could affect the shareholder's individual tax calculation. The separately stated items include capital gains and losses, § 1231 gains and losses, charitable contributions, tax-exempt interest, depletion allowances, and passive losses. The non-separately stated items include all other items of income, gain, loss, and deduction. The non-separately stated items are aggregated and used in calculating the S corporation's taxable income or loss which is then passed through to the shareholders in accordance with their shareholdings.

The separately stated items which are passed through from the S corporation are then aggregated by the shareholder with any individual amounts of such gain, loss, or deduction in the particular category passed through. The individual tax rules regarding the allowability and character of such gains, losses, and deductions then apply to the aggregated amount on the shareholder's individual 1040 tax return.

Problem 29–1

Sharon and Bob each own 50% of the shares of Mountain Bike, Inc. It rents mountain bikes. A property filed S election is in effect. The rental business generates net income of $20,000 for the year. All income and expenses of the business are non-separately stated items. During the year, the corporation sells real property it owns, generating a capital gain of $30,000. Bob has also, during the year, incurred an $8,000 capital loss on the sale of stock.

1. What is the corporation's income as reported on its 1120S?
2. How is the capital gain treated?
3. What will be reported on the K–1 forms of Sharon and Bob?
4. What will Sharon's personal return (1040) look like, assuming no other income or loss?

5. Does Bob benefit from the retention of the capital gain character of the separately stated item passed through to him from the corporation?

2. PASSIVE ACTIVITY RULES

While the focus of this Chapter is primarily on profitable S corporation operations, the application of the passive activity loss rules in the context of an S corporation must be noted. The passive activity loss rules of § 469 characterize all income, gain, loss, deduction, and credit as either passive or non-passive. Passive income or loss is that derived from a trade or business activity in which the taxpayer does not materially participate. Passive losses may not be deducted against non-passive income. The characterization of both income and loss as either passive or non-passive is important. Passive income can shelter passive losses of the taxpayer.

The passive activity loss rules do not apply directly to S corporations. They do, however, apply to S corporation shareholders. The S corporation shareholder must first examine the various business activities which occur at the corporate level. The passive activity rules apply to each separate activity in which the taxpayer is a participant. Reg. § 1.469–2T(e)(1). This activity determination is made at the corporate level. Each shareholder is then treated as though he or she owned an undivided interest in that corporate activity. The income or loss of that activity is determined by an allocation of corporate expenses and income. The shareholder must then determine whether he or she has materially participated in any of the corporation's activities. If so, the income or loss from the activity will not be passive. If not, the income or loss from the activity of the corporation will be passive. If the *income* of the activity is deemed to be passive income at the shareholder level, it may, subject to the other rules of § 469, be offset by other passive losses of the shareholder. If the activity's *losses* attributable to the shareholder are passive, they may be nondeductible under § 469 even though they would otherwise be deductible. Even if non-passive, the losses may still be denied in the event that the shareholder is not at risk with regard to the losses under § 465 or has insufficient basis to deduct them, pursuant to § 1366(d)(1).

Problem 29–2

Henry, June, and Ann each own 1/3 of the stock of Hejuan, Inc., an S corporation. It owns a building. The ground floor is a fast food restaurant operated by the three shareholders as their full-time employment. The upper four floors are apartments which are managed by an outside real estate company. The shareholders do not participate in the management of the apartments. During the taxable year, the food operation generates $90,000 of income, with no separately stated items of income or loss. The apartment rental operation, because of vacancies, yields a loss of $30,000.

1. What items will be separately stated on the 1120S?

2. What will each shareholder's K–1 form show?

3. Can the apartment rental loss be offset against the restaurant gain?

4. June has $7,000 in passive income from a separate real estate investment. What will her individual return reflect?

5. What if Henry dropped out of the restaurant operation and devoted all of his time to managing the apartments?

6. What if Henry divided his time between the two activities?

3. DISTRIBUTIONS

A final consideration in reviewing the taxation of S corporation operations is the treatment of distributions by an S corporation to its shareholders. As in the case of a partnership, a distribution by an S corporation to a shareholder may take several forms. If a shareholder has performed services for the corporation, the distribution could be treated as wages or other compensation to the performing shareholder. The same distribution could, on the other hand, be treated as a shareholder's proportionate share of corporate profits.

As will be seen in the next chapter, issues often arise in C corporations as to the reasonableness of the compensation paid to shareholder/employees. In a C corporation, the shareholders may be attempting to avoid the corporate level tax by creating a purportedly deductible payment to a shareholder/employee which is actually in excess of the value of the shareholder's services. If challenged by the Service, such payment may prove not to be fully deductible. In the S corporation context, there generally is no corporate level tax. There are, however, employment taxes (FICA, FUTA, and state taxes) on wages paid to employees which often do not apply to profit distributions to business owners. Thus, in the S corporation arena, the Service's position is reversed. The Service has held that a shareholder cannot take *inadequate* compensation from a corporation in order to avoid employment taxes. Rev.Rul. 74–44, 1974–1 C.B. 287. This issue is particularly prevalent in the case of corporations owned by a sole shareholder who is also an employee of the corporation when the corporation's income is at or below the Social Security wage ceiling.

Setting aside the issue of whether the distribution to a shareholder should be treated as wages for employment tax purposes, the *income* tax treatment of distributions of an S corporation can be quite complex. Particular problems arise for an S corporation which previously has been a C corporation. These are discussed in the next section of this chapter. Corporations which have always been S corporations do not have to deal with the C corporation concept of accumulated earnings and profits and therefore do not generate dividend income on distribution to shareholders of their cash or other assets. Like a partnership, the taxable income of an S corporation is attributable to its shareholders regardless of whether cash is distributed to them. The amount of the reported income, however, under § 1367(a)(1), increases a shareholder's basis in the stock he or she holds in the S corporation. This increase in basis is favorable to the S corporation shareholder. Amounts distributed from an S corporation without accumulated earnings and profits to its share-holder are treated, under § 1368(b), as a return of capital to that shareholder to the extent of his or her stock basis. Thus, they are not taxable. Any distribution in excess of the stock basis is treated as capital gain to the recipient shareholder. These rules are easily applied when the S corporation without accumulated earnings and profits makes a distribution of cash. As discussed in Chapter 32, a corporation which distributes appreciated property, including an S corporation, however, will generate additional income at the corporate level since the corporation must recognize gain under § 311(b) as if the property had been *sold* to the distributee. This item of corporate income would then be passed through to the shareholders in accordance with their shareholdings on the K–1 which they receive from the corporation at the end of the year.

D.   S CORPORATIONS WHICH WERE FORMERLY C CORPORATIONS

An S corporation election made by a corporation at its inception means that such an entity would not be subject to the C corporation rules as regards distributions. Such a situation occurs when a newly formed corporate business immediately elects S status or when a business is transferred to a newly formed S corporation by a sole proprietor-ship, partnership, or limited liability company. However, when a business operating as a C corporation elects, mid-stream, to make the S election, special rules apply. Specifically, a C corporation which elects S corporation status may be subject to various "penalty" taxes as it continues its operations, including: (1) the penalty tax on built-in gains; (2) the penalty tax on excessive passive investment income; and (3) the potential dividend status of corporate distributions.

1.   PENALTY TAX ON BUILT–IN GAINS

Section 1374 imposes a corporate-level tax on the "net unrealized built-in gains" that are recognized by a former C corporation during the first 10 taxable years that the S election is in effect. The tax rate is the highest applicable corporate rate in force at the time that the built-in gains are recognized. The net recognized built-in gains of the corporation (net of corporate-level taxes payable) are then passed through to and reported by the corporation's shareholders.

The rationale behind § 1374 relates to the abolition of the *General Utilities* doctrine for C corporations which took place in 1986. Following the repeal of that doctrine, as discussed at Chapter 32, a C corporation recognizes gain on the distribution or sale of its appreciated assets at the corporate level. The built-in gains tax is designed to prevent a C corporation from avoiding that corporate-level tax on unrealized appreci-ation by making an S election prior to selling or distributing its assets. The effect of the built-in gain tax is to reinstate the concept of double taxation (tax at both the corporate and shareholder level) as to those S corporations which have appreciated assets at the time of their conversion from C to S status. The practical effect of the rule is to require that any C corporation converting to S status obtain an appraisal of its assets as of the first day of its first S election year. The built-in gain is comprised only of appreciation which exists on that date, and not appreciation which accrues thereafter. The amount of tax actually paid at the corporate level is passed through to the shareholders as a loss under § 1366(f)(2) and may be deducted by them in proportion to their shareholdings. If the corporation is able to wait 10 years following the date of its initial election, § 1374 is inapplicable and the gain on the appreciated asset (whether accruing before or after the date of the S election) would be taxable only at the shareholder level.

APPLICATION OF THE BUILT–IN GAIN RULES OF SECTION * * * 1374 OF THE CODE TO INSTALLMENT SALES

NOTICE 90–27
1990–1 C.B. 336.

* * *

3. *Installment Sales and Section 1374*

Section 1374 of the Code, imposes a corporate-level tax with respect to certain gain recognized by an S corporation. Generally, the tax is imposed for any taxable year beginning in the recognition period of an S corporation in which the corporation has a net recognized built-in gain. Under section 1374(d)(2)(A), the term "net recognized built-in gain" means the lesser of (i) the amount that would be the taxable income of the corporation if only recognized built-in gains and recognized built-in losses were taken into account, or (ii) the corporation's taxable income (determined as provided in section 1375(b)(1)(B)). If, for any taxable year, the lesser amount is the corporation's taxable income determined under section 1375(b)(1)(B), the amount by which the excess of recognized built-in gain over recognized built-in loss exceeds taxable income is treated as recognized built-in gain in the succeeding taxable year. Section 1374(d)(2)(B). The amount of the net recognized built-in gain taken into account under section 1374 for any taxable year is limited to the excess, if any, of the net unrealized built-in gain over the net recognized built-in gain for prior taxable years beginning in the recognition period. * * *

Section 1374(e) of the Code provides that regulations shall be issued as may be necessary to carry out the purposes of section 1374. In addition, section 337(d), in part, provides that regulations shall be issued as may be necessary or appropriate to carry out the purposes of the amendments under the Act made to section 1374, including regulations to ensure that such purposes not be circumvented through the use of any provision of law or regulation. The Service has determined that the purposes underlying the repeal of the General Utilities doctrine and the related amendments to section 1374 would fail to be carried out in certain cases if an S corporation disposes of an asset either prior to or during the recognition period in an installment sale reported under the installment method.

Accordingly, the Service will issue regulations governing the treatment of installment sales under section 1374 of the Code, including regulations providing that, in certain cases, section 1374 will continue to apply to income recognized under the installment method during a taxable year ending after the expiration of the recognition period. Under the regulations, if a taxpayer sells an asset either prior to or during the recognition period and recognizes income (either during or after the recognition period) from the sale under the installment method, the income will, when recognized, be taxed under section 1374 to the extent it would have been so taxed in prior taxable years if the selling corporation had made the election under 11 section 453(d) not to report the income under the installment method. For purposes of determining the extent to which the income would have been subject to tax if the section 453(d) election had not been made, the taxable income limitation of section 1374(d)(2)(A)(ii) and the built-in gain carryover rule of section 1374(d)(2)(B) will be taken into account.

Example 1. In year 1 of the recognition period under section 1374, a corporation realizes a gain of $100,000 on the sale of an asset with built-in gain. The corporation is to receive full payment for the asset in year 11. Because the corporation does not make an election under section 453(d), all $100,000 of the gain from the sale is reported under the installment method in year 11. If the corporation had made an election under section 453(d) with respect to the sale, the gain would have been recognized in year 1 and, taking into account the corporation's income and gains from other sources, application of the taxable income limitation of section 1374(d)(2)(A)(ii) and the built-in gain carryover rule of section 1374(d)(2)(B) would have resulted in $40,000 of the gain being subject to tax during the recognition period under section 1374. Therefore, the regulations will subject $40,000 of the gain recognized in year 11 to tax under section 1374.

Example 2. In year 1 of the recognition period under section 1374, a corporation realizes a gain of $100,000 on the sale of an asset with built-in gain. The corporation is to receive full payment for the asset in year 6. Because the corporation does not make an election under section 453(d), all $100,000 of the gain from the sale is reported under the installment method in year 6. If the corporation had made an election under section 453(d) with respect to the sale, the gain would have been recognized in year 1 and, taking into account the corporation's income and gains from other sources, application of the taxable income limitation of section 1374(d)(2)(A)(ii) and the built-in gain carryover rule of section 1374(d)(2)(B) would have resulted in all of the gain being subjected to tax under section 1374 in years 1 through 5. Therefore, notwithstanding that the taxable income limitation of section 1374(d)(2)(A)(ii) might otherwise limit the taxation of the gain recognized in year 6, the regulations will provide that the entire $100,000 of gain will be subject to tax under section 1374 when it is recognized in year 6.

These regulations shall not apply for purposes of the application of section 1374 of the Code as in effect prior to amendment by the Act.

The Service will also issue regulations to provide rules similar to those described in this Notice for regulated investment companies and real estate investment trusts that elect to be subject to rules similar to the rules of section 1374 of the Code. See Notice 88–19, 1988–1 C.B. 486.

2. EXCESS PASSIVE INVESTMENT INCOME

Section 1375 imposes a penalty on an S corporation's "excess net passive investment income." The penalty tax applies only if the S corporation has (1) passive investment income in excess of 25% of its gross receipts, and (2) the existence of C corporation earnings and profits from years before the S election took effect. The purpose of the tax is to encourage an S corporation with earnings and profits from its C corporation days to distribute them. The amount of the penalty tax is the highest corporate tax rate, multiplied by the lower of the corporation's "excess net passive income" (computed under § 1375(b)(1)(A)), or the S corporation's taxable income (computed under § 1375(b)(1)(B)), as if it were a C corporation (without net operating loss carryovers and certain other deductions). A practical method of avoiding this tax is to have the S corporation distribute the amount of its C corporation earnings and profits as dividends. If the C corporation's earnings and profits are eliminated so that none remains at the end of the year, the penalty tax does not apply.

Passive investment income generally includes gross receipts from royalties, rents, dividends, interest, and annuities, as well as net gains from the sale or exchange of stock or securities. If the former C corporation has no earnings and profits or if it distributes those earnings and profits as dividends, there are no restrictions on the amount of passive income that can be earned by it, as an S corporation, without penalty. If, however, the S corporation has some amount of C corporation earnings and profits, the tax applies. It should also be noted that significant passive income may jeopardize the S corporation election. Under § 1362(d)(3), excessive amounts for three consecutive years may result in a termination of that status.

3. DISTRIBUTION TO SHAREHOLDERS—THE AAA

When an S corporation has no accumulated earnings and profits, the taxation of distributions is totally dependent upon the shareholder's basis in his S corporation stock. Such stock basis is increased by the shareholder's proportionate share of income and by his or her contributions of cash or property to the corporation. It is decreased by distributions of cash or property from the corporation and by losses passed through from the corporation to the shareholder.

The rules are considerably more complicated if the S corporation has earnings and profits. Generally, such earnings and profits arise in an S corporation which was previously a C corporation. When the C corporation elects S status, its earnings and profits are essentially frozen. If an S corporation has accumulated earnings and profits, tax-free distributions can be made to the corporation's shareholders only to the extent of the corporation's accumulated adjustments account ("AAA"), as defined in § 1368(e). The AAA generally consists of the corporation's income for all S corporations' years which is taxed to shareholders, less the amount of such income distributed to shareholders in prior years. To the extent of the AAA, distributions are treated the same as if they had been made by a corporation without accumulated earnings and profits ("E & P"). Therefore, if the AAA exceeds shareholder basis and the corporation distributes amounts equivalent to the AAA, shareholders must recognize capital gain to the extent of such excess, but not dividends. Any amounts distributed in excess of the AAA *will* be treated as a dividend to the extent the distribution does not exceed the corporation's accumulated E & P. If distributions for a year exceed the AAA, § 1368(c) provides that the AAA is to be allocated pro rata to all distributions during the year. This precludes distributions from being tax-free in the early part of the year and fully taxable toward the end of the year. After the AAA account has been depleted and all accumulated E & P has been distributed, any excess distributions are treated as a return of capital and a reduction of stock basis. When stock basis is reduced to zero, any further distributions are treated as capital gain under § 1368(c)(3). Section 1368(e)(3) provides that an S corporation may elect, with the consent of all its "affected shareholders," to treat distributions made during an S year as dividends out of E & P rather than a tax-free distribution out of the AAA. Such an election generally would be made to allow the corporation to eliminate its accumulated E & P in order to avoid exposure to the tax on passive income or the passive income termination rule. If the election is made, it is a "all-or-nothing" election and any distribution subject to it is treated as a dividend to the full extent of E & P. The S corporation cannot treat part of the distribution as coming out of AAA.

Problem 29–3

Lorraine is the sole shareholder of a C corporation which owns and operates parking lots adjacent to a major league stadium and sports facility. The corporation is operated as a C corporation and has accumulated earnings and profits of $75,000. The assets of the corporation include a parcel of undeveloped real estate which has a cost basis of $100,000. On January 1, 1997, Lorraine makes a valid S election on behalf of the corporation. At the time of the S election, the value of the undeveloped real property is $200,000. For the taxable year 1997, the operations of the corporation generate income of $150,000. On December 31, 1997, the undeveloped property is sold to a third-party purchaser for a total purchase price of

$225,000. Also on December 31, 1997, the corporation makes a cash distribution of $100,000 to Lorraine.

1. Is there any corporate-level tax due for the tax year 1997?

2. How much taxable income is reported by Lorraine on her individual return for 1997?

3. What is the character of the gain reported by the corporation and Lorraine?

4. What are the accumulated earnings and profits of the corporation as of December 31, 1997?

5. What is the amount of the corporation's AAA account as of January 1, 1998?

Chapter 30

AVOIDING DOUBLE TAXATION
IN C CORPORATIONS

Code References: §§ 1(a)–(d); 11; 106; 119(a); 162(a); 179; 274(a), (c), (d); 7872(c).

Regulation: §§ 1.162–7, –8, –9, –17(a)–(c); 1.274–1, –2(a), –5T.

A. INTRODUCTION

Small businesses often elect not to use the C corporation as an operating entity because of the specter of double taxation. Many small businesses, however, have operated for years as C corporations, disdaining the S election and the more recent LLC alternative. This is because, as a practical matter, very few small businesses operating as C corporations incur any significant double taxation. There are two obvious strategies for avoiding double taxation: (1) eliminate corporate income; or (2) eliminate individual income. Historically, the former alternative has been the strategy of choice. With current maximum individual rates exceeding those of corporations, however, the latter may become increasingly popular.

The typical method of avoiding corporate tax is the generation and orchestration of corporate-level deductions which minimize or totally eliminate corporate taxable income. A typical small business filing its Form 1120 (the C corporation annual income tax return) will show little or no taxable income. At a minimum, the goal of such a business is to reduce corporate taxable income to less than $100,000 so that the lower graduated corporate rates apply. The most common and flexible method of eliminating corporate income is through the payment of salaries and bonuses to shareholder/employees of the corporation. A corporation facing $150,000 in taxable income on December 31st might declare a bonus of $75,000 to each of its two 50% shareholder/employees in recognition of their fine job performance during the year. The resulting compensation deduction would eliminate corporate income and cause the profit of the business to be taxed only at the individual level, just like an S corporation, a partnership, or an LLC. More subtle deductions may also be available to the corporation during the year and at year-end. Contributions to retirement plans, the payment of deductible fringe benefits, permissible prepayments of anticipated expenses, net operating loss carryforwards, and investment in depreciable assets or in other businesses which may pass losses through to the C corporation are commonly employed techniques. These techniques will be examined in more detail later in this chapter. In addition, the Code contains certain tax incentives which are designed to specially benefit small businesses by granting favorable tax treatment aimed at minimizing tax at the corporate level.

The second method of avoiding double taxation is that of eliminating tax at the individual level. If the corporation has income upon which it pays tax, the profit remaining after that payment need not be distributed to the shareholder/employees where it would normally be subject to a second tax. In the case of a growing business, the net corporate profit might be reinvested in additional corporate assets rather than distributed to shareholders. Those investments, in and of themselves, could give rise to corporate tax benefits. Another technique used with varying success by closely held corporations involves the corporation *loaning* after-tax profits to its shareholder/employees. Since loan proceeds are not income, the second level of tax is theoretically avoided.

The Service is not unmindful of the techniques utilized by closely held corporations and their shareholders in attempting to avoid or minimize double taxation. Litigation at both the corporate level and the shareholder level, with the Service attempting to maintain the integrity of the federal corporate income tax, has been prolific. The tax adviser for a small business operating as a C corporation must be aware of this body of law.

B. CORPORATE DEDUCTIONS

1. SALARIES AND BONUSES TO SHAREHOLDER/EMPLOYEES

In those corporations where the shareholders are actively involved in the operations of its business, the payment of salaries and bonuses is the most frequently utilized deduction to reduce or eliminate corporate taxable income. There are, however, limits. Section 162 allows as an ordinary and necessary business expense "reasonable ... salaries or other compensation for personal services actually rendered." If payments to shareholder/employees are obviously excessive and appear solely designed to eliminate taxable income at the corporate level, they will be attacked by the Service as "unreasonable compensation." If compensation is unreasonable, it is not deductible by the corporation, thereby yielding an increase in corporate taxable income. The payments remain fully taxable to the recipient, however, as dividend income. Numerous factors relating to the resolution of this issue have been developed in the Regulations and in court decisions. Not all of these authorities focus simply upon whether the amount paid is excessive in relation to the services performed. Specifically, the courts have considered whether the payments to shareholder/employees are in proportion to shareholdings (making them look like dividends), whether dividends have actually been paid by the corporation to its shareholders during the year, and whether the compensation is paid at the very end of the corporation's year (when its officers and directors can accurately estimate the corporate profits that must be eliminated). These are all factors considered in determining whether a corporate distribution is a deductible salary or bonus or, rather, a nondeductible dividend.

In determining whether the amount of a payment to a shareholder/employee is excessive in comparison to the services rendered by such employee, other factors have also been developed. These include (1) the salary history of the shareholder/employee (does the distribution dramatically increase his or her compensation in a year when the corporation is profitable?); (2) the salary scale for other employees in the corporation (is the corporation generous to all employees and not just shareholder/employees?); (3) industry-wide salary scales for employees performing like services in similar businesses; (4) the education, business experience, and leadership ability of the shareholder/employee; (5) the contribution by the shareholder/employee in question to the success of the business; and (6) the formality and timing of the corporate action (approval by outside directors, etc.).

Advanced planning in this area is crucial. If the tax adviser fails to provide proper guidance to the corporation as to its distributions, a subsequent Service audit could have devastating effects. That is, the corporate income for a prior year could be dramatically increased, causing the corporation to incur additional taxes, penalties, and interest. Such unbudgeted amounts would have to be paid from corporate assets available at the time that the audit is completed and the assessment made by the Service.

HOME INTERIORS & GIFTS, INC. v. COMMISSIONER

73 T.C. 1142 (1980).

SIMPSON, JUDGE: * * *

The only issue to be decided is whether the amounts paid by Home Interiors & Gifts, Inc., to three of its officers, constituted reasonable compensation for services rendered within the meaning of section 162(a)(1) of the Internal Revenue Code of 1954. * * *

OPINION

The sole issue for decision is whether the amounts Home Interiors paid to Mrs. Crowley, Mr. Carter, and Mr. Horner from 1971 through 1975 constituted reasonable compensation for services rendered within the meaning of section 162(a), which, in part, provides:

(a) IN GENERAL.—There shall be allowed as a deduction all the ordinary and necessary expenses paid or incurred during the taxable year in carrying on any trade or business, including—

(1) a reasonable allowance for salaries or other compensation for personal services actually rendered;

The parties focused their evidence and arguments on the question of whether the compensation paid to the executive officers of Home Interiors was reasonable within the meaning of section 162(a)(1). * * *

The reasonable compensation provision, now appearing in section 162(a)(1), was first enacted in 1918. In 1943, Dean Griswold sought to discover the purpose of the provision. He found that there was a dearth of legislative history illuminating its purpose; he concluded that the legislative objective was to enact the limitations which had appeared in the Treasury regulations denying a deduction for payments which were in effect dividends or gifts to shareholders or their relatives. However, later research led Dean Griswold to a different conclusion: He found that the language of the 1918 Act was similar to the language of earlier excess profits tax regulations and that such language had been included in such regulations to allow a deduction for reasonable compensation for officers even though no such compensation was actually paid. Thus, he concluded that the provision was not designed as a limitation on the deductibility of compensation. Despite Dean Griswold's research, the law has developed otherwise. The reasonable compensation provision has uniformly been considered by the courts to be a restriction on the deductibility of compensation; nevertheless, Dean Griswold's research helps to point the way in deciding the scope of the restriction.

In deciding reasonable compensation cases, the courts have established the propositions that whether the compensation was reasonable is a question to be resolved on the basis of an examination of all the facts and circumstances of the case. The determination of the Commissioner is presumptively correct, and the burden of proving the reasonableness of the compensation is upon the petitioners. The factors considered relevant in determining reasonableness of compensation include: the employee's qualifications; the nature, extent and scope of the employee's work; the size and complexities of the business; a comparison of salaries paid with the gross income and the net income; the prevailing general economic conditions; comparison of salaries with distributions to stockholders; the prevailing rates of compensation for comparable positions in comparable concerns; the salary policy of the taxpayer as to all employees; and in the case of small corporations with a limited number of officers the amount of compensation paid to the particular employee in previous years. No single factor is decisive; rather, we must consider and weigh the totality of facts and circumstances in arriving at our decision. Where officers-shareholders, who are in control of a corporation, set their own compensation, careful scrutiny is required to determine whether the alleged compensation is in fact a distribution of profits.

At trial, the Commissioner and the petitioners presented expert testimony to support their positions. The Commissioner's expert and Hay Associates which employs him are recognized experts in designing plans of executive compensation, and the expert presented a carefully prepared report and testimony on the compensation which he considered reasonable for the officers of Home Interiors. His conclusions were primarily based on a type of analysis which is known as the "Hay method." Under such method, the expert first interviewed Mrs. Crowley, Mr. Carter, and Mr. Horner to learn about the operations of Home Interiors and the roles they performed in such operations. Then, with that information, he determined, from a survey of approximately 800 companies, the highest amounts those companies paid to employees in positions requiring similar skill, responsibility, and creativity. To check the results obtained by use of the Hay method, the expert also conducted a "market price analysis" of 6 other direct selling companies and 10 other high growth companies with respect to which information was available. He computed the ratio between the compensation paid to the chief executive officers of such other companies and the sales and profits of such companies, and he applied that ratio to the sales and profits of Home Interiors. As a result, he found that the compensation which would be payable to the officers of Home Interiors under the market price analysis was substantially less than the amounts of compensation which he had found by use of the Hay method. Finally, the Commissioner's expert was of the opinion that the following amounts represented reasonable compensation for the officers of Home Interiors:

Year	Mrs. Crowley	Mr. Carter	Mr. Horner
1971	$198,000	$159,000	$ 88,000
1972	248,000	190,000	96,000
1973	268,000	218,000	108,000
1974	338,000	265,000	143,000
1975	411,000	293,000	173,000

The petitioners' experts adopted a different approach. They did not undertake to determine what specific amounts of compensation were reasonable for the officers of Home Interiors; instead, they examined the financial reports of Home Interiors, and compared the amount of compensation paid to its officers with its sales and profits. They selected 18 other companies which they considered to be comparable because those companies were of medium size and involved managers with unusual skills. When they compared the amount of earnings which Home Interiors allocated to the payment of executive compensation with the similar information of the other companies, they concluded that Home Interiors was not paying excessive executive compensation. In reaching their conclusion, the experts also pointed out that Home Interiors' performance over the years was extraordinary.

We have here a most unusual case: the amounts of compensation paid the officers of Home Interiors were very large, but their efforts produced extraordinary results for Home Interiors and everyone connected with it. However measured, the success of Home Interiors was very impressive. Its gross sales in 1968 were $4,284,456 and in 1975, $97,583,835; thus, during such period, the gross sales increased almost 23 times, or at an average annual rate of 57 percent. The after-tax earnings of Home Interiors in 1968 were $60,094 and in 1975, $6,858,-947; thus, during such period, such earnings increased 114 times, or at an average annual rate of 110 percent. When the performance of Home Interiors is compared with the growth in the GNP and with sales of retail establishments generally, the results are equally impressive: in 1971 through 1975, the GNP increased about 43 percent; retail store sales generally, about 44 percent; but Home Interiors' sales, 360 percent. What is more, we are convinced that the extraordinary success of Home Interiors was no accident, nor was it merely due to the generally favorable economic conditions prevailing in the 1960's and 1970's.

Mrs. Crowley spent most of a day on the stand as a witness, and it is clear that she possesses rare talent. The profitability of Home Interiors depended upon its sales, and after hearing her describe her policies and practices in leading Home Interiors, we can understand how she was able to recruit a sales organization of over 17,000 by 1975, why the organization was motivated to produce such exceptional results, and why there was little turnover in personnel. We doubt that she could have been replaced.

Mr. Carter also made immense contributions to the success of Home Interiors. Its greatest increase in sales and profitability occurred from 1968 through 1977, a period beginning shortly after he assumed a significant role in managing the affairs of the company. His responsibilities were many and varied. He assisted significantly in conducting the rallies and other activities designed to inspire the sales organization, and he wisely managed the inventory and arranged for the design of products which would have a wide appeal.

Mr. Horner's responsibilities were more limited, but his compensation was also considerably less. He was unrelated to Mrs. Crowley and Mr. Carter, and he was employed, in an arm's-length transaction, to assist them in managing the affairs of Home Interiors. He did perform a wide variety of activities which contributed to the success of a very successful company. He had only an insignificant ownership interest in the company, and there is no reason to believe that the company would pay him more than his services were worth to it.

Though Mrs. Crowley, Mr. Carter, and Mr. Horner received large amounts of compensation, the other key employees of Home Interiors also received munificent compensation during the years in issue. In our findings of fact, we included information concerning the compensation of the area and branch managers. That information shows that in 1975, one area manager received $295,000 in commissions and that the average commissions received by an area manager in that year were $226,-000. Similarly, the highest commissions of a branch manager in that year were $271,000, and the average for a branch manager for that year was $141,000. Although the area and branch managers were required to pay most of their business expenses out of their commissions, we have found that those expenses averaged around one-third of such commissions; thus, even when those expenses are subtracted, those managers were left with very handsome compensation. Moreover, the compensation of those managers actually increased at approximately the same rate during the years in issue as did the compensation of Mrs. Crowley, Mr. Carter, and Mr. Horner: the aggregate nondeferred compensation of Mrs. Crowley, Mr. Carter, and Mr. Horner rose from $954,091.74 in 1971 to $2,223,384 in 1975—an increase of approximately 133 percent. Whereas, the average commissions of an area manager increased from $103,000 in 1971 to $226,000 in 1975—an increase of 119 percent; and the average commissions of a branch manager increased from $59,000 in 1971 to $141,000 in 1975—an increase of 140 percent.

In judging the reasonableness of the compensation received by Mrs. Crowley, Mr. Carter, and Mr. Horner, it is also significant that all key employees of Home Interiors were compensated on the basis of commissions and that the use of such method of compensation was a longstanding practice of the company. Section 1.162–7(b)(2), Income Tax Regs., provides in part:

> Generally speaking, if contingent compensation is paid pursuant to a free bargain * * * before the services are rendered, not influenced by any consideration on the part of the employer other than that of securing on fair and advantageous terms the services of the individual, it should be allowed as a deduction even though in the actual working out of the contract it may prove to be greater than the amount which would ordinarily be paid.

When Home Interiors was first organized, it decided to compensate Mrs. Crowley and Mr. Amon, its key officers at that time, primarily on the basis of commissions at 2½ percent of sales. At such time, there was no way of knowing the amount of income that would be produced by such commissions. The company continued to pay Mrs. Crowley commissions at that rate through the years while it was experiencing modest success. The rate of her commissions was never increased; but it was decreased in 1973 and again in 1975 when Home Interiors was experiencing such extraordinary success. The rates of commissions paid to Mr. Carter and Mr. Horner were also established before Home Interiors' great success; those rates too were never increased, but the rate paid to Mr. Carter was also reduced in 1974 and again in 1975.

It is true that each year the board of directors of Home Interiors could have changed the rates of commission paid to these officers, but in view of the sharply increasing profits of the company and in view of the fact that the other shareholders were receiving increasing benefits, the board of directors had no reason to reduce such commissions. It is also true that Mrs. Crowley and Mr. Carter, together with their families, owned slightly more than 50 percent of the stock of Home Interiors; but there were many unrelated shareholders, and together, they held a substantial block of the stock. Thus, this is not a situation in which Mrs. Crowley and her family were free to do as they wished in running the affairs of the company. The company was achieving earnings which must have been gratifying to all of its owners, and all of them had reason to favor continuing the arrangements which had resulted in such success.

Moreover, although the commissions actually received by Mrs. Crowley, Mr. Carter, and Mr. Horner increased greatly from 1968 through 1975, those commissions represented a sharply declining percentage of the earnings of Home Interiors. In 1968, Mrs. Crowley's nondeferred compensation represented 97 percent of the pre-tax earnings of the company; Mr. Carter's, 67 percent; and Mr. Horner's, 22 percent. However, by 1975, Mrs. Crowley's compensation was equal to only 8 percent of the company's pre-tax earnings; Mr. Carter's, 8 percent; and Mr. Horner's, 2 percent. Thus, a declining percentage of the company's earnings was allocated to compensation of its executive officers.

Over the years, the shareholders of Home Interiors participated handsomely in its earnings. From 1971 through 1975, the average return on equity was 49 percent. From 1968 through 1975, the dividends distributed to shareholders increased dramatically: in 1968, the aggregate dividends were $17,800; in 1971, $63,549; and in 1975, $544,895. Thus, the dividends in 1975 were approximately 9 times the amount in 1971 and approximately 30 times the amount in 1968. The dividends per share increased in an equally impressive manner: in 1969, the dividends were 10 cents per share; in 1973, $1 per share; and in 1975, $1.80 per share.

We recognize that the percentage of after-tax earnings distributed as dividends declined over the years in issue. However, the decline was not the result of the payment of higher compensation to the executive officers; it resulted from a decision to retain additional earnings in the business. Such retained earnings increased from $864,445 at the close of 1970 to $15,333,203 at the close of 1975, and as a result, the book value of Home Interiors stock rose from $1.27 per share at the end of 1969 to $26.62 at the end of 1975. On this record, it is clear that an investment in the stock of Home Interiors was very attractive and that the shareholders were receiving their fair share of the profits of the business. Under such circumstances, there is no ground for concluding that the compensation paid Mrs. Crowley, Mr. Carter, and Mr. Horner represented an arrangement for them to draw off more than their fair share of the profits of the business.

The testimony of the Commissioner's expert was persuasive. We were impressed by the thoroughness of his study, and we are convinced that his conclusions as to the reasonable compensation for Mrs. Crowley, Mr. Carter, and Mr. Horner represent the norms for their services. Yet, such conclusion is not dispositive of the issue in this case. Section 162(a)(1) was not designed to regulate businesses by denying them a deduction for the payment of compensation in excess of the norm. The payment of abnormally high compensation does warrant a careful scrutiny of the arrangement to be sure that the payments were in fact made for services actually rendered. However, in view of the extraordinary services furnished by Mrs. Crowley, Mr. Carter, and Mr. Horner, we are convinced that they earned large compensation. When their compensation is compared to that received by other employees of the company, it is clear that the compensation of the executive officers was not disproportionate. Also, when the return to shareholders in the form of dividends and appreciation in the value of their stock is examined, it is apparent that the exceptional prosperity of the company was shared with the stockholders.

It is true that the compensation received by Mrs. Crowley and Mr. Carter exceeded the compensation paid to the chief executive officers of many other corporations with much larger sales, more employees, and greater profits; but those other corporations did not experience the superb growth achieved by Home Interiors in sales, in earnings, and in return to shareholders. Moreover, in these times of unparalleled inflation, our concept of reasonable compensation must take into consideration such inflation, and as appears in the Forbes information, some other companies were also paying their chief executive officers extraordinary compensation, which might have been considered excessive in other times. Accordingly, after very careful analysis of all the facts and circumstances and careful weighing of those circumstances, we conclude and hold that the compensation paid Mrs. Crowley, Mr. Carter, and Mr. Horner in the years 1971 through 1975 was reasonable within the meaning of section 162(a)(1).

Decisions will be entered under Rule 155.

Problem 30–1

Phil and Jack are equal shareholders in a personal injury law firm which is operated as a C corporation. They have one associate, Phyllis, who is paid a fixed annual salary. On December 26, Phyllis settles a large contingency fee case upon which she has been exclusively working, collecting a fee of $250,000. The other gross income of the firm for the year has been $400,000, offset by $200,000 in expenses (including Phyllis' salary), and $100,000 each in salary to Phil and Jack. On December 31, Phil and Jack, in their capacity as officers and directors of the corporation, declare and pay themselves each a bonus of $125,000. No dividend is paid to Phil and Jack in their capacity as shareholders.

1. Is the bonus payment deductible to the corporation?

2. What if the funds were received and paid out earlier in the year?

3. What if Jack and Phil each were paid $25,000 as a dividend, with the remaining $100,000 each as a bonus?

4. What if $100,000 were declared as a bonus to Phyllis and $75,000 each to Jack and Phil?

5. What if Jack and Phil had also worked extensively on the case yielding the settlement?

6. What if Jack were paid $200,000, in recognition of his position as a Managing Director of the firm, with Phil receiving only $50,000 as a bonus?

7. What if the bonus were paid on January 1 of the next year?

2. FRINGE BENEFITS

In addition to salaries and bonuses, a corporation may pay to, or on behalf of, its shareholder/employees other amounts which directly or indirectly benefit them. If such expenses are deductible, the corporation avoids corporate tax on the income it has generated to fund such deductions. In addition, the employee may, in certain cases, take the position that the benefit received is not income to him or her since it was provided in connection with the performance of duties as an employee for the corporate business and not for personal reasons.

In certain cases, the tax treatment of these payments is mandated by statute. Section 106 allows an employer to pay the medical insurance premiums or medical expenses of its employees and deduct such payments. In turn, the benefit received by the employee does not constitute income. Similarly, § 119 allows meal and lodging expenses which are provided on an employer's business premises and for such employer's convenience to be deductible expenses by the corporation and not included in the income of the employee.

The most common form of nonsalary/nonbonus payments to shareholder/employees, which are deductible by the corporation and not included in the income of the employee, are contributions to a corporate pension and/or profit-sharing trust made by the corporation on behalf of the employee. Such contributions are deductible to the corporation under § 404(a). They do not constitute immediate income to the employee. Extremely complex rules have arisen as to the permissible amounts of such contributions, the required coverage of nonshareholder/employees in such a qualified plan, the timing of the vesting of the corporate contributions, and the utilization of the plan proceeds pending their ultimate distribution upon the retirement of the employee on whose behalf they were contributed. Despite these complex rules, many small businesses achieve significant tax benefits from a year-end contribution of excess profits into a pension and profit-sharing trust for the benefit of its shareholder/employees. As an added tax benefit, the amount contributed to the qualified trust accumulates income on a tax-deferred basis until it is ultimately distributed to the employee upon his or her retirement or at certain specified ages. The ultimate distributions are taxed as ordinary income at the time of such retirement or other distribution. While pension/profit-sharing contributions remain an enormous tax benefit to small business owners, the maximum size of contributions and the ability to exclude non-shareholders has been extremely limited by recent legislation. A complete discussion of the rules relating to such qualified deferred compensation payments is beyond the scope of this work.

Historically, corporations have attempted to deduct many types of benefits provided to shareholder/employees on the theory that they are ordinary and necessary corporate business expenses, qualifying for deduction at the corporate level under § 162. In turn, the shareholder/employee receiving the benefit would normally not include the value of the benefit received into personal income on the theory that it was merely incident to the performance of corporate business. Corporate payment of travel expenses, entertainment expenses, vehicle expenses, and club dues and expenses were primary examples. The Service initially fought these deductions on the ground that the payments were not ordinary and necessary business expenses under § 162 but rather personal, non-business benefits paid on behalf of the shareholder/employee. As such, the Service's position was that the payments were nondeductible dividends at the corporate level and taxable income to the recipient shareholder/employee to the extent of their value. Beginning in 1978, Congress began coming to the aid of the Service, initially with the enactment of § 274 which imposes strict verification of business purpose and recordkeeping requirements and prohibits entirely the deduction of expenses incurred with respect to entertainment facilities which include yachts, hunting clubs, fishing lodges, and the like. Section 274 has been gradually broadened to severely limit the corporate deductibility of entertainment expenses and to eliminate entirely the deductions for club dues of any kind. Even when meal and entertainment business expenses are allowed, the corporate deduction is now limited to 50% of the amount paid.

Despite the increasing restrictions placed upon the corporate deductibility of various items, there remains fertile ground for dispute with regard to certain types of expenses frequently deducted by a corporation, particularly in the area of business travel, expenses for business vehicles, and the payment of other similar expenses on behalf of an employee who is performing duties for the corporation, but also may personally benefit from the corporate expenditure.

Problem 30–2

Mary is the sole shareholder of Classics, Inc., a book store. The corporation incurs an expense of $4,000 to send Mary to the Book Seller's Convention in New York. The amounts paid are for travel, meals, and lodging.

1. Are the expenses deductible to the corporation?

2. Are they includable in the income of Mary?

3. What if the corporation also paid $1,000 in extra expenses so that Mary's husband, a non-employee of the company, could attend?

4. What if the expenses included a side trip, taken by Mary to visit her sister in Boston?

5. What if the expenses included a Broadway show for Mary and one of her book suppliers?

6. What if Mary flew first-class?

3. PAYMENTS TO PERSONS OR ENTITIES OTHER THAN THE SHAREHOLDER/EMPLOYEE

A corporation may also reduce its taxable income by deducting payments for goods and services provided by persons other than its shareholder/employees. Payments for cost of goods sold, rental of the business premises, interest on corporate business debt, salaries to non-shareholder/employees, and other similar items, are deductible from the corporation's gross income in determining its taxable income. In addition, Congress has provided small businesses with certain incentives to encourage investment in property used in the trade or business. The most commonly used of these incentives is § 179 which allows a small business to currently expense, rather than capitalize and depreciate, property purchased by the business for use therein up to $17,500 per year. Thus, the business may invest in capital expansion to that extent and receive an immediate tax deduction for its expenditure. See discussion at Chapter 2.

Other expenses incurred by a business may be of less clear deductibility. "Gifts" to customers of the business are limited to an annual deductibility of $25 per donee. Section 162(c) mandates that no deduction is allowed for a business expense which is a direct or indirect payment of an amount constituting an illegal bribe or kickback. Professional fees paid to attorneys and accountants are normally deductible so long as they are ordinary and necessary in nature and connected with the trade or business of the corporation. To the extent that they constitute fees for advice relating to the personal matters of a shareholder/employee, or to the extent that they are incurred in connection with a capital expenditure, however, they may be either nondeductible or required to be capitalized.

As noted in Chapter 28, a corporate taxpayer with extraordinary taxable income in a given year may seek to defer all or a portion of such income into the following year by deferring income or accelerating the deduction of expenses through prepayment of trade payables. While such techniques still have some usefulness, their availability has been significantly restricted (particularly for accrual-method taxpayers) by the "economic performance" rules of § 461(h).

C. AVOIDING INDIVIDUAL TAX ON CORPORATE DISTRIBUTIONS

There are two basic methods of avoiding double taxation while operating as a C corporation. The prior sections of this chapter have focused upon the traditional methods utilized to avoid the corporate tax, generally resulting in distributions of what would otherwise be corporate taxable income which is then taxed to the individual shareholder/employees of the corporation. With the advent of individual rates which are higher than those of C corporations, however, additional incentive is provided to avoid tax at the individual shareholder level. One method is to simply retain and not distribute corporate earnings. This strategy has its own complications, however, including potential penalty taxes on retained corporate earnings as discussed in Chapter 33. Of more practical importance, the shareholder/employee of a small business corporation may need the funds to meet personal obligations which cannot be paid by the corporation. Thus, the adviser must focus on tax planning at the individual level for taxable corporate distributions.

1. SHELTERS

Prior to 1986, a shareholder anticipating income from a corporate distribution could essentially "purchase" losses through various "tax shelters" which were, if not sanctioned, at least tolerated by the Code. Such schemes often had no real economic substance and were designed purely to provide a taxpayer with tax losses to shelter his or her taxable income from other sources. Implementation of the passive activity loss rules through the enactment of § 469 in 1986 virtually eliminated this tax strategy. A taxpayer who earns income in one business or activity generally cannot offset it with losses of another unless the taxpayer materially participates in the activity generating the loss. In the case of most small business owners, participation in two going concerns is not possible.

With the availability of tax shelters severely curtailed under current law, each shareholder/employee's tax situation must be examined to determine whether he or she may have legitimate losses or deductions which might be utilized to offset the corporate income distribution. Individual deductions for home mortgage interest, charitable contributions, alimony, employee business expenses, and other allowable deductions may be used to shield tax on an otherwise taxable distribution made from the corporation. In summary, prior to determining the effect of the corporate distribution upon the individual distributee, his or her personal tax situation must be reviewed.

2. LOANS FROM THE CORPORATION

A strategy which has been used over the years by small business corporations seeking to avoid a taxable distribution to their shareholder/employees has been the making of loans from the corporation to the shareholder/employee. Loan proceeds are not taxable income and there is no direct statutory prohibition against loans between related parties. If the loan is actually a bona fide debt, the recipient avoids individual tax. On the other hand, the loan disbursement is not deductible to the corporation and the interest received thereon generates taxable income to the corporation. Thus, if the debt is not bona fide, it will be included in the income of the recipient as a dividend distribution, thereby resulting in the very double taxation which most small business corporations seek to avoid. Alternatively, the Service could assert that the loan distribution is compensation to the shareholder/employee, in which case, it would at least be deductible against corporate income (unless it were unreasonable in nature), although taxable to the individual. If the interest rate on the loan is below market, it may generate income to the shareholder either as compensation or in the form of forgone interest under § 7872(c)(1)(B) or (C).

In determining whether a distribution is recognized as valid corporate debt for tax purposes or as a disguised dividend or compensation, the Service asks such questions as: (1) is there a promissory note or other written evidence of indebtedness?; (2) is commercially reasonable interest charged?; (3) is there a fixed schedule for repayment?; (4) is there adequate security or collateral as would be required by a commercial lender?; (5) are repayments actually made?; and (6) was the borrower solvent at the time the advance was made? See *Alterman Foods, Inc. v. United States,* 505 F.2d 873 (5th Cir.1974). If the small business owner is not vigilant in maintaining the indicia of bona fide debt, the Service will prevail in its position that the distribution is actually a dividend or compensation and therefore taxable to the shareholder/employee. The Service may also look to other factors peculiar to the specific corporate situation at hand, such as whether the recipient employee actually was paid reasonable compensation over and above the debt distribution, whether there was a business reason for the corporation to make the loan to the shareholder (such as a higher rate of interest than it could earn on other investments), and whether loans are made to shareholders on a pro rata basis in accordance with their shareholdings (therefore, making them appear to be a substitute for dividends). From a practical standpoint, the most significant factor in such cases (since the Service is viewing the facts in hindsight at the time of the audit) is whether repayments of principal and interest have actually been made by the shareholder/employee. If not, even a debt which might have appeared initially to have been a bona fide debt may, upon review, be treated as a taxable distribution.

Chapter 31

EXPANDING A CORPORATE BUSINESS THROUGH ACQUISITION

Code References: §§ 354(a); 356(a)(1); 358(a); 361(a), (c)(1); 362(b); 368(a)(1)(A)–(C), (a)(2)(B), (a)(2)(G); 1060(a)–(c); 1032.

Regulation: §§ 1.354–1(a); 1.368–1, –2(b)–(d).

A. INTRODUCTION

The owners of a successful small business often seek to expand its scope of operations. Reasons for expansion include the acquisition of competitors, opening branches in new locations, acquiring suppliers to ensure a fixed-cost of raw materials, and expanding into a related business.

When the business seeking to expand its operations by acquisition is a corporation, a variety of techniques are available. This is particularly true when the business targeted for acquisition is also operated as a corporation. Alternative acquisition methods exist when the target is a partnership, limited liability company, or sole proprietorship. In those situations where a corporate business is the acquisition target, the negotiating parties must first decide whether the acquisition will be of the assets of the business or, in the alternative, the stock of the corporation which operates the business. Traditionally, the acquiring corporation would prefer to acquire assets, rather than stock, for several fundamental reasons. First, the buyer can pick and choose which of the assets it desires, rather than acquiring all assets of the corporation which is the result of acquiring its stock. Second, the acquiring corporation may achieve a tax advantage by acquiring appreciated assets if it takes a "cost" basis (for the purposes of depreciation, amortization, or resale) in the assets acquired to the extent that the purchase price is allocated to that asset. Stepping up the tax basis of the acquired assets is more difficult, and sometimes impossible, if the stock of the acquiring company is purchased rather than its assets. Third, when assets are purchased, the acquiring company does not necessarily acquire the contingent liabilities (which may lie in either contract or tort) of the selling corporation. When stock is acquired, the purchasing entity will acquire assets of the target subject to the "skeletons" of the corporate operations, thereby subjecting them to the claims of such contingent creditors.

On the other side of the negotiating fence, the owner of the target corporation may be more inclined to sell stock than assets. The sale of stock will generally yield a single capital gain tax to the selling shareholder. The sale of the corporate assets followed by a liquidation of the corporation in order to distribute the sale proceeds to shareholders can result in taxable income (which may be ordinary) at the corporate level and an additional tax on the distribution of the net funds by the corporation to its shareholders. Payment of such taxes obviously results in significantly less net proceeds to the selling shareholder. In an effort to placate the purchaser, the selling shareholder may seek to effectuate a sale of his shares (rather than assets) by personally indemnifying the buyer against any contingent liabilities of the corporation. This indemnity might be secured by an escrow of a portion of the purchase price for a period of time or by a right of offset by the purchaser against any deferred payments due to the seller of the shares in the event that such contingent liabilities should arise.

Once the purchaser and seller agree as to whether assets or stock will be acquired, the next step is to determine the purchase price and the terms of purchase. In the case of an acquiring company which is a corporation, the consideration available is diverse. The corporation could pay the purchase price from its own cash funds or, in the alternative, with borrowed funds from a lender. Another possibility is to pay the acquisition consideration in whole or in part with the notes or other deferred obligations of the acquiring corporation. In this latter case, the owners of the acquired business might seek a personal guarantee from some or all of the shareholders of the acquiring corporation, depending upon its financial condition.

The acquiring corporation might also pay the price of acquisition by transferring to the target corporation or its shareholders newly issued shares of the acquiring corporation's stock. The utilization of the stock of the acquiring corporation to pay for the assets or shares of the target corporation can be effectuated through several vehicles: (1) a statutory merger under the state law of the jurisdiction in which the transaction takes place; (2) a non-merger asset acquisition utilizing the acquiring corporation's stock as consideration; or (3) a tender offer to the shareholders of the target corporation in which they would transfer their shares to the acquiring corporation in exchange for stock in the acquiring corporation. The result of the third technique is that the target corporation becomes a subsidiary of the acquiring corporation. The effect of all of these stock techniques is that the "selling" business owners continue as partial owners of the combined enterprise. The utilization of the acquiring corporation's stock as consideration for the acquisition of the target corporation's assets or stock can be a tax-advantaged transaction under § 368. Each of the acquiring techniques described above may qualify as a "corporate reorganization" which allows the owners of the target corporation to receive the shares of the acquiring corporation without incurring any immediate tax. This favorable result occurs only if the various rules regarding corporate reorganizations are strictly complied with. While merger and tender offer techniques are often utilized by publicly traded companies to effect mergers and acquisitions, essentially the same rules apply to small business corporations which seek to expand. The stock of a closely held, non-traded company, however, is usually less attractive to a selling business owner than that of a publicly traded company, since it lacks the "exit vehicle" of liquidity. It is also important to note that the corporate reorganization rules of § 368 apply only to the acquisition of a corporate business. Different, and often less favorable, rules apply when an expanding corporation seeks to acquire the assets of a partnership, limited liability company, or sole proprietorship utilizing its own stock as consideration.

B. ASSET ACQUISITIONS

In most scenarios, when a corporation acquires the business of a target company by acquiring its (the target's) assets (rather than its stock, partnership interests, or other participation interests), the acquisition will be taxable to the acquired entity or its owners. In certain cases, however, where the targeted business is itself a corporation and its owners do not desire to "cash out" their investment, the acquisition transaction may be structured in such a way that the assets of the target business are acquired with qualifying stock of the acquiring corporation so that the resulting transaction is a reorganization which is not taxable to the target corporation or its shareholders.

1. TAXABLE ACQUISITIONS

The most straightforward method of acquiring a target business is for the acquiring corporation to purchase the assets of that business for cash or its promissory note or a combination of the two. The source of such a cash payment could be working funds available within the acquiring corporation or cash borrowed for the purpose of making the acquisition. If a promissory note of the acquiring company is utilized, the seller's focus in negotiation will relate to the value and liquidity of the collateral offered by the buyer to secure payment of the promissory note. The seller may or may not want the purchased assets as security. In some purchases, the amount to be received by the seller varies depending upon the performance of the acquired business following the acquisition (i.e., an "earn out"). In addition to the actual assets of the target company, the acquiring entity may be willing to pay for a noncompetition agreement and/or continued employment or consulting agreements which bind the key employees of the target.

The structure of the purchase price and related payments have significant tax ramifications to both the acquiring and target businesses. If the target business is a pass-through entity (such as an S corporation, a partnership, or a limited liability company), the tax effects of the sale will, with certain exceptions, be visited upon the owners of the business rather than the entity itself. In the case of a taxable acquisition of assets from a C corporation, the tax considerations also apply to the target entity itself. If the C corporation liquidates following the asset sale, the shareholders will have their own additional tax calculations to make. As to the acquiring corporation, the payment of the purchase price and its allocation to the various assets and/or the payment of sums under employment or noncompetition agreements will have a significant effect upon how the cost of the acquisition is ultimately treated for tax purposes.

In general, the acquiring corporation's basis in the assets acquired in a taxable transaction will be equal to the sum of (1) the cash paid, (2) the full principal amount of any deferred obligations (such as the buyer's promissory notes), and (3) the amount of any liabilities assumed from the target entity. It is important to note that the acquiring entity receives full credit for its deferred obligations by assigning tax basis to the acquired assets in the full face amount of those obligations, even though the payments to be made are not due until some future date. A notable exception to this rule is that, if the future obligations of the acquiring corporation are contingent (as in the "earnout" scenario described above), no part of such obligation is included in basis until the amount of the contingent payment is either specified or paid. When a corporation purchases an ongoing business, it will normally acquire a variety of assets which require differing treatment for tax purposes. These generally include depreciable real property improvements, depreciable tangible personal property, nondepreciable land, inventory, and amortizable intangible property such as patents, trademarks, or the value of the ongoing operation or reputation of the business (i.e., goodwill). Separate amounts may be paid for ongoing employment agreements and covenants not to compete. These latter amounts may be paid at the time of the sale transaction or, in the alternative, over the period of the employment or noncompetition agreement.

As to the business assets, the acquiring corporation (as discussed in Chapter 2) will generally seek to allocate the purchase price among the assets acquired which will be most quickly deductible for tax purposes. For example, amounts allocated to inventory are recovered when the inventory is sold; amounts allocated to depreciable property are recovered over the useful life of such property in accordance with the Accelerated Cost Recovery System rules of § 168; and amounts allocated to nondepreciable property, such as land, are generally recovered only when the property is sold or otherwise disposed of. Amounts allocated to intangibles, such as goodwill and going concern value, are amortizable under § 197 over a 15–year period. Payments under noncompetition agreements are also covered by § 197 and are therefore amortizable over a 15–year period regardless of the life of the noncompetition agreement. Payments under employment and consultation agreements are deductible at the time that the services are performed.

Historically, sellers have attempted to allocate little or no portion of the purchase price to goodwill or going concern value since, prior to the enactment of § 197 in 1993, such amounts were neither depreciable nor amortizable. Even with the enactment of § 197, the 15–year amortization period is not the most favorable write-off period to the purchasing entity. Because of § 1060, however, which generally applies to all taxable acquisitions of a trade or business, it is often difficult to avoid allocating a significant portion of the purchase price to the goodwill factor of the target business. Section 1060 mandates a "residual method" of purchase price allocation which must be made in accordance with a specified system of priorities. The priorities apply to both the buyer and the seller and basically are enumerated in the Regulations, as impacted by the enactment of § 197, as follows:

(1) The aggregate purchase price is first reduced by the amount of cash, demand deposits, and similar assets which are part of the acquisition;

(2) The next allocation is to government securities, readily marketable securities, foreign currency, and other similar items, in accordance with their relative values. No amounts are allocated in excess of such values;

(3) The third class is a broad class, including all assets not included in the first two classes except for § 197 assets, including goodwill and going concern value. Thus, this category may include depreciable and nondepreciable assets. This category includes many of the business assets acquired. A portion of the purchase price is allocated to these assets in proportion to their relative fair market values, except that no basis may be allocated to any asset in excess of its fair market value; and

(4) The remainder of the purchase price is allocated to all § 197 assets, including goodwill and going concern value.

Item (4) is the "residual" aspect of the allocation system. Obviously, this system places a premium on the valuation of the assets in the third category, since the higher their value is determined to be, the lesser the amount of the purchase price remaining to be allocated to the § 197 assets, including goodwill and going concern.

From the point of view of the acquiring corporation, there may be a clear tax advantage if a portion of the overall acquisition cost is diverted away from the assets acquired and toward a consulting or employment agreement for the key employees of the acquired corporation. Amounts which, if included in the asset purchase price, might be allocated under § 197 to goodwill and deductible only over a 15–year period would be deductible when paid pursuant to an employment agreement under § 162. A noncompetition agreement provides no such tax advantage, however, since, as noted, the amount paid must be amortized over a 15–year period, just like goodwill. The deliberate diversion of asset purchase funds to an employment agreement may, however, be disregarded by the Service if the amounts paid under the guise of such an agreement are in excess of the value of the services performed and/or if the amounts paid for the purchased assets are clearly below their true value. In addition, the shareholder/employee of the target corporation may be unwilling to accept a purchase price reallocation to a consulting agreement since the amounts received thereunder are treated as ordinary income and possibly subject to employment taxes whereas the proceeds of the sale of assets may be a nontaxable return of basis or treated as capital gain, depending upon the basis and character of the assets sold.

The tax adviser to the owners of the target company must review other tax considerations. The basis allocation required under § 1060 applies to the seller as well as the buyer. As discussed at Chapter 3, the allocation of the purchase price to inventory or depreciated assets may result in ordinary income to the seller. Allocation to goodwill, however, which may be required under the residual method, would generally yield capital gain to the selling owners. The receipt of consulting fees or employment fees are ordinary income to the recipients. Similarly, payments received under a covenant not to compete are ordinary income. If the seller receives an installment obligation or deferred payment obligation of the purchaser, the benefits of the installment sale reporting will normally be available to the seller under § 453, thereby allowing the seller to report the income under the note gradually as the payments are received.

JONES v. UNITED STATES

65 F.3d 168 (6th Cir. 1995).

Per Curiam.

Plaintiffs, Sam and Louanna Jones, contend that the United States improperly allocated $100,000 of taxable income to them for the tax year 1981. They filed a complaint in the United States District Court for the Northern District of Ohio, seeking a refund of the corresponding federal income taxes, interest and penalties which they paid to the Internal Revenue Service.

The district court entered summary judgment in favor of the Government, finding that the $100,000 was properly attributed to Mr. and Mrs. Jones as income and therefore, that they are not entitled to the requested refund.

Mr. and Mrs. Jones have appealed that ruling, arguing that the district court erred in granting summary judgment because there exists a genuine dispute about the proper allocation of the $100,000.

Finding the arguments of Mr. and Mrs. Jones unpersuasive, we affirm the district court's entry of summary judgment in favor of the Government.

I.

Sam B. Jones owned one hundred percent of the stock in the Bryan F. Jones Agency, Inc. ("the agency"), an Ohio corporation which was in the business of selling insurance. Jones also owned interests in several other businesses, including a minority interest in Alliance Underwriters of Ohio Agency, Inc. ("Alliance"). As president and sole shareholder of the agency, Jones entered into a contract to sell the assets of the agency for the total purchase price of $539,000. The purchase agreement identified Allan Stoessner as the "Buyer" and Sam Jones and the agency, collectively, as the "Seller." Of the total purchase price, $100,-000 was specifically designated as consideration for the Seller's covenant not to compete.

With regard to the covenant not to compete, the agreement provided:

> Whereas the Seller desires to sell to Buyer all of the assets and interest in and of the Bryan F. Jones Agency, Inc., a business engaged in the sales of insurance policies and programs in the general area of Portage County and immediate vicinity, including expiration lists, office furniture, fixtures, goodwill, the use of the name "Bryan F. Jones Agency" and a covenant by the seller, Sam B. Jones, not to compete as set forth in more detail below....

> * * *

> .F. The Seller, either Sam B. Jones, individually, or The Bryan F. Jones Agency, Inc., shall not, directly or indirectly, for a period of three years from the closing date [compete against the Buyer].

> * * *

> e. In connection with the foregoing, it is understood that the Seller will maintain and continue to pursue business in the entity known as Alliance Underwriters of Ohio Agency, Inc., provided, however, that in pursuing that business the Seller may not violate or infringe the covenants contained in F. a. through d. of this agreement.

Although $439,000 of the purchase proceeds was reported by the agency as income, the $100,000 designated as consideration for the covenant not to compete was reported neither on the tax return of Mr. and Mrs. Jones nor on any of the tax returns of the businesses with which Mr. Jones is affiliated.

When the Internal Revenue Service determined that the unreported $100,000 should be attributed to them, Mr. and Mrs. Jones paid the entire tax, plus penalties and interest, and subsequently filed this suit seeking a refund....

III.

It is well-established that the amount a buyer pays a seller in exchange for a covenant not to compete is taxable as ordinary income to the seller. In order to challenge the unambiguous allocation of the purchase price among assets in an asset purchase agreement, a party must demonstrate that the contract is unenforceable due to mistake, undue influence, fraud, or duress.

Where the contract terms regarding the allocation of the purchase price to a non-compete covenant are ambiguous or where there is no contract, the Danielson rule does not apply. In such a situation, the court, in determining the proper allocation of the purchase price, will consider the mutual intent of the parties at the time of the agreement. However, the "Danielson rule" precludes the court from considering the parties' mutual intent unless it is first established that material terms of the contract are ambiguous.

Mr. and Mrs. Jones do not allege that the sales agreement is unenforceable or ambiguous. Instead, they simply contend that the $100,000 should be allocated not to them, but to Alliance, the insurance agency in which Mr. Jones is a minority shareholder. They present two arguments in support of that proposition: (1) that Alliance was bound by the covenant not to compete; and (2) that Alliance ultimately received the $100,000.

A.

Although the sales agreement provides that only Mr. Jones and the Bryan F. Jones Agency will not compete against the buyer for a period of three years, Mr. and Mrs. Jones allege that Alliance also was bound by the covenant not to compete. In support, they point to paragraph F(e) of the sales agreement which allowed Mr. Jones to maintain his minority interest in Alliance, provided that he did not violate the covenant not to compete. They argue that this paragraph necessarily bound Alliance to the non-compete agreement, although they concede that neither alliance nor its other shareholders were signatories to the contract. Mr. and Mrs. Jones further allege that Alliance possessed the ability to compete with the buyer, and that Mr. Jones believed it was his obligation to ensure that Alliance did not do so. Finally, they contend that Alliance did comply with the covenant not to compete.

It is undisputed that neither Alliance nor any of its other shareholders was a signatory to the non-compete agreement. Under Ohio law, it is axiomatic that a corporation is a wholly separate legal entity from its shareholders, such that it cannot be bound by the independent action of any of them. Therefore, a minority shareholder's assent to an agreement cannot bind his or her corporation to that agreement.

Further, the sales agreement is not ambiguous. Absent any ambiguity, extrinsic evidence regarding the parties' intent is not admissible.

B.

Finally, Mr. and Mrs. Jones argue that the $100,000 is taxable to Alliance because Alliance ultimately received the money which was paid by Stoessner.

It is well-established that a taxpayer cannot assign a portion of his income to avoid tax liability thereon. Indeed, "[t]he power to dispose of income is the equivalent of ownership of it. The exercise of that power to procure the payment of income to another is the enjoyment and hence the realization of the income by him who exercises it."

IV.

The district court found that it was undisputed that Mr. Jones personally gave the covenant not to compete and that he alone possessed the power to direct disposition of the $100,000 received therefor. Accordingly, the district court's entry of summary judgment in the Government's favor was not in error.

Affirmed.

Problem 31–1

Stephan owns a business, Hotel Managers (HM), which manages hotels and motels. One of Stephan's primary competitors is Phyllis, who operates her business as a corporation, known as Superior Hotel Services, Inc. (SHS). Stephan proposes a transaction whereby he would buy the business of SHS for $1 million in cash. He proposes to pay $500,000 for the ten hotel management contracts owned by SHS (which have an average remaining duration of two years); $100,000 for the furniture, fixtures and equipment (FF & E) owned by SHS; $250,000 for a two-year consulting agreement whereby Phyllis is obligated to assist HM in absorbing the 10 new management contracts and to seek their renewal on its behalf; and $150,000 to Phyllis, payable at closing, for a five-year covenant not to compete in any area in which HM manages hotels.

1. What is the tax result to Phyllis if the proposal is accepted and closed?

2. What result to her corporation?

3. What if SHS liquidates following the sale and distributes the net proceeds of sale to Phyllis?

4. What if SHS were an S corporation?

5. How are the payments made by HM amortized or deducted?

6. What if Phyllis negotiated a reallocation of the sales proceeds so that the consulting agreement paid $500,000, and the covenant not to compete $300,000, leaving only $100,000 allocable to the management contracts?

2. TAX–DEFERRED ASSET ACQUISITIONS

An entrepreneur who seeks to expand his corporate business through the acquisition of another corporate business may not always have the available funds nor the borrowing power to do so with cash.

On the other hand, a corporate owner who seeks to sell the business to an acquiring corporation may not be in a position to pay tax on consideration received from the sale and/or may wish to maintain a stake in the combined business. If these situations exist, the goals of the purchaser and seller may often be achieved through the utilization of the provisions of § 368 (sometimes referred to as the "tax-free reorganization" provisions). However, this section more properly is called the "nontaxable reorganization" or "tax-*deferred* reorganization" provisions.

These favorable acquisition rules apply only to a combination of *corporate* businesses. The fundamental requirements for achieving a nontaxable acquisition are that the seller shareholders maintain a "continuity of interest" in the ongoing combined business and that the "buyer" corporation inherits the tax basis of the seller in the acquired assets, regardless of the value of the consideration paid. The basic format of a nontaxable acquisitive reorganization is that the selling corporation transfers its assets to the acquiring corporation with the consideration being paid to the selling corporation's shareholders in the form of the acquiring corporation's stock. The two basic acquisitive reorganization vehicles available under § 368 to achieve this result are the "A" reorganization which is the "statutory merger" described in § 368(a)(1)(A) and the "C" reorganization which is the "stock for assets" reorganization described in § 368(a)(1)(C). Although these statutory vehicles are precisely those utilized by major public companies to effectuate large asset acquisitions on a nontaxable basis, they also apply to two corporations in which the stock of each is owned entirely by one shareholder. In order to qualify as either an A or a C reorganization, certain specific statutory requirements must be met.

a. The Statutory Merger—A Reorganizations

An A reorganization is defined in the Code merely as a "statutory merger or consolidation." The statute referred to in this definition includes each of those contained in the corporate codes of the various states. All states have provisions allowing a merger or consolidation of two corporations. When two corporations are merged, the assets and liabilities of the merged corporation are transferred to the surviving corporation by operation of law. No deeds or other conveyancing documents are necessary. The consideration received by the shareholders of the merged corporation, which consideration is generally the stock of the surviving corporation, is transferred directly to the shareholders of the disappearing corporation. It does not pass-through the disappearing corporation.

In order to qualify for favorable reorganization tax treatment, the merger must strictly comply with the local law requirements of the state in which the merger takes place. This involves filing articles of merger with the secretary of state, the issuance of new shares to the shareholders of the disappearing corporation, appropriate plans of merger, resolutions, and related documents. If the state statutory requirements are met, the statutory merger is the most flexible acquisitive reorganization from a federal tax standpoint. This is so because the acquiring corporation may utilize any type or class of its stock as consideration for the acquisition. As will subsequently be seen, in a B or C reorganization, the *voting* stock of the acquiring corporation must be utilized. In addition, in an A reorganization, the acquiring corporation is not required to acquire "substantially all" of the assets of the target corporation (as it is in a C). Thus, the target corporation can distribute or "spinoff" unwanted assets prior to the merger.

Finally, the acquiring corporation in a merger may give cash or other nonqualifying property to the target shareholders in addition to its stock, so long as the judicial "continuity of interest" threshold is met by the "selling" shareholders. The nonqualifying consideration in such a transaction is known as "boot." While the extent of boot which may be given in an A reorganization without disqualifying its tax deferment is not entirely clear, there is significant authority that boot may constitute as much as one-half of the total consideration received by the target shareholders. In this situation, the boot is taxable to the shareholders to the extent of the gain (value over basis) inherent in their target shares, but the acquiring corporation stock received will not generate additional gain.

The transfer of the target corporation's assets to the acquiring corporation is not taxable in a merger, but the basis of those assets will be "carried over" from the target corporation to the acquiring corporation under § 362(b). The basis of the acquiring corporation's stock received by the target corporation shareholders will generally be that basis which those shareholders had in their relinquished stock of the target corporation under § 358(a). If boot is received by the target shareholders, it will have a basis equal to its fair market value. If boot is received in the form of money, the stock received in the merger will have its basis reduced by the amount of money received and increased by the amount of taxable gain recognized on the transaction.

In a "pure" merger, where no boot is present, the entire transaction should be tax-deferred since the acquiring corporation will acquire the assets of the target corporation with no tax to the target corporation and will carry over the target's basis in those assets. Similarly, the shareholders of the target corporation will receive stock in the acquiring corporation in exchange for the cancellation of their shares in the target corporation. The basis of the acquired corporation's shares in the hands of the target shareholders will be the same basis as their basis for the target corporation stock.

b. *Stock for Assets—C Reorganizations*

A "stock for assets" C reorganization essentially achieves the same tax result as a statutory merger, but is considerably more complex and has more restrictive requirements. The definitional requirements in § 368(a)(1)(C) dictate that the target corporation transfer "substantially all" of its properties to the acquiring corporation in exchange for the *voting* stock of the acquiring corporation. Thus, in a C reorganization, the stock of the acquiring corporation travels first to the target corporation itself (rather than its shareholders) in exchange for its assets and is only subsequently distributed to the shareholders upon a liquidation of the target corporation. Unlike a statutory merger, the assets of the target corporation do not pass to the acquiring corporation by operation of law and, consequently, conveyancing documents relating to the assets are required. Similarly, the acquiring corporation's stock must be assigned first to the target corporation and then reassigned to its shareholders in liquidation.

In addition to the mechanical complexities of a C reorganization, the requirements necessary to preserve its tax-free nature are also more restrictive. The acquiring corporation must use its voting stock as consideration and the acquiring corporation must acquire "substantially all" of the target corporation's assets. This has been interpreted to mean virtually all of the operating assets of the target and the Service, for the purposes of issuing letter Rulings, considers 90% of the net assets of the target corporation to be the minimum portion that is considered substantial. See Rev.Proc. 77–37, 1977–2 C.B. 568; Rev.Proc. 86–42, 1986–2 C.B. 722. In addition, since the statute requires that the assets of the target corporation be acquired "solely for voting stock," the utilization of any form of boot in a C reorganization will generally jeopardize the entire tax-free nature of the reorganization transfer. It should be noted that the shareholders of the target corporation may still receive boot in the transaction even if it is not provided by the acquiring corporation. That is, any assets not transferred to the acquiring corporation, but subsequently distributed to the target shareholders in liquidation of the target corporation, will be treated as taxable boot to them.

Because of these various restrictions, a C reorganization is generally less useful than a statutory merger. The C reorganization may still be used, however, in the event that the corporations do not wish to comply with the merger laws of the state of reorganization or in the event that the acquiring corporation does not desire to acquire all of the liabilities of the target corporation. In a statutory merger, the liabilities of the target become those of the acquiring corporation by operation of law; whereas, in a C reorganization, the acquiring corporation may pick and choose the liabilities of the target corporation which it assumes.

If the C reorganization meets the statutory requirements, the tax results are similar to that of the A reorganization. That is, the transfer of appreciated assets by the target corporation will not be a taxable event. The assets received by the acquiring corporation will have their basis carried over from that of the target corporation. The basis of the shares received by the target corporation shareholders will be the same as the basis of the stock given up in the liquidation exchange. Where boot is involved, the basis of the stock in the acquiring corporation is decreased by the value of the boot received and increased by the amount of any taxable income or gain realized because of the boot. Boot property other than cash takes a basis equal to its fair market value.

PENROD v. COMMISSIONER

88 T.C. 1415 (1987).

The issues for our decision are: (1) Whether the exchange of stock of corporations owned by the petitioners for stock of McDonald's Corp. (McDonald's) qualifies as a tax-deferred reorganization under section 368, I.R.C. 1954.

FINDINGS OF FACT

* * *

Prior to May 15, 1975, petitioners Robert A. Penrod (Bob), Charles E. Penrod (Chuck), and Ronald L. Peeples (Ron), together with Jack Penrod (Jack), owned stock in a number of corporations which operated McDonald's fast-food restaurants in South Florida. Jack Penrod and petitioners Bob and Chuck Penrod are brothers. Petitioner Ron Peeples was the brother-in-law of the Penrods during the years in issue. Jack, Bob, and Chuck Penrod and Ron Peeples will sometimes be referred to collectively as the Penrods. * * *

By May 1975, the Penrods had acquired franchises for 16 McDonald's restaurants in South Florida. In all cases but one, a separate corporation was formed to hold each franchise and to operate each restaurant. In one case, a single corporation owned and operated two McDonald's restaurants. * * *

By 1975, the Penrods had built an unusually successful and efficient organization. On February 20, 1975, Jack was visiting McDonald's corporate headquarters near Chicago, Illinois, when McDonald's president, Fred Turner, told Jack that he wished to acquire the restaurants owned by the Penrods. In subsequent discussions, McDonald's management indicated that the company wanted to use the pooling of interest method of accounting for the acquisition on its financial statements. Accounting rules then in effect prevented McDonald's from using the pooling of interest method if McDonald's purchased the Penrod corporations for cash. For such reason, McDonald's management contemplated the acquisition would be achieved through an exchange of the stock owned by the Penrods for McDonald's common stock. At no time did Jack request cash for the Penrod stock; at all times, he agreed to the acquisition in exchange for McDonald's stock.

* * *

The final agreement and plan of reorganization (the agreement) called for McDonald's to issue its unregistered common stock in exchange for the stock in the Penrod corporations. Since SEC rules required that stock such as that received by the Penrods be registered before it could be sold in the first 2 years, Mr. Reed insisted on provisions in the agreement giving the Penrods incidental and demand registration rights with respect to their stock. The incidental rights were set forth in section 6.4 of the agreement, which required McDonald's to give written notice to the Penrods of any proposed registration of stock and to include any of the Penrod stock in such registration if requested to do so. The demand registration rights were contained in section 6.5 of the agreement, which provided that a majority of the Penrod stockholders could inquire whether McDonald's proposed a registration of stock and, if McDonald's did not, could demand that McDonald's register their stock. The demand registration rights could first be exercised in mid-August 1975 and expired on May 15, 1976. The expenses of a registration were generally to be paid by McDonald's. It was Mr. Reed's practice to negotiate for such registration rights on behalf of his clients each time he represented shareholders in a corporate acquisition. The Penrods made no express request that he negotiate for registration rights.

After Jack and McDonald's agreed on the basis for the acquisition, the Penrods' attorneys drafted a proposed ruling request to be submitted to the IRS, in which the Penrods requested a determination that the acquisition would be treated as a reorganization under section 368. Representatives of McDonald's informed the Penrods' attorneys that McDonald's was anxious to close the acquisition quickly and that there was not sufficient time to wait for a ruling from the IRS; therefore, no ruling request was ever submitted to the IRS. Instead, the Penrods obtained an opinion from their attorneys that the merger qualified as a reorganization under section 368. The opinion included the statement that:

Our understanding of the circumstances under which the reorganizations will be accomplished is as follows:

* * *

12. * * * McDonald's has no claims or agreements to reacquire any of the McDonald's shares issued to the shareholders of the Companies, and the shareholders have no present intention to sell or otherwise dispose of the McDonald's stock to be received in the reorganizations.

* * *

On May 15, 1975, McDonald's and the Penrods executed the agreement, which transferred ownership and management of the Penrod corporations to McDonald's. In exchange for the stock of such corporations, the Penrods received 106,464 shares of McDonald's unregistered common stock. Of such amount, Jack received 79,266 shares, Bob received 15,833 shares, Chuck received 7,648 shares, and Ron received 3,717 shares. As required by the agreement, 10 percent of the shares received by the Penrods, or 10,646 shares, were held in escrow to cover any claims or liabilities of the acquired corporations which arose after the closing.

After May 15, 1975, Bob, Chuck, and Ron continued to work in the restaurants. However, it became apparent that McDonald's intended to change the management of such restaurants. McDonald's brought in new supervisors and managers, transferred managers who had worked for the Penrods to other restaurants, and remodeled and installed new equipment in several restaurants. Employees who had worked for Bob before the merger complained to him about such changes and expected him to represent their interests with the new management. After Bob voiced the concerns of such employees to McDonald's management, he was told to simply stay home and collect his McDonald's paycheck, and to stay away from the restaurants. Despite these warnings, Bob continued to visit the restaurants.

* * *

Sometime in 1974, Jack began to plan the development of a chain of restaurants to be known as "Wuv's." Jack intended Wuv's to compete in the fast-food market and expected his competition to be other fast-food restaurants such as McDonald's, Burger King, and Wendy's. In August 1974, Jack engaged a Washington, D.C., attorney to conduct a trademark search to determine whether the name "Wuv's" was available for use as a fast-food service mark. * * *

In mid-August 1975, McDonald's common stock closed at approximately $44 per share on the New York Stock Exchange; by November 11, 1975, the price had risen to $58 per share. On that day, Mr. Reed sent a letter to McDonald's management, pursuant to section 6.5 of the agreement, inquiring as to whether McDonald's intended within 60 days to file a registration statement with the SEC which would allow the Penrods to register their McDonald's stock for sale. Such letter further stated that, if McDonald's did not intend to file such registration statement, the Penrods as a group desired to sell approximately 60,000 shares received from McDonald's pursuant to the acquisition. By reply letter dated December 3, 1975, McDonald's informed the Penrods that it did not plan to file a regular registration statement and that it was preparing to file a registration statement on the Penrods' behalf to be effective after January 1, 1976. Such letter further reflected McDonald's understanding that the Penrods had decided, subsequent to Mr. Reed's November 11 letter, to sell all of the shares received by them in the acquisition, except for those held in escrow. On December 3, 1975, McDonald's common stock closed at approximately $54 per share on the New York Stock Exchange. When the registration statement for the Penrods was filed with the SEC, the number of shares to be sold by them had increased to 96,554.

McDonald's stock covered by the registration statement for the Penrods was sold on January 12, 1976, for approximately $60 per share. Bob, Chuck, and Ron appointed Jack as their agent in negotiating for such sale. As of January 14, 1976, the Penrods owned 10,646 shares of McDonald's stock, all of which was held in escrow by McDonald's pursuant to the agreement. Jack owned 7,927 of such shares, Bob owned 1,583 shares, Chuck owned 765 shares, and Ron owned 371 shares.

* * *

Wuv's had its principal office in South Florida. By December 31, 1975, Jack had opened three Wuv's restaurants. One such restaurant was in Boca Raton, Florida, and another was in Deland, Florida. By December 31, 1976, approximately 20 Wuv's restaurants were opened. Ordinarily, it takes a minimum of 12 months to plan, obtain zoning variances and building permits, and actually construct a fast-food restaurant such as Wuv's. In assembling his management team at Wuv's, Jack hired three important regional employees of McDonald's. All of those individuals were hired to work in the same or similar capacity as that in which they worked for McDonald's.

* * *

On his Federal income tax return for 1976, Robert Penrod reported the gain on the sale of his McDonald's stock as long-term capital gain. In like manner, Charles and Mary Penrod and Ronald and Carol Peeples reported such gain as long-term capital gain on their Federal income tax returns for 1976. McDonald's treated its acquisition of the Penrod corporations as a taxable purchase on its Federal income tax returns.
* * *

In the notices of deficiency sent to the petitioners, the Commissioner determined that the exchange of stock of the Penrod corporations for McDonald's stock did not qualify as a reorganization under section 368, due to the absence of a continuity of interest on the part of the Penrods. Accordingly, the Commissioner determined that the petitioners should have recognized an immediate gain from the exchange of their shares on May 15, 1975. * * *

OPINION

The first issue for decision in this case is whether the exchange of stock owned by the petitioners for stock in McDonald's qualifies as a reorganization under section 368. The parties agree that the transaction constituted a statutory merger that was in form eligible for reorganization treatment under section 368(a)(1)(A). However, the Commissioner determined that such exchange of stock did not qualify as a reorganization because the petitioners failed to maintain a sufficient equity interest in McDonald's after the exchange.

It is well settled that, in addition to meeting specific statutory requirements, a reorganization under section 368(a)(1)(A) must also satisfy the continuity of interest doctrine. The continuity of interest doctrine has developed from the fundamental principle of tax law that the substance of a transaction, and not its form, controls its tax consequences. Because the reorganization provisions are based on the premise that the shareholders of an acquired corporation have not terminated their economic investment, but have merely altered its form, the continuity of interest doctrine limits the favorable nonrecognition treatment enjoyed by reorganizations to those situations in which (1) the nature of the consideration received by the acquired corporation or its shareholders confers a proprietary stake in the ongoing enterprise, and (2) the proprietary interest received is definite and material and represents a substantial part of the value of the property transferred.

The entire consideration received by the Penrods pursuant to the May 15, 1975, merger consisted of McDonald's common stock. Thus, the parties agree that, in form, the nature and amount of such consideration satisfied the continuity of interest test. However, they do not agree on the effect of the Penrods' subsequent actions.

The Commissioner argues that the acquisition and the subsequent sale of McDonald's stock by the Penrods was part of an overall plan to "cash out" their investment in the acquired corporations and that, therefore, the two events should be considered to be, in substance, one transaction. The consequence of his position would be to treat the petitioners as having received all cash on the date of the acquisition, and therefore, the acquisition would fail the continuity of interest test. On the other hand, the petitioners argue that their decision to sell their McDonald's stock was based only upon events which occurred after the acquisition and that the acquisition and subsequent sale should therefore be treated as separate transactions. * * *

In the present case, there was no binding commitment by the Penrods at the time of the acquisition to sell their stock. However, we need not decide whether the absence of a binding commitment, standing alone, is sufficient to prevent the application of the step transaction doctrine; after carefully examining and evaluating all the circumstances surrounding the acquisition and subsequent sale of the McDonald's stock received by the Penrods, we have concluded that, at the time of the acquisition, the Penrods did not intend to sell their McDonald's stock and that therefore the step transaction doctrine is not applicable under either the interdependence test or the end result test. * * *

In this case, Jack was unquestionably the leader of the Penrod group. He owned not less than 60 percent of the outstanding stock of each of the Penrod corporations at the time of the acquisition. Further, Jack was solely responsible for negotiating the terms of the agreement with McDonald's, and the petitioners appointed him as their agent to negotiate the terms of the sale of their McDonald's shares. Thus, we shall focus our analysis on the intention of Jack at the time of the acquisition and subsequent sale of McDonald's stock.

The Commissioner argued vigorously that Jack intended to sell his McDonald's stock when he acquired it because he planned to organize Wuv's, a competing fast-food restaurant chain. The evidence shows that Jack began thinking about a fast-food restaurant to be named Wuv's in 1974. At that time, he was enough interested in the idea to employ an attorney to research the trademark. Yet, he was then engaged in operating 16 McDonald's restaurants, and there is absolutely no evidence that he planned to sell or otherwise terminate his interest in those McDonald's restaurants at that time. In fact, Jack testified that it was the president of McDonald's who first mentioned the possibility of McDonald's acquiring the restaurants in February 1975. Jack did not initiate the proposal to exchange the stock of the Penrod corporations for McDonald's stock; it was McDonald's that took the initiative. Moreover, Jack never asked for cash for his restaurants. McDonald's proposed to issue unregistered common stock in exchange for the stock of the Penrod corporations, and Jack never questioned that proposal. This evidence shows that, at the outset, Jack expected to operate his Wuv's restaurants without any liquidation of his interest in McDonald's.

In March 1975, the deal was struck—Jack and the management of McDonald's agreed on the exchange and on the amount of McDonald's stock to be issued for the Penrod stock. Only the details of the agreement remained to be worked out by the lawyers. Hence, in March 1975, Jack knew that he was going to terminate his operation of the restaurants to be acquired by McDonald's. He then, with Bob's assistance, apparently moved ahead on his plans to organize Wuv's, and on the day after the closing of the acquisition agreement, he arranged for the incorporation of Wuv's. He had approximately 2 months to make such arrangements after the deal was struck with McDonald's. Yet, while the agreement was being negotiated, Jack led his lawyers to understand that he intended to continue to hold the McDonald's stock to be acquired.

In August 1975, the Penrods could have demanded registration of their McDonald's stock, but they did not. In October 1975, Jack arranged to borrow $2 million from the Dania Bank to finance the operations of the Wuv's restaurants. Before securing such loan, Jack calculated that he could open 30 restaurants with $1,500,000 of funds supplied by him. Such estimates may, or may not, have been realistic, but there is no dispute over the fact that Jack made such calculations and believed that such funds would be sufficient to open the Wuv's restaurants. In connection with the loan from the Dania Bank, Jack's representative advised the bank that Jack planned to sell enough of his McDonald's stock to pay off $1 million of his loans and to pay his taxes on the sale. He then planned to retain approximately $2 million of the McDonald's stock. This evidence reveals that by October 1975, Jack had decided to sell some of his McDonald's stock; yet, if the evidence correctly reflects his intention at the time, he would have retained enough of the McDonald's stock to constitute a substantial interest in McDonald's, and the continuity of interest requirement would have been satisfied.

We do not know why the Penrods did not demand registration of their McDonald's stock at the earliest opportunity; we do know that the value of the stock was depressed in August 1975 (approximately $44 a share) and that the value had risen to $58 a share on November 11, 1975. On that day, the Penrods took the first public action to sell their McDonald's stock. At the outset, they planned to sell 60,000 shares, but by December 1975, they increased the number to 96,554. In December, the value of the stock had dropped slightly, but the general trend was upward. They received $60 a share for the stock when it was sold in January 1976. It may be that by the fall of 1975, Jack decided to sell his McDonald's stock in part because he wanted the funds to open the Wuv's restaurants and in part because the market for the stock was favorable. Yet, a review of the record of events that occurred in 1975 supports Jack's testimony that he did not intend to sell his McDonald's stock when he acquired it and that he expected to be able to continue to hold that stock and to operate the Wuv's restaurants simultaneously.

In addition, Bob, Chuck, and Ron all testified that they intended to hold the McDonald's stock when they acquired it, and the circumstances corroborate their testimony. They all continued to work for McDonald's, and each of them hoped to acquire his own McDonald's franchise. Conflicts between them and McDonald's, particularly involving Bob, resulted in the relationship between them and McDonald's souring. In time, they either left McDonald's or were fired. The record of those events supports the testimony that they intended to hold the stock when it was acquired and that their decision to sell it arose because of subsequent events.

Disputes also developed between Jack and McDonald's after the acquisition. Jack hired some of the key employees from McDonald's and opened competing restaurants. McDonald's took the position that such activities constituted violations of the provisions of the acquisition agreement. Those disputes were eventually settled. If they have any bearing on the issue before us, they tend to support the conclusion that the decision by Jack to sell was an independent transaction.

For these reasons, we have concluded that Jack and the other Penrods intended to continue to hold the McDonald's stock acquired by them in the acquisition. Accordingly, in our judgment, the acquisition of the stock and its subsequent sale were not interdependent steps, nor were they steps in a plan the end result of which was to cash out their interests in the restaurants. Under such circumstances, we hold that such transactions should not be stepped together, that the Penrods' ownership of the McDonald's stock satisfied the continuity of interest requirement, and that the acquisition of such stock constituted a reorganization within the meaning of section 368(a)(1)(A). * * *

Problem 31–2

Bart owns all of the issued and outstanding stock of Gusher, Inc., a corporation in the business of owning and operating oil well drilling rigs. Bart's primary competition in the oil drilling business comes from Alpha Corporation, the stock of which is owned solely by Norm. Norm has significant taxable income and available cash. He does not need more money, but he desires to sell his business to pursue other interests. He would like to continue to participate in the fortunes of the oil well drilling industry through potential stock appreciation. Gusher, Inc. offers to acquire all of the assets of Alpha in exchange for newly issued shares representing 49% of the equity of the combined company.

1. Can the proposed transaction be structured as a statutory merger?

2. Could the proposed transaction be structured as a C reorganization?

3. Would the answers to questions 1 or 2 change if Norm negotiated to take 50% of the "purchase price" for his company in cash and 50% in the voting stock of Gusher?

4. What if Gusher, Inc. wanted Norm to have appreciation rights but not voting rights, and consequently issued nonvoting common stock?

5. What if 50% of the stock of Alpha were owned by Norm's brother, Phil, who needed cash. As a result, Gusher, Inc. issued voting stock to Norm and cash to Phil in exchange for their respective shares in Alpha. Could an A or C reorganization still be utilized?

6. If Norm had a $10,000 basis in his Alpha stock and received cash in the amount of $500,000 and stock with a value of $500,000, what would be the tax basis in his newly issued Gusher stock?

7. What if Alpha, prior to the acquisition, distributed to Norm the office building which had been used in its operations, and then transferred all of its remaining assets to Gusher, Inc. in exchange for voting stock of Gusher?

C. STOCK ACQUISITIONS

Perhaps the simplest method of acquiring a corporate business is to purchase the stock of its shareholders for cash. In corporate acquisition jargon, the offer to purchase the shares of a target corporation from its shareholders for a stated price is known as a "tender offer." As discussed in the context of an asset acquisition, an acquiring corporation may sometimes lack the cash to make a tender offer and/or the shareholders of the target corporation may desire to avoid the tax cost inherent in selling their shares for cash at a profit. In such cases, § 368(a)(1)(B) permits the acquiring corporation to exchange its stock for that of the target corporation. An offer to do so is commonly referred to as an "exchange offer." If accepted, the shareholders of the target corporation receive stock of the acquiring corporation on a tax-deferred basis and the target corporation becomes a subsidiary of the acquiring corporation.

1. TAXABLE STOCK ACQUISITIONS

An acquiring corporation may seek to obtain the shares of a target corporation by purchasing them for cash from the target shareholders. The cash for such an acquisition may come from available corporate cash of the acquirer or borrowed funds. If the offer is successful, all of the target shares will be purchased by the acquiring corporation, thereby making the target a subsidiary of the acquiring corporation. The payment of cash by the acquiring corporation to the target shareholders is a taxable transaction.

In some cases, a selling business owner is willing to endure the tax bite of a cash sale of his shares in order to dispose of his or her business. The stock held by the target shareholder is usually a capital asset, thus yielding favorable capital gain rates to the selling shareholder, and no tax at the corporate level since no corporate assets are being sold. In rare cases, the share sale may qualify for the additional 50% exclusion provided by § 1202. The single capital gain tax payable by the selling shareholder may be the most economical exit vehicle available to a retiring owner. This may be particularly true if the selling shareholder has capital losses or net operating loss carryforwards to offset the gain or if § 1202 applies. The gain recognition may also be deferred through an installment sale of the stock under § 453. Such a deferred payment sale would allow the selling shareholder to "invest" the entire proceeds of his sale, through the receipt of interest on the entire unpaid portion of the purchase price, until the purchaser's payments are made, rather than receiving only the net after-tax proceeds of sale and subsequently investing them. Moreover, if the corporation has been properly structured and maintained under state law, the sale of its shares relieves the selling shareholder of the liabilities and claims which may exist against the corporation, except to the extent that he or she was personally responsible for or personally guaranteed such liabilities and claims.

While the acquisition of target shares for cash is simple, it may have adverse consequences to the acquiring corporate shareholder. The amount paid for the acquired shares will be their tax basis in the hands of the acquiring corporation. The purchase price of the shares is not reflected in an increase or decrease in the tax basis of the individual assets of the acquired corporation. Thus, such assets will retain their historical basis within the target corporation for the purposes of depreciation, amortization, inventory cost, resale, etc. Therefore, in addition to the purchase price paid for the shares, the acquiring corporation may pay a second price equal to the tax on the appreciation in the assets of the target corporation upon their ultimate disposition.

2. TAX–DEFERRED ACQUISITIONS

A corporation seeking to acquire the stock of a target corporation in a tax-deferred acquisitive reorganization may do so under the provisions of § 368(a)(1)(B). This is known as a B reorganization or an "exchange offer." If successful, the target corporation emerges from the transaction as a subsidiary (at least 80% of its stock owned) of the acquiring corporation and the former shareholders of the target corporation become shareholders of the acquiring corporation.

The statutory requirements mandated for a B reorganization are different than those for an A or a C reorganization and are stringent. The statutory language requires (1) that the target corporation stock be acquired by the acquiring corporation "solely in exchange for the voting stock" of the acquiring corporation, and (2) that "immediately after the exchange," the acquiring corporation must "control" the target. As discussed in connection with a C reorganization, the solely for voting stock requirement precludes the use of other types of stock of the acquiring corporation. It also precludes the use of any type of boot, i.e., cash or property. The control requirement has been defined in § 368(c) as (1) stock possessing 80% of the combined voting power of all stock of the target entitled to vote *and* (2) 80% of the number of shares of each class of the target stock not entitled to vote.

a.   *Permissible Consideration*

The tax adviser to the acquiring corporation in a proposed B reorganization must be extremely vigilant as to the type of consideration given to the target shareholders in the transaction. The solely for voting stock rule has been strictly applied. If the target shareholders receive nonvoting stock of the acquiring corporation, cash, other property, or other consideration of any kind, the *entire* transaction will be taxable. In such event, the combined value of the voting stock and the nonqualifying consideration will be the amount realized by the target shareholders and will constitute gain to the extent it exceeds the basis of the target stock surrendered. A violation of the solely for voting stock rule can be inadvertent. For instance, the payment by the acquiring corporation of transactional expenses of the target corporation's shareholders might be deemed to be boot, thereby causing the transaction to be taxable. See *Helvering v. Southwest Consolidated Corp.*, 315 U.S. 194 (1942). Similarly, the payment of shareholder debts by the acquiring corporation is clearly boot which will cause the transaction to be taxable. Obviously, the payment of cash or other nonvoting consideration to the target shareholders would have a similar result.

In a B reorganization, the liabilities of the target corporation are, in essence, "assumed" by the acquiring corporation's group, although the creditors of the target are normally limited in their collection efforts to the assets of the target. Because of the continued existence of the target corporation, the "assumption" of the liabilities of the target in a B reorganization is not deemed to be additional consideration which would violate the solely for voting stock requirement.

In some situations, an acquiring corporation may have initially acquired a minority stock interest in the target stock for cash and then subsequently seek to acquire control of the corporation for its voting stock. The issue in these cases is whether the initial acquisition of stock for cash is "old and cold" or whether it is part of an integrated acquisition transaction. If the transactions are integrated, the initial acquisition of target stock for cash will taint the entire transaction and make it taxable. See Reg. § 1.368–2(c).

b.   *Control of the Target Corporation*

The second fundamental requirement of a successful B reorganization is that the acquiring corporation emerge from the transaction with control of the target corporation. If the target corporation has only one class of stock, as many small businesses do, this simply means the acquisition of at least 80% of the shares of the target. In most cases, the acquisition will result in the acquiring corporation obtaining 100% of the stock of the target corporation, making the target a wholly owned subsidiary of the acquiring corporation.

In the event, however, that the target corporation has more than one class of voting stock, or has nonvoting stock, the job of the acquiring corporation's tax adviser becomes more difficult. As to the voting stock, it is clear that the acquiring corporation must acquire 80% of the total combined voting power of all classes entitled to vote. As to nonvoting stock, the Service has interpreted the statutory requirement to mean that the acquiring corporation must acquire 80% of each class of nonvoting stock of the corporation which is outstanding. Rev.Rul. 59–259, 1959–2 C.B. 115. While this test is purely mechanical, the due diligence efforts of the acquiring corporation and its attorney must ensure that there are no classes of stock in the corporation outstanding which go unacquired.

c. *Other Requirements*

Unlike a C reorganization, there is no requirement under a B reorganization that "substantially all" of the assets of the target corporation be acquired. Thus, a target corporation could spin-off or distribute to its shareholders unwanted assets prior to the acquisition. Similarly, after the acquisition, the acquiring corporation would not be risking a violation of the B rules by selling a substantial portion of the assets of the target corporation. The tax planner must take care, however, that any amounts paid to the target shareholders by the target corporation prior to the acquisition are not, in fact, sums which flow from the acquiring corporation and therefore violate the solely for voting stock rule. For instance, if the target shareholders were distributed a promissory note payable on demand prior to the acquisition and the note was subsequently satisfied by means of a cash injection from the parent to the subsidiary immediately following the acquisition, the distribution of cash to the shareholders could be deemed to flow from the acquiring corporation and therefore violate the solely for voting stock requirement of § 368(a)(1)(B).

AMERICAN POTASH & CHEMICAL CORPORATION v. UNITED STATES

399 F.2d 194 (Ct.Cl.1968).

The facts are not in dispute. Taxpayer is engaged in the production and sale of industrial and agricultural chemicals. Between September 1954 and November 1955, Potash acquired all of the outstanding stock of Western Electrochemical Company (hereinafter referred to as Wecco) in exchange for 66,662 shares of its voting stock and $466.12 in cash paid for fractional shares.

Between September 28, 1954 and November 3, 1954, Potash acquired 48 percent of the Wecco stock in exchange for 33,367 shares of

Potash plus $466.12 in cash. On November 30, 1955 Potash acquired the remaining 52 percent of Wecco stock in exchange for 33,295 shares of Potash.

Potash made two separate offers to purchase all of the Wecco stock. In August, 1954 it offered each Wecco stockholder one share of Potash (selling at approximately $60 per share) for 6.5 shares of Wecco. For shares not evenly divisible by 6.5 it offered $9.23 per Wecco share (on the basis of $60 per Potash share). That offer expired on November 18, 1954, and some 52 percent of Wecco shareholders did not accept it.

In November, 1955 Potash again approached the Wecco shareholders with a new offer of one Potash share (now selling at $90 per share) for seven shares of Wecco. There were no fractional shares involved. The remaining 52 percent shareholders accepted this offer, and Potash acquired complete ownership.

Plaintiff admits that both of these stock acquisitions were to further its ultimate purpose—obtaining the Wecco assets—and that if it could not have obtained the remaining 52 percent ownership it would have sold the 48 percent interest acquired in 1954.

Potash did not acquire either 80 percent of the total combined voting power of all voting stock or 80 percent of the total number of shares of all other classes of stock during any 12–month period between September 1954 and November 1955.

For seven months, from December 1, 1955 to June 30, 1956, Wecco was operated by Potash. During that period taxpayer advanced $646,-293 to Wecco for working capital and other miscellaneous current operating needs. On June 30, 1956, Wecco was completely liquidated and all of its assets were distributed to (and its liabilities were assumed by) Potash. The fair market value of the assets distributed to Potash was $10,843,023. The liabilities assumed were $4,934,448 which, together with the $646,293 advanced, totaled $5,580,741 in liabilities.

For 1957, 1958, 1959 and 1960 fiscal tax years Potash computed its depreciation deduction for the depreciable assets received from Wecco on an adjusted basis of $7,085,551. This was its "cost" of the depreciable assets. That "cost" included the value of the 66,662 shares transferred in acquiring Wecco stock, the liabilities assumed on the liquidation and the cash advanced during the seven months that it operated Wecco. Immediately prior to the liquidation Wecco's basis in these assets was $3,788,779.

On audit of Potash's 1956 and 1957 tax returns the Internal Revenue Service determined that the correct basis of these assets was $3,788,779, the basis in the hands of Wecco prior to the liquidation. Taxpayer's adjusted basis was reduced by $3,296,772 and, accordingly, its yearly depreciation deduction was reduced by $100,843 per year. Taxpayer paid the 1957 deficiency on May 19, 1961. It adjusted its 1958, 1959 and 1960 tax returns, and the increased tax was included in the taxes paid for those years.

Claims for refund for 1957 and 1958 were filed on May 17, 1963. The claims for 1959 and 1960 were filed on September 5, 1963 and September 11, 1964, respectively. The 1957, 1958 and 1959 claims were denied on June 10, 1964, and the 1960 claim was denied on May 25, 1965. Suit was timely filed on June 7, 1966.

For the purpose of this motion, both plaintiff and defendant agree that the stock acquisition of Wecco and its liquidation were undertaken for the purpose of obtaining the Wecco assets, i.e., plaintiff purchased the stock to reach the assets.

I.

The government, in support of its motion for summary judgment, argues that, as a matter of law, a carryover basis is required because either the entire transaction was a reorganization under section 368(a)(1)(C) of the Internal Revenue Code of 1954 or alternatively, if the stock acquisition can be separated from the liquidation, the assets received in the liquidation are subject to a carryover basis under sections 332 and 334 as assets received by a parent (Potash) in the process of liquidating its wholly-owned subsidiary (Wecco). * * *

II.

Section 1012 provides that the basis of property is its cost except where otherwise provided. Section 362(b) requires a carryover basis for depreciable assets received in "connection with" a transaction which qualifies as a reorganization as defined in section 368(a)(1). Defendant concludes that a C reorganization has occurred and, therefore, a carryover basis is required for the assets.

A C reorganization, in general, is a transaction whereby one corporation (the acquiring corporation) acquires substantially all of the property of another corporation (the transferor corporation) as part of an exchange in which the acquiring corporation gives solely its voting stock (or the voting stock of its parent) to the transferor corporation in exchange for the transferor corporation's assets. Under certain limited circumstances, money or other property in addition to voting stock may be exchanged.

Before a transaction can be classified as a C reorganization three basic factors must be present. These are (a) an acquiring corporation gives *stock* to another corporation, and (b) receives *in exchange* for that stock (c) substantially all of the *properties* of the transferor corporation.

Defendant argues that taxpayer has not *purchased* Wecco's stock for cash and liquidated but has *exchanged* its stock for Wecco stock and then liquidated Wecco pursuant to its plan and intent to obtain Wecco's assets. Plaintiff, defendant continues, has therefore exchanged its stock for Wecco's assets, a transaction which qualifies as a C reorganization. Defendant contrasts a *purchase* of stock followed by a liquidation (in which the stockholders of the acquired company do not have any stock interest in the acquiring company) with an *exchange* of stock for stock followed by a liquidation (in which the stockholders of the acquired company become stockholders of the acquiring company). In the latter situation, defendant argues that there is a continuity of ownership, which, together with the basic intent to obtain assets establishes that the entire transaction was a reorganization.

Taxpayer's intent is considered in determining the existence of an overall plan to accomplish a particular result by a series of steps and in determining the existence of a plan to reorganize. The existence of either a plan to reorganize or a plan to accomplish a particular end result, however, does not necessarily mean that the particular route chosen to accomplish the desired result qualifies as a reorganization, as that term is defined in the statute.

A continuity of ownership and of interest are elements of a reorganization which must be present in addition to the specific exchange provided for by the statute. See: Reg.Sec. 1.368–1(b). The existence of either one or both elements does not establish that the particular process through which continuity was achieved is a reorganization. Nor does the end result of a transaction establish the presence of a reorganization. The existence of a continuity of ownership indicates only that one element of a reorganization is present. The particular transaction must meet all of the specific requirements of the statute before we can conclude that a reorganization occurred.

A regulation under section 368 (Reg. § 1.368–1(b)) explains the purpose of the specific requirements of the reorganization provisions. It states:

> * * * *In order to exclude transactions not intended to be included, the specifications of the reorganization provisions of the law are precise. Both* the *terms* of the specifications *and the underlying assumptions and purposes* must be satisfied in order to entitle the taxpayer to the benefit of the exception from the general rule [gain or loss must be recognized on the exchange of property]. [Emphasis supplied.]

We note that defendant admits, and we agree, that the form of this transaction—a transfer of Potash stock to the shareholders of Wecco in return for the stock of Wecco—resembles, and would seem to invoke the provisions of, section 368(a)(1)(B), if any reorganization provision were applicable. Without question, the basic transaction was a stock for stock exchange (B reorganization) rather than a stock for asset exchange (C reorganization). Potash transferred stock to, and received stock from, the Wecco shareholders. It did not transfer stock to the Wecco corporation in return for a transfer by the corporation of its assets.

In our view the transaction does not meet the requirements of a B reorganization but only because control of Wecco was not obtained by a series of stock for stock exchanges within a 12–month period (as is required by the applicable regulations, infra). This is an aspect of the attainment of stock control by "creeping acquisitions" rather than a single stock for stock exchange.

The creeping acquisition of control problem arose under the 1939 Code in a B reorganization when an acquiring corporation owned some stock of the corporation to be acquired but less than control. To resolve any lingering doubts about the validity of classifying successive stock for voting stock exchanges as a B reorganization, the 1954 Code specifically approved its use in the context of a B reorganization.

By its regulation (Reg. § 1.368–2(c)), which echoes S.Rep. No. 1622, supra, the government provided:

> Such an acquisition [B reorganization] is permitted tax-free in a single transaction or in a series of transactions taking place *over a relatively short period of time such as 12 months*. [Emphasis supplied.]

The infirmity, in this case, is that the entire transaction took place over a period of 14 months, and plaintiff never obtained control within any 12–month period. Defendant has not urged that this was a B reorganization. * * *

Defendant argues that despite its form (stock for stock) the entire transaction should be tested as a C reorganization because plaintiff has stated that it intended to obtain Wecco's assets. This position is premised on our integrating and collapsing the several transactions which began with the first acquisition in 1954 and ended with the assets received in the June 1956 liquidation into a "single transaction". That "single transaction," defendant argues, is a reorganization when measured against the provisions of section 368(a)(1)(C). Plaintiff's intent, as mentioned above, is relevant to the existence of a plan to obtain the assets and is an important factor when we are faced with denying independent tax significance to a liquidation which follows a reorganization. It does not establish that a reorganization occurred, or that *stock* was, in fact, *exchanged for assets* as is required in a C reorganization.

The issue before the court is whether we can transform a stock for stock exchange which does not itself qualify as a B reorganization, into a C-type stock for asset exchange by finding that the subsequent liquidation and distribution of the assets of the acquired corporation had no tax significance and that Potash, therefore, exchanged its stock with the Wecco corporation for the Wecco assets. The issue before us is not whether a liquidation which follows a valid B reorganization is to be given independent tax significance. In this case we are faced with the more basic problem; i.e., finding if a reorganization occurred. We cannot find any decision which has transformed a non-qualifying B-type exchange into a valid C reorganization by concluding that a subsequent liquidation of the acquired corporation was without significance. Defendant has not urged that this transaction was anything other than C reorganization. Courts have concluded, under comparable circumstances, that the property received in the post-reorganization (qualifying) liquidation was property received in connection with a transaction which separately qualified as a B reorganization. Other courts have concluded that an assets transfer was a mere change in the identity or form of the corporation and, therefore, a reorganization occurred. (Both of these possibilities will be explored at a later point.)

Defendant would have us create a C reorganization out of the substructure of an unqualified B-type exchange and a subsequent liquidation. We find that there was no reorganization to which we might attach the liquidation and that the liquidation itself does not transform the non-qualifying B-type exchange into a valid C reorganization.

The C reorganization subsection evolved as a "practical merger" alternative and was designed to permit corporate combinations which did not meet the applicable state requirements for a merger or consolidation. The Revenue Act of 1921, 42 Stats. 227, 230, provided, in section 202(c)(2), that:

> The word "reorganization" * * * includes a merger or consolidation (including the acquisition by one corporation * * * of substantially all the properties of another corporation) * * *

The parenthetical exception was construed as permitting combinations which were "effective mergers."

Corporations may choose between a stock for stock exchange or a stock for asset exchange to effect a combination. Typically, in a C reorganization the transferor corporation is divested of its assets (and usually is liquidated). A B reorganization results in the acquisition of a subsidiary.

One important reason for choosing a B rather than a C exchange is that gradual exchanges of stock may be accomplished in a B "creeping" reorganization. The acquisition of assets in a C reorganization should be accomplished in a single exchange transaction. In addition, the transferor corporation in a C reorganization must obtain stockholder approval before transferring its assets. In a B reorganization, however, each stockholder can, independently, exchange his stock for the stock offered by the acquiring corporation.

There is no evidence that Potash or Wecco could have obtained the approval of Wecco shareholders, and the presence of a dissenting majority during the first series of acquisitions would seem to imply that Potash could not have chosen a C reorganization. Potash states that it was *forced* to seek the Wecco assets by an acquisition of stock because it could not otherwise obtain the assets.

The practical merger aspect of a C reorganization precludes multiple stock for asset exchanges. A creeping asset acquisition is not permissible in a C reorganization as it would be impermissible in a statutory merger.

The stock for stock exchange series in this case would have qualified as a B reorganization (a "creeping acquisition") if control had been obtained within 12 months. Were we to conclude that a C reorganization had occurred because the B reorganization was followed by a liquidation, we would approve a *seriatim* creeping acquisition of stock control which, by virtue of a subsequent liquidation, becomes a *seriatim* acquisition of assets. The latter is not permissible under the statute, and in addition it contradicts the basic "merger equivalence" of a C reorganization.

* * *

Problem 31–3

Travis owns all the shares of BankTwo Corporation, which owns and operates a commercial bank. Sylvia owns all of the shares of BankThree Corporation, which owns a competing bank. Travis offers to acquire all of Sylvia's stock in BankThree Corporation in exchange for the issuance to Sylvia of voting shares by BankTwo Corporation which, when issued, would equal 35% of BankTwo's total outstanding stock.

1. Would the proposed transaction qualify as a B reorganization?

2. What if, in addition to the stock transferred to Sylvia by BankTwo Corporation, BankTwo agreed to pay Sylvia's legal fees in the transaction?

3. What if, prior to the transaction, BankThree Corporation distributed to Sylvia a Cadillac which was owned by BankThree but had been utilized by Sylvia in connection with her banking duties?

4. What if, 10 years earlier, BankTwo Corporation had purchased for $50,000 cash, nonvoting stock of BankThree Corporation which it still holds?

5. What if, as part of the transaction, BankTwo Corporation agreed to pay a personal loan of Sylvia owing to BankFour Corporation?

6. What if the loan in question 5 to BankFour Corporation was owned by BankThree Corporation, but personally guaranteed by Sylvia, and assumed by BankTwo Corporation as part of the transaction?

7. What if, immediately following the transaction, Sylvia redeemed a portion of the stock received in the transaction in exchange for cash from BankTwo Corporation?

8. What if, immediately after the transaction, Sylvia sold a portion of her BankTwo stock received in the transaction to a third party for cash?

Chapter 32

DISTRIBUTIONS BY A C CORPORATION TO ITS SHAREHOLDERS

Code References: §§ 243(a)–(b); 301(a)–(d); 311(a)–(b)(2); 312(a), (b), (k), (n)(5); 316.

Regulations: §§ 1.301–1(a), (b), (j); 1.312–6, 5(a); 1.316–1, –2.

A. INTRODUCTION

It is relatively simple for a shareholder of a newly organized or ongoing business corporation to transfer property to that corporation without significant state law or federal tax consequences. This is so whether the transferred property is cash, appreciated inventory, fixtures and/or equipment, or other assets.

As to assets held by an operating corporation (whether originally contributed by the shareholders or subsequently acquired by the corporation), however, tax problems arise when the corporation seeks to distribute them to shareholders. In short, it is much easier, from a tax standpoint, to place assets into a corporation than to draw them out.

This chapter deals with the distribution of property (in cash or in kind) from an operating C corporation to its shareholders. It examines the effect of such distributions, both on the corporation and the recipient shareholder. "Distributions" are those which are either made, or deemed to be made, "with respect to the stock of the corporation." This latter phrase refers to property transfers made to shareholders in their capacity as shareholders rather than as employees, contractors, or creditors. This chapter does not examine distributions which are made *in exchange* for the stock of the recipient shareholder, either as a stock redemption of a particular shareholder or in liquidation of the entire corporation. Such exchange distributions are addressed in Chapters 34 and 35.

A tax adviser reviewing the balance sheet of a C corporation which is planning to make a distribution to shareholders may well conclude that the tax costs of the potential distribution make it economically unsound. He or she will often conclude that, from a tax standpoint, certain of the assets should never have been placed in the corporation in the first place. In this case, the creative tax planner may develop alternatives to the actual distribution of money or property to a shareholder. As discussed below, when such creativity exceeds certain boundaries, a "constructive distribution" may be deemed to have occurred.

B. THE DIVIDEND CONCEPT

In the context of publicly traded corporations, a dividend is generally viewed as a distribution of the corporation's income to its shareholders essentially constituting a return on their stock investment, paid in accordance with the number of shares they own. State corporate laws often restrict the source of such distributions to the earnings or "retained earnings" of the corporation. Typically, such distributions may not be made from the stated capital of the corporation. The federal tax law embraces a similar concept. As usual, however, it has rules of its own regarding what constitutes a "dividend."

Under the statutory combination of §§ 301(a), 301(c), and 316(a), the tax definition of a dividend is a distribution by the corporation to a shareholder with respect to his or her stock which is made from either the accumulated or current "earnings and profits" of the distributing corporation. When a distribution from a corporation to its shareholders is a tax dividend under this definition, it is not deductible to the corporation in determining the corporation's taxable income and it constitutes ordinary income (as opposed to preferentially treated long-term capital gain) to the recipient shareholder. The earnings and profits of a C corporation are generally its profits *after* the payment of the corporate-level tax.

When distributed as dividends, these after-tax profits will again be taxed to the recipient shareholder at individual rates. As discussed in Chapter 28, the combination of these two taxes can provide an extremely high overall tax rate on the dollar of profit initially earned by the distributing corporation. For instance, if a C corporation earned $100, taxed at a corporate rate of 34%, and distributed the remaining $66 to an individual shareholder, taxed in the 39% bracket, the total tax cost would be approximately $60, leaving the recipient shareholder with only $40. Traditionally, this double taxation was the federal tax cost for the privilege of operating under a state limited liability entity structure. With the advent of the S corporation, the limited liability company, and other limited liability partnerships, however, such a cost may be irrational or at least excessive. In these "pass through" entities, the taxable income is calculated at the entity level, but taxed only to the individuals. In an S corporation, for instance, the $100 corporate profit would normally be "passed through" the entity and taxed only to the individual owner at the 39% rate, for a total tax cost of $39. The entire $100 cash would be distributed from the entity to the shareholder. After payment of the personal tax, $61 would remain.

In order to determine whether a distribution to a shareholder from a C corporation is a dividend for tax purposes, it must first be determined whether the distributing corporation has earnings and profits as required by § 316. While earnings and profits roughly equate to the accounting concept of retained earnings, they are not entirely identical. In order to analyze earnings and profits, the distributing corporation must make two calculations. First, it must determine whether it has accumulated earnings and profits. Accumulated earnings and profits are those accumulated at any time since March 1, 1913 (the advent of the federal income tax). If such accumulated earnings and profits exist on the date of distribution, the distribution will be treated as a dividend to the extent of those earnings and profits. The second calculation, of current earnings and profits, relates to earnings and profits of the corporation in the year of the distribution. Even if the corporation has a deficit in its *accumulated* earnings and profits, if there are, at the *end* of the year of distribution, current earnings and profits, then any distribution during that year (regardless of when during the year the distribution or the earnings occurred) will be a dividend to the extent of those year-end earnings. This is true even though the current year's earnings are less than the deficit in accumulated earnings. Distributions from earnings and profits are deemed to be from current earnings and profits to the extent thereof and thereafter from accumulated earnings and profits.

The actual calculation of earnings and profits is extremely complex. Section 312 requires adjustments to earnings and profits for such exotic items as distribution of government insured loans, construction period carrying charges, and LIFO inventory adjustments. In the small business context, however, the usual practice in computing earnings and profits is to begin with taxable income. Even in this case, however, the adjustments necessary to convert taxable income to earnings and profits are quite significant. Adjustments may be different for accrual method taxpayers than for those on the cash method. Corporate taxpayers are not allowed, in determining earnings and profits, to use such tax return permitted conventions as percentage depletion, installment reporting, and accelerated depreciation methods. Rather, the earnings and profits of the corporation are increased to reflect the amount that the corporate taxable income would have been had the corporate taxpayer used cost depletion, noninstallment reporting, and straight-line depreciation. When the fair market value of property distributed by a corporation exceeds its adjusted basis, the corporation, under § 312(b), increases its earnings and profits by the amount of the excess and, in turn, after determining the amount of the dividend, decreases its earnings and profits by the fair market value of the property distributed, rather than by its adjusted basis.

By way of example, assume that a corporation has taxable income of $100 and pays tax of $34. Assume further that, in computing its taxable income, the corporation reported a sale of property on the installment method, reporting a gain of $10, but deferring an additional gain of $30 under § 453. Assume further that the corporation, in determining its taxable income, claimed accelerated depreciation of $10 when a straight-line method would have yielded a depreciation deduction of only $3. The corporation's earnings and profits for the year would be calculated by taking its taxable income of $100, less its taxes paid of $34, plus the deferred installment sale gain of $30, plus the accelerated portion of its depreciation of $7, yielding a total "current" earnings and profits for the year of $103.

In practice, a tax attorney seeking to determine the effects of a potential corporate distribution will contact the accountant for the corporation and have the accountant calculate the current and accumulated earnings and profits (or deficits) of the corporation. He or she can then determine what portion of the distribution, if any, will be a dividend. Small business corporations rarely intentionally declare dividends. As seen in Chapter 30, one of the primary tax planning techniques utilized in connection with small business corporations relates to the distribution of their profits in ways which are deductible to the corporation. That is, the corporate income is distributed to the shareholder in his capacity as an employee, contractor, or creditor of the corporation, thereby not constituting a "distribution in respect of stock." Small business corporations may, as a strategic matter, declare minimal dividends in order to illustrate to the Service that they have a "dividend policy" designed to reward the shareholders for their investment in the corporation. Larger distributions, however, are usually made as deductible payments to the employees, contractors, and service providers of the corporation, even though such persons happen to be shareholders as well.

A corporation with excess funds, whose shareholder/employees have already been adequately compensated with salaries and bonuses, may seek to provide benefits to its shareholders without actually making distributions. Making loans to shareholders, the acquisition of corporate property for use by shareholders, and payment by the corporation of shareholder debt or other obligations, may be viewed by the Service as, in reality, shareholder distributions. If so, the Service will argue that these "constructive dividends" are taxable as actual dividends to the shareholders to the extent that the corporation has earnings and profits. As noted later in this chapter, if the constructive dividend is a deemed distribution of *appreciated* property (rather than money) from the corporation to the shareholder, the tax effects can be significant. In such a case, not only could the value of the property be deemed ordinary income to the recipient shareholder, but the distribution would generate taxable income to the corporation under § 311(b) to the extent of the appreciation in the property.

REVENUE RULING 74–164

1974–1 C.B. 74.

Advice has been requested concerning the taxable status of corporate distributions under the circumstances described below.

X corporation and *Y* corporation each using the calendar year for Federal income tax purposes made distributions of $15,000 to their respective shareholders on July 1, 1971, and made no other distributions to their shareholders during the taxable year. The distributions were taxable as provided by section 301(c) of the Internal Revenue Code of 1954.

SITUATION 1.

At the beginning of its taxable year 1971, *X* corporation had earnings and profits accumulated after February 28, 1913, of $40,000. It had an operating loss for the period January 1, 1971 through June 30, 1971, of $50,000 but had earnings and profits for the entire year 1971 of $5,000.

SITUATION 2.

At the beginning of its taxable year 1971, *Y* corporation had a deficit in earnings and profits accumulated after February 28, 1913, of $60,000. Its net profits for the period January 1, 1971 through June 30, 1971, were $75,000 but its earnings and profits for the entire taxable year 1971 were only $5,000.

SITUATION 3.

Assume the same facts as in *Situation* 1 except that *X* had a deficit in earnings and profits of $5,000 for the entire taxable year 1971.

SITUATION 4.

Assume the same facts as in *Situation* 1 except that *X* had a deficit in earnings and profits of $55,000 for the entire taxable year 1971.

Section 301(a) and 301(c) of the Code provides, in part, that: (1) the portion of a distribution of property made by a corporation to a shareholder with respect to its stock which is a dividend (as defined in section 316), shall be included in the shareholder's gross income; (2) the portion of the distribution which is not a dividend shall be applied against and reduce the adjusted basis of the stock; and (3) the portion which is not a dividend to the extent that it exceeds the adjusted basis of the stock and is not out of increase in value accrued before March 1, 1913, shall be treated as gain from the sale or exchange of property.

Section 316(a) of the Code provides that the term "dividend" means any distribution of property made by a corporation to its shareholders out of its earnings and profits accumulated after February 28, 1913, or out of its earnings and profits of the taxable year computed as of the close of the taxable year without diminution by reason of any distribution made during the year, and *without regard to the amount of earnings and profits at the time the distribution was made.*

Section 1.316–2(a) of the Income Tax Regulations provides, in part, that in determining the source of a distribution, consideration should be given first, to the earnings and profits of the taxable year; and second, to the earnings and profits accumulated since February 28, 1913, only in the case where, and to the extent that, the distributions made during the taxable year are not regarded as out of the earnings and profits of that year.

Applying the foregoing principles, in *Situation* 1, the earnings and profits of *X* corporation for the taxable year 1971 of $5,000 and the earnings and profits accumulated since February 28, 1913, and prior to the taxable year 1971, of $40,000 were applicable to the distribution paid by it on July 1, 1971. Thus, $5,000 of the distribution of $15,000 was paid from the earnings and profits of the taxable year 1971 and the balance of $10,000 was paid from the earnings and profits accumulated since February 28, 1913. Therefore, the entire distribution of $15,000 was a dividend within the meaning of section 316 of the Code.

In *Situation* 2 the earnings and profits of *Y* corporation for the taxable year 1971 of $5,000 were applicable to the distribution paid by *Y* corporation on July 1, 1971. *Y* corporation had no earnings and profits accumulated after February 28, 1913, available at the time of the distribution. Thus, only $5,000 of the distribution by *Y* corporation of $15,000 was a dividend within the meaning of section 316 of the Code. The balance of such distribution, $10,000 which was not a dividend, applied against and reduced the adjusted basis of the stock in the hands of the shareholders, and to the extent that it exceeded the adjusted basis of the stock was gain from the sale or exchange of property.

In the case of a deficit in earnings and profits for the taxable year in which distributions are made, the taxable status of distributions is dependent upon the amount of earnings and profits accumulated since February 28, 1913, and available at the dates of distribution. In determining the amount of such earnings and profits, section 1.316–2(b) of the regulations provides, in effect, that the deficit in earnings and profits of the taxable year will be prorated to the dates of distribution.

Applying the foregoing to Situations 3 and 4 the distribution paid by *X* corporation on July 1, 1971, in each situation was a dividend within the meaning of section 316 of the Code to the extent indicated as follows:

SITUATION # 3

Accumulated Earnings and Profits (E & P) 1/1	$ 40,000
E & P deficit for entire taxable year ($5,000) Prorate to date of distribution 7/1 (½ of $5,000)	(2,500)
E & P available 7/1	$ 37,500
Distribution 7/1 ($15,000)	(15,000) taxable as a dividend

E & P deficit from 7/1–12/31	(2,500)
Accumulated E & P balance 12/31	$ 20,000

SITUATION # 4

Accumulated E & P 1/1	$ 40,000
E & P deficit for entire taxable year ($55,000) Prorate to date of distribution 7/1 (½ of $55,000)	(27,500)
E & P available 7/1	$ 12,500
Distribution 7/1 ($15,000)	(12,500) taxable as a dividend
E & P deficit from 7/1–12/31	(27,500)
Accumulated E & P balance 12/31	$(27,500)

C. TAX TREATMENT OF DIVIDEND DISTRIBUTIONS TO THE DISTRIBUTING CORPORATION

If a corporation with either accumulated or current earnings and profits makes a dividend distribution to its shareholders, the distribution will not be deductible to the corporation in determining its taxable income for the year of distribution. If the distribution is of cash, it will have the effect of generating a dividend to the extent thereof and reducing (but not below zero) the corporation's earnings and profits for the current year. If there are no earnings and profits for the current year, such distribution will have the effect of reducing (but not below zero) the corporation's earnings and profits which have accumulated since March 1, 1913. Should a current deficit in earnings and profits arise, it will reduce the corporation's accumulated earnings and profits. If the earnings and profits of the corporation disappear, shareholder/distributees may receive subsequent distributions without dividend treatment. Additionally, under § 311, the distributing corporation itself is not subject to tax on a distribution of cash, since cash is not appreciated property.

Prior to 1986, the corporation could distribute appreciated property to its shareholders as a dividend without generating corporate income. That is, although the value of the property distributed would not be deductible to the corporation in determining its income for the year of distribution, the appreciation inherent in the distributed property would not be taxable income to the distributing corporation. Since the statutory repeal of this doctrine in 1986, through the amendment of § 311(b), such appreciation constitutes taxable income to the distributing corporation. At the end of the year, such taxable income will, when added with the other income and deductions and attendant tax liability of the corporation, be relevant in determining whether the corporation has earnings and profits for the current year. The gain generated by the distribution of the appreciated assets will generate taxable income and hence create earnings and profits for the corporation. After determining the amount of the dividend, under § 312(b)(1), the distributing corporation's earnings and profits are reduced to the extent of the value of the property distributed. The basis of the distributed property to the shareholder is its fair market value under § 301(d).

When a small business corporation deducts compensation, benefits, or services provided to its shareholder/employee as deductible compensation which the Service successfully asserts to be either "excessive" or simply nondeductible, the corporation loses the deduction. As a result, it will have increased corporate taxable income. The amount of the increase in taxable income less the attendant tax liability will, in turn, constitute earnings and profits for that year. Thus, the nondeductible portion of the compensation will normally constitute a dividend since the corporation, which anticipated no earnings and profits in accordance with its filed tax returns, has earnings and profits because of the denied tax deductions.

An S corporation generally has no difficulty with distributions out of earnings and profits since, under the S corporation rules, all of its "earnings and profits" are passed through and reported by its shareholders on an annual basis. Under § 1371(c)(1), an S corporation generally has no earnings and profits. An exception exists for those S corporations which were formerly C corporations. A C corporation which has accumulated earnings and profits at the time of its conversion to an S corporation will retain those earnings and profits on its books. As noted in Chapter 29, distributions in excess of corporate taxable income reported by the S shareholders will constitute dividends to the extent of those earnings and profits.

D. SPECIAL TREATMENT OF DIVIDEND DISTRIBUTIONS TO CERTAIN SHAREHOLDERS

The distribution of a dividend from a corporation to an individual shareholder constitutes ordinary income to the recipient shareholder. Such amount is not subject to the preferential treatment for long-term capital gain and cannot be viewed as a return of the shareholder's capital. Normally, the shareholders in closely held small business corporations are individuals. If, however, a corporation is a shareholder of the distributing corporation, all or a portion of the dividend may be excluded under § 243. The effect of such exclusion, however, only relates to taxable income and the distribution would still increase the earnings and profits of the recipient corporation. Thus, a distribution from the recipient corporation to *its* individual shareholder would subsequently be a dividend provided that there were no other activities in the recipient corporation to offset the earnings and profits generated by the dividend.

E. CONSTRUCTIVE DIVIDENDS

As noted above, in a closely held corporation the ultimate determination of a dividend distribution may not be obvious from the books, records, or tax returns of the corporation. In the case of excess compensation, for example, the tax issue arises primarily at the corporate level since the recipient shareholder will have reported the salary or bonus received as ordinary income, the same as if it had been a declared dividend. The issue is whether the corporation is entitled to a deduction for the payment. In the case of services, property, or benefits provided by a corporation to its shareholder, the corporation may or may not have deducted the value provided to the shareholder/employee. The shareholder, however, would normally not have reported as income the benefit received. In such a case, the corporation may be denied the deduction *and* the shareholder may be required to report the value of the services or property received as ordinary income. In the case of loans from a closely held corporation to a shareholder, the corporation will normally not deduct the amount of the loan made and the shareholder will not take it into income. The theory is that the loan proceeds are not income because they are offset by an obligation of the shareholder to repay the loan to the corporation. If the loan is recharacterized as a dividend, the corporation may be able to justify a deduction to the shareholder on the grounds that the loan is actually compensation. However, such a justification is particularly difficult if the shareholder is a passive investor who performs no services for the corporation.

In the case of small business corporations with multiple shareholders, a distributee shareholder might take the position that a distribution made to him or her by a corporation, even though it had earnings and profits, was not "with respect to stock" since the other shareholders did not receive similar distributions. The Service, in facing this issue, will search for offsetting benefits or for prior or subsequent distributions through which shareholders seek to proportionalize their total revenue from the corporation with stock holdings. Even if the distributions of the corporation, including substitutions for distributions such as compensation, benefits, and other services provided to the shareholders, cannot be tied to stock ownership, the shareholders making such arguments in the closely held corporate context have generally been unsuccessful in convincing the courts that such distributions are not "in respect of stock."

F. NON–DIVIDEND OPERATING DISTRIBUTIONS

If the corporation has no current *or* accumulated earnings and profits, the tax effects of a shareholder distribution are governed by § 301(c). Under that section, the distribution to a shareholder may be treated as a reduction in the basis of the stock to the extent of such basis. Once earnings and profits have been exhausted and the shareholder's basis in the stock recouped, the remainder of the distribution is treated as gain from the sale or exchange of property. The "sale or exchange" treatment provides the ground upon which the recipient shareholder can claim capital gain treatment.

The tax adviser must be careful, however, in assuming that a distribution is not from earnings and profits. As noted above, earnings and profits can be retroactively affected by adjustments to the taxable income of the corporation made by the Service on audit or through successful litigation. This is particularly true in small business corporations when certain items deducted by the corporation, such as excess compensation to shareholder/employees, are determined to be nondeductible to the corporation. Thus, even a distribution which apparently avoids dividend treatment under § 301(c) may subsequently turn out to be a dividend.

ASHBY v. COMMISSIONER

50 T.C. 409 (1968).

* * *

FINDINGS OF FACT

The petitioner Ashby, Inc. (hereinafter referred to as the corporation), was incorporated on September 30, 1946, under the laws of the State of Pennsylvania. Its principal office at the time the petition herein was filed was at Erie, Pa. It is engaged in the business of printing, lithographing, binding, publishing, making photo-offset plates, assembling and selling books, calendars and promotional materials, and operating a general printing business. It filed its Federal income tax return for the taxable year ended March 31, 1964, with the district director of internal revenue, Pittsburgh, Pa.

* * *

The petitioner is, and was during the period involved herein, president of the corporation, its sales manager, and the owner of over 98 percent of its outstanding stock.

On July 20, 1961, the corporation purchased a secondhand boat, the *Jed III,* for $60,000. It is documented through the U.S. Customs Service and is identified as a 55–foot Chris Craft Constellation. It can carry a total of 28 persons, and has sleeping accommodations for 10 persons. It is registered as the property of the corporation. The petitioner is the boat's master, acts as its engineer, and operates it without any crew assistance. He is the only employee of the corporation allowed to run the boat.

The *Jed III* is kept at the Erie Yacht Club, Erie, Pa., during the boating season, being laid up in the main building at Lund's Boat Works the rest of the time. Petitioner lives within 5 minutes' driving time of the Erie Yacht Club, and is a member of such club. In addition, he is a member of Port Dover Yacht Club of Port Dover, Ontario, Canada, Zem

Zem Temple (Masonic Shrine), Kahkwa Club (a golf club with facilities for swimming and tennis), and the Erie Club and Aviation Country Club, both private dining clubs.

Petitioner has had a personal interest in boats and has enjoyed operating them for a number of years. Prior to the purchase of the *Jed III* by the corporation, he had individually owned a number of yachts and boats. In 1948 he bought a 30–foot boat for the use of his family. However, he took guests out on the boat and, found this to be helpful in his business. Subsequently, he bought a 36–foot boat and after that a secondhand 46–foot boat. Then the *Jed III* was purchased by the corporation.

In the calendar year 1963 the boat was launched on May 3 and was laid up ashore on November 2. During that period the petitioner frequently used the boat to entertain various guests. The guests included personal friends of the petitioner and persons who represented companies which had done or later did business with the corporation. Generally, the petitioner took the guests for rides on the boat and sometimes served food and drink aboard. Sometimes the boat would be used to travel to some point at which guests would be entertained ashore at lunch or dinner. The boat was used on one day for a meeting of the sales personnel of the corporation and on another day for entertainment of the corporation's employees. Occasionally, when the boat was docked, petitioner's friends would visit him aboard the boat and play cards.

The petitioner kept weekly expense reports in which he made entries at the end of each week showing the dates on which the boat was used, the names of the guests entertained, and the amount of expense incurred for the entertainment. Such reports show that the boat was used on 68 days during the period May 3 to November 2, 1963. However, except for the two instances when the personnel of the corporation were aboard, such reports do not show whether any of the guests had any business relationship to the corporation, nor does it show the nature of any discussions held between any of the guests and the petitioner or any other representative of the corporation.

In its return for the taxable year ended March 31, 1964, the corporation claimed deductions of $5,400 for depreciation on the boat, $8,999.46 for repairs and maintenance of the boat, $100 and $25 for dues paid to the Erie Yacht Club and the Harbor Island Club, respectively, $1,547.71 for entertainment in connection with which the boat was used, and $1,174.26 for boat interest expense. In such return the corporation reported earned surplus and undivided profits as of the beginning and end of its taxable year ended March 31, 1964, in the respective amounts of $125,109 and $137,833.

* * *

Opinion

The petitioners contend on brief that 75 percent of the use of the boat owned by the corporation was devoted to the corporation's business[2] and that therefore 75 percent of the cost of entertainment in connection with which the boat was used, 75 percent of the cost of repairs and maintenance of the boat, and 75 percent of the dues paid to the Erie Yacht Club and the Harbor Island Club are deductible as ordinary and necessary business expenses of the corporation under section 162 of the Internal Revenue Code of 1954. They also contend that 75 percent of the depreciation sustained on the boat should be allowed as a deduction to the corporation under section 167 of the Code. The respondent maintains that the corporation is not entitled to deduct on account of entertainment in connection with which the boat was used more than $707.30, the amount which he allowed. He further maintains that the corporation is not entitled to any deductions on account of depreciation, repairs, and maintenance on the boat, or for dues paid to the Erie Yacht Club and the Harbor Island Club, on the ground of failure to substantiate business usage of the boat and the clubs.

Section 162 of the Code allows as a deduction all the ordinary and necessary expenses paid or incurred during the taxable year in carrying on any trade or business, and section 167 of the Code provides for the deduction of a reasonable allowance for exhaustion, wear, and tear of property used in the trade or business. However, by the Revenue Act of 1962 Congress added a new provision to the Internal Revenue Code of 1954, namely, section 274, applicable to taxable years ending after December 31, 1962, which provides that no deduction otherwise allowable shall be allowed for an item with respect to an entertainment activity or with respect to a facility used in connection with such an activity, unless the taxpayer meets certain requirements set forth in such section. * * * We accordingly approve the respondent's disallowance of deductions claimed by the corporation for depreciation on the boat, and for costs of its repair and maintenance. We also approve his disallowance of the deduction for dues paid to the Erie Yacht Club and the Harbor Island Club. There is no evidence upon which we can determine what portion of the use of such clubs, if any, was in furtherance of the corporation's business.

There remains for consideration the question whether, as determined by the respondent, the petitioner received from the corporation additional income in an amount equal to the deductions disallowed to the corporation, namely, boat entertainment expenses ($840.41), dues paid to the Erie Yacht Club and the Harbor Island Club ($125), repairs and maintenance of the boat ($6,021.64), depreciation on the boat ($4,050), plus boat interest originally disallowed but now conceded to be deductible ($880.60). In the notice of deficiency the respondent's position was that these amounts represented personal expenses paid on behalf of the individual petitioner. On brief the respondent takes the position that these amounts constituted constructive dividends.

---

2. This is based on the contention made in the original brief that 51 of 68 days of boat use, or 75 percent, was for business purposes.

It is well established that any expenditure made by a corporation for the personal benefit of its stockholders or the making available of corporate-owned facilities to stockholders for their personal benefit may result in the receipt by the stockholders of constructive dividends. As pointed out above, the respondent disallowed as a deduction to the corporation $840.41 of the $1,547.71 of entertainment expense and charged the petitioner with income to that extent. The petitioner has not established that such $840.41 was not paid for his benefit and we approve the respondent's determination in this respect. We also approve the respondent's determination that the dues of $125 paid to the two clubs is taxable to the petitioner, since there is no showing that such amount was not paid entirely for the benefit of the petitioner. However, we are of the opinion that the individual petitioner should not be charged with dividend income in the full amount of the remaining items set forth above, which relate to the boat. Even though we have approved the determination of the respondent in disallowing as deductions to the corporation the full amounts claimed for depreciation and repairs and maintenance of the boat, the reason therefor was the failure of the petitioner to substantiate, in accordance with the requirements of section 274, that the boat was used *primarily* for the furtherance of the corporation's business. This, of course, does not mean that such facilities were not used to some extent for a corporate business use. The fact that the full amounts have been disallowed as deductions to the corporation does not necessarily mean that the full amounts are to be treated as dividends to the individual petitioner. We are satisfied from the evidence that as much as 20/68 of the use of the boat was for corporate business purposes and accordingly are of the opinion that only 48/68 of the depreciation and costs of repairs and maintenance of the boat and the same percentage of the boat interest constituted amounts paid or incurred for the benefit of the individual petitioner. The precise amounts to be included in the income of the individual petitioner as constructive dividends will be computed in the recomputation under Rule 50. The petitioner has not shown that the benefits conferred upon him by the corporation had a fair value less than such amounts. Furthermore, it has not been shown that the corporation did not have sufficient earnings and profits available for the payment of taxable dividends in such amounts.

Decisions will be entered under Rule 50.

Problem 32–1

S & J Interiors, an accrual method C corporation, is owned equally by Sally and her sister, Jean, who is a Canadian citizen. The company, which is in the business of providing interior design services for residential properties, has been in business for five years. Its past operations have accumulated losses of $400,000, with the two sisters taking only minimal compensation for their services. In 1997, the corporation lands a contract to provide interior design services for the newly constructed mountain mansion of an oil-rich Saudi prince. The corporation realizes fees of $500,000 in that year against expenses of only $150,000, yielding current earnings, before salaries, of $350,000. Based upon past practices and industry standards, the maximum salary which Sally and Jean could take under Service guidelines is $75,000 each.

1. What tax result to the corporation, Sally, and Jean if each shareholder is paid $75,000 in salary and distributed $100,000 on December 31, 1997?

2. What result if the dividend distributions are made on January 1, 1998?

3. What result if Sally and Jean are distributed the additional $100,000 as a "performance bonus" rather than a dividend?

4. What result if the corporation forgoes $200,000 of its fees and accepts as a substitute a mountain condominium from the prince valued at $200,000? What if the condominium is distributed, on December 31, to Sally and Jean as joint tenants? What if the actual value of the condominium is $300,000?

5. What if the corporation loans the $100,000 to Sally and to Jean? The loan is reflected on the books of the corporation as a loan but is not evidenced by a promissory note, is unsecured, and has no specified repayment date or interest rate.

6. What if the corporation invests the $200,000 in a yacht which is to be used exclusively by Sally and Jean?

7. What if no distribution is made and no salaries are paid at all?

Chapter 33

CORPORATE PENALTY TAXES: THE ACCUMULATED EARNINGS TAX AND THE PERSONAL HOLDING COMPANY TAX

Code References: §§ 531; 532(a); 533; 535(a), (b)(1), (c); 537(a); 541; 542(a); 543(a)(1)–(7); 544(a); 545(a), (b)(1), (5); 547(a), (d); 561.

Regulation: §§ 1.535–2(a)–(b), –3; 1.537–1, –2.

A. INTRODUCTION

As discussed in prior chapters, the primary tax planning objective for a small business operating as a C corporation is the avoidance of double taxation. Combined taxes on corporate income and on the distribution of that income to shareholders yields a significant tax rate. One method of avoiding double taxation is to simply not take the second step of distributing the corporate income to shareholders. That is, the after-tax corporate funds would be accumulated and retained in the corporation rather than being distributed as compensation or a dividend. This strategy is particularly appealing, as is presently the case, when the corporate tax rate is lower than the maximum individual tax rate. Assuming that the individual shareholders of the corporate business do not need the income generated by the corporation or can, alternatively, indirectly utilize those corporate funds to benefit themselves, it is now less costly to pay the single corporate tax than to have the funds taxed in an individual capacity through deductible corporate distributions or through utilizing a "pass-through entity." Since the inception of the corporate income tax, the tax laws have contained provisions to prevent the accumulation of corporate income and profits in an effort to avoid the double tax structure. Under current tax law, the provisions designed to prevent corporate accumulations of income are the "accumulated earnings tax" and the "personal holding company tax." Each is designed to force a C corporation to either distribute its taxable income to its shareholders or suffer a penalty tax, over and above the normal corporate tax rates. The existence of these two penalty taxes is yet another reason why the C corporation has suffered a steady decline as the entity of choice for small business operations. The S corporation, limited liability company, limited liability partnership, general partnership, and sole proprietorship are not subject to these penalty taxes. As a practical matter, public corporations or corporations with a diverse shareholding group are also rarely the subject of these taxes. Rather, the two penalty taxes apply most often to closely held corporations in which the officers and directors controlling the financial fortunes of the corporation are also its shareholders.

B. ACCUMULATED EARNINGS TAX

The basic structure of the accumulated earnings tax is set forth in §§ 531–537. These provisions impose a special surtax on corporate taxable income which is accumulated rather than distributed to shareholders. The Code imposes a 39.6% surtax on accumulated taxable income. This is a surtax over and above any normal corporate tax paid under § 11 on the earnings of the corporation. Pursuant to § 535(c)(2), each corporation is entitled to a credit of $250,000 ($150,000 for personal service corporations) which it may accumulate without penalty. In addition, a corporation is not penalized if it can illustrate that the amounts in excess of the credit have been accumulated for the "reasonable needs of the business." The reasonable needs of the business is an ephemeral concept which may vary depending upon the type of business conducted by the corporation, the perception of its officers and directors, and the views of the Service. Most litigation in this area takes place in connection with whether legitimate reasonable needs of the business are being provided for by a corporation's accumulation of taxable income.

1. MECHANICS OF THE ACCUMULATED EARNINGS TAX

The tax applies to a corporation's "accumulated taxable income" for the year in which the tax is asserted. In order to determine accumulated taxable income, the starting point is the taxable income of the corporation which is then reduced by the normal § 11 taxes payable upon such amount and certain other minor adjustments. It is then increased by the amount of any dividends received deduction and any net operating loss deduction claimed by the corporation in determining its taxable income. The resulting amount is then reduced by a credit for any dividends paid to shareholders during the year or within two and one-half months after year-end. Only pro rata dividends (as opposed to preferential stock distributions) count towards the dividends paid credit. A "consent dividend" may be utilized to achieve the credit if the shareholders and corporation agree that a specified amount is to be taken into income by the shareholders, but that the actual funds are to be retained by the corporation. In addition, the accumulated taxable income is reduced by a credit equal to the amount which the corporation in question can justify as being retained by the corporation for the reasonable needs of the business. Regardless of the determined amount, a minimum § 535 credit ($250,000 or $150,000 in the case of personal service corporations) is generally provided. If there remains any accumulated taxable income, it is taxed at a rate of 39.6%. Although the tax is limited to the amount of accumulated taxable income in the particular year or years in question, prior accumulations are relevant in determining whether current-year retentions are necessary for the reasonable needs of the business. That is, if cash is on hand from prior-year accumulated earnings, it may be less reasonable to retain additional funds from the year in question to meet the reasonable needs of the business.

2. REASONABLE NEEDS OF THE BUSINESS

There are no hard and fast rules for determining whether an accumulation is validly made for the reasonable needs of the business. Often, reasonable business purposes spring into existence in close proximity to the time when the excess accumulation is asserted by the Service. The Service has certain procedural advantages in that an accumulation of taxable income is *presumed* to be for tax avoidance purposes unless such assumption can be rebutted by the corporate taxpayer. Such rebuttal, however, can take many forms. The conservative fiscal policies by a given corporate board will be considered. Reserves and accumulations for specific projects may be made in certain situations. Such accumulations, however, must actually be utilized for such legitimate business purposes and not diverted to individual purposes such as shareholder loans. In reviewing whether accumulations are made for business needs rather than personal needs, various factors are considered including: (1) whether shareholder loans are extant; (2) the dividend history of the corporation; (3) investments by the corporation in unrelated businesses; (4) investments by the corporation in businesses of the shareholders which are unrelated to the corporate business; (5) whether funds accumulated to redeem stock in the future are retained for legitimate corporate business purposes or rather for the tax or economic benefit of the shareholder to be redeemed; and (6) the favorable or unfavorable tax situation of an individual shareholder in the event that a dividend were declared.

In addition, if the corporation in question does not itself conduct an active business but is rather a mere holding company or investment company, the presumption of tax avoidance is even more firmly imposed by § 533(b).

Although the statute references accumulated taxable income, the issue in actual practice focuses upon the amount of working capital the corporation accumulates in excess of its business needs. Justification for the retention of working capital can be made in many ways. The economic cycle of the particular business involved may require the buildup of funds for the purchase of raw materials, the costs of manufacturing and delivery, and the potential delay in collecting receivables. In addition, (1) the replacement of obsolete equipment, (2) the expansion of an existing business or diversification into a new business, (3) the accumulation of funds to pay off debt, (4) the investment of equity or debt funds into suppliers and customers, (5) reserves for potential extraordinary expenses, such as costly litigation or loss of revenues from pending termination of a significant customer, and (6) accumulation of funds to pay deferred compensation to officers of the corporation who are under contract to receive such deferred compensation, have all been sustained as valid reasons for accumulating funds. The traditional indicia of a tainted buildup of funds, deemed *not* to be for the reasonable needs of the business, is the existence of shareholder loans or investments in institutions or businesses unrelated to those of the corporation.

A corporation may attempt to justify the buildup of funds through the generation of corporate minutes reflecting monetary concerns and the necessity for various reserves. Such minutes may be advantageous but can also work against the taxpayer if they are obviously self-serving and provide a flag to the Service auditor of excess cash buildups. The extent to which the minutes can be bolstered with additional documentation (such as plans and specifications for a proposed building) is helpful.

As noted above, corporate investment in an unrelated business has historically indicated that the reasonable needs of the corporation's existing business do not require that the funds be retained in the corporation. However, with the modern business strategy of diversification, which exists in small business corporations as well as large conglomerates, this government argument appears to be less valid. This is particularly so if the diversification is into a business operated by the corporate officers and employees rather than a passive investment in the new business.

FABER CEMENT BLOCK CO. v. COMMISSIONER

50 T.C. 317 (1968).

Tannenwald, Judge:

The sole question for our consideration is whether petitioner was availed of for the purpose of avoiding Federal income taxes with respect to its shareholders.

Findings of Fact

Some of the facts have been stipulated. Those facts and the exhibits attached thereto are hereby incorporated by this reference.

Petitioner, Faber Cement Block Co., Inc. (hereinafter referred to as Faber Block), is a New Jersey corporation engaged in the business of manufacturing and selling cement and cinder blocks. It had its principal place of business at the time the petition herein was filed at Paramus, N.J. Petitioner's books and tax returns are kept and filed on the calendar year, accrual basis. Timely Federal corporate income tax returns were filed for 1961, 1962, and 1963 with the district director of internal revenue, Newark, N.J.

The minutes of a board meeting held December 19, 1963, contained a resolution to the effect that Faber Block proceed "to engage such expert assistance as might be necessary to prepare plans for expanding the plant facilities in Paramus, it appearing that Paramus was the most logical location." Petitioner had been somewhat skeptical about expanding the existing Paramus plant, mainly because it was a nonconforming use under the local zoning ordinance and, consequently, a variance had to be secured before any expansion could be undertaken. Despite the objections and resistance displayed by neighboring residents, Albert Faber was convinced that the necessary variance could eventually be obtained. He had discussed petitioner's proposed expansion at various times since 1961 with the Mayor of Paramus, who had recommended deferring application for a variance until local opposition had toned down.

In addition to plans for expansion of petitioner's plant, there was recognition of the need to acquire more modern equipment for existing facilities, as reflected in the minutes of meetings of petitioner's board of directors as follows:

Mar. 1, 1961 . . . . Four trucks plus ancillary equipment—no cost stated.

Mar. 28, 1962 . . . . Loader, cement bin and conveyor, trucks and trailers—estimated cost $85,100.

Oct. 3, 1962 . . . . Grinding machine and trucks—estimated cost $29,500.

Dec. 19, 1963 . . . . Review of acquisitions made during 1963 having an aggregate cost of $130,000.

Upon advice of its general counsel, petitioner embarked on a program of building up the commercial character of the property contiguous to the existing plantsite. It was hoped that such program would provide a "buffer zone" of friendly neighbors around petitioner's plant to counteract the pressure of complaining neighbors and thus help to change the tides of local opposition to the dust and noise emanating from petitioner's operations. Pursuant to this plan, additional land was purchased and developed for commercial tenants by Faber Bros., Inc. (hereinafter referred to as Faber Bros.), a New Jersey corporation whose stock was held 50 percent by Albert Faber and 50 percent by Gerhardt and Elsie Faber. The land acquired by Faber Bros. had a large potential future increase in value. Faber Bros. also owned the land upon which petitioner's plant was located and received rent therefor from petitioner. The "buffer zone" acquisitions were financed in part by interest-bearing loans from petitioner to Faber Bros. The outstanding principal balance on such loans at December 31, 1961, 1962, and 1963, was $155,000, $180,000, and $165,000, respectively. By December 31, 1966, the principal balance had been reduced to $80,000.

The following shows comparative balance sheets of Faber Bros. at December 31, 1961, 1962, and 1963 (rounded to the nearest thousand):

	12/31/61	12/31/62	12/31/63
Cash	$11	$34	$18
Notes and accounts receivable	1	3	8
Buildings	674	786	864
(Reserve)	(189)	(211)	(239)
Land	86	86	86
Other assets	5	6	9
Total assets	589	704	746
Accounts payable			$2
Federal income tax	$16	$18	22
Mortgages, notes, and bonds	297	380	390
Other liabilities	6	11	6
Capital stock	32	32	32
Earned surplus	238	263	294
Total liabilities	589	704	746

Throughout their experience in the block business, Albert and Gerhardt Faber have striven to maintain a "no-borrowing" policy, and, with limited exceptions, have managed to finance the business internally through earnings. In addition to the $85,000 mortgage secured in connection with the Monsey plant in 1960, petitioner in 1967, because of a shortage of cash, borrowed $200,000 in connection with the completion of the Paramus expansion program.

It has also been the policy of petitioner to pay its raw materials bills promptly in order to take advantage of cash discounts available upon early payment. The following reflects the data relevant to such practice during the years in issue:

			Inventory		Trade accounts receivable	
Year	Purchases	Discounts	Jan. 1	Dec. 31	Jan. 1	Dec. 31
1961	$1,748,735	$123,326	$102,739	$135,044	NA	$412,534
1962	1,337,171	45,267	135,044	144,846	$412,534	365,546
1963	1,363,587	49,005	144,846	141,132	365,546	445,213

For several years, including those in issue, petitioner has maintained for its employees a program of financial aid, pursuant to which loans (typically non-interest-bearing) are made to help employees through difficult periods or to enable them to purchase homes. Over the years, Faber Block has enjoyed a good relationship with its labor force and has experienced only a minimal amount of turnover.

Petitioner has also found it necessary to finance some of its customers for extended periods, sometimes as long as 120 to 150 days. A substantial portion of petitioner's accounts receivable is typically over 90 days old. Loans made by petitioner to customers were reflected by outstanding notes receivable totaling $63,781.65, $78,854.62, and $86,-253.87 at December 31, 1961, 1962, and 1963, respectively. On infrequent occasions, petitioner has charged interest of 3 to 3½ percent on such loans.

In May 1960, following a trip to Germany by Albert Faber to investigate the cement-block truss industry, the Faber brothers and others connected with the block and building industries formed the United Filigree Truss Corp. (hereinafter referred to as United Filigree). United Filigree manufactured steel trusses which are used with cement blocks for roofing and flooring. Effective use of the truss serves to reduce the time and costs of construction. Petitioner, during the years in issue, advanced substantial sums to United Filigree, which sums appeared as "Loans Receivable" on its balance sheet in the following amounts at the dates indicated:

December 31—	*Amount*
1961	$30,000.00
1962	104,000.00
1963	84,564.30

Prior to 1966, petitioner owned no equity interest in United Filigree.

Beginning in 1959, petitioner started negotiations for the purchase of Hy–Way Cinder Block Co., Inc. (hereinafter referred to as Hy–Way Block). One James Swales, the owner of another New Jersey block company, agreed to join petitioner in the purchase of Hy–Way Block on a 50–50 basis. In late 1959, contracts for this proposed acquisition were prepared by petitioner's attorney. It was contemplated that the total purchase price would be $1 million, with $150,000 payable in cash and the remaining $850,000 payable over a period of 8 years with annual interest of 5 percent. Consummation of such agreement, however, was prevented because of internal strife between the related owners of Hy–Way Block—an uncle and his nephew. Throughout the years in issue, periodic discussions were held between the interested parties, but the uncle would not agree to sell. In 1964, the nephew began legal proceedings to force him to sell, but by this time Swales' interest in the venture had waned. Petitioner, however, did remain interested and continued negotiations in the hope that the family differences could be resolved. Counsel for Hy–Way Block last contacted petitioner with regard to the sale in 1967.

During the years in issue, the possible death of Albert Faber, petitioner's chief administrator, was of great concern. Albert suffered from recurring heart trouble, underwent major surgery as well as two minor operations which resulted in further complications and, between 1960 and 1963, was forced to spend a good deal of time in the hospital. On May 14, 1959, petitioner entered into a "Stock Retirement Agreement," the effect of which was to obligate the company, upon Albert's death, to purchase from his estate that portion of his interest in the corporation necessary to pay various death taxes. It was estimated that such agreement would ultimately cost Faber Block somewhere between $200,000 and $300,000. At least in part, the agreement was to be funded by a $20,000 insurance policy held by the corporation on Albert's life. The agreement was terminated pursuant to a corporate resolution on December 19, 1963. On the same date, it was decided that steps should be taken to secure as much as $500,000 insurance on the lives of Albert and Gerhardt in order to indemnify petitioner for financial loss upon the death of either and assist the survivor in the continued operation of the business. After investigating the matter, however, petitioner was unable to obtain the desired insurance.

OPINION

Once again we are called upon to determine whether a closely held corporation has been availed of by its shareholders for the purpose of avoiding personal income tax via improper accumulations of earnings and profits. While the proscribed purpose of tax avoidance must be found in every such case, section 533(a) provides that, unless petitioner can prove to the contrary by a preponderance of the evidence, the very fact that its earnings and profits were permitted to accumulate "beyond the reasonable needs of the business" will be determinative of such purpose. Section 537 defines the term "reasonable needs of the business" to include the *reasonably anticipated* needs of such business. By complying with certain statutory conditions prescribed in section 534, the petitioner in an accumulated earnings case may shift the burden of proof regarding reasonable needs to respondent. But petitioner herein has not attempted to meet these requirements and must thus bear the burden.

* * *

We now turn to the critical question involved herein, namely, whether petitioner's accumulated earnings and profits were sufficiently committed to assets currently tied up in its business and required to meet the reasonably anticipated needs of its business so as to justify the conclusion that the surtax on such earnings and profits should not be imposed. Noting that the question of whether accumulations go beyond the reasonable needs of a business (including reasonably anticipated needs) involves essentially a factual determination, we think the accumulations herein did not exceed such needs during the years involved.

We are not unmindful that, in the first instance, it is for the corporate officers and directors to determine the reasonable needs of a particular business. Consequently, we are reluctant to substitute our business judgment for that of corporate management unless the facts and circumstances, buttressed (in the absence of a proper statement under section 534) by the presumptive correctness of respondent's determination, dictate that we should do so.

There is little doubt but that, through consistently successful operations, petitioner had accumulated a substantial surplus and continued to prosper during, and subsequent to, the years involved herein. For the years here relevant, its net income after taxes was $172,197 (1961), $137,419 (1962), and $184,069 (1963), and its earned surplus account showed beginning balances of $1,426,259 (1961), $1,598,186 (1962), and $1,716,486 (1963). As we have previously pointed out, however, the critical factor is not the monetary size of the accumulated earnings and profits but the liquid position of the tax payer and the relation of that position to current and anticipated needs.

In this vein, as to the outstanding loans receivable from Faber Bros. and United Filigree, the evidence in support of their relationship to the business requirements of petitioner is far from clear. With respect to the loans to Faber Bros., while there was some general testimony about the hoped-for benefit to petitioner from a "buffer zone" of friendly tenants, it seems clear that the potential future increase in the value of the land acquired was large and that the benefit from such increase to Albert, Gerhardt, and Elsie as the shareholders of Faber Bros. was, in all likelihood, a strong motivating factor for the acquisitions. With respect to the loans to United Filigree, Albert testified that they were made "more or less not for ourselves (petitioner) as much as * * * for the association (members of the cement block and building industries)." Moreover, even if these loans were business related at the time they were made, it does not necessarily follow that they can never be considered as liquid assets available to meet the reasonable needs of the business. In this connection, we note that petitioner itself considered them as current assets. In any event, for purposes of decision, we will assume that these loans were liquid assets.

Having thus determined availabilities, we now turn our attention to the offsetting reasonable needs of petitioner's business. While petitioner claimed a variety of factors as giving rise to such needs, as we view the situation, it will suffice to concentrate on only some of them:

1. *Working–Capital Needs.*—Respondent's regulations specifically provide that earnings may be retained to provide for working capital requirements. While neither of the parties directed their attention at the trial to the question of petitioner's working-capital requirements, we think it obvious that such requirements existed during the taxable years at issue. On brief, respondent calculated petitioner's need for working capital at $513,957 at the end of 1961, $462,384 at the end of 1962, and $490,957 at the end of 1963. Our own calculations, in terms of expected costs for a single "operating cycle" under the so-called Bardahl formula are approximately the same—$432,000 (1961), $173,000 (1962), and $503,000 (1963).

2. *Proposed Plant Expansion.*—Respondent contends that, during the years here relevant, petitioner did not have adequate plans for plant expansion in the claimed amounts of $500,000 to $750,000 so as to fall within the scope of section 537 and the regulations thereunder. We disagree.

Section 537 was designed to enable a corporation to accumulate earnings and profits without investing them immediately, "so long as there is an indication that future needs of the business require such accumulation." See S. Rept. No. 1622, 83d Cong., 2d Sess., pp. 317–318 (1954). The committee reports also state that "where the future needs of the business are uncertain or vague, or the plans for the future use of the accumulations are indefinite, the amendment does not prevent application of the accumulated earnings tax." Such plans, according to respondent's regulations, must be "specific, definite and feasible." Under the particular circumstances herein, we think that petitioner has met these requirements.

Because its operations constituted a nonconforming use under the local zoning ordinance, petitioner was faced with practical difficulties regarding expansion at the existing site in Paramus. Such difficulties, however, were not insurmountable, as is indeed attested to by the fact that in 1957 a variance to build a new plant had been secured under the same ordinance. By proceeding patiently and by carefully timing their application for a variance, the Fabers had good reason to believe that they would ultimately secure permission again to expand. In point of fact, this is precisely what happened, for in 1966 the desired variance was granted. Admittedly, such variance might not have been granted. Yet, the mere fact that expansion plans are contingent upon the outcome of certain local political action will not result in a blanket bar of accumulations made pursuant to such plans. Taking note of the fact that local zoning matters typically abound with political nuances, we do not think it our province to second-guess the optimism of the Fabers, especially when we are not even in a position to claim the benefit of hindsight.

Concededly, a finding that petitioner reasonably expected to secure a variance does not of itself guarantee that the expansion would in fact take place. Thus, respondent suggests that the variance obstacle was set up as a convenient smokescreen behind which petitioner could accumulate substantial earnings without ever having any fixed intention to use such accumulations when and if the smoke cleared.

Unquestionably, as respondent points out, the minutes relating to the proposed plans for expansion are flavored with tax planning; they were concededly prepared by petitioner's tax counsel and are replete with boilerplate statements which exude concern over the possible assertion of an unreasonable accumulation challenge. But the aura of tax consciousness does not destroy the fact that the minutes contain evidence of plans to expand. Contrariwise, these minutes in and of themselves will not serve to immunize petitioner. Mere words in corporate minutes, if unsupported by further evidence of actual implementation, or the likelihood thereof, will carry little weight.

We also recognize that petitioner's plans for expansion were not set forth in the minutes or other documentary material with precision or in detail. But the requirement of "specific, definite, and feasible" plans does not demand that the taxpayer produce meticulously drawn, formal blueprints for action. The test is a practical one, namely, that the contemplated expansion appears to have been "a real consideration during the taxable year, and not simply an afterthought to justify challenged accumulations." The decided cases, which admittedly cover a variety of factual situations, indicate that in applying this test the courts primarily take into account evidence of actual implementation in evaluating the specificity of plans as they existed during the critical period, provided that some evidence of plans is adduced.

We are satisfied on the basis of the record herein that (1) petitioner had plans to expand well before the end of 1961, the first taxable year involved herein; (2) the prospective cost of such expansion was between $500,000 to $750,000; (3) a reasonable need for such expansion did in fact exist; and (4) active steps were in fact intended to be taken during the years in issue to implement the announced objectives.

Further, we are satisfied that sufficient steps were in fact taken by petitioner towards implementing the proposed expansion. Most significant in this regard is the fact that petitioner actively sought out alternatives to expanding the existing Paramus plant, fully aware that the zoning board might not act favorably. For various reasons, such alternatives were rejected, but it was not until they had been exhausted that petitioner finally designated the existing plant site in Paramus as the locus for expansion. Under the circumstances, the fact that the exact location of the proposed expansion was temporarily unknown has little significance.

Finally, we cannot and will not ignore the ultimate fruition of petitioner's expansion plans—accomplished within a reasonable time after the years in question at a cost closely in line with the amount originally estimated. While not controlling, evidence of what petitioner in fact did in subsequent years certainly affects the weight to be given its declared intention during the years in issue.

3. Machinery and Equipment.—Clearly petitioner had continuing need for funds to cover substantial annual outlays for additional and replacement machinery and equipment. Upon the basis of the amounts of these items as contemplated to be and in fact purchased, we think it reasonable to allocate $100,000 annually out of availabilities for this purpose.

Thus, petitioner had far less availabilities than were required to meet the current and future reasonable needs of its business as they existed during the years at issue. The deficit in these availabilities was sufficiently large that our conclusion would not be changed even if we were to take into account petitioner's bright financial future at the close of each year, confirmed by a continuing high level of profits—a procedure which might well be open to question.

The substantial deficits in availabilities make it unnecessary for us to consider other items for which petitioner claimed the necessity of retaining earnings and profits. We note in passing, however, the following:

(a) Although, by our method of determining availabilities herein, we have largely discounted petitioner's claimed need for funds to make short-term loans to employees, finance customers, and obtain purchase discounts, the fact is that petitioner needed modest, continuing cash reserves for these purposes.

(b) Throughout the years in question, petitioner was considering the acquisition of Hy–Way Block Co., which would have required an initial cash outlay of $75,000 plus an additional amount of $425,000 payable over an 8–year period with interest at 5 percent. The record is unclear whether this acquisition was considered by petitioner as being in addition to, or in substitution for, the expansion of its own facilities at Paramus, although the disparities in dates and in the potential amount involved possibly point in the former direction.

(c) As to the possibility that funds would be required to redeem petitioner's shares in the event of Albert's death, we recognize that the courts tend to look askance at such claimed need for the purposes of the accumulated earnings tax, particularly where, as is the case herein, there is no evidence that there were dissenting or competing shareholder factions which threatened the corporate health. Moreover, the testimony herein reflects no more than the vaguest sort of estimates as the amounts involved. Similar considerations apply to the claimed need for keyman insurance on the lives of Albert and Gerhardt, which was in fact never procured and, in light of Albert's poor health, was unlikely ever to be procurable as far as he was concerned.

While the record herein is not as neat and tidy as it might have been, we are left with the firm conviction that, during the taxable years involved herein, petitioner had proven business needs and that it had the requisite plans to meet those needs. Our conviction is reinforced by the critical fact that both the needs and the plans therefor were actually implemented to a very large degree. Under these circumstances, even if there are residual doubts, we would not be justified in substituting our business judgment for that of petitioner's officers and directors. We thus conclude that petitioner has fully sustained its burden that the accumulation of all its earnings and profits during 1961, 1962, and 1963 was required by the reasonable needs of its business. Such being the case, we have no need, in light of the credit provided for in section 535(c)(1), to consider whether the proscribed purpose of avoiding income tax may have existed.

Decision will be entered for the petitioner.

Problem 33–1

Leslie and John own equal shares of stock in Fidelity Title Insurance Company, a C corporation in the business of insuring title to real estate. The business has been relatively successful and has accumulated earnings of $200,000 which John and Leslie have left in the corporation as a "cushion" against potential future claims. Because of a residential real estate boom, the corporation has $1,000,000 in profits in 1997. In addition to their salaries for the year, John and Leslie declare a $200,000 bonus payable to each of them, which bonus is distributed on December 31, 1997. The remaining $600,000 in profit is retained in the corporation.

1. Will the corporation be subject to the accumulated earnings tax? To what extent?

2. What is the amount of the accumulated earnings tax credit for the corporation?

3. What if, because of the number of policies issued, it is actuarially determined that a reasonable reserve for claims against the large number of policies issued in 1997 is $300,000?

4. What if, at the board of directors meeting on December 31, 1997, in addition to issuing bonuses, the directors authorize the officers of the corporation to explore the possibility of building a new office facility for the corporation?

5. What if the board, consisting of Leslie and John, foresees a strong downturn in the residential real estate market, causing potential losses to the corporation in the years 1998 and 1999?

C. PERSONAL HOLDING COMPANY TAX

1. INTRODUCTION

The second penalty tax in the Internal Revenue Code affecting small businesses operated as C corporations is the personal holding company tax. This tax was originally instituted in the mid–1930's when the individual tax rates became significantly higher than those of corporations. Like the accumulated earnings tax, the provision was designed to prevent the retention of taxable income in the corporate entity, thereby incurring only the lower corporate tax rate and avoiding the higher individual tax which would be paid if the corporate earnings were distributed. The lower corporate rate may also be viewed as an advantage over the higher individual rates assessed upon the owners of "pass-through" entities. Unlike the accumulated earnings tax, the determination of whether a corporation is a personal holding company and, if so, whether it owes a personal holding company tax is determined on strictly objective bases. The nebulous issues surrounding the directors' and shareholders' subjective intentions regarding the reasonable needs of the business do not exist in the personal holding company context.

If taxable personal holding company income exists, the penalty tax rate is the same 39.6% as the accumulated earnings tax. Unlike the accumulated earnings tax, however, the personal holding company rules provide an escape hatch whereby a distribution of the tainted accumulation can be made after the fact (including after an audit by the Service), thereby allowing avoidance of the penalty tax at the corporate level. The accumulated earnings tax does not apply to personal holding companies. If, however, it is determined that a corporation which was thought to be a personal holding company is not, the accumulated earnings tax may, if its rules apply, be used as an alternative weapon by the Service.

Once again, the application of the personal holding company tax is less significant to small businesses than in prior times because fewer of them operate as C corporations. The tax may still catch the unwary C corporation, however, particularly if the entity is used as a mere receptacle for passive investments. Such a situation may arise, for example, when an operating business corporation has sold its active business and either taken a purchase money note or invested the cash sales proceeds in passive investments pending liquidation. In addition, the tax may apply to certain personal service corporations where proper measures to prevent its application are not taken.

2. BASIC REQUIREMENTS OF APPLICATION

The personal holding company rules apply primarily to closely held corporations. The rules do not apply at all unless a small number of shareholders control the corporation (the "stock ownership requirement"). If the stock ownership requirement is met, the corporation is treated as a personal holding company only if a required percentage of its "adjusted ordinary gross income" is "personal holding company income" (the "gross income requirement"). While the stock ownership requirement is relatively straightforward, a determination of whether the gross income requirement is met may require technical and precise calculations depending upon the various types of income which the corporation realizes.

a. The Stock Ownership Requirement

The stock ownership requirement is met if five or fewer individuals control (directly or indirectly) a majority of the *value* of the stock of the subject corporation. The control requirement relates to the value of all stock outstanding. Thus, if five shareholders controlled all of the corporation's common stock but more than five unrelated parties controlled preferred stock which was of greater value, the owners of the common stock would not meet the stock ownership requirement. Stock ownership is that which exists at any time during the last half of the corporation's taxable year. Extensive attribution rules apply under § 544. These attribution rules are distinct from other attribution rules in the Code and apply only to the determination of the stock ownership requirement in the personal holding company context. As a practical matter, most small business corporations have only one class of stock and fewer than five owners, so the stock ownership requirement is generally met.

b. The Gross Income Requirement

In order for a corporation which meets the stock ownership requirement to be a personal holding company, it must also meet the gross income requirement. The gross income requirement, simply stated, is met if at least 60% of the corporation's adjusted ordinary gross income is personal holding company income. While this requirement may appear simple, it is extremely complex in application. In practice, corporate owners who fear personal holding company status must cause their accountants to make calculations which will lead to the determination of this crucial ratio.

The denominator of the fraction is the company's adjusted ordinary gross income. The primary peculiarities in determining the adjusted ordinary gross income of a corporation are as follows:

(1) The starting point for service corporations and for rental businesses are the gross receipts of the business. In the case of a manufacturing or production business, however, the starting point is the gross receipts less the cost of goods sold or, what is normally known in accounting parlance as the gross profit. Thus, the denominator of the fraction in a manufacturing or production business may, before adjustments, constitute a relatively low number if the gross profit margin in that particular business is low.

(2) The starting point described in the prior paragraph is then adjusted to determine the denominator of the fraction. The main adjustment is to remove from gross income any corporate capital gains for the year. In addition, rental income and certain oil and gas income are reduced by certain tax deductions allowed for depreciation, taxes, interest, and depletion. Certain interest income is also removed from the figure, particularly interest earned on condemnation awards and tax refunds.

The resulting figure constitutes the denominator of the fraction.

Determining the numerator of the fraction is more difficult. The calculation is designed to identify certain types of passive income realized by the corporation. The statute, however, is broad and includes types of income which would not normally be viewed as passive. The numerator figure clearly includes corporate income from dividends, interest, and the taxable portion of annuities owned by the corporation. In addition, it may include the personal service income earned by the corporation if a person other than the corporation (such as the recipient of the services) is permitted to designate the corporate employee who actually performs the services and that designated individual is a 25% or greater shareholder of the corporation. While this provision was originally aimed at incorporated actors and entertainers, it also applies to physicians, attorneys, accountants, and other professionals operating as a corporation. Such professional corporations may achieve personal holding company status under these rules unless they are careful that no individual client or patient has the contractual right to designate an individual within the corporation to perform services.

Certain rents and royalties earned by the corporation are also included in the numerator as personal holding company income. The rules regarding this type of potentially passive income are extremely complex. Royalties earned by active computer software companies are generally excluded. In the case of other rents and royalties, however, the tax adviser must carefully review the Regulations to determine whether they will be included. Payments made for the use of corporate property which benefits shareholders will generally constitute personal holding company income. This is true even in situations where, if such amounts had been paid by outside parties, the proceeds would not constitute personal holding company income.

Once the numerator is calculated, if it equals or exceeds 60% of the denominator, and the stock requirement is met, the corporation is a personal holding company for the year.

REVENUE RULING 75-67
1975-1 C.B. 169.

Advice has been requested whether, under the circumstances described below, a corporation will be considered to have received personal holding company income within the meaning of section 543(a)(7) of the Internal Revenue Code of 1954.

B, a doctor specializing in a certain area of medical services, owns 80 percent of the outstanding stock of L, a domestic professional service corporation. B is the only officer of L who is active in the production of income for L, and he is the only medical doctor presently employed by L. B performs medical services under an employment contract with L. L furnishes office quarters and equipment, and employs a receptionist to assist B. P, a patient solicited the services of and was treated by B.

Section 543(a)(7) of the Code provides, in part, that the term personal holding company income includes amounts received under a contract whereby a corporation is to furnish personal services if some person other than the corporation has the right to designate, by name or description, the individual who is to perform the services, or if the individual who is to perform the services is designated, by name or description, in the contract.

In dealing with a professional service corporation providing medical services, an individual will customarily solicit and expect to receive the services of a particular physician, and he will usually be treated by the physician sought.

A physician-patient relationship arises from such a general agreement of treatment. Either party may terminate the relationship at will, although the physician must give the patient reasonable notice of his withdrawal and may not abandon the patient until a replacement, if necessary, can be obtained. C. Morris & A. Moritz, *Doctor and Patient and the Law* 135 (5th ed. 1971). Moreover, if a physician who entered into a general agreement of treatment is unable to treat the patient when his services are needed, he may provide a qualified and competent substitute physician to render the services. *C. Morris & A. Moritz, supra,* at 138, 374-75.

Thus, when an individual solicits, and expects, the services of a particular physician and that physician accepts the individual as a patient and treats him, the relationship of physician-patient established in this manner does not constitute a designation of the individual who is to perform the services under a contract for personal services within the meaning of section 543(a)(7) of the Code.

If, however, the physician or the professional service corporation contracts with the patient that the physician personally will perform particular services for the patient, and he has no right to substitute another physician to perform such services, there is a designation of that physician as the individual to perform services under a contract for personal services within the meaning of section 543(a)(7) of the Code.

The designation of a physician as an individual to perform services can be accomplished by either an oral or written contract. See Rev.Rul. 69–299, 1969–1 C.B. 165.

Moreover, if L agreed to perform the type of services that are so unique as to preclude substitution of another physician to perform such services, there is also a designation.

Accordingly, since in the instant case there is no indication that L has contracted that B will personally perform the services or that the services are so unique as to preclude substitution, it is held that income earned by L from providing medical service contracts will not be considered income from personal service contracts within the meaning of section 543(a)(7) of the Code.

3.   THE PERSONAL HOLDING COMPANY TAX

If a corporation is determined to be a personal holding company pursuant to the stock ownership and gross income tests described above, the personal holding company tax may or may not apply. The tax is *not* a tax upon the personal holding company income of the corporation (the numerator of the crucial fraction). Rather, it is a tax based upon the "adjusted taxable income" of any corporation which constitutes a personal holding company.

The starting point for determining whether the tax applies is the taxable income of the corporation. Such income is reduced by accrued income taxes attributable to it and a broader charitable deduction, if applicable, is allowed. The taxable income of the corporation, reduced as set forth above, is then increased by the amount of any dividends received exclusion claimed by the corporation under § 243 during the year and any net operating loss carryforward deduction except that for the prior year. There also may be minor upward adjustments for excessive business deductions relating to property owned and operated by the corporation.

The primary reduction allowed in calculating the taxable income of the corporation for this purpose is the dividends paid deduction. The taxable income of the corporation, adjusted as described above, may be reduced by any dividends paid by the corporation during the year. The dividend, however, must be (1) paid rather than merely accrued, (2) pro rata, and (3) included in the income of the recipient shareholders. The corporation is permitted to make a consent dividend which reduces personal holding taxable income to the extent it is agreed upon by the corporation and the shareholder, who receives no cash but must take the dividend amount into income. A consent dividend is then treated as being immediately contributed to the capital of the corporation by the "recipient" shareholder. In addition, the personal holding company income of the corporation may be reduced by the amount of certain "excessive" shareholder distributions made by the corporation in the prior two taxable years. All of these amounts may serve to reduce or eliminate the personal holding company taxable income of the corporation, thereby avoiding the penalty tax, even though the entity meets the personal holding company definition.

In addition to the potential reductions in personal holding company taxable income described above, the Code provides one last escape hatch for a corporation facing the personal holding company tax for a prior year. This is the unique concept of the "deficiency dividend" which allows a corporation to make a distribution to its shareholders in a year long after the year in which the personal holding company status is determined. The distribution is treated as a reduction of personal holding company income in the prior year, but constitutes income to the recipient shareholders in the year they receive it. The deficiency dividend rules require the corporation to make such payment to its shareholders within 90 days following the determination of its personal holding company status for such prior year. That determination may be reached through a Tax Court decision, a Closing Agreement, or an agreement with the District Director of the Internal Revenue Service. Such determinations are often made three to five years after the tax year in question. The deficiency distribution reduces personal holding company income for that prior year, but does not count as a dividend distribution in determining personal holding company income of the distributing corporation in the year of distribution. While the deficiency dividend procedure eliminates the personal holding company tax for the prior year, it does not eliminate interest and penalties on that tax.

REVENUE RULING 86–104

1986–2 C.B. 80.

Issue

Can a personal holding company be granted an extension of time pursuant to section 1.9100–1 of the Income Tax Regulations in order for a distribution of dividends to qualify as "deficiency dividends" under section 547 of the Internal Revenue Code?

Facts

X is a corporation all of whose issued and outstanding stock is owned by one individual. Because its income consists of interest and dividends and more than 50 percent in value of its outstanding stock is owned by one individual, X is a personal holding company within the meaning of section 542 of the Code. During the taxable year X failed to pay any dividends to its shareholder and as a result had a large amount of undistributed personal holding company income. *X* and the Internal Revenue Service reached an agreement concerning *X's* liability for the personal holding company tax imposed by section 541. After receiving *X's* signed acceptance of the terms of the agreement, the district director sent a registered letter to *X* evidencing acceptance of the agreement by the Internal Revenue Service and setting forth the procedures for the distribution of "deficiency dividends" as defined in section 547(d)(1). However, *X* failed to make such a distribution within 90 days after the date of registration of the letter.

Law and Analysis

Section 541 of the Code provides that in addition to other taxes imposed by this chapter, there is imposed for each taxable year on the undistributed personal holding company income (as defined in section 545) of every personal holding company a personal holding company tax equal to 50 percent of the undistributed personal holding company income.

Section 547(a) of the Code provides that if a determination (as defined in section 547(c)) with respect to a taxpayer establishes liability for personal holding company tax imposed by section 541 (or by a corresponding provision of a prior income tax law) for any taxable year, a deduction shall be allowed to the taxpayer for the amount of deficiency dividends (as defined in section 547(d)) for the purpose of determining the personal holding company tax for such year, but not for the purpose of determining interest, additional amounts, or assessable penalties computed with respect to such personal holding company tax.

Section 547(c) of the Code provides that, for purposes of section 547, the term "determination" means: (1) a decision by the Tax Court or a judgment, decree, or other order by any court of competent jurisdiction, that has become final; (2) a closing agreement made under section 7121; or (3) under regulations prescribed by the Secretary, an agreement signed by the Secretary and by, or on behalf of, the taxpayer relating to the liability of the taxpayer for personal holding company tax.

Section 547(d)(1) of the Code provides that, for purposes of section 547, the term "deficiency dividends" means the amount of the dividends paid by the corporation on or after the date of the determination and before filing a claim under section 547(e), which would have been includible in the computation of the deduction for dividends paid under section 561 for the taxable year for which the liability for personal holding company tax exists, if distributed during such taxable year. No dividends shall be considered as deficiency dividends for purposes of section 547(a) unless distributed within 90 days after the determination.

Section 1.547–2(b)(1)(v) of the regulations provides that a determination under section 547(c)(3) of the Code may be made by an agreement signed by the district director or such other official to whom authority to sign the agreement is delegated, and by or on behalf of the taxpayer. The agreement shall set forth the total amount of the liability for personal holding company tax for the taxable year or years. An agreement under section 1.547–2(b)(1)(v) that is signed by the district director (or such other official to whom authority to sign the agreement is delegated) on or after July 15, 1963, shall be sent to the taxpayer at the taxpayer's last known address by either registered or certified mail. If registered mail is used for such purpose, the date of registration shall be treated as the date of determination, unless the dividend is paid by the corporation before the postmark date.

Under section 1.9100–1 of the regulations, the Commissioner has discretion, upon a showing of good cause by a taxpayer, to grant a reasonable extension of the time fixed by the regulations to make an election or other application for relief in respect of tax under subtitle A of the Code. The extension may not be granted if the time for making the election or application is expressly prescribed by law.

Rev. Proc. 79–63, 1979–2 C.B. 578, sets forth certain considerations that the Internal Revenue Service generally will use to determine whether, under the facts and circumstances of each situation, good cause for granting an extension of time fixed by the regulations to make an election or application has been shown and the other requirements of section 1.9100–1 of the regulations have been met. Section 3 of Rev. Proc. 79–63 provides that the scope of that revenue procedure is limited to requests for extensions of time fixed by the regulations for making an election and to applications for relief, in accordance with the specific language of section 1.9100–1. Thus the revenue procedure does not apply to requests for extensions of the time fixed by the Code for making an election or to applications for relief from statutory deadlines.

Section 547(d) of the Code sets a fixed period (90 days) within which the taxpayer must act following any of three types of determination, as defined in section 547(c). Section 1.547–2(b)(1) of the regulations merely clarifies when the determination occurs. Thus, it is the statute and not the regulations that fixes the time within which the dividend must be distributed if the personal holding company tax is to be avoided. The Commissioner has authority to clarify ambiguity in a statute by regulation (for example, the date on which a determination occurs and the 90–day period begins). However, the Commissioner does not have authority to extend a time period specified by statute unless the statute confers such authority. For an example of such authority, see section 338(g)(1).

Holding

The personal holding company cannot be granted an extension of time pursuant to section 1.9100–1 of the regulations in order for a distribution of dividends to qualify as deficiency dividends under section 547 of the Code.

Problem 33–2

Alex is the sole owner of the shares of a manufacturing company ("OldCo") which he has operated as a C corporation for many years. He accepts an offer to purchase the company in December, 1996. The corporation receives, in exchange for its assets, cash of $1,500,000 plus a promissory note from the purchaser in the amount of $2,000,000. The corporation pays a $500,000 federal income tax on the cash sale proceeds. Alex has a low basis in his OldCo stock. In order to postpone the capital gain which he would recognize on a liquidating distribution of the net sale proceeds and promissory note until 1997, he maintains the corporation in existence. In 1997, the corporation earns $70,000 in interest on the $1,000,000 net cash sales proceeds; receives a $500,000 installment payment on the purchase money note which constitutes $100,000 of interest income, $100,000 of capital gain, and $300,000 of return of basis. The corporation had no other income in 1997. The corporate income tax attributable to the income earned in 1997 is $85,000.

1. Is OldCo a personal holding company?

2. If no distributions are made, what is the amount of the personal holding company tax payable by OldCo for 1997?

3. What if the corporation declared and paid a $100,000 dividend to Alex on December 31, 1997?

4. What if the Service audited OldCo in 1999 and determined that personal holding company status applied? What would be the effect of the payment of a $100,000 deficiency dividend at that time?

5. What if the $100,000 income portion of the 1997 installment payment received by the corporation were ordinary income (not personal holding company income) rather than capital gain?

Chapter 34

REDEMPTIONS OF CORPORATE STOCK

Code References: §§ 302(a)–(d); 303(a); 311(b); 312(n)(7); 318(a).

Regulation: §§ 1.302–1, –2, –3, –4.

A. INTRODUCTION

Chapter 32 examined the tax effects of a corporation which makes a distribution of property to a shareholder "with respect to its stock." That scenario contemplated a corporation distributing its property or cash (but not its own stock) to shareholders without consideration passing back to the corporation. To the extent the corporation has earnings and profits, such a distribution results in a dividend.

This chapter examines the tax effects of a corporate distribution of property made to a shareholder *in exchange for* his or her stock. In the absence of a complete liquidation of the corporation, such transfers are known in tax parlance as "redemptions." If certain statutory requirements are met, such a distribution is not treated as a dividend but rather as a sale or exchange by the shareholder of his or her stock to the corporation. Sale or exchange treatment is generally more favorable than dividend treatment for three reasons: (1) the selling shareholder reports gain only to the extent that the corporate distribution exceeds the tax basis of the corporate stock surrendered; (2) providing that certain holding period requirements are met, under § 1222 the sale or exchange characterization will qualify for long-term capital gain treatment which is taxed at rates more favorable than those applicable to dividends; and (3) capital gain can be offset by otherwise potentially unusable capital losses of the shareholder taxpayer, unlike dividends which cannot be so offset.

Since tax treatment as a redemption distribution may be significantly more favorable to the shareholder than that applicable to a dividend, the Service and the Congress have been careful to set forth specific rules to distinguish between the two. Shareholders of a closely held corporation have often sought to qualify for redemption treatment for a distribution which is more akin to a dividend. For instance, if a shareholder holding 100% of the shares of a corporation with earnings and profits surrendered half of the shares in exchange for cash, the distribution would be essentially equivalent to a dividend since the shareholder would own 100% of the outstanding shares of the stock of the corporation, both before and after the distribution. He or she would still have total control over the corporation; the only difference being that he or she would hold a lesser number of shares after the distribution. In such a case, the tax law will not permit redemption treatment. Rather, the cash received by the shareholder would be taxed as a dividend. Similar, less obvious, variations on this theme may be generated by creative tax planners. Consequently, specific rules have been set forth in the Code which govern redemption treatment.

Section 302 authorizes exchange treatment for four particular situations in which a shareholder conveys his stock to the corporation in exchange for its cash or property. The transfer is treated as a redemption:

> 1. If the effect of the distribution is "not essentially equivalent to a dividend";

> 2. If the exchange is "substantially disproportionate";

> 3. If the redeeming shareholder's interest in the corporation is "completely terminated"; or

> 4. If the distribution in redemption of the stock of a noncorporate shareholder is in "partial liquidation" of the corporation.

If the transfer qualifies under any of these categories, an exchange exists and gain or loss is recognized by the shareholder under § 1001. If the distribution fails to qualify under one of the four categories, the income recognition rules of § 301, described in Chapter 32, apply. In either event, if the corporation distributes appreciated property in such an exchange, § 311(b) requires it to recognize gain as if the property were sold to the distributee at its fair market value. Thus, regardless of whether the distribution is treated as a dividend, redemption, or a return of capital, the corporation will recognize gain on the distribution of appreciated property to its shareholders.

In the context of a closely held corporation, the potential for favorable tax treatment afforded to qualifying redemptions has many practical uses. For instance, the buyout of a deceased, disabled, or retiring shareholder/employee of the corporation may be structured to allow such departing shareholder sale or exchange treatment upon the redemption of the stock by the corporation, whether pursuant to a shareholder's buy/sell agreement or otherwise. The redemption of a shareholder's stock for cash may be used as a vehicle to reduce a corporation's net worth, thereby allowing an outside purchaser (such as a key employee) to purchase remaining shares at a more affordable price.

Such a redemption might also provide a portion of the purchase price (from the corporation's own funds) which would allow an incoming buyer to meet a seller's targeted purchase price. The redemption of stock in exchange for property may also be utilized to rid a corporation of unwanted assets prior to an acquisition. In certain situations, the redemption of stock may provide an inexpensive source of funds from which the distributee shareholder repays a debt owing to the corporation. When a key employee shareholder dies, the utilization of the redemption may allow the corporation to acquire the shares from such shareholder's heirs or estate without them having a continuing interest in the business. In this particular situation, the special rules of § 303 may apply. That type of redemption may also be particularly advantageous to the successors of the deceased shareholder since it can provide liquidity at a low or no tax cost in order to meet death taxes and other obligations of the decedent's estate. Redemptions of stock in a family corporation may also be important in separating the interests of a husband and wife who are involved in a divorce. The redemption of the stock of the nonparticipating spouse may be crucial to the continued success of the corporation and may provide a tax-advantaged vehicle for such spouse to liquidate his or her share of the family investment.

As will be seen in subsequent discussions, when dealing with family corporations, the attribution ownership rules of § 318 come into play in determining whether the distribution qualifies as a redemption or, rather, will be treated as a dividend. Each of these concepts is more fully discussed and illustrated in the materials to follow.

B. STATUTORY SCHEME

In determining whether a given distribution in exchange for stock qualifies for redemption treatment, §§ 302(b)(1), (2), and (3), each focus upon the distributee shareholder(s) before and after the distribution. Section 302(b)(4), on the other hand, examines the corporation itself to determine whether a "partial liquidation" has occurred and § 311(b) focuses on the corporation's distribution of appreciated assets.

1. SHAREHOLDER ANALYSIS

The first three subsections of § 302(b) focus on the distributee shareholder. Section 302(b)(1) is subjective, applying if the distribution is not essentially equivalent to a dividend. Although the primary emphasis is on the distributee shareholder, corporate characteristics, such as existence of earnings and profits, are also taken into account.

Section 302(b)(2) provides an objective mathematical analysis relating to proportionate shareholdings of the distributee shareholder before and after the distribution. Section 302(b)(3) also appears to be a straightforward objective analysis of whether the distributee shareholder's interest in the corporation is terminated. When the remaining shareholders of the corporation are unrelated to the distributee, this termination analysis is simple and straightforward. Where the remaining shareholders are family members whose stock is attributed to the distributee under § 318, however, the analysis is more complex. In addition, § 302(c) allows a waiver of family attribution in certain situations, which makes the entire termination analysis much more difficult in the case of a closely held family corporation.

From an analytical standpoint, it is easiest to examine these three sections in the reverse of their statutory order, taking § 302(b)(3) first.

a. "Completely Terminated" Redemptions

As noted above, § 302(b)(3) appears straightforward. It states that the favorable "exchange" treatment of § 302(a) shall be afforded to a distributee shareholder if "the redemption is in complete redemption of all of the stock of the corporation owned by the shareholder." Thus, assume corporation X is owned equally by shareholders Alice and Beth who are unrelated. X distributes $1,000 to Alice in exchange for all of Alice's stock in the corporation. Regardless of the earnings and profits of the corporation, the distribution to Alice in complete termination of her interest will be treated, under § 302(b)(3), as an exchange of her stock for the $1,000. Alice will have capital gain or loss to the extent that the $1,000 distribution exceeds or is less than her basis, under § 1001. If desired by the parties, X may pay the consideration to Alice on an installment basis and Alice may report her gain (if any) under § 453 as the payments are received. Courts have held that this treatment is permitted even though the redeemed shares are held in escrow as security pending the full payment of the corporate note. See *Lisle v. Commissioner*, 35 T.C.M. (CCH) 627 (1976).

An interesting practical issue arises in the context of whether a shareholder, such as Alice, has completely redeemed all of her stock in the corporation. As was seen in Chapter 25, debt owing from a corporation to a shareholder may, in certain circumstances, be deemed to be stock when it has more characteristics of equity than debt. Thus, if Alice in the above hypothetical were to transfer all of her outstanding stock in the corporation back to X but retain a debt owing to her from X, she could conceivably be deemed *not* to have met the termination requirement if the debt were recharacterized as equity.

Most of the analytical difficulties under the complete termination provision of § 302(b)(3) arise in situations where the shareholders of the corporation, other than the terminated distributee, are family members of the distributee. In determining stock ownership for the purposes of § 302, § 318(a)(1) attributes to the distributee the stock ownership of his or her spouse, children, grandchildren, and parents. Thus, in the hypothetical above, if Beth were Alice's daughter, Beth's shares would be attributed to Alice under § 318(a) and Alice's stock interest in the corporation would therefore not be terminated because of her constructive ownership of Beth's stock.

Section 302(c), however, provides a waiver of family attribution in certain situations. Such waiver applies only to *family attribution* and not to the other categories of attribution described in § 318. Section 302(c), however, exacts a price from the distributee shareholder in exchange for the waiver of the attribution rules. That is, the distributee shareholder must comply with the good behavior rules of § 302(c)(2)(A) for a period of 10 years following the distribution. During that time, the distributee may have no interest (except as a creditor) in the corporation. This means that the distributee shareholder cannot, during that period, become a stockholder in the corporation nor become an officer, director, or employee of the corporation.

In addition, § 302(c)(2)(B) contains a "look-back" rule which a distributee desiring to utilize the family attribution waiver rules must also meet. Under that section, the distributee must not have acquired any portion of the redeemed interest from a family member (as defined in § 318(a)) within the 10–year period prior to the redemption. Finally, the redeemed shareholder must not have *conveyed* any stock ownership interest in the corporation to a family member within a 10–year period preceding the distribution (except in the same redemption transaction). These latter two rules are waived if the principal purpose of such conveyances is other than tax avoidance. Thus, with the addition of this final rule, what apparently is an objective termination test becomes significantly more subjective in family situations.

It is important to remember that the complicating rules regarding the waiver of family attribution apply only if such attribution is present in a particular redemption. The rules do not apply in the event that there is no attribution or attribution from a source other than the family. Thus, in the initial hypothetical set forth above, where Alice and Beth are unrelated, Alice could reacquire an interest in the corporation following the redemption since Beth is not a member of her family. Unless the reacquisition were deemed to be some form of step transaction, the initial redemption would be unaffected by the subsequent interest acquisition.

REVENUE RULING 77–293
1977–2 C.B. 91.

Advice has been requested concerning the Federal income tax treatment of a redemption by a corporation of a retiring shareholder's stock under the circumstances described below.

Corporation X had 120 shares of common stock outstanding, all of which were owned by A, its president. A's son, B, had been employed by X for many years as its vice-president and general assistant to the president. Realizing that the future successful operation of X required a thorough knowledge of its operation, products lines, and customer needs, A had trained and supervised B in all phases of the business so that upon A's retirement B would be able to assume responsibility for managing the business.

As part of A's plan to retire from the business and to give ownership of the business to B, A gave 60 shares of X stock to B as a gift, and not as consideration for past, present, or future services. Shortly thereafter, *A* resigned and *B* assumed the position of chairman of the board and president of *X*. *X* redeemed the remaining 60 shares of stock owned by *A* in exchange for property. Immediately after the redemption, *A* was not an officer, director, or employee of *X* and no longer had any interest in *X*. *A*'s gift of stock to *B* was for the purpose of giving *B* complete ownership and control of *X*. The earnings and profits of *X* exceeded the amount of the distribution in redemption of the *X* stock.

Section 302(a) of the Internal Revenue Code of 1954 provides, in part, that if a corporation redeems its stock and if section 302(b)(1), (2), (3) or (4) applies, such redemption will be treated as a distribution in part or full payment in exchange for the stock. Section 302(c)(1) provides that section 318(a), relating to constructive ownership of stock, will apply in determining the ownership of stock for purposes of section 302.

Section 302(b)(1) of the Code provides that section 302(a) will apply if the redemption is not essentially equivalent to a dividend. Section 302(b)(2) provides that section 302(a) will apply if the redemption is substantially disproportionate with respect to the shareholder. Section 302(b)(3) provides that section 302(a) will apply if the redemption completely terminates the shareholder's interest in the corporation. Section 302(d) provides that if section 302(a) does not apply, the redemption will be treated as a distribution of property to which section 301 applies.

In the instant case, neither section 302(b)(1) of the Code nor section 302(b)(2) applies since *A,* through the constructive ownership rules of section 318(a), owned 100 percent of the stock of *X* both before and after the redemption. Therefore, there was no meaningful reduction under section 302(b)(1) or a substantially disproportionate reduction under section 302(b)(2) of *A*'s stock ownership.

Section 302(c)(2)(A) of the Code provides that for purposes of section 302(b)(3), 318(a)(1) will not apply if (i) immediately after the distribution the distributee has no interest in the corporation (including an interest as an officer, director, or employee), other than an interest as a creditor, (ii) the distributee does not acquire any such interest (other than stock acquired by bequest or inheritance) within ten years from the date of such distribution, and (iii) the distributee files an agreement to notify the district director of any acquisition of any such interest in the corporation. However, pursuant to section 302(c)(2)(B)(ii), the provisions of section 302(c)(2)(A) are not applicable if any person owns (at the time of the distribution) stock the ownership of which is attributable to the distributee under section 318(a) and such person acquired any stock in the corporation, directly or indirectly, from the distributee within the ten-year period ending on the date of the distribution, unless such stock so acquired from the distributee is redeemed in the same transaction. However, section 302(c)(2)(B)(ii) will not apply if the disposition by the distributee did not have as one of its principal purposes the avoidance of Federal income tax.

The structure and legislative history of section 302 of the Code make it clear that the purpose of section 302(c)(2)(B) is not to prevent the reduction of capital gains through gifts of appreciated stock prior to the redemption of the remaining stock of the transferor, but to prevent the withdrawal of earnings at capital gains rates by a shareholder of a family controlled corporation who seeks continued control and/or economic interest in the corporation through the stock given to a related person or the stock he retains. Application of this provision thus prevents a taxpayer from bailing out earnings by transferring part of the taxpayer's stock to such a related person and then qualifying the redemption of either the taxpayer's stock or the transferee's stock as a complete termination of interest by virtue of the division of ownership thus created and the availability of the attribution waiver provisions.

Tax avoidance within the meaning of section 302(c)(2)(B) of the Code would occur, for example, if a taxpayer transfers stock of a corporation to a spouse in contemplation of the redemption of the remaining stock of the corporation and terminates all direct interest in the corporation in compliance with section 302(c)(2)(A), but with the intention of retaining effective control of the corporation indirectly through the stock held by the spouse. Another example, which would generally constitute tax avoidance within the meaning of this provision, is the transfer by a taxpayer of part of the stock of a corporation to a spouse in contemplation of the subsequent redemption of the transferred stock from the spouse.

Whether one of the principal purposes of an acquisition or disposition of stock is tax avoidance within the meaning of section 302(c)(2)(B) of the Code can be determined only by an analysis of all of the facts and circumstances of a particular situation. Here, the gift of X stock by A was to B who is active and knowledgeable in the affairs of the business of X and who intends to control and manage the corporation in the future. The gift of stock was intended solely for the purpose of enabling A to retire while leaving the business to B. Therefore, the avoidance of Federal income tax will not be deemed to have been one of the principal purposes of the gift of stock from A to B, notwithstanding the reduction of the capital gains tax payable by A as a result of the gift of appreciated stock prior to the redemption.

Accordingly, if A files the agreement specified in section 302(c)(2)(A)(iii) of the Code, the redemption by X of its stock from A qualifies as a termination of interest under section 302(b)(3). * * *

Problem 34–1

Craig and Dave own equal interests in a corporation which operates a clothing store. The two are unrelated and have held their stock for five years. The corporation has not elected to be taxed as an S corporation and has been successful, accumulating earnings and profits over the years.

Craig would like to retire, but Dave does not have sufficient personal funds to buy out his interest. It is agreed that the corporation will acquire all of Craig's stock in exchange for an initial payment of $10,000 and an installment note in the amount of $90,000, payable $10,000 per year for the next nine years with interest at the prime rate. The note is secured by Craig's stock in the corporation which is placed in escrow pending the payment of the promissory note by the corporation. Craig's tax basis for his corporate stock is $50,000, representing his initial investment in the corporation.

1. Does the acquisition of Craig's stock qualify as a redemption under § 302(b)(3)? If so, how much gain does Craig report in the year of sale?

2. What if Craig and Dave were brothers?

3. What if Craig is Dave's father, and (a) Dave received his stock as a gift from Craig five years prior to the redemption; (b) Craig signs a consulting agreement with the corporation during the installment redemption period; or (c) Dave acquired his stock through a contribution of his own funds and Craig takes no part in the business, as an officer, shareholder, director, or in any other capacity following the redemption?

4. What if the terms of the promissory note from the corporation to Craig are that it is unsecured, bears no interest, has no due date, and is payable if, as, and when the corporation has the available funds to pay it?

5. What if Craig, in addition to the redeemed shares, also has 20 shares of nonvoting, preferred stock which he received in exchange for making an advance to the corporation in prior years?

b. *Substantially Disproportionate Redemptions*

The most objective of the statutory safe harbors through which a redeeming shareholder may obtain sale or exchange treatment is that provided by § 302(b)(2). A corporate distribution will be treated as a sale or exchange under the substantially disproportionate redemption rules if (1) a shareholder's percentage ownership of *voting* stock in the corporation is reduced, immediately after the redemption, to less than 80% of the shareholder's percentage ownership in such stock immediately before the redemption; (2) the shareholder's percentage ownership in the outstanding *common* stock of the corporation (both voting and nonvoting) is similarly reduced to less than 80% of that before the redemption; and (3) immediately after redemption, the shareholder owns less than 50% of the total combined voting power of the corporate stock.

While the three tests which must be met in order to qualify under this provision are mechanical and arithmetic, the calculation can be somewhat tricky. In applying the 80% tests, it must be remembered that the denominator of the fractions which are examined after the redemption (both as to the total number of shares and the total number of voting shares outstanding in the corporation) is reduced by the number of shares redeemed. In addition, the attribution rules of § 318 apply in determining the 80% ratios as well as the less than 50% requirement. The attribution rules cannot be waived as they may be under § 302(b)(3). On the other hand, if the mechanical tests of the substantially disproportionate redemption are met, there are no good behavior rules restricting the shareholder's participation in the corporation's activities following the redemption. That is, the rules of § 302(c)(2) apply only when the redeeming shareholder is seeking to qualify under the complete termination haven of § 302(b)(3). The simplest application of these rules can be illustrated by the following example:

Assume that Alan and Bruce each own 50% of the voting common stock of X corporation. It is the only class of stock outstanding and Alan and Bruce are unrelated. Alan sells 12 of his 50 shares to the corporation in exchange for cash. Alan would clearly meet the third statutory requirement of § 302(b)(2) since he now holds less than 50% of the total voting power of the corporation. As to the first two requirements, however, he would fail. His percentage of ownership before the redemption is 50%. His percentage of ownership after the redemption is 43% (Alan would still own 38 of the remaining 88 shares outstanding). Since Alan's post-redemption ownership (43%) is more than 80% (it is 86%) of his pre-redemption ownership (50%), the amount of cash received would be treated as a distribution in respect of his stock and taxed under § 301. The minimum number of shares which Alan could redeem and still qualify under the 80% test would be 17. In that situation, Alan would own 39.7% of the corporate shares following the redemption (33 of 83) as opposed to 50% prior to the redemption. The resulting fraction is less than 80% and the distribution in exchange for the 17 shares would qualify for sale or exchange treatment.

If the corporation has both voting and nonvoting stock, the 80% test must be applied to the voting stock individually and to the total stock ownership of the redeeming shareholder as well. The substantially disproportionate rules also deny sale or exchange treatment to any shareholder who remains in control of the corporation following the redemption by holding 50% or more of its voting stock. Such voting control may exist through direct ownership or through attribution. In addition, control may exist if certain debt held by the shareholder is treated as stock. In such a situation, the shareholder may be able to qualify under the more subjective rules of § 302(b)(1) by claiming that, although the safe harbor of a substantially disproportionate redemption is not met, the distribution is not essentially equivalent to a dividend under § 302(b)(1).

Finally, if a shareholder ostensibly qualifies under the substantially disproportionate rules, but the redemption is found to be one of a series of redemptions to various shareholders, the net result of which does not meet the requirements of § 302(b)(2), the individual steps in the series will be disregarded under § 302(b)(2)(D).

REVENUE RULING 77–237

1977–2 C.B. 88.

Advice has been requested whether, under the circumstances described below, a redemption of nonvoting preferred stock will qualify as an exchange under section 302(a) of the Internal Revenue Code of 1954 by reason of section 302(b)(2).

X corporation had outstanding 100 shares of voting common stock and 100 shares of nonvoting preferred stock, * * *. The 100 shares of X voting common stock were owned in equal part by individuals A and B, who were not related. The 100 shares of X nonvoting preferred stock were owned by C, who is the father of A. C held positions as vice-president and a member of the board of directors of X, which positions he maintained subsequent to the redemption of the nonvoting preferred stock.

X redeemed for cash all 100 shares of the X nonvoting preferred stock held by C and 20 shares of the X voting common stock held by A.

Section 302(a) of the Code provides, in part, that if a corporation redeems its stock, and if section 302(b)(1), (2), or (3) applies, such redemption will be treated as a distribution in part or full payment in exchange for the stock instead of a distribution of a dividend as provided for in section 302(d) and section 301.

Section 302(b)(2) of the Code provides that section 302(a) will apply the redemption substantially reduces the voting power of the shareholder, but that section 302(b)(2) will not apply unless immediately after redemption the shareholder owns less than 50 percent of the total combined voting power of all classes of stock entitled to vote.

For purposes of section 302(b)(2) of the Code, the distribution is substantially disproportionate if the ratio that the voting stock of the corporation owned by the shareholder immediately after the redemption bears to all of the voting stock of the corporation at such time, is less than 80 percent of the ratio that the voting stock of the corporation owned by the shareholder immediately before the redemption bears to all of the voting stock of the corporation at such time.

Also for purposes of section 302(b)(2) of the Code, no distribution will be treated as substantially disproportionate unless the shareholder's ownership of the common stock of the corporation (whether voting or nonvoting) after and before the redemption also meets the 80 percent requirement of the preceding paragraph.

Section 318(a)(1)(A)(ii) of the Code provides that an individual will be considered as owning the stock owned, directly or indirectly, by or for the individual's children, grandchildren, and parents.

Section 1.302–3 of the Income Tax Regulations provides, in part, as follows:

Section 318(a) (relating to constructive ownership of stock) shall apply both in making the disproportionate redemption test and in determining the percentage of stock ownership after the redemption. The requirements under section 302(b)(2) of the Code will be applied to each shareholder separately and will be applied only with respect to stock which is issued and outstanding in the hands of the shareholders. Section 302(b)(2) only applies to a redemption of voting stock or to a redemption of both voting stock and other stock. Section 302(b)(2) does not apply to the redemption solely of nonvoting stock (common or preferred). However, if a redemption is treated as an exchange to a particular shareholder under the terms of section 302(b)(2), such section will apply to the simultaneous redemption of nonvoting preferred stock (which is not section 306 stock) owned by such shareholder and such redemption will also be treated as an exchange.

While section 1.302–3 of the regulations states that section 302(b)(2) of the Code does not apply to the redemption solely of nonvoting stock, the redemption of nonvoting stock actually owned by C and of voting common stock constructively owned by C is a redemption of both voting and nonvoting stock for purposes of these regulations. The redemption of C's preferred stock will therefore be treated as a payment in exchange for the stock if the requirements of section 302(b)(2) are satisfied.

In applying the provisions of section 302(b)(2) of the Code to the redemption of C's nonvoting stock, C is deemed to have owned 50 percent of X's voting common stock prior to the redemption and approximately 38 percent of X's voting common stock subsequent to the redemption such stock ownership being attributed to C from A under section 318(a)(1)(A)(ii)). Thus, C's percentage ownership in X's voting common stock after the redemption is less than 80 percent (78 percent) of what such percentage ownership was prior to the redemption. Therefore, the 80 percent requirement in section 302(b)(2) defining substantially disproportionate is met. Also, as required in section 302(b)(2)(B), after the redemption C owns less than 50 percent of the total combined voting power of X.

Since the terms of section 302(b)(2) of the Code are met with regard to the voting common stock constructively owned by C, that section applies to the redemption of C's nonvoting preferred stock. This treatment is consistent with the rule set forth in section 1.302–3 of the regulations that if a redemption is treated as an exchange to a particular shareholder under the terms of section 302(b)(2), such section will apply to the simultaneous redemption of nonvoting preferred stock * * * owned by such shareholder and such redemption will also be treated as an exchange.

Accordingly, the distribution by X to C in redemption of the 100 shares of X nonvoting preferred stock is substantially disproportionate within the meaning of section 302(b)(2) and, therefore, the redemption qualifies under section 302(a) as a distribution in full payment in exchange for the stock. The redemption of A's voting common stock likewise meets the requirements of section 302(b)(2).

Problem 34–2

Pam, Bob, and Ted are equal one-third owners of a sporting goods store which is operated as a C corporation. The three are unrelated and have held their stock for a period of five years. Ted needs cash and is willing to relinquish a portion of his ownership in exchange for a distribution from the corporation. Prior to the distribution, each of the shareholders holds 25 shares of common stock in the corporation, which are all the shares outstanding. The corporation redeems 10 of Ted's shares in exchange for $10,000.

1. Does the redemption of Ted's 10 shares in exchange for $10,000 qualify as a redemption under § 302(b)(2)?

2. What if Bob were Ted's father?

3. What if Bob were Ted's father but, following the redemption, Ted took no part in the business and had acquired his shares with his own funds?

4. What if the reason for Ted's redemption was that he had incurred a capital loss in an unrelated transaction and, if he could achieve a capital gain on the redemption, he would pay no tax because of the deductibility of the otherwise unusable capital loss?

5. What if, one month following Ted's redemption, Bob redeemed 10 of his shares for $10,000 and one month following that, Pam redeemed 10 of her shares for $10,000?

c. Redemptions Which are Not Essentially Equivalent to a Dividend

The most subjective of the three shareholder-focused redemption tests is that of § 302(b)(1) which states that a redemption will qualify for exchange treatment if it is "not essentially equivalent to a dividend." Attempting to qualify under this portion of the statute carries significantly more tax risk than under the two more objective rules discussed above. The essential equivalence test requires an examination of the facts and circumstances of each particular distribution. Like the other two tests, however, the primary focus of this third test is whether there has been a meaningful reduction in the shareholder's proportionate interest in the corporation. Although there are no mechanical or arithmetic tests to apply, it is clear that the attribution rules of § 318 will be considered in determining whether this test is met. It is also clear that a redemption of the shares of a sole shareholder is always essentially equivalent to a dividend. On the other hand, where a given redemption fails to qualify as a complete termination or as substantially disproportionate, the not essentially equivalent to a dividend category may provide the redeeming shareholder with the salvation of exchange treatment in certain situations, or at least afford an argument to that effect.

The cases and Rulings in this area have focused on whether the reduction in corporate stock ownership is so significant that the rights and influence of the redeemed party, in his or her capacity as a shareholder, are reduced to a meaningful extent. In the landmark case of *United States v. Davis,* 397 U.S. 301 (1970), which follows, the Court ruled that the presence or absence of a corporate business purpose for the exchange is not taken into account in determining whether the redemption is essentially equivalent to a dividend. The focus is rather on the shareholder's equity position. The analysis of whether a shareholder's influence in the corporation has been meaningfully reduced can be extremely complex in situations where there are various classes of stock. In these situations, courts focus on different voting rights, different preferences to earnings and assets, and all other rights and obligations attaching to a particular class of stock in determining shareholder status before and after the redemption. While the attribution rules affect the determination of whether a meaningful reduction has occurred, it is clear that the good behavior rules of § 302(c) are not specifically applied to automatically disqualify a redemption from exchange treatment under this test. A redemption that fails under § 302(b)(2) or (3) may still qualify under the not essentially equivalent to a dividend exception. Thus, the final shareholder redemption qualification provision of not essentially equivalent to a dividend may be available in situations where the shareholder is unable to qualify under the more objective rules of § 302(b)(2) and (b)(3), particularly when such nonqualification flows from the attribution rules of § 318. See generally Postlewaite and Finneran, *Section 302(b)(1): The Expanding Minnow,* 64 Va.L.Rev. 561 (1978).

UNITED STATES v. DAVIS

397 U.S. 301 (1970).

[*Facts*]

Mr. Justice Marshall delivered the opinion of the Court: In 1945, taxpayer and E.B. Bradley organized a corporation. In exchange for property transferred to the new company, Bradley received 500 shares of common stock, and taxpayer and his wife similarly each received 250 such shares. Shortly thereafter, taxpayer made an additional contribution to the corporation, purchasing 1,000 shares of preferred stock at a par value of $25 per share.

The purpose of this latter transaction was to increase the company's working capital and thereby to qualify for a loan previously negotiated through the Reconstruction Finance Corporation. It was understood that the corporation would redeem the preferred stock when the RFC loan had been repaid. Although in the interim taxpayer bought Bradley's 500 shares and divided them between his son and daughter, the total capitalization of the company remained the same until 1963. That year, after the loan was fully repaid and in accordance with the original understanding, the company redeemed taxpayer's preferred stock.

In his 1963 personal income tax return taxpayer did not report the $25,000 received by him upon the redemption of his preferred stock as income. Rather, taxpayer considered the redemption as a sale of his preferred stock to the company—a capital gains transaction under § 302 of the Internal Revenue Code of 1954 resulting in no tax since taxpayer's basis in the stock equaled the amount he received for it. The Commissioner of Internal Revenue, however, did not approve this tax treatment. According to the Commissioner, the redemption of taxpayer's stock was essentially equivalent to a dividend and was thus taxable as ordinary income under §§ 301 and 316 of the Code. * * *

I. The Internal Revenue Code of 1954 provides generally in §§ 301 and 316 for the tax treatment of distributions by a corporation to its shareholders; under those provisions, a distribution is includable in a taxpayer's gross income as a dividend out of earnings and profits to the extent such earnings exist. There are exceptions to the application of these general provisions, however, and among them are those found in § 302 involving certain distributions for redeemed stock. The basic question in this case is whether the $25,000 distribution by the corporation to taxpayer falls under that section—more specifically, whether its legitimate business motivation qualifies the distribution under § 302(b)(1) of the Code. Preliminarily, however, we must consider the relationship between § 302(b)(1) and the rules regarding the attribution of stock ownership found in § 318(a) of the Code. * * *

Taxpayer, however, argues that the attribution rules do not apply in considering whether a distribution is essentially equivalent to a dividend under § 302(b)(1). According to taxpayer, he should thus be considered to own only 25 percent of the corporation's common stock, and the distribution would then qualify under § 302(b)(1) since it was not pro rata or proportionate to his stock interest, the fundamental test of dividend equivalency. See Treas.Reg. 1.302–2(b). However, the plain language of the statute compels rejection of the argument. In subsection (c) of § 302, the attribution rules are made specifically applicable "in determining the ownership of stock for purposes of this section." Applying this language, both courts below held that § 318(a) applies to all of § 302, including § 302(b)(1)—a view in accord with the decisions of the other courts of appeals, a longstanding treasury regulation, and the opinion of the leading commentators.

Against this weight of authority, taxpayer argues that the result under paragraph (1) should be different because there is no explicit reference to stock ownership as there is in paragraphs (2) and (3). Neither that fact, however, nor the purpose and history of § 302(b)(1) support taxpayer's argument. The attribution rules—designed to provide a clear answer to what would otherwise be a difficult tax question—formed part of the tax bill that was subsequently enacted as the 1954 Code. As is discussed further, *infra,* the bill as passed by the House of Representatives contained no provision comparable to § 302(b)(1). When that provision was added in the Senate, no purpose was evidenced to restrict the applicability of § 318(a). Rather, the attribution rules continued to be made specifically applicable to the entire section, and we believe that Congress intended that they be taken into account wherever ownership of stock was relevant.

Indeed, it was necessary that the attribution rules apply to § 302(b)(1) unless they were to be effectively eliminated from consideration with regard to §§ 302(b)(2) and (3) also. For if a transaction failed to qualify under one of those sections solely because of the attribution rules, it would according to taxpayer's argument nonetheless qualify under § 302(b)(1). We cannot agree that Congress intended so to nullify its explicit directive. We conclude, therefore, that the attribution rules of § 318(a) do apply; and, for the purposes of deciding whether a distribution is "not essentially equivalent to a dividend" under § 302(b)(1), taxpayer must be deemed the owner of all 1,000 shares of the company's common stock.

II. After application of the stock ownership attribution rules, this case viewed most simply involves a sole stockholder who causes part of his shares to be redeemed by the corporation. We conclude that such a redemption is always "essentially equivalent to a dividend" within the meaning of that phrase in § 302(b)(1) and therefore do not reach the Government's alternative argument that in any event the distribution should not on the facts of this case qualify for capital gains treatment.

The predecessor of § 302(b)(1) came into the tax law as § 201(d) of the Revenue Act of 1921, 42 Stat. 228:

> "A stock dividend shall not be subject to tax but if after the distribution of any such dividend the corporation proceeds to cancel or redeem its stock at such time and in such manner as to make the distribution and cancellation or redemption essentially equivalent to the distribution of a taxable dividend, the amount received in redemption or cancellation of the stock shall be treated as a taxable dividend. . . . "

Enacted in response to this court's decision that pro rata stock dividends do not constitute taxable income, the provision had the obvious purpose of preventing a corporation from avoiding dividend tax treatment by distributing earnings to its shareholders in two transactions—a pro rata stock dividend followed by a pro rata redemption—that would have the same economic consequences as a simple dividend. Congress, however, soon recognized that even without a prior stock dividend essentially the same result could be effected whereby any corporation, "especially one which has only a few stockholders, might be able to make a distribution to its stockholders which would have the same effect as a taxable dividend." In order to cover this situation, the law was amended to apply "(whether or not such stock was issued as a stock dividend)" whenever a distribution in redemption of stock was made "at such time and in such manner" that it was essentially equivalent to a taxable dividend.

This provision of the 1926 Act was carried forward in each subsequent revenue act and finally became § 115(g)(1) of the Internal Revenue Code of 1939. Unfortunately, however, the policies encompassed within the general language of § 115(g)(1) and its predecessors were not clear, and there resulted much confusion in the tax law. At first, courts assumed that the provision was aimed at tax avoidance schemes and sought only to determine whether such a scheme existed. Although later the emphasis changed and the focus was more on the effect of the distribution, many courts continued to find that distributions otherwise like a dividend were not "essentially equivalent" if, for example, they were motivated by a sufficiently strong nontax business purpose. There was general disagreement, however, about what would qualify as such a purpose, and the result was a case-by-case determination with each case decided "on the basis of the particular facts of the transaction in question."

By the time of the general revision resulting in the Internal Revenue Code of 1954, the draftsmen were faced with what has aptly been described as "the morass created by the decisions." In an effort to eliminate "the considerable confusion which exists in this area" and thereby to facilitate tax planning, the authors of the new Code sought to provide objective tests to govern the tax consequences of stock redemptions. Thus, the tax bill passed by the House of Representatives contained no "essentially equivalent" language. Rather, it provided for "safe harbors" where capital gains treatment would be accorded to corporate redemptions that met the conditions now found in §§ 302(b)(2) and (3) of the Code.

It was in the Senate Finance Committee's consideration of the tax bill that § 302(b)(1) was added, and Congress thereby provided that capital gains treatment should be available "if the redemption is not essentially equivalent to a dividend." Taxpayer argues that the purpose was to continue "existing law," and there is support in the legislative history that § 302(b)(1) reverted "in part" or "in general" to the "essentially equivalent" provision of § 115(g)(1) of the 1939 Code. According to the Government, even under the old law it would have been improper for the Court of Appeals to rely on "a business purpose for the redemption" and "an absence of the proscribed tax avoidance purpose to bail out dividends at favorable tax rates." However, we need not decide that question, for we find from the history of the 1954 revisions and the purpose of § 302(b)(1) that Congress intended more than merely to re-enact the prior law.

In explaining the reason for adding the "essentially equivalent" test, the Senate Committee stated that the House provisions "appeared unnecessarily restrictive, particularly, in the case of redemptions of preferred stock which might be called by the corporation without the shareholder having any control over when the redemption may take place." This explanation gives no indication that the purpose behind the redemption should affect the result. Rather, in its more detailed technical evaluation of § 302(b)(1), the Senate Committee reported as follows:

"The test intended to be incorporated in the interpretation of paragraph (1) is in general that currently employed under section 115(g)(1) of the 1939 Code. Your committee further intends that in applying this test for the future that the inquiry will be devoted solely to the question of whether or not the transaction by its nature may properly be characterized as a sale of stock by the redeeming shareholder to the corporation. For this purpose the presence or absence of earnings and profits of the corporation is not material. Example: X, the sole shareholder of a corporation having no earnings or profits causes the corporation to redeem half of its stock. Paragraph (1) does not apply to such redemption notwithstanding the absence of earnings and profits."

The intended scope of § 302(b)(1) as revealed by this legislative history is certainly not free from doubt. However, we agree with the Government that by making the sole inquiry relevant for the future the narrow one whether the redemption could be characterized as a sale, Congress was apparently rejecting past court decisions that had also considered factors indicating the presence or absence of a tax-avoidance motive. At least that is the implication of the example given. Congress clearly mandated that pro rata distributions be treated under the general rules laid down in §§ 301 and 316 rather than under § 302, and nothing suggests that there should be a different result if there were a "business purpose" for the redemption. Indeed, just the opposite inference must be drawn since there would not likely be a tax-avoidance purpose in a situation where there were no earnings or profits. We conclude that the Court of Appeals was therefore wrong in looking for a business purpose and considering it in deciding whether the redemption was equivalent to a dividend. Rather, we agree with the Court of Appeals for the Second Circuit that "the business purpose of a transaction is irrelevant in determining dividend equivalence" under § 302(b)(1).

Taxpayer strongly argues that to treat the redemption involved here as essentially equivalent to a dividend is to elevate form over substance. Thus, taxpayer argues, had he not bought Bradley's shares or had he made a subordinated loan to the company instead of buying preferred stock, he could have gotten back his $25,000 with favorable tax treatment. However, the difference between form and substance in the tax law is largely problematical, and taxpayer's complaints have little to do with whether a business purpose is relevant under § 302(b)(1). It was clearly proper for Congress to treat distributions generally as taxable dividends when made out of earnings and profits and then to prevent avoidance of that result without regard to motivation where the distribution is in exchange for redeemed stock.

We conclude that that is what Congress did when enacting § 302(b)(1). If a corporation distributes property as a simple dividend, the effect is to transfer the property from the company to its shareholders without a change in the relative economic interests or rights of the stockholders. Where a redemption has that same effect, it cannot be said to have satisfied the "not essentially equivalent to a dividend" requirement of § 302(b)(1). Rather, to qualify for preferred treatment under that section, a redemption must result in a meaningful reduction of the shareholder's proportionate interest in the corporation. Clearly, taxpayer here, who (after application of the attribution rules) was the sole shareholder of the corporation both before and after the redemption, did not qualify under this test. * * *

2. PARTIAL LIQUIDATIONS

The fourth category of statutory distribution from a corporation which may qualify as a redemption is set forth in § 302(b)(4). This provision focuses at the corporate level on whether the distribution effectuates a "partial liquidation" of the corporation. The partial liquidation concept has gradually been reduced and restricted as part of the tax law. It has minimal application to the average small business corporation.

In order to qualify as a partial liquidation, an analysis is made of the distributing corporation itself. First, the distribution must not be essentially equivalent to a dividend as determined at the corporate, rather than shareholder, level. Secondly, the distribution must be pursuant to a plan of partial liquidation and must occur within the taxable year in which the plan is adopted or within the next succeeding taxable year. A distribution will be *deemed* to qualify as not essentially equivalent to a dividend if the distribution is attributable to the corporation ceasing to conduct a "qualified trade or business" or if it consists of the assets of a qualified trade or business and, immediately after the distribution in question, the corporation remains actively engaged in the conduct of a qualified trade or business. A qualified trade or business is one which the company actively conducted throughout the five-year period ending on the redemption date and which was not acquired by the corporation during that period in a transaction in which gain or loss is recognized in whole or in part.

If the distribution qualifies as a partial liquidation, it appears that § 302(b)(4) will override the traditional redemption categories of §§ 302(b)(1), (2), and (3). The rules will apply if the assets of the qualified business are actually distributed or if the proceeds of sale of the qualified business are distributed. In the former case, however, the corporation may recognize gain pursuant to § 311(b) if the distributed assets are appreciated.

C. DISTRIBUTIONS AND REDEMPTIONS OF STOCK TO PAY DEATH TAXES

Superimposed over the rules discussed in the prior portion of this chapter is a special, relatively limited, rule governing the redemption of stock of a deceased shareholder to the extent of his death taxes and funeral administration expenses. Where the stock redeemed is included in the gross estate (for federal estate tax purposes) of a deceased shareholder and the other conditions of § 303 are met, the redemption is treated as a sale or exchange of stock and not a distribution. While somewhat limited in scope, the provisions of § 303 can provide an important provision in the taxation of closely held corporations.

In order to apply, the value of all of the stock of the corporation which is included in the decedent's gross estate must be more than 35% of the value of the shareholder's adjusted gross estate. For the purposes of the 35% test, the stock of two or more corporations may be treated as the stock of a single corporation if 20% or more in value of such stock in each corporation is included in the decedent's estate.

The favored redemption treatment is available to the executors or administrators of the deceased shareholder or to his or her heirs. It is not available to purchasers or transferees of those persons. It is also not applicable to any person unless that person bears, to some extent, the financial burden of the estate or inheritance taxes or administrative expenses. The amount of the redemption which is accorded sale or exchange treatment under this provision cannot exceed the sum of the estate, inheritance, and other taxes imposed because of the decedent's death, plus the amount of funeral and administrative expenses allowable as a deduction under the federal estate tax laws. Any distribution in excess of this amount will be treated under the normal redemption rules of § 302. While the stated sums provide a ceiling on the redemption treatment allowed under § 303, it is not necessary that the redemption proceeds be actually needed or used for such purposes.

Chapter 35

CORPORATE LIQUIDATION

Code References: §§ 267(b); 331; 332; 334; 336(a), (b), (d); 337(a); 453(h).

Regulations: §§ 1.331–1; 1.332–1, –2, –3, –4.

A. INTRODUCTION

This chapter addresses distributions to shareholders from a corporation which has ceased to do business in corporate form and is distributing its assets in liquidation of the corporate entity. In determining whether a liquidating distribution occurs, the focus is on the corporation. In the case of nonliquidating distributions, such as dividends, return of capital, and stock redemptions, the shareholder's status generally is examined. In such nonliquidating distributions, either the shareholders surrender no stock, only part of their stock, or only some of the shareholders surrender all of their stock. In a liquidating distribution, all of the shareholders' stock interests are extinguished, the corporation ceases to do business, and the corporation distributes to the shareholders either its operating assets or the proceeds from the sale of such assets.

The federal tax effects of liquidating a C corporation exemplify the double tax concept. If the corporation sells its assets as a prelude to distributing the proceeds in liquidation, the corporation is taxed on any gain recognized upon the sale of such assets. Similarly, if, rather than selling its assets, the corporation distributes them to its shareholders in a liquidating distribution, any appreciation inherent in the assets at the corporate level is treated as gain to the corporation as if a sale had taken place. In the latter case, the assets are treated as having been sold at their fair market value.

At the shareholder level, those who receive a liquidating distribution are treated as though they have sold their shares to the corporation in exchange for the value of the distribution. Thus, if the fair market value of the assets (including the amount of any cash) distributed exceeds a shareholder's basis in his or her corporate stock, a second tax is exacted at the shareholder level. The resulting combined tax rate is rarely less than 50%. The basis of the assets received by the shareholder is their fair market value.

A relatively minor (in the small business context) exception to the general treatment of gain recognition for both shareholder and corporation occurs in cases where a parent corporation is liquidating a subsidiary (80% or more owned by the parent). In such a case, there is generally no tax at either the corporate or shareholder level and the tax basis of the assets is carried over from the subsidiary to the parent.

There are numerous business reasons which may dictate a corporate liquidation. The controlling shareholder(s) of a business may die or retire and therefore stop doing business. The owners of the business may desire to sell the business to a third party. In order to limit liability exposure, most buyers prefer to purchase the assets of the corporate business rather than the stock held by its shareholders. The sale proceeds received for the corporate assets are then generally distributed to the shareholders in a liquidating distribution. Finally, an ongoing business may desire to cease doing business in corporate form. With viable pass-through entity alternatives, including limited liability partnerships, the limited liability company, or the well-insured sole proprietorship, a C corporation may no longer be the best entity choice.

One of the fundamental tax concepts in the Code has been to not tax businesses when they are merely changing their form of operations. Under this timeworn principle, assets may generally be moved into or out of a partnership or limited liability company without significant tax considerations. They may also be moved *into* an S or C corporation. However, in the context of moving a business *out of* a C corporation, and to a lesser extent an S corporation, the mere change of form concept does not apply. Since the repeal of the *General Utilities* doctrine and former § 337 in 1986, a business operating in corporate form is often "locked in" to that entity configuration. The tax costs of liquidating, even if such liquidation has the legitimate business purpose of seeking to operate in a more favorable form of entity, may prove prohibitive. This key distinction between a corporation and other business entities is often a significant factor which militates against the use of a corporate business vehicle in the first place.

B. STATUTORY STRUCTURE

1. TAX TREATMENT OF LIQUIDATING CORPORATIONS

The basic tax treatment for a corporation making a liquidating distribution to its shareholders is set forth in § 336(a). That section provides that "gain or loss shall be recognized to a liquidating corporation on the distribution of property in complete liquidation as if such property were sold to the distributee at its fair market value." Thus, the distributing corporation compares the fair market value of the asset transferred to the shareholders against its tax basis in such asset. The difference is generally recognized to the corporation as either a gain or loss. The rule applies to all assets distributed by the corporation in liquidation, including intangible assets. Thus, the fair market value of the goodwill inherent in a going concern will normally have some value, particularly if the business is ongoing and to be continued in noncorporate form. Generally, the tax basis of such goodwill or going concern value is zero. Gain will consequently be recognized by the corporation.

The character of the gain or loss recognized by the corporation is subject to normal tax rules. Thus, a capital asset in the hands of the corporation will generate capital gain or loss. More importantly, however, the rules relating to recapture under § 1245 and those relating to related-party transfers under § 1239 will apply. A distributee shareholder will often be a "related party" under § 1239 because, in the small business corporation context, the distributee shareholder often "controls" the distributing entity, either directly or through attribution. Consequently, certain gains which would otherwise be capital gain are converted to ordinary income for the corporation. Even though there is currently no differentiation between the corporate ordinary income and capital gain rates, this distinction remains important because of the limitation that otherwise nondeductible capital losses can be offset only against capital gains. If § 1239 is applicable and produces corporate ordinary income, the opportunity for offset would be lost.

As a practical matter, the "consideration" received by the corporation from shareholders in the deemed sale mandated by § 336(a) is its own stock. Consequently, no cash is generated to the corporation with which to pay the corporate tax due. The corporation may have to retain separate cash reserves to pay any tax resulting from the liquidating transaction or, in the alternative, sell a portion of its assets to third parties, rather than distributing them to shareholders, in order to generate the required cash with which to pay the tax due under § 336(a). Such potential sales to third parties may, themselves, also yield a tax liability, leaving only the after-tax net proceeds of sale available to pay the tax due from the corporation on liquidating distributions to shareholders.

There are certain relatively minor (at least in the small business context) exceptions to the gain recognition requirement of § 336(a). If the liquidating distribution is made to a shareholder corporation which owns 80% of the distributor and such distribution is in complete redemption or cancellation of all the stock of the liquidating corporation pursuant to a plan of complete liquidation, § 332 overrides § 336(a). No gain or loss is recognized. Asset bases are generally carried over pursuant to § 334(b). An 80% distributee is a corporation that, on the date of the adoption of the plan of complete liquidation and at all times thereafter until the receipt of the distributed property, owns stock in the liquidating corporation possessing at least 80% of the total voting power of such corporation and at least 80% of the total value of the stock of such corporation. If those requirements are met, § 332 dictates that no gain or loss is recognized by the liquidating corporation. This subsidiary liquidation provision is of limited application in the small business corporation context.

Of more general application, however, are the rules of § 336(d) which limit the recognition of *loss* to the liquidating corporation in certain situations. Under these rules, no loss may be recognized by a liquidating corporation on the distribution of property to a related person within the meaning of § 267 if the property is "disqualified property" or if it is distributed to the shareholders on a non-pro rata basis. Disqualified property is property which is acquired by the liquidating corporation in a § 351 transaction within five years of a period ending on the date of distribution. The definition also includes property which was traded for disqualified property in a substituted tax basis transaction (such as a tax-deferred exchange pursuant to § 1031). A shareholder related to the corporation is an individual who owns, either directly or by attribution, more than 50% in value of the outstanding stock of the corporation and any corporation which is deemed to own more than 50% of the total combined voting power or more than 50% of the value of the stock of the distributing corporation.

Similarly, under § 336(d), any property which was contributed to the corporation with a tax avoidance purpose (essentially defined as property which has a built-in loss at the time it is contributed to the corporation) may not generate a loss deductible to the corporation when it is distributed to the corporation's shareholders. Property contributed to the corporation within two years of the date upon which the corporation adopts a plan of liquidation will generally be treated as having been contributed for tax avoidance purposes unless the taxpayer can show the absence of such a motive.

Losses generated by non-pro rata distributions to related parties are also, under § 336(d)(1)(A)(i), denied to the corporation. This provision may cause obvious practical problems if multiple shareholders wish to divide corporate properties by each taking separate assets, rather than an undivided interest in each corporate asset.

Losses denied to the corporation under § 336(d) are lost to the corporation forever. In addition, there is no basis adjustment to the assets distributed in the hands of the distributee shareholder and no loss allowed to the original contributing shareholder of the property.

2. TAX TREATMENT TO DISTRIBUTEE SHAREHOLDERS

Section 331(a) requires that "[a]mounts received by a shareholder in a distribution in complete liquidation of a corporation shall be treated as in full payment in exchange for the stock." Thus, the distributee shareholder must compare the cash and net fair market value of the property received in the liquidating distribution against the tax basis of the stock surrendered. The net fair market value is the fair market value of distributed assets reduced by the amount of any corporate liability that the shareholder assumes or takes subject to. The basis to the distributee shareholder of the property received is, under § 334(a), its fair market value.

If a shareholder has acquired his shares in the corporation at different times and for different prices, each distribution must be applied to the respective blocks of stock owned by the distributee shareholder and allocated based upon the number of shares in such block. Rev.Rul. 68–348, 1968–2 C.B. 141, as amplified by Rev.Rul. 85–48, 1985–1 C.B. 126. Within each such block, a cost recovery concept is applied to staggered liquidating distributions, with the full basis of each block recovered before any gain is recognized. No loss is recognized until the final liquidating distribution is made. If the stock held is a capital asset, the gain may be long-term for one block of stock and short-term for another, depending upon the holding period of the taxpayer for such shares.

There are certain limited exceptions to the gain recognition provisions of § 331. If the distributee shareholder is an 80% corporate shareholder, § 332 will prevent recognition of gain or loss to the shareholder.

Section 453(h) allows a shareholder who receives certain corporate-owned installment obligations in a liquidating distribution to avoid immediate tax upon the value of the note distributed. Rather, the payments received on a qualifying installment obligation are treated as payments in exchange for the shareholder's stock when they are received by the shareholder from the note obligor. These rules apply only to obligations acquired by the corporation with respect to the sale or exchange of its property during the 12–month period beginning on the date of adoption of the plan of complete liquidation and only if the liquidation of the corporation is completed within such period. They apply to inventory sales only if such inventory is sold in bulk to one person in one transaction.

In certain rare situations, a distributee shareholder may claim application of the open transaction doctrine, asserting that the value of the asset distributed cannot be valued with reasonable certainty at the time of liquidation. See discussion at Chapter 2. In such a case, the distribution is not taxed until the shareholder receives a full recovery of the tax basis in his stock and then only when, if, and as received. The Service takes the position that it generally is able to place a value on a distributed asset and that a transaction will qualify as open only in rare and extraordinary circumstances.

RECOGNITION OF GAIN OR LOSS ON LIQUIDATING SALES AND DISTRIBUTIONS OF PROPERTY (*GENERAL UTILITIES*)

PRIOR LAW
Overview

As a general rule, under prior law (as under present law) corporate earnings from sales of appreciated property were taxed twice, first to the corporation when the sale occurred, and again to the shareholders when the net proceeds were distributed as dividends. At the corporate level, the income was taxed at ordinary rates if it resulted from the sale of inventory or other ordinary income assets, or at capital gains rates if it resulted from the sale of a capital asset held for more than six months. With certain exceptions, shareholders were taxed at ordinary income rates to the extent of their pro rata share of the distributing corporation's current and accumulated earnings and profits.

An important exception to this two-level taxation of corporate earnings was the so-called *General Utilities* rule. The *General Utilities* rule permitted nonrecognition of gain by corporations on certain distributions of appreciated property to their shareholders and on certain liquidating sales of property. Thus, its effect was to allow appreciation in property accruing during the period it was held by a corporation to escape tax at the corporate level. At the same time, the transferee (the shareholder or third-party purchaser) obtained a stepped-up, fair market value basis under other provisions of the Code, with associated additional depreciation, depletion, or amortization deductions. Accordingly, the "price" of a step up in the basis of property subject to the *General Utilities* rule was typically a single capital gains tax paid by the shareholder on receipt of a liquidating distribution from the corporation.

Although the *General Utilities* case involved a dividend distribution of appreciated property by an ongoing business, the term *"General Utilities* rule"[43] was often used in a broader sense to refer to the nonrecognition treatment accorded in certain situations to liquidating as well as nonliquidating distributions to shareholders and to liquidating sales. The rule was reflected in Code sections 311, 336, and 337 of prior law. Section 311 governed the treatment of nonliquidating distributions of property (dividends and redemptions), while section 336 governed the treatment of liquidating distributions in kind. Section 337 provided nonrecognition treatment for certain sales of property pursuant to a plan of complete liquidation.

Numerous limitations on the *General Utilities* rule, both statutory and judicial, developed over the years following its codification. Some directly limited the statutory provisions embodying the rule, while others, including the collapsible corporation provisions, the recapture provisions, and the tax benefit doctrine, did so indirectly.

Case law and statutory background

Genesis of the General Utilities rule

The precise meaning of *General Utilities* was a matter of considerable debate in the years following the 1935 decision. The essential facts were as follows. General Utilities had purchased 50 percent of the stock of Islands Edison Co. in 1927 for $2,000. In 1928, a prospective buyer offered to buy all of General Utilities' shares in Islands Edison, which apparently had a fair market value at that time of more than $1 million.

---

43. *General Utilities & Operating Co. v. Helvering*, 296 U.S. 200 (1935).

Seeking to avoid the large corporate-level tax that would be imposed if it sold the stock itself, General Utilities offered to distribute the Islands Edison stock to its shareholders with the understanding that they would then sell the stock to the buyer. The company's officers and the buyer negotiated the terms of the sale but did not sign a contract. The shareholders of General Utilities had no binding commitment upon receipt of the Islands Edison shares to sell them to the buyer on these terms.

General Utilities declared a dividend in an amount equal to the value of the Islands Edison stock, payable in shares of that stock. The corporation distributed the Islands Edison shares and, four days later, the shareholders sold the shares to the buyer on the terms previously negotiated by the company's officers.

The Internal Revenue Service took the position that the distribution of the Islands Edison shares was a taxable transaction to General Utilities. Before the Supreme Court, the Commissioner argued that the company had created an indebtedness to its shareholders in declaring a dividend, and that the discharge of this indebtedness using appreciated property produced taxable income to the company under the holding in *Kirby Lumber Co. v. United States.* Alternatively, he argued, the sale of the Islands Edison stock was in reality made by General Utilities rather than by its shareholders following distribution of the stock. Finally, the Commissioner contended that a distribution of appreciated property by a corporation in and of itself constitutes a realization event. All dividends are distributed in satisfaction of the corporation's general obligation to pay out earnings to shareholders, he argued, and the satisfaction of that obligation with appreciated property causes a realization of the gain.
* * *

Statutory law and judicial doctrines affecting application of General Utilities rule

Recapture rules

The nonrecognition provisions of sections 311, 336, and 337 were subject to several additional limitations beyond those expressly set forth in those sections. These limitations included the statutory "recapture" rules for depreciation deductions, investment tax credits, and certain other items that might have produced a tax benefit for the transferor-taxpayer in prior years.

The depreciation recapture rules (sec. 1245) required inclusion, as ordinary income, of any gain attributable to depreciation deductions previously claimed by the taxpayer with respect to "section 1245 property"—essentially, depreciable personal property—disposed of during the year, to the extent the depreciation claimed exceeded the property's actual decline in value.

A more limited depreciation recapture rule applied to real estate. Under section 1250, gain on disposition of residential real property held for more than one year was recaptured as ordinary income to the extent prior depreciation deductions exceeded depreciation computed on the straight-line method. Gain on disposition of non-residential real property held for more than one year, however, was generally subject to recapture of all depreciation unless a straight-line method had been elected, in which case there was no recapture.

A number of other statutory recapture provisions could apply to a liquidating or nonliquidating distribution of property, including section 617(d) (providing for recapture of post–1965 mining exploration expenditures), section 1252 (soil and water conservation and land-clearing expenditures), and section 1254 (post–1975 intangible drilling and development costs). * * *

Judicially created doctrines

Under prior law, the courts applied nonstatutory doctrines from other areas of the tax law to in-kind distributions to shareholders. These doctrines also apply under present law. For example, it was held that, where the cost of property distributed in a liquidation or sold pursuant to a section 337 plan of liquidation had previously been deducted by the corporation, the tax benefit doctrine overrode the statutory rules to cause recognition of income. The application of the tax benefit doctrine turns on whether there is a "fundamental inconsistency" between the prior deduction and some subsequent event.

The courts also applied the assignment of income doctrine to require a corporation to recognize income on liquidating and nonliquidating distributions of its property.

Reasons for Change

In general

Congress believed that the *General Utilities* rule, even in its more limited form, produced many incongruities and inequities in the tax system. First, the rule could create significant distortions in business behavior. Economically, a liquidating distribution is indistinguishable from a nonliquidating distribution; yet the Code provided a substantial preference for the former. A corporation acquiring the assets of a liquidating corporation was able to obtain a basis in assets equal to their fair market value, although the transferor recognized no gain (other than possibly recapture amounts) on the sale. The tax benefits made the assets potentially more valuable in the hands of a transferee than in the hands of the current owner. This might induce corporations with substantial appreciated assets to liquidate and transfer their assets to other corporations for tax reasons, when economic considerations might indicate a different course of action. Accordingly, Congress reasoned, the *General Utilities* rule could be at least partly responsible for the dramatic increase in corporate mergers and acquisitions in recent years. Congress believed that the Code should not artificially encourage corporate liquidations and acquisitions, and that repeal of the *General Utilities* rule was a major step towards that goal.

Second, the *General Utilities* rule tended to undermine the corporate income tax. Under normally applicable tax principles, nonrecognition of gain is available only if the transferee takes a carryover basis in the transferred property, thus assuring that a tax will eventually be collected on the appreciation. Where the *General Utilities* rule applied, assets generally were permitted to leave corporate solution and to take a stepped-up basis in the hands of the transferee without the imposition of a corporate-level tax. Thus, the effect of the rule was to grant a permanent exemption from the corporate income tax.

Anti-tax avoidance provisions

In repealing the *General Utilities* rule, which provided for nonrecognition of losses as well as gains on distributions, Congress was concerned that taxpayers might utilize various means (including other provisions of the Code or the Treasury regulations) to circumvent repeal of the rule or, alternatively, might exploit the provision to realize losses in inappropriate situations or inflate the amount of the losses actually sustained. For example, under the general rule permitting loss recognition on liquidating distributions, taxpayers might be able to create artificial losses at the corporate level or to duplicate shareholder losses in corporate solution through contributions of property having previously accrued ("built-in") losses. In an effort to prevent these potential abuses, Congress included in the Act regulatory authority to prevent circumvention of the purposes of the amendments through use of any provision of law or regulations. In addition, it included specific statutory provisions designed to prevent avoidance of tax on corporate-level gains through conversions to subchapter S corporation status and unwarranted recognition of losses at the corporate level.

Problem 35–1

Dave and Craig have operated a retail clothing store in a location which is no longer popular because of the opening of nearby shopping malls. Their C corporation has operated for ten years. Craig and Dave have each held 50% of the stock of the corporation since its inception. They decided to cease doing business and liquidate the corporation. At the time of this decision, the corporation's assets are as follows:

	Basis	Value	Original Cost
Inventory	$ 50	$100	$ 50
Furniture & Equipment	$ 25	$ 60	$ 50
Cash	$ 25	$ 25	$ 25
Investment Real Estate	$100	$ 75	$100

The shareholders adopt the appropriate corporate resolutions and make the proper filings under state law to effectuate the liquidation. In all circumstances, the corporation retains the cash for the payment of any tax liability which it is assumed equals the amount thereof. What tax results to the corporation and the shareholders (each of them has a $5 basis in his corporate stock) in the following situations:

1. The corporation sells the inventory at its fair market value. The proceeds of such sale and the remaining assets other than cash are distributed to the shareholders, in equal proportions as to each asset, in complete liquidation of the corporation.

2. The furniture and equipment, real estate, and inventory are sold and the resulting proceeds of sale other than cash are distributed equally to the shareholders.

3. All of the assets including the inventory, other than cash, are distributed on a pro rata basis to the two shareholders.

4. The inventory is sold, after reserving $25 to pay corporate taxes, and the cash and proceeds of inventory sale are distributed $57.50 to Dave and $42.50 to Craig. In addition, the furniture and equipment is distributed to Dave and the real estate is distributed to Craig. What if Dave is Craig's father?

5. What if the real estate had been contributed by the two shareholders to the corporation one year prior to the adoption of the plan of liquidation and, upon liquidation, it is distributed pro rata to them?

6. What if the real estate were sold for $150 on an installment basis following the adoption of the plan of liquidation and the resulting buyer's note were distributed to the shareholders, pro rata, within 12 months following the adoption of the plan of liquidation, in complete liquidation of the corporation?

C. SPECIAL LIQUIDATION SITUATIONS

1. LIQUIDATION OF S CORPORATIONS

Pursuant to § 1371(a)(1), the rules relating to C corporation liquidations generally apply to S corporations except as specifically otherwise provided. Thus, as with a C corporation, a distribution in liquidation of a shareholder's interest in an S corporation is treated as gain to the distributee shareholder to the extent that the cash and value of property distributed exceeds the tax basis in his corporate shares. The basis of the property received by the distributee shareholder is its fair market value. The liquidating corporation recognizes gain to the extent that it sells its appreciated property prior to liquidation or makes a liquidating distribution of such property which is taxed under § 336(a) as though a sale had taken place. Thus, on its face, it would appear that S corporation liquidations generate the same tax results as do C corporations.

In practice, however, the likelihood of double taxation upon liquidation is significantly diminished in an S corporation. This is so because the corporate gain on the sale or distribution of its appreciated property is passed through to the shareholders in accordance with their shareholdings under §§ 1366 and 1367. Such gain increases the basis of the distributee shareholders' shares to the extent of such gain recognized. Accordingly, there is less income under § 331 at the distributee shareholder level when the corporate assets are distributed because of increased basis in the corporate shares. Consequently, for S corporations which have always been S corporations, the double taxing effect of § 336(a) is minimal. The basis increase in the distributee's shares will either reduce the shareholder's gain on liquidation or produce an offsetting capital loss. This offset may, however, be imperfect if the corporate gain on the sale or distribution occurs in one year and the capital loss to the shareholders on the liquidating distribution is recognized in the next. Similarly, if the gain to the corporation is ordinary but the loss resulting from the increased basis for the stock is capital, the offset may not be available at all.

If a liquidating S corporation has previously been a C corporation, avoidance of double taxation upon a liquidation is less likely. This is because § 1374 applies a corporate penalty tax to any built-in gain which is recognized by the S corporation upon liquidation. Such gain does *not* increase the distributee shareholder's tax basis in his or her shares. One of the reasons for the enactment of the § 1374 penalty was to prevent C corporation shareholders from avoiding double tax by making a "one-shot" S election in anticipation of liquidation. Under § 1374, the S election must be made ten years prior to the liquidation in order to avoid the penalty tax. To the extent that the corporation's gain is not built-in gain, as in the case of appreciation in corporate property which occurs after the S election is made, the penalty tax will not apply and the double tax effect of § 336(a) will be mitigated by the shareholder basis increase discussed above.

There are special rules for S corporations which distribute installment notes in complete liquidation. Section 453B(h)(1) provides that the distribution of certain notes does not constitute a disposition of the installment obligation. Thus, the S corporation does not recognize installment obligation disposition gain as a result of the distribution and the shareholder is required to report the gain attributable to the note only as the payments are received. As with C corporations, only installment obligations acquired from the sale of property by an S corporation during the 12–month period beginning on the date that a plan of complete liquidation is adopted may qualify for this special treatment and only bulk sales of inventory qualify, even within the 12–month period. Finally under § 453(h)(1)(C), a sale of depreciable property will not qualify if it is to a greater–than–50% shareholder of the S corporation.

Problem 35–2

In 1985, Jerry and Connie each contributed $500,000 to Realty Corporation, a C corporation, in exchange for 50 shares each of its common stock. The corporation utilized the contributed funds to purchase an office/retail building, and the underlying real estate, for a total purchase price of $1,000,000. On January 1, 1991, Jerry and Connie made an S election on behalf of the corporation. At the time of the election, the real estate had an adjusted basis of $800,000 and a fair market value of $1,800,000. The corporation continued to operate the property until January 1, 1997, at which time the corporation was liquidated and the property distributed to

Jerry and Connie as joint tenants.   At the time of liquidation, the real estate had an adjusted basis of $600,000 and a fair market value of $2,500,000.   On the date of liquidation, Jerry and Connie each had an adjusted basis in their corporate stock of $400,000.

1. What is the tax consequence of the liquidation to the corporation?

2. What is the tax effect to Jerry and Connie individually?

3. What if the fair market value of the building at the time of the S election had been $800,000, an amount equal to its adjusted basis?

4. What if the liquidation did not take place until January 1, 2002?

5. What if, in February of 1997, Jerry and Connie sold jointly owned General Motors stock, generating a capital loss of $1,500,000?

*

Index

References are to pages

References are to pages

†

0–314–06603–9

90000

9 780314 066039